Also by James McCourt

Queer Street

W. W. NORTON & COMPANY · NEW YORK · LONDON

Rise and Fall of an American Culture, 1947–1985

Queer Street

by James McCourt

EXCURSIONS
IN THE MIND
OF THE LIFE

Photo spreads researched, edited and designed by Vincent Virga with Rubina Yeh.

Portions of Chapter 10 appeared previously in *Performing Arts Magazine*. Portions of
Chapter 20 appeared previously in *Vogue*, *Film Comment*, and *The Yale Review*. Portions of
Chapter 22 appeared previously in *Review of Contemporary Fiction*.

Grateful acknowledgment is made for permission to reprint lines from: "Lexington Avenue
Subway, 1941" from J.D. McClatchy, *Hazmat*, Alfred A. Knopf, 2002; "Notes on 'Camp'"
from Susan Sontag, *Against Interpretation and Other Essays*, Farrar, Straus and Giroux,
1966; "'Man Who Beat Up Homosexuals Reported to Have AIDS Virus'" from Richard
Howard, *Like Most Revelations*, Pantheon, 1994; "February," "Fabergé," "The Crystal
Lithium," "Hymn to Life," "The Mourning of the Poem" and "A Few Days" from James
Schuyler, *Collected Poems*, Farrar, Straus and Giroux, 1993, and from the Estate of James
Schuyler. "Among My Souvenirs" by Horatio Nicholls and Edgar Leslie. Copyright © 1927
Lawrence Wright Music Co., Ltd. Copyright renewed, assigned to Edgar Leslie
(administered by Herald Square Music, Inc.) and Chappell & Co. All rights reserved.
Used by permission, Warner Bros. Publications U.S., Inc., Miami, FL, 33014.

Manufacturing by The Haddon Craftsmen, Inc.
Book design by Rubina Yeh
Production manager: Anna Oler

Library of Congress Cataloging-in-Publication Data
McCourt, James, 1941–
   Queer street : rise and fall of an American culture, 1947/1985 : excur-
sions in the mind of the life / by James McCourt.— 1st ed.
      p. cm.
Includes bibliographical references and index.
   ISBN 0-393-05051-3
   1. Gays—United States—History—20th century. 2. Gay
communities—United States—History—20th century. 3. Gays—United
States—Social conditions. I. Title.
   HQ76.3.U5M383   2004
   306.76'6'0973—dc22
                                                        2003016112

W. W. Norton & Company, Inc.
500 Fifth Avenue, New York, NY 10110

W. W. Norton & Company Ltd.
Castle House, 75/76 Wells Street, London W1T 3QT

1 2 3 4 5 6 7 8 9 0

To my brother David,
who let me know what manhood is

and

To Elaine Markson,
who insisted there was a call for it

And on the way to somewhere else—
he can't think of the stop, the stops—

. . . .

He'll ask this nerveless dark angel of age
again what he did, what he did wrong.

—J.D. McClatchy, "Lexington Avenue Subway, 1941"

Contents

PART THREE: BREAKING OUT

PART FOUR: EXPATRIATES

PART FIVE: RETURN ENGAGEMENTS (POSTQUAM REARRIVED)

PART SIX: DEAD RECKONINGS

PART SEVEN: LOST ANGELES (INSIDE STORY)

Acknowledgments

Without the editorial persistence and executive dexterity of Robert Weil, the disparate threads of *Queer Street* could never have become a book.

Without Vincent Virga's picture edit the pattern of the narrative would have remained a closely guarded secret.

John Yohalem, in copyediting, saved the author more than just occasionally from acute prose thrombosis.

The author's heartfelt thanks go out for the enthusiasm and composure of two very sharp editorial assistants, Jason Baskin and Brendan Curry; the ingenious and innovative book design concepts of Rubina Yeh; the patient, welcoming and always authoritative production supervision of Nancy Palmquist and Anna Oler; and David Hawkins, Adrian Kitzinger and Don Rifkin, for additional editorial work.

More than any other works cited in *Queer Street*, George Chauncey's *Gay New York* and Robert Dawidoff's writings on homosexual rights seen as manifest in the fabric of the American Constitution inform this book.

The author is deeply grateful to these benefactors for helping *Queer Street* come about: Susan Sontag, Harold Bloom, John Hollander, J.D. McClatchy, Wayne Koestenbaum, Victoria Wilson, Donald Lyons, George Haas, Darragh Park, Kathleen and Hugh Howard, Ann Mahon Fuller, Catherine Bolger De Martino, Laureen Campbell King, Tracy Young, Robert Cohen, Tim Robinson, Lester Glassner, John Paradiso, Chris Felver, Chip Kidd, William Moses Hoffman, Michael Silverblatt, Eric Garber, Jack Burlison, Gary Johnson, Suzannah Lessard, Noel Brennan and Greg Zabilski, and to the following deceased, who must here represent in memory whole legions of bright-light, quick-witted anonymous contributors who might have made (and still might make) life for us all a freer, truer and finer thing than all too many others told us it could ever be: Richard Mahar, Harry

Blair, William Corley, Ralph Tardi, Carmen Delgado, Robert (Aubrey) Tarbox, Jarry Lang, Leo Lerman, James Schuyler, James Merrill, Richard Rouilard, Jerome B. Fierman, Neil Cunningham and Dorothy Dean.

And lastly, to his constant and wonderful friends in the Publishing Office of the Library of Congress, and in particular to W. Ralph Eubanks, Margaret E. Wagner, Evelyn Sinclair, Linda Osborne, Blaine Marshall, Iris Newsome Sara Day, Heather Burke, Susan Reyburn, Alex Hovan, Gloria Baskerville-Holmes and Clarke Allen.

Queer Street

PART ONE

Origination

CHAPTER ONE

Predicament

> "I can imagine a book made up entirely of examples."
> —Wittgenstein
>
> "When did you first get the idea you were queer?"
> "Two weeks into the first grade, January, 1947."
> —interview with the author

In which times, places, weather conditions, and descriptions of what people were (so to speak) wearing come of necessity into figurative play.

Who, what, when, where (there's no why but why, because). In the beginning it had no name, and no extension either. The street. What the canonical calendar is to the working fiction of time (generally speaking, cyclical time: the seasons of the year, any year, in any liturgy, from sowing-reaping to Advent-Pentecost and beyond), so is the canonical map to the working fiction of place: generally speaking, the mandala place, including mazes. Examples: the Monopoly board and the Map of Queer Street.

Queer Street is our Broadway, replete with impressions to which a clever boy responds with force, traversed by seven parallel avenues (easy reference, the Seven Ages of Man), and on the grid by any number of names, letter and number streets (a sort of mix of New York, Los Angeles and the District of Columbia), all out of sequence and Oz-like willy-nilly. (Note: We could, if necessary, quote the text of Jacques's "All the world's a stage" Seven Ages speech from *As You Like It*, trusting that the emendations to the names be taken as read. Or not.)

The Avenues:
Fathers' Arms
Shining Morningside
Sighing Furnace*
Reputation
Ancient Sayings
Pantaloon
Mere Oblivion

*New York queers, who consider themselves, especially in respect of Los Angeles, orig-
inary in all things (including the importation of tropical plants and floral exotica into both
public and private space), insist on Third Avenue (even without the El) to signal Third
Sex, Third Leg, Three-Dollar Bill and the Trinity (referred to in Irish Catholic intellectual circles, as in the West of Ireland, as The Three Gay Fellas).

Some cross streets: Attitude, Camp, Jewelry, Lipstick; P, D and Q and
Promising, Deep, Meaningful and Talented, 7, 11, and Boxcars, 69 and 4/4
(as in "She did the figure 8 the hard way: two fours"). The convergence of
Queer Street—the intersection of whatever avenue and any of these cross
streets—creates a little neighborhood of its own. Other streets terminate in
circles, nine of them, rather than cutting all the way across the grid and
others still (such as Moribund) are hardly more than a block long (like Gay
Street in the real Village), curving like bent hooks and spilling into culs-de-
sac of each other lanes (such as Memory). Finally, there are little mews
courts (corresponding to the real Sniffen and Patchin, Milligan Place and
Pomander Walk) with names like Seclusion, Betrayal and Go-to-Hell.
Replete with impressions to which a clever boy (one consumed with ambition, a salient feature of which is to be admitted—"Blesh you dahling!"—
into Tallulah Bankhead's dressing room: no mean feat, even for one
accustomed to the camerini of numerous star headliners at the Metropolitan
Opera, considering both the taxing rigors imposed by Miss Bankhead's
honor guard and the alarming celerity with which her vehicles opened and
closed on Broadway) responds with force.

The Major Monuments:
Orestes: intersection, Queer Street/Fathers' Arms
Alexander: intersection, Queer Street/Shining Morningside
Beloved Disciple: intersection, Queer Street/Sighing Furnace
Michelangelo: intersection, Queer Street/Reputation
Shakespeare: intersection, Queer Street/Ancient Sayings

Beethoven: intersection, Queer Street/Pantaloon

Melville: intersection, Queer Street/Mere Oblivion

Author walking, hearing the voices—the hawking cries of random Queer Street vendors. Stopping in front of the shop windows, pausing: at which time cartoon bubbles appear over Queer Temperament's head. Eventually these accrue, in strict obedience to the peculiar laws attaching to the phenomenon "bubble cluster," into something like a collection of essays. These essays, brought to the point of completion years after their inceptions on strolls along Queer Street, are presented in windows inserted in the non-fiction *roman fleuve* which *Queer Street* finally is.

As recently underscored by the philosopher Thomas Nagel, "The stream of consciousness is what we all live in. The expression is now associated with a literary form in which a character's inner monologue of thoughts and associations is presented accurately and is very different from the orderly outward forms of his life in the world. But the true stream of consciousness is far richer and far less verbal than anything described in *Ulysses*. Think about what happens to you during any two minutes spent walking on a city street— the flood of sensations, perceptions, and feelings that courses through you, most of them hardly drawing your attention. The multiplicity and density of detail is far greater than even the richest collection of verbalized thoughts or conversations with yourself that may have been going on at the same time. The process by which the world impinges on us at all times and the constantly shifting apprehension of our relation to it are too enormous for us to fully grasp" (*The New York Review of Books*, April 11, 2002).

Put another way, Author's essays are no more nor less than a congeries of echoes of years of overheard and vis-à-vis opinion and commentary (Other Voices, Other Rooms over Strange Interlude). Each topic that occurs to Author (as Queer Temperament, QT) along the way and over the years may be elaborated like a character. QT's ideas in any case are initially all amalgams of and reactions to things others said; however, this state of affairs must be overcome. This is called becoming original, a seeming oxymoron, but there are no born originals.

Imagine trying to make a book out of voice cards—the book a house of cards—one strong puff—but all memory is an inhalation; followed by a holding of the breath—and the one strong puff that blows its house of cards down is the exhalation that resumes life.

Marcel Proust refused to exhale—to recommence life—and died of emotional asthma.

Premonition is the circumstance in which "when then" usurps the position of "then, when." It entails the confidence of the manner in which reading or writing a book is life-like: there is no present in it; the client is occupied with seeking to come to terms with what has simultaneously not yet and already happened.

Thus at a certain point in life, Author, modeling his enterprise on the devices of Gestalt therapy and the practices of innumerable meditative verbal musicians working in both verse and prose, becomes the mentor to the younger self. As if in dream time, he revisits the locale, the scene of the crime, the topos of Queer Street to instruct himself as the young Augustine was instructed in language: through mimicry. Thus the impression created is a literary one rather than a sociological one, as if Queer Anonymous had been channeled, incorporating T.S. Eliot, W.H. Auden, Tennessee Williams, Truman Capote, Paul Bowles, Gore Vidal, James Baldwin, William Burroughs, Coleman Dowell, Alfred Chester, and later Frank O'Hara, James Schuyler, John Ashbery and James Merrill, together with Boyd McDonald (redactor of the notorious Straight-To-Hell testimonies of toilet-wall queer America), John Rechy and the amazing and anomalous literary shipwreck that was Gordon Merrick.

Display, response and the significant scene.

Other voices in other rooms (and often other doorways, other park benches, other lobbies, other cafeterias) constitute the Whitmanian New York topos. Introduction of the Ventriloquies, likening them to the Convolutes of The Arcades Project (and to the author as a lesser Lypsinka *avant la lettre*). Sometimes the Ventriloquy in the mouth of a distinct character, sometimes an anonymous "voice" Author QT has heard in his head, referencing all the while the French Ventriloquist from *All About Eve* ("There was nothing he didn't know").

Ultimately, the presentation derives from the image of regression, with pointed reference to Freud as recalled by William Maxwell, "When we talk about the past, we lie with every breath we take."

Author: "So what?"

Whereby the essay is another note toward a supreme court-of-final-appeal fiction. One sees, or remembers, oneself propped up in a lap, looking around a room, being taught to thrive by parroting, by imitation—an image that metamorphoses easily in Author's mind into the Show Business story of the ventriloquist's dummy who "takes over" the brain of the ventriloquist (or, like Pinocchio, becomes a real boy), both scenarios versions of the essential Oedipal conflict idea of supplanting.

The melodrama of the Ventriloquies is thus predicated, so that each time Author, seemingly on his own, formulates a set of ideas it is as if he is climbing down off some lap and walking across another room, another voice in the Forensic Society that is consciousness. Not to mention Author's habit of indulging in masking patterns which regularly find subsidiary parts clouding the picture by bleeding into the foreground.

—◦—

Queer Street. Queer Street. It doesn't start anywhere; there isn't a beginning. We won the war; the warriors came home, those who did, to find everything the war changed changed, is one opening.

Viewed by homosexual men of the era—combat veterans and their undecorated coevals alike—as the newly legitimated grasping of an existential option between the World of Day (with its ordinal American criteria delimiting life, liberty and the pursuit of happiness) and the World of Night (the New York–Los Angeles Night, seen as other than American, with its deep, insatiable passions, accessed through the portal of twilight, as paradigm).

It (the street, the history) doesn't start anywhere. Viewed by the world of straight America (primed to rescind the liberty and license vouchsafed queers under grueling combat conditions), it becomes the radical inverse of the renewed moral and civic duty prescribed in the triumphalist Republic: as a deeply suspicious communal existence (in the dawning American age of the suburban single-family unit dwelling, to each his own), a communality of mutually enraptured, timeless, self-stimulating purposelessness (observers citing regularly the homosexual's obsession with beating back the signs of aging: spending as rumor had it half his life in wardrobe, hair and makeup). Viewed as such and denounced alike by organized religion, by Metropolitan High Culture (and by its secular creed, a tortured, straightjacketed, prescriptive Freudian psychoanalysis) as a design for living redolent of depraved luxury, recalling such practices as the Biblical sin of onanism (seen perforce as thwarting pro-creation, and therefore as a wilful slap in the face to the mass-chant agitprop politics of the Baby Boom).

It doesn't start anywhere; there is simply no big bang for anybody's buck. Nevertheless performance subsists in time and material space: the performance is recorded; the performers are studied, often obsessively. ("It's like she was studyin' you, like you were a book or a play or a set of blue-prints. How you walk, talk, think, eat, sleep."—Birdie Coonan [Thelma Ritter] to Margo Channing [Bette Davis] in Joseph L. Mankiewicz's *All About Eve*—20th Century Fox, 1950.)

And, in an update, Queer Theory is on the march, proffering an anti-essentialist ontology: how concepts of gender and desire have been constructed in Western discourse in an attempt to deconstruct the pernicious effects, particularly on the bodies of women and sexual dissidents.

Anti-essentialist means existentialist, cutting into Queer Street exactly at war's end, coinciding not accidentally with the explosion of existentialist philosophy in Europe and its immediate and irreversible effect upon post-war American culture. We'd won the war—and the winning of it (as brilliantly and meticulously detailed in Alan Berube's *Coming Out Under Fire*) homo-sexual men and women played a more than merely significant part; morale was vital and, as was reflected even in such mainstream post-war entertain-ments as Rodgers and Hammerstein's *South Pacific*, both tolerance of dif-ference (as dutifully versed in "You've Got To Be Taught") and the liberating exuberance of drag shows (as exuberantly demonstrated in "Honey Bun"), were an essential component. So were other forms of tolerance, some of them directly countervalent to the armed forces code of discipline.

As Hal Call remembers, in Eric Marcus's *Making History: The Struggle for Gay and Lesbian Equal Rights*, "I had absolutely no sexual activity in the armed forces with anyone, because I knew it was a no-no. Besides, when you became a commander and an officer, you didn't carry on with the troops. There were some who were carrying on, and we'd hear of it now and then, but we'd never try to investigate it. You have to consider the circumstances. You were in the South Pacific, down on Espiritu Santo. You came from a combat operation in the Marianas and were going up to a combat opera-tion in the Ryukyus. The men had not been home or had a furlough or any-thing like that for two or three years. Years, not months. They were under the stress of war, and they were going into combat again where a lot of them were not going to come out. So if they went up under the coco' trees and sucked a little cock and jacked off together or something like that, so what? Who was harmed? Nobody. That's the way the armed forces should look at it. The armed forces could not operate without homosexuals. Never could. Never has. And never will."

Everything the war changed, which did seem to be altogether everything.

All the tight lids seemed to have come off at once (a phenomenon which homosexuals who could easily be privately consulted—an elite—did not, from their seemingly secure positions, view with feelings of unmixed delight). There had occurred in wartime a relaxation of moral surveillance, so that, for example, when the Under-Secretary of State Sumner Welles was caught *in flagrante delicto* with a Pullman porter on the presidential train returning from Hyde Park to Washington, not a breath of scandal was allowed to hit the cold winter air. Similarly when the eminent composer-critic Virgil Thomson and the venerable Senator Walsh of Massachusetts were both hauled into night court, following a raid on a male cat house in Brooklyn's Carroll Gardens district (the site having been staked out for months through telescopes by ardent Catholic parishioners nearby, giving the police no choice but to act) neither personage was prosecuted (although the brothel keeper did do hard time).

What transpired in the Asian jungle went as well for London in the Blitz—particularly, according to the consensus, when the Yanks landed to beef up the expeditionary forces for the Normandy landing (D-Day, June 6, 1944), and by a sort of back-formation extension for New York, under the blackout curtains that never quite dropped in an actual attack (but all the same—).

As the intrepid homosexual traveler and commentator Tobias Schneebaum points out in his 1979 memoir *Wild Man*, the post-war homosexual novel could be published and reviewed openly in newspapers and periodical journals only if the protagonists (always pathetically unhappy, utterly at a loss, alcoholic and happen worse) were seen to come to criminal peculation and a dread end. He cites two forthright examples: Gore Vidal's *The City and the Pillar* and Fritz Peters's *Finisterre* (neglecting to include Charles Jackson's *The Lost Weekend*, which although it is not often so recalled, did in fact address both alcoholism and homosexuality, indeed rendering the two as syzygetic indispositions), and even the cyber robot-art porn fictions of William Burroughs first published underground by Maurice Girodias in his Olympia Press Travelers Companion series.

Later, in Allen Drury's *Advise and Consent*, winner of the Pulitzer Prize for fiction for 1960, the character unfortunate enough to have succumbed to a homosexual wartime liaison (in the South Pacific, although not ostensibly up in the cocoa trees), fearing disclosure a decade later, kills himself. Defiance dared not rear its head out of doors until 1963, in John Rechy's best seller, *City of Night*, savagely reviewed by the vermillion-wigged washout

Alfred Chester in *The New York Review of Books*. Alfred Chester was, of course, how the West Side liked its queers in the '60s. Defiance—a thing not seen again (and more apocalyptically) until 14 years later in the milestone *Dancer from the Dance*, in which from the pseudonymous genius of Andrew Holleran the charismatic balls-ass warrior queer Sutherland sprang up whole from the metaphorically blood-drenched plowed queer earth.

Whereupon, as if to reinforce his picture of the immediate post-war zeitgeist, Schneebaum complements his observation with the true-life story of a dissolute pair of outré sodomites in Mexico. Two climactic paragraphs from this interlude serve as well as anything written at greater length to illustrate the prevailing view of the homosexual in the late 1940s, well before the determining effect of McCarthyism on queer life in America in its unstoppable imperial years.

"By the time these liberties [as valet, defined in somewhat shady terms] were extended to open attendance on his body, Lynn's drinking habits were already affecting his sexual abilities and he became impotent. He coughed incessantly and learned he had cancer of the throat. He smoked additional cigarettes each day and drank himself senseless at night. We never talked of this and I didn't even know of his illness. I was already back in New York when he shot and killed himself; I learned it through a letter from Nicholas, describing the gruesome necessity of cutting off Lynn's feet before his long body could fit into the coffin.

"Nicholas left Ajijic years after I did and went to California, where he worked as an interior designer. He came to visit me once in my eleven-dollar-a-month apartment in New York. I opened my door to find him dressed more elegantly than ever; Brooks Brothers suit, shirt with button-down collar, Sulka tie, bowler hat, a silver handled cane. He laughed at the way I lived, and when we walked down the six flights of stairs, he pointed out the trash on steps; the puddles of urine and their smells, the disreputability of the building. I never heard from him directly again, but I knew he lived alone in Los Angeles, rich, isolated and introspective. Zoe wrote me to say that he had died mysteriously after losing his job; he had been discovered sitting in a chair three days after his death."

A baleful look (covert but definitive) at the post-war New York homosexual was offered in Alfred Hitchcock's *Rope* (1948; screenplay by Arthur Laurents from the play by Patrick Hamilton). The picture famously shot in eight ten-minute invisibly stitched takes, literally can't take its eyes off the proceedings, as a pair of rather-too-intimate young Upper East Side "bachelor" roommates tantalize their airily befuddled guests with chirpy, macabre chit-chat, play sinuous Poulenc on the piano, and nearly get away with murder as the sun goes down over New Jersey and night falls on Gotham.

It was in that same city in the same year that the hot Broadway ticket was for Marlon Brando's naked torso and Tennessee Williams's bared queer soul together on view in *A Streetcar Named Desire* that the archbishop of New York, Francis Spellman—known to the host of his beleaguered handlers as Bess—and the director of the Federal Bureau of Investigation, J. Edgar Hoover—known at large in New York clubland as Mary—held separate sway and made communal hay, that the critically bloodied but unbowed Tallulah Bankhead, artist, star and errant night-owl daughter of a former Speaker of the U.S. House of Representatives, reigned as lesbian Lord of Misrule over what was then called the Rialto, and to cap it off, that the notorious Kinsey Report, *Sexual Behavior in the Human Male*, was published, categorically declaring, among so many other explosive things, that ten percent of the male population was predominantly homosexual between the ages of sixteen and fifty-five; that 8 percent was exclusively homosexual for at least three years between the ages of sixteen and fifty-five; and that 4 percent of white males had been exclusively homosexual after the onset of adolescence up to the time of the interviews.

At the same time (allowing as queer parlance might have had it for the clocking shift), while Hollywood, in the wake of its all too brief if sentimental fling with film noir and the socially conscious problem picture (scored right from the beginning by conservative can-do America as demoralizing and communistic), set about, in the sunshine decade of the 1950s, its business of projecting the fevered American dream of a victor's paradise, in which the likes of Marlon Brando, James Dean, Anthony Perkins and Paul Newman (out of the New York milieu) and Rock Hudson, Tab Hunter, Troy Donahue and Charlton Heston (along with several less successful specimens of the sort of home-bred Hollywood beefcake habitually found draped in studied attitudes around George Cukor's pool on Sunday afternoons) attempted a Technicolor, wide-screen redefinition of the American male, a collection of stalwart types from real-life Los Angeles (an exploding metropolis of raucous vagrants policed by, hands down, the most corrupt force in the nation) set about casting changes—changes generated mainly by two particular parties from the legacy of names, Harry Hay and Dr. Evelyn Gentry Hooker.

Harry Hay, who died in 2002, was movie star material—or more exactly the kind of real California man the stars were confected to call to mind. His story (rather than, for example, that of actual movie star Billy Haines, who, refusing to renounce his lover Jimmy Shields, stood by his man and chucked a promising career to reinvent himself as one of Hollywood's most successful interior decorators) became the wisdom-literature this is the way it must have been of what later would be called Gay Liberation.

It doesn't start anywhere. Harry Hay would disagree. In his own words (to James A. Dubro, for ICON, reproduced at gaywave.com), "It all begins in 1947/48/49, when we [on the radical Left] had the feeling that the country was beginning to move toward a police state. We had loyalty oaths; all the teachers had to take loyalty oaths. The House Un-American Activities Committee was tearing at all the leaders of the trade unions, attempting to destroy them. And I thought to myself at that moment, you know this time the scapegoat they will use as an organizing tool to scare the populace will not be the Jews, because the Holocaust is much too fresh in everyone's mind. They won't be using the blacks, because the blacks are now being organized by the trade unions and there are all kinds of community organizations starting up—the NAACP and the ACLU are handling their cases with the Supreme Court, and so on. It will be us."

The Mattachine Society, a name derived from the Arabic *mutawajihin* in Moorish Spain, and chosen by Hay to recall groups of Renaissance Italian and French maskers who assumed behind their disguises the clamant court-jester and carnival prerogatives of speaking the truth and indicating with impunity, was founded in Los Angeles in November 1950, when five men, Hay, Bob Hull, Chuck Rowland, Dale Jennings and "R" met at Hay's home.

"In the first Mattachine Society," Hay reports, "we figured that the way we would come together and confide in each other was to come out to each other—absolutely unheard of, because most of us until that time had been so bedeviled by police stool pigeons on the one hand and blackmailers from the other side. Any names or addresses given to the newspapers would be published on the front page and all of us automatically would lose our jobs; we would lose our cars, lose our lodging; we'd be wiped out. This was the life and the terror under which we lived, so the whole idea of coming out to each other and learning who we were for the first time was something marvelous. We had a feeling of golden brotherhood." The whole movement began to develop by leaps and bounds. *ONE* magazine (from Thomas Carlyle's "All men together in a society of one") became the official organ of the Mattachines.

The second, and indeed finally more commanding hero of homosexual liberation, is Dr. Evelyn Gentry Hooker (what's in a name?), a Nebraska-born psychiatrist who demonstrated initially to her own and finally to significant others' satisfaction that the "projective testing" (and particularly the notorious Rorschach testing) routinely done on both avowed (usually felonious and collared) homosexuals and on those presumed to be in need of a correct diagnosis regarding the curve of their libidinous drives was so badly skewed as to prove fundamentally worthless. A professor of psychology at UCLA, married to Edward Hooker, an English Department Dryden specialist, and living in Santa Monica Canyon, she was brought up short by the realization that the derogatory remarks made about practicing homosexuals in pathology textbooks were assumed to apply to her neighbors Albert Grossman, Charles Aufdeheide, Gerald Heard and Christopher Isherwood—whose *Berlin Diary* had made his name in intellectual circles—holding a particular significance in light of her own earlier residence at the Institute for Psychology in Berlin, where she witnessed firsthand the Nazi accession of 1933. As a result, urged on by Isherwood ("She never treated us like some strange tribe, so we told her things we never told anyone before") and the philosopher Heard, and after an enlightening trip to San Francisco to see Finocchio's renowned drag show, she applied for and received from the National Institute for Mental Health the funding necessary for a series of substantive controlled experiments.

Her first difficulty was to find a sample of heterosexual men in California on equitable par in terms of commonly agreed cultural level with her pre-selected homosexual sample. Then, in 1953, the Mattachine Society and *ONE* helped her recruit seventy-four exclusively homosexual men who had never been in psychotherapy or in trouble with the law. That done, when asked to evaluate her result by acknowledged experts certain they could identify homosexuals from testing alone, and submitting matched pairs of Rorschach, TAT and other blind tests, the results proved that two more of the homosexual than of the heterosexual men were classifiable as well adjusted. Her results were published in the *Journal of Projective Techniques* in 1957 and 1958 as "The Adjustment in the Male Overt Homosexual."

Her earlier (1956) "Preliminary Analysis of Group Behavior in Homosexuals" in the *Journal of Psychology* examined the ways in which the so-called Gay Community lent support for those deprived of it in their background, thus improving their behavior and attitudes. "The most striking finding of the three judges," Hooker wrote, "was that many of the homosexuals were very well adjusted. In fact they agreed on two-thirds of the group as being average to superior in adjustment. Not only do all homosexuals not have strong feminine identifications [in those times constitutive of passive and passive-aggressive trait formations] nor are they all 'somewhat paranoid,' but according to the judges, may not be characterized by any demonstrable pathology."

Evelyn Hooker was appointed in 1967 by Dr. Stanley Holles of the National Institutes of Health to lead a Task Force on Homosexuality, a report buried by the Nixon administration. (Holles himself was fired.) She is rightly considered the originator of the battle to remove homosexuality-as-such as a pathology from the diagnostic manual of the American Psychological Association, finally effected in 1972 in Chicago. (Subsequently the University of Chicago set up the Evelyn Hooker Center for the Mental Health of Gays and Lesbians.)

In 1986 Evelyn Gentry Hooker was made the Grand Marshal of the Christopher Street West parade. She called this the high point of her life. She died at the age of ninety in 1997.

HAVING DISENTANGLED THE PREDICAMENT

Queer Street:

It doesn't start anywhere; it doesn't end there, either. Any attempt to suggest a beginning is necessarily arbitrary, and, as Yogi Berra famously decreed, it ain't over 'til it's over.

Instead, a congeries of argument, such as could be heard in those days at any hour of the day or night in clusters incessantly forming, dispersing, reforming and heading elsewhere, in Union Square, Washington Square, Bryant Park and the unofficial speakers corners in any saloon or cafeteria in town. Prime locations on the Queer Street map include:

The northwest corner of Queer and Attitude, just as Queer debouches into Fathers' Arms.

On all sides of the Alexander Fountain at Queer and Morningside.

Benches anent the Beloved Disciple mens' convenience at "Five Points" (convergence of Queer, Camp and Sighing Furnace).

Michelangelo Park at Queer and Reputaton.

"69" at 69 Lipstick (east side), four doors south of the intersection of Lipstick and Jewelry.

The Horn and Hardart on Promising, just off Pantaloon.

Suckers Alley, between Boxcars and Deep, in the Theater District.

The Shmooze Cafeteria, just off the southwest corner of Shmatta and Queer, in the Garment District.

The Free Woman Hall, in the cul-de-sac on Mortified.

The Bramble (a.y.o.r.) in Centaur Park.

The Standing-Room Line at the Metropolitan Opera House.

CHAPTER TWO

The Wherewithal

> "In storytelling there is an element that is deeply opposed to mortal judgment, that skirts its coercive side, eludes the descending knife. Storytelling is a going forward and a turning back, a wave-like movement in the voice, a continual cancelling of borders, a dodging of sharp spears. (And of horror vacui.)"
>
> —Roberto Calasso, *The Ruin of Kasch*

To begin the author's life in The Life with the official beginning of his life in The Life is neither, from the point of view of the strictest historical accuracy on the psychological plane, possible, nor what he wants. To begin at the beginning of his life proper, it would be necessary, in view of what is to come out, to declare unequivocally that he was *born that way*. He was, no question. Hence his nomination in the pages of *Queer Street*: Queer Temperament, or QT, as *on the*.

What he wants. (Who he is, where he comes from, what he wants, and where he's going: the four essential questions Stanislavsky required his actors to answer, scene for scene for every character in every play they played.)

He wants to parallel his attempt with "440," a painting he admires made by his friend Darragh Park who, when faced with eviction from the premises at 440 West 22nd Street, Chelsea, where for a generation he had made his home and conceived about half of his picture output (the urban motifs), and so forth—

ANATOMY IN A ROOM

A room not exactly rendered, not really presented, neither catalogued nor particularly coped with; what then?

We look at the picture; what we see (one way and another) is what we get: model of all epistemological situations (of time, of place, of situation, of predicament) in a fallen (disremembered) world, while the picture (two simultaneous views in an entangled state: a long view addressing momentum and a cross section addressing position) asks itself the question even the painter (of uncertain principle) is at a loss to answer: what's in it for me?

Focused light produces halation of highlights, propagated by beams reflecting off shiny surfaces. The hot pursuit of light generates more light. As the room lights up, the operations of memory, rumor and innuendo on the motif can be likened to trawling up the past in the maw of a gouger, destroying it to get at a few morsels—but these morsels, linking perception and reflection, make of voluntary seeing a vehicle of involuntary thought. Eyes see not only what passes across the field but also what is atomized in the room blurred by the collision in which field elements at one place-time-situation-predicament must interact with field elements in all other place-time-situation-predicaments. Images of things enacted according to the amplifying capacity (intrinsic spin) of the viewer's vehicular imagination and of the soluble-media envelope—emblematic of the mystery of origins, according to styles of measurement, now particular, now vague. (One of the illusions in the method is that the aqueous *facture* never dries—this is working the trapeze without a net.)

A parallel: The book as sliding panels: esthetic parallel to the layers of "440." So past and present may be slid one behind, or in front of the other. This happens in fact when a book is remembered; it may be remembered sequence-upon-sequence, but seldom *in* sequence beginning to end; more often out-of-sequence (the way a motion picture is shot), each scene according to the topic, or matter, it recalls to mind. For instance, Chelsea then and now, or the paradigm shift in Queer Street itself, recalling Thomas Kuhn's own emendation of the word *paradigm* to the word *exemplar*, itself a motion tacitly recognizing the emergence of a politics.

Marvelous journeys offered more than just pleasure, satisfaction of curiosity, amusement, escape, terror and thrills; they offered a more thorough explanation of the whole of reality than was available anywhere else. And they were complicated and otherwise modified—by stop-offs, by sidetracks—by a religious apprenticeship to the business of viewing motion pictures: the continual filmic communion with New York image after New York image on the post-war silver screen. Patterns of expectation were thereby forever set.

Events conspired; disembodied voices in the sempiternal New York night were, variously, alternate, some sites simultaneously menacing, powerless in the grip of obsession, salvific and lethal—epitomized in the voice of the faceless assassin we all learned to fear—hanging up the telephone as poor Barbara Stanwyck lay strangled in her bed on Sutton Place and the BMT rumbled over the Queensboro Bridge—announcing "Sorry, wrong number." (The ultimate homosexual truth: rejection equals death.)

The whole of the journey is the length of a room—an Appian Way of temples and shrines and other way stations (all evoked by, embodied in, furniture, pictures on the walls, tschotschkes, memorabilia). Pacing the room a reactivation of the ordeals of travel. Beckett's "the siege in the small room" (writing a book) and other comparisons of exteriors to interiors—or moments of claustrophobia balanced against a progressive agoraphobia: all characteristic of the melodrama of remembering and recording—in which, the Sufis maintain, the being who sighs with nostalgia is, while sighing, in sighing, identical to the being toward whom his nostalgia sighs. One and the same ardent desire is the cause of the manifestation and the cause/occasion of the return.

Thus on the walls of the room pictures of the street (in which the solitary recorder registers and mediates between his travel anxiety and his wanderlust) and, as it were, on the walls of the street, pictures of rooms (rooms seen through windows: the traveler mediating between his desire to cover the beat as an observer and his desire to *belong* as a participant within).

Two kinds of *tell-all* books have become familiar in reading rooms of the serious minded. Putatively self-revealing books by lonely crazies who don't get around much any more, and books of self-involvement by intensely committed gadabouts. Words every day between engagements.

Each appeals to an integral part of the fundamentally schizoid temperament of the common reader, who for the most part has lately come to favor the small book of consoling thoughts over the Grand Design treatises on self-improvement. (Wittgenstein's *Philosophical Investigations* is widely read, his *Tractatus Logicus-Philosophicus* is not.)

The voice of the author, Queer Temperament (QT) switches back and forth from one to another historical self—what happens in fact when a book is remembered: selective scene by selective scene (something is always missing, in the memory of the book in relation to the whole text as whole text in relation to the subject matter—see Harold Bloom's *A Map of Misreading*).

Whether or not there is or isn't a past (the Faulknerian denial), there is certainly no real past, or future either, in a book, although the illusion of both is easily sustained by flipping pages in one direction or another. Thus when it comes to ideas, developments, stories, the illusion of sequence is very easily dispensed with by rearranging narrative. There are ideas and stories told in voices QT hears as if from forty years ago; they come to a conclusion, or at any rate stop, at varying points in the trajectory of the late twentieth century.

Required of the author: accomplished narration; thick description, drawing on rich stores of classical and general literary recollection, refreshed upon occasion in a moderate way by invention. Queer Temperament thus attempts a grand *tour d'horizon* of queer life in America since the Second World War. Viewed by homosexual men as the grasping of an existential option between the Day World, with its ordinal criteria, and the Night World, with its deep and insatiable passions, accessed through the portal of twilight. A Night World viewed ordinal heterosexual society as the radical inverse of moral and civic duty—viewed it in fact as a sort of timeless communal existence of mutually enraptured, self-stimulating nothingness, akin to autism as Julia Kristeva might say.

Put another way, the author's window essays, like the similar work of most investigators, betray accretions of years of overheard and vis-à-vis opinion and commentary. Each topic that occurs to QT along the way and over the years is elaborated like a character. QT's ideas in any case are initially all amalgams of and reactions to things others said ("Most people are other people; they have other people's ideas, and come to other people's conclusions," said Otto Fenichel, who might well have added, especially writers.) However this state of affairs must be overcome: this is called becoming original, a seeming oxymoron, but there are simply no born originals, and that's that.

Queer Street proposes adopting Feynman's path-integral, sum-over-histories approach: all possible paths at once, including the enantiodromic, in order to: create particles with identical mass but opposite charge and spin.

The matter of the high school Forensic Society, in default of track and field and of swimming, because Author, at fourteen, would not consider giving up smoking Lucky Strikes right in the face of those street thugs he no longer encountered on the way home, a consequence of staying long hours in Brooklyn doing extracurricular activities.

Under the rubric of two meanings: the two meanings of forensic. Investigative reporter on the eighth Manhattan daily. Detail: vice.

Subcategory: homosexual. The snappy Big City remark, when entertained by a writer-temperament soon extends itself, but a kind of perpetual *esprit de l'escalier* and exuberance of structural invention into the long loop of the idea, and from there into the developed essay. Untenable, really, for point-scoring social conversation, but as in the example given by Oscar Wilde, who turned his epigrams into curvilinear one-liners and more in the late nineteenth century, eminently suitable for the increasingly dense late-twentieth-century private art form, the Theater of Oneself in Retaliation. (Gabriel Harvey in the sixteenth century spread his books out on a sort of Lazy Susan—or a roulette wheel—and spun them around copying out quotations, nearly willy-nilly, picking the ones he liked for his commonplace book and later reworking them.)

So, awake is back on the rack, the roulette wheel, or ferris wheel, or rotary Syntopicon.

Queer Street: a memoir of Somebody Thinking Out Loud. The Odyssey of a Temperament. QT becomes little by little Queer Theorist (Queer Temperament grown up, gone out and gotten some kind of certification). In place of the taxonomy of class, kin and ancestry, a kind of democracy, a certain preference for anonymity and the strenuous application of the principle of elective affinity. (Gore Vidal's admiration for Aaron Burr is tantalizing: Aaron Burr, of whom John Adams said that he had the strongest prejudice of any man in the country in favor of birth, parentage and descent, manifest in Vidal's high-anxiety personal myth of descent from an elevated American position, both social and political, and of the substitution in queer life of election for descent, not to merely mention, but to underline, Burr as outlaw and gunman, or duelist supreme, the echo of a more robust time, and a dressier bit of identification for the homosexual outlaw that any common killer would be.)

Wherefore, to write it up in a straight declarative-sentence way is a betrayal of what one thinks (or thinks one thinks): a compendium of what one has chosen to remember. And this too is a fiction: there is no evidence to support the idea of formal decision in this regard. Better to say what it has befallen one to remember: what is one's remembered lot.

Thus Queer Street is not a place anybody can walk down easily: they are forever digging it up, blocking off sections of it for publicity shoots, throwing up scaffolding, and such. Wherefore sites of contestation to which the Chorus of Queer Street Voices moved in the early years; Eighth Street, Greenwich Avenue, the Cherry Lane, Lenny's Hideaway; Mary's, Julius's,

Danny Monk's, The Modern, the Ninth Circle; the St. Marks Baths, the Everard Baths, the Metropolitan Opera standing-room line between 39th and 40th on Broadway, the Astor Bar "Flit" Side—and the infiltrated "Straight" Side at the opposite end—the other side of the mirror. Dozens of subway and Department of Parks mens' toilets (the "tea rooms"), the Ramble in Central Park, the Metropolitan Museum of Art, MoMA, the Frick Collection. Duffy's and the Sea Shack in Cherry Grove, on Fire Island, the Belvedere (the grandest beach house in the Grove), the Cherry Grove Playhouse.

Meanwhile, the text pitches a delicate and complex paradoxical and polemical dogma, composed of a putatively balsamic mixture of heady eroticism and ultimate renunciation. ("Some Enchanted Evening," "Hello, Young Lovers," "This Nearly Was Mine.")

In the Beginning was the Word on the Street, both spoken and written in chalk at timely spaced intervals, recorded then and there and recollected. The admonitory handwriting wasn't always scrawled on the tea room walls; sometimes it was done in chalk on the pavement, in between rainstorms, near the curb on the rim of the gutter. Sitting there, when we weren't looking up at the stars, we studied it, some harder than others.

If the role of objects is, as Samuel Beckett has insisted, to restore silence, what then is the proper function of lists? To jump-start the argument, as such.

1. Midway in a life stretch—stationed (here one is
   in the darkling City of Uncounted Souls)
   between the buff boys of the Chelsea night, ripped
   all, like Alpha-male delicatessen, work
   of Paul Cadmus, and Charles Demuth. What would you
   do? Pray—pray like there was no tomorrow, as
   if End Time were nigh (the odds are with you,
   all told). Do it.

2. Notice to the sensitive and musical:
   Take this Down: The poem is the story
   of the poem: imagine it free of association.
   But then the feeling that the sides are falling
   off? Wing it, it's only words.
   Oh, no it's not and you know
   it's not. Metaphor's one thing, but simile?

One thing is never much like
another—see the poetry of James
Schuyler. Wise up. (Oh, and while I have you,
yodeling into the word-warp's
not writing poetry either. Now you know.)

3. Thus was each new
    link in the chain
    of generations opened—no genealogy of kings
    but this linking of scores of faggot stories
    E Hoie—
    The Mattachines, *Physique Pictorial, ONE*
    And *A Star is Born.*
    (Overheard at Carnegie Hall—and don't ask,
    you know what night: "Homosexual life as
    we live it today, dates from the release of
    A Star is Born.")

4. Reason so many of these political queens are so
    desperate to be taken *seriously* is
    this: their chances of being seriously
    taken are next to nil. Do you care if there's
    a gay gene? Do you care, really, if there are
    queer giraffes? Get over it. (Now isn't that
    the ultimate get-tough Statement of The Life.
    But if anybody ever *did* get over it, what would
    life be? This is sacred eschatology?)

5. Our take on the collective narcissistic
    pathos of the Committee is: Misery
    loves company, but it just *hates*
    competition. Queer life is a bit like jazz
    styles: in New York it tends to be that much more
    pulsory. In Chicago and the Midwest
    it's inclined to emphasize coloration.

6. The cruel irony of "I Will Survive." All those wild
    orebaisia dancing boys taking every drug there
    was in the world to go on
    (with the self-regard theretofore thought proper

exclusively to noumena) in the terrible and
apparently incessant floor show their lives
had become. (As a consequence, we've always
assumed that most of the leashed pig boys we see
around Town are off-duty investment bankers.)

7. AC/DC/B.C./A.D. A-E-I-O-U.
   AM/FM/AM/PM/SM/UPS/COD
   And if livin' for myself is
   what I'm guilty of, go on and sentence me,
   I'll still be free.
   Oh, really?

8. The point is, either you did see Tanaquil
   Le Clercq in action or you did not, and if
   you did not, you are that Next Generation
   not simply beset by anxiety, but
   excuse me, there's no tactful way to put this,
   crippled with it; period. And Tanaquil
   Le Clercq is only the beginning: she heads
   the list of everything else you missed. Sorry.

9. What is Fame? The Renaissance-Reformation
   corruption of the medieval doctrine
   of sanctifying grace.
   And Power? The Renaissance-Reformation
   corruption of the medieval doctrine
   of actual grace.

10. What are the four last things?
    The thing of it.
    The thing to do.
    The sweet young thing.
    "That my thing was on the floor."

11. This just in: *Noun, Nauni, Amoun, Amauni*
    (No, darling, not Armani, *Am-a-uni*).
    The second movement of Samuel Barber's
    Violin Concerto is the most sublime
    piece of music yet composed by a homosexual

in America. Nothing written by any other
homosexual in America comes
even close (although certain parts of the Piano Quintet
of Amy Marcy Cheney Beach . . .). And meanwhile,
Eleanor was the end gorgeous in *Vanessa*, not to
mention *Knoxville: Summer of 1915*.

And that's when the fight started—or so they said.

CHAPTER THREE

Certain Shades of Limelight

> "Yes, and we are easy to find. Under bridges, at the back end of piers, in parks when parks are closed, in the shadows of others, in the night."
> —Jamie O'Neill, *At Swim, Two Boys*

Wherein amid murmurs of the darkening of the American '50's sunlight vision—in big book fiction in William Styron's Lie Down in Darkness *and* Set This House on Fire, *in James Gould Cozzens's* By Love Possessed, *on the Broadway stage in Tennessee Williams's* Cat on a Hot Tin Roof, *William Inge's* Picnic, *Robert Anderson's* Tea and Sympathy, *and onscreen in Alfred Hitchcock's* Vertigo, *and Douglas Sirk's* Written on the Wind *and* Imitation of Life, *the* Time *magazine restlessness of the Beat Generation and the consequent apparition of queer culture in mainstream life—the author, styled as Queer Temperament, first encounters openly queer street life on Eighth Street and Greenwich Avenue.*

Queer Street, while imagining itself Quality Street, experiences itself as Back Street and the penumbral Boulevard of Broken Dreams, whole stretches of which most resemble the Coney Island board-walk. The street, like queer identity itself, evolves over the decades into a post-modern, non-linear cluster-fuck event construction, a sexual Potemkin village, a metaphoric Warners back lot, and its Sibyls and high priestesses (Lana Turner to Louis Calhern in *The Prodigal*: "Just remember, you may be the high priest, but I'm the high priestess"), from Bert Savoy (famously struck by lightning on that very Coney Island promenade when during a summer storm he talked back to a thunderbolt, declaring, "That'll be enough out of you, Miss God!"), down through T.C. Jones, Charles Pierce to Charles Ludlam, Charles Busch, Ethyl Eichelberger and the amazing Lypsinka. And especially with what went on underneath that promenade (in the days when you'd see kids peeking through the slatted boards and night cops full of giddy mirth running flashlights over them and crying "Meow").

The Big City had two entirely different meanings for straight and queer children.

The former were as likely to be excited by it, and plan for it, but what they were planning by and large was working the daytime city. (Night porters, night clerks, night doorman and nightclub personnel might be jobs taken while working their way through college, but the goal was a corporation day position). They might live in it, raise families in it (or in its accessible leafy suburbs), but they would generally (unless we could snag them at cocktails) be home for supper, and if out again afterwards, certainly be home (unless, again, we could induce them to miss their trains, call home and bunk with a—"you and him once, honey"—buddy in downtown) not so long after midnight (on weekdays).

The latter were driven to wonder about and begin (very often early on via the seductive availability of rapid transit) to seek out if not yet the City of Night, then certainly the City of Twilight. This was part of getting one's message, and knowing that the Guiding Light is of hermetic provenance, designed according to the rules of art, and antipathetic to the oppressive sunlight with which the workaday world contends.

A hermeneutics, however, for which closet cases in church choirs, living at home with aging parents, perhaps teaching in high schools, provided no keys, no evidence. As observed these might take in a matinee with mother (something no doubt with the Lunts in it), which alerts us to the fact they held supposedly advanced ideas about the way heterosexuals behave, and even lunch at the Stork Club or 21. But the story was, if they came out, or if we were thinking of doing likewise, that peril wasn't the half of it; almost certain annihilation, like the girl model victim in *The Naked City* (1948, Jules Dassin), in the way of hooking up with the Fatal Stranger was if not absolutely, then reckoned so statistically more certain as to rate as a terror in contemplate.

(The girl's parents are being quizzed by police, while out the police station window the New York skyline looms. The mother, crazed with anger at the victim for having left home somewhere out there in the Midwest to come to the big city, pours out invective while the silver fortress glistens, mocking, in the daylight.

"Bright lights, Theaters! Furs and nightclubs. Why didn't she stay at home?!")

The city is by reputation hard, cruel and cynical, but the author's New York is somewhat softened, at one and the same time by its native familiarity and by the mythical vision of it set out by Hollywood, in those days still its client state, in which Barbara Stanwyck, in *Golden Boy*, promises William Holden "You could make all that your carpet to walk on." In which, in *The Fountainhead* (1948, King Vidor), Gary Cooper builds its fabulous futuristic skyscrapers; in which Central Park becomes a fantasy dancing ground for sailors (in *On the Town*) and Joseph Cotten and Jennifer Jones, in *Portrait of Jennie* (1948, William Dieterle), enact a symbolist melodrama of the city as lost girl and forsaken dream.

Queer viewers were able to cross-identify: with the yearning female element as well as with the ill-defined male trace, or vestige, and also to determine a coign of vantage on the oblique (as they were able to do also in two directions—uptown and downtown—through Hitchcock's *Rope*: its coffin-centered killers' lair the emblem of the most nearly explicit homosexual melodrama of the immediate post-war period).

The world pictured onscreen, viewed again on the bias by the penumbral and ambiguous figures such as fight trainers and promoters, swishy makers of snide remarks, loner cowboys featured as the heroes' sidekicks, bachelor sergeants in war pictures and furthermore.

And in those days, in summer, other voices in other rooms spilled out into the street, in the Village often giving out an invitation to a bottle party. Stylish New York intrigue was largely an indoor business, an *acquis communitaire* negotiated behind the windows in the skyline's million slits. Gene Tierney's and Clifton Webb's apartments in *Laura* (1944, Otto Preminger), Bette Davis's penthouse loft in *Deception* (1947, Irving Rapper), all skylight view and grand piano (and said to be modeled on Leonard Bernstein's first New York loft apartment), Joan Crawford's modest Village flat in *Daisy Kenyon* (1947, Otto Preminger).

To the author, thinking back decades later but fixing on the vantage point of 1950, the city revealed itself as the Matter of prose romance chiefly through the prismatic lens of a single career studded with New York roles: in 1978, to honor the seventieth birthday of Bette Davis in *Film Comment*, he assembled a New York-through-the-years-as-seen-by the protean persona of a great Hollywood star.

Bette Davis. The suppressed hysteric with the pinwheel strut appeared in pictures over the space of two decades, playing out the dream of the rise to the top by way of the dewy ingenue opposite an improbable, but convincing, George Arliss in *The Man Who Played God*, and speaking of improbable, as the completely recessive good girl in *Three on a Match*, then the gal reporter in *Front Page Woman*, followed by the earnest, hard-working brick-of-a-gal in *The Girl from Tenth Avenue*. Finally, in *Dangerous*, she unleashed her inner '30s neurotic, in her first Oscar-winning performance, the down-and-out Broadway actress (modeled on Jeanne Eagels, dead at forty in 1929), followed quickly by the more multidimensional nightclub-moll-beaten-to-a-pulp-and-turned-States-Evidence witness in *Marked Woman*, on up to Long Island-cum-Gotham socialite Judith Traherne, in *Dark Victory*, the performance of her career. As the aging old-money narcissist Fanny Trellis Skeffington opposite the great Claude Rains in *Mr. Skeffington* and, in the long home stretch, as the renowned Gotham author Kit Marlowe ("I know practically everyone in New York") opposite the hilarious Miriam Hopkins in *Old Acquaintance*, the concert pianist-murderer Christine Radcliffe in *Deception*, both painter-good twin Kate Bosworth and no-good freelance home wrecker Pat Bosworth in *A Stolen Life*, exquisite poet Susan Grieve in *Winter Meeting*, fashion magazine editor-in-chief Linda Gilman in *June Bride*, and finally, and consummately, as the fabulous Margo Channing in *All About Eve*, reigning supreme over a swarm of hectic comedians ("You're in a beehive, pal; we're all busy little bees, full of stings, making honey").

As a consequence, it was an article of queer faith that Bette (or more exactly Margo Channing) knew all the trouble every faggot went through. She loved us for them (in particular the older among us, for whom, from the seventies on, the New-York-is-not-what-it-was blues set in). They imagined Margo returning from time to time, stalking the old locations, sitting alone in winter, a shopping-bag lady in a sable coat, in the pocket park where the Stork Club once stood, and skulking through decrepit Broadway byways where she had swaggered not all that long ago, then quietly boarding the Brewster train at Grand Central for "that little place just two hours from New York" that used to be on her list of things she would never understand, like collecting shrunken Indian heads.

Bette/Margo understood us all: we were our woe, our woe was us, like Jesus Christ. ("Am I a Jew?" Pilate asked. "Your people and your chief priests have delivered you to me. What have you done?" We reply, "A fucking lot more than you, Mary!" "Your chief priests have made accusations." "Concerning my erotic proclivities? They don't like it, they could shove it up their ass.") Something terribly grand had come over us: the wild, reckless grandeur of captured ill-treated things. Royalty sent into exile.

Freud's myth of descent from a high place came into it. Like Euripides's Ion, one was a changeling prince, and although not necessarily splenetive (we all wanted to play Hamlet, especially after seeing Donald Madden do so at the Phoenix Theater in 1961), one was rash and did have in oneself something dangerous.

In the line of looking back through the years, sometime in the early '80s, the author, interviewed for *Christopher Street* by the poet and critic J.D. McClatchy, was asked,

"When did you first twig to the fact you were queer?"

"Two weeks into the first grade, January 1947."

"That sounds snappy, but really."

"But really. Look, I played doctor with the girl up the block and got caught. I played doctor with the boy down the block and didn't. So there I am, sitting in the first grade wondering how many boys I can play doctor with and not get caught."

"Moving right along, what were you doing in the nineteen-fifties?"

(This and all the following replies, perhaps a little neon, nevertheless fairly encapsulates a not atypical New York homosexual temperament of the period.)

I was aging from going-on-ten to going-on-twenty, the way the family said I always did everything: the hard way. Going to parochial school, going to church, going steady. Reading through "the columns" of seven New York dailies. Getting tickets for Broadway shows (for some of which, such as *The Rose Tattoo, Cat On a Hot Tin Roof, Orpheus Descending, Picnic,* one neither wrote up reports for the high school newspaper, nor attempted discussion at the dinner table). Hanging out in Shubert Alley and on the standing-room line at the Old Met. Working summer jobs. In an artists' materials store in the Village—the famous Delsemme's, patronized both by members of the 10th Street Cedar Tavern crowd and the sort of painters whose works ended up draped all over Washington Square in the outdoor exhibits of the period—and in the office of a stevedoring contracting firm on lower Broadway, dispatched from there as a paymaster on assorted piers on the New York waterfront. (Years later, standing in the daylight in front of these, fallen into dangerously dilapidated condition and employed as a twenty-four-hour queer fuck pit, Author mentioned casually to one companion in particular, "I used to hand out pay envelopes from a cubbyhole in there to the real versions of the trade in the longshoreman costume they all like to go down on with such vehemence.")

Observation on the author:

"Butter wouldn't melt in that mouth."

"Butter wouldn't get the chance."

Acting in school plays, reading, at first intermittently and then incessantly, rather ostentatiously sitting out crucially forensic intermissions at the opera to signal the strong commitment to print life. Traveling around America on Greyhound buses. Hanging out at Rockaway and Riis Park, then, past sixteen "getting away" with friends (queer code for lying about one's companions, in whose company one was categorically jail bait) for weekends in East Hampton and Fire Island. Going to nightclubs and gay bars: dancing with girls, dancing with men, and all the while carrying torches for boys in high school and college—boys with flawless insouciant New York techniques for reciprocating just enough to make matters worse. Suffering like a Christian.

McClatchy: The usual neighborhood taunts?

Author: Yes, but with an even more unnerving twist.

> Chorus of Threatening Voices:
> Cause you're a fag
> The way you walk,
> Talk, smoke, dance, You're
> A fag. Stay off
> The street. Stay home.
> You come out, fag
> You'll get the teeth
> Kicked outta your
> Fuckin' head. Stay
> Home indoors, fag.
> Don't make a move.

How he walks, how he talks. Were these barbarians studying him, like he was a book or a play or a set of blueprints? Not fucking likely; they're going with the rumors.

Which is really just terribly unfair. Is he down the cellar behind the Polk movie (the local temple of cinematic art—further afield: the Corona, the Jackson, the Colony, the Boulevard, the Granada, the Valencia, the

Sunnyside, the Triboro, the Flushing, the Prospect, et cetera) in the circle jerk with them, saving up shot spunk in communal milk bottles? It's manners to wait till you're asked; he hasn't been asked.

On the other hand, friendless, alone and alert, might he become even better equipped to take in the message and devise queer readings for such epochal transmissions to come as *The Prodigal*—Edmund Purdom crawling back to Daddy to be good again, having debased himself in thrall to that tramp of tramps Miss Lana Turner. (And later on down the pike wasn't it really she what stuck the shiv into Johnny Stompanato's flabby guts on that Holy Thursday night in godless Hollywood, letting daughter Cheryl take the rap?)

From *Rebel Without a Cause*: James Dean, the archetypal troubled '50s god-boy worshipped not at all from afar, but from extremely close quarters, by Sal Mineo, with the affection reciprocated yet.

And from *The Egyptian*: Bella Darvi, as a vengeful Fata Morgana: queer soul identified with her leprosy, forecast of all future STDs. Visionary queer pharaoh— Akhenaton—finds God. Dumb hustler Edmund Purdom is brought low by Fortune. Smart military hustler Victor Mature accedes to ultimate corrupt power, as successor pharaoh to queer visionary.

They're also giving one another blow jobs. They're talking about fucking one another. And he's a fag. They can eat shit. He should call the *News* and *Mirror*. And the news is they have a mirror. Everything they do they do in the mirror.

None of this sprang up unbidden out of nowhere, however, although were these activities brought to the attention of the rectory, murmurs of diabolic possession would undoubtedly be heard, and the diocese might well be brought into it.

No, it all seems to have started with the building super. Lonely guy, keeps himself to himself, you know. Started letting them use the cellar last summer to play poker in, and of course because it was so hot and there was no air conditioning anywhere in those days except in the movie theaters, poker turned into strip poker in nothing flat.

In return he's allowed to take Polaroids of the whole gang at it.

This is the guy (not at all a bad-looking guy, not at all like the hoople pervert the FBI is warning every parent in the country against) who last year started taking the whole gang, the author among them, all the way to Brooklyn on the subway, to swim in the Olympic-regulation-size pool at the St. George Hotel in Brooklyn Heights, and also introduced them to the invigorating practice of going into the steam room and the hot room after swimming. (Author remembers a line from *All About Eve*, "The little witch must have sent out Indian runners to barrooms and steam rooms and wherever else critics hang out.") Whereupon much was gleaned concerning certain proclivities of ugly older naked men.

Also he reads to them, Author has been informed, from the *Kinsey Report*, *Sexology* magazine and all the latest journals, how the whole guy-guy thing is only a phase, one he wants to help them get through, and teach them how eventually to get tantric about it: whereby you can plug it into her and go forever without coming, making her scream, hit the ceiling and become your sex slave for life, or however long you want it to last, it'll be your call, and meanwhile document the progress for his M.A. in Sociology (from CCNY).

The Polaroids he can have copied for a nominal price, and meanwhile they can wear paper bags over their heads with the eyes and mouths cut out and funny crayon marks on them, like Halloween masks (or, as Author remembers years later, the famous Saul Steinberg shoot of his friends in masks he designed). The bolder among them say, "Fuck it, man, show our faces—who gives a shit." What guys. Hilarious.

As Jo Van Fleet told James Dean in *East of Eden*, "That's pretty funny—if you don't think that's funny, you better not go to college."

So this sociologist tells them he's teaching them lots of different ways to play at fetch. That's what he says, play *at* fetch, not play fetch, like getting the dog to fetch the newspaper—which almost nobody in the neighborhood knows anything about anyway except from Andy Hardy movies, as paper boys are dying out fast in Jackson Heights; there's only one paper boy job still going strong, for the *Long Island Star Journal*, a really shitty rag, and everybody gets the *Journal-American*, the *Daily News* and the *Daily Mirror* at the candy store, even the little fag who buys the *New York Times* and delivers it to the nuns.

Anyway this guy, this mentor as he calls himself, is teaching them to play at fetch and, believe it or not, actually photographing them in dog collars with leashes attached to them, and does Guido Gavone not dig it the most to get down on all fours and bark when somebody shoots. Fetch in, get this, the Victorian sense—as if anybody in the neighborhood ever heard of Queen Victoria or even saw Irene Dunne in *The Mudlark*, and explaining to them how they can find this *original meaning* as he calls it in the CCNY library, or in the main reading room of the New York Public Library on 42nd Street.

Author has been there; it's not far from Shubert Alley, on which he has, consequence of attending Broadway shows with parents and older brother, a fairly sophisticated take, right down to getting certain men he talks to there to buy him tickets for shows he would have the same trouble getting into by himself as he has had getting into condemned movies like *Smiles of a Summer's Night, I Am a Camera, The Young and the Damned* and *Bitter Rice*.)

Only you have to be careful, warns sociologist mentor and dog trainer, of the place and the park behind it, Bryant Park, named for the author of a great American poem "Thanatopsis," all about death, because in the men's can right across the hall from the catalogue room where the *Oxford English Dictionary* is, and in the mausoleum-like convenience in Bryant Park, it's exactly like the pool at the St. George Hotel—see above—or in any of the subway men's rooms on every platform they pass along the way. There are slimy sick old perverts in both places, plus plainclothes cops posing as young perverts in the line of duty to catch these slimy sick fucks and put them away in Sing Sing, where they have to be locked away in a special cell block to keep the normal criminals from slitting their throats—which they get to do regularly anyway, in mess hall or in the showers, only it never makes the papers.

Oxford for these boys can mean only one thing, and that's shoes, oxfords and cordovans (they buy theirs at Thom McAn's, whereas Author, instructed by his brother gets his father to take him to McCreedy and Schreiber on West 44th Street, not far from Shubert Alley, to get the genuine article, onto the heels of which, following the current fashion, he has the shoemaker nail steel taps), which are pretty much the same thing, and that makes Author, who knows Oxford and Cordova are places, in England and Spain respectively (*A Yank at Oxford, They Came to Cordova*), think about words and learning and his ambition to go around the world (which is funny, because that's another thing—going around the world—that this mentor has promised to teach his cellar-sex Boy Scout troupe this summer).

Thus when the Big Guy offered to take them camping in the spring—out in the Plandome woods, and photograph them doing it bosky, he started calling them the Boy Scuts (which in an Irish Catholic parish had the same resonance it would have had in the the Old Country, where *scut* was the word the priest used, chasing you out of the confessional with a blackthorn stick, if you dared fill his ears with more filth than he could reasonably be expected to absolve). Author can just imagine them writing little compositions about this, whatever it is, when they get back to school after Labor Day.

A love of punning had already arisen from an earlier instance of linguistic confusion. At the opera, on the way out of the broadcast matinee *Salome*, in which the wayward flame-haired Bulgarian diva Ljuba Welitsch had created a more than merely vocal sensation, the author had heard a voice on the sidewalk—a voice addressing a mixed-gender clutch of opera goers at the head of the long standing-room line waiting to go in to the evening performance—proclaim, "Mary, what a *camp*." At home he asked what it means and was told, "I haven't any idea; they're starting to let a lot of riffraff into that place, and you can't tell what's going to come out of their mouths." *Riffraff* in the opera house. Standing room. Hm. *Riffraff* was a movie with Jean Harlow, lately featured in *Life* in a big spread on Marilyn Monroe. Harlow died at twenty-six. He'd be twenty-six in fifteen years.

So: Fetch. Author makes his way to the aforementioned card catalogue room of the New York Public Library on 42nd Street and looks up all the senses historically recorded in the *Oxford English Dictionary* of "fetch," and there it sort of was, between the entries "to make the butter come by churning" and "to fetch the pump: to obtain a flow of water by priming." You had to be a little attuned to language to get it. He is, of course, unique among his fellows (former fellows, for he has been thrown down, thrown out and threatened by them all), no stranger to the New York Public Library on 42nd Street (or as a matter of fact either to the men's room upstairs anent the Main Reading Room, or to the mausoleum in Bryant Park). He has for some time now been seen going in and out of Central Circulation a couple of times a month, taking out the Burns Mantle annual *Best Plays* anthologies and memorizing the plots of all the ones—most of them—he hasn't seen, so as to lie about having been in the audience sometime in the future. (He doesn't know quite when, but he knows as well as he knows his own by now three names that he will.)

Yes, he has three names now; he has been confirmed—he took John, for the Beloved Disciple, also said back then to be the author of the Fourth (the best) Gospel and of the Apocalypse (forbidden to be read by Catholics except under the supervision of a priest; he of course tried it anyway and couldn't get into it).

He has also gotten drunk for the first time in his life at his Confirmation party, a second rite of passage rather more sophisticated than the sacrament (although, like the amorous Queen of the Fairies in Gilbert and Sullivan's *Iolanthe*, he may not say so).

Moreover, apropos rites of passage, he too has felt the pangs of love, and may not say so much about that either (or more exactly may say so much, and be gently and mockingly cheered up by family and friends, so long as he lies and says it was a girl). Nevertheless his knowledge such as it is of the doings down the cellar (or, as also happened, up the roof) is none of it practical information. The dissemination of this information (he's already into puns) could leave the informer seriously maimed.

And learn to walk quiet—get the taps off the shoes.

What next?

A life, all told, crowded with incident, semi-veiled in secrecy and run on edgy bravado. Not perhaps a genuinely happy life—they were difficult years of severe and mounting trouble—except that it was being led in New York in a time which was even then in no uncertain terms recognized as epochal. One became interested in, relied upon, revelations—the four-star late night final, *in alles was der Fall ist,* in great men and turning points.

McClatchy: A couple of years ago they were saying the '80s are like the '50s. I'll be you don't think so.

Author: The they who were saying that were trying to say something that could not be said about the American post-Vietnam, schizo-affective depression prevalent in the first Reagan administration like anything else said about America at any period, it could have had next to nothing to do with the facts of New York life as we know them. As we know them now, we know them in large part in terms of what's missing. The Rialto. The waterfront. The Lunts. Cardinal Spellman. Dorothy Kilgallen. Hitchcock. The Old Met, the old Pennsylvania Station. Maria Meneghini Callas. Judy. Merman.

THE HIERARCHIES

McClatchy: The hierarchies? What about them?

Author: The Renaissance idea of the Great Chain of Being, exploded in modernism and early psychoanalysis, has been replaced in our time of postmodernism and late psychoanalysis, for as long a time as anyone can envision, by the notion of the Immense Grid of experience. Everything about the vertical—aspiration, hierarchies, from Chartres to the Chrysler Building—is being replaced by modular ideation in the immense Los Angeles interlock. We still dream in and of New York, but the paramount aggregate has gone L.A. Which of course is the cabalistic meaning of the accusation the Girl

Who Calls Herself Phoebe (and why not) puts to Eve Harrington (née Gertrude Slescynski) in the climactic scene in the hotel room.

"You're going to Hollywood, aren't you?"

"Uh-huh"

"From the trunks you're packing you must be going to stay a long time."

"I might."

(Which in itself is a screen reply, the true meaning of which is, I might as well.)

When there were hierarchies, there were rubrics. In later years advanced queer politics would deploy an extensive rhetoric to deplore two things:

1. Oedipal Reliance on Bette.

Let's forget gay sensibility, shall we? Let's forget the novels of Mildred Watson Drake (*Married in June, Geraldine, Girl Afraid, Lingering Love,* etc.), the single novel of Kit Marlowe (*Bury My Soul*) and Kit Marlowe's Broadway play in which Julia Broadbent stars (*Nostalgia in Chromium*). The two plays of Lloyd Richards's that Margo Channing starred in and the one she dropped out of, allowing Eve Harrington to shoot to stardom in the role of Cora (*Remembrance, Aged in Wood* and *Footsteps on the Ceiling,* respectively). Let's forget all that and so much else and just talk a little about queer perspective. Then, later, we'll get back to Millie and Kit and *Old Acquaintance,* and to Margo and Bill and Karen and Lloyd and Addison and Miss Caswell, to Max Fabian and Birdie Coonan's memories of the French Ventriloquist, as the sun sets beyond Hell's Kitchen, while the sun shines bright in Eve Harrington's Los Angeles.

2. The plotting of queer dream life along the lines of the heterosexual paradigm, essentially decrying the sloppy seconds approach: the double-dating queer dreaming the Impossible Dream, longing to snatch the other boy on the excursion for himself and head out with him—without leaving the Big City—for The Territory: a feat quite impossible to bring off—quite outside the range of actual possibilities for all but the bi-located glorified body sketched in the Baltimore Catechism. But where was the queer boy to meet Prince Charming, if not somehow, at the prom—some prom? The problem with annihilating the mirror-fantasy approach was simple: what could be imagined without something to mirror. Only dark places and groping, almost certainly unsanitary hands: thrilling enough to entertain for a time (like a '30s horror movie) but not something to dwell on, to fully imagine the way things were fully imagined back then, in glorious Technicolor, breathtaking CinemaScope and stereophonic sound.

All About Eve: itself something of a nostalgic way station midway in his cinematic ontogenesis between the violent childhood fantasies engendered by saturation (at the Polk theater) in film noir and Hitchcock's *Rope* and the even more volcanic disruptions brought on (an exacerbation of pubescent upsurge, hardly required, but a royal flush is a royal flush) by the Technicolor melodramas of Douglas Sirk and Nicholas Ray, *Magnificent Obsession, All That Heaven Allows, Written on the Wind, The Tarnished Angels, Imitation of Life, Rebel Without a Cause, Johnny Guitar* and *King of Kings*.

(Many years later Author would retroactively and on the bias incorporate into his meditations James Merrill's "The Black Swan," written in 1947, published in the same year as Salinger's *The Catcher in the Rye*, as the most elegant expression of his own rather inelegant feelings in this period of adjustment.)

Essentially however *the* events of 1956–1957 were the Metropolitan Opera debut of Maria Meneghini Callas and the release of Douglas Sirk's *Written on the Wind*. The Callas impact was immediate, but it took another few years (and the publication of the auteur theory) for the author to understand how one director had been responsible for changing his life.

(Years later again, when he met Douglas Sirk, wearing that Persian lamb-collared coat indoors at a party given by MoMA's film department, all he could say was "I'm so happy to meet you, *Written on the Wind* changed my life."

"Oh? How?")

To begin with, it was not really the content—or the redemption of the content (of the weepies, or women's pictures) or even Sirk's and Ross Hunter's casting of superior screen actresses (Jane Wyman, Dorothy Malone, Agnes Moorehead, Lauren Bacall) to buttress the central argument: the redemption of America through male suffering in peacetime, or even his and the great Russell Metty's unique handling of the Rock's amazingly photogenic American-hunk ambiguity. (Sirk read T.S. Eliot to him, presumably to get him a little misty.) It was first and foremost the formal disposition of the Sirkian frame: the impression in set-up after set-up of austere isolation in the all-too-overcrowded '50s wider screen, letting the viewer know that in spite of prosperity, in spite of the trumpeted comforts of conformity in the postwar paradise on view, this director believed the core truth of American life to be what it has always been: radical estrangement, radical loneliness.

That being the case, being alone not only like Rock Hudson but, against all the odds in the world, *with* Rock Hudson, beat out being alone with

Christ in Gethsemane hands down (that is, until the early '60s, when Nicholas Ray cast Jeffrey Hunter and Robert Ryan as Christ and John the Baptist in *King of Kings* and in so doing, perhaps unwittingly, invested American Christianity with a blazing new glamour not even Billy Graham had mustered).

Magnificent Obsession and *All That Heaven Allows*—two blindness pictures, in the first of which Rock, as reckless playboy turned godly eye surgeon and strapping benefactor of mankind, literally gives Jane Wyman back the sight in the loss of which he had been recklessly instrumental, and in the second, as neo-Thoreauvian seer in the guise of arborist colliding with a well-off country-club widow with two grown but regressed children and a well-meaning but thickheaded neighbor ("Carrie, your gardener?" "He's not my gardener, Sarah, he comes to trim the trees") and deciding to see to it she ends up seeing for herself and knowing on her own terms what is essential in life.

In *Magnificent Obsession*, Jane Wyman is blind and that's that. It is a picture in which the camera does nearly all the acting; in which Rock and Jane are really voice-overs for a ninety-minute sequence of exquisitely rendered rooms and enclosed exteriors—the two finally meeting in the operating theater and (in the most perfect match of interior and exterior in one shot in all of '50s Hollywood cinema) the recovery room of a private clinic in the middle of the Arizona desert (vibrating out the window). In *All That Heaven Allows*, Jane inhabits a tight little world in a tight big house with room dividers and latticed front windows barring her from a new life. She is widowed, worried, trapped, resigned, riddled with decency and alone. (Situations that, were they calculated to do so, could not be improved upon as devices for driving a "sensitive" adolescent over the edge or into a novitiate.) Rock, the tree man and barn-renovating builder, possesses the ultimate in demure strength (somebody, or something, likely the astral Genius of Hollywood Itself, must have remembered Richard Barthelmess) of a frank and open, but quite white, nature; innocent of cerebral guile, blessed with patience. Galahad to the rescue, the lady rescued. America, had she listened to Thoreau. It is Sirk's most wistful picture; it says "would that it were."

Which led straight to author's queer adaptation of certain movies: a *Magnificent Obsession* in which the son becomes the doctor's love object and the mother—still Jane Wyman, but a more finally accepting Jane Wyman—becomes the surprise guardian angel, a Gay Pride mom *ante literatem*; Hitchcock's *Vertigo* rethought as *Pervertigo*, but still starring Kim

Novak, as a boy. Only in New York that boy had better not try jumping into the East River under any of the bridges; the East River, not a river at all, but a turbulent strait, would sweep him away in two seconds; he wouldn't even get to be fished out, the way Ida Lupino was in *The Hard Way*.

In this same way (as a presentiment of Harold Bloom's great *Map of Misreading* insight) many versions of the same essential private strategy were adopted by every homosexual who avidly sat through heterosexual melodrama after heterosexual melodrama, evidence in spades of the mind's scope (especially the scope of one of Norma Desmond's wonderful people out there in the dark), equal in every instance, in freedom, flexibility and special effects to anything served up there on the screen.

And even without the plot-wrenching, the author was able to identify in no time at all with Jane Wyman as she was in *Magnificent Obsession* and *All That Heaven Allows*, and with Dorothy Malone (about whom you couldn't in your right mind alter a single quality) in *Written on the Wind* and *The Tarnished Angels*, both of which ladies changed his life. And how.

CHAPTER FOUR

Identity and the Masks of Enclosure

(THE EXISTENTIAL QUEER)

> "Man is least himself when he talks in his own person. Give him a mask and he will tell you the truth."
> —Oscar Wilde, *The Critic as Artist*
>
> "Darling, in faggotry there is absolutely no distinction between fiction and fact—none. A true story is simply one that hasn't yet turned on the teller. 'Believe that one and I'll tell you another' is absolute faggot gospel, and make it come true the one and only authentic, heartsick, heartfelt faggot prayer. Slow curtain, the end."
> —Diane DeVors, to the author

JACOB, THE PUBLICAN AND THE GOOD THIEF
(Narcissism and Dissembling in the Usurper)

Jacob and the Publican (who comes into it only sideways) were two tales, one a lush, exotic Old Testament saga illustrated in polychrome in Bible Stories, the other a severe New Testament vignette, Luke's parable of silence, exile and cunning illustrated in stained glass in our parish church. These operated on me, the second son, with a kind of intertextuality, although I read neither of them the way I read the Oz books or the *Odyssey*, and neither was made into a motion picture—a lack lately redressed, to no avail, by Turner Television. (Billed as a vibrant "holiday" release, *The Story of Jacob* was a caper that would have been hooted off the screen in my youth. No wonder

Americans resort to Bible theme parks. Is there a Jacob's Ladder ride some-where, or are we fabulists to hold out for the fine tuning of Virtual Reality?)

Jacob was one of the many stories read out by exuberant nuns, one's pri-mary school teachers (given to notions of angels and of dreaming), and one of the two sources of Bible intelligence, the other and far less compelling, source being the Gospel and Epistle fragments upon which the priests' rou-tinely deadly Sunday sermons were pegged. Catholics did not read the Bible at home. All Catholic families then were (happily) alike. All Protestant families were (unhappily) different, perhaps because of their reading and interpretation of the Bible. (The fact is, that the pact made in the seven-teenth century between the American Protestantisms—increasingly Deist Southern aristocratic and increasingly diluted New England Puritan mer-chant—pulled New York neither way. New York, rather, set off on its own course of the Manhattan-Mammon bread-and-circuses, shopping/play-going/opera-going/brotheling, etc. This erased the old European idea of gestural redemption through the sacraments, adorned with fetching Latin incantations, with government through the Word, expressed in the undeni-able perfection of the Authorized Version.) Thus to us part-Americans— both by virtue of our being Catholics and of our being New Yorkers—Bible study seemed to advertise an aura of Close Encounter with The Lord in the Garden (a maneuver we might attempt meditatively in the first sorrow-ful mystery of the rosary but, having the Eucharist, not otherwise ambi-tiously pursue).

Old Testament plots and New Testament "fulfillments" of them were read at Sunday Mass as pretexts for homiletics. Called "chapters" in the earlier church, their praxis was identical to that of segments of low-budget thriller serials—also called chapters—given us at Saturday matinees, along with Movietone News, westerns and biblical epics. We got our goods, worldly and heavenly, on the installment plan. My problem was that in the cliff-hanger serials the hero always got away—got away with it—whereas I must be arrested, mocked, scourged, spat upon and crucified with Christ to be redeemed.

Perhaps because they'd often told me truth was stranger than fiction and always to keep away from strangers, I tended to opt for fable, and so, finally opening the Bible, looked on it as escapist fiction and read it companion-ably, aided by Hollywood (which furnished if not exactly exegesis, then surely eroticism, and exegesis without Eros is bread without salt). Catholics left real Bible interpretation (Old and New Testaments respectively) to the Jews and to the American College in Rome. (The chief mystery of the Jews was that, as God's Chosen People, they hadn't chosen to become Christian. Clearly a manifestation, the more liberal theology of the '50s suggested, of the difference between the Will of God and the wishes, even wish-fulfillment fantasies, of The Second Person of the Blessed Trinity in His human nature.)

Finally I became as intellectually anti-Protestant as I was culturally philo-Semitic. If you were Irish Catholic and wanted a career other than one in the metropolitan clergy, it was necessary to assimilate to something else, and given a choice between the dowdy, self-appointed American elect and the worldly (clothes, show business), cultured (book publishing, music), liberal and sexually tolerant *mishpocheh* of New York Jewry, neither horns nor dilemma compromised the transaction.

(A purely imaginative exercise. I'd surely have made a weak Jew, given to capricious readings of the Torah, a virtue that is no virtue as the exegete Rashi insists, rather than to the conscientious study of Mishnah and the Talmud. I settled for the cultivation of Yiddish idioms and that gorgeous, and a little tasteless, sense of humor, for no New Yorker who writes about New York and neglects them can be on the qui vive.)

These predilections were the product of anxiety in the face of assimilation to the WASP ascendancy. Their like had accounted for the simultaneous enlistment in various underworld and civic brigades that made nineteenth-century American Irish both the most blatantly criminal element in New York life and the majority on metropolitan police forces (and was later manifested in the flirtation of the Kennedys with both the Sicilian Mafia and Hoover's FBI). It created untoward resistance in me to the intentions of the Framers, the Movers and the Shakers, and excluded me from the enthusiasm of my fellow educated Americans for the Authorized Version (the very idea of a Father *which* art in heaven!). We read the Douay-Rheims Bible. Also for Milton (we were thoroughly Spencerian, in full, gorgeous, perhaps a little tasteless sacramental and ceremonial panoply) and for Emerson.

One was an estranged boy, yet Jacob's fusion with Israel spoke one's singular identification with America. It is the peculiar affectation of those born, as I was, on the Fourth of July, that they can become something of another stripe—as it turns out, sadly for the Catholic, always the result of self-inflicted, and therefore by definition protestant, lash marks. Hawthorne, born on the Fourth of July, wrote of being branded. George M. Cohan set the condition to music. Roberto Calasso, in *The Ruin of Kasch*, says of would-be originators Freud and Nietzsche, "Then they discovered origin as deception, thus choosing the form of deception into which they wanted to fall—and which would bedevil them to the last."

The Bible was the Word of God. That word was passed along, and the exact wording of the written form was of far lesser consequence than the understood intent of a man who had given you his word: no gentleman required it as part of the agreement. When later I surveyed God's literary career, I found him a revisionist author whose first book, Genesis, if not his best, was certainly his most original, and who thereafter, under pseudonyms ranging from The Jahwist to The Divine, suffered the anxiety of his own influence to a degree he failed to tolerate, until at last he blew a gasket in Revelation.

It was to DeMille and Nicholas Ray and not to Milton we turned for elaboration: to *Samson and Delilah* and to *King of Kings*. In the tale of Samson and Delilah, male sexual prowess and the ability to bring the house down met its match in Woman, especially when Risë Stevens sang Dalila at the Met, outdoing Hedy Lamarr as a Biblical wanton hands down. Being struck blind was allegory: it was perhaps wise to turn a blind eye to Woman. In *King of Kings* we all met our match in Jeffrey Hunter's Jesus.

The Bible was not sincere. As Oscar Wilde pointed out, sincerity is the hallmark of bad poetry, and the Bible is great poetry. Moreover, it takes only the merest glance at the *Oxford Dictionary of English Etymology* to understand that if the Bible were sincere, it would require no exegesis, no hermeneutics, no John the Divine breaking the seven seals to get at the big ending.

The notion that the Bible is sincere was born in some long, wet chilly Northern European Protestant winter and unhappily exported to America, where it devolves into fundamentalist schizophrenia. To think that the Bible is sincere is finally impudent: it argues for a reciprocal God whose outpouring of favors procures love, and as two great writers on dulcet resignation, St. Teresa of Ávila and Baruch Spinoza, understood, to love God is the supreme command (as health is the primary duty) of life. They who do so with all their hearts have no such impertinence as to expect to be loved by God in return.

Not sincere, and yet God's word. (And two senses of word were operative under the rubric of the Logos: this sense of bond or promise—"He's as good as his word"—and the sense of "What's the good word?" as in the *on-dit*, the noise.) Therefore the Voice of God in the Bible is the Voice of the Trickster. It addresses the devout (particularly the devout in uniform, in canonical, or clerical dress) in much the same way and delivers much the same message as that vouchsafed Cary Grant (in the uniform of the Salvation Army) by the salvific American genius Mae West: "You can be had." The great promise of the Old Testament can be summed up in one line: every valley shall be exalted; and that of the New in another: the last shall be first. What can this be but God saying: if you take to this idea—this will be that: the opposite will obtain—then only a little thought will yield the notion that in what you call the afterlife, every existent will be non-existent . . . and this means you. The East of course has touted this famously relaxing ambiguity for nearly three millennia, but Western Man's harking to it seems epitomized by the dismaying success of dharma bums out to relieve consumer depressives of their spare bucks, abated only by the odd touchdown visits of true illuminati to their credent sects to contemplate with them the *atman-brahman.*

Jacob the Trickster is the third member of the Jewish Trinity of Patriarchs, and (since we always thought in trinitarian terms) the one aligned with our Holy Spirit. Also Three Sheets to the Wind if ever there was one.

Abraham was so clearly the Father, and Isaac the Son, both sacrificed and spared, that Jacob had to be the mysterious third, who proceeded from the love between the father and the son, for even though the Old Testament was full of strong women, we still imagined patrilineally, and of progeny as mental, as arithmetic, as multiplication tables.

I like the fact that Harold Bloom, before he decided to designate the author J. a supremely smart woman, thought of designating the text as Jacob's signature work, which would have fit it well with the Elohist's later dressing up the tale with angels (a garlanding that has made the gospels into greeting card scenarios for Yuletide carols and major oratorios and upon which Revelation greatly relies). It means for me that if Jacob might be thought of as the writer disguised as this holy *shnorrer*, then I . . . well, as Bloom writes, "The Blessing gives more life, awards a time without boundaries and makes a name into a pragmatic immortality, by way of communal memory." (Now, if this isn't precisely what a writer either wants instinctively or is early taught is the only possible anodyne for his incurable narcissistic wound . . . but it is.) "Indeed the Blessing in J. cannot be distinguished from the work of memory. And yet, in J. the Blessing is always partly ironic and frequently attended by fraud." (Which is to say revision: it didn't happen that way; it can't have. This is how it must have been, or I die now.)

I also deem appropriate a later aperçu of Professor Bloom's. It seems to apply absolutely to the re-making stress suffered by Marcel Proust, and will therefore do nicely. (A Catholic writer might carry it in his wallet in case of accident, in lieu of the famous "I am a Catholic; please call a priest.")

"And yet to call J.'s Jacob that [hypocrite, that is] is at once coldly accurate and wildly misleading, since he has just won the new name Israel in an astonishing exhibition of persistence, endurance, even transcendental heroism." (And "new name" is crucial. Ask Marcel Proust, James Joyce, Virginia Woolf or William Faulkner; they'll tell you. The name stamped on their books is a pseudonym, as surely as George Eliot, George Sand, Stendhal or Shakespeare.)

Jacob's consorting with angels in the dream signals an identification. Jacob is an angel, a good boy (not as to his purity—the thief of the birthright is in a sullied existential position—but as to aesthetics: he broadcasts the message).

The propensity of the mother of the queer is to enlist the son against the father, seeing the son as her chief rival in the world. This may be why God put straight men in charge of politics and war, and women and queer men in charge of fashion and manners. And why, when the two camps join forces, as in fifteenth-century Florence, sixteenth-century Spain, Elizabethan England, the France of Louis Quatorze, Hollywood in the 1930s and 1940s, and New York in the 1950s and 1960s, renaissances occur.

Rebecca encourages Jacob to put on some older male hair, the exterior of the firstborn; to beguile (seduce) his father Isaac—in my queer reading himself the near victim of his father's terror in reaction to homosexual attraction, saved only by the angel of the Lord.

Jacob's deception is tantamount to donning a wig, becoming a transvestite (or transsexual) and having his way with the father, old and blind to the truth: the way queer boys in anguish always see their fathers. Whether they, the fathers, are good to them or bad to them, they, the queer sons, are conditioned to take the old man for a ride.

Jacob is therefore both the Trickster and the Trick himself, a smart operator, a smoothie. A lustrous pre-adolescent boy of angelic countenance (without body hair). There is no way he can become Israel until he butches up his act: be a man, go out and kill something. The mother will cook it: men slay, women cook up the results. And if he wants to do that he has to imitate his brother, and, by doing so, supplant him—or kill him.

Jacob's mother helps him pose as a man, cooking up and dressing the event. Jacob wears not only a goat skin but Esau's dirty old clothes: the old goat's sense of the smell of his own favorite kid delivers the kicker erotic charge. There is nothing more effective in certain situations, every hustler knows, than cheap scent. For me it is as telling as a boxer skipping rope. Jacob was like that cheap scent, that boxer. I'm reminded of the late Glenway Wescott's advice to a cadet, and how the older homosexual addressing the younger would habitually say, "Now listen to your mother." Wescott advised, "It's best not to fight, but if you have to, if you feel you must, then for pity's sake, fight dirty."

This ability of the mother to act as Fixer, to rearrange the dictates of any order, a bow to the capricious power of Nature, is carried into Christianity in the radical veneration of the Mother of God in Mediterranean countries and in Ireland, where it is accepted that to get to Him you go through her, the Mediatrix of all grace. Jesus of Nazareth's first miracle, changing the water into wine at the marriage feast of Cana, was done at the express request of Mary, over his objection that his time had not yet come. She said in effect, "I'll be the judge of that."

The mother of the queer son is ambivalent as she dispatches him. Saying, with Rebecca, "My son, any curse would be mine. My voice guides you— only follow," she is confident the husband-father will be charmed by him, but also torn between the fear that he, *fructus ventris*, will succeed, displacing her and rendering the role of woman ancillary to the parthenogenic rule of celibate men (the story of Jesus Christ) and that he will fail, arousing the wrath of the father, and be rejected. (The same story, ending in the naked outcry *Eloi, Eloi, lama sabachthani?*)

The story is also the great sadomasochistic turnaround of father-son and master-servant, realized lately by Samuel Beckett in the Pozzo-Lucky second-act switch of *Waiting for Godot*, in which Pozzo, beaten down by life, no Godot, enters, blind.

He also detected in Esau and Jacob an echo of the *Dioscouri*. Although Jasper Griffin, in a recent *New York Review of Books*, assures readers that the Hellenic Greeks, whose manners Jews adopted, were "cheerfully ignorant" of Hebrew literature, there is surely a resemblance between the older Greek story of the twins, one mortal, one immortal, and that of Esau and Jacob. As surely as Esau is ordinary, mortal, and (perhaps therefore) susceptible to being tricked, so Jacob, by virtue of tricking, wrestling with God and becoming Israel itself, achieves what for the Jews is the only acceptable immortality: memorial fame, attached, not as for the Romans (and for our time) to violence and publicity and glamour, but to fecundity and stability and guile. It has often been pointed out that the chief glory of Greek expression is its celebration of the fleeting moment (the one-time life), and in the Democratic Age, Greece has now come into its glory, but all along there has been the other lurking thing: the mortal and immortal self (or strain of self, or strain of self-similarity; the latest version, DNA). The Hebrews, in their foundation (Jacob/Israel), had, it seems to me, a grip on the immortal self, the same grip characteristic of the maritime Celts, who had no literature before Church Latin gave Irish an alphabet, but an epic oral tradition as old as the Phoenicians and still operative in the West of Ireland.

The second son seemed to have tricked his way through childhood on a curious alternation of savage hysteria and winsome ways, then crashed, spending an uncomfortable if eventful year of adolescence as a bullied boy, adopting for the siege a manic-depressive (or visionary-abject) defense against this reopened breach in the narcissistic defense: somehow glorying in the shame to self and family that the unfortunate sociological shift in Jackson Heights (the element coming in) afforded. It was in that time that he began to pine after memories of Jacob, Oz and latency, and made fast on his identification with the publican (any promise of relief) and replaced Oz in his fantasies with extraterrestrials (sci-fi pictures were plentiful) and peer rejection with replays of the "special and invisible friend" stage fantasies of one's guardian angel's friends (guardian angels were dogma). He developed attachments to Method acting in the New York theater, to foreign films, to the Metropolitan Opera, the New York City Ballet, Martha Graham (who worked her magic in summer—creating many of her greatest pieces at a place in the country called Jacob's Pillow), to Lucky Strike cigarettes, alcohol, and the orchestral music of Bruckner, Mahler and the Second Viennese School. (Literature, however, was at first another kind of bully.)

He learned the thing to do in lobbies at intermission was sparkle: to seem not merely one who belonged, but one who had become himself significant and a little mysterious, one whom the Lord had found wandering in the wilderness forty-five minutes from Broadway and had led in to Shubert Alley and to the Metropolitan Opera House and kept as the apple of his eye, as God had Jacob.

Later still, in Identity Crisis (ages twenty-eight through twenty-nine), he came to view Jacob as the first analysand, his pillow as the first analytical couch, his vision the first exercise in free association, his wrestling the first fight against the death instinct. ("But Jacob's cunning," writes Harold Bloom, "is the defense of a survivor, and while it guarantees the continuation of his long life, it does not protect him from suffering.") Analysis replaces the imaginary angelic friend with whom one wrestled gaily in the assurance of no resentment and finally, as with Jacob and his angel, of the kindly blessing, with the match against the Introject.

Analysis, popularly supposed a wrestling with demons, actually reveals the difference between one's angels and one's demons to be chiefly one of dress-up: the engagement, the embrace, the agon is what matters. As Baudelaire wrote:

> *Ange ou Sirène, qu'importe si tu rends . . .*
> *L'univers moins hideux et les instants moins lourds?*

Or, the aim of psychoanalysis is to replace neurotic suffering with ordinary unhappiness: the Tragic Sense of Life by day; Camp sensibility by night.

Hence although aperçus, epiphanies and orgasms came one upon another in sequence (and sequins) trotting up and down night ladders, they had a uniform resemblance, like Ziegfeld girls on that spot-lit stairway to paradise. I realized this was what was called aestheticism, something in those days to be tempered with a diet of red meat: political commitment . . . social concern. . . . But I was hooked. Jacob was the Great Aesthete and Judaism the type of the lost "original" religion for which one had been greatly longing.

THE GOOD THIEF
(Fantasy of Rough Trade)

Unnamed in the gospel, he was called by the Church St. Dismas, and a special emphasis was put upon him, as it was upon all exemplars of the grace of conversion. We prayed to him, as I recall, for benignity, a virtue akin to humility (we prayed for that to the publican in the same evangelist's parable of the publican and the Pharisee) but more guilelessly energetic.

And there were two other malefactors led with him to be put to death (Luke 23:32).

And one of the malefactors which were hanged railed on him, saying, If thou be the Christ save thyself and us.

But the other answering rebuked him, saying, Dost thou not fear God, seeing thou art in the same condemnation?

And we indeed justly; for we receive the due reward of our deeds: but this man has done nothing amiss.

And he said unto Jesus, Lord remember me when thou comest into thy kingdom. And Jesus said unto him, Verily I say unto thee this day shalt thou be with me in Paradise (Luke 23:39–43).

The story in this form is unique to Luke the physician (and psychologist, the Chekhov of the gospelers). In Matthew and Mark, both thieves rail at Jesus along with the chief priests, the Pharisees and the rabble. Luke calls them, unspecifically, malefactors, and John simply records two others, but John, uniquely present as the Beloved Disciple was, it may be presumed, too enrapt by the stunning glamour of Jesus's direct address to him in the matter of the care of Mary the Mother (John 20:25–27) to attend to a competitive discourse. And after all, "Look after this, will you, dear?" and then the God/man turning to not-so-much-a-disciple-never-mind-a-minion-but-the-nearest-mouth-full-of-kind-words and directing: "You come with me" constitutes the kind of erotic contretemps one would hardly either brave or record.

But what about the grace of benignity? It was deemed, as has been said, more dynamic, more candid than humility—a stance that often seems ravenous with studied deserving—by those aligned with the virtue of simplicity, and at root with the idea of salvation through Faith, evidenced by a demure, stricken quality cognate to the meekness that would inherit the earth.

My grace is sufficient for you, my power is made perfect in weakness (2 Corinthians 12:9).

Nuns had it sometimes, and those downtrodden (or never prosperous) unaccountably good secular Americans (glamorized on the screen from *Tol'able David* through *Meet John Doe* right down to *Forrest Gump*), players often represented as dealing from less than full decks or rolling incompletely dotted dice, who make the Game of Life's winners seem commonplace and mean. (Underlying sense: purely good works are categorically impossible in a fallen nature and would in any case add nothing to God's estimation of a soul, an estimation undeceived, radically severe and infinitely merciful.) Holden Caulfield, with his baseball cap on backward, was bewitchingly benign. Reckoned a mysteriously inherent quality in its possessors, nevertheless it was important for us to believe we could come to it, and so strive accordingly, although it, or the proof of it, might be vouchsafed only at the very end, as it did to Dismas. Or, in an indelible impression of death-row salvation from my early childhood, to Jimmy Cagney being dragged screaming to the electric chair in *Angels With Dirty Faces*: pretending to be a yellow-bellied punk so as to help priestly Pat O'Brien convince the kids back in

Hell's Kitchen that crime doesn't pay. The unnamed thief, toughing it out, would have spat in Pat's face.

Author seems always to have had a particular predilection for the matter of the sexuality of priests—not ministers, priests. And not Episcopal priests but Roman Catholic priests. Also, it is a commonplace, by no means restricted to the Catholic Church, that sexually frustrated women habitually work out their incest fantasies on ministers and priests. In the Catholic Church that melodrama is very potent indeed, and everybody loved a good tear-jerker about the wife whose husband is either a drunk or an executive power freak seeing to corporate matters on Madison Avenue in the late afternoons, but what they don't know is that while Missus is mooning over Father Shenanigan (who probably even as she doesn't speak is either getting reacquainted with his fist, not for the first time that day, or mooning over one if not all three of her darling sons, all altarians), what she was really doing—all, it must be said, unbeknownst to herself—is carving away at all the boyos' unmannerly privates at once, and mixing and measuring carbolic soap enemas into the bargain. (They want to take it up the ass? Try this. Perhaps I needn't tell anybody how popular that trope—High Colonic Water Sports—became. And why not?)

There is a fixed suspicion in that branch of Catholic moral theology opposed to Counter-Reformation Jesuit triumphalism (which paradoxically in the late twentieth century the Jesuits themselves came to embrace, as Liberation Theology) concerning the Protestant value put on both exemplary social demeanor and good works, seen to have spawned in the modern world aggressive industry, aggregation and pollution of land, capital gains and delusory self-aggrandizement. (Consider the emaciated ecstatic abnegation of primitive-Christian, agape-driven, syncretic and pentecostal Latin America in relation to the corpulent religious-affiliate bravado of Protestant United States and Canada.) A fixed suspicion and a conviction derived from Jansenism and its offshoots that even the hoarding of spiritual capital is a mark of avarice. The lilies of the field are the emblem of this (mainly French) habit of soul, its most famous twentieth-century European exemplars Charles Péguy and Simone Weil, and its paramount aesthetic mirror the films of Robert Bresson (*Pickpocket, Mouchette, Balthazar, Le Diable, Probablement*). The American version, redolent of Jansenism and of the even earlier Montanists and Cathars, is best summed up by a wacky title from the '50s (I don't remember what it was attached to): *Embezzled Heaven*. The preeminent American models were Peter Maurin and Dorothy

Day (the most glamorous Magdalen, or good girl thief, of her era). The characteristic witness of adherents in my youth was feeding, clothing and consorting with the unwashed under the banner of the cardinal virtue Charity, hoisted by the strong scrubbed arm of the gleaming Miss Day, appearing to grovel just a little, dreaming not of being Americans in Paris but barefoot pilgrims to Chartres and espousing the existential angelism of Gabriel Marcel.

I did it all. More important, I came to an understanding of the intrapsychic melodrama the story of the two thieves represents. All three of the crucified on Calvary are Christ, who, suffering unto death, is confronted with two reactive personae, and must first abide the negative before embracing the positive. For what is the bad thief's railing but the mirroring, the doubling, of Jesus's own *Eloi, Eloi, lama sabachthani?* (Matthew 27:46; Mark 15:34) and the resignation of self in the good thief the doubling of "Father, into thy hands I commend my spirit." The moral lesson, a reiteration of the Redeemer's own dictum "Unless you become like little children" is not to expect the fulfillment of motive (the kingdom of heaven) before helplessness, infantile wailing and even the failure of recognition (an undoing parallel to the formation from helplessness through rage to some sense of functional autonomy in the first part of life) has been undergone. The anomaly that it is self-referring man's fate to negotiate successive stages of maturation (storing up treasure), only to fall backward through them again before the apocalypse of the distinguished thing, is the unanswered question. Chekhov, ending his last, greatest play wrote, "If only we knew."

CHAPTER FIVE

How It Got to Be So

(STUDY PERIOD)

> "All we have to go on being the clue,
> Clumsier than what was of what was is."
> —Douglas Crase, "Felix Culpa Returns From France"

Wherein the author, having accepted the double identification Jacob/Dismas tries to come to grips with the following theological paradox:

Angelic ladder (or stairway to paradise) = cross and crucifixion.

And the thrilling but desperate agon of wrestling together with Christ (Christ A as he might be called) the demons of rage at being abandoned by the father ("Eloi, Eloi, lama sabachthani?") and actually wrestling, as in hitting the mat with Christ B himself, whose demand to be loved in and through other men is impossible absent sexual enthrallment.

Men are not angels; to imagine they are is to become psychotic. Get your rocks off.

Concerning foundation myths and dating schemes, it has been pointed out that when counting ahead, we don't start with zero, but with one, whereas when counting backwards, when we get to one, that one is the first day, month, year or epoch after the beginning of it all. The beginning of it all is always a zero: queer lives always spring out of a void, thus controverting the raw evidence of a natural birth from two human beings who have necessarily engaged in the last one provisionally defining heterosexual act, intercourse for the purposes of procreation as prescribed by the Natural Law.

Concerning the inveigler's trajectory: from the alleyway to the dressing room to the orchestra seat (row G on the aisle) to the supper at Sardi's or the party in the star's duplex on Sutton Place, the ambition is uncluttered; it is to become Something Called a Temperament and still look plausible in pants and brogues and coats that button right over left.

(Overheard in Shubert Alley, after a matinee of T.C. Jones's extremely successful one-man drag revue *Mask and Gown*, in 1956: "I adore T.C., darling, but while seeing him provides a couple of hours respite from weal and woe, it hardly helps a homosexual solve life's central problem. After all, whether done well or not so well, impersonating a woman comes more or less naturally to us. What we need to study more closely is how to impersonate a *man*, or at least something like one—you know, the way Tony Perkins does.")

As a consequence of the above outlined theological dilemma, elements of Christian rhetoric obtained, particularly sermons of proof.

In which the diachronic, narrative time of the *exemplum* combines with the retrospective and eschatological time of the *auctorites* (essentially, passages from Scripture) and with the atemporality of the *rationes* (Thomas Aquinas out of Aristotle).

To begin with: a human sinning (or suffering) and overhearing narratives.

The message. As someone accessing the great canonic repository of queer New York demotic phraseology would assert of a young article who'd just arrived on the opera line, or might be walking like *that* up Greenwich Avenue of a summer afternoon, "That one has not gotten his message."

It was heard all over the neighborhoods too of some kid who held his schoolbooks in both arms, for example, instead of on one hip—generally the left—braced with one hand. Nobody ever of course used a book bag or slung a belt around the books and carried them over a shoulder: such form was strictly from Archie comics. Such further evidence—observation of the way you lit your cigarette and the way you looked at your nails when ordered impromptu to do so—began to be accumulated in the sixth grade to make up a test for which you couldn't find the Regents guide, to fail at which marked you, unless you skipped town, for life. For the record, observant Author passed them all (which ought to have been its own message). Even so the closesness of the call made him determinedly connect on associative grounds with the anti-message crowd, especially apropos intent in literature, music, painting, et cetera. (If you want to send a message, call Western Union.)

A curious paradox worked from childhood up through middle adolescence. On the one hand to the extent that Author was lucky (or skilled) enough to play his cards right, he felt quite at home (imagining himself like many others to some degree a Holden Caulfield) on the streets, in the subways, in taxi cabs. He talked to anybody who would talk back, people streaming in and out of offices, movie theaters, bowling alleys, restaurants. Case of pure prelapsarian Whitmanian innocence. It wasn't until he made that single gossipy mistake concerning the revels of that New-York-neighborhood-real-boy-all-boy sex club that the axe fell.

That New-York-neighborhood-real-boy-all-boy sex club from which he had been pointedly excluded on formal grounds: imputation of incapacity in respect of starter's orders and the manly expedition of the drill (No Beginners: mooncalf applicants referred to Self Abuse 1A, private instruction available on strictly quid pro quo basis, schoolyard, afternoons), Author having when tested early in his fourteenth year (late summer, 1954) having demonstrated an insufficient degree of experimental savvy (or grasp) of that which, when they all went to confession and told, automatically elicited the query "With yourself or with others, son?" Referred to in weirdly jocular fashion by the participants themselves, lately enlightened as to phase specifics by their avid mentor the super, as *fag shit*.

If only they'd waited another six weeks. (But was it not the close reading by the midnight oil, reader propped up with pillows in the bottom bunk bed, of those same articles of dismissal, in bitter recollection soothed only by the downing of three or four tumblers of Hennessy V.S.O.P. in the quiet of the night, turned into a reliable service manual indeed, which when coupled with the intense and perversely erotic isolation visited upon the subject—now as regularly oiled by midnight as any lamp might be, and running in his musical mind as the obligatory background soundtrack the haunting theme from Douglas Sirk's *Magnificent Obsession?* Liszt's étude "Consolation"—which became the very circumstance that propelled the issue to . . . issue? It was.)

By which time something rather more existential than felt alienation (called definitive extrusion from the tribe) had irrevocably occurred.

Then it was that in tree-lined streets the chant came not from within (although it was difficult not to assimilate the content) but from hostile conspecifics, the Voices in the Neighborhood.

'Cause you're a fag

The way you walk,

Talk, smoke, dance, You're a fag.

Stay off the streets. Stay home indoors. Don't make a move.

Bruta sorte. Nasty (if ironic turn).

Boy hero of his own story ostracized, his continuance imperiled, merely for inquiring too closely into . . . fag shit. Of course it was known to be a volatile subject, in the nation as much as in the neighborhood, in spite of the fact that the noise was you got off easy enough in the confessional unless you fell in with some fanatic who gave a whole fucking rosary and a stiff lecture on the rain of fire on Sodom, weeping angels and the bleeding whiplashed Christ you were doing it to all over again with each, er, stroke.

It had also lately come to be mysteriously connected with atheistic Communism emanating out of godless as-yet-unconverted Russia. And yet surely those Irish Catholic boys (plus Guido Gavone) weren't up to *that* down in that cellar. You could go to the *chair* for fucking Commie shit; the Rosenbergs just had.

Going to the chair was a very bad idea, a really gonza *bruta sorte*. And as for it and Commies, et cetera, even the once revered Senator Joseph McCarthy, a crusader, had gotten his ass burned looking too closely into the combination (for what reason exactly nobody had ever sufficiently explained, certainly not the *New York Times*. Maybe it wasn't fit to print).

Meanwhile, stay home doing what, exactly? Playing solitaire Chinese checkers? Watching the *Million Dollar Movie*, and on weekends *The Late Show* and *The Late Late Show* alone? (One had gotten into the habit of doing that, and so much else, if not as yet fag shit, with others.)

"Don't make a move" actually meant don't make a detectable move. Time then to hop on the English racer and investigate adjacent Jackson Heights sectors out of radar range.

Jackson Heights, immortalized in Ronald Firbank's unfinished last novel *The New Rhythum* in the following passage, set at Bertie Waldorf's rose-viewing matinee on Riverside, and concerning the first spat of a newly engaged couple.

"He intends that they shall remove and go and live on Jackson Heights. Nothing on earth, she avers, would induce her to go and live on Jackson Heights."

Broadway and 74th Street (another, lesser Broadway, another, lesser 74th Street), the transfer point from the overhead IRT Flushing Line to the Independent Subway, on what had by then become one's daily route to high school.

And high school itself was, of course, a salvation. One learned Latin, finding Caesar's *De Bello Gallico* amazingly sexual, and started all over, resolutely determined to:

1. Keep any and all opinion like that concerning *De Bello Gallico* under his hat, and

2. Not to make the same flannel-mouth-fag mistake.

And one succeeded brilliantly, becoming, with next to no alteration of either strut or swagger rather than a fag a zany, and a zany moreover with brains and even, *mirabile dictu*, sports ability (in track and field and in swimming) and what was readily accepted as negotiable diocesan Catholic secondary school bonhomie. This to such an extent that, in a seemingly miraculous switch clearly and unequivocally effected by the disciplined attention and support of his extremely popular, much older brother, back from Korea, about to be married (and to move to the Pacific Northwest, so time was of the essence), he was able not only to fit in, but to become almost immediately the trusted-with-every-confidence best pal of the carrot-top prince of a guy who would in a short year become the varsity tennis ace. What a guy; what a pair of guys.

Broadway and 74th Street, Jackson Heights. A nodal point with its all-night Bickford's, its many racy-looking bars, some with bright neon signs the equal of anything along (the real) Eighth Avenue (one of which in particular had for some time been catching Author's eye: the Floradora) and its taxi rank where neighborhood swells who wished to make the last hop home from Manhattan could grab a cab to the door, a facility that had become important as Author, now moving along in high school, had starting going out on big-city dates with girls who took along a little "mad money." Seeing them home from 74th Street in a taxi was very much the gentlemanly thing to do, reassuring the parents he was a considerate gentleman (who walked on the curb side).

Dating girls, and even going steady, was really more than cover; New York girls were fabulous, smart, glamorous, vulgar, sophisticated well beyond their years, Rosalind Russell pals, and for all these reasons delightful. And the prospect of forming a sustainable dyad could really be put off for years, at the very least until some time after graduate school, or early in the (advertised) advertising career.

Floradora was the household-word famous name of a turn-of-the-century Broadway musical extravaganza grandfather still talked about, legendary for its lineup of "Floradora girls" and for the hit song lyric, "Tell me, pretty maiden, are there any more at home like you?" "There are a few, kind sir, but simple girls, and proper too." (The sheet music lay there in the music cabinet at home, a Floradora girl and her gentleman canoodling on the cover: a precious relic of the age of Stanford White, Evelyn Nesbit, Harry K. Thaw and the risky, raucous Rialto of their day.)

The discovery made soon after the making of Alfred Hitchcock's *The Wrong Man*. QT mentions this the first time he is in the place.

Response: "Fascinating."

Second try. "We spent a lot of time around here last year trying to get into *The Wrong Man*."

Response: "Really? You could've saved yourself the effort by coming in here then, 'cause that's all you're ever gonna find in here, honey, the wrong man."

Author as a consequence, something significantly short of referential background beyond the *Life* magazine spread on Pollock, a certain chroma (derived from hanging out in and around Shubert Alley), a nearly encyclopedic culling of the columns and, most reliably, several eventful years' exposure to the standing-room line at the Metropolitan Opera, began to examine life according to rubrics derived point-for-point from the script of *All About Eve*.

While concurrently, in high school, befriended (and thrillingly, secretly in love with) the tennis ace, and able with the most exhilarating duplicity which didn't feel like anything of the sort to double date, dance the night away with a real girl (so long as *he* was dancing with another real girl nearby), subject to the attention of a succession of sympathetic English teachers, one religious, two secular.

The first of these a very handsome Italian hardly ten years older than the author, who, in order to scotch dirty sniggers in the classroom, once walked in, wrote "blow job" on the blackboard and invited discussion of the topic. "What, show and tell?" a bold voice (belonging of course to a hip Italian kid from Bensonhurst) quickly followed. In those days, show and tell had not been widely promulgated, and Author suppressed the urge to go into his (entirely hearsay) file on the cellar in Jackson Heights, which was wise, because in a very few minutes the discussion, become lively, had naturally focused on girls, revealing to him a truly shocking fact. Girls gave blow jobs. Such a thing had never come close to entering his mind. Necking was necking, and petting was petting, but *that*?

Suddenly a joke popular in Little Italy and told him by his cousin was being retold, by the "show and tell" boy.

Two Italian girls are coming out of Our Lady of Pompeii Church after confession late on a Saturday afternoon. The first girl stops at the holy water font, and instead of just dipping in her fingers and making the sign of the cross, she plunges her whole hand in.

Second Italian Girl: Whaddya doin' that for?

First Italian Girl: It's part of the penance; I told him I jerked my boyfriend off and he told me to dunk my whole hand in the holy water.

Second Italian Girl: Move over, I gotta gargle.

The second English teacher, who uséd to tear with gusto into Lady Macbeth, a bit of a ringer for Emil Jannings in *The Blue Angel* (1930, Josef von Sternberg) and the subject of one of Author's not-very-original schoolboy pranks: the caricature on the blackboard of the mustachioed English teacher in Lady Macbeth drag (intuitively omitting the idea of the comic-book dialogue bubble "I have given suck"; this man might be razzed, but he was far too respected to be cravenly insulted). Amused, cool reaction of the teacher (a very smart and dedicated man of Slavonic extraction who too had served honorably in the Pacific), then tore right into the sleepwalking scene.

(Flash to the funniest of T.C. Jones's routines in *Mask and Gown*, relayed across America on *The Ed Sullivan Show*: Bette Davis as Lady Macbeth, lighting the cigarette from the candle and narking, "*Screw* your courage to the sticking place!")

Also the two-fisted De La Salle Christian Brothers (pointedly not those Irish ruffians poor James Joyce spent time with and tried unsuccessfully to erase from his recall).

(Flash forward seven years later to Bruce Ritter, O.F.M., an amazing Joel McCrea–like specimen of that burgeoning platoon, the queer men of God. Not Francis Cardinal Spellman types—Camp swish pinchers and patters of altar boys' behinds—but manly priests and ministers of the higher churches as well as the queer Elmer Gantrys who drove the country boys to get in the Greyhound and head for Gotham, ill-defended from their conflicts by the Roman Catholic hierarchy, and inflamed Saturday afternoon after Saturday afternoon by the cunning little confessions adolescent boys would make, about their failure to stop doing "it" alone and with others, these breathy set-ups would drive the poor hearers on the other side of the grille to distraction and such late-night practices as would have them up and at one another at the crack of Sunday dawn to confess to and be absolved by one another, in a weird parody of Schnitzler's classic Viennese comedy *Reigen*, translated in the early '50s to the French screen as *La Ronde*, to enjoy a long and profitable run in New York in spite of being the number one condemned picture on the Legion of Decency list. Sad, really.)

A SAMPLE FREE-ASSOCIATION '50S QUEER SYLLABUS

Bette Davis
All About Eve
Claude Shannon ("Play the Liebestraum.")
Mae West
Barbara Stanwyck
Joan Crawford
Maria Montez (*Cobra Woman*: "Young men, young women,
    children—all must go!")
Irene Dunne
Carole Lombard
Ida Lupino
Gloria Grahame
Paula Wessely
Zarah Leander
Lyda Roberti
Paul Robeson
Pearl Bailey
W.C. Fields
Bert Savoy
Gloria Swanson as Norma Desmond in Billy Wilder's *Sunset
    Boulevard*
Tallulah Bankhead
Jeanne Eagels in *Rain* (1922) and onscreen in *The Letter*
    (1928), shown occasionally at MoMA
Marlene Dietrich
Rancho Notorious (A fine and true woman would rather die than
    come between two men who belong together.)
Edith Piaf
Eartha Kitt
Valentina
Jacques Fath
Ceil Chapman ("Mix 'em and match 'em.")
Charles James
Charles Lisanby
Pauline Trigère
Edward Carpenter ("Homogenic Love")

Magnus Hirschfeld
Leonardo da Vinci
Michelangelo Buonarroti
Michelangelo Merisi da Caravaggio
Ludwig Wittgenstein
T.S. Eliot ("Yes, darling, the Moment in the Rose Garden.")
T.C. Jones
The New York School
Jackson Pollock
Jasper Johns
Samuel Barber
Leonard Bernstein
Marc Blitzstein
Uncle Virgil [Thomson]
Vladimir Horowitz
Sviatoslav Richter
Arthur Gold and Robert Fizdale
Francis Poulenc
Reynaldo Hahn
Ned Rorem
Gene Moore
Dick Banks
Marcel Proust's *À La Recherche du Temps Perdu* (in French; fake it).
The novels of Colette, most especially *Chéri* (ditto).
The poetry of Verlaine, Rimbaud and Paul Valéry (don't try faking it)
William Beckford
Vathek
John Mahaffey
Gerard Manley Hopkins
Baron von Gloeden
Aleister Crowley
D.H. Lawrence
Lawrence of Arabia
Lytton Strachey
John Maynard Keynes
Bloomsbury

Virginia Woolf
Vita Sackville-West and Harold Nicolson
Paul Cadmus
Charles Demuth
Marsden Hartley
Glenway Wescott
David/Jonathan
Christ/The Beloved Disciple
Achilles/Patroclus
Orestes/Pylades
Elektra/Chrysothemis
Aristophanes
Kit Marlowe
Edward de Vere, Earl of Oxford
Henry Wriothesley, Earl of Southampton
John Keats/Benjamin Robert Haydon
Abraham Lincoln/Joshua Speed
Herman Melville/Nathaniel Hawthorne ("Eat your heart out.")
Billy Budd/Claggart/Vere
Alexander the Great
Julius Caesar
Brutus and Cassius
Nero
Hadrian/Antinoüs
Vespasian (and the urinals)
Marcus Aurelius
Montaigne/Michel de la Boëtie
Baron Corvo (Frederick Rolfe)
Clyde Fitch (though you may not think so)
Max Beerbohm
E.M. Forster
J.R. Ackerley
The Benson brothers—the novelist and the Archbishop of
    Canterbury
Federico García Lorca
Jean Cocteau/Jean Marais
Luchino Visconti
Porgy and Bess

Show Boat
James Whale (*Frankenstein*; *Show Boat*, 1935 version)
Helen Morgan (in *Show Boat* on Broadway and the 1935 film)
Polly Bergen
Ruth Etting
Doris Day
Johnny Ray
The Everly Brothers (held for questioning)
Carmen and Aurora Miranda
Carol Burnett ("I made a fool of myself over John Foster Dulles.")
Carol Channing
Tom Lehrer
New Faces of 1952 and *1956*
Gary Cooper and Randolph Scott
Franklin Pangborn
Clifton Webb
Billy de Wolfe
Lizabeth Scott
The novels of Ronald Firbank in Grove Press editions (with
    covers by Andrew Warhol)
The stories of Kay Boyle
Carson and Reeves McCullers
Paul and Jane Bowles
Clark Kent and Jimmy Olsen
Bruce Wayne and Dick Grayson
Captain Marvel
Wonder Woman
The Golden Apple
The Boy Friend
The Peabody
The Madison
Paul Stuart
Da Pinna
Saks
Kaye Ballard
Elaine Stritch ("Bingo, bango, bongo, I don't want to leave the
    Congo.")
Upstairs at the Downstairs

Dody Goodman (as Salome: "I'm so bored with Judea." "I think
    Daddy is a sissy.")
Emmett Kelly
J. Edgar Hoover ("Mary")
The Kennedys
Allard Lowenstein
Beatrice Lillie ("Not Wanted on the Voyage")
Emily Dickinson
Martha Graham
Agnes de Mille
Aaron Copland
Billy the Kid (balletic paean to queer cowboys)
Billy Budd
Walt Whitman
Hart Crane
Eudora Welty
The plays of Enid Bagnold
George Balanchine, Lincoln Kirstein and the New York City
    Ballet
The tragedy of Tanaquil Le Clercq
Edward Villela
Les Ballets Russes de Monte Carlo
The Marquis de Cuevas Ballet
Sadler's Wells
Margot Fonteyn
Moira Shearer
Svetlana Beriosova
Edwige Feuillère
Gérard Philipe
Maria Casares
Robert Bresson's *Les Dames du Bois de Boulogne* and *Journal
    d'un Curé de Campagne*, *Pickpocket* and *Un Condamné à
    Mort S'est Échappé*
The Theatre Nationale Populaire
Marie Bell
Phèdre
Anna Magnani
Kim Stanley

Geraldine Page

Julie Harris

Jean Arthur (as Peter Pan)

Jean Seberg (in *Bonjour Tristesse*)

Marlon Brando

Ralph Meeker (the second Stanley Kowalski, star of Robert
   Aldrich's *Kiss Me Deadly*)

Uta Hagen (the second Blanche Dubois, later to create the role of
   Martha in Edward Albee's *Who's Afraid of Virginia Woolf,*
   rewriting and rethinking the script to keep the audience from
   leaving the theater)

Stella Adler, teacher of Marlon Brando

Paul Newman and Joanne Woodward

Donald Madden

Rock Hudson

The plays of Terrence Rattigan

Roddy MacDowell

John Gielgud

The Oliviers

Montgomery Clift

Anthony Perkins

Larry Kert

Joel Grey

Billie Holiday

Judy Holliday

Billy Strayhorn

Chet Baker ("My Funny Valentine") and Gerry Mulligan: the
   way they wrapped their lines around one another

Jackie (Moms) Mabley

Frances Faye

Chris Connor

Ethel Merman

Mary Martin ("Now Mary, y' know Ah love ya, but not like that!")

Burr Tillstrom (*Kukla, Fran and Ollie*)

Marjorie Main

J.K. Huysmans

Tennessee Williams

William Inge

Donald Windham ("You Touched Me!")
Jean Genet
William Burroughs's *Naked Lunch* and *The Ticket that Exploded*
Jack Kerouac and Neal Cassady
Allen Ginsberg
Truman Capote
Newton Arvin (his rise and fall)
Alfred Chester
Coleman Dowell
Gore Vidal
W.H. Auden and Chester Kallman
James Merrill and David Jackson
Kimon Friar
Sherman Billingsley
Richard Kolmar and Dorothy Kilgallen
The Windsors
Jimmy Donohue
Francis Cardinal Spellman
And always and forever, Judy

Elaborations: A compilation of the lines spoken by Bette Davis, from "I'd love ta kiss ya, but I just washed my hair" through "Don't let's ask for the moon, we have the stars" to "Fasten your seat belts, it's going to be a bumpy night" and "But ya, are, Blanche, ya are in that wheelchair!" come very close. The thing is, less has never been more in queer life, and Bette's lines are merely spoken, whereas Judy's are sung.

The ultimate Judy lyric is from "Alone" and of course echoes the parting words of the two most queer-identified heroines in American drama, Miss Alma in *Summer and Smoke* and Blanche Dubois. "Whoever you are, are you alone on this night that we two could share?"

Bette Davis/*All About Eve*. Had Claudette Colbert, as was intended, played Margo Channing, the picture would come first. As it was, is and ever shall be, Margo may be many queers' idea of the absolute incarnation of Bette Davis, whereas in fact Bette Davis is one of the very few genius American auteur actors whose impact on the culture was and is such that not only billing over the title but utter and complete independence of the personal intelligence and charisma from identification with any and every role, even the role of Bette Davis, is an absolute.

Judy Plus (The Elaboration of Doom).

You could adore Judy—eyes welling up with tears in "Somewhere Over the Rainbow," chin to the wind in "The Trolley Song"—all you wanted to—needed to—for before, during and after the rainbow and all the while the trolley rolled along on its track, did not the essential question she put to the world echo in your ears, did it not become the essential question of your life: how could you ignore the boy next door: how were you ever going to be able to do so—in fact how were you ever going to be able to keep your mind on anything else in life for fifteen minutes at a time?

Thus adoration of Judy, strutting in sequined toreador pants across the stage at Carnegie Hall, became a true religion, lasting down to our own day, when what has become known as the "Judy dump" is a particular round in the Office of Identification of the Oppressed.

Judy Garland proof texts: "The Man That Got Away" and "If Love Were All" ("Heigh-Ho").

Subsequently, and peaking in the last torrid week of June 1969, in the Stonewall riots, the tension between the one-time-only historical Judy and the evolving interpretation of her significance could no longer be tolerably sustained.

Older queers set special store by the all-too-brief period in which Judy lived, sang, acted, suffered, wisecracked, did drugs, died and went to heaven. It was a super-sacred time both in Show Business itself and in twentieth-century queer history, and Judy's songs did and do still constitute a unique canon of queer proof texts of despair and fulfillment the like of which no other single entertainer's can match. You could dig Ella and the divine Sarah, even dote on Doris Day and Peggy Lee—after all, some of the elders had been wild about the likes of Dolly Dawn. Even do an imitation of Eartha Kitt singing "Santa Baby"—but you absolutely, in New York, had to more than just appreciate Miss Lee Wiley, Miss Mildred Bailey, nearly above all Miss Mabel Mercer, and the *sine qua non* and final statement as all wrapped up, finally, in Lady Day, singing such hymns to martyrdom and isolation as "Strange Fruit" and "God Bless the Child," in the white gardenia in Miss Billie's hair, in her lowdown report of covering the waterfront and her lamentation concerning the wearing of last year's love. (The most important trope of all: it all had to start with lost love.)

And you had to know the lyrics to all the songs of *The Golden Apple, House of Flowers, The Boy Friend* and *Valmouth*, most especially "It's a Lazy Afternoon" and "I Could Be Happy With You." And if you ever said things like "irregardless" and "being that," you'd better be unequivocally gorgeous, otherwise, the heave-ho.

Everybody read Hart Crane. Brooklyn Heights, the Brooklyn Navy Yard, so forth. The author QT, deciding to make something out of the Queensboro Bridge, which his grandfather had helped build, used Crane's making something out of the Brooklyn Bridge (undeniably the lovelier span, but what to do?) as a model. Again invokes the great *Sorry, Wrong Number* metaphor: the BMT lumbering over his bridge at midnight as Barbara Stanwyck is strangled in bed. Identification with career illness ("I'm a hopeless invalid") à la Marcel Proust. ("Go to bed and write a book.") Robert Louis Stevenson's "The Land of Counterpane" ("counter-pain").

The guilt complex and Baudelaire's *L'heautontimoroumenos*, the self-terrifier again.

Also immersion in J.K. Huysmans's *À Rebours* (translated as *Against the Grain*, later *Against Nature*, and said to be the last book read by Nathan Leopold before the murder of Bobby Franks in Chicago in 1924).

The other Huysmans books: *Là-bas* and *La Cathédrale*.

But before, during and after until now, always the charter myth of *All About Eve* ("And in the last analysis, none of it's any good unless—"), the focal crossroads of two generations (that of Carl Van Vechten, Glenway Wescott, Virgil Thomson, Francis Poulenc and Benjamin Britten, and that of Leo Lerman, Arthur Laurents, Leonard Bernstein and Ned Rorem) released in 1950, at the exact point at which queer culture was poised to take over the New York theater, remake show business and fuck everybody.

Head Queer: Leonard Bernstein.

Prince Regent: Arthur Laurents.

Mediating figures: Leo Lerman and Gray Foy.

All About Eve. The last view of the black-and-white old-school homosexual theater world (soon to be replaced by the razzle-dazzle Technicolor Hollywood world of *A Star is Born*). The picture with everything, from High Camp recherché European info, like the divinity of Paula Wessely (a sort of Austrian Edwige Feuillère with something of a singing voice), to an exact reading of the core-essential American-career myth of the first half of the century, the driven migration to New York.

Eve as desperate gay boy from the Heartland, with the inevitable stained past. ("She never proved anything." One of a collection of titles for unwritten queer short stories all based on sample lines.) Some others:

"Something Called a Temperament"
"Everything But the Bloodhounds"
"The Copacabana School of Dramatic Art"
"That's How You Met Me—in Passing"
"Unhappy Rabbits"
"Now You Want an Argument"
"The Things You Remember (and the Things You Don't)"
"In Wilkes-Barre"
"So Much Better Theater Too"
"A Part That Good"
"Nobody's Fool—Least of All Yours"
"I've Heard of Them"
"Slow Curtain, The End"

Margo Channing as all-wise queen ("And in the last analysis . . . slow curtain, the end").

Addison DeWitt as perversely heterosexual evil queen ("That I should want you at all strikes me as the height of improbability, but that in itself is probably the reason").

Karen Richards as girl sidekick of the type unkindly called fag hags, who, after all, sometimes are driven to empty the gas tank on purpose, and may never tell. The watcher with a developing hard edge ("The cynicism you refer to I acquired the day I discovered I was different from little boys"). Such a woman in queer life will always see her tormented gay men as little boys (and see to it that they do too; it's her only chance with them).

Bill Sampson, ace director, as butch trick (sometimes a straight man, often married, now increasingly the one willing for the sake of a little peace in the house to take on the role of husband, and who thrills the partner by saying the equivalent of "my beautiful junkyard").

Lloyd Richards as the trusted and stable brother. (Eve's great transgression is in trying to seduce him—a terrible and damning violation of the incest taboo.)

Birdie Coonan as the auntie who'll always have a bed for you—but don't ever cross her—she reads you like nobody else ever has or will.

And what were the things all queers wanted more than anything? Margo Channing's fire and music. To live, so they imagined, in an inflamed state of consciousness. (Nevertheless, a piece of general advice parceled out at receptions went something like this: "Nothing too brilliant, darling, nothing at all incandescent; it bewilders them; standard candle is what gets stamped re-entry.")

Concerning theatrical parlance and Queer sex venues (together with the sex carried on in them). The places and the doings were always called scenes (as in "they got a good scene goin' up in the Park").

MARKING TIME

The Queer Revolutionary Calendar of 13 Moons: Vaseline, Stevedore, Partouze, Dexamyl, Amyl, Attitude, Mascara, Revenge, Judy, Balenciaga, Syphilis, Penicillin and Frottage.

Radical Activists in the 1970s, exploiting the tension of inheritance and the performance anxiety-of-influence manifest in the career of Liza Minnelli, tried unsuccessfully to have Judy changed to Stonewall, echoing the raging controversy between Thermidor and Fervidor in the days of the Directoire.)

There were but two seasons of the Revolutionary Queer Year, Summer and Winter, as there were but two time frames, Now and Next, in the culturally determined queer universe. Now and Next were not, as concepts, correlative to Then, as Then implied one of two things: consequence-futurity (abhorrent to the homosexual under siege) or the covered past (shameful, sepulchral, Caravaggiesque and inevitably compromising to him).

The four stages of the ordained queer life, adapted to a four-step routine for the prosecution of each episode of emotional entanglement, from The Four Stages of a Woman's Career as sardonically laid out by the brilliant Mary Astor (Bridget O'Shaughnessy in *The Maltese Falcon*, Academy Award best supporting actress of 1941 for the *The Great Lie*, the picture she and her co-star Bette Davis re-wrote, at Davis's insistence, to beef up the Astor part).

The Four Stages:

"Who's Mary Astor?"

"Get Mary Astor."

"Get a Mary Astor type."

"Who's Mary Astor?"

and boiled down from Erik Eriksson's eight stages of the heterosexual paradigm (both homosexual and homosexual life ending with Old Men Burdened with Winter):

Get Down.
Get It On.
Get Off.
Get Over It.

◄o►

All told, and despite their much vaunted espousal of the Greek ideal, *ataraxia* was not a high priority among them. The quiet life of reason was too much associated with staying in, and in the words of one dedicated every-nighter, "Plenty of time to stay in when you're dead."

The author makes note of structural tenets.

Things most likely happed this way—but may have happened otherwise.

Repetition of the familiar story with minor variations.

The fluidity and porosity of texts before they become canonical.

Nostalgia flashpoints: Charter myths: Ever since the Old Met. Ever since the Everard. Ever since Stonewall. Ever since (*All About*) Eve.

PART TWO

Investigations

Forensic Society

The reverse of coming out of the closet: secrecy was paramount; camouflage (good clothes) required to enter from the cold winter streets, the wayside parks, the bus station, the subway toilets, haunted by Margo Channing's damning dismissal of autograph hounds—spied in Shubert Alley while buying a ticket for Tallulah Bankhead in *Eugenia*—"They're nobody's fans. They never see a play or a movie even—they're never *indoors* long enough!"

Some Shubert Alley palaver:

"New York's sometimes fierce crosstown winds are emblematic or the world city as a cyclonic zone, drawing in so many different currents."

"You mean New York's a bit like Kansas after all?"

"New York is both Kansas and Oz, dahling, both black-and-white and technicolor, with wicked witches on both sides of town, and good ones too, showing up in bubbles, every so often—if you know how to blow them."

"The bubbles or the witches?"

"Either one."

Eighth Street in the summer of '57: a real stretch of the imaginary *Queer Street* metropolis. The Eighth Street Bookshop, the Whitney, the Bon Soir and the Village Barn. The Walgreen's on the northeast corner of Eighth Street and the "Avenue of the Americas" (don't-cha know). The Eighth Street (at Broadway) men's toilet (the uptown side). One was not to be pointed in the direction of Canal Street under any circumstances, and the correct access to the Wall Street/Broad Street come-all-ye of forms not found

in art or nature was by way of the downtown IRT caught at Astor Place).
Washington Square, NYU, the Coach House, the Gramophone Shop.

Once finished at (or flushed out of) the men's, catch the BMT up to
either 34th Street for Macy's or for the Metropolitan to Times Square,
40th Street end, and the "curtain-call" flower stall where, at bargain prices,
great bouquets suitable for flinging across the footlights could be found. And
if to Macy's, in the front door on Herald Square and a beeline for the men's
department (and its adjacent facility) to finger a few ties and spritz on a
little free Yardley from the samplers, then over to the Dixie Bus Terminal
across from the General Post Office, then back to Broadway and straight
up to the Great White Way.

"Broadway's on the diagonal!" somebody cuts in. So was he. The diagonal, they'd been taught in geometry, is in relation to the straight sides irrational incommensurate, as is the square root of two. (This made some sense,
particularly when one considered the odiousness of measuring up in general and if the two sides in question stood for the two lives being led, the
schoolboy life and the jail-bait life.)

Therefore a social strategy, beyond being picked up and taken indoors.
Talk to him, get him to talk about himself. Ask him how, for instance, he's
spending the week: work, theater engagements, his musical life . . . all that.
Be demure: wait for him to suggest a further engagement. It might be a party
on Bank Street. Lo and behold, it *is* a party on Bank Street, which as it
turns out is quite literally an open house: the doors have been thrown open,
the word has echoed down the acoustic length of Greenwich Avenue to the
Avenue of the Americas (*"Mi casa su casa, chicos!"*), liquor and food have
been carted in and nobody in the place knows more than half a dozen of the
others. All the same (and taking note of the phenomenon: you just go into
a bar, drink up and find the party, which is by no means always a queer
party *as such*) there is that about going in with an actual invited guest which
bolsters confidence. *They* then are the dress extras; you are at least for the
night a contract player.

UNITS AND OBJECTIVES

*"Do you recall, at one of our first lessons, when I asked you to go out onto the
bare stage and act? You did not know what to do and floundered around help-
lessly with external forms and passions."*

But they're all doing exactly that. Listen.

"'I cahn't wear this wig, Noel, it's like peeking out of a Yank's arsehole!' She actually *said*—"

—◄○►—

"No, dahling, I did not get sick all the time, stay in bed and play with dolls, I got sick, stayed in bed as much as I could and played with toy soldiers. Get it? I never played with little girls or their dolls, and I never let them within a yard of me, O.K.?"

"How gladly, with proper words, the soldier dies."

"Sez who?"

"Wallace Stevens."

"Oh, her!"

"Don't you just adore hearing *poem* pronounced correctly, in two syllables?"

And what kind of party is this (or are the others)?

There are four paradigms; three from movies and one from the record he listened to over and over in the Jackson Heights Public Library all those (four? five?) years ago, before . . . what?

"What did you do before?"

"Before what?"

"Before . . . the jewels."

"I wanted them."

—Charles Boyer and Hedy Lamarr in *Algiers*

The four parties: from *Laura*, from *Rope*, from *The Bachelor Party* and from *The Cocktail Party*.

Added to which: a week-long crash program derived from intense after-school study (in the Reading Room of the New York Public Library at 42nd Street) of Konstantin Stanislavsky's *An Actor Prepares*, the bible of all serious aspirants in the theater:

Monday: Units and objectives.

Tuesday: Faith and a sense of truth.

Wednesday: Emotional recall.

Thursday: Adaptation.

Friday: Inner motive forces (Ruth Draper "Earth ray thought forces," *errth raay thawt fawces*).

Saturday afternoon (before the dinner date, at the Finale on Commerce Street and the party afterwards): The Super-objective.

(Home on Sunday: double emphasis, indicating, bombast and fuck them all, What are they anyway? A pack of cards. Oh? And what exactly are you, other than loaded dice?)

—◄o►—

"We all need beauty, serenity and nice surprises in our lives."
"Surprise me, Jane, I love surprises . . . I *do*!"

—◄o►—

"My soldiers died gladly, for me, in 'The Land of Counterpane.'"
"Huh?
"Robert Louis Stevenson's *A Child's Garden of Verses*. The toy soldiers in 'The Land of Counterpane.'"
"Listen, in my neighborhood, Queens—"
"Sssh—for God's sake don't mention Queens!"

—◄o►—

"Poetry, dear? There's not much to starting in—rhyming and timing for fun and profit, although not quite so much perhaps as there used to be, except in advertising."
"Hmmm."
"Yes, dear, well put. The first thing you must do is go out and get your-self a rhyming dictionary, which ought to keep you occupied for a few weeks.":
"A rhyming dictionary?"
"Oh, yes—unless of course you want to jump in at what these new freaks consider the deep end and just start *expressing* yourself. Yes indeed, an invaluable tool, one of those—not the freaks, dear; they're almost literally a dime a dozen or at any rate ten cents a dance. No, the dictionary. Start, for example, with rhyme itself. Let's see, crime, dime, I'm, lime, mime, rhyme, slime, time. There you are, dear, that's either the octave to a sonnet or some scraps for a *pantoum*. Kicky little form the *pantoum*—irrepressibly gay. Anyway, now you're off and running."

-◄o►-

"I grew up in the aftermath of World War II, watching boys play Burn Down Hitler's Bunker, and Iwo Jima with some of the soldier's faces painted yellow. I brought my older brother's soldiers as a contribution, but when he found out, he said he'd *macerate* me if any of them got burned: he'd arranged them on playing fields when the war headlines, the radio broadcasts and the newsreels were new, and they'd survived, and if I—so I withdrew, until the reissue of *Gone With the Wind*, in the late '40s, and then I went out and got—or sent for from offers on the backs of cereal boxes—a collection of Civil War soldiers, uniformed blue and gray-with-yellow-sashes, but by then boys were interested in buying blue caps and gray caps and wearing blue dungarees and black dungarees bleached out to gray and going off into the vacant lots to play Wilderness and Antietam, whereas I went out and bought little Christmas trees from Woolworth's to represent the wilderness and set up hospitals and bandaged the wounded, and would out the soldiers from different sides down on pallets together, enacting rituals of reconciliation."

"I call that *sweet*."

-◄o►-

(Over against the wall: two commentators):

"Who is that boy?"

"Oh, I don't know, somebody new."

"He's very young—he can't be legal, can he?"

"He has a draft card—it's probably a fake."

"Unusual boy, curiously compelling."

"Now watch it, professor, don't get run over."

"What do you mean?"

"Only that if you were thinking of taking him to Jersey—Asbury Park for the roller derby—you should remember the Mann Act."

"Me, a pedophile? Dahling, perish the thought—yes, *perish* the thought!"

"Of getting caught."

"You are deeply terrible. You will come to a bad end."

-◄o►-

All right, they were looking over at him, talking about him.

We find many objectives on the stage, and not all of them are either necessary or good.

"*I should define the right objectives as follows,*" said he.

1. They must be on our side of the footlights. They must be directed toward the other actors, and not toward the spectators.

―◁○▷―

"Seduction, persuasion, conversion, or whatever else you choose to call it, I say with head held high—"

"For a gay change—"

"With head held high, that I have gladly done my part whenever called upon to carry the message to the mistakenly married."

"Gaga's life is an open book, fallen off the remainder table."

―◁○▷―

2. They should be personal yet analogous to the character you are portraying.

―◁○▷―

"It's more than an easy metaphor, darling, flute playing. Only when you have mastered double tonguing and flutter tonguing, and not before, are you ready to open for business."

―◁○▷―

"Girl Trouble, I have clocked your m.o. from Jump Street—there is no turn you can 'gin up I ain't seen.'"

"A formidable woman."

―◁○▷―

"The fact is, dahling, there are good days and bad days, and this is one of them."

"I don't know—but I'll tell you one thing, I'm getting very tired of these young fairies forever talking out of the sides of their mouths. You never know

which side, you never know who's talking to whom in a crowded room—
and you can't possibly put them down at a dinner table without incurring collisions: it's worse than setting right- and left-handed eaters side by side. I
blame the situation comedies on television."

—◄o►—

3. They should have the quality of attracting and moving you.

—◄o►—

"Balked of allies in the present, more elastic climate, she persists."
    "In?"
    "Attempted constriction."
    "Ah."
    "Hinting of royal blood and family madness."

—◄o►—

" 'And so,' says she—and you know how grand she does get after handing
out her old tomatoes—'I was borne out, which gave me great—no, enormous—satisfaction.' Whereupon up pipes this little queen who hadn't whispered a syllable all night. 'Gee, honey, ya must come from tolerant people.'
'I'm afraid,' sniffs the Baroness, 'I don't know what you mean.' 'Well, honey,
I was born out too, and I admit it was easier that way, not having to come
out, at work for instance—which anyway in display isn't what you could
call a big deal—but I wanna tell ya it was hell in the neighborhood growing
up.' "

—◄o►—

4. They should be active, to push your role ahead and not let it stagnate.

—◄o►—

"So he goes out to Universal, signs for the one picture, makes it, and it looks
like he's got something—this is just before the Wasserman purge, understand. So he diddles around on the contract and wonders out loud could

he get a piece of the property. An actor. I said 'Who do you think you are, darling, Bette Davis? in *A Stolen Life?*' Anyway, he was so stupid that the agent, just to keep him smiling, said 'I think I might be able to get you a small percentage—of the net of course.' Of the net. Hilarious."

"Because there is no net—is that what you mean?"

"You might say that. When it comes to the net, darling, it's rather like the Life. You slip off the high wire and *sayonara*—followed by a sickening thud."

—◄○►—

An objective should have attraction for the actor, make him wish to carry it out. This magnetism is a challenge to his creative will.

Objectives which contain these necessary qualities we call creative. Rehearsals are taken up in the main with the task of finding the right objectives, getting control of them and living with them.

—◄○►—

"Queer. A word like Mesopotamia, the responses to which are mainly emotive. Much depends on so much else—as in contract bridge, in which a cardinal rule is you must always interpret your partner's signal as attitude unless it is unmistakably suit preference."

"In faggot lore the iceman cometh with the postman, always twice."

"Our wound, dahling, has become our poetry—witty, stylish, poignant, mordantly comical and—yes, terribly sad."

"Plus which, due to the rise in general knowledge and social education faggots receive from *The New Yorker* and the better fashion magazines—well, it cannot be denied we are beginning to have a real influence."

"Do you think so? I do not. In my opinion the homosexual clerisy lays noisy, dressy claim to a power it ultimately fails to obtain—for the very same brute reasons women in pants fail similarly. Whereupon both project a fiction for that same power into separate realms—the homosexual into the realm of the aesthetic and the women in pants into the realm of the sexual. The realm of power is neither aesthetic nor sexual: in it persuasion is never the product of a response, and force is neither an accoutrement nor a titillation, it is a determinant—*the* determinant."

"Any culture is a system which limits or denies individual agency."

—◄○►—

The important question today is how to draw an objective from a unit of work. The method is simple. It consists of finding the most appropriate name for the unit, one which characterizes its inner essence. Have you any conception of what a really good name for a unit represents? It stands for its essential quality. To obtain it you must subject the unit to a process of crystallization; for that crystal you find a name.

(Aha! Essence *succeeds* existence: process of crystallization. *That's* why the Russians are the true existentialist actors.)

—◄○►—

"Does a dedicated masturbator worry about the demonstrable psychological import of digit ratio? I think not."

"The boy has—how shall I put it, dear—linguistic capacities."

—◄○►—

"Nietzsche said it best. 'Each of us carries around within him a productive originality which is the very core or his being—' "

"Yes, dahling, in sizes small to XL, available in an array of dazzling designer shades."

"'—and if he becomes aware of this originality, a strange aura, the aura of the extraordinary, shapes itself around him.' It's true—we are turned on, dahling, by romanticism, daydreams, introspection and perplexity—what the world calls sin."

"Nietzsche. Didn't Nietzsche invent Superman?"

"Yes, he did, dahling, you're quite right—everything but the cape; Travis Banton invented that."

—◄○►—

"Fucking smart-ass—everybody's a fucking smart-ass. It's the fucking smart-ass capital!"

"Well, my analyst is an existentialist. They don't believe in traits at all— they consider traits superstitious nonentities of a no longer viable game plan.

They believe in multifarious experience and its sedimentation—and in internal kinetic convulsions brought on by vicious exertions of the superego."

"Go to jail, go directly to jail—do not pass Go, do not collect two hundred dollars."

—◄o►—

(Multifarious experience and its sedimentation, crystallization. So, *I'm an existentialist.*

And I've only known me five minutes.)

—◄o►—

"What about Gore Vidal?"

"What *about* Gore Vidal?"

"Is he, well, queer?"

"Gore Vidal is the smart-ass of smart-asses—the *president.*"

"He'd love the last part of that."

"Fat chance—and anyway he'd be terrible."

"Gore Vidal may be queer, but he thinks there is no such thing as homosexuality *per se.*"

"*Per lui,* I think you mean—it doesn't *apply* to him."

"He says there are only homosexual acts, no matter who—"

"—is committing them, yeah, yeah. I'll tell you something better, dahling. There are a lot of men who commit only homosexual acts no matter who they think they're fucking."

"Oh, well. He says it's only a construction—something out of Oscar Wilde."

"Constructed truth; very much in vogue these days. Construction workers too."

—◄o►—

Step by step, with the aid of questions and explanation, Torsov led us to the conclusion that there are two kinds of truth and sense of belief in what you are doing. First, there is the one that is credited automatically and on the plane of actual fact. Second, there is the scenic type, which is equally truthful but which originates on the plane of imaginative and artistic fiction.

—◄O►—

"If you mean by McCarthyism the drunken ravings of the sweaty senator from Wisconsin, whose fear of faggots and passion to extirpate them from Foggy Bottom so endears him to Mary-Mary Hoover and the Federal Bunghole of Inverts, then I sympathize with your anguish, darling, but I am far less worried by all of that than by the McCarthyism of the liberal left, by which I mean the product of the ugly mind of Mary-Mary McCarthy, from whose vile snatch issue such propaganda pieces as that little *investigation* of fag culture in the Village that ran some years ago in no other rag but that oh, so libertarian, egalitarian and compassionate *New York Post*. And you can quote me!"

—◄O►—

"Well the rumor is he was *furious* over that nellie fag Capote getting the *New Yorker* assignment to *do* Brando when *he*, a real man's man, with a *background*—"

"Oh, honey Glory and her *background—quel camp*."

"Well then, what about Brando—is he or not?"

"What is a man?"

"Exactly."

"What we do know, darling, is that Brando is just a bit more *embrangled* than Alfred Lunt."

"Well, I thought that *New Yorker* profile was actually terribly illuminating."

"That profile was made up out of a very few, very tentative statements that set the fevered brain of a ballsy queen who terrified his subject into overdrive, period."

"Lil goes way back with Brando—she remembers Mama's Truckline Café."

—◄O►—

You must use a lever to lift you onto the plane of imaginary life. There you will prepare a fiction analogous to what you have just done in reality. Properly envisaged "given circumstances" will help you to feel and create a scenic truth in which you can believe while you are on the stage. Consequently in ordinary life truth is what really exists, what a person really knows, whereas on the stage it consists of something that is not actually in existence but which could happen.

"Well one thing at least Gore said makes a lot of sense to me, and that's never pass up a chance either to have sex or be on television."

"Glory would like to kill two birds with one stone—doing both at once."

"Glory should really go on *What's My Line?*—but as panelist or mystery guest?"

"Lilies are not stalked on weeds, darling, although they may sometimes stand among them."

"Actually Tennessee, Glory and Truman should all go on together; as the Unholy Trinity."

"Oh, darling, they wouldn't last a minute, not with La Kilgallen. They may all be friends of Dorothy, but not *that* Dorothy."

—◄o►—

"Eliot is *the* poet, my dear—even Eartha Kitt knows that."

"Well, Eliot *is* monotonous—Miss Kitt knows that much all right."

"Poetry today is monotonous, true, and monotony is poetry."

"I think poetry should pay attention to the world. Courting an audience is not the same as paying attention to the world. Walt Whitman paid attention to the world."

"Whitman was a careerist swish. Oh, captain, my captain indeed. *Hullo, sailor* is more like it. *Melville* is the most deeply, desperately, definitively homosexual writer of the nineteenth century."

"But I love Hart Crane."

"He certainly was poetic. In the sense that poetry is conspicuous, he was poetic."

—◄o►—

"Emerson isn't for us, darling. I mean, can you seriously conceive of a two-fisted, self-reliant homosexual without an active petitionary prayer life? No, Thoreau is for us."

—◄o►—

"Lum and Abner are homosexual lovers, and that is *that*."

—◄○►—

"There are no great men, child, there never were; what there are are great stories about men—and that's something they've got to hand us, we do know that; that's what our irony is all about, at bottom. We are like valets—and you are I hope familiar with the saying concerning so-called great men and their valets, who, if the truth be known were, and still are, under it all, fags."

"Under it all . . . at bottom . . . categorical statements are, I always think—"

—◄○►—

Of significance to us is this: the reality of the inner life of a human spirit in a part and a belief in that reality. We are not concerned with the actual naturalistic existence of what surrounds us on the stage, the reality of the material world. This is of use to us only insofar a it supplies a general background for our feelings.

—◄○►—

"That boy over there—he *is* musical? He *is* so?"

"He's musical all right, but I don't know if he's *so* or *so-so*."

"Does *he*?"

"Oh, darling, your mother really is not up to reading a whole string of beads tonight. One presumes he has had intimations, inklings, perhaps even experiences, whatever they are."

"Experiences are—oh, but you probably didn't mean it that way."

—◄○►—

In those days the question was still asked, is he *musical* or so. He was so musical he knew he belonged on Broadway (although probably not at the address between 39th and 40th streets) and mostly to 42nd Street: naughty, bawdy, gaudy—yes, the Deuce. From the New York Public Library Central Circulation all the way over to the big new Port Authority bus terminal. Nobody had to tell him—and a good thing too, because there were no leads in the seven New York dailies—to make straight (hah! hah! *hah!*) or the gentlemen's, shall we say, *lounge.*

For open secret tea-room ceremonies. Tea ceremonies are properly held in tea *houses,* true, but the tea room at Port Authority was the size of a half-floor in the fabled Dakota Apartments overlooking Central Park West. (He found that out almost immediately, chance happening transformed into destiny by a single occurrence of popular demand.) Two seemingly endless rows of urinals, as many as at Radio City Music Hall—with as many semaphoric penises as a full kick line of Rockettes' legs . . . and in the stalls, you might say, apropos tea ceremonies, there was a kind of Zen operating insofar as the meditator was summoned to contemplation of a symmetry without the burden of any attendant meaning.

"So he's in the tea room at 59th and Lexington, of course on the uptown side, and he sees scribbled on the stall wall, *For a nice acomodation, call Regent 4———,* and for the first time in his life is impelled to scribble a reply: *There are two c's and two m's in* accommodation, *Mary.*"

◄○►

If you only knew from within how important self-study is! It should go on ceaselessly, without the actor even being aware of it, testing every step he takes, for who will guarantee that having rid himself of one lie, another will not immediately take its place?

◄○►

George Chauncey's summary of the ethos and praxis of the tea rooms cannot be matched. From *Gay New York: Gender, Urban Culture and the Making of the Gay Male World 1890–1940*:

"Most commonly the vice squad hid policemen behind the grille facing the urinals so that they could observe and arrest men having sex there or in the stalls. . . . The observers' need to hide was significant; as even the police admitted the men they observed would have stopped having sex as soon as they heard someone beginning to open the outer door.

"The men who used subway washrooms tended to be relatively poor and to have relatively little access to other kinds of private space, either because of their poverty or because their own homes were unavailable to them for homosexual trysts.

"It would be wrong, though, to suppose that only poor men frequented the tea rooms, for many other men visited them as well. Indeed the constant sexual activity in the city's public restrooms involved thousands of men for whom the encounters had widely varying meanings. Even among gay men, views about the propriety of such visits varied enormously. Some men, particularly those who who were professionally successful in jobs that required them to pass as straight, found it astonishing that anyone in their circles would risk going to a tea room, given the threat of arrest and the availability of alternatives to men highly integrated into gay society. Others were as likely as the anti-vice squad to regard such encounters as shameful; for they expected the same level of romanticism, monogamy and commitment to be involved in gay relationships that bourgeois ideology expected of marriage."

◄○►

It was a time of voyages to lower hemispheres; of whale-shit shipwrecks too. Tea-room culture was both a driven, muddied thing and a source of heart-healing joy in zones of pregnant (if peculiar) resonance, albeit in small doses, and not at all sufficient unto nightfall.

They had a right to feel low down, a right to hang around, down around the river.

One's social performances in subway toilets could not really be said to have thrived under the watchful gaze of an intelligent, controlling long-range purpose—in fact mental health professionals, in league with the American Psychiatric Association, described them as floridly decompensated schizophrenic behaviors—but they were nevertheless invariably soothing, and they did render one, if not secure, then at any rate refreshed, and ever more patient and observant.

◄○►

("*I shall not undertake to form a definition of it,*" said the director Torsov, "*all I can do is help you feel what it is. Even to do that requires great patience, for I shall devote our whole course to it. Or to be more exact, it* will appear by itself *after you have studied our whole system of acting and after you yourself have made the experiment of* initiating, clarifying, transforming *simple everyday human realities into crystals of artistic truth,* and this does not happen all in a minute.")

-◄�o►-

It was exhilarating: total immersion learning, in at the deep end, like under-water hockey, where the only thing between the player and the score is the need to breathe, the only mission in life to raise the effect of allure to the level of agony. New York was, from Pearl Harbor until the McCarthy fag witch hunts a decade later, not unlike what one heard reported of the Weimar Republic. Everything went topsy-turvy. Amid much laughter and even more screaming, men danced together, and women too, in the large hope of bond-ing across social differences. Of course we in the Eisenhower years, inher-itors of all that, were fools thinking we could build on such foundations, particularly when it came to bagging the married ones. Remaking *Back Street* over and over (and dreaming of the musical), we told ourselves we were having affairs because they were, but whereas they were being unfaith-ful to true women (one of the things that, in summing it all up, gave *The Boys in the Band* such weight), we had absolutely nothing to be unfaithful to, unless you count parental guidance, such as it had been.

However, speaking of the underground of which the tea rooms were the emblematic locus, there was that little something extra (besides fire) one could always be sure of finding down below, in what censorious social queers, sounding like the public prosecutor, called *those* places.

From a discussion at Hector's Cafeteria, 42nd Street, off Seventh Avenue, south side:

"That little something extra. O.K., I'll bite."

"Ouch."

"Cheerleaders, dear—although there are no sidekicks in the tea rooms; everybody is a star."

"Old cops always called the tea rooms the nickelodeons."

-◄o►-

You will see actors who are gifted with magnificent powers of expression in all phases of human emotions and the means they use are both good and right. Yet they may be able to transmit all this to only a few people, during the inti-macy of rehearsal. When the play goes on and their means should grow in vividness, they pale and fail to get across the footlights in a sufficiently effec-tive theatrical form.

—◄○►—

"I've never understood how anybody can do business in such places, with express trains roaring by at regular intervals, inhibiting conversation—never *mind* the ever-present danger of being hauled in and charged with indecency, outrage and affray."

"Which only goes to demonstrate that the Post Office has nothing on us when it comes to the swift accomplishment in all weathers of our appointed rounds, or the Church either, in terms of devotion. For we too have our fathers, and maintain their faith in spite of fire, dungeon and the sword. And that for all that, there are those such as you, dear, the censorious, who prefer the more, shall we say, *leisurely* occupation of following snaky-looking barefoot androgynes, slender, smooth and hyacinthine, down overgrown garden paths to gothic chambers mystical with chimes and incense."

—◄○►—

If ordinary people employ a large variety of adaptations, actors need a correspondingly greater number because we must be constantly in contact with one another and therefore incessantly adjusting ourselves. The quality of the adjustment is crucial: vividness, colorfulness, boldness, delicacy, shading, taste.

—◄○►—

"Whereupon one is at any rate securely and properly indoors, and relatively serene. There are certainly necessary estimates in precise degrees to be made in the arena there, but really, compared to the number of harassing calculations necessary in a career of exhaustive trawling on Rapid Transit—"

"Oh, I don't know. After all, if they take you to an old hotel on Third Avenue—"

"You're dating yourself, dahling—get a smart grip! Since the El came down, there are no more interruptions—no more mass audiences hurtling past your window at regular intervals. They've planted sycamore trees on Third Avenue: by 1960 it'll look like the Boulevard St. Germain, and the only eyes that scope you being seen to on the second floor will be the little eyes of nesting sparrows."

"And in the harried calculations department pretty intricate work—particularly when you are dealing with clean-cut pay dirt."

"Good thing that Arthur Murray taught you dancing in a hurry."

"The tea-room tango. I had a week to spare—one did in those days, Mad in pursuit, and in possession so / Had, having, and in quest to have, extreme."

"You bring up a good point about the subsequent occurrence of metaphysical debasement. Metaphysics is an essential part of tea-room culture—particularly that branch of it dealing with the penetration of heavy disguises, and most particularly in winter, with so much gorgeous clothing coming into play. Why, by the time one does get down to pay dirt—if one does, before Lily Law comes swaggering in to call time out—one has inevitably fingered one's way though a representative sample of the merchandise available at De Pinna, Paul Stuart, Brooks Brothers, Saks and the lesser emporia. And if one doesn't, one learns again and all too well indeed that something heavily camouflaged is there even if one can't see it: there even more so, consequence of one's knowing pretty exactly, within reasonable, measurable limits, what it would be like to see it independently of seeing it unconcealed. It's a dialectic, darling, that can indeed prove truly lacerating."

◄○►

"You already know how important it is to choose the right name for an objective. You remember that we found the verb form preferable because it gave more impetus to action. The same is true to an even greater extent in defining the super-objective.

◄○►

"Plus which, one is required by prudence and the circumstances of municipal ambience to give oneself up to long, hard, patient scrutiny—and to give a certain dignified, stately form to the things one says, the feelings one expresses. Scrutiny, for instance, of the inscriptions all over a typical tea-room partition's metal walls—in which activity we resemble adepts of the ancient world's magical religions, who lived by the inscriptions carved on magical gems: etched with little or no regard for appearance, but with an iron determination to get the necessary words and patterns, somehow or other, onto the stone."

◄○►

The main inner current of a play produces a state of inner grasp and power in which actors can develop all the intricacies and then come to a clear conclusion as to its underlying fundamental purpose.

◄◦►

"Indeed, speaking of the tea room in the Eighth Street BMT—downtown side—I have never forgotten the inscription made during the war by the sharp edge of some diamond on the mirror over the sink there. *GNOTHI SEAUTON.* Know thyself—of course one night some mad queen in a Benzedrine rage smashed the mirror. A palsied wretch regressed to the wild-mind state that is our natural naked condition—for our minds are at root wild, animal minds, shaped by a terrible history of environmental pressures. To know one's self is to know the beast. As the wise old academic hag who brought me out at Amherst maintained, we are all prime examples of Baudelaire's *l'heautontimoroumenos*—self-terrifiers, darling, gnawing away our whole lives at the *palaion penthos* that marks us.

"For which we try to compensate by turning our lives into a vital art—one that springs, as Yeats proclaimed art must, from the argument we have with ourselves. It's no mystery at all why three-quarters of the queens in this room identify so absolutely with Margo Channing. Although hardly beautiful women, they are all terribly intelligent and talented ones at the peak of their careers—or if perhaps, as time accelerates, just past the peak, but still not to be had for the price of a martini, like a salted peanut. They have every reason for happiness—except happiness.

"And, in addition to serious *agraphia*, there is always the wit—of which I have always treasured two enchanting examples: the gloss on a message carved by a penknife on a wooden partition in the men's room opposite the Main Reading Room of the New York Public Library at 42nd Street. Under the boastful advertisement of that carver's gargantuan penile endowment was daubed in bright red nail polish the admonition, 'Important, if true!' And second the following little dialogue:

'My mother made me a homosexual.'
'Will she make me one if I give her the wool?'

"We are good sports; sex is salvation enough."

◄◦►

*If all the minor objectives in a part are, because of tendencies, aimed in differ-
ent directions, it is of course impossible to form a solid, unbroken line. Consequently
the action is fragmented, uncoordinated, unrelated to any whole. No matter
how excellent each part may be in itself, it has no place in the play on that basis.*

◄○►

"*Gnothi seauton.* Know thyself indeed. I shall never understand how the
homosexual world has been able to sustain the idea that knowing oneself is
the same as spotting one's own kind. Oh, well, as Stella Adler tells her students—she calls them all *dahling*—if all else fails, substitute."

"You meet a lot of public relations types in tea rooms."

"Yes, but have you noticed they tend not to call them tea rooms, but
things like *facilities*? It's touching."

"What you meet a lot of in tea rooms, talking of touching, is cops. There
is a much better than even chance that on any given evening spent adventuring
under the streets of New York, your scented little tryst will be suddenly interrupted quite unceremoniously and to your disadvantage by Muss 'Em Up
Donovan and company."

The tea rooms, where under the rubric *Cometh the hour, cometh the
man*, and to the repeated humming of the strains of their theme song, "As
Time Goes By," the celebrants of this worldwide religion clocked significant portions of their lives. "Anybody got the time?" a voice would call out
from a stall.

"Anybody who doesn't better wise up!"

"I mean literally; I've got an appointment."

"If it's with destiny, Mary, you've had it."

"No, really, I need to know the exact time."

Whereupon an acerbic answer would be given, in the manner of Lloyd
Richards to his wife Karen in that mysteriously broken-down car on the
road to Brewster, "When you asked a minute ago it was five forty-two, it is
now five forty-three. When you ask again in a minute's time—"

"All right, all right!"

"All of which means, I'm afraid, that if your cutie was due at two-to-two
today, you've missed him by exactly three and three-quarter hours."

"Sitting here hour on hour as we do, you'd think we could at least talk
about something."

"There are occasions, dear, that go beyond words."

"Somerset Maugham declared that conversation is only possible when men's minds are free from pressing anxieties."

"Owing to the cult of more violent sensations, contemplation is undervalued."

"Speaking of which, whatever happened to wipe, do not blot?"

Sometimes there would be a little song, sweet and plaintive like:

> "Won't you tell him please to follow my lead,
> Swallow some speed.
> Oh, how I need
> Someone to put up with me!"

Thus the scenes, the roller-coaster ride the tea-room circuit was (although underground) and the reminiscence by older queens of the time when the roller coaster was called the scenic railway.

Tea-room Graffiti:

MULTIPLE UNIT RECREATIONAL FACILITY

SOME RAN COMING

AND SO IT IS WE ENTER THE BROKEN WORLD, TO TRACE THE VISIONARY COMPANY OF LOVE

◄○►

A Quiz:

Lars Proscenium by the nine gods of Clusium swore what, exactly?

Who was Lars Proscenium?

Who are the nine gods of Clusium?

What was the point?

Answers (written upside down and backwards):

He'd never be hungry again.

Nils Aster's demon lover.

Porthos, Athos, Aramis, D'Artagnan, Groucho, Harpo, Zeppo, Vladimir, Estragon.

Point Lookout.

Gloss: The proper translation of Clusium is Closet Room (Bonus Points if asked and correctly answered).

"THE EXPENSE OF SPIRIT IN A WASTE OF SHAME."

("SPRINKLES EXTRA")

Sic ego perire coepi
Agnosco veteris vestigia flammae
Sunt lacrimae rerum, et mentum mortalia tangunt.

Really? Get Over It.

The exposure of clandestine origins, vexations and spumes. The guttering failure of the faggot's life.

Seasonally adjusted expectancy predictions.

A graffito dialogue over some days:

> "In meditation, booth by booth
> We ponder the hard lines of Truth
> And witness through door-cracks forsooth
> Th'ungirdling of the loins of Youth
> (Apologies to W. Pater)"

You needn't apologize for that old queen; she closed the first half for eleven years and she never let anybody forget it.

I said *to*, not *for*.

Oh, did you? Sorry, dear, I get my boxing terms confused.

◄o►

TRAVEL TIP: The Santa Maria Atocha *Caballeros* shrine—located in the very underground pit where the charred remains of heretics, Jews and sodomites were thrown to the scavenging dogs following the *autos-da-fé* in the reign of Philip II. In this holy precinct male sex monks perform the sacred transformative rituals of cock worship and communion of both species, flesh and hot spunk.

Male sex monks? A pleonasm, I'd have thought.

◄o►

Apocryphal tea-room story. In a late-night cop raid, after the opera, the ballet and the theater crowd had long gone home, as the pursued felons dispersed, haring down platforms, leaping over turnstiles, jumping down onto the tracks and disappearing in the tunnels full of sewer rats, where they hoped to be spared death by oncoming local trains, one voice calling wildly, "Stay alive—I'll find you!"

Fascinating, all of it, but there must be a way to access The Life upstairs in the open air.

> *facilis descensus Averno:*
> *noctes atque dies putet atri ianua Ditis:*
> *sed revocare gradum superasque evadere ad auras,*
> *hoc opus, hic labor est.*
>
> —Virgil, *Aeneid*, VI, 126–29

> "Easy enough the descent to Avernus;*
> Night and Day** the door of dark Dis lies open
> But to retrace your step, to escape into
> The upper air, this is the task, the labor."
>
> *a snap in fact
> **(*you are the one*)

◄○►

"Aw rocks, tell us in plain words."

> —Marian (Molly) Bloom (née Tweedy)

This narrative records varieties of consensual relations between a male minor and any number of male adults.

Up from the Eighth Street BMT toilet, upstairs to Eighth Street itself, and as a result of another immediate encounter so to finally make it indoors, and up in the elevator to the open fires in the living rooms, with the views over the park, or of the river (and of the bridge over which one had come to Manhattan).

The half-divine apostle (or john or agent or shill), mirroring the stars' admixture of human and divine, perceives the sin (or suffering) and begs for intercession ("When you wish upon a star"). The john (or agent or shill), in praying to the stars, draws the readers' attention to stardom's manifold virtues—eroticized out of the primal gnosis as Deep Mingling, Undecaying Union, Self-existent Pleasure and Only-begotten Happiness. (Note: the reader of the omens "I'm gonna read you your beads, little faggot.")

The john performs a miracle (cosmetic) on the prospect (akin to raising the dead or curing epilepsy) to astonish the populace. Somehow the author connects this to *Shazam* and the entire homosexual subtext of the crippled newsboy/Captain Marvel fantasy.

The miracle impresses the sinner, the crowd and the readers. And so, they are humbled as the sinner (sufferer) begs for admission to the ranks. The request is granted.

The prospect is bought out—in town. At the theater: *Auntie Mame* was one big attraction for this for a particular reason: the john could be seen to be innocently imitating the chin-to-the-wind valor of Rosalind Russell, a great favorite of faggots for all the best resaons, not least because she had taken the male part of Hildy in *The Front Page*, made him into woman in *His Girl Friday*, and still succeeded in providing a frame—smart lip fault-lessly delivered, city-editor gray pinstripe-skirted suit drag, competition with Cary Grant, a fag—and actually take the "uncle" part for an afternoon in all-seeming innocence.

Or, the yearling is taken to Fire Island.

And on Fire Island, the ungirdling of the loins of youth. Baptism and Confirmation, Eucharist ("scheduled maintenance on us") and a foretaste of Extreme Unction.

First Old Queen: "How long are you out, my dear?" "Two months, since the beginning of summer." "Go back! Go *back*!"

Second Old Queen, remonstrating with FOQ: "Quit whining, willya—ya knew it was dangerous work when ya took the job."

—‹o›—

Never lose yourself on the stage. Always act in your own person, as an artist. You can never get away from yourself. The moment you lose yourself on the stage marks the departure from truly living your part and the beginning of false acting. Always and forever, when you are on the stage, you must play yourself, but it will be in an infinite variety of combinations of objectives, and given circumstances which you have prepared for your part, and which have been smelted in the furnace of your emotional memory. This is the best and only true material for inner creativity. Use it, and do not rely on drawing from any other source.

—‹o›—

The most sought-after transaction in queer life is the brokering of affection with a stranger.

Why wasn't the trusted friendship of the high school tennis ace sufficient? Impossible to say, but the conviction was that when they'd heard the song "Tonight You Belong to Me"—a bit hit that season—the beloved was not having the exact same response the secret lover was having, and that there was nobody to blame for it, and nothing, short of ruining everything and returning to a state of terrified torment, to be done about it, upped the ante on sweet sorrow to the degree of a swoon, and then, only way out of a swoon was cold water in the face, and cold water was all that ran out of the faucets in subway toilets. Or ran in the brook in the Ramble.

"I get vertigo in the Ramble, dear—all those precipitous declivities."

"A rugged boy has the bracing appeal of all natural hazards."

"Hitchcock is out at Universal making a picture called just that."

"*Precipitous Declivities?*"

"No, you idiot, *Vertigo.*"

The following were the short- and long-division operations in relation to Queer Life in the 1950s. Take the figure six (from the seminal almost-but-not-quite-sacred book, *The Sixth Man*). Better still, make it seven for handicap and call it a good luck number. Divide into a sample population of males. Then take that result, representing, let's call them qualitatively homosexual men, and do long division, putting the result under (or into, same difference) that same general male population, and that result will perhaps give some indication of the outside number of homosexuals perhaps likely to live their lives, badly scarred, but possibly walking around standing up, and eventually collecting something in the way of veterans' benefits.

The elders propound a history: of the evolution of deep structures and of the vexation of art in queer life.

Right away the young Queer Temperament catches intimations of the propensity for temple tales and potentially oppressive power, but when it's been put on display in Tiffany's corner window by the great Gene Moore, not to buy into it (or, more exactly, accept its bright coin in his hot fist) would be idiotic.

Along with becoming fiercer lesson by lesson, one day finding oneself in a position to declare, not necessarily in song but with the menacing insouciance of the great Risë Stevens as Carmen at the Metropolitan Opera,

> "Quand je vous aimerai?
> Ma foi, je ne sais pas.
> Peut-être jamais, peut-être demain,
> Mais pas aujourd'hui, c'est certain."

Fade-out . . . fade-in. And before dawn you found out in what exact way it was completely unnecessary to go all the way up to Harlem to do the uptown lowdown.

It was not a good idea at all to signal a need, much less to indicate a cost. One was by definition jail bait anyway, the merest suspicion of any further ability to or predilection for creating collateral damage was stupid. ("Wounded time does not heal itself, darling—that is a lie.") Free to go home was the better ad.

—◄○►—

"I am glad you have mastered yourselves, but although you have given evidence of will power in your actions, that is not sufficient for my purposes. I must arouse in you something more lively, more enthusiastic, a kind of artistic wish. I want to see you eager to go on the stage full of excitement and animation."

—◄○►—

The author responds, "I'm aroused, Professor Tostov; watch my smoke."

CHAPTER SEVEN

A Sample Progress on Queer Street

> "It is not a joke, the great clang of New York. It is the sound of brassy people at the party, at all parties, pimping and doing favors and threatening and making gassy public statements and being modest and blackmailing and having dinner and going on later."
>
> —Harold Brodkey

Wherein the author (clearly under the influence of Alfred Hitchcock's greatest picture, Vertigo) becomes habituated to leading a double life, until the double life (considerate curbside young heterosexual gentleman vs. The Other One) became a strain and when felonious queer reality hit that high-carat idea from the European arsenal, Alienation in the Metropolis, and one began one's career in brokering of affection with strangers, ever after clouding the original picture of the Edenic abode.

THE CIRCUITS

Carnegie Hall: pivot of the uptown circuit (favored by serious contenders). Carnegie Hall to the Russian Tea Room to the Plaza to the Sherry-Netherland to the Angel of the Waters. . . .

Across the boat lake into the Ramble, back past the Belvedere Castle to the Dakota and the Apthorp; segue to the Mais Oui, then back to the Osborne (diagonally across from . . . Carnegie Hall).

An essential strand of the elders' history, deep-structures category, always figures in the stories of mettlesome queers who "came out under fire" in

World War II and, as a societal sop, were indulged by the nation in the post-war years, emboldening the firebrand Harry Hay, the Mattachines, and *ONE* magazine to pitch more than just a few camp tents coast to coast. This all took place until the unholy alliance of the hard-line New York Freudians (wielding their powerful electro-and-insulin shock therapy wands) and the McCarthy–Army-State Department scare, compounded by the actions of the ever-resourceful *Confidential* magazine and Universal Studio's purge of queers, resulting in Universal's preservation of the fiction of Rock Hudson's heterosexuality by having him marry Phyllis Yates, thus making it possible, inter alia, for Rock to appear in the Sirk melodramas. This Unholy Alliance raised the national hysteria against the Queer Menace to a pitch that brought on nervous seizures in show dogs (a low blow).

In reaction to all of which, the author, QT, confected and retained for personal use the brawny bathhouse image of the gorgeous manly Harry Hay and his bronzed Los Angeles Mattachines, and of a Queer Street stretching underground from coast to coast, accessible in QT's imagination (and then some) through secret passageways in myriad Greyhound bus station toilets.

While closer to home, moving along at warp speed from a single encounter on Eighth Street (the Other Circuit, where those beyond contending slummed and spawned their hardy guttersnipe offspring) QT was ferried to what Auden nailed as the Uptown Manhattan Homintern, finding himself, improbably—but that in itself was probably the reason—present at Sunday matinee receptions at which, like Beckett's *Godot* (all the rage, but who'd ever seen the play except on television?), Gore Vidal, Arthur Laurents, James Baldwin, Truman Capote, the Ancients of Days: Carl Van Vechten, Glenway Wescott, and Leo Lerman (then only in his middle forties, but already Augustan beyond the common measure) were always expected and seemed never to show—or if they did, they'd leave, like the sable-enveloped Hollywood star at Margo Channing's coming home party for Bill Sampson in *All About Eve*, with half the men in the joint, leaving the host to remark, "The trouble with inviting every suspect in New York to a party is they tend to come."

Sunday matinee party talk was divided largely between two branching topics, decoration/display/music/theater and Abstract Expressionism. From the first would ramify, inevitably, all the latest Lenny Bernstein, Jerry Robbins, John Latouche and Company dish—such as who had really been at the opening night party for *Candide*, who really had seen *The Golden Apple*, *House of Flowers* and James Dean in *The Immoralist*, and for those who insisted on chewing old cud as if it were licorice sticks, or James Dean's last pair of socks, who really had been there at the opening night of *The Cocktail Party*? Nearly always next—following a few nods toward the literary (Must we really read *By Love Possessed*? Do we freely admit we devoured *The Fountainhead*?) the most minutely detailed give-and-takes concerning the preparations for the drag-flotilla that sailed once a year, at season's end, from Sayville across Great South Bay to Cherry Grove: show boats packed to the gunwhales with Du Barrys who were no ladies bent on making this the Year of Years on Fire Island to remember all year long back on the uptown Bird Circuit (the Blue Parrot, the Coq d'Or) and downtown at the Café Finale and the Cherry Lane on Commerce Street, at Lenny's Hideaway and the Modern.

From the second topic inevitably, the *on-dit* on Jackson Pollock, as rumored rough trade guesting at Mary's and how de Kooning threatened to beat him up for it if it was true, never mind the measurable difference in size or stature, or vertical extension up from the plane of earth between them.

On the boys at MoMA, on the burgeoning New York School: Frank O'Hara, John Ashbery (absent on official leave in Paris), Kenneth Koch (he's straight, thank God) and James Schuyler (the crazy one, but one of these days . . . watch out) or Edwin Denby and what *exquis* he'd just penned for *Ballet News*, on the go-betweens Rudy Burkhardt, Joe Le Sueur, Morris Golde, on certain painters besides Pollock and de Kooning, on the fabulous Patsy Southgate (back from Paris in peak form).

Certain post-modern tenets come retrospectively into play right about here. The parable is itself performative, a case of circular, or self-propagating information transfer. Fiction/non-fiction: free-association. The prophecy is self-fulfilling. The jig is up. The fleet is in. The price is right; the time is now. (The Bronx is up and the Battery's down.) You might as well live.

Thus more of the Romance of the Authority Figure, which utterly P.C. homosexuals, gasping for tenure-plus-treats, have learned with ease to call identifying with the oppressor. What I say is, if you're looking to convey a message, put it on a bumper sticker like the one I saw that afternoon coming back on the ferry from Cherry Grove to Sayville: Feel Safe Tonight/Sleep With a Cop.

The author's avidity became entirely a matter of connection to older queer New York: *res gestae* of a raucous past (toot, toot) and his self—image that of the Solovox, the instrument, precursor to the Moog synthesizer, in which eight instruments could be simulated one at a time by pressing switches, becoming now the cello, now the horn. And as an instrument how do you get to Carnegie Hall? Practice, practice, practice.

Every queer coming of age in America, who developed the ambition to be metropolitan, was instructed the same way: the goal is the penthouse overlooking the river, or the Park, or midway between the two, but uptown, far away from the 14th Street fault line. (Nowadays it's Chelsea, a little close for comfort, but home of the pre-cast façade: gyms, clubs, cafés, housed in those cast-iron buildings that made New York what it was a hundred and fifty years ago: The Metropolis of the pre-cast façade.) Every queer who instead opts for the house off Mulholland Drive, or hanging precipitously over one of the better canyons, likes to think he has the po-mo edge over his Eastern Seaboard coeval, but knows his house and all that goes with it is likelier with each day that passes to be, if not burnt off the hill, then swallowed up by the restless earth on which over the centuries he has had less than good luck wandering.

Then there was the enemies list, headed by the awful Norman Mailer solemnizing and slandering in politico drag, investing in hip. But possibly, originally, Emerson and everybody in his thrall, including, sadly the infantilized Hart Crane, who in "passages" yearned for an improved infancy, but in any event, without question, the *Partisan Review* mafia and the terrible Trillings, plus conflicted "self-reliant" liberals in the business who were if anything worse than the pinko straight (as Allard Lowenstein and Bayard Rustin, for two, discovered to their grief). So that when today, when some leftist hectors the author for his interest in the Log Cabin Republicans, saying, "Don't those assholes know their party is out to destroy them?" he tells him, as if he were Ayn Rand or somebody like her (the director of the Federal Reserve, for example), to check his premises.

For some years prior to the publication in 1964 of Susan Sontag's "Notes on 'Camp'" (a breakthrough) in *Partisan Review*, the issue of the Jews and the homosexuals as two subversive agencies was back in the news—even as queer historian-activist Richard Plante tried without any real success until the 1970s to make the equivalence-in-suffering vivid with his revelations of the Pink Triangle in Auschwittz.

Timely icon: the Jewish heterosexual sympathizer ("No, but some of his best friends are").

QUEER MUSIC

Prior to all contenders and to any declarations of relative worth, and historically exemplary in both the aesthetic and the moral sense, Henry Cowell is American Queer Music's Apollo. Sprung from the late nineteenth century's San Francisco Bay Area Bohemian milieu, promulgator of the rule-shattering tone cluster ("Natural sounds, such as the wind playing through trees or grasses, or whistling in the chimney, or the sound of the sea, or thunder, all make use of sliding tones"), author of the highly influential *New Musical Resources*, and teacher of George Gershwin, John Cage and Lou Harrison, he was an innovator, a rebel and a genius (and not incidentally a victim of the stringent sodomy laws in force throughout the land and only finally—if not in perpetuity—rescinded on June 27, 2003, by the United States Supreme Court in *Lawrence and Garner v. Texas*).

Samuel Barber, the single genius (the violin concerto, the string quartet, *Knoxville: Summer of 1915*; *Vanessa* at the Metropolitan Opera).

Gian-Carlo Menotti (late-late verismo: Zandonai for Broadway and television).

Ned Rorem, salon fritillary and fashion victim; musical ideation derived from singing French ventriloquists, pitched as something on the level of Poulenc, actually a watery combination of "Chopsticks" disguised as "Gymnopédie" and endless sub-Reynaldo-Hahn elaborations of "Ah, vous-dirai-je, maman?").

Uncle Virgil Thomson (the plain Jane of plain Janes) who koshered Gertrude Stein into Protestant American plainchant in *Four Saints in Three Acts*, and who, it was said, wrote to assure Mary Garden concerning Maria Callas's impending Metropolitan debut, that he'd been told she, Callas, was a fake.

Leonard Bernstein, triumphant composer of *On the Town*, *Candide* and the immortal *West Side Story*, an expert if undiscriminating master of musical derivation and pastiche—in which respect he imagined himself the American Stravinsky, but as exquisite and self-effacing as was Stravinsky's "serious" musical decorum, so did Bernstein's become coarse, and narcissistic.

Ned Rorem, then, as always, at the height of his career.

Lou Harrison. Uncle Virgil said of him, "It was Mozart's boast that he could master any musical style within a week and by the end of that time compose in it adeptly enough to deceive experts. Lou Harrison has something of that virtuosity himself . . . and he mixes things with infallible imagination." A later generation recognized in him the very alchemical genius Uncle Virgil had so devoutly wished for in himself—to make American music anew in according to the very "melting pot" principle upon which the Republic, if not exactly founded, has been, since the end of the Civil War, sustained. Chances are it could only have happened in California.

-◄o►-

And everywhere and always the self-styled (and he made it stick) Petronius
Arbiter of the official shirt-and-tie counter-culture, Gore Vidal ("Gloria
Vitriol," and to the chic known as *Madame Sans-Gêne*): his trump card,
the ceaselessly repeated until virtually canonized Blatant-Male-Sexuality-
Incarnated-For-The-First-Time-In-The-Culture-By-Marlon-Brando hypothesis. This was contested by the venerable with forensic defenses of pre-war
and wartime erotica: Valentino, Richard Barthelmess, Ramon Novarro and
Francis X. Bushman in *Ben-Hur*, Paul Muni in *Scarface*, Johnny Weismuller
as Tarzan, William Holden in *Golden Boy*, John Garfield (the sexiest yid
on film till Paul Newman, who is anyway only half) in *Body and Soul*, Burt
Lancaster in anything, not to mention the thousands of images of near-naked
fighting men in the Pacific with which the newsreels created as many ripple
effects as there were women and queers.

All supplemented by the action features in which dozens of young, toothsome American males of varying histrionic capabilities revealed the aggres-
sively sexual male in his most characteristic environment, war: essentially
farm boys transformed by the glamour of the camera into the warriors of
classical mythology.

All these men paved the way for that undeniably volcanic appearance
in 1947 at the Ethel Barrymore, an event which certainly rocked Gotham,
in which the boy Nils from *I Remember Mama* (who'd also been Katherine
Cornell's Marchbanks in Shaw's *Candida* and had even done a stint opposite Tallulah Bankhead in *The Eagle Has Two Heads*, and of whom some
queens insisted they'd seen it in him all along) suddenly tore his shirt off
and bellowed "Stell-aaa!" (With particular vehemence, some said, to please
his famously emphatic teacher, Stella Adler.)

Followed in the next decade (the great chrysalis decade of twentieth-
century American homosexuality) by the sensitive boy on Broadway. Tony
Perkins as Eugene Gant in *Look Homeward, Angel* (wags crowed, "Look, a
homo angel!"), Roddy MacDowell (former boy idol and emblem of Ganymede
pluck) and Dean Stockwell (resolutely heterosexual but heart-stopping opposite Errol Flynn as Kipling's *Kim*, and in Joseph Losey's late-'40s "difference" melodrama, *The Boy with Green Hair*) tearing up the proscenium as
the fictionalized Leopold and Loeb in Meyer Levin's *Compulsion*. Stockwell
was the Leopold giving the most delirious rendition of homosexual passion

since definitions were applied. And Off-Broadway, the legendary formance given by James Dean as the Arab Boy in *The Immoralist.*

"Ah, oui, chéri, guider mon ombre aveugle en ces rues que j'aime."
—The French Ventriloquist

The eleven blocks walk of destiny: down Broadway from the Old Met ("The Yellow Brick Brewery on Broadway") to the Everard Baths. Broadway is on the diagonal and so was the author, QT. Broadway is an old Indian trail that cuts across the superimposed Manhattan grid. At the southwest corner of 28th Street, turn right into the old Tenderloin. The Everard Baths. The two green lamps made it look like a precinct entrance. It *was* a precinct entrance—since everyone did say it was owned and operated by the Patrolman's Benevolent Association.

Everybody went to the Everard Baths ("We have all walks of life in here, my dear, and some of death"). From Alfred Lunt and Lorenz Hart to Charles James dressed up in a long sheet tied into a 1913 hobble skirt to Gore Vidal to Nureyev. Et cetera! The place reeked of the experiences of men caught up in history, of the destinies of their own kind, of war and chemistry and a life truly lived.

The Everard in evening clothes: The Metropolitan Opera Club (reserved seating in the Grand Tier), an all-male bastion presided over genially by Francis Robinson, the Assistant General Manager, a true Southern gentleman who applied all the finesse of an Eleanor Belmont to lightly pinching teen-boy cheeks and trawling the Family Circle score desks for "guest listeners" and was the nicest possible old daddy a young person with musical ambitions could want to know. On a first-name basis with all the divas, current and retired, although he never addressed Ponselle or Jeritza, Novotna or Milanov, as anything but "Madame."

And behind the opera house, on Seventh Avenue, the outdoor tarpaulin covered the scene dock: metaphor of the queer life: scene upon scene all slotted together to be carried off in the back of a truck (and later that night: the scene among the trucks along West Street). Truckers and the scene dock became synonymous with Ljuba Welitsch ("It's a short show; wait for me across the street in Bill's"). Then they would frolic in her dressing room while the lucky guy's colleagues good-naturedly struck the set.

The Opera Line, Shubert Alley, the Museum of Human Oddities, the Astor Bar: all side turns off the main drag. The tour bus from Eighth

Avenue. Author imagines a queer version, for newcomers who might like to look at what they're getting into before deciding. Even so, it probably wouldn't work—cause of that Potemkin Village–Warner Brothers–back-lot quality of façade construction.

At the opera Gotham queers preferred *Don Giovanni* to *The Marriage of Figaro*, the *Don* being the one opera most undeniably pliable in a queer reading (although the queer immolation opera of all time remained Bellini's *Norma*), most especially in the character of the Don himself, who, like some lockerroom Lothario jock, carries his cocksman reputation on stage but is never once seen to succeed in seduction during the course of the evening (and believed by queers, before he attempts to seduce Zerlina, to have his eye squarely set on a *ménage-à-trois* with Masetto, whom he trusts will pursue and be cajoled into consenting).

In *Don Giovanni*, the intrigues of the wicked city were imprinted on them the way Beaumarchais's intrigues, analogous to country-house party weekend, could hope to be. And *Don Giovanni* was the one opera that had really gotten to Freud. Features included the easy elision of the ear from *ragazza* to *ragazzo* in the champagne aria, so Cesare Siepi and George London, both big butch guys, could be imagined without undue paranoiac strain as, for a gag, dropping in at a gay bar, or even at a stretch, the Everard.

Don Giovanni, all in all, the opera most complicated for queers—much more so than the tortured readings of *Tristan* that imagined Tristan really in love with Kurvenal, or anything at all by Verdi or anything else by Mozart. Donna Anna was gay vengeance itself—Ljuba Welitsch and Eleanor Steber as oracular women—and Donna Elvira was a gay boy's madonna—the intro music, "Povera Elvira!" to the "Mi tradí" the most piercing lament in the whole opera.

At the author's first opera queen party, the floating symposium on the question of the opera of *Gone With the Wind* to open the new opera house ran on all night. Scarlett O'Hara must be a mezzo, Melanie Hamilton a lyric soprano, Ashley Wilkes a lyric tenor. The only agreed-upon piece of casting: Eleanor Steber as Belle Watling.

An evening full of the antics of (male) parlor divas dressed up in low drag doing Santuzza, Amneris, Leonora, Ortrud, Cio-Cio-San, Liu, Lady Macbeth, in sync with the Meneghini—a camp trend that culminated a generation later in the creation (by Ira Siff, tenor star of the inspired queer oratorio compositions of the wonderful Rev. Al Carmines) of the sublime Vera Galupe-Borszkh, and her La Gran Scena opera troupe. But it was also from such crossover soiree performances that the gift of David Daniels, countertenor superb, would be brought to light.

The Old Met Standing-Room Line came further out. Barber's *Vanessa* at the Metropolitan and Carlysle Floyd's *Susannah* at City Opera became the encoded queer operas of the age (augmenting *Norma* and *Salome*). *Vanessa* was the pink-tea queen's fantasy of betrayal, and Eleanor Steber, its star, a great gay icon right down to the 1970s when, a resident of the fabled Ansonia Hotel at 73rd Street and Broadway, she came all the way down in the elevator, in a gorgeous recital gown, and sang to the men in the then-regnant Continental Baths, located in the subterranean passages of the Ansonia's basement, joining such successor luminaries as Bette Midler and Holly Woodlawn to constitute a triple goddess of quality queer vaudeville.

Susannah was the encoded story of all the hundreds (later thousands) of boys who ran away from religion and preachers with hot hands that were not just layin' on the Holy Spirit. Particularly, they were Catholic boys from dioceses of Brooklyn, New York, Newark and Philadelphia, bearing the secret of having been raised up to more than sanctifying grace in the sacristy and through the confessional grille.

And not just grand opera. There wasn't a queen worth the salt she took her truth with who didn't identify absolutely, not only with Judy and The Man That Got Away, but also with that Weimar relic, Lotte Lenya, singing "Surabaya Johnny" from *Happy End*. You heard them singing it on the opera line and in the corridors of the Everard.

In due time, *West Side Story* became the supreme encoded queer Broadway musical. The deconstruction of "I Feel Pretty" for queers: "See that pretty girl in the mirror there!" Chorus: "What mirror, where?" "Who can that attractive girl be?" and so on. The "absent" but "ever present" mirror of the queer narcissistic experience: in the shop windows; in the windows on the subway; in the tea-room window—*Vide Supra*—copied in the shiny stone and finally glass façades of the new skyscrapers replacing the look of the '20s boom with the "mirror look" that dominated and defined first New York then every other American city in the next four decades.

Before *West Side Story*, people who called Leonard Bernstein a genius were confusing a pathological narcissist with an abundance of talent with the real thing. After *West Side Story*, Bernstein joined the company of Victor Herbert, Irving Berlin, Jerome Kern, George Gershwin, Cole Porter, Richard Rodgers, Frederick Loewe and Frank Loesser as a Broadway legend. *West Side Story*, if not the greatest musical ever, (*Show Boat, South Pacific, Oklahoma!* vie with it), but it certainly stands at the pinnacle of American musical theater.

In theater, the self-identified queer playwright drew upon and replenished the queer culture to a far greater extent than the queer novelist. The narcissism inherent in the predicament inducted gay boys into a theater: to have a look at themselves in the company of others far more successfully, from their point of view, than sitting home, in that most dreaded of all queer circumstances, alone, reading a book. Without question they got bangs for their bucks in their theater: at home with a book they might have been forced to whimper. They'd tell you they'd read the latest—but you daren't attempt to quiz them on the contents. As for the latest spectacle by—they could give it back to you, blow by blow, and the lower the blow the better the bite.

All very curious to recall, when in today's queer-karaoke theater, playwrights, actors and directors staining the world with the beauty of their sin have been virtually replaced by the sinning public itself, the club promoters and the most po-mo-homo creature of them all, the dj, who engineers that apotheosis of attention-deficit disorder and the cocaine aesthetic of discontinuous jump-cut discourse, the mix. As a rising dj star recently told *HX*: "The number one thing is to be representative of the people. They're the ones who put you there. Once you have their attention and respect, you can educate them." Presumably out of their deficits.

A central conflict then of '50s queens, looking back at the earlier Golden Age of the '40s, was this: whether to be Judy singing the Trolley Song all the way to the end of the line or Blanche Dubois taking the streetcar named Desire, then transferring to one called Cemeteries and getting off at Elysian Fields. But the haunted woman was not Judy or Blanche—it was Kim Novak in *Vertigo*.

On *Vertigo*

Vertigo is Alfred Hitchcock's retelling of a primordial theme (Pandora, Eve), Man's Great Fall Through Woman's Wiles.

A man may conceive of his father as the author of his life, but if so, he can never deny that his mother is the publisher. For a filmmaker this translates as follows: he may be the author/father of his oeuvre, but the distributor/mother is certainly the captain of The Industry—and Hitchcock is the artist he is in large measure because he has been able to marshal his fear and aggression to seduce The Industry (and its clientele the paying public) in ways that, for instance, Orson Welles, his artistic equal and companion paranoiac has never mastered.

Vertigo's conscious register is, as its creator told Peter Bogdanovich, to "play on his fetish (of the protagonist, played by James Stewart) in creating this dead woman and he is so obsessed with the pride he has in making her over."

But what is a fetish? A pliable stand-in (the physical utensil that corresponds to screen memory) for the exact reverse tendency: so that in the unconscious register (to which the audience responds with anxiety and ambivalence, components crucial to effective catharsis) the protagonist betrays the shame he has in annihilating this living woman—a stand-in for every living one—and the shame he feels in undoing her body and soul. And this is what surfaces so memorably in the best acting Stewart does in the film: the reaction to the barbed indictments of the sitting judge in the inquest scene and the unconscious undertow of reluctance he manifests as his goal comes closer and closer in sight and Kim Novak's Judy Barton turns back into Madeleine Elster.

Vertigo is operatic, never more than in the gaping plot holes vaulted over (without a downward glance) by gestural rhetoric. Early commentators in that supposedly Freudian age seem to have missed the point of the title credits, concentrating on the apparent or given image of the woman's eyeball swirling into a vortex: the first emblem of the one dangerous open window of the heroine's soul (through which the hero lives in terror of falling to his psychic death). Then, within seconds of the running credit sequence, a Bernard Herrmann canonic theme begins doing its part to induce imbalance in the viewer-listener. The score is the third major actor in *Vertigo*, starting out like *Rheingold* and evolving through the second act music of *Tristan und Isolde* and Schoenberg's *Verklärte Nacht* into a carousel tune at the point of Hitchcock's orgasmic 360-degree pan.

The eye quickly evolves into the whorl which will later be revealed as the back knot of the heroine's coiffure, but is initially perceived as first a conch shell—emblem of the "oceanic" female, the mermaid, Lorele-Undine that the heroine will, impersonating so much else, impersonate as well—and then finally as what it has been reaching toward all along, the vagina.

These creatures—the undines, willis, and sprites, also the enchanted swans or nightingales or birds of paradise—are called by esotericists *egregore* beliefs. As the anonymous author of *Meditations on the Tarot* writes:

Like the belief in the Canaanite Moloch, who demanded the bloody sacrifice of the (male) firstborn, and like the Tibetan *tulpas*, they are created by a collective imagination infatuated with the thrill of fear, in a three-part process involving

1. the creation of a *tulpa* through concentrated and directed imagination,
2. the evocation (romancing) of these, and
3. the freeing of consciousness from their hold on it by an act of knowledge which destroys them.

The theme cannot thereafter be easily ignored. Barbara Bel Geddes (the extraordinarily gifted Method actress, creator of Maggie the Cat in Tennessee Williams's *Cat on a Hot Tin Roof* on Broadway) as Midge (whose diminutive name—and emotional diminution by Scottie—denotes her status as girl "buddy" in this grim buddy picture) is sketching the design for a brassiere on the principle of the cantilever bridge. (So the identification between San Francisco—a city reached by bridges—and the terrain of the female body is established, to be played out over and over as Scottie pursues Madeleine over the city's hillscape.) In one of those instantaneous cuts that Hitchcock might have designed for analysis, three letters out of "cantilever" read in bold face: EVE.

Scottie's depressive character is an inversion of James Stewart's career-making "sensitive boy" roles and a perverse fulfillment of his suicidal George in *It's a Wonderful Life*. The vacancy of his bewilderment, which made him an American icon, is here cannily registered as precisely the reaching out for validation of a man who believes in nothing definite—the typical American stance after the Great Depression and World War II proved beyond suspicion that nice guys finish behind last. Scottie's real name is John, really the American name for Adam: Midge calls him "Johnny-O" as if to underscore the point, which also points to the viewers' realization that Stewart at first glance is too old by fifteen years for the part. As the picture progresses, however, it becomes clear that arrested development is a key essential in the psychic action. Similarly, the actor seems at first temperamentally unsuited to sadistic aggression—the signal American gesticulation—but Scottie typically retreats into passive aggression against Midge. And in Barbara Bel Geddes, Hitchcock found one of the supreme masochistic female temperaments in looks and voice of the depressed-at-home-housewife era.

Another thing established in the Scottie-Midge dialogue (and Hitchcock pictures rely so very little on dialogue to define anything at all that whenever they do so it is important) is that the condition, the fall (in the prologue)— so far as the surface, or legal-moral plane, is concerned—"isn't your fault." "I know," Johnny-O replies. "That's what everybody says." Meaning he does not believe it—and neither does Catholic Hitchcock. He is clearly willing to have the argument garlanded with Freudian Newspeak and imagery. (He was willing to do the same, for somewhat similar but more superficially melodramatic purposes, in *Spellbound*. By the time he came to make *Vertigo*, as again in his late masterpiece *The Birds*, he was determined to scale the heights, not look down. Both pictures program stop-dead, irresolute closure, although *The Birds* hints at the possibility of escape and renewal.)

We resort not entirely to dialogue for the set-up of Scottie's "bad boy" (unconscious homosexual) pact with Elster. Scottie and Midge were engaged back in college (easily finessed historically by imagining Scottie as a mature GI Bill student). "You were the one broke it off, remember?" Cut to Midge, whose look is one (as they used to say) pregnant with possibilities, and the next point is "Do you remember a guy called Gavin Elster?" (Midge's responses tend to be gnomic, like a sister's, but after that look there is a good enough case for thinking she remembers all right.) In the next sequence, in the meeting between Scottie and Elster, where the plot starts spinning— centripetally, like that eye vortex—the relation established between the two old friends (and new accomplices, one conscious, one unconscious) is initially presented as a little dance of exchanging positions—standing and sitting (who is on top, who is underneath)—and proceeds again by means of plot line and dialogue to establish Madeleine's connection with the uncanny (control from beyond the grave), and from the look on Stewart's face it is further stressed that everything murky, inexplicable and dangerous is associated with women. (One cannot help noticing that a remake of *Vertigo* set in San Francisco today would be untenable: there is almost no one in California who does *not* believe in channelling and retrieved memory from former lives: Social acceptance there is well on its way to being determined not merely by who you are now but who you were lately.) This unconscious pact is again reinforced in the critical inquest scene, when, in the grisly and detached manner Hitchcock always employs when dramatizing courtrooms, Scottie is publicly exonerated by the sitting magistrate (read superego) but implicitly condemned for Madeleine Elster's death, and Gavin Elster approaches his hapless accomplice and says, "It's no use, Scottie, they'll never understand. Only you and I know who killed Madeleine."

Whether we like to think so or not, as often as not cathartic feelings of pity and terror are engineered in us by accomplished artists who are outside the exhilarations of their art fairly pitiful and terrified human beings, and this is as true of the very greatest American motion pictures as it is, for example, of the American novel and of bluegrass music.

The first sight of Madeleine—with the husband on the way to the opera—is of her bare back and signal conch-shaped bun (once more, as in Botticelli's "Birth of Venus," known vulgarly as "Venus on the Half-Shell," symbol of woman born of the sea). Thereafter, at the McKittrick Hotel, in the filtered light of the garden of the Mission Dolores, in the museum at the Presidio, in the noon glare of the Mission San Juan Bautista, and most of all deep in the redwood forest, Madeleine impersonates the kind of blonde, utterly chaste heroine of a highly evolved spiritual cast of mind that Wagner lit on for his early kitschy knight-errant operas—Elsa in *Lohengrin* and Elisabeth in *Tannhäuser*—but all the while the "real" brunette Judy Barton from Salina, Kansas, Gavin Elster's cat's paw, lurks behind the scene with all the malign force of Ortrud the witch and the pagan Venus in the same operas.

From her first words (waking in Scottie's apartment after the plunge into San Francisco Bay)—"What am I doing here?"—Kim Novak treads the fine line between the ridiculous and the sublime. There was at the time not another actress in Hollywood whose reading of the line would have dared the audience to laugh the way Kim Novak's reading does. Indeed the essential quality of the Kim Novak persona—entirely in tune with her career trajectory: she very quickly grew to despise stardom, and gave it up as soon as she could—was best expressed in the very question: What *was* she doing there? Apart from the epicene beauty common to Poles (beautiful males and beautiful females of that nationality are, so far as facial features are concerned, nearly identical), Kim Novak always seemed both there and not there, even as the earthy Judy, tentative in a way that is absolutely perfect for *Vertigo*. It is nevertheless true that she was not Hitchcock's first choice and he was not happy with her. ("Miss Novak," he told François Truffaut, "arrived on the set with all sorts of preconceived notions I couldn't possibly go along with.") It is one of the great ironies of film art that either because of that, or in spite of it (and who can tell those things apart?), not only is she far and away the most effective female in the Hitchcock oeuvre (I would put Tippi Hedren not far behind her), but it is her very physical obstinacy—the neck and shoulders are particularly marmoreal, Nike-like and static—that goes a long way toward making *Vertigo* the universal masterpiece it is. She is the plumb line which grounds the aesthetic: without her *Vertigo* might have been some kind of strange combination of the depressed and the hysterical that the late *Frenzy* was; with her it achieves that balance between ratios of *kenosis*, demonization, ascesis, and *apophrades* (return of the dead) that places it at the very center of the American visionary sublime.

Kim Novak's abstracted readings and sullen aura, which Hollywood tried desperately to cover with adjectives like ethereal, make her—always excepting Marilyn Monroe—the most interesting leading female player in fifties American motion pictures, and in an amazing way the very reverse of the coin of which Marilyn is the obverse. (Compare the smoky approach-retreat intonation Kim Novak gives—in answer to Stewart's "I hope we do meet again." "We just have."—with Marilyn's classic contribution to social small talk in *All About Eve*. "I believe you know Miss Caswell?" George Sanders as Addison de Witt offers. "I do not," Bette Davis as Margo Channing replies. "We've never met, maybe that's why," Marilyn rebounds.)

Madeleine next appears at Scottie's apartment in the middle of the night, again dressed in the highest mannequin mode, again embodying (whenever clothed) the American female as the creature of advertising, a living emblem of what the late Harold Brodkey has called our optimism and hopefulness, our "American fondness for advertising and our dependence on it cultur-ally to represent not what works or is worth preserving but what is worth our working for." When Judy/Madeleine later comes to Scottie's door in a histrionic panic, having been tutored in the story of the Spanish church seen in a dream, and Scottie equates that dream landscape with the real, local Mission San Juan Bautista, what he says is "You're going to be all right now, Madeleine. Don't you see, you've given me something to work on." This is the high point of Scottie's hubris—pretending, as it were, against cast-ing, to embody the kind of wisdom and to work the kind of magic that Ingrid Bergman had worked on Gregory Peck over a decade before in *Spellbound* (It has often been pointed out that Hitchcock was most intrigued and obsessed with police and priests. The psychoanalyst is, of course, both, and to have an out-of-commission—impotent—cop play the dupe, in the guise of mental detective, was perhaps the filmmaker's most ironic achievement.)

In other (Freudian) words, Scottie acts out our wish fulfillment. It is the depressive and effectively impotent Scottie's wish to find and see destroyed the perfect embodiment of woman, and he is willing to work very hard indeed to see it happen. For his vertigo is, in the manner of screen words, a screen fear, a defense directed against its opposite: not the terror of falling but the terror of mounting. Of course, the "dream" scam works, and leads to the (off-camera and problematical) murder and the turning point in the picture or, really, the "ending" of the first picture, for the unique genius of *Vertigo* is that it is the perfect mirror film: two in one, the second the exact reverse angle of the first.

To emphasize this point there is the high-angle view of the mission tower bisecting the screen. On the left, the crowd gathers around (the real) Madeleine Elster's fallen body. On the right, running away from the scene, is Scottie—so as to be unable to verify the corpse, of course, but more importantly, thematically, so that he is disassociated from both the action and the passion, and falls into the mirror-world half of the picture, into a hopeless torpor, which is the true reflection of his inner state.

Hitchcock subscribes to a universe in which man is charged with the organization of space and time, and woman (the latecomer) with the propagation of both (unto chaos). Thomas Mann nervously attributed to Beethoven, whose *Fidelio* is another kind of a story of a woman in purposeful disguise (but as a man), "articulating time, filling it up, organizing it." The paranoiac ailment free fall (vertigo) is thus emblematic of male *failure*. (Of the four great film masters, Hitchcock and Welles were paranoiac, and Griffith and Ford were purely grandiose.) The chaotic profusion of contexts (unweeded gardens, propagation rampant) is dramatized in the *apophrades*, in this case the Judy who impersonated Madeleine, who unwisely and willfully has stayed in San Francisco after the murder has been committed, who must then again (by compelling, merciless fate) be undone, destroyed. Thus this Kim Novak antiheroine (or vamp) is variously Madeleine (the Magdalen, or Holy Whore), Carlotta (name not only of the "sad" character, buried at the Mission Dolores, she pretends to believe she has reincarnated, but of the mad hapless Empress of Mexico—an association resonant in the world of Spanish California that is *Vertigo*'s ground) and finally Judy Barton. (Judy is the trickster of the Punch and Judy show—the English reduction of the Italian *commedia dell'arte*—but also the diminutive of the great Biblical castrator and avenger Judith.) Thus, the most dramatic overall aesthetic configuration in *Vertigo* is related to Freud's latest and most compelling formulation, from *Beyond the Pleasure Principle*, the compulsion to repeat.

Robin Wood, the most astute of the English Hitchcock critics, writes (in *Hitchcock's Films*): "Hitchcock is throughout the first half of *Vertigo* using his audience's escapist expectations, the fact that they go to the cinema to see a 'hero' with whom they can identify."

Contrary feminist theory would hold this statement evident hostage to the classic psychology of under half of the human race—and not incidentally of Hollywood market research, which results in the industry targeting product to an audience of middle-to-late-adolescent males. It would point out that the continuous female orgasm—the reverse of vertigo—renders such psychic formulations more than merely dubious, and (compare classic Buddhism, Aristophanes's *Lysistrata*, and early Christianity) that it is the organized suppression of that information that is responsible for the forging both of Western civilization and of its discontents.

Elster had to train Judy to be Madeleine, so Scottie does it all over again—reinforcing the male pact—and this time it is he who succeeds in murdering *his* femme fatale, with the same unwitting accomplice. The view that here Judy becomes as trusting as Desdemona is, I think, not far-fetched, nor is the observation that Judy's allure, both physical and temperamental, is far greater than Madeleine's, who was after all a zombie.

Scottie discovers Judy walking on the street with a group of girls—in sharp contrast to the elegant restaurant where he first sighted Madeleine in the company of Elster. Judy has dark brown hair, but she is carelessly wearing a dress the same color as Madeleine's car. The dress is clinging, common wool jersey, the polar opposite of Madeleine's carapace couture costume. He follows her—on foot, as befits this lowly reality and not on expensive wheels as before—as he had followed Madeleine, and she, just as Madeleine did, enters a hotel—only this time, when he goes to find her, she is indeed in her room, not the evanescent will-o'-the-wisp, or the elusive swan, but a sitting duck. In rebuffing him, she tells him she works at Magnin's—where Madeleine would have shopped regularly—and so the mental associations begin to build up in the audience, along with the suspicions, until, in the picture's great departure, the audience is let in on just who—or more exactly what—she is: the female not as mate but as accomplice.

The moral crux, however, is ambiguously delineated in the silent replay (behind Judy's trapped gaze, full front to the camera) of the murder of the real Madeleine Elster. Just as Judy, pursued by Scottie, reaches the top of the bell tower stairs at the Mission San Juan Bautista, Elster is waiting with the already strangled corpse of his wife, Madeleine. Judy registers not the excitement of a true accomplice, but the shook of a woman who has agreed, for money, to take a charade up to a crucial point without being aware of the full scenario. Nevertheless, in Hitchcock's picture, she must die at the end. In the fatalistic, paranoid and obsessive Hitchcockian mind, an essentially cruel mind allied to one of the great geniuses of cinema, the merely fallible woman—the cat's paw of the hero's degradation—must be destroyed: not existentially, for her actions, but for what she essentially is.

The "second" Madeleine is made by Scottie out of his grotesque idea of Judy and is as surely murdered by him as the first was by Elster, thereby completing by duplication, or compulsive repetition, the misogynist pact between the two men. Greatly resembling both the ordinary exploited call girl and indeed the victims of male perpetrators generally, she conforms more directly to the configurations of the cabalistic tradition of Lilith—Adam's perfidious first wife (Eve's dark side). Whereas the Fall of Man is initially attributed to the serpent who first seduces Eve, the "second" and all-pervasive corruption of the race is given over in a progressive sense to the perennial Lilith, the ageless female, the vampire, embodied in *Parsifal*'s Kundry. Robin Wood adduces Keats's Lamia, placing the matter in the exact referential constellation—youth:truth:beauty:death—and also observes of *Vertigo* that "to object that the characters' motives are not explained in terms of individual psychology is like demanding a psychological explanation of the sources of evil in *Macbeth*." By "individual psychology" he intends the rationalist literary expression of character developed in the Renaissance and exemplified by Shakespearean soliloquies. The answer we have to come to prefer in this post-Renaissance, post-Enlightenment and particularly post-Romantic time lies, as does the explanation of the sources of the evil in *Macbeth*, in the force of evil once projected onto women as witches, but from all ages generated in the psyche of disjunct and paranoiac man.

CHAPTER EIGHT

Mirror, Mirror: Same Difference

(FROM THE FILE ON THE ASTOR BAR)

"And what is truth?"

—Pontius Pilate

Wherein a landmark environ (school for scandal and lair of big male cats of many varying stripes) on Seventh Avenue at 44th Street (southwest corner, one half block north of the fabled Paramount Theater) off the lobby of the flagship Hotel Astor, quite belatedly immortalized by Cole Porter in "Well, Did You Evah?" from the motion picture High Society.

At the Astor, the "flit side" and the straight side reflected sideways at one another in the long mirror behind the oval onyx bar, a uniformity of setting suggestive of more than nothing imposed by the skyline of bottles ranged the mirrored length of the high altar.

From the straight side where women talk about their analysts and men about their women or their promotions, but attention has been known to stray:

"It's real holiday for strings over there tonight, wouldn't you say?"

"They don't bother me—in fact, I hardly notice; but I was in the army with them."

"Oh? In what outfit—the Fighting Powderpuffs?"

"I'll ignore that. Actually, as a bunch, they were pretty gutsy."

"It's true, standards were relaxed during the war. Guys found themselves doing the old in-and-out with virtually anything that crawled."

"Didn't you know, baby? Life is a curve ball!"

The lady pouts: "Life isn't about any of that, darling—life is about love!"

"The idea was, if he could make himself interesting to the right people, he wouldn't have to work for a living—and so he does, and so he doesn't."

"A harlot high and low."

"Yeah, high on Dexamil and low on talent."

"No artist tolerates reality, Camus said—and we're all potential artists, my friend—all turning what we say into the fantasy of what we are telling one another. 'Going around telling people' you hear people say. 'Telling people what?' you ask. 'Things—does it matter what?' It doesn't. People are energized and fascinated by the possibility alone. Mark my words, one day in the very near future there will be a Nobel Prize for publicity."

"Look, slice it any way you want, advertising isn't meaningful work!"

◄०►

"Emergent complexity, my ass—those are screen words for 'Beats me.'"

◄०►

"Allowing the earth is round, it is absolutely unnecessary to know where Archimedes places his lever."

"That, if I ever heard one, is a truly subversive remark."

"—devastating attacks with the doubling cube—absolutely uncanny for a woman."

"If."

"What do you mean, if?"

"Just what I said, babe, if. The middle word in Life. The word featured on all those graduation cards—on the scroll with the mortarboard on top. Kipling or somebody. They put out one for boys and another one for girls."

◄०►

"Leslie Fiedler says there were such homo-social couples as Nisus and Eurylaus, Castor and Pollux, Achilles and Patroclus—or much later, Ishmael and Queequeg, Huck and Jim. Couples who have in common not necessarily overt, covert or latent homosexuality, but who are entirely representative of the transgressive paradigm of male intimacy—a heterodox ortho-sexuality that seeks to challenge and subvert the soulless, misogynistic, competitive scrotal-control construction of masculinity in which the axiomatic moment of ontological trust is necessarily followed by aggression—dictated by mid-twentieth-century market capitalism."

What's he trying to do? Make the girl by appearing sensitive? Possibly.

"Very interesting—and what about Chopin in the mid-nineteenth century? Chopin and his pen-pal Tytus Woyciechowski, to whom he would send, by way of complimentary close, wet kisses on the mouth?"

"You'd have to know more about Polish customs before drawing any—"

"It's American customs, not Polish ones, that worry me. Have you read Frederick Wertham, *The Seduction of the Innocent?* He absolutely proves that Batman and Robin are homosexual—that Batman comics are the wish dream of two homosexuals cohabiting—and Wonder Woman is the obvious lesbian counterpart."

"—aiming at himself. It means we're all homosexual."

"Anybody says Hemingway is a fag, I'll deck him!"

"The fact of the matter is, there is no such thing as homosexuality per se, and there never was. It is purely by a spurious metaphysical dialectics spawned out of the social energies of late capitalism that its necessity has been deduced and its operational plane situated. The queer, as queer is wholly and entirely the subject of a passive verb, he who by desiring himself imagines himself desired—and that is very sad."

Zoom in on the guy who calls everybody "sweetheart" and "darling":

"Let me let you in on a little something political, darling. Politicizing queers is as stupid and dangerous as politicizing Jews—and you can see where that is leading us! Jews and queers are Culture warriors—or so they'd have us believe—and if Culture is the new religion—which it clearly is—then it makes no more sense to make political animals out of queers and Jews than it ever did to make soldiers out of priests. And don't tell me about the Jesuits, sweetheart, I know all about the Jesuits—or about that fat little fag Spellman, putting on fatigues and humping it to Korea, which was sickening."

"'The archer is aiming for himself.' Does anybody realize the implications?"

"Actually, I don't know about culture, sweetheart, I leave all that to the French-cuff boys with hairdos, but I'll tell you another thing for sure—fags have got a hammerlock on Broadway. All the successful Broadway playwrights are fags—Tennessee Williams, Bill Inge, Gore Vidal. . . ."

—◄o►—

"The *osculum nefandum*—the serpent taught Eve how to rim."

"And Shanghai Lil taught the Duchess of Windsor."

". . . axiomatically, not on evidence. I absolutely can't buy it—not even at the discount they're giving."

—◄o►—

"Women have multiple orgasms, men have continuous thought; it's a deal."

"Really? Is that a truth universally acknowledged? I don't know how you can honestly call ricochet continuous thought, and the only deal I know is, first they hand you a bat and tell you to keep it in your pants. Then when you can't stand that any more, they put you up and start you swinging. First you get to first base, then you get to second base; then you get to third base, and then you make the run for home plate—and it turns out home plate is a trap door. That's the only deal I know about, sweetheart!"

(Therefore since all sex is aggressive, all aggression sexual, there is really no such thing as heterosexuality or homosexuality: there are merely circumstantial object combats; which tilts the scientific categorization habit of the late nineteenth, early twentieth century.)

"Every explanation which does not ultimately lead to a relation of which no 'why' can be further demanded—homosexuality being a prime example—stops at an accepted *qualitas occulta*. And Freud, who certainly had what you would call a sufficiently dim view of the whole of humanity, seems to have held for homosexuals a peculiar sympathy."

"The overwhelmingly expressive effect of skewed features; the secret calculus of the human heart; the deepest—"

"Oh, give it up!"

—◄o►—

"Well, that little encounter sure blew his proximity fuse—no shit."

━◄○►━

"Please don't talk to me about Ernest Fucking Hemingway. I've got my own novel to write. I've got the title and everything. *And the Sun Goes Down in the West—And That's It.* Why don't-cha come up sometime—see me; I'll tell ya the plot."

They look over at the flit side.

"You can't really tell who's over there in this light—only that they're over there . . . whoever they are."

"*Perspeculum in aenigmate.* Shadows."

"Going around telling people."

"They're over there, like missionaries, recruiting—they do it at all hours of the day and night. Their antennae vibrate at large, in all directions at once—identifying objectives, projecting goals—"

"Tangling tonsils."

"I wouldn't be surprised; in this light you can't really tell. I do know, however, they like to tongue one another's ears."

"—forging plans to reach them, organizing, monitoring; judging consequences to see it's all accomplished as intended. They're as active at it, as driven, as that Army recruiting office across the street. Since they can't breed, they recruit—they call it 'bringing a prospect out.' And even if it isn't biological, they still relate it to some kind of damned evolutionary process—seed, breed and generation—like when the first hominid crossed over and became—"

"Homo sapiens!"

"Exactly! They even forge genealogies related to who-brought-who-out, so it ends up sounding like racing—you know, like Seabiscuit from Man o'War through Hard Tack."

"'I got the horse right here, and man this horse is queer,' huh? The sport of queens."

"Exactly. *Guys and Dolls*, only with guy dolls."

"It's 'the horse right here, his name is Paul Revere.'"

"So it is, darling, but the whole world knows that Paul Revere was queer."

"Homosexuals, having no progeny and therefore no future, and affectively compromised by things themselves, are pathologically overinvested in the memories of things."

"A queer is a set of attributes that constitutes an absence—some grim state I call it."

"Be thankful for a tankful—that's what I say."

"Interesting—because the phrase that comes to mind when I think of queers is what-not."

"Queers think three is an even number, which divided by two gives one-and-then-some."

"Anyway, this place is one of their prime hangouts, famous on their grapevine. They trawl Eighth Avenue—between the Dixie Bus Station and the 50th Street one—for young colts arriving. Then they bring the stuff here, to their paddock—their saddling enclosure—and break it in.

"He felt the horse's barrel, expanded between his knees. The horse lifted its head, neighed and reared on its hind legs. Et cetera."

"And the interesting thing is, though some of the prospects are geldings, not all of them are. It's higher-order purposeful behavior, all right."

"Higher order and purposeful indeed. Not to my mind, they aren't. To my mind they are merely busy. Infantile—in fact, hebephrenic; visions of sugarplums dance in their heads."

"What is hebephrenic? It sounds like some kind of Jewish psychosis."

"Oh, really!"

"I am sure that is not meant as an anti-Semitic remark—merely one that indicates how aware you are—as we all should be, really—of the, shall we say, convergence of interest prevalent between Jews and homosexuals. For instance, the phenomenon of the great pianist. It has been rightly said that to be one or the other seems almost a prerequisite, and to be both makes it an almost moral duty."

"If it's true that in order to achieve consciousness we must become the objects of our own perceptual systems, then who can ever be more conscious than the homosexual?"

"What I want to know is, do they feel the things we do? Do they feel anxious, happy, sad the way we do? They put on pain-racked faces, but do they suffer? Because I really can't tell. And I can't tell because I'm accustomed to read the facial expressions and bodily movements that indicate states of mind according to a pattern related specifically to two sexes, and their facial expressions and bodily movements are so mixed together—some like boys', more like girls'—that what it comes down to is, I can't tell are those expressions simply mismatched copies of the ones we make, without the underlying feeling?"

"Lamont Cranston—The Shadow; ask him—he knows."

"My analyst says that what they have, more than feelings, is feelings about their feelings—and that operation in them is continuous—like I was saying about orgasms in women. They can't help it, and it makes them completely crazy in less than half a normal lifetime."

"Really. Like that other thing they used to say stunts your growth and makes you crazy?"

"More or less, yes. Also too few of them are happily socialized to the peculiar rules of their interpretive community—consisting almost entirely of learned and rapid-fire commentary."

"Well, my analyst calls them 'from the psychic womb untimely ripped.'"

"Hey, that's not bad—not bad at all."

"The fact is, they are paranoid schizophrenics in regression, pure and simple and nothing else. Not hebephrenic at all—which although once employed was a rather fanciful and romantic diagnosis and has virtually disappeared from the diagnostic manual. Their gesticulations are in fact frantic, beseeching signals of a longing for their opposite, stasis, which, because they understand only too well that process will be the death of them, they see as their only hope."

"You don't mince words."

"I've come to the conclusion, when all's said and done, that psychoanalysis is, by and large, really only a subcategory of *Jugendstil.*"

"I always think people are interesting when seen through another's eyes."

"Really? Dawn Powell points out, in *Turn, Magic Wheel,* anybody seen literally in another's eyes is extremely diminutive and upside down."

"Lamont Cranston—a fag?"

"Absolutely."

"Listen. why don't we just admit it; we're jealous of them. They have their cake and eat it too; we hate that."

"Did you say cake?"

"Hey—wordplay! You boys in advertising are so clever."

"Listen, I don't care what you say—I find them disgusting."

"Really? You know, Darwin called disgust a specific feeling excited by anything unusual in the appearance, odor or nature of our food."

"Whatever that's supposed to mean, I don't think—"

"You're interested in eating them. I don't either—not exactly. In any case, among subjects tested, disgust always seems to have to do with food, body products and sex—particularly when the normal exterior envelope of the body is felt to have been somehow breached or altered."

"So?"

"So, all I really mean I guess is that, in the anthropological sense—and especially since the establishment of diffusionist criticism and the fieldwork tradition—the inescapable moral relationship between the observer and the observed precludes anything but a highly colored and ambiguous relevance to any observation."

"'Once more into the breach.' Didn't Shakespeare say—"

"Egregious fag—bent as Hook's crook. Those sonnets, man! Once more into his britches is more like it, you ask me."

"Food left untouched, for instance, on the plates of strangers, won't—"

"My point exactly—those specimens over yonder will pick a strange plate clean, so to speak."

"What do you mean by fieldwork? I never go near—"

"I'm sure you don't, but for those who sometimes do, and can talk about the experience calmly and without undue prejudice, it is quite clear that behind the whimsy and the irony, the clutter of analogies and the multiple asides—which certainly does put one in mind of Durkheim's notion of social effervescence—there is not only a very clear example of *le fait social total*, but also some powerful and exciting mentation. Particularly as they are wont to communicate in special signs—a sign being defined in anthropology these days as a transmission or construct by which one organism affects the behavior or state of another in a communication situation on any of three levels, the syntactic, the semantic and the pragmatic."

"Now look here, bottom button—"

"Such as the transmission of the clap—result of a pragmatic communication situation in the raw, as an anthropologist might put it."

—◄○►—

"In my day close men friends were called adhesive."

"It would seem God made queers for the hell of it."

—◄○►—

From the flit side:

"He developed this routine. He'd stand by a taxi stand looking, you know, all wan and lost. Inevitably some mark would come along, take a cab, and before closing the door, ask 'Can I drop you?' 'I don't know why not—everybody else has.' Worked every time."

"Over there, up against the bar. One of those bewildered Philadelphia Main Line boys commutes from the other side after he's had a few, tells you right out he's from the City of Brotherly Love, and how Whitman lived right across the river in Camden. You know the type—spent his entire adolescence drifting past Eakins's 'Swimming Hole' in the Museum down there."

"We used to call 'The Swimming Hole' the queer 'September Morn.'"

—◄○►—

"'There are no words to express the abyss between isolation and having one ally.' Chesterton, dear."

"Yes, dear, a dream right out of *Faust*—the real *Faust*, not the ghastly opera. The doorman hands me a little gold key—I was, am still, Phi Beta Kappa. 'That little thing,' I object. 'Hold it in your hand.' . . . 'Faust,' you understand, means 'fist' in Old German."

"*Oooh!*"

"Yes. 'Hold it in your hand and watch it grow. It has an instinct for the right place—follow it down the stairs to the place of the Fathers.'"

"The fathers, and the uncles, and the brothers, and the nephews."

"Then I woke up. It's such a comfort to be educated."

—◄○►—

"For once there was something found that Agrippina would rather have been than what she was: that something was a soldier boy."

—◄○►—

"Marc was down there anyway, under the sheltering palms, sending back ecstatic postcards to all and sundry about the Caribbean moon, the intoxicating flora, the sha-sha-sha of the casuarinas, when in a single evening he succumbed to a fatal mishap of an unspecified nature."

"A gay knock, dear."

"Succinctly put—and borne out by the nature of the injuries."

—◄○►—

"The only faggot composers worth talking about are Sam Barber and Henry Cowell."

"Not Lenny?"

"Lenny's a fake, but he isn't a fraud; there's a difference."

"I would throw myself at his feet."

"Really? A woman who meant business would aim a little higher."

—◄○►—

". . . the accurate slicing of fragile structures."

"Exactly."

—◄○►—

"Queers in the Bible, dear? Ubiquitous—starting with Adam's off ox. Jacob, for instance—queer as Dick's hatband."

"No!"

"Yes."

—◄○►—

"Let's face it, dahling, more passionate kisses have been given to GIs by French generals."

"Or to T.S. Eliot by Jean Verdenal—*mort aux Dardenelles*."

"Well, as to that, dahling, we've all had our Phoenician Phlebases, dead or dying in our arms."

"Have we?"

—◄○►—

" 'I fucked his brains out. . . . I fucked his brains out.' He kept on insisting like that. 'Really,' I finally said back, 'hardly the work of an evening, was it? How did you pass the rest of the time you'd purchased—reading to him aloud from *Huckleberry Finn*?' "

◄○►

"If Camp is my language, it is so only in a complex, contested and painful way."

"Oh, darling, we've noticed that—you are so brave!"

◄○►

"The line from *Mildred Pierce* I've never forgotten is Jack Carson's. 'You know me, Mildred, I see an opportunity, right away I start in cutting myself a piece of throat; it's an instinct.'"

"It woke you up to the world, huh?"

"It did just that."

◄○►

"See him? One of a pair of divinely beautiful identical twins who never go anywhere except, it's said, home to bed, together. In society's night sky they alternate, dear, like Castor and Pollux—and, get this, the one over there is regularly seen shadow-boxing at the West Side Y—not exactly sparring with his social equals—while the other is to be found daily—mounted—on the horsepath in Central Park. Très gay!"

"An investor, don't-cha know. A big brute on the Street. She regularly wakes up screaming from such nightmares as being drowned in the Great South Sea Bubble Bath!"

◄○►

Pan in on the straight side:

"It's a cute setup. When the curtain goes up, one is sitting at the piano playing Chopin and the other is sitting on the couch reading Schopenhauer. Get it?"

"They're so clever up in Cambridge, aren't they."

"Too much is banned in Boston. I prefer New York and its immediate vicinity. Everything from Ibsen to burlesque, and back on the ferry for the late show at Upstairs at the Downstairs."

"Chopin and Schopenhauer—I don't know if I do get it."

"I would've preferred New York in the Gay Nineties—Stanford White and all that. Do you know they even had boy burlesque!"

"You think they'll ever have boy burlesque again?"

"In another hundred years, perhaps."

> "'Zip—I was reading Schopen*hauer* last night,
> Zip—and I think that Schopen*hauer* was right.'"

—◁○▷—

Back to the straights:

"Schopenhauer believed that in the rapt contemplation of the sculptured essence of man, men escape the restless striving of their own souls, the innumerable temporal vanities of individual men. His delineation of the characteristic dilemma of the romantic will, which can never get what it wants and never love what it gets, is unsurpassed in the history of thought. His pages on the insight of genius and the quality of esthetic perception, his luminous—"

"The sculptured essence of man—meaning statues?"

"Statues, or those muscle magazines you see. *Physique Pictorial* and all."

"Ah."

"His luminous writing on music, his dramatic rendering of the pity and negation which constitute the lives of saints—is too much."

"For television?"

"Schopenhauer said women had long hair and short ideas—that doesn't sound very faggy to me. Fags play up to women on purpose—it's how they score against us."

"Some fags—well, maybe most fags—play up to women, but a lot of them play up to us, thinking we won't know they're fags. Anyway, Schopenhauer had the bitch mother of all time—she hated his guts—threw him down a flight of stairs, in fact—so you can't go by that; he's still a fag. His philosophy—and Nietzsche's too, is fundamentally the philosophy of the *tête-à-tête* in the mirror—and nobody has mirror *tête-à-têtes* like fags."

"Categorical statements are, I always think, similar to the point of congruity. They are all more or less like the statement that all games played with bats and balls—or sticks and stones—are unequivocally phallic. Difficult to impossible to refute—being the product of dogmatic minds alarmed at the operations of a thinking which obeys only the imperatives of its own internal norm, they are all by and large confessions of cognitive failure."

"Well, that explains it. George Sand—who by the way was a hermaphrodite—used to throw Chopin down the stairs all the time—on Majorca, you know. You can read all about it in his letters to the Polish boyfriend. Laura Riding Jackson did the same to Robert Graves."

"A fag, without question—he admitted it."

"Excuse me, George Sand was not a hermaphrodite; George *Eliot* was a hermaphrodite. The second husband jumped out the window in Venice, into the Grand Canal, on the honeymoon."

—◄○►—

"Laura Riding Jackson is John Ashbery's favorite poet, speaking of Cambridge. He's gone to live in Paris—possibly forever, or that's the noise."

"I'll bet Frank O'Hara hopes so anyway."

"Anyway, all this hip versus square crap is bullshit. Hip, square—two sides of the same coin . . . kind of a symbiosis. The only interesting life is the double life. Lie to everybody—Jekyll-Hyde. One face for the daylight, another for the night."

"Straight white males are vestigial? What the fuck's that supposed to mean?"

"Like endangered—like striped dolphins in the Mediterranean."

"Let's face it, Freud was a fag—I mean he admitted it too for chrissakes—admitted he was in love with that other fag who was into noses."

"Interesting—if not quite immitigably convincing."

"'Teeth, throat and bowels are objectified hunger.' That's all I remember of Schopenhauer. Pretty depressing, really."

"I remember a little more—two consecutive sentences actually, from *The World as Will and Idea*. 'The occasion of an erection is a motive, because it is an idea, yet it operates with the necessity of a stimulus: it cannot be resisted. This is also the case with disgusting things, which excite the desire to vomit.'"

"I rest my case."

"Y'know everybody says that in here—the place is a regular Case Dormitory."

"So far as Schopenhauer goes, Freud put paid to his vogue. There are no ideas and there is no will; there are introjects and there are cathexes—that's it."

"I disagree absolutely. Freud is Schopenhauer redux, in fancier German.

Schopenhauer's thing on subduing assimilations, on no victory without con-flict—lower *Vorstellungen* brought into subjection by higher. Freud took it all, rendering it, I grant you, in better German, but so what, when it has been translated into a grotesque English with words like 'cathexis' and 'introject' and 'abreaction.'"

"I don't know about translations, but he's right about the will, so far as fags are concerned. Does anybody realize how many of them die intestate? It's pretty amazing."

Someone has observed that Kinsey has set up a volunteer booth on the mezzanine floor of the hotel where you can go and volunteer information.

"Everybody lies!"

"'What is truth?' asked Pilate—getting his nails done in that beauty parlor on the mezzanine."

"Yeah, well, they've been leaking information to the press, and get this. Turns out queers have statistically bigger cocks than straight guys."

"Only statistically?"

"It's not funny. You know how guys are about their—"

"Dimensions, yes."

"And sometimes they exaggerate."

"You don't say. So, they—oh, I get it. If they do, then they—"

"Exactly."

"There's simply no getting around it—it's encoded in the language: in both oral and anal sex, the passive role is degrading. Look at Egyptian hiero-glyphs of captured soldiers taking it up the ass, and tell me otherwise."

"An interesting particular, if not an immitigably convincing one. In point of fact, the language we speak and read is rather closer to Greek than to Egyptian hieroglyphs—and on Greek vases it looks like something rather more complex than degrading. All roosters proffered as love gifts by the *erastes*, the whole tradition of pederastic *paidaia*—"

"As Thomas Mann, for example, was at pains—"

"Well, Thomas Mann was a fag; fucked his own son—that was the word."

"Like that guy in the Paul Bowles story."

"'Pages from Cold Point'—wild story."

"Fags are committed to a deep-seated disequilibirum, and that's that. For instance, take the case of Flaubert."

"Flaubert was a fag?"

"No, Flaubert was not a fag. I'm talking about the appreciation of his work. We all know what his masterpiece is, right? *Madame Bovary*, but go and listen to the fags and you'll be told it's really *Salammbô*."

"Interesting, because down at NYU—"

"You mean N.Y.Jew, don't you?"

"Oh, come on, didn't you ever see *Gentleman's Agreement*?"

"You'll have to cross to the other side for those arrangements."

"Jews and homosexuals, not exactly a novel insight."

"I never read novels—except maybe by the likes of Flaubert."

"But some of your best friends do."

"Yes, and at NYU they have this new thing, intertextuality, whereby they read two books together, like *Ulysses* and *Finnegans Wake*, or *Moby-Dick* and *Billy Budd. . . .*"

". . . or *Lie Down in Darkness* and *Set This House on Fire*."

"And they are now reading *Madame Bovary* and *Salammbô* like that."

"Madame Salammbovary. Cute."

◄○►

"Teeth, throat and bowels—depressing; cripplingly so."

"The homosexual's highly stereotyped attack strategy is narrow, fixed in its repertoire and seemingly unaware of any object in the larger environment—weaving webs, ambushing anything resembling a prey, no matter where it is, showing no signs of adaptation to the larger scenarios of a wider world. Domain-general regulatory capacities seem entirely beyond their understanding—which leaves them immersed in streams of raw episodic experience from which they can gain no significant distance."

"On the other hand, single-mindedness is what won the West."

"The West, the war, the contract for Pepsodent. . . ."

"The paradigm, you understand, specifies detailed declarative knowledge of the world."

"So it says here in small print."

"Look, the cognitive system of the homosexual on the prowl, his verbal stun gun, loaded and cocked, is fixed to respond automatically, with practically no possibility of withheld response."

"Busy little bees, full of stings—"

"Making honey—but honeybees, you know, despite their utilization of nervous systems of great complexity and the execution of dances of amazing precision, do not, by any criterion I am aware of—*pace* Maeterlinck—

possess consciousness. One cannot extrapolate—in honeybees or in social-climbing homosexuals—directly from neural complexity—or neurotic activity—to awareness. Awareness arises from some very specific design features of particular kinds of nervous systems."

"Hard-as-nails ones?"

"That's one variety, surely. In any case, the controlling insect mind is distributed—like the homosexual's—across many rudimentary minds; it constitutes a social-cognitive system which makes no exigent demands on any individual brain, and which few would suggest as an appropriate model for human culture."

"Chanel called Cocteau an insect—an unspeakably vile pederast who never did anything his whole life long except steal things from people."

"I can't really accept that honeybee-dance analogy. Have you ever seen bees lined up to do the Madison, or executing knife-edge box-turns in the Peabody the way they do out in Cherry Grove? We taxi over from Kismet just to watch them—they're fantastic!"

"... and of course they have their own fraternities—campus to campus."

"Do they get pinned?"

"Pinned? They get nailed—and not only by the cops either. Among themselves, I'm told, they go in for re-enacting the Crucifixion."

"Of the Nazarene—yes, I've heard those stories."

"You want to carefully sift through the ER admissions records at Mass General some time."

"I don't know that I do, really."

"Anyway, I spell the Crucifixion C-R-U-C-I-F-I-C-T-I-O-N."

"A girl always won the eighth-grade spelling bee."

"Queers are, despite their evident solipsism, flocking creatures, with next to no ability to cultivate and build on individual relationships. They respond, each of them, to his own proprioceptive somatic enclosure with the rapt self-absorption of cats washing themselves, but ask them to give a kid a bath—well, you wouldn't do that anyway, but you do follow the drift, I hope."

—◁○▷—

"Obviously there's a homosexual element in *Godot*, and in *Endgame* too—no question. That doesn't mean—"

—◁○▷—

"The whole Islamic world is bisexual. They have a proverb, 'For children, a woman; for pleasure, a boy; for delight, a melon.'"

"A melon?"

"That reminds me of the time back in college when I was in the fraternity and we used to pass around these—you know, pictures—and in one of them that was supposed to be funny the guy was doing exactly that: fucking a canteloupe with a hole bored in it. He was either a very weird guy— which I suppose you would have to be in the first place to pose for such things—or else trained by Stella Adler, a very good Method actor, you know, because his eyeballs were rolling up into his skull and he was obviously either coming or, as I say—"

"I was in a fraternity too—and the same pictures were passed around, only we had one guy who was Italian, raised on Long Island, and he confessed to fucking cantaloupes regularly out of his father's garden as a teenager. Also something he called a ga-gooz, which he said was almost as good as the cantaloupe if you put in a little olive oil first."

"Excuse me boys, I hate to spoil the fun, but what the proverb means is the sublime delight in eating a melon."

"Oh . . . well. . . ."

"Please don't—I just had a delicious dinner."

". . . of a like mind—a beguiling phrase, really."

"Sweetheart, will you let a Madison Avenue mandarin let you in on something deep, dark and disgusting? When Norman Mailer rails against toothpaste being marketed, not so much to clean the teeth as to fend off the irresistible urge to fellatio—"

"Is he really doing that?"

"I thought he was talking about that shit Pepsodent used to say was in their—*irium*? Raymond Chandler once called it just another name for the ineffable."

"Irium is what the professor put in Bugs Bunny's carrot to make him Super Rabbit."

"The thing I always wondered about Bugs Bunny was why he didn't have a girlfriend. I mean, aren't rabbits supposed to fuck—I mean isn't it proverbial?"

"The early Bugs had a girlfriend, but they got rid of her."

"Bugs is a fag. That's why he says 'What's up, Doc?'"

"Oh, really!"

"Anyway, he isn't talking about the housewife, he's talking about himself."

"Bugs? Always. That's another way we know that he's a fag."

"Norman Mailer says *Ulysses* is not obscene because its express intent is not pornographic. What's express intent?"

"Express intent, sweetheart? Express intent speeds by on the middle track and gets you there a lot faster than local intent."

"Hah-hah!"

"Norman Mailer's not queer, is he?"

"Nor do you want him to be."

"Norman Mailer, no. Rock Hudson, supposedly. Bugs Bunny, maybe. I could go for Bugs, if I could get around the teeth, and probably, in circumstances, for Rock. The way he cried in *A Farewell To Arms*. You never see a guy cry on the screen like that; it was kind of beautiful. 'Scuse, me Honeybunch, I'm usually more careful around women, but being even a little bi-lateral is a strain in this culture, where the nance element holds sway in matters Platonic."

"Holds sway, indeed. Swing and sway with—Rock Hudson, eh? Would you throw on the duck sauce? You don't have to answer that: we don't want to make you cross to the flit side, not without your flit gun, anyway, in case the fruit flies are in evidence."

"Platonic. That's ancient Greek isn't it? Everybody in Ancient Greek was queer, right?"

"Not exactly; in ancient Greece they were what you'd call Homer-sexual."

"A comedian. Everybody's suddenly a comedian."

"It's television. Anyway, fuck Norman Mailer. When he isn't bawling about reverence and poise and the quality of the felt life, or about the free play of the vital intelligence."

"Hah! *C'est à rire.* The cheap feel and the free ride are more his style—him and his GI bill of goods. Nietzsche is the only one who knew anything about the felt life—although they say Kinsey is still trying to find out about it, upstairs in the mezzanine."

"Who?"

"Kinsey—*Doctor* Kinsey. Still at it you know, on the mezzanine."

"On the mezzanine—what is he, your dentist?"

"Kinsey drew a line with seven points—the degrees of inversion."

"Seven is a big queer lucky number—seven and eleven. They all claim to have at least seven inches and dream of going down on at least eleven."

"Inches."

"Suspects—per day; each with eleven inches."

"Arithmetic evidence overwhelms me."

"Seven inches, eleven suspects, *The Sixth Man*—it's all just roulette."

"And the lady gambles."

"Too-shay."

"You know, James Dean cried in *East of Eden*—and in *Rebel Without a Cause*, too. Plus which, he lived over at the Iroquois before he went to Hollywood."

"Listen, Valentino, Monty Clift, James Dean, Rock Hudson—all those heartthrob boys."

"Lived over at the Iroquois before they went out to Hollywood."

"Very funny."

"Mental autonomy vis-à-vis the environment is the principal criterion for judging an advanced mentality."

"The Museum of Human Oddities. I asked directions for that place once; they sent me here."

"Probably figured you wouldn't make it to the Blue Parrot."

"So you want to be famous—anything else?"

"Well, relationships . . . people; in the object field?"

"I wouldn't worry, if I were you, about your object field. You can always put those award-winning projections where your object field ought to be."

"I haven't won any awards—not as yet."

"Oh, but you will, buddy, you will! You cannot conceivably miss. The more your being just happens to happen, the more the mystery of its self-disclosure self-discloses. And nobody need ever know you flunked the Minnesota Multiphasic Personality Inventory or that you appear so deceptively open precisely because you are so fundamentally defended. You will be a star, darling, and I for one promise to stare at you as you go by."

"I'm not from Minnesota, I'm from Wisconsin."

"Of course you are, darling, and so are the Lunts."

"I don't understand a word you've been saying."

"Teeth, throat and bowels—kind of thing can ruin your life."

"Let me tell you the true name of this city, baby; this city is called Men-da-city."

CHAPTER NINE

The Sunday Matinee

> "As song commences, as glasses fill, as the wind comes up,
> a room fills with conversation; dialogue
> like breaking waves . . . and there is Saladin raising his hand
> to bid on the irresistible, pre-owned Joseph."
>
> —Jalal al-din Rumi
> (free translation)
>
> "Many an empire has been run by drunken men wearing makeup."
>
> —Alexander Cockburn

Following the route of the steadfast landed one at Sunday afternoon at-homes, called matinees, where conversation percolated for pleasure and profit along strictly governed Gotham ha-ha lines.

Lillian Nassau was the emporium, and Tiffany glass the new rage. No TO THE TRADE ONLY sign hung in the window; the queer East Side descended en masse, casting off contemporary and making out of hundreds and hundreds of objects out in Corona at the turn of the century, objects that had been gathering dust for two generations or more in attics across the country, investments for the future that paid off big time.

One opulent decorator queen, native of someplace upstate, carried parts of his trove of windows from his New York apartment, where they'd been stacked up in the maid's room off the back stairs (the stairs one was firmly instructed to use when leaving of a morning after) to his Cherry Grove, Fire Island, beach house each summer, an environ strictly reserved for the beautiful, the consistently amusing and the deeply trusted.

The annunciation of the high point of this culture was made in the year 1961, together with the first clear indications of mourning (of rigor in performance strongly grounded in method, in theories of both pathos and hilarity) and the grim forecast of swift decline. Laugh tracks had, for some years, been prevalent on television; the slovenly practices thus engendered were relentlessly seeping into Sunday at-home matinees, making havoc of timing. Conversations had become unremarkable (citing sociological experiments done at City College and at NYU in the Science of Persuasion) indicating the ways in which, among the common run, anybody can be made to laugh or weep. Quite suddenly the word went out—in an onanistic sort of way—that all excellence in performance is a contract not between performer and audience but the result of sudden and repeated renaissances of interest in formulations originally made among the performers (and priests) themselves.

In the simultaneous decline of the East Side and the West Side, this pattern of persuasion, already abstracted as something called marketing (which no longer meant shopping at Gristede's, either for Wheaties or Kix), would be progressively employed as an end in itself, mainly to create jobs, a spurious activity of the handlers to convince the ultimate powers-that-be to wholly redefine money, power and prestige, essentially entailing the printing of more of each on speculation, with a view to scooping up the results as hard coin. Eventually marketing would prove itself able to sell anybody anything, including an identity.

THE SUNDAY MATINEE TRANSCRIPTS

"I'm afraid there's no doubt about it, my dear, the Church of Rome categorically loathes us, despite the fact there are so many of us dangling her sacramental keys. That odious harridan the Cardinal, for example—pixilated on the unpotable swill she affects to transform into the blood of Christ, and daydreaming of the *seises*, the dancing altar boys of old Seville, of teaching his own little captive snotnosed chicklets to execute grave minuets on Corpus Christi. To her—the Church of Rome, that is, not Fanny Spellbound—we are the unnatural descendants of gesticulating man, on whom medieval clerics looked with such odium, reminiscent to them of the actors in the pagan theater as well as of bodies possessed by the devil."

"Between the universe apprehended by pure intelligence and the universe perceptible to the senses, there is an intermediate world, the world of Ideal Images, of archetypal figures, of subtle substances, of immaterial matter: the world of the motion picture. Homosexuals live almost exclusively in this world, in which visionary events and symbolic histories appear in all their truth and beauty, becoming, whatever else they may need to know, all they can bear to behold."

"The power of positive thinking is not your average fairy's forte. We're very nineteenth century, really, in our amatory calculations and in our sense of cost and retribution. Let's face it, all it takes is a couple of strong doses of the clap—front and back, dear—and at least one of the syph, or a couple of weeks off the sauce and on penicillin or something even more aggressive to nip those girls in the bud—so they won't come back in thirty days or thirty years to rot out your brain the way they did Schubert's and Schumann's and Nietzsche's and God knows how many other *fedeli d'amore*—to pretty much convince our kind they are living lives mired in unyielding filth. And no matter how many times you sit through *The Barefoot Contessa* and identify with Ava's feet in the mud—well, the idea just can't help sinking in, and that I'm afraid is all there is to it."

"Michelangelo adopted a maternal role with young men—"

"So did Leonardo da Vinci."

"To overmaster the effects of maternal deprivation."

"Leonardo complained his protégés all ran off to be with the Swiss Guards, hunting with slings for birds in the Roman ruins."

"Michelangelo's passion for boys was permeated by nurturant maternal qualities derived from overzealous identification with the lost mother—a condition of which queers are haplessly reminded each and every time they have to recite, along with their Social Security numbers, her maiden name, to re-establish their own identities."

—◦—

In bringing a boy out, they took a leaf out of the debutante's handbook and got him to talk about himself (and of lost love), reinforcing identifications with humble warnings hence, as if they desperately wanted one to turn out, if not straight at least enough like the straight boys at cotillion to pass muster.

Suddenly one was "the mousy one," in out of the rainy alley warming up backstage with a calculated agenda, hearing Lloyd Richards invite one to "Tell us about it, Eve." Not of course the agenda—not the answers to the second two of the first set of crucial questions—What do I want? Where am I going?—but as much might allow of the first two, Who am I? Where do I come from?

And the voices continue, forming two successive little dialogues in author's head:

Admonitory Voice:

And don't say, If only I knew how. You know how, or you wouldn't have had the gall to show up here in the first place with all these other contestants desperately trying to seize the imagination of a restless world. Moreover, as Martha Graham advised her aspirants, "You are in competition with nobody but yourself—either do the work as it was meant to be done, or get out and don't ever come back."

Secure a return engagement. Begin.

The negotiation quickly became a trafficking in scents: the smell of folding money as over and against the smell of fresh boy, (which they went for even more than the Eau Sauvage, the Pour Un Homme and the Vetiver they favored in those turbulent and dangerous years). The trick was to get them to bestow a dusting of the former on the foundation of the latter, to let them know you were made happy by little things: cufflinks, collar pins, stickpins, shirt studs, and at Christmas (or if you were very bold, at graduation) by modest wristwatches in white gold. These you would keep quite separate from the family gifts, and put on only to wear to those Sunday afternoon parties, theater and gallery openings, and on those special excursions.

Old queens spoke admonitions, like "Decide, darling, what you want in a john: how much scope. The steady ones keep to the circuit: opera, ballet, theater, Carnegie Hall. The Metropolitan, the Frick. It's the territory they understand. Beyond, there be drag queens—and drag queen slayers."

If you worked out—nothing to do with pumping iron in those days, an activity earmarked in the queer mind for that quaint set of ambiguous calisthenics freaks and working-class habitués of the Sheridan Square Gym—and by extension for homoerotic background shots in fight pictures, in which young specimens of robust ethnic manhood on the hoof were carefully appraised by slightly bent trainers and their masters, pretenders-to-class wearing camel hair coats and sporting diamond stud pinky rings on manicured fingers with clear-polished nails—if you worked out, if you were reckoned to be iridescent, intense, you might be taken out to Fire Island in summer, or if you were very good indeed, invited to frolic in distant places, down among the dancing date palms (cha-cha-cha).

Commentary (overheard in the pantry) offered another newcomer besides Author QT, by an older (likely of legal age) contestant who'd evidently been through the ropes.

"You're quite a guy."

"Think so?"

"Makeup's a little heavy."

(Mental note: in future save lavender eye shadow for candlelight soirees.)

Back in the living room, an older sympathetic queen, known as Prudence, takes the reins. Author QT senses a kindness in the man akin to that of his by-now-collegiate English teachers.

"There is a battle you have been steeling yourself for, darling, day after day all the years of your life, praying all the while it may never be joined. Your prayers are not unprecedented; indeed they are components of an ancient liturgy. It was the same with us before the war—the actual war: what the world called war—and in point of fact the war the world called war took our minds off the inner war and the terrible wounds we bore in silence, going to *Parsifal* and making comparisons, reading T.S. Eliot and fabricating a way of life.

"What we found out, darling, in the world's war in which we served with distinction—have you seen Michael Curtiz's *This Is the Army*?—did, however, help us when we were mustered out of that man's army only to be reconscripted into the war at home: helped us especially in the face of existentialism. That there were no answers we had been prepared to accept, but that there weren't even any reasons? We have, all told, faced up to that one far better than the straights, no question.

"In the world's war we might have been killed in some way reckoned glorious, whereas in our own, if we didn't kill ourselves first or get bumped off in some dark place, we'd have begun to die before we ever got back home. In point of fact we'd never get back home, because whether or not anybody can ever go home again, we emphatically cannot."

"Do not imagine anyone comes in here to lick his wounds, for we are altogether wiser stigmatics than that. The reason the wounded animal so employs its tongue is well known to science, but your faggot is a rather special case of wounded animal, whose tongue has too often found itself lodged in such insalubrious places that it can have retained few antiseptic properties—rather the reverse. And few indeed are the tongues of others that would serve. Seeking out mother's is a very big mistake, and father's, which might do the trick, is never available since, despite the lurid and sentimental fantasies of our more exuberant pornographers, eons of incest taboo restrictions still apply with stringent force.

"Which leaves fag hags—the very worst resort, cause of which being the universal truth, impossible to either deny or ameliorate, that the fag hag's tongue is yet more steeped in venom and bile than is the faggot's, thus reinfection of the wound becomes certainty itself."

An exchange at the window.

"We post-war homosexuals are the avant-garde of suffering—the chorus that calls up famous sorrows. Our lives are marginal scribbles in the battered Book of Life. Henry James is our prophet, preferring the presentation of events not as they happen—because whatever happens, darling, is going to happen dead against us—but as refracted, deflected and analyzed in conversation that touches upon them."

"Maybe so. All the same, for there to be dance, there must be something needing to be danced. A social existence entirely picturesque and decorative is no longer enough."

"Hold it right there—let us have no derogation of decorators. As you are all in the way, either by destiny or choice become heathen, it may be necessary to let you know that in the Book of Genesis, of the six days of creation, fully three are given over to the Works of Decoration. I have my own little gnosis on the situation, I believe it can be demonstrated on evidence that the chief decorator was the archangel Gabriel.

"Whatever of that, do you know the story of René Duchez? René Duchez was a decorator, in the town of Caen, who just happened also to be a member of the *maquis*—the Resistance. The Nazis, who undoubtedly thought a decorator no threat to them, hired René Duchez to do up the HQ, and while he was about it, René Duchez discovered—and sequestered—a map labeled Special Blueprint: Top Secret. He may have read German, which would be less surprising in a decorator—*Jugendstil*, and all that—than reading French would have been in a Nazi German, or he may have simply twigged to the importance of any map lying around on a desk.

"At any rate, as a result of René Duchez's find—an elaborate plan of the obstacles to invasion—tank traps, minefields, barbed wire, gun installations, known as the Atlantic Wall, the invasion of Normandy—D-Day— was, if not exactly made easy, dear, certainly made significantly less deadly."

"But was he queer?"

"Whether he was or wasn't, one thing is certain: some of his best friends were. And of course you know, don't you, it was a queer name of Alan Turing who broke the Enigma code and saved England. And for a thank-you, they drove him to suicide—wouldn't they just. Poor darling ate a poisoned apple—can you beat it?"

"Because you see, dear, it's the same with our kind as with the cryptologists. We too have developed the ability to scope out the enemy—indeed have come to know the pattern of his every move nearly before it is made. But we live in mortal terror of wielding our power, of acting upon the intercepts, lest our secrets be discovered in return—and so we go with half a life about our ways."

"*Veramente—brava questa prudenza.*"

Two amblers through vestibules:

"Reminds me of the Claude Rains character in *Casablanca*—definitely queer."

"Yes, discovered typically by some young husband who's tarried a little too long at the Astor Bar—oh, not on the flit side, you understand, but over there, safe among his comely peers in the onyx mirror. Or maybe he's found his way down to Julius's on Tenth Street—just to soak up a little atmosphere, don't-cha know, with the rest of the sporty guys who frequent that snug little alcove of self-deception, and who, when it comes their turn to pony up at the office party, report their funky little egress-and-tell impressions. At any rate a fellow who's missed that last train from Grand Central home to Happily-Ever-Afterville Larchmont. Whom we've befriended for the night—bedded down on the sofa, given all the comforts of home, including a hot shower in the morning, a nice breakfast, possibly even the "loan" of a Paul Stuart shirt . . . you get the gist."

Prudence to the author:

"Yes, dear, as it plays out, you see, we're like a lot of terribly clever cripples, reinventing wheels for wheelchairs, who for their thanks are rolled over a cliff.

"The beautiful circuit and subterfuge of our thought and our desire. That's Henry James, darling, an illustrious faggot of yesteryear—not perhaps as picturesque and decorative as some, but he got asked out nevertheless, and made much of what he heard tell of.

"And speaking of getting asked out, it is absolutely the distinguished thing we live for. In these little cenacles of ours we meet week after week to present for one another's close inspection our lives as open books—but there is always that one bit of telltale information scribbled late along on the flyleaf of the presentation copy, and concealed likely for all time by the date stamp slip pasted on by Central Circulation.

"We like to come on as frank and honest—but you know the old joke.

'Let me be frank.' 'Oh, not again—you were Frank last night!' Thus are we warned against the current cant that advertises the courage of one's convictions. Darling, to a faggot, the very word conviction can only mean one thing. It happens in night court and, although it's often celebrated, it ain't distinguished."

—◄o►—

"Sodomy—it troubles me, I admit it."

"It is the sin, dear, that makes the angels weep. And do you know why? Exactly because in the state in which they find themselves and despite the urgent prompting of the most dynamic love there is said to be, they can't *do* it. Your guardian angel can *almost* do it. That is, he can watch you do it, and whisper to you to be kind and considerate while you're at it, and afterwards offer a cigarette or accept one if it is offered—by you or your partner, that is; your guardian angel doesn't smoke, either; but otherwise . . . any questions?"

"No kind of life worth living can be defined—it must be, as Coleridge believed, assumed."

"The world of thought and word is not, my dear, the world of deed."

"All that intellectual what-have-you is, I suppose, valuable, if it makes you feel better about who and what you have—but ask yourself honestly, which would you rather get for Christmas, a divine new boyfriend and all the heartburn that goes with him, or the latest edition of *The Oxford Companion to the Mind*?"

Somebody strongly identifies and the topic of lost love burgeons.

"I sympathize with your predicament, darling, indeed I do, but didn't you see the sign in the vestibule? 'We regret we cannot assume responsibility for lost or stolen articles.'"

The Speaker protests that he's talking about a person.

"So much the worse."

"That is a matter of opinion, darling. When I was young—well, younger anyway—I used to think somebody stealing my tricks was the worst thing that could happen. Until one night some trick stole my Cartier watch. I never believed in deterministic prediction until that moment; since then I'm afraid I believe in nothing else."

"What is a somebody, anyway? What does this terrible star-gazer public relations culture of ours with its incessant bouts of self-appraisal and its relentlessly empty flash acts add up to in the end? The so-called strong personality is not necessarily the more spiritually advanced, nor has it ever been. There are such qualities as finesse and sensibility, and gravitas, and Wordsworth is not just a boring old fart out of step with the pace of modern life beloved of underpaid high school English teachers. The meek shall inherit the earth. And although today's sophisticates may hiss at that beatitude and say, in effect, 'All that means is, the meek will be buried, period, whereas the aggressive have a chance at least to achieve apotheosis,' what is apotheosis? There is an older and a better magic in a sympathetic attachment to the earth than has ever been made manifest in aggressive sky religion."

"The meek shall inherit the earth is Dorothy Day's favorite saying."

"Dorothy Day hates faggots."

"Dorothy, who has the patience of Job fused to the temperament of Medea, does not hate faggots. It is merely that they exasperate her—and God knows the ones she gets buzzing around her mystical honeypot would drive a saint to distraction, the way they seem to confuse peace of mind with the prolonged avoidance of life's clear harsh truth. Dorothy knows that a true lover remains perplexed in love, exposed to every peril."

"Yes, a somebody. Should I try the Bureau of Missing Persons?"

"You're in the Bureau of Missing Persons, pal. We're all busy little missing persons with lonely terrifying gifts, hallucinating whereabouts. All subatomic particles, having neither identity nor location until an act of measurement—accidental or intentional—forces us to declare ourselves to ourselves as we pluck our dark rebellious eyebrows in the mirror—the better to achieve that ironic look so necessary in our dealings with that world which offers us no survival advantage."

"There was a message picture came out just after the war—maybe you remember it, I've never forgotten, *The Boy with Green Hair.* Joseph Losey. All about being different. Dean Stockwell was in it. There's a divine scene where the boy runs into the woods and the posters of all the displaced persons come alive to deliver the message."

"I haven't yet gotten over Dean Stockwell in *Compulsion*—and he's absolutely straight."

"We are all of us boys with green hair, darling."

"Whatever of that, we are the reverse of all the people in the Wanted posters in every post office. Queer folk are the Not Wanted people—'Not Wanted on the Voyage,' as Auntie Bea declared."

—◄○►—

" 'Doll,' I said, 'you are played out. You must lie low; you must rest, regroup your forces, absent thee from publicity awhile.' "

"Work fascinates me, darling, although I know only its result."

—◄○►—

"I'm a sucker for bastards with inner wounds."

"I like the ones from the city, in off the streets—I like how they grew up playing stick ball and stoop ball and all those other street games."

—◄○►—

"Jerry Robbins never had a single original idea—he steals everything from everybody. DeMille, Tally Beatty, Donald MacKayle—everybody. In the world."

—◄○►—

"I suppose Callas is unprecedented; she's a cross between Lina Pagliughi and Lina Bruna-Razza, and nobody ever thought of that before."

"Well, whoever thought her up, I don't like her at all—the voice is absolutely lacerated. And her fans! My dear, in my own personal opinion, they bear all the hallmarks of that crazed Bolognese flagellant cult, the *battuti*, for whom, according to Meyer Shapiro, a follower of Cimabue painted the 'Scourging at the Pillar' at the Frick."

"I understand there are lots of followers of Cimabue at the Frick. Don't know how many of them are flagellants, but it would be interesting to find out, no?"

"I adore Cimabue—he's just so, erotic!"

And at the center of things were the Roman Catholic Dancing Wu Li Masters of the New York Lavender Night. Art was their life, their sensibilities so many flare paths through the darkness that abounded. Their tastes were so elevated they would regularly trot over to 47th Street, to St. Malachy's, sit through high mass and get themselves invited to one of the specifically Catholic matinees. There they would comport themselves the way people did in the Italian Renaissance. They would read a little St.

Augustine, something out of *Jubilee* magazine, passages from Ronald Firbank's *The Flower Beneath the Foot* and *Concerning the Eccentricities of Cardinal Pirelli*, down lots and lots of old fashioneds while simultaneously repenting of their lives, like publicans in the parable, like Jansenists at Port Royal.

They'd listen to recordings of Gregorian chant, sing old show tunes or put on a tape featuring both, simultaneously. Then they'd spin a few pre-war platters and dance the Peabody, all before recessing to catch the five o'clock Exposition of the Blessed Sacrament by the pharisee Jesuits at St. Ignatius Loyola—those talkers of smooth things, who were to a man so understanding, so inspirational, you could positively emulate them all, especially perhaps the notorious silver-tongued orator who knocked them flat every Sunday like clockwork, and who after Saturday night confession would take boys right into the rectory, show them the love he vowed that Christ showed the Beloved Disciple (*delicias Domini*: cynics said "Yes, dear, the Lord's little bit of delicatessen—salami"), discuss with them the cyclical simultaneity of sin and repentance, of the Fall and the Resurrection, then absolve them and put them in a taxi with the fare home . . . no shit.

"I myself am a woman of extremes, I frankly admit it—a lifelong victim of devotion. For instance, in *The Magic Flute*, I only go into the auditorium— I'm in the club, you know, so it's really easy to slip in and out at will, which always make me think I'm in one of those wonderful nineteenth-century costume pictures, where, you know, all the intrigue is done at the opera. Like *Camille*, or this Venetian thing Tennessee wrote for Visconti and Farley Granger put in opposite Valli. You remember, it was supposed to be for Brando and Bergman, but then she went to Stromboli with Rossellini and he went completely Hollywood? Anyway, darling, nowadays at *The Magic Flute* I slip into the auditorium only to listen to the Queen of the Night and Sarastro."

-◄◦►-

"I think this '20s revival we're going through suits us. I mean, so far as we are concerned, darling, it is definitely still Prohibition. Every place we foregather is by definition a speakeasy, and the gangsters and the tommy guns and the clean-cut FBI boys just dying to be corrupted, and even the boys in high places breaking whatever versions of the Volstead Act there are across the land forbidding us."

—◄○►—

"She kept going on about being stabbed in the back, stabbed in the back, until finally I said 'Darling, how did they find your back? I've never seen anything of you but varieties of fronts and sides.' She pouted."

—◄○►—

Prudence deposed by the District Attorney:

"Our kind is better off with ideas than with facts. The Stagirite is not our guide, his mentor is. Read the *Phaedo*, youngling, and the commentaries of Porphyry on *The Odyssey*. Then realize that the East and North rivers, with a little assistance from the Harlem Ship Canal, ring Manhattan island exactly as Phlegethon and Cocytus ring Hades, and that we are all of us alive on this island of fallen souls. We entered under Cancer—the island's sign—and must depart under Capricorn, in the cold of the year and the dead of the night. Read your Plato and your Porphyry, dear, and know that all tales of hell are tales of this earth. The phrase 'hell on earth' is a pleonasm, a redundancy, as are, each and every one of them, the days of our incarceration in the body of this death, and all the twisted ways of our lives.

(Two eavesdroppers walking away:

"I'm no intellectual, darling, but I thought Fay-dough was French—wrote screamingly funny plays. I saw one once, translated by Noël Coward. *Look After Lulu*. Laughed my head off.")

"You cannot save up your youth to use in old age—no, you cannot bank your youth, but you can broker it. No one has a right to happiness, or a living—only to a chance to hustle both."

At which point the author rose and walked to a high window, looking across the East Side toward the Queensboro Bridge (and the places across the river beyond its extension from which he'd come) over which the BMT trains had sometime since ceased to rumble. Nevertheless the question came to him, who among these men were prime candidates for reenactment of Barbara Stanwyck's awful fate in *Sorry, Wrong Number*? How many keys were there to this, and to how many other apartments like it, and wasn't it true that the doxy of the night ("Theaters! Furs!") gets rubbed out with the designated victim? Tricky.

And while he was there, at the window, watching plane after plane make its seemingly lazy descent into La Guardia (and remembering them all—the family—going up Sundays to have lunch and watch the fabulous Lisbon clippers take off), he thought about the airport beyond, at the other side of Rockaway, Idlewild. Gay name, for sure it was from Idlewild that you boarded Air France for the only other city on earth worth scheming to get to. Time enough, of course, but all the same, as he was beginning to understand just what lust was. . . .

—◄o►—

"Intellectual camaraderie of course, darling—in return for furs and jewels."

"Well, my solemn belief is, if the gift blesses the giver, then who am I to endanger the prospect of anyone's beatitude?"

"And of course flowers by Max Schling—nobody else will do."

"And this above all—in the *Symposium*."

"Oh, yes, translated as *The Cocktail Party*."

"I used to read all that metaphysics, dear, and such other meditations as the heart did prompt—until I discovered Wittgenstein. Now I only read him. A fairy with a mind is such a fabulous thing, and his stuff is so sensible. You could write it on the tea-room walls: I wouldn't be at all surprised if in the next generation that is exactly what happens—in the BMT Eighth Street Station, for example."

CHAPTER TEN

A Performance to Give

(THE FIRST CALLBACK)

"So rapid in fact was the rhythm of his inward drama that the quick vision of impossibility produced in him by his hostess's direct and unexpected appeal had the effect, slightly sinister, of positively scaring him. It gave him a measure of the intensity, the reality of his now mature motive. It prompted in him certainly no quarrel with these things, but it made them as vivid as if they already flushed with success."

—Henry James, *The Wings of the Dove*

"The attempt to reconcile your 'dream' momentum—as the subjective element in the dialectical image—with the conception of the latter as model has led me to some formulations. . . ."

—Theodor Adorno to Walter Benjamin

Wherein the author presents his set piece, a tale of first love he calls

SUMMER WISHES, SUMMER DREAMS

"I think your mother is very brave," T.'s mother said, cooking breakfast. "All the way to California, with two teenage boys, by bus!"

"My brother is only twelve," I replied, probably intending to score my mother's scheme with the mark of recklessness, even parental irresponsibility, although I'd certainly approved the plan at first. It was going to take me to Los Angeles, and from there perhaps as far south into film noir terra incognita as Ensenada, in Baja, where Barbara Stanwyck got that perfume she didn't know the name of, the one that drove Fred MacMurray crazy in Billy Wilder's *Double Indemnity*. But that morning in August 1956, I wasn't approving anything that would take me from the splendor of Candlewood Lake and away from T., the varsity "seeded" carrot-top tennis star with whom I was in love, the way the wise tell you you are just once in your life, almost always in summer.

—◄○►—

On our last afternoon together, T. and I were lolling wordless in the boat, adrift in one of the lake's innumerable coves. T. had turned the Evinrude outboard motor off and tipped it back. Each of us was scanning a different stretch of landscaped shoreline. We'd been laughing about the difference between two high school sophomore classmates' lives (our lives), as illustrated by their parents' (our parents') disparate boy-rearing philosophies. Neither of us had or wanted sisters, nor did we care to know just then at the age we were, fifteen, how differently different girls were bred; it was the shared assumption and conceit of our fitful stabs at maturational communication that when we married and fathered we'd do as our fathers had done: we'd father boys. I envied T. his position as the teenage son of parents who still joked about turning forty, in a "sane" American family—even as I tended to think it was a family right out of television, whose interactions were nothing but auditions compared to the intramural histrionics I'd cut and gnashed my teeth on.

We'd compared the kinds of summers we'd experienced for the last several years. In childhood, after World War II, I'd lived much the way he had. I'd spent long vacations in Northport on Long Island, in Windham in the Catskills, at the Jersey shore in settlements called Lavalette and Vision Beach. I'd picked berries, swum from Saint James Beach across Northport harbor to the Vanderbilt seaplane hangar in Centerport, and walked on the beach, it was later revealed, where Eugene O'Neill had sat in declining health, glaring into a camera lens. I'd drifted too far out off Vision Beach on a rubber surf raft, on the sunny day after the rainy day spent looking at Marilyn Monroe play crazy at Richard Widmark in *Don't Bother to Knock*, while the rain pattered on the Quonset-hut movie theater's tin roof. I'd been rescued, and been taken, as if being placated, as if the escapade on the raft had been some kind of threat, to the Roller Derby up in Asbury Park.

These were our "normal" vacations, before my mother decided, in 1951, to improve on the situation by packing my brother and me and her sophisticated and talkative bachelor-girl pal Flo (an executive secretary at American Tobacco) into the Chevrolet and heading out to see the U.S.A., because America was asking us to call. (It was always understood that we, as New Yorkers, did not really inhabit America, either at home in Jackson Heights or in our various vacation locales.) Not even I myself, the Yankee Doodle Dandy, born on the Fourth of July, inhabited America. So, in fact, we had to go see America: the Eastern Seaboard, its battlefields, its monuments, its restored, renovated and maintained towns, its plantations. Salem, Plymouth, Lexington, Concord; Gettysburg, Williamsburg, Charleston, Atlanta. Charlottesville, Monticello, Mount Vernon. We "did" them all, and in the evenings we played quartet canasta.

T. always idealized my family: my faintly mysterious, dapper, "cool" father, who worked as a timekeeper on the New York waterfront, knew Toots Shor personally and brought home things like cases of Hennessy V.S.O.P. that, as they say, "fell off" the ships. My sophisticated, "bohemian" mother, also "cool," who played Broadway show tunes from memory on the piano at parties, of which my family had always thrown more than anybody else's. What T. didn't know about, I'd tell him, were the arguments between us, between parties. Arguments chiefly over what I read—*Bonjour Tristesse*, in French, for example, which she'd dug out from under the French 2 grammar in a pile on my private desk. Arguments about where my "life" was apparently headed, featuring remarks like "You can't shock me. I read Maxwell Bodenheim's *Naked on Roller Skates* and all the rest of it!"

T. had never been caught reading compromising literature; he might safely stash the paperback of *Peyton Place* anywhere out of sight in his room, without fear of parental investigation, but neither did he get to go anywhere, except in order to play championship tennis, because his kid brother was still too young.

"You've been to Texas."

"But not by bus."

We reviewed the week, a more manageable subject than parents, *Peyton Place*, *Bonjour Tristesse*, or sex per se.

The first day, the boat flipped over, and we'd come up under it at opposite ends, each fearing to find the other cut to bloody ribbons by the Evinrude's blade.

The swimming race across the widest part of the lake, which I'd astonished T. by winning by several lengths.

"Why aren't you on the varsity?"

"They said I'd have to give up smoking and drinking both."

"Bullshit!"

"Seriously!"

The double dates with the "fast" public school girls from New Milford. (We'd heard, and compared, the verdicts. On me: "He's skinny, but he's cute with that crewcut, those red Bermuda shorts and those white bucks. But he reads on the beach!" On T.: "He is an everlovin' livin' doll cute, smart, athletic . . . and he can kiss!") We were both, T. and I, cheating on steadies back home, in Jackson Heights and Flushing, and the song that week was "Tonight You Belong to Me," sung by Prudence and Patience.

T. liked to comment on my imminent conquest of fabled California.

"You won't come back. You'll transfer to Hollywood High. They'll give you a swimming scholarship, and you'll train in Olympic pools in Beverly Hills. They'll let you smoke and drink all you want, and you'll get to drive to Las Vegas on the weekends."

"I can't drive; you can't either. They had to drive us to the drive-in, remember? They thought it was 'a panic.'" (We saw *Rebel Without a Cause*, which we'd been seeing together on double dates all sophomore year, time after time, tracking it from theater to theater, in Jackson Heights, Flushing, Bayside and Jamaica, until our steadies refused to sit through it one more time.)

"You'll be driving in a week. In convertibles. Just don't go drag racing on the cliffs in Malibu. You'd get your sleeve caught in the goddam door. You're like that genius: two left sleeves."

"T.! Jimmy!"

"It's Mac." (T.'s older brother, whose given name was James.)

"T.! Jimmy! C'mon! You're gonna miss the train!"

Neither of us made a move to look at one another, or to tip the outboard motor down, until T.'s father's voice:

"Come on in, you guys; the party's over! It's train time!"

"We better go. I gotta get to practice, and you gotta get to California...."

—<o>—

By the middle fifties, everything in our dog-tagged American lives was either brand new or "newly renovated": the bus stations, the buses, the roads, the idea of summer itself. We did not, for example, make the stop that summer morning we'd made in earlier years, at Edelstein Bros. in Long Island City, to stash the silverware and my mother's topaz dinner ring. (Scorpio birthstone) in pawn. We were flush in 1956, heading out, with traveler's checks and sporty new Samsonite luggage, from the Greyhound bus terminal at 50th and Eighth (the one immortalized, just before they demolished it, by Audrey Hepburn and Buddy Ebsen in Blake Edwards's *Breakfast at Tiffany's*). Walking into the elevated rear saloon of the Greyhound Scenicruiser, we were dressed as if we were sailing on the *Ile de France* or taking off on TWA from Idlewild. I was "collegiate casual," in regulation pressed chinos, new white bucks, button-down powder-blue polished cotton shirt with sleeves rolled up three flaps and "throw-over" white high school sweater emblazoned with a purple-bordered gold L. Forensic League, the arms encircled with purple stripes. The ads said, "Leave the driving to us," but the subtext read, "And while you're at it, dress the way these passengers you're looking at in this commercial are dressed: as if you're going someplace, to meet somebody."

We'd scarcely cleared the Lincoln Tunnel before my mother, the New York Archdiocesan parochial sixth-grade teacher, launched into conversation with two opposite numbers from the New York public school system, Staten Island division. My brother pulled out his EC and Donald Duck comics, and I, a seat apart, dove back into what I'd been reading on the beach at Candlewood Lake: Dostoyevsky.

"I see you're reading *The Brothers K.*," remarked one of the teachers, who looked and sounded so much like Nancy Culp on *Love That Bob* that, positive she was kidding me, I lost my composure.

"I'm trying to." What I meant (I thought in a matey way) was something like "If Marilyn can get through it . . . ," whereas what came out obviously gave her the green light to clock me as a snotty little contraption whose Vaseline brush cut and existentialist horn rims might have them fogged in at home in Jackson Heights but (I realized as we crossed the Passaic Plain and headed into what I'd been trained in Gotham smart-talk to regard as the Midwest) wasn't fooling this cookie for a hot second.

Abashed, I skulked down in my seat and took out the other book: *On the Road*. The paperback, just out, was the sensation of the the nation (having replaced *Bonjour Tristesse*) and, as far as I'd found out, was all about the road the road we were on had effectively replaced: the road running somewhere out there, as it were (but not exactly), parallel to ours, and all about the year (1947) I'd started grammar school, and all about sub fusc sex (speaking of

me in the first grade: latency had, it seemed, come late into my development, to last for exactly seven years).

All this by way of saying that while I was on that bus on that road at the
end of that summer cruising along those great Middle Atlantic States turnpikes of that bemused and benighted era comprising a ribbon-road prologue
to the strategic Civil Defense thoroughfare We the People would come to
know as the Interstate: emblem and occasion, metaphor and setting of so
much of everything there is to say about Nothing in the U.S.A., I was ever
more so page by page (having disappeared at a crossroads rest stop into the
Twilight Zone) hunkered down in the back seat of that car in the winter of
1947, on that road that had already become the road of the broken-down
motels (Vacancy!), crumbling road houses, fast drug deals and nimble sex
behind billboards: the underbelly of American Life, immortalized a generation later in queer life by the Straight-to-Hell masterpieces of Boyd
McDonald and the films of Joe Gage, the Douglas Sirk of queer male porn.

Like my new idol, Jack, "We flashed past the mysterious white signs in
the night somewhere in New Jersey that say South (with an arrow) and
West (with an arrow) and took the south one, from the dirty snows of 'frosty
fagtown New York' as Dean called it, all the way to the greeneries and river
smells of old New Orleans at the washed-out bottom of America."

I was already hooked, I wanted to be with Jack; fuck the other bozo. I
wanted to be listening to *The Lone Ranger* with him and telling him how
Kimo-sabe means "cocksucker" in Navajo and "living to the blank tranced
end of all innumerable riotous angelic particulars that had been lurking in
our souls all our lives."

As for us, we were sleeping on the bus the first night, staying in St. Louis
on the second, sleeping aboard on the third, stopping on the fourth at the
Grand Canyon; then heading into twilight and overnight through the Painted
Desert, veering off 66, up to the Hotel Sal Sagev in Las Vegas. ("The Sal
Sagev!" I'd crowed. "That's like staying at the *Serutan*!") Finally, coming
down through Bakersfield, California, we'd be docking downtown in Los
Angeles, a week to the day after leaving New York, and going to stay in
Beverly Hills (on the right side of Wilshire Boulevard, as it turned out),
our hostess, my mother's old Yorkville acquaintance, a former operetta and
tall-hats vaudeville soprano, for whom she had on and off in the twenties
played rehearsal accompaniment on the Strand Roof, at a time, we were let
to know, when Ruby Stevens, before she turned herself into Barbara
Stanwyck, was frequenting the same hall.

I'd gotten through the first-night, 4 a.m. somewhere-in-central-Ohio rest stop and all, and had awakened into a morning that ought to have been washed in the kind of serenity evoked by the following (recently found elsewhere than in the memory):

"The bus rolled westward across the farmlands as the wheat, corn and oats bent easily in the summer breeze. Barns and silos shrank before the vast sea of soil and grain that stretched as far as he could see."

(How I've always sometimes wanted things to align themselves with the evangelical, American-summer-ripened simplicity of that paragraph.)

As far as I could see, that morning on that Greyhound bus, on the banks of the Ohio, summer was a show I could pay a minimum of attention to and still review. ("I had a very good time.") We'd come a long way from tending the Victory Garden in Northport to tossing a block of Birds Eye into the double boiler at the end of a busy big-city day, and that was, metaphorically, what had become of summer too.

In the meantime, as far as I could tell from what I saw of, and in, any and all seasons (and their signal effects on the Something Called a Temperament I'd decided to become): reading was one of only two ways there were or ever had been to keep me from going completely crazy from the radical, and thoroughly unsatisfactory, difference between Life and Motion Pictures, and the other way between movies and segments of reading was rigorous concentration on One's Own Performance, and on the fixity of one's self-installation, on the security of one's coign of vantage. Otherwise the bastards would so to speak shake the full-leafed sycamore you'd foolishly imagined would hide and protect you in summer, until you fell out of it at their feet and broke your attractive neck.

‐◄○►‐

The speeding, air-conditioned Greyhound bus was a perfect, armored perspective, safely away from the summer beaches where year after year I'd spent far too many overexposed afternoon hours in the sun that did my fair skin no good, longing for ten or twenty minutes in cool shade. There in the rear, reading, I could do more comfortably what I'd always done, wait for the summer night and sing to myself, "One summer night I fell in lu-uv," or "The day is my enemy, the night is my friend," depending on how sophisticated I felt like getting, how deep I felt like drawing on the Luckies, and whether the offer of a genuine cocktail (or a slug out of the bottle of Hennessy

V.S.O.P. my mother kept tucked away as a specific against "travel cramps") could be described in the offing.

On the Road to Manhood-Delayed definitely indefinitely. Forsaking all other ambitions than digging it. Instead, every time I'd look out the Scenicruiser's window, I'd see road for the sake of road and torment myself with fantasies of Jack, trying when they became overbearing, to float in my mind the Russian steppes, another plenitude of Nothing, hard to dig, but negotiable. For I had decided, somewhere west of Paramus, to become Dostoyevsky's Alyosha Karamazov. My father's middle name was Aloysius—T. even found that cool—but I was cross-casting the beatific A.K. with the Jesuit mascot Aloysius Gonzaga, whose role it seemed, was edifying boys over eleven towards resisting reaching through the holes they'd poked in their pockets to do that thing that those two back there On the Road were doing, you just knew it, incessantly . . . even more incessantly, it was whispered, in summer.

As the sun set so far ahead of us on its own eventful (and fated) way to California, I put down *The Brothers Karamazov* and resumed *On the Road*.

What close reader can ever forget that penetrating exchange not in the front of the fag Plymouth (the effeminate car with no real power and no pickup) but later in the journey in the (how much more fitting) back seat of that old, cool, battered Hudson Terraplane?

They had it goin' on, those two, in their mobile-unit holding room; more-over, it was conducive. The two big road warriors, Mack and Truck, leaving confusion and nonsense and the terribly unflattering street lamps of Fagtown all snuffed behind them and barreling down the highway to pursue their four-point existential program: to charm, to cheer, to endear, to adorn. Or trying to, each feeling out the other's way, shape and form, testing the shock absorbers although, as you feel when you read the book, actually not moving at all but only sitting there while America jiggled by in back projection. Hunting yonder clouds in shapes of great white whales and dreaming of: one, ending up together on a Wheaties box; and two, riding in triumph through Pocatello, while playing truth-or-dare pocket pool like the pair of pothouse buffoons they were. Mack the holy hustler, looking for satori, an American Dostoyevsky seeking subliminal fusion with the Thing itself, *dans une seconde l'infini de la jouissance* at the very limits of the namable. And Truck, a down and dirty, horny, ball-baring, rope-a-dope Benzedrine slob, who whacked it without waiver half a dozen times a day when all else failed, and even when it didn't.

Then they'd pull over under the stars and piss together in twin streams, copious and unending, which would really froth up Mack's love bubbles (his beautiful man's body matched only by his simple child's mind), but Truck would immediately drop off into the deepest, most unfrothed and inconsiderate of sleeps. Then Mack, lying there crying softly, would hear Truck in his sleep moaning "Thanks for the buggy ride" and he would wonder . . . and pretend.

Oh, and then there were the dress extras, If, And and But: the two college kids intended to mirror Jack and Neal at an earlier more-unripe stage, and the Designated Fag, whom the deranged duo, out of the kindness of their pounding hearts, didn't roll in the hotel room in Sacramento. It is Jack who drives the fag Plymouth which somewhere they leave behind and pick up the Cadillac of the gods . . . but narrative continuity, which, beyond the certainty of syntax, builds space and time and reveals the mastery of an existential judgment over hazard conflicts, was hardly Jack's show.

Fact was he was never able to decide if the one divine event to which the whole of creation moves toward the ends of being and ideal grace was the moment of the sunrise, the moment when the hit off the bong first kicks in, or that double-trill-sonata moment of reciprocal scrotal contraction when you and your buddy, talking, finally do get one another off . . . and stars fall on Alabama.

It was farther west of St. Louis, on what I ever after called "The Nightbus to Tulsa," that both the trip's vehicle provenance and its wardrobe contour swerved into alarming "Ozark" disarray. Up till then, in one long first act, the deluxe Scenicruiser conceit had held: all along the great turnpikes, with their gleaming Formica-table way stations installed with portfolio jukeboxes wailing Elvis Presley and the Everly Brothers, the great ship of the road had sailed. Through that vast sea of soil and grain: the waving wheat that sure smelled sweet, right out of *Oklahoma!* But I preferred the smell of paperbacks, of Luckies, of Hennessy, and finally, in a wild, yearning, Kansas-in-August seizure of American sentiment, my fellow man. (He's come aboard in sailor whites, and was talking to, of all people, my little brother, still only twelve, asking to borrow a Donald Duck comic book.)

Then, suddenly, in a town I never knew, a breakdown, a deposition of baggage out onto the curbside of a dark and shuttered Main Street, whereupon we passengers were hustled from the wet heat of a southern Missouri August night into the musky claustration of a late-forties-model Greyhound, its steamlines rust-pocked and dented, the kind of bus Barbara Stanwyck took out of town in *Clash by Night*, telling them she'd send for her things. I was beside myself. I'd been flung into the only America I'd ever believed in: the America of film noir, of Edgar G. Ulmer's *Ruthless*, of Russell Rouse's *Wicked Woman*, land of a decade of my troubled dreams. It was frightening, more frightening than summer, but I belonged there, more than I'd ever belonged, or would belong, in *The Brothers Karamazov*. . . .

Nobody wearing coordinated separates was boarding the bus at any stop along the road to Tulsa. The gospel of mix 'em and match 'em had evidently not been carried west of the Mississippi. A lot of women got on wearing dungarees, halter tops, ballerina "flats" and nothing else, and carrying only handbags. Men boarded wearing overalls. . . .

A woman got on with two small children; she was carrying very little luggage, nothing capacious enough to stash below. My mother started a conversation. They were laying over in Albuquerque, then moving on somewhere, she wasn't sure where. All she was sure of ("All's I do know") was they weren't ever going back where they'd come from, and they sure as hell were through with him. He'd kept her "barefoot" in winter, but she'd been able to put by in the spring without his catching on, and now, in summer, they were cutting loose, getting so far away he wouldn't bother to look. They were of course headed west; everybody knew there was no percentage in going east. . . .

The sailor, having drifted to the last row, was beached opposite me, stretched out, legs spread apart, engrossed in Donald Duck. I kept smoking Luckies and reviewing the situation of the night in my mind, until the tide rushed in: a complex fantasy of vampirism, schizophrenia and sex, accompanied by the voiceover of Vivien Leigh as Blanche Dubois, taunting "at the 'Tarantula Arms,'" in counterpoint with another, more sepulchral voice from the same work, "*Flores para los muertos . . . Coronas para los muertos. . . .*"

The philosopher Ludwig Wittgenstein has said that of that which we cannot speak, we must perforce remain silent. The 1947 Vincent Sherman film noir *Nora Prentiss*, starring Ann Sheridan, issues the same directive, and so does the Tennessee Williams shocker *Suddenly, Last Summer* (which appeared some seasons following the events under consideration here). To invoke another authorial precedent: William Maxwell, an American who writes definitively about, among many other things, adolescence, says somewhere, "When we talk about the past, we lie with every breath we take."

It may just be I've already lied to the absolute limit of suspiration. I can, however, designate, as in parables we're taught to do (always remembering to paraphrase Maxwell again that time has already, significantly, darkened it), the exact (metaphoric) nature of the lie of that night's ramble East of Eden, in the Land of Nod. I'll call it the very rapture of brain fever. Or, snatching another telling title, Henry Roth's *Call It Sleep.*

So cut to the chase, to Recto and Verso, the big boys, and (in my mind) their touching be-bop mutual orgasms in Elijah's battered Cadillac with Rosenkrantz and Guildenstern. And and But, huddled together in the back seat just like me and my sailor (and Donald Duck), as Chicago looms in the offing.

And I was thinking of Jack more and more. Later in life, after his untimely death, I would come to understand the degree to which overstrained, aim-inhibited, energy-consuming and inexpedient sex was the cold curse of poor Jack's days on this troubled earth. But who was it who said *"Il n'appartient qu'aux grands hommes d'avoir de grands defauts"* or as we put it in the English, "The bigger the cheese, the bigger the holes."

For, as became apparent to me in my subsequent investigations (so bordering on obsession that when it came time to delegate a camp name, there was only one possibility for mine: Mardou, the heroine of Kerouac's *The Subterraneans*, he was, as all who knew him insisted, a saint, with kindness in his eyes, warmth in his laughter and a delicate benevolent mischief in his parish-priestly smile.

"She'll land on her feet; those women always do," my mother pronounced authoritatively, walking out of the Hotel Sal Sagev into the hallucinatory neon glow of downtown Las Vegas. "What I'd like to know is what happened to that poor soul the bus didn't wait for at the Grand Canyon. . . ."

When I'd remarked out loud of the Grand Canyon, looking down from a guard-railed protuberance into that apotheosis of concavity, that it reminded me of a megatonic bomb crater somebody had decorated with colored chalk, I was glad the sophisticated Staten Island schoolmarm was already a day ahead of us on her itinerary because, although only dimly aware why (or lacking the requisite actual grace or existential male fortitude to embrace an overwhelming *horror vacui*), I definitely wanted to be taken seriously, most especially by myself.

—◦—

"In *The Leviathan* . . . prose can still rise above itself and in a flash burst into a sort of poetry with some grim image or digression"—Stuart Hampshire on Hobbes's *Leviathan*, in "Vico for Now," *The New York Review of Books*, November 3, 1994.

More desperate even than Kerouac to rise above himself, the author became determined then and there, and not for the first time either, not only to commit like Jack to grim images and digressions of every provenance but to a prose that would burst in flashes into poetry itself (and never mind the qualifier *sort* either): a prose that was to American metric verse (so over-determined by Oxbridge English Newdigate-Prize English) what the music of Debussy's *Pelléas et Mélisande* was to Purcell's *Dido and Aeneas*. And apropos *The Leviathan*, the Leviathan was the Biblical whale, and what was for him the ultimate American book, if not *Moby-Dick*, and who was not only the great beauty of American Letters (*pace* the Hawthorne party) but also the supreme verbal musician if not Melville?

I was thinking about Thinking About Art, Art "threatened" by Nature. Years later I'd write, and hold, "I prefer a picture of a tree to a tree. Does that give you a problem?" I had so far failed to learn the enduring lessons of faith, to acquire the humility evoked by high and wild places.

I was thinking about construction sites in Manhattan, places my maternal grandfather, one of those legendary ironworkers who built twentieth-century New York, had brought me to on warm sunny days as soon as I could walk, and I was imagining the Grand Canyon serving as the foundation excavation for the celestial-terrestrial city, a futuristic Ripley's Believe-It-or-Not Nineveh of my imagination. I was thinking of the toy I'd played with in summer on the beach at Northport, a yellow metal tractor, and of the tract-housing construction site behind the carriage house we'd lived in, the postwar image and situation that replaced the Victory Garden the same summer after the Summer of Hiroshima we'd first heard the words "harbor pollution" spoken in the village.

I was thinking of all that then, and then of Sorrow (in sunlight).

But even so, parish-priestly smile or no, it was all still frightfully disintegrating for Jack and a matter of no small concern to oneself because, after all, what does the queer, or homo-social boy have to offer—what are we to call him? hetero-social boy? homo-anti-social boy? Consolation once in a while or, if he gets lucky, the consolation prize?

But it was worse even than that, for while Jack thought Neal was a living, breathing oneiric text way beyond butternut-wack, Neal suspected Jack of being *au fond* rather commonplace, or maybe it was just he found him suspiciously fond of emotive fondue, which is to say, a faggot after all, a saint and a faggot being not so very easy for even a Schopenhauer speed-freak surveillance officer and virtuoso in the hermeneutics of surmise to tell apart. Not only that, but Jack was paying too much attention.

William James had written, "In paying attention to your life history, I must temporarily turn my attention from my own." Now this was not a Neal deal, in fact inconceivable, and he mistrusted anyone else's attempt at it. Jack was suddenly no longer consigliere to Neal's capo in the Cosa Nostra of the Great Experiment, in which Neal would get the idea and Jack would tell him if the idea was bangin', but a ravenous-demon-gorging-himself-on-the-very-marrow-of-Neal's-soul who if allowed to continue would be responsible for the death of a beautiful subject.

Thus unnerved, Neal began declaring his disquiet re Jack's erotic score card, spreading confusion in the jerk circle, pitching the question: were the girls inhibited by his aura not passing the mustard or was it the case that Jack just couldn't cut it?

Which was frightfully unfair, because Jack did like girls as pictures (graphic registration of their early sufferings), although he found them lacking in . . . stability. As companions they bored him, but he liked having them curl up in his saintly arms to fondle and get all humid *con espuma che dura,* whereupon he would jack their text broadside, tapping their earthy sides and drawing from them deep, carnal laughter, then commiserating with them *comme si de rien n'était* over people's insincerity, the *à quoi bon* of life itself, the disturbed chemistry of the unsatisfied, the heartbreak of psoriasis and the square of the correlation, his feelings vibrating in sync with theirs until fork-tender.

‒◦‒

Las Vegas is either the Apotheosis of the Midway or a detention camp for vaudevillians, or both. Its moon-crater desert situation and its grotesque night-for-day *mise en scène* made it for me the great grotesque parody of American Summer, a kind of hallucination, conflating Coney Island's Luna Park, Rockaway's Playland, Lou Walter's Latin Quarter, and Toffinetti's on Broadway and 43rd Street. No wonder the Mafia invented it; it is the great barococo revenge of the Excluded-from-the-Quite-White-American-Society Deer Park. Nobody brought up in New York, I decided, could take it seriously for an evening. It was worse than television; it was color television, a Mecca for enraged, depressive morons. And the gambling looked ridiculous: it had neither the sexual allure of Damon Runyon's back-alley Broadway (as designed by Jo Mielziner and staged by Abe Burrows in Frank Loesser's *Guys and Dolls*) nor the dextrously fabricated insouciant frisson of Nice and Monte Carlo (where, in those fabulous fifties, Grace Kelly, a Philadelphia girl out to show people, had made *To Catch a Thief* for Alfred Hitchcock and then snared herself some kind of Camp-Royal croupier).

That said (about Las Vegas), we had a very good time. I had never before actually seen, in true car flesh, either an Edsel or a heliotrope Thunderbird, and that night we saw a lot of both. We went out to a "Night of the Stars" in a stadium there, and later collected matchbooks from the lobbies of those entertainment hotels better known nationally than the Sal Sagev.

I was feeling better and better about the West because, west of Oklahoma, both elegant gleaming buses and carefully detailed costuming had come back. Native Americans, still Indians then, had boarded wearing silver and turquoise bracelets, and the getups on weathered white people, cowboy hats and snakeskin boots: the watchword was "bedizened," made them look what I called Western. Although nobody slung a gun, there were suddenly men coming down the aisle of the bus actually carrying lengths of looped rope. The Petrified Forest and the Painted Desert overlaid the Russian steppes in my fraught mind, and I forgot about being Alyosha Karamazov. By the time we reached Bakersfield, I was very nearly convinced (as I have been time and time again, the moment always a reckless moment, I crossed the California state line) that reading was not necessarily the way.

When we pulled out of Bakersfield in the white-on-white heat of a California summer midday, I was in love with heat as I had never been in oppressive, humid, sweaty summer New York. ("It's why they called California 'California,'" declared Mac, the driver. "They named it after the heat.") I knew that Marilyn Monroe was California, was summer, and I knew too why she'd come east to stand, legs spread apart, over the subway grating. . . .

We didn't go to look at any battlefields in California that summer, but that night in Los Angeles, my mother's friend and her husband took us out on the town to (or at any rate past) the Brown Derby, Ciro's, Mocambo and the Coconut Grove, and on subsequent occasions on location at the Planetarium in Griffith Park, high on Mulholland Drive, on the cliffs at Malibu, and all along Sunset Boulevard, where the canonized James Dean finally, fairly, in ghostly single combat, once and for all vanquished his rival, the canonized Aloysius Gonzaga, in the war for my soul and spare parts. I began to envision this melodrama in moompix sports newsreel terms as a hand-wrestling saga, shot on Venice Beach, between James Dean, as himself in a sailor suit, and Sal Mineo as Aloysius Gonzaga in cassock and surplice. Natalie Wood wasn't cast. . . .

I began to understand how it might come about that T.'s joking prediction about me in California would come true. (In the worried last scene of *All About Eve*, Barbara Bates, as the plaintive Phoebe, asks Anne Baxter, as Eve Harrington, if she plans to stay long in California. She's told, "I might.")

Even James Dean and Marilyn Monroe, working singly or as a team, couldn't have done it to me all by themselves; it was the sets more than anything else: the sets and the decoration of the sets. It was the streetlamps of Beverly Hills; it was the perfume of the night-blooming things fluorescent in every canyon. (There was no need to go to Ensenada.) It was, of course, the view, from Mulholland Drive, of the Grid lit up, stretching across Immensity to the shore of the Pacific, like the central-and-autonomic nervous systems of a supine, ultra-sentient, intergalactic Somebody. . . .

I went back east to face T., Jack, and the others, and to commence dissembling, methodically, with increasing guile. I found it necessary to do so, and I credit California with showing me how.

I still don't drive.

CHAPTER ELEVEN

Stipulations

(POST-MORTEM WITH THE PARTY IN FULL TILT)

"The purpose of myth is to provide a logical model capable of overcoming a [real] contradiction."
—Claude Lévi-Strauss

"**D**o you suppose all that actually happened to him, my dear?"

"Well, it *occurred* to him; isn't that enough?"

"Might be, but it does sound as if he watched the whole thing through a glory hole."

The older queen they call Prudence approaches the author, QT.

"Well-told, dear. You have a curious talent beyond your years, and a soul which seems to understand, with the divine Oscar, that though the gorged asp of passion, has it not already done so, must one day rise to feed upon your young boy's heart, yet have you burst the bars, stood face to face with Beauty, and known, if not the love that makes the earth move—which, by the way, unless he ever jerked off near a blasting site, nobody really believes Miss Hemingway has either—then indeed the love which moves the sun and all the stars."

Prudence—pronounced the French way, from the aging whore in the Cukor/Garbo *Camille*, played by Laura Hope Crews, whose most famous line is "I'm thirty-six!" and who, when Garbo as Marguerite Gautier suffers her first collapse at the party at which she meets Armand Duval, instigates the callous exit from the premises, carrying all the food, to continue the festivities at her place.

"I've been listening to you, darling, and watching you, and thinking about you, and, frankly, worrying a little about you all the afternoon. And I have come to the conclusion that you are a boy with a brain in your head—moreover, a boy a little bit more infused, if I may say so, than the general run of pert, ruthless, animated porcelain that trots its way through this alcove of a typical Sunday.

"You have an appealing thumb-swatch, rough-molded quality, and in addition, I might add—plus which, as they do like to say around here—the makings of a decent human being. But I must tell you—I must—in all candor and in the nicest possible way—as I hope you'll remember, and report later, when you speak of it, and you *will*—that for a not-yet, you talk far too much. The fact of the matter is, you are quite clearly still reeling—like a boy in a spangled costume just shot out of a cannon—with the shock of sudden emergence from what the Master, in *The Wings of the Dove*, so wisely called 'the obscurity of extreme youth.' And although you absolutely must not let what happened to Milly Theale happen to you—to fall in love in order to save your life and have it fail to do just that—you do apparently share her great ambition, adjusted for gender: you want desperately to be the hero of a strong story. And so you talk too much. Attractive talk in its way—actually you are the sort of boy one might just, braving the terrible risk of neighborhood surveillance, apprehension and prosecution on morals charges, take to bed just to hear what things you talk about in your sleep.

"You also have in my opinion an interesting jagged edge—particularly in the matter of narration—a broad-brush treatment of an anguished background that's almost Abstract Expressionist—which in this milieu, characterized as it is, you'll have noticed, by the superimposable type, is, well, something. Only a very few ever come to understand that it is non-super-imposability that opens the door to interactions that yield something more than snug fits of the congruous.

"Yes, attractive talk, and not talk out of turn—not yet. And that's to the good—the mark of a ripening political *astuce*—and that is why I am speaking to you. Because newcomers who talk out of turn do not make call-back, and I would like to see you here again some other Sunday.

"Aristotle let it be known that a good life has the inherent value of a skilled performance. Well, to recast the Aristotelean in vaudeville terms—where for our crowd it emphatically belongs—there are no double acts on Queer Street. If that looks like a couple, one of them is the dresser. No, darling, we are all singles, like the French Ventriloquist—or if not, we're part of the animal act. I gather both from that sweet little impersonation you gave before of Eartha Kitt doing 'Santa Baby' and from the story you told of your lost love—which I may say betrayed the vestiges of the exemplum or edifying anecdote that flourished in the Era of Faith—that you understand this already.

"Moreover, we are all, whether we admit it or not, cruel boys. We tell one another we are the refugees and survivors of the cruelty of boys, and the fact that refugees have since the war become so chic in New York bumps us up another notch in our own esteem. But all boys without exception are cruel, and that means us, darling, because none of us, not even the nelliest, was ever a girl. Nobody born with a dick, darling, is ever going to be a girl.

" 'There is a time of apprehension which begins with the beginning of darkness, and to which only the speech of love can lend security.' Kay Boyle wrote that, dear.

"Take it from an old pro—an old slag, some say, who has made enough mistakes in her life to start a whole new world: when you find yourself in an influential environment, like this one, listen to everybody in it, not just to the weary likes of me. But I think you will do that on instinct, because I think you know you are where you belong. There's no getting away from it when you're Irish. And you are not in the least like that white boy Jimmy Baldwin writes of in *Giovanni's Room*, everything in him screaming no and the sum of him sighing yes. Sum and substance seem to me to be one in you, dear, and it is screaming that silent eye-scream yes, yes, yes, yes, she said, yes. You are one boy who will not have to go to Paris to find himself—although of course it is to Paris you must go, as surely as we all did after D-Day.

"Queer life, when it comes down to it, is a biological system, and biological systems operate like effective economies, thriving best on decentralized and diffuse guidance. Think of it not in terms of a setting with a cast of characters—unless all you want is to become one taking up space in the other—but as a scene of transformation; it can be that. But it is a risky sea to navigate.

"Heterosexual boys, you realize, proceed in life's journey according to ephemerides—firmly established and corrected tables calculating the future positions of the sun, moon, planets and fixed stars of a universe of determined courses and pre-booked destinations. Whereas our kind move on, blind in the night.

"Excuse me, I wasn't—"

"Listening—I know. A mistake—not the inattention, dear, the admission of it: far too risky. It gives the game away. When one is in the position of calculating one's next advance, it is as well to appear to be listening. Which brings me to something important.

"The problem in putting you over, dear, as I see it, is just this: you're a good turn—indeed in my considered opinion as good a turn as has come along in many a Sunday—but you are just a little too aware of your own allure.

"You can whistle up a story of yourself—that much is clear. In fact as I sit here listening it occurs to me you are probably capable of whistling up some version or other of the story of all of us here this afternoon, and holding on to it for years—so that, long after we're gone, you may end up representing us in the manner of that Shakespearean sonnet, concerning giving life to the beloved. Yes, you might—putting such words in as will by then be old dead mouths that people will wonder, 'Did anybody ever really talk that way?' And you must tell them all we did. You must go on talking the way you do, and tell them once upon a time we all talked that way. This way—because, of course we all know this way is fast becoming obsolete. There aren't ten years left—there may not be so much as five—in the era of this discourse.

"But in order to do all that, you must learn one or two things. First, to periodically regroup your forces and stop confusing the procedural with mere display. You must decelerate to a stately pace when sharing your experiences. I have no doubt you were a whopping great success in comic parts in school theatricals, but the watchword hereabouts, darling, is *festina lente*. I'd be more than happy to take your timing in hand.

"It's a bit like the bonds of marriage, darling. This today in your case was the first time of asking. Following two further auditions—relax, you needn't spill another bean; in fact it's best you do not. If nobody comes forward—except it's done behind your back—to read you out, you'll have earned free entry.

"Another essential thing: don't go trying to be a little whore. For one thing it isn't you, I can tell, and for another, in my experience, it's whore today, gone tomorrow, with very few exceptions—and you wouldn't be one of them; you wouldn't allow yourself to be—and that, if you care, is a compliment.

"So if he takes you into his study, shows you his Marsden Hartley and Charles Demuth reproductions and his George Platt-Lynes photographs, do try to keep your particulars zipped into your pantaloons, won't you? Because, corny as it seems, he's giving you his little test—you might risk the pun and say his testicle.

"Oh, I've seen them come and go, darling—come and go with absolutely dizzying celerity. The feature of the season, the theme of every tongue—and then it's 'Oh, hello! Haven't seen you for ages. Call me, do—we'll have lunch, go to a MoMA screening, or something.' They come in from small towns, and from farms out in the middle of absolutely nowhere, and from carnivals they ran away with and then ran away from.

"Like Jeanne Eagels, dear—do you know about Jeanne Eagels? I suppose everybody thinks they know about Jeanne Eagels now, because of that rather fanciful movie with Kim Novak. Although it was, of course, considering the talent pool out there, an acute piece of lavender casting—for Jeanne Eagels was, along with Nazimova, Cornell and Le Gallienne, one of the great Sapphics—but I saw Jeanne Eagels, dear, stand on the stage of Maxine Elliot's theater in *Rain* and tell the preacher to go to hell, and that was a few years ago to be sure, but somehow the boys who come in here continue to remind me of Jeanne Eagels telling the preacher to go to hell in *Rain*, and very, very few of them, my dear, can carry it off, and so after a very few times I stop seeing them, and I do wonder what becomes of them.

"And as for Maxine Elliot, dear, well, she was perhaps even more interesting than Jeanne Eagels, although they'll never make a movie out of her life because she didn't die of a heroin overdose. All she did was act a little in the Gilded Age, fuck J.P. Morgan, get him to teach her all about money, get filthy rich, get fat and go live with a lot of queer spongers on the Riviera.

"But back to you and clever boys like you and what is to become of them in the Life. Yes, yes, it's lovely to be given an education; to be able to read books—to be really good at it and to get so you can call that a living. To be able to come out of the opera or the ballet or the theater or the better movie theaters—the ones where you've been downstairs and drunk black coffee before the feature starts—and go on at length. On the other hand there is the workaday world. Display, for example, is in certain of its aspects sweated labor, but we like to emphasize the creative in it—and it is too one of the last great apprentice crafts, and if you're good at it, darling, and willing to be supervised, you can before very long be pulling down a hundred a week, plus treats.

"But of course you're going to be a writer, aren't you? Still and all, you could do worse than attend to display.

"And speaking of the French Ventriloquist, I am now going to address you in French—assuming you have studied that language in the good high school from which I am told you have recently graduated with honors, and that you have read *Bonjour Tristesse* in the original.

"Not that I am going to speak about the *bande à* Sagan or the Tropeziens, about whom you have undoubtedly read all in *Paris Match*, a publication I am sure you peruse weekly at Hotaling's International News Stand in Times Square, and who, I feel quite sure, are less interesting all told than were the Kirstein gang out at Cherry Grove—indeed probably not even as interesting as the Sunday afternoon regulars at Riis Park.

"No, I am going to speak to you about Julien Green, the American in Paris, whose work, if you don't know it, you must become aware of immediately. Julien is emphatically *de la vraie souche*. I met him during the war—oh, yes, dear I was in the army, and yes, I liberated Paris, and yes, yes, I sat with the rest of the more advanced GIs at the feet of Gertrude Stein, who used to be the American in Paris. Julien Green is the American in Paris now—or in truth one of two, the other being Bricktop.

"We were sitting together in a little café on the Quai d'Orsay, talking about Simone Weil and Charles Péguy—"*Le Mystère de la Charité de Jeanne d'Arc*" and "*Le Mystère des Innocents Saints*"—and I said quite simply, '*La vie s'en roule, Julien.*'

"'*C'est vrai, mon vieux,*' Julien me disait, en gardant, comme on peut dire, ses perles—tout en observant le tact et la correction qu'il est inutile de rappeler à des Françaises. 'Oui, c'est vrai. Les reputations s'anéantissent si vite . . . si vite. Voilà comme la vie nous avait tout épaissis, tout alentis, et nous sommes ici, au milieu du vingtième siècle, deux vénérables vieillards chrétiens dans un café aux quais de la Seine, comme Saint Antoine et Saint Paul, assis au bord d'une source, étourdis par le grouillement de monstres sataniques qui l'entourent: ces larves, ces vampires, ces êtres hybrides, les jeunes Parisiens.*'

"'*Ça vous dérange, bien alors,*' a harsh voice interrupted, unbidden, at this point, '*de vous mêler avec le peuple?*'

"'*J'aime ces types silencieux,*' Julien continued, as if the voice had never spoken, '*aux allures des hommes torpilles. Ils me semblent comme des personnages allégoriques du* Roman de la Rose: *Bel Accueil, Douce-Merci, Faux-Semblant, Danger, Honte, et Peur. Ils vont toujours jusqu'au bord de l'abîme pour voir. La contemplation d'eux arroche ma pensée à mon corps et la transporte en un lieu hors de l'espace d'où il n'y a perspective ni point de vue. L'espace s'outre. La mesure de l'espace ordinaire de la perception est remplacée par une infinité à la deuxième ou quelquefois troisième puissance!*' '*Embrasse-moi, donc,*' je veux dire, '*et prend cette bourse qui me gêne.*' Ils m'enfollent, tout à fait."

Eavesdroppers:

"Don't you hate it when faggots talk French like that?"

"I don't mind people talking French. French is a beautiful language. Racine made quite a thing of it—Baudelaire did too—and still told nothing but the truth."

"Racine . . . Baudelaire . . . Proust . . . Colette. Colette called happiness a kind of wisdom."

"Don't talk to me about Colette—Colette was a monster who wrecked people's lives. I grant you she wrote attractive French—as does, for example, that young Françoise Sagan creature."

—◁○▷—

"She came East as soon as she realized two key things. First, that for the type of *réclame* she was after, she was, in Kansas City, although a crazy little woman, surely, just as surely the wrong color, and second, that there were no pearls to be found in prairie oysters."

—◁○▷—

"He falls easily into a rage—calls it his Achilles tendency."

"The dear!"

—◁○▷—

Prudence again:

"And remember, darling, you are the music while the music lasts.

"And now it is time for me to toddle home. Speaking of vaudeville again, Birdie Coonan boasted she closed the first half for eleven years; I've been closing it for nearly twenty—it makes listening to the post-mortem bearable, if not exactly like attending to the Gospel of John. For you see, dear, the fact of the matter is, the future may not need the likes of me, but the past emphatically does."

And at the door:

"And do remember what I told you, won't you? Bide your time, and time will reward you. As it stands now, you're rather too instant—too—how shall I put it—Nescafé. But if you really want it, there is an alchemy that can turn you into a really good, strong regular grind—espresso, not percolator.

"Listen, listen, and go on listening and chances are you'll end up lasting. And you want to last—it's a rotten feeling, dear, really it is, being plowed under."

◄o►

Commentary from the Chorus:

"Poor Pru's light is flickering—her sorrows lie heavy upon her."

"She was sure lookin' you over old fashioned."

"She used to send minions ahead—'my beaters,' she called them—to forecast her entrance. Alas, her beaters have bit the dust—in that she is a true survivor."

"High noon thus passed, her time decayed."

"The poor darling has dwindled to a vestige. A great exponent, nevertheless over the years of the covered dish matinee. Tell us, dear, what was under her lid this afternoon? What was she filling your shell-pink ears with of a Sunday—the story of her life?"

"Telling me all about Jeanne Eagels in *Rain*."

"Jeanne Eagels in *Rain*? That was before the *flood*!"

"Actually, darling, it was just as the flood was getting underway. Prudence made it into the ark in time; poor Jeanne Eagels didn't."

"Jeanne Eagels in *Rain* at Maxine Elliot's theater. About Maxine Elliot too—how she got rich. Then about somebody called Julien Green. He says he's the American in Paris."

"Pru has a passion for the cultural history of late antiquity."

"Reason possibly being she *is* the cultural history of late antiquity."

"Or pretends to be—and by and large gets away with it. Personally, I'm skeptical of her texts, as highly readable as they are. I find them not, shall we say, composite. Rather, in the manner of the genre known as medieval forgery, replete with direct altered borrowings, reflection of sources, doubtful attributions and whole cloth inventions, the pattern of which is hers alone to know. In short, the woman is a mint of information."

"There must have been a time when—"

"Oh that there was, and the story is not without interest or meaningful ramification. Actually, we know all about her fixation on Jeanne Eagels in *Rain*. Sometimes we call her 'Suzy Rain'—she is such a bossy thing.

"To put it in allegorical terms, you could say she'd been given a ticket for the front row in life, but stopped off for cocktails with the wrong set, unwisely skipped dinner with the right people and arrived at the show somewhat the worse for wear. Seems they were already well into the second act—in point of fact the second act dream ballet. She started out hectoring everybody for a plot summary—confusing the power to part a room with the ability to empty one—and when push came to shove, she got the heave-ho into the alley.

"Badly shaken, reeking of social flop sweat, she nevertheless rallied, considered strategy and tactics, and made it, *en grande tenue*, in a Checker cab across town from the theater district to the smart East Side, where she's held forth ever since. Her latest little revelation concerns the Tower of Babel. She sees skyscraper New York as it, and New Yorkers of the present generation as desperate to climb the dizzy heights of Olympus."

"Isn't that mixing metaphors?"

"She mixes what she likes—and after she's mixed a few more than she ought to mix, having rattled at some length about her salad days in a finer time—rubbing elbows with Noël and Gertie and Ina Claire and Grace George, while the pianist played "How About You?" until you're ready to scream—she's apt to try to introduce you to a leg of lamb, so don't be alarmed. Anyway, lately it seems she sees God's terrible punishment being visited upon us all every night, as we stagger home, each of our self-constructed towers demolished, our Jacob's ladders thrown down, each of us left alone and babbling an unknown language in our dreams."

"Bible study is absolutely fascinating—particularly study of the Old Testament, which is why I profit so greatly from going up to Jacob's Pillow with Martha and the company. Martha is very severe—very Old Testament."

"Everybody's always talking about Martha. I wish people would talk more about Isadora, and Ruth St. Denis and Doris Humphrey."

"Religion is supposed to be a comfort—Violetta Valéry says so."

"So does Simone Weil."

"Darling, you cannot seriously compare a whore and a mystic, even if both died of consumption."

"Simone Weil, darling, went in for a kind of elevated pouting—I wouldn't call it mysticism—although, you know, I once tried to convince Martha to do a piece on her. I mean, by any existential definition Simone Weil was Camp, and Martha's genius redeems camp; it is for that reason we have deified her."

"Yet they are alike—not pouting and mysticism, but Violetta Valéry and Simone Weil. We were talking earlier of lost love, well, Violetta Valéry's story speaks for itself of course—or sings for its supper, if you prefer—but Simone Weil was in my opinion the high priestess of lost love, properly understood in our time."

"Noël Coward is amusing, but hardly innovative or trenchant. I mean what is that *Design for Living* thing? Two queens and a fag hag. Boring and ridiculous. I do like *Blithe Spirit*, but then I have a thing for the dead—particularly dead women. My analyst says—well, never mind what she says. I hardly ever do."

Parting shots.

"All told, darling, we have decided, as a self-confessed opera queen and a former member of the High School Forensic League, you are already in an advantageous position as regards facing American life. By all means go to college, but be aware that it will make not the slightest bit of difference—unless of course you become an academic, and frankly we don't see that in your cards.

"Because you see, American is, as presently constituted and will be for as long as anyone alive can foresee, exactly two things: a talk show and a soap opera. Therefore, since as Aquinas points out the higher form possesses the lower form virtually, so the Forensic Society governs the talk show and, strange as it may seem at first but according to the rigorous rules of logic, governs soap opera—and musical comedy, too."

"So listen to your mothers—we are giving you an identity free of charge—or nearly: all we ask is lifelong allegiance, a few kind words now and then, and a martini at lunch."

Followed by The Fall Decision to be an intellectual. The heritage of the religion and an education.

SPECIAL ISSUE

PARTISAN REVIEW

ROBERT LOWELL
        My Kinsman, Major Molineux (a play)
SUSAN SONTAG   Notes on "Camp"

R.H.S. CROSSMAN   Radicals on the Right

MURIEL SPARK   Four Poems

MAX KOZLOFF
        The New York Avant-Garde
GEORGE LICHTHEIM   On David Riesman

Reviews by Marshall Berman, Reuben A. Brower,
Paul de Man, Stephen Donadio, Mason W. Gross,
Philip P. Hallie, and John Simon

SOME COMMENTS ON GOLDWATER
Daniel Bell, Martin B. Duberman, George P. Elliott,
Richard Hofstadter, John Hollander, Jack Ludwig,
Hans J. Morgenthau, William Phillips, Richard
Poirier, Philip Rahv, Richard Schlatter, and William
Taylor

FALL
1964

$1.50

9/–

PART THREE

Breaking Out

FROM DRAGS TO RICHES
SAT., SEPT. 12, 1964

CHAPTER TWELVE

Dirty Boulevard

(ORIGINATING AT THE MEETING OF CLEARASIL AND EYE SHADOW)

Wherein the story of the darkening of the American '50s sunshine vision unfolds, the author as an NYU graduate student encounters Queer Street life on Greenwich Avenue and is caught up in the dizzy whirl of the Everard Baths's celebrity glory days.

Elsewhere, the *Life* photo essay on the flaming queens of Greenwich Village (Summer 1964, the Goldwater year), the political undoing of Allard (never stop running away) Lowenstein and Bayard Rustin, these very twin tintypes, white and black, of the closeted self-immolating queer politico, and the beginnings of public discourse and, in the wake of the passage of the Civil Rights Act, of the civic defiance that will culminate in Queer Bastille Day, the Stonewall Riots (June 28–30, 1969).

Convergent: the downtown queer theater explosion. Al Carmines's *Home Movies* and *Faggots*, LaMama, the Café Cino and the emergence of the renegades Harry Koutoukis and Jackie Curtis, leading later to the works of Robert Chesley and the Glines playwrights, of Larry Kramer, Terrence McNally and William Hoffman and, as Ira Siff spun off from Carmines, the glories of *La Gran Scena di New York* and the fabulous diva Vera Galupe-Borszkh.

It is just as likely as anything is that Gay Liberation, like women's liberation, was the result of the psychological atmosphere, by prosperity which was ushered in by the simultaneous introduction of non-violent child rearing (not to mention the notion that children could, in fact, be treated as children) and the Baby Boom birth ratio. For two decades, 1946 through approximately 1965, there was a great surge in birthrates, and then a reversion to earlier patterns. Before these two developments, there were always—more or less so—many children to rear and but one sure way prevalent among the working classes, brought from Europe, to do so: break them, physically and spiritually, exactly as you do horses.

Quite suddenly, in the aftermath of two World Wars, victorious America decided to treat its children the way it had decided to treat the conquered Japanese. And chief among the rules was the substitution of surplus consumption for what had become superfluous work-ethic industry, exhausted by war production.

One had to be cautious whom one cruised on the street as well, as certain grinning souls, eyes merry, would slip the cuffs on (and this not fetish but vocation) at the first hint of suggestion . . . even if, wary from some sixth or seventh sense, one had neither suggested nor hinted. "Hello there." "Uh, hello." Busted. And the tanks never so romantic as Genet, in prose or film, would have them.

Telephone numbers circulated—two of the tops of the Finest were just fine, don't-cha know, and if called, would (might) spring the friends of friends of friends (and Dorothy in there somewhere), charges dropped, record clear.

The young don't believe it, but so it was: you risked a night in stir, a record ever stained, by smiling on the street, especially toward the end of the month when the boys had a quota to fill. It was not pleasant. It was not ever pleasant. The fear cannot be designated tang.

It put rather a bite in one's resentment of the liberal established, who seemed never to *get it* about gay rights and civil rights, were ever apt—prone—supine—to justify, with circular reasoning, flat prejudice. And no one believes *that* now.

An interesting history might be compiled, the columns and articles and the bonniest mots of the well-intentioned, on that *one group* that never was, never could be, accepted with total equanimity. Fascinating. They believed it, and they believed they were good.

This prevalence of cultural narcissism, as it were, came simultaneously with the dawning of the "Great Age of Publicity"—the Kennedys as sexual libertines, putative queer icons and political heavyweights, along with Marilyn Monroe's shady death in 1962 and Judy Garland's near death on television.

It was an era in which queer boys from the Ivy League (mind you, never would we hear *them* utter "darling," at least never in public) just lived for football weekends, and dreamed, like Cole Porter wannabes, of "making the team," all the while their hearts were primed for Daddy. It was the age when a real homosexual Hamlet (Donald Madden at the Phoenix) was actually unveiled: in love with Father and Horatio and drawn madly to Claudius and Laertes, while remaining coldly callous to Gertrude, a pest. Sentimentally attached to Ophelia, his better soul, and thus reviling her in an act of self-mutilation. Hamlet as Orestes.

And on the town, after the theater, as naturally as the sun had set over the Hudson, the Everard Baths.

THE FILE ON THE EVERARD BATHS

Thing about the Everard is, it was just rooms and beds, tiny rooms and tiny beds. No tile and marble glories (much less divas warbling within), no "fetish rooms" like the Club and Man's Country in the years to come. Barebones bodies. A little steam, for tradition's sake. But they made their own heat.

You could imagine boys coming here just to bathe—the tub in the kitchen being full of dirty dishes.

There was *no music*—so one could sleep if one had a mind (or had lost it). And the walls of the rooms did not reach the ceiling—you could hear everything—you couldn't *not* hear everything. Slurping and moaning and everybody's dish about everybody else. A salon, dear, in Purgatory—with partitions more palpable than masks. You could pretend you didn't know who was doing what. You could pretend you knew. Everyone knew.

Of a patron, staggering down the halls:

"They say he has a kind of falling sickness."

"We all have the falling sickness in here, Leda. Grand mal, the Fall of Man. The collective experience *dans cette maison particulière de grief soupir* is in three parts: tonic, colonic and coma—something to do with endocrines. Paresis Hall. The entrance is a dream of cartoons, and after descending the imaginary pillowed stairs, you will scream irrepressibly in front of a series of distorting mirrors that make you look like a fat man on one side and the world's thinnest on the other. Maybe you thought you'd come to that psychiatric instution, Creedmoor? You have come instead to this degraded corner of unveiled vice, and those aren't mirrors, they are merely mirror-selves! Here we undergo, each of us in his nocturnal prowl, garbed in tatters, the base contamination of a hundred palms, as we execute over and over with tango passion here on the dark canyon floor the night-long mating dance of the deadly scorpion. The wonder is why we don't collectively swallow our tongues and choke to death, but even if we did—on our own tongues, or on something a bit thicker—our tongues would go on flapping. They could cut them out of our heads, and still they'd flap, in nervous miseries, like little spastic creatures on the filthy floor, born of spilled spunk, the get of unholy lust. We are not hearsed, but make our ghost home here among the soul-shrunk lost."

"I think that is the most depressing instance of self-hatred I've heard in enormous years. Base contamination, indeed—wash it off!"

"That's the spirit, woman—go on!"

"I shall. I cannot be patient of such waste of shame. In the first place, it is natural for man to reach the intelligibilia through the sensibilia. That's Thomas Aquinas, darling. And if you insist on calling certain sensibilia sinful, there is this to be said for sin, it is a terribly vigorous form of human potential. And in the second place, this place, necessary product in these dangerous times of a civic conspiracy of masculine silence, is vital not only as a refuge from killing cares, harassing anxieties, unforeseen reversals and hopes blasted, but as an academy conducive to the education in matters of proportion, probability and degree of the many who want what some few have, and will go to any lengths to get it. Here one may not only closely read society itself, its historical and monumental aspects, its rich and authoritative consciousness, its shifting values and transgressions anatomized, but frequentation of the rituals enacted in these hallways, in the swimming pool, the massage parlor, the steam room, and particularly of the conversation in the coffee shop intended to while away long hours in the loiter, also contributes a very great deal towards brightening many a life and alleviating the despondency caused by feeling one is a fish out of water in the world."

"You're not serious!"

"Freak-went-ation is the word—a freak a minute, at least."

"I am entirely serious. Where else in lavender New York, I ask you, may those big-boned, dolichocephalic shit kicker halfbacks pouring in from the idyllic, if improvident countryside—creator of vigorous loins but stifler of the imagination—encounter for the first time in their lives the magic of New York—reckless, dizzy, ecstatic—flexing their hard, urgent thighs in the giant diesel hum of street and harbor traffic, the sweet music of danger, the voices of deathless tonight-only love and unrepeatable, intoxicating adventure. Where can such as these, together with those smaller, altogether more delicate but equally toothsome inhabitants of cities, toilers trained merely in unsupervised street trades whom unkind fate has relegated to streetcars, whisky bars and permanent proletarian status, whose music is that of steam engines, machinery and shrill whistles, whose exertions of spirit are so inextricably bound up with sweated labor—where else can these, these and the higher class of mechanic—all desiring a benevolent association for their mutual assistance, and justifiably wary of the Odd Fellows and the Philomathean Lodge—"

"Talk about user illusion. Meanwhile, darling, *streetcars*? Get a gay grip!'

"—mix with their cosmopolitan betters of a wider and more mobile nature in the middle walk of life and beyond, thinking larger-than-life-thoughts in an environment lifting them out of the tumult of everyday existence into the serene atmosphere of dignified discourse—one palpable hope springing from many hearts—in free and frank exchange of opinions and aspirations, *en alterance*, indulging without fear of reprisals at the hands of their originating captors—"

"Hands and feet, darling, hands and feet!"

"Well put. At the hands and feet of their originating captors, in comforting displays of knowledge, prudential considerations and taste relative to the trammels of human vice and the rigors of human virtue?"

"Oh, Mary—Man-soul delivered from Diabolus, by Emmanuel and his regiment, here in the fucking baths! Re-runs nightly of Horatio Alger—scenes right out of *Ragged Dick* and *Struggling Upward?*"

"The woman is completely out of control!"

"Now do you really think you are still in the Century Club? Do you imagine you see the souls of the righteous being instructed by Cato in the law? Ridiculous—although I will agree that wide and mobile natures abound here—often hanging weirdly from hooks in the ceiling and making extravagant rotating gestures with far-flung open arms."

"I was taken to lunch at the Century Club last week. There is the prettiest picture hanging in the second-floor library there of Henry James as a youth. Fuckable—absolutely."

"And if you like philosophy, darling, here's a little Nietzsche for you that pegs this place just perfect. It concerns the eternal return—maybe you saw the Cocteau film? Anyway, Nietzsche says, 'Whatever condition this world may reach it has already reached, not once but innumerable times. The whole of your life, mankind, is like an hourglass, always being inverted and always running out again.'"

"Oh, we all saw that—in *The Wizard of Oz*."

"Indeed. Indeed, and when you see some queens crawling out from under the pileups in the dormitory, ragged dick is exactly—"

"Hush up with that—we're discussing Nietzsche, it's serious! And I must say that although it is true that once I came in here I could never look at a man in a Hart, Schaffner and Marx suit in the same way again, I am all the same less than enthusiastic about such mixing, or about the idea that vital emanations from men of the lower orders may affect the minds and bodies of their betters."

"I know just what you mean—anybody, even Nietzsche, could get the clap."

"I rest my case."

"That's good—both you and your case deserve a rest."

"Nevertheless—or is it therefore—hope springs eternal."

—◁○▷—

"Darling, the Patrolman's Benevolent Association, which everyone says owns this place, always always give notice of raid, and tonight's not a night—not even to control the Micks."

"I love the New York police—they look after their own."

"You said a mouthful there, queen! A little more lenity to lechery—for a gay price, dear."

"I go to a policeman's funeral whenever I can—and a fireman's, too. To my mind they are our unsung heroes. I was at a firemens' double funeral only last week; women wept in the streets, dear, and burly men clenched their jaws."

"Oh, I love it when burly men clench their jaws!"

Richard Plante, an early activist, consciousness-raiser and proselytizer for recognition of the Nazi slaughter, along with the Jews and the Gypsies, of enormous numbers of homosexuals of the Weimar era, perambulates arm in arm with a protégé. Somebody whispers aside:

"*Mensch gib acht—was die tiefe Mitternacht!*"

RP: Did you know about the pink triangles at Auschwitz and Dachau? I know there is something in you that would not be surprised, really, if suddenly they sent the National Guard in here with rifles—or padlocked the place and burned it to the ground with all of us here in it. In fact, *that* they could probably get away with—the feds, I mean; I'm aware the premises are the protectorate of the New York PBA. But don't ask me to get sentimental over it.

—<o>—

"Call me idealistic, sentimental or whatever you like, but I like to believe the rugged numbers I do for trade remember, from time to time, with fondness, the moments we've shared."

"You mean all your little reindeer games. Would you settle, Miss Vixen, for senile demented?"

"Yes, it's true, they call me the White Sister. All love is white, didn't you know?"

"Yeah, sure, like all the sheets on the beds in here."

—<o>—

". . . the men who do each other eat—the *anthropophagi.*"

"Fresh seafood: an amenity essential to any metropolis worthy of time."

"Yes, dear, Marge has left us—on the *Ile de France.*

'To sail beyond the sunset, and the baths.
Of all the western stars.'

You'll say that in that case she's sailed in the wrong direction, but she's always found her own way, if you take my meaning."

—<o>—

"Is one being interrogated in form?"

"Darling, really! You never have entirely gotten over it, have you—the wartime raid on that tomcat house in Red Hook, when you and Virgil Thomson and that senator from Massachusetts were hauled into Night Court on Joralemon Street and given the gay fright of your lives."

"Perhaps not. One was, after all, a senator's private secretary—and not that it matters I suppose, but the establishment in question was not in point of fact located in Red Hook but in Boerum Hill. Virgil is still inclined to make quite a point of that."

—<o>—

Not Cato dispensing laws, but we do have a little thing we call, after our favorite founding father's favorite woman, the Dolly Madison code system of sexual gourmandise. We collate flavors with, well, *façons*, with *pratique*. Vanilla is j.o., double vanilla: mutual dry, French vanilla, mutual with unguents; butterscotch is fellatio, butterscotch twirl, *soixante-neuf*; almond and or butter pecan, vanilla fudge, rimming; ganache, Hershey Highway; you may work out acordingly. Strawberry is nibbles and frottage raspberry ripple: 69 nipple sucking. Pistachio is water sports; tutti frutti: partouze. High colonic ramifications we do not endorse.

From many an open door, overhearing, many a different possible construction.

Further remarks on Richard Plante and the protégé:

"So what is that in there—a tutorial?"

"A tutorial, a confession—or perhaps an audition."

"This place is nothing but auditions."

"Like television."

"Very. Variety shows (no dear, Ed Sullivan is not our kind), soap operas, big city melodramas—all in flattened and diminished scale, in shades of black and white and gray, lacking depth of field and subject to capricious interference."

—◦►—

"That a whole culture's mating, food-finding, navigational and social behavior should converge at a single point on West 28th Street in New York City is certainly notable."

"This place does seem to be another dimension, where parallel lives converge."

"Our lives aren't parallel, darling, they're pick-up sticks dropped on the floor by a madman."

"Make that bent pick-up sticks, dear, while you're at it."

—◦►—

". . . strong, charmed links to the insane. I like that."

"I said the unseen, not the insane. Really!"

"Everything is failing—eyes, ears, the nether parts."

—◄o►—

Somebody being read to sleep from Patrick Leigh-Fermor's *Mani*: intercut with other dialogue in the halls:

"The phallus-wielding Bounariots of Tyrnavos . . . the Cretan fellaheen of Luxor . . ."

Two queens passing by:

"What's a *fellaheen*, darling?"

"Not what you think, you single-minded woman."

". . . the little bootblacks of Megalopolis . . . the boys kidnapped for janissaries . . . the Ralli Brothers of India."

"The Loubinistika-speakers of the brothels . . . the Hello-boys back from the States . . . the Phanariots of the Sublime Porte . . . and a solitary Arab I saw years ago in Domoko."

—◄o►—

"A what?"

"A *vestige*, dear—a nonfunctional trace of something that once existed or was once more important than it is now."

"The crust!"

"The term has a wider meaning—referring broadly to any remnant of the past that endured, whether it is functional or not."

". . . that combination of aloofness and charm which used to be attempted in my generation by those who had often looked upon Cornell."

—◄o►—

". . . what song the Sirens sang, or what camp name Achilles assumed when he went AWOL among women."

"I don't know a thing about Achilles among the women, but the sirens, so far as I know, only ever sing one song, and that's 'Get Out of Town.'"

—◄o►—

"Oh, sweetheart, God doesn't mind atheists. Pure atheism—not that French existentialist crap, which is just dimestore cologne in a whore's twat cooked up by ex-altar boys who got sick on frankincense—no, pure atheism is simply the diastole to the mystic piety of the likes of Thérèse of Lisieux, Charles Péguy, Simone Weil and—"

"Piaf?"

"Oh, sweeheart . . . yes, if you like. Yes, Piaf, yes, yes, yes."

—◄o►—

"She's inside, dear, hosting a private party—for her private parts."

"Be that as it may, I fear she is an epileptic."

"You've been peeking again than through the glory hole at her!"

"She is inside there twitching like Theresa in ecstasy—instinct and alive with certain terrible emotions."

(Another passes.)

"Do not read poor Miss Tick out—she is a heedful woman and has authentic visions!"

"Of sugarplums?"

"Of the gay saints—and sometimes of the gay Lord!"

"The Pope has those."

"Miss Tick is more pious even than the Pope. She is a big white girl in search of God."

"So, what does she want, us to send up a flare?"

"Take no notice of the woman. Believe me, she is not of sound mind, nor has been since the Army-McCarthy hearings."

"She claims the long wide tongue of the Buddha has licked her into shape."

"Really! Presumably she means the great Indus. Whoever took her there, I wonder—or has she been ushering in newsreel theaters again?"

"Well, whatever, it certainly beats her wailing last year, when they fished her out of the drink over at the Circle Line—where she'd been approaching tourists, weeping and assuring them, 'Penny Candy' was written for me—it was!"

"It is more than that with which a girl can cope."

"What ails Miss Trial?"

"Carburetor trouble, I suppose—the curse."

—◄o►—

"He is a very important executive, my dear, with endless collateral and absolutely enormous globular responsibilities."

"*Oooh!*"

"Pre-existence doesn't live—it hasn't time!"

—◀○▶—

"Rouse yourself, lethargic woman—burst the bonds of mind and body. Masturbate. Masturbation is the key to life; it nourishes the vital essence and the blood, it invigorates the brain and promotes intelligence, particularly if ejaculation is postponed until sunrise—at which time a good spout relieves the propensity toward convulsion and calms the endopathic wind."

—◀○▶—

". . . and a social purpose too. By fostering, as we do, the mass production and lavish scrapping of so much high-type American spunk, we stand the harried husband to sweet respite from his melancholy baby-boom mission—levering up the livestock birth rate in the missionary position."

"Whatever of that, I still think all this mixing with a view to some imagined betterment brings nothing but harm. As St. Paul says in I Corinthians 7:25, 'In view of the impending cataclysm, it is well for a man to remain as he is.'"

"Clement of Alexandria assures us laughter is the prelude to fornication."

Doggerel on a cubicle wall,

> *Cogito ergo sum* is
> a hallucination
> that turns me into a figment
> of my own imagination.

—◀○▶—

In another cubicle: IMPOSSIBLE VENIR. MENSONGE SUIT.

—◀○▶—

"He is something to behold, all right. At the debut Monday night—in the Grand Tier of course, guest of one of the clubhouse gang—and even earlier as he swaggered in, redolent of *uomo* and flush from the ballet and who knows what *intime* supper—well you would have thought it was a younger Jean Marais you were looking at. The maquillage, dear—the *facture* of it, at once so free and yet so necessarily densely wrought—as the years have piled onto the original *esquisse*, the boy face there was, time out of mind— the freight of a very ambitious career. But, now, Vera, after a couple of hours swirling around in this in this hell hole, he looks like Death's Own Head on Stilts right on time for Halloween!"

"What you say is true, but I must say I have never felt the glamour of the person. Indeed I feel the difficulty in appreciating him goes beyond display conditions."

◄○►

"'Teach me not the art of remembering, but that of forgetting—for I remember things I do not wish to remember, but I cannot forget things I wish to forget.' Themistocles to Simonides, dear, as reported by Cicero."

◄○►

"I shouldn't be here tonight—I belong home, doing my closets."

◄○►

". . . a soundstream classifiable as language only by the most strenuous. . . ."

◄○►

"He ordered a *mazagran*. 'What on earth,' I thought to myself, 'is a *mazagran*?' but I ordered a stinger and said nothing."

◄○►

"Amore . . . sudore . . . odore . . . dolore!"
    "Ya gotta blister, sister? Get some Unguentine!"

◄○►

Sign on a closed door: BEAUTIFUL, GIFTED, AND RESTING, and on another
NATURE IS A HYPOTHESIS.

Two queens reading out a number cruising the hall with their requisi-
tion white cotton robes untied.

"Would'ja look at the size of that! Hang on a minute, lover, this'll take
some special negotiating. Anybody in the joint take it up the *nose*? What?
Oh, yeah? Hey, you're in luck, stun-gun, sister has a hankerin' t' be with ya—
soon as she finishes snortin'. Takes all kinds, don't it, but that's what I love
about this terlet: we got all kinds. The lewd bawds and naughty-packs of
all the world! As P.T. Barnum's partner Mildred Bailey put it, there's a
cocksucker born ev'ry othuh minute—and that was before the population
explosion!"

◄○►

Once again out in the air: on the way to breakfast:

The senescent, semi-derelict pensioned-off civil servant queer from one
of the many residential hotels in the neighborhood is sitting on the bench a
mere two blocks south in Madison Square, at six on a summer morning.
Sex still rages in the bushes and up against the trees, and particularly significantly in the thicket behind the Saint-Gaudens statue of Admiral Farragut
("Damn the torpedoes—full speed ahead!") with his flaring long coat,
pedestal and chair.

Beginning *in medias res* while, patting the bench, inviting an audience,
the pensioner says:

". . . who, in his tenderloin years finds some newlovely thing, his hope
runs high and he flies on manhood's new wings. Better than riches are his
thoughts—but the growing season of man's pleasure is a short one, and falls
to ground as quickly when an unlucky twist of thought loosens its roots.
That's Pindar.

We want to talk about Donald Madden's Hamlet at the Phoenix, but
the old fuck says he remembers only the comedies now. *Twelfth Night*, for
example.

"'Yet hath my night of life some memory / My wasting lamps some fading
glimmer yet.' That speaks to an old fuck as the evening sun goes down over
Jersey and young bloods troop down to Chinatown to kick the gong around,
hah-hah!

"Yes, the Bard. So much more refreshing to go up the Central Park and see him played by young hopefuls than to come upon men enacting unseemly rituals of death and resurrection under those self-same trees. They do it here too, of course, all night long, behind the statue of Farragut—barely noticing the cops cruising by.

"But then this square has definitely hit the skids, although there is some fading glimmer yet of what was once the center of it all.

"'Some fading glimmer yet.' Yes, as Ouspensky declared, today's events were yesterday's ideas, and tomorrow's events lie today in *aulum ingenti memoriae*—in someone's irritation, someone's hunger—even such a simple hunger as you two stylish bravos choose, in the fashion of the young, to appease with simple proletarian fare.

"I repeat history as history repeated itself to me, when the tenants of the Rialto of my youth would sit up all night reading late reviews in the cafeterias of Broadway, and hearing from their elders wonder tales of the original Rialto, with the Hippodrome on one end and Madison Square Garden on the other, the Tenderloin between; a flower and willow world co-inhabited by the hardworking geishas and Hell's Angels of their day as well by as every variety of gender-rebellious value theoretician and punk.

"The round world shook veritable lions into the civil streets, and such dissentious numbers too to pester them—and for variety such redeemed and putatively redemptive street angels as the cunning little Evelyn Nesbit, who sometimes dressed as a boy, but who as the Girl in the Red Velvet Swing brought on a broil with the most erotic show ever seen in New York, before or since. Freud, had he seen it, would have fainted dead away before Jung made him do so—homosexual paranoia, you know. For her swing act positively flaunted the coded gestures of equilibrial eroticism, by which female masturbation to multiple, oceanic orgasm, is always signified—and, as we all know, led eventually to murder, mayhem and the violent spectacle of celebrities in frenzy."

"Really?"

"Oh my, yes. Veritably. As the crowds sat there, not like you two lithe specimens, radiating the cool narcissistic, *négligé* aplomb of choir boys while bearing the traces, the stains, of some love that dare not speak its name on greeting cards, but bulbous and veiny plutocrats.

"Majestic wealth, said Juvenal, is the holiest of our gods.

"Veiny plutocrats and their fancy women together with their scrubbed-up off-duty shills on the cops, all stuffed from their eight-course meals at Delmonico's and Rector's, loosening their buttons and stays to get a whiff

of freedom from the wretched excess that all their gluttony cried out for—
dietum descrescere in parvis moribus—like the gorged in hell. The men in their
boiled shirtfronts, shoo-in candidates all for the sudden burst of valve arte-
rial in the noble parts—had they but such—looking up at her, Evelyn Nesbit,
sailing back and forth across the auditorium right over there, yes right here
in Madison Square Garden, enacting in one single arc both their sense of
imprisonment in the horizontal expression of vertical longings and her own
true freedom from their well-deserved fears of exploding. Every father among
them knowing that every time a man pushes a little girl in a swing. . . .

"Yes, you might say the taint of imbecile rapacity blew through the whole
city, like the whiff of some corpse, fretting like a weevil at its very fabric.
Boss Croker ruled New York, and was fond of handsome horses. His many
enemies in polite, reform-minded society declared him guilty of innumerable repeated and varied obstructions of justice, garnished with gaudy public
and private lies, vicious slanders, tactical blunders, gross errors of judgment,
hypocritical displays of conciliation, affronts to conventional morality and
parental authority, and desecration of revered civic symbols and regalia. In
short, of presiding over a moral charnel house in which glances both overt
and covert betrayed uneasy, nay, desperate estimations, hushed conspira-
cies, loud, grating boasts of power, mistrust, dissimulation and betrayal.

"Well, 'charlock on the fallow will not twice arise!'

"It was all too much for Stanford White, and poor Clyde Fitch too,
queer as he was, even though in all paranoia there is always the cool, detached
observer. No, nothing ever done later—not Eva Tanguay shimmying to 'I
Don't Care,' or Bert Savoy strutting in feather-boa drag, hand on hip, assuring the world 'You don't know the half of it, dearie!' (as Charles Baudelaire
had done and said a half-century earlier, strutting all over Paris in *his* feather
boa), or all the antics of the many who later paraded on the uptown Rialto
or stomped down to opium-den Chinatown—none of them were a patch on
Evelyn Nesbit, who wore no underwear when she went up in the air so high
in that swing. Her act was not out of *A Child's Garden of Verses*—as the
Irish say, Robert Louis Stevenson wasn't in it. Although she sang her
songs—old and plain they were, as Shakespeare calls his own in *Twelfth
Night*—in an innocent little voice such as spinsters and knitters in the sun
and free maids that wove their thread with bones did use to chant. It was
silly sooth and did dally with the innocence of love."

"They knew how to have a good time, huh?"

"Indeed they did, you bright, inquisitive, contemporary boy, with your flowing finger-combed hair, heraldic amber kiss-curls clustered at the nape and your generation's penchant, I ween, for saying either everything at once or nothing at all.

"Yes, indeed, banquets, bard-jive, the best life has on offer—excluding contract bridge. They kept their plot lines rolling like clowns in the circus— pulling scarfs, rabbits, white doves and what not else out of their pockets. The curtain never rose on their little scenes, in the alcoves at Delmonico's for instance.

"I will now tell you the story of Miss Tammany Hall, who replicated the Evelyn Nesbit red velvet swing act—up in the air in no underwear—save that Miss Tammany Hall was a boy, and flapped not only a full bush but a full set of the family facsimiles into the bargain, at all the gentlemen at Club Paresis."

(We remarked then, as often later, how the Inquiring Photographer always went after the wrong people in New York, asking all the wrong questions on all the wrong topics.)

"Still, one must not live in the past, on one's too-often-ill-advised designs and misdirected investments. As the Bard says, 'What custom willed in all things should we do it / The dust on antique time would lie unswept.' Ah, *Twelfth Night*! The paean to good gone times. 'Dost think that because thou art virtuous there shall be no more cakes and ale?'

"In the Italian *commedia*," he continued, waving a big bony hand, "the curtain fell—dropped from above the proscenium, like a pair of the silk drawers Evelyn Nesbit never wore on that swing, and was pulled in a trice off into the wings. Yes, young man, they knew how to invoke the gods and make a reverberating song and dance for those to come! But the Gay Nineties, and all the cultural and societal gold, coarse and fine, nuggets and trace minerals mined therein, were doomed—by the privatizing, standardizing, domesticizing, misogynist-homophobic social arrangements of corporate industrial capitalism, the mother country's terrible bequest to break the back of man, the heart of monster.

"Ah, England! So much is made of what was donative in that bright realm—of the legacy of due process, habeas corpus and gin—and scarcely anything of the godmother country's abundant gifts. And yet from France came savoir faire, champagne and the Statue of Liberty, forthwith adapted to our own devices. Emma Lazarus wrote the uplifting poem, 'Give me your tired your poor, etc. Send these the homeless tempest-tossed to me, I lift my lamp, et cetera,' but the WASP captains of industry said right back, 'Yes, you do that, and we'll turn them into swine feeding at the trough of free market Gilded Age capitalism!'

"Lillian Russell, Diamond Jim Brady, Ada Rehan and their lower companions—and a generation later the great transvestite Julian Eltinge. There was a woman as beautiful as Ada Rehan; the public adored him. Of course it all had to end. By the time the psychoanalysts got around to ripping the drag off and exposing the boy-man, the era of great dressing—and of great lingerie—which was the key to it all, then as now—had passed. Sad, really, but then to heap insult on injury, they were told the garments were only symbolic substitutes for the penis—although how that can have been so, when the penises were all too real, if pressed down . . . and that they wanted to be looked on and loved as women because, unable as men to formulate solid relationships, develop effective communication skills and realize personal authenticity, their primal sadism had been turned against their egos and they needed to suffer masochistic tortures. Really! Try telling that to Julian Eltinge, the great beauty of the age whose worst masochistic torture was passing up a second helping, darling, of *riz à l'Imperatrice*, or would it have been *crème au chocolat*, at the Waldorf, and cream in the coffee if you please.

"But you boys wanted to talk about Hamlet, as in '. . . and it must follow as the night the day.'

"Well, night follows day—day does not night. The hour of the wolf intervenes—which is the instant of death. Then the dawn, which is the resurrection. All this has only just happened again, but the homosexual denies it. Oscar Wilde charges Ada Levinson when she comes to take him from Reading Gaol, 'Sphinx, you can't have got up, you must have stayed up!' This is the homosexual stance par excellence. Up through the night, from *l'heure bleu*, when a delicious *tristesse* supplants the terror occasioned by the sun going down, the homosexual rules the night, as does Oberon, who defies the fear of death, which he feels much more acutely than the heterosexual. Why? Because the heterosexual takes immense comfort in his progeny: the homosexual, should he have them, is more terrified of them than anybody else.

"What is love, darling? What is creation? What is longing? What is a star? *Also Sprach Zarathustra*."

"What a guy, huh?"

"You may say so. Yes indeed. Of course you might say the same thing about Zarah Leander; in fact, *Also Sprach Zara Leander* would undoubtedly sell more copies today—at least in Germany, even in Wittenberg, what with the way the old bag still plays to the Krauts—and to a certain sort of *musical* GI too, dear, if you take my meaning.

"She has her own take, you might say, does *die Leander*, on the will to power, dumb Swede that she is, and she'd give old Zarathustra a run for his money, particularly in the song department. In fact 'The Night Song,' 'The Dancing Song' and 'The Tomb Song' are all her meat, and not only because of the timbre of her instrument either, but because as Douglas Sirk remarked on the set of *La Habanera*, '*Die Leander war nicht interessiert im Politik, sie war interessiert im . . . Musik.*'

"And she knows, as does her more subtle sister Marlene Dietrich, that the holy pronouncement of 'yes' is a camp. Ja, ja, as Elisabeth Schwarzkopf, opera's own Marlene Dietrich, yawns as she segues off screen in *Der Rosenkavalier*—playing just now, dear, if you're interested, up at Carnegie Hall.

"Nietzsche asks a fascinating question. He wants to know if the *wave*, having greedily penetrated the rocky cleft, now seen retreating rather more slowly, all foaming still, is disappointed. Well, the poor dear drove himself mad trying to figure things out. You know what happened to him at the end, in Turin? He began to pay close attention to his wardrobe and to sip coffee in public squares. 'I do not in the least want anything to become different,' he declared. 'I want everything to stay the same, most especially myself.' And then the landlady caught him through the keyhole dancing seriously naked in front of a long mirror.

"You know, dear, apart from the fact that I haven't got what you would exactly call a landlady, although the night clerk does partake of a certain wan maternal charm, I share Nietzsche's sentiments absolutely and I do all those things Nietzsche ended up doing, and nobody has yet come to throw the net over me and haul me up to Ward's Island. America, land of the free, ain't it grand!

"What are life's milestones other than the tombstones of our illusions? You know, don't you, that Houdini's publicity used to boast he'd triumphed over every kind of threat to masculine integrity—bondage, imprisonment, insanity and death. They never mentioned castration, which is obviously, if you will pardon the pun, the key. What a sad waste of time, a career like that, devoted to the pathetic denial of absolute reality—even considering the money made.

"In any case, in order for you to come to understand homosexual life in our time, it is absolutely necessary to understand—to dig, as the Beats would have it—both Schopenhauer and Nietzsche. Between them they have identified, catalogued, explicated and suffered everything that is fundamental to homosexual existence. Nietzsche's insistence on enhancement, for instance. . . ."

The tower clock at Metropolitan Life struck the early hour. The author, looking up, remembered how Barbara Stanwyck convinced Gary Cooper not to jump, in *Meet John Doe*. Long ago somebody convinced this Kenmore Hotel–park bench polymath queer John Doe not to jump. Good.

CHAPTER THIRTEEN

The File on Fire Island

> *"I must explain why it is that at night, in my own house*
> *Even when no one's asleep, I feel I must whisper."*
> —Reed Whittemore, "Still Life"
>
> *"The waves broke on the shore."*
> —Virginia Woolf, *The Waves*

Wherein the author encounters:

Fire Island: drag queens: The Little Revue *at the Cherry Grove*
Playhouse (and reads Carlyle's The Clothes Screen*).*

The "Goncourt Sisters" (recorders of scenes at the Grove and in the Pines).

Belvedere, the great house of Cherry Grove; its host His Whorishness,
the Pontifex Maximus of Misrule, midnight mass, the sedia gestatoria *and*
the flabelli *(mopped from the Met production of* Aida*). Also: reenacted:*
the procession of the volto santo *in Lucca.*

The two Memory Theaters of the homosexual dispensation: the Cherry
Lane on Commerce Street in Manhattan and the Playhouse at Cherry
Grove.

And the waves' resounding voices as they break on the shore.

"**S**he was expelled, dear, for supporting the Queen's oath against transubstantiation."

A comment on a performer who'd lately muscled his determined rag trade way into *The Little Revue*:

"Darling, I wouldn't plonk down good Protestant money to watch that woman leave a *damp stain*."

—◦—

"She thought she was being so intellectual, backing up her predilections and tastes in slap and drag with citations from a groovy English celebrity mind, whereas all she was doing was wondering would they *read* her at Bemelmans Bar when she sashayed in with her escort, and toss her, body and soul, back into the street."

"My dear, she thinks the eight-fold path is that maze of thicketed lanes between the Pines and the Grove known to the unenlightened as the Meat Rack."

◄○►

"Edith Wharton discovered what it means to be a happy woman when for the first time in her life, she couldn't read. I have never been a happy woman."

◄○►

"Never in the onomasticon of places was ever a place so well named as Cherry Grove—and it doesn't have what to do with trees, although ripe for the picking are words that spring to mind the minute that boat pulls out of the dock in Sayville."

◄○►

"He is extravagant in hose, the darling."
    "In how many outfits does the god appear!"

◄○►

"To me it's really amazingly simple: if a girl executes the gestures of happiness, she becomes happy."

◄○►

"What agreement?"
    "The agreement to ignore the abyss, dear."

◄○►

"She is a hard and reckless rider to the hounds."

—<o>—

"Cruelty, darling, is one of the oldest festive joys of mankind."

"Any custom, dear, is better than no custom at all—and the same goes for customers. Society is and ever was threatened far less by man's unbridled passions than by the prospect of paralysis attendant upon their suppression."

—<o>—

"Nobody gets what they want, pet, on Fire Island, except the deer. Check the faces on the ferry on the way back: there ought to be a branch of the Department of Welfare with a passport photo apparatus to snap head shots on the Friday afternoon and again on the Sunday evening—before and after, as in the ads for AYDS, the reducing candy. The idea that candy can lead to weight reduction is no crazier than canonizing the idea that a weekend in Island Pines can lead to happiness. Never have I seen so much unavailing untold want, such fruitless longing as on the dance floor, along the meat rack and in the drugged hollows of Island Pines."

—<o>—

"She's in wardrobe, or in makeup, or in hair, or in retreat."

"She lives in serene certainty of her entitlement to certain *égards*. She'll have you know, for instance, she spent the whole of last summer in drag in Atlantic City, as one of Harry Hackney's lobster waitresses—they're a legend, darling—winning first prize in the Boardwalk Beauty Pageant. All in red—a lineup of a dozen lobsters with tits, arms encased in huge lobster claws. Is that a camp?"

—<o>—

". . . striding up the gravel path, practically shouting, 'No, I don't know them at all, but people are always glad to show their house if it's a really nice one.'"

—<o>—

"... a proposed adjustment to reciprocal procedure between the Sayville constabulary and the Grove vigilante committee."

"Involving the exchange of, shall we say, stash."

"The Sayville constabulary is, we find, in, under the circs, that understanding."

◄○►

"The borrowed light of the moon is light enough for Sissy."

◄○►

"Crashed to the floor in a faint. People made room—cleared a little space marked off by two hurricane lamps—and the dance went on, switching to the Madison, the lines on either side of the comatose heap—deciding she'd have wanted it that way."

Overheard at dawn at the meat rack:

"You begin early, my dear—or do you perhaps continue late?"

"I'm lookin' for lark's eggs, sister—got any?"

◄○►

"All these little slime trails, darling—they were bright silver in the moonlight; they are not quite that now—do not betoken snails, much as the gourmet queens hereabouts do love to swallow the creatures . . . snails, that is."

"You know, sister dear, you really are too clever for words."

"So shut up, right?"

"Did I say that?"

◄○►

"She said, 'I said "my own merry little way," not "my little Mary-Ann way." He-whore cock *sucker*!'"

◄○►

"So I said to Jimmy Baldwin, 'Baby, you really hadda oughta get *ovuh* that terrible black Hamlet complex of yours—protestin' vainly through the smart of hot tears how all Caucasians do inform against you—or else just sit your-self down and start writing converting ordinances like your papa preached.'"

"Miz Baldwin is a formidable, defiant woman—you could take her off pork chops and put her back on fatback and beans, she would ever retain her regal demeanor."

—<o>—

"I love the silence of the morning here on the Island. Who was it said, under all speech that is good for anything lies a silence that is better."

"Better—better for anything?"

"Virtually anything—anything but serious shopping, or getting a divorce."

—<o>—

"I want to meet somebody both intense and mystical—very physically and compellingly so, yet with strong, charmed links to the unseen."

—<o>—

"Caravaggio, of course, but did you know, dear, that Velázquez once went onstage in drag? Isn't that divine?"

—<o>—

At Max Patrick's beach house over in Island Pines. Max, the renowned Milton scholar with the apartment on Washington Square West. Big, crazy sixtyish redhead stripped down to his shorts, interviewing his students while plugged into the Relaxacisor machine, and reciting from Comus, voicing his unwillingness to play the lead and "deflower" Author. Then at his beach house over in Island Pines amending *Paradise Lost*:

"In this Paradise, baby, when a bright sleep falls on Adam, he's bar-gained for no Eve."

Max to Author QT:

"You find the cackle and quack out here bracing, I suppose—like the legendary salt air?"

"Well, speaking of the legendary Saltaire. . . ."

"Not this weekend, you little tart—in fact not this season. After I've engineered your debut in the PMLA. This weekend we take you to see the great Diane DeVors, starring in *The Little Revue* over in the Grove."

Max is telling the author he must read the *Thalia Rediviva* of Henry Vaughan. Another academic guest whispers (for the host is more than a little deaf), "Max is quite irretrievably *dirigiste*, but a great-hearted old sodomite."

Max advises the author to patch up the holes in his intellectual armor by tackling the Great Books and the Great Books Syntopicon (Vol I: From Angel to Love; Vol II: From Man to World). Author is grateful for a practical suggestion but, alas, is no scholar.

Conversation at cocktails (*l'heure bleu-rose*):

"—turns to me out of the blue, declaring, '*Nemo potest personam*,' Seneca insists, '*diu ferre fictum*.' 'Seneca? Really?' I replied—reflectively, y'know, the way I can over stingers—'That does seem strange.' Apparently, he never met a drag queen, which I suppose says something about the austerity of Latin tragedy. Perhaps one shouldn't be too surprised; apparently Arthur Miller never has met one either."

"Too many are being educated, in too much of a rush."

"They can all fuck, and lots of them are pretty, but the time comes when they've got to be asked the really important question—do they play bridge?"

"Well, I know a few who will play *on* the bridge."

"Me too—once you've gone through their little toll booth."

"Which, if you hear them talking, they call the *troll* booth."

"Really, can none of you women conceive of the notion that such motives might seem—might be—unworthy of souls whose lofty designs are concerned solely with things celestial?"

"It's a sweet thought—like you find in fairy tales."

"What you find in fairy tales in the principle of penalty."

"Thank you, Marianne Moore."

"The candles are listing, darling, the hot wax dripping all over."

"Will you shut up!"

◄○►

"Berenson said apropos looking, one moment is enough, if the concentration is absolute. He was, of course, absolutely full of shit—and a nasty woman into the bargain."

—◄○►—

"Her proudest possession, Geoffrey Scott's *A History of Time*, a slim volume, dear, bound in Moroccan vellum; exquisite, and *very expensive*."

—◄○►—

"I mean lesbians, darling, don't hold a hot-flash candle to fag hags as lethal, lacerating Kundry mothers, devouring your anguish with cannibal zeal—into which scenario and praxis many vengeful queens, who behave as though they never had a dick at all, fall.

"In the immortal words of the final chorus of *Oedipus Rex*, recast for today, 'Call no woman happy until he is dead.' 'So this is bliss,' she whispers when, disengaging her compact mirror from its accustomed use, she slips it under those hated nostrils and sees no mist of breath ripple its surface."

A Story of Fag Hag Revenge:

The john always took his tricks to Fire Island and confided everything to a certain fag hag whose apartment in the Village (on Bank Street) he used so as not to compromise his reputation with his doorman in Beekman Place, and on whose shoulder he always cried when the tricks would go off with younger or richer johns. Until one boy—a sixteen-year-old Italian originally from Jersey City—with whom he became completely besotted, perversely insisted on Asbury Park for the Roller Derby, Atlantic City in winter so he could be rolled up and down the boardwalk and go hear Lillian Roth at the Steel Pier.

That summer they took a place together in some Mafia-protected shore town. The fag hag he left behind at Cherry Grove got crazy drunk and unwittingly informed on him to an undercover cop trawling for gossip at Duffy's. They nabbed the john and the kid coming back through the Holland Tunnel from Jersey and charged the john under the Mann Act (which caused an uproar on more than Beekman Place, mind you). The john went up the river, the boy went into fight training for the Golden Gloves, and the fag hag, after unsuccessfully taking a bottle of aspirin and slitting her wrists, was held in custody for misprision of a felony, and when released didn't leave her apartment for a year except to go to Gristede's. She became addicted to soap operas and talk shows and the *Million Dollar Movie*, then finally hitched up with the Met opera line, where she found forgiveness and salvation in the cult of Zinka Milanov.

The boy meanwhile chucked the Golden Gloves, ending up in Lincoln Hall, the reformatory run by the Christian Brothers up the Hudson, where he was completely turned around, went to Manhattan College and Fordham Law, and became a public prosecutor.

"And the john?"

Now, that's a very interesting denouement. They found a body in that faggoty-50s penthouse apartment, sloshing around in a pink bath, with, I give you, the face eaten away—teeth and all. Two tiny scraps of gold gleaming at the bottom of the tub, like two funky earrings sunk in a pool of pink champagne.

All Cruella's i-d—we called her that: Cruella de Bourbon, in that she was one mean drunk—present and accounted for in the bedroom, on the bed—which was the single piece of furniture in the place. Not stick or stone other than—absolutely. Zilch. And Tilly had had a lot of shit in that apartment—Tiffany, Baccarat, Lalique, a collection of Balenciaga frocks—a lot of shit.

The police called it a brutal Mafia rubout, but the true story was somewhat otherwise. The mob cut a deal—took half Tilly's shit, put the rest in the hold of the *Leonardo da Vinci*, put Tilly—not in a Balenciaga but, we were told, in a Ceil Chapman get-up—called her the Principessa Trapani, and off she went to Genoa, where she disembarked, trained down to Rome and made straight for the Via Veneto.

Soon enough she was employed at Cinecittà, and if you take the trouble you can spot her in *La Dolce Vita*. It's a heartwarming story.

" 'Well, what is truth?' asked Pilate's wife, plucking her arched eyebrows, in make-up at Cinecittà."

—◁◦▷—

Pollock was homosexual. All homosexual means is hung up on men. Pollock was as hung up on men, exactly, as de Kooning was hung up on women; anybody who doesn't know that knows nothing. Whatever accommodating affectionate and social arrangements Pollock made do nothing whatever to cancel the central fact. That he loved and needed his wife was apparent.

"I never said Lee was a man; she wasn't—but she very definitely was a guy."

"As in guy rope."

"If you want to put it that way, I'll co-sign."

"The queer artist of genius has always made the figure 8 the hard way: two fours. The drip and the poured painting was, you understand, the apotheosis of masturbation."

"Well, all that is over—all that abstraction. Faces are back."

"But, darling, have you never seen the face in 'Full Fathom Five'? Look hard and you can't miss it: a vulnerable, haunted, sensitive, face—male of course—bespectacled. Nails Pollock. And you know, really, Pollock was always painting depositions—abstract depositions . . . as in from the cross."

"Exactly. So that a title like 'Distressed Queen' will make its way directly to my innermost heart; it is simply another way of saying 'Weeping Mary,' and that's that."

—◄○►—

"It's terribly relaxin' list'nin' to you dear, gettin' the highbrow lowdown. One knows just how Mae West feels having Freud read to her by Theodor Adorno out on the veranda in Santa Monica."

"I dream't I dwelt in marble halls, darling, only to wake up in a Formica toilet."

"Anyway, what's there to say about life—thanks for the memory?"

"Until the semantic field of the word queer has been circumscribed—"

—◄○►—

"The correlation between the sense of time suspension in the orgasm and the idea of eternity is attested in all major religions."

"George Herbert, who so unforgettably likened swaddling clothes to winding cloths, said when boys go first to bed, they step into their voluntary graves. Now let me be."

"'A thing of beauty is a boy forever,' said Carlo Van Vechten, right in my living room—of course I'm not so silly as to suppose he didn't say it elsewhere too, but I've got it on tape!"

"A beautiful boy is like a dry-cell battery, in which the captive energy is restless under the casing—restlessness producing a raging galvanic attraction—"

"To make the love muscle of a dead frog twitch."

"A leg muscle, darling, I believe—but it's a gay thought."

"—as impossible to resist and as potentially dangerous as the hot, persistent arcing of sparks across a gap between two split wires. The history of the human race fairly swarms with examples of intelligent and learned men, forbidding, stately heroes who dreamed wild dreams of flight and transformation, of exaltation and escape, only to become transfixed and brought thuddingly to earth by the ensorcelling energy in a boy's glance—exquisite product of the intricate computational cranial circuitry that controls the manipulation of captive objects, formerly known as the soul. The holy King David proved one such willing victim of the condensing properties of a boy's eyes when he took unto himself and onto his satin whoopee cushion the beautiful young Jonathan."

—◄○►—

A discussion by elders on the beach about giving QT a Camp name. Everybody had a Camp name, most often conferred on the recipient but sometimes self-proclaimed

"I call myself Phoebe."

"And why not."

At Belvedere, the manciple manages the guest list (and a history of the Camp names).

Camp names were always supposed to have an edge, as when Auden dubbed Chester Kallman and James Schuyler "Fiordiligi" and "Dorabella" after the fickle sisters in Così fan tutte. Often the recipient was less than happy with his name. Schuyler said that anyone who had the impertinence to call him Dorabella in his later years would get slugged—and people believed him.

One old queen of mystical gnostic bent summed the practice up thus:

"Sigmund Freud, dear, by way of his Oedipus complex, divined a pivotal dilemma among the heterosexuals he analyzed, which Lévi-Strauss has lately made much of. They actually could not reconcile the idea of birth from one parent with the idea of birth from two parents. Well, we at heart have no belief in birth from any parents at all. We give birth to one another as magical siblings, darling, and to the next generation as both uncles and aunts—including the very important fixing of Camp names. We are the originators, the inhabitants and the inheritors of our own myth.

"Our naming practice echoes Adam's—note, dear, Eve named no

names—and the history of it is indeed a pathetic text, which serves to remind us forcefully of the primordial sadness of the Divine Names, or archetypes, anguished in the expectation of beings who will name them—that is, make them manifest in the world, together with the divine compassion of the Nameless Supreme, who knows that all naming is the seal of death."

"It certainly was in front of the House Un-American Activities Committee."

"Has anybody except me, I wonder, realized that in all probability Camp comes from the theories of Maxime de Camp?"

CHAPTER FOURTEEN

The Theater

> "Want to know what the Theater is? A flea circus. Also opera. Also rodeos, carnivals, ballets, Indian tribal dances, Punch and Judy, a one-man band— all Theater. Wherever there's magic and make-believe and an audience— there's Theater."
> —Joseph L. Mankiewicz, All About Eve

Let us begin, yet again, with the story of Diane DeVors, starring just then in The Little Revue *at the Cherry Grove Playhouse.*

Diane DeVors was the stunningly authoritative Camp identity of William (Jarry) Lang, genius photographer, stage manager for Leonard Sillman's legendary *New Faces of 1952* and *1956* and intimate of Kaye Ballard, by virtue of her rendition of "Lazy Afternoon" in the in-show of in-shows *The Golden Apple*, music by Jerome Moross, book and lyrics by John Latouche, the essential in-singer for out queers (Judy Garland having long since transcended categories).

In between sightings at Duffy's and the Sea Shack of Auden, Janet Flanner and her Italian Countess, and a host of other glamour inverts of the decade, QT drank stingers and sidecars and Singapore slings, and gin milk in the mornings, smoked a little opiated hashish and dozens of packs of Lucky Strikes, dreaming along in lonely shadows under the boardwalk, while on the deck of the Belvedere *tout* Cherry Grove quacked on and on in one endless-summer relay marathon of Jacob's Ladder (the Bible story, the place in Massachusetts), of dancing the Madison with the big boys (it was vouchsafed in the end, before the Labor Day weekend) and of having worked with Diane DeVors in Hollywood in the 1930s.

DIANE DEVORS, THE FILMOGRAPHY

1. *Samoan Love Song.* Warner Bros. 1929. d. Wm. Beaudine.
   Cast: Charles Bickford, Anna Mae Wong, Willie Fung.
   D deV played (in debut) small role as victim of white slavers.

2. *Leftover Ladies.* Warner Bros. 1930. d. Lloyd Bacon. Cast:
   Wynne Gibson, Helen Vinson, Herbert Marshall, Lyle
   Talbot, Edmund Lowe, Cecil Cunnigham. D deV was cast
   as innocent victim of jealous older women.

3. *Pert* (Working Title: *Perky*). Paramount. 1930. d. Wm.
   Beaudine. Songs: Robin & Rainger. Cast: Johnny Downs,
   Eleanor Whitney, Joe Morrison, Leif Ericson, Richard
   Denning, Maude Eburne. On move over to Paramount,
   D deV was third-cast as Homecoming Queen and General
   Disruptor of the campus in this college semi-musical.

4. *Boardwalk Melody* (A Musical History of Atlantic City).
   Paramount. 1931. Songs: Gordon & Revel. d. Mitchell
   Leisen. Cast: Eddy Duchin & His Orchestra. Johnny Downs,
   Eleanor Whitney, Phillips Holmes, George Burns & Gracie
   Allen, Betty Furness, Leon Errol, Lillian Bond, Louise
   Beavers. D deV in her first leading role aged from teenager to
   septuagenarian in this tune-filled, fast-stepping historical trib-
   ute to Atlantic City. She introduced the now-standard songs
   "Loop-The-Loop" and "Would You Wish On A Star?"

5. *Eighteen and Dangerous.* Paramount. 1932. d. Dorothy
   Arzner. Cast: Donald Cook, Paul Lukas, Mary Astor,
   Gene Raymond, Noel Francis, Astrid Allwyn, Kent Taylor,
   Arline Judge. In her first dramatic lead, D deV played a girl
   from the wrong side of the tracks who climbed society's
   ladder on the arm of an older man.

6. *She Learned to Lie.* Paramount. 1933. d. Raoul Walsh.
   Cast: Fredric March, Edward Arnold, Mona Maris, Jack
   Oakie, Gertrude Michael, Natalie Moorhead, Toby Wing.
   D deV played a madcap heiress in this screwball comedy
   about a dog mix-up.

7. *Tawdry.* Paramount. 1934. d. Ernst Lubitsch. Cast: Herbert Marshall, Phillip Reed, Edward Arnold, Bruce Cabot, Laura Hope Crews, Charles Ruggles, Helen Jerome Eddy, Sheila Terry, Ann Sheridan. In this wryly satirical drama, D deV, in her first over-the-title billing, played a courtesan, who, after ruining several tycoons, settles for love with a poor boy. She received her first Academy Award nomination.

8. *The Story of Lorna Lang.* RKO. 1935. d. Rouben Mamoulian. Songs: Levant & Fields. Cast: Francis Lederer, George Brent, Mary Astor, Paul Kelly, Robert Benchley, Anne Shirley, Claire Dodd, Merna Kennedy, Jane Darwell, Beryl Mercer. D deV's first great dramatic triumph. The story of a streetwalker who commits murder to save her daughter from a similar fate. D deV sang the title song, "Lorna." Her second Academy Award nomination.

9. *The Unvarnished Lie.* RKO. 1937. d. William Wyler. Cast: Fred MacMurray, Ralphy Bellamy, Gail Patrick, Claude Rains, Jerome Cowan, Edward Everett Horton, Jack Carson. A divorced couple involved in the murder of his fiancée (mistress).

10. *The Most Beautiful Woman in the World.* M.G.M. 1937. d. George Cukor. Song: Freed & Brown. Cast: Melvyn Douglas, Robert Young, Walter Pidgeon, Frank Morgan, Tala Birell, Edna Mae Oliver, Diana Lewis, Reginald Owen, Henry Hull, Charles Coburn, Cecilia Parker, Ann Rutherford. The role for which D deV won her Academy Award. She played the role of the richest and most beautiful woman in the world (inspired by Barbara Hutton), her tragedies and eventual happiness. D deV sang the bittersweet love song which also won an Academy Award, "Penny For Your Dreams."

Diane deVors was born in Pleasant Ridge, Michigan, in 1911. Her grandfather was of Spanish royalty, but she has always refused to discuss her origins. She made only ten films and retired in 1937, some say due to the Countess di Frasso scandal. She has been married three times and is extremely wealthy due to excellent investments mainly in real estate. She has refused all offers (including some of a million dollars or more) to return to films. She refuses all interviews and has been known to verbally attack photographers. She has been rumored to have been in ill health recently. She lives in Manhattan, Paris, Taormina, Palm Springs, London and Long Island.

(Reprinted from *Films in Review*)

◄o►

"DeVors is in the great, the classic tradition. She has never made the mistake so common to the drag queens out here, who think that because they have in some way gone further than their great predecessors, they have on that account surpassed them. 'Knowledge of the identical in different phenomena,' she has often insisted, 'and of the differences in similar phenomena, is, as Plato so often remarked, a sine qua non of philosophy.'"

◄o►

After a party after an opening at the Cherry Grove Playhouse, a season guest addresses the author:

"Darling, you probably think you have reached the pinnacle of homosexual society out here this weekend, but you haven't, not even close. You are about halfway out on the train ride. When you have ridden all the way to East Hampton, have snaked your way through the hedges into The Creeks and have attended, or perhaps taken a small dress part in, one of Alfonso Osorio's *tableaux vivants*, and when that curiously powerful little ex-chorine Ted Dragon—he who guards the castle, darling—has somewhat approved of you, then and only then will you, mixing with the art crowd, largely heterosexual, by the way—do you think you can handle that? Listening to sad tales of the death of Jackson Pollock, all from eyewitnesses, as it were—then and only then will you have arrived as a cultivated homosexual, as opposed to the darling of staple-gun dreck and television faggots in flashy drag.

"I remember I was at a party after the opening of something—it could have been *Streetcar*—and I came out with 'All the world's a'—and suddenly a fat pink hand was clamped over my mouth. I remember the hand smelled of Sortilege, and the pinky ring, a pavé diamond, grazed my teeth. Then the face gave the word.

"'All the world is not a stage, baby—have you learned nothing from the play? All the world is a pinball machine, and life, or the imitation of life, is a pinball game, and most poor sons of bitches who think they're players are nothing but pinballs. You can without much effort figure the rest—the knobs and knockers, bells and flashing lights. Just realize that no matter, whether players or pinballs, no matter what score, there is not one bit of difference you can ever make to the logistics of production. If you get to be a player, secure a modest place in the dance world in which your arc of energy is released— or maybe score high, making one perfect swing on the high trapeze—then "Gay gown." You've become what the existentialists call authentic.

" 'Martha is an existentialist; she's forever saying movement never lies. Of course she's conveniently forgetting that movement is life itself, and if life isn't one big lie, darling, I simply don't know what else it can be called.

"In any event, darling, whatever your moves, you understand, the machine is unaffected. You make no difference—none whatever in this sad world— to the pre-set rules or to the bounce of the game itself. Which consists mainly of long and, to hear it told by those who have benefited from it, exhilarating sequences of copyright infringement, breach of contract, defamation, verbal abuse, invasion of privacy, theft and the hurling of heavy objects.' "

Theda Barracuda Holds Forth (A Weatherbeaten Sibyl Reads the Author Out)

"Listen to your mother, darling, and learn from her costly mistakes. There is no Oz, no Tara, and no *Belle Rive* either; there never were. There are only tornadoes, Sherman's March to the Sea, and dark rising Mississippi flood-waters. Oz and Tara and Belle Rive are the names of houses out on Fire Island, representative of the tissues of lavender lies faggots pay dearly for in the bazaar, in which they wrap their pathetic illusions, to stash in closets with the muscle magazines. As Freud put it, correcting the self-enchanted Shakespeare, 'What a piece of shit is man.' The end.

"Or almost the end. First comes El Death. You know, as in '*Flores, flores, para los muertos!*' He enters—usually right after the paper boy, that prince out of the *Arabian Nights*. You are of a philosophical mind, have faced his coming with equanimity and are serene.

"Serene? Don't bet on it. Depressed, maybe, by Mass Culture, urbanization, unstable public affairs, the vastly growing Entertainment Industry, hectic everyday cares, the superficial character of intellectual life: all these enter into it.

"All these others you convinced yourself you cared about—they don't fool me, or anybody. They made you waste your time—suffer for nothing, speaking of them, when all along, to reach Go, you should have spoken of you and you alone.

"And as for you in some relation to them—something that might play a night in a theater. It's *Grand Hotel*. Not only are the pearls cold, not only have you never been so tired, when you check out, somebody else checks right in, and takes your bed—*finito*. [Pause.]

"And in case you think you're talking to the bellhop, darling, you're talking to the concierge—who sees you, darling, sitting in the lobby, while the endless room-service charges get chalked up at the front desk, where nothing becomes something and vice versa, and this means you, darling. And don't worry about your luggage: it's been sent on ahead, and you're preboarded. [Another pause.]

"You know, your problem with all that, as I see it, is this: you seem to believe yourself, now as always, at the turning point of your career—whereas a man exists at peak form for, at the most, a season—or the length of a pinball game, remember? All the rest is simply banging at the front door to be let in, then later standing there at the top of the service stairs—remember Hollywood parties? And what else, darling, has your life been? A celebration of the tender receptivities of the exquisitely sensitive?

"You think you were educated in the gay ontologies of Aristotle—that you came out with some kind of *Phronesis* or, better yet, *Sophia*? Sophia Loren, maybe, or Anna Maria Sophia Kalogeroupoulos, a.k.a. the Meneghini. And now you sit momentarily expecting what, darling, a remake of your career? The musical? The motion picture? I don't think so.

"Get over it, darling—get over yourself. El Death holds up a piece of paper. He says, 'Do you recognize this? It's your résumé.'

"El Death reads out to the Recording Angel your roster, personality profile and curriculum vitae. 'Philosophical. That's a hot one. Yes, so it says here in small print. Thinks deep thoughts. Well, used to, anyway.'

"He shows the Recording Angel something you copied out. 'Going down is different from ending. Every going down is sheltered in an uprising.' 'Impressive,' he admits. 'I'm sure everyone you ever went down on would agree.'

"'Well, now, darling, while I have you, still thinking, wrap your mind, such as it is, around this one: *Seinvergessenheit.*' Whereupon, El Death tears your résumé to pieces, turns his back on you and spits, 'And now, get lost.'"

(Author connects the pinball machine with his writing. Each steel ball a subject, but instead of obeying the rules set down in composition class, he fires one after another up the shoot into the pinball box and watches it bang around the arena until TILT.)

◄◦►

"Transgression, obsession, self-immolation—how can these things be good for us to ponder?"

"Rather reminds one of the ending of *Morocco*—another of those so-called revelations fairies in their collective deluded agitated depression—which perfectly matched the country's in 1936, the year the picture came out—decided to live by—indeed virtually decided to build an entire Works Progress Administration around. Sudden seizure in exotic climes, resulting from unexpectedly sensitive moment in otherwise overexuberant floor show. Vulnerability as absolute value. True love springs miraculously from apparent mismatch. Terrible words scrawled on dressing room mirror—a version of the handwriting on the wall—turned as if by magic from indictment of a life wasted into the revelation in the burning bush. The climax of the broken string of pearls—a whole monograph could be written for fairies on that broken string of pearls."

◄◦►

"I don't trust any kind of woman. I say, anything that bleeds for three days and doesn't die can't be trusted."

One dove into it—the fast talk. It became clear that it was all part of a masque. "A suite of speeches," as Thomas Warton exulted when speaking of Milton's *Comus*, "perpetually attracting attention by sublime sentiment [or often enough, anyway], by fanciful imagery of the richest vein, by an exuberance of picturesque description, poetical allusion and ornamental expression."

He began to emulate the fat pinky rings until, quizzed by Max on his abilities and told he will be given, on the basis of his essay on Inversion in Herrick's Oberon poems, the chance to climb the ladder of academic success, QT, recalling the religious discussion, the gnostic's attribution of sorrow to the divinity, the Jacob's Pillow–talk and the Graham dictum, "You are in competition with nobody but yourself," declines.

Max asks QT what he wants to do. QT says he wants to record the talk, but also to go away and be alone and think up essays. Max counsels: do both. He wants to know what QT was like in college. QT pleads fatigue, retires and sits up that night composing a few scenes from a play he has been writing in his head while cruising the halls and lying in the dark at the Everard. In the morning, he decamps early, while Max is working in his study, and leaves two scenes of a script behind. With a note saying:

Dear Max,

So, from the Dakota to Fire Island—yes, the Cherry Grove Little Theater Revue. I dreamed of playing in it—my solo turn adapted from the Japanese ghost story called *Kanegamesaki* and from an incident in recent life. Intercut *Kanegamesaki* with *Vertigo* and the double-Madeleine.

Kanegamesaki: A girl falls in love with a hermit as he travels to worship at the shrine of Kumano. He spurns her love. Relentless, she pursues him through the region until he finds shelter beneath the great bell of Dojoi Temple. Driven mad by passion, she jumps off a cliff. (pause) I've been rehearsing on the beach, jumping off the lifeguard's chair, like Peg Entwistle screaming "I can't go on!" Just like the *Vertigo* girl—but Madeleine wasn't really Madeleine; her name was really JUDY!

The *Vertigo* girl was tripped up by a piece of jewelry.

I am an intricate system of assumed persona and dramatized selves

(And all but all) yours,

James

P.S. Now that you've become my father confessor, not quite replacing Halcyon, the one onstage in the scenes you're about to read, remind me to tell you about how the one who was came to be college chaplain just as I was leaving. One Bruce Ritter, a blond Franciscan hunk of man who loves rolling up his cassock sleeves so the gold hairs on his wrists glisten in the sun and talking about

Jesus as a man's man. Haly thinks he's danger money, and the general opinion among the more fastidious is "confess elsewhere."

"In case you think it's easy." Harry says that: Harry is "Haly's" real name, Harry Blair. He's every bit as smart as you are, Max, and twice as elegant, although I do love your zany old queen performance: it's how I think I'd probably be at sixty (the problem being I'll never live to be sixty).

SO: POSTSCRIPT AS PREFACE TO *THE NIGHT THE DAY* THEATER IN A LONELY ROOM

Presents

THE NIGHT THE DAY

—new comedy—

SCENE: The lights come up. The bar. CHRISTOPHER and HALCYON together. In the background the jukebox and the noise of the bowling machine.

BAR VOICE

"To hell with the truth! As the history of the world proves, the truth has no bearing on anything. The lie of the pipe dream is what gives life to the whole misbegotten mad lot of us, drunk or sober."

THE BARTENDER

Ain't it the truth.

[A group of male voices starts singing "A Hundred Bottles of Beer on the Wall." A second cuts in with "Heart of My Heart."]

CHRISTOPHER

Take me away from all this.

HALCYON

You seem troubled—more troubled than usual.

CHRISTOPHER

They come to me . . . tell me . . . then go and sing songs.

HALCYON

Poor Kit, poor . . . (*to the bartender, waving an empty glass*) Patrick, could we do this again?

CHRISTOPHER

If you loved me, you'd take me far, far away—

HALCYON

"If I Loved You" is a song. (*pause*) I do love you.

[On the jukebox, Billie Holiday, singing "As Time Goes By."]

CHRISTOPHER

When they've stopped—do we all go back to your place?

HALCYON

More than troubled—terrified. Can you tell me?

CHRISTOPHER

"Terror can become a kind of beauty too
When two fellows stand up to it together."

HALCYON

There are too many songs being sung at once. . . .

[The lights dim to near-blackout.]

━◦━

SCENE: CHRISTOPHER at the mirror.

CHRISTOPHER

I am not a well woman—that is a fact, demonstrable from first principles, correctly syllogized.

Yet philosophy is barren—where is the jism in a syllogism? I have enemies—they who stuck my face in the dirt.

I go to the Metropolitan *Opra*. Also to the *theatuh*. The New York City Ballet. I have seen the greatest dancer of our time, Tanaquil Le Clercq. At the City Center Theater I walk up the left side stairs—not distracted by the sound of Irish dancing in the basement—to the Second Balcony, and get in free, fabulous as I am in the company I keep. I watch *Agon*, for which I have constructed a rigorous psychoanalytical scenario. At the opra I have been seen walking on—in *Aida*. I have prayed myself—what the hell—to *immenso Ptah*, and have dreamed that I too am the *figlia di Faraoni*. (*he sings, falsetto*) "*In cor ti lessi—tu l'ami!*"

VOICE FROM THE HALL

You're wanted on the telephone, Madame Callas!

CHRISTOPHER

You are too kind. (*aside*) The poor fool thinks the Meneghini is a mezzo. Not that she's not, but while it's true that she's not not, it is not true that she is. But just try explaining existential paradox around here! (*aloud to the hall*) Tell the caller that Madame is indisposed—who is it anyway, Joe, some carhop, some dress extra? Love?

VOICE FROM THE HALL

Dunno—your mother . . . your girlfriend. . . .

CHRISTOPHER

My mother? Necessity is—and I am the invention of Halcyon. My girl-friend? All women call me friend—foolishly—but Love does not know this boy's name. *Ich habe deine Mut geküsst, Jokanaan! Ich habe. . . .* (*pause*) Kill that woman! (*to the messenger in the hall*) Cause the woman, who'er she may—to desist; to quit me. Say I'm in meditation. In hair. In wardrobe. I'll call her back tomorrow—or the next day. I'm on the line to the coast—the seacoast of Bohemia, my country. (*pause*) Not well . . . not well.

[The lights dim.]

CHRISTOPHER ("acting")

The voice of a temple bell sounds in the quiet dark. The great bell harbors myriad malices, struck at midnight, it echoes the teaching of Nirvana . . . slow curtain, the end, amen.

Who am I? Where do I come from? What do I want? Where am I going?

Remember death. What is life to me without me? Where is the light? The way out is the way in. What must I do? Not send to know for whom the . . .

VOICE OF THE BELOVED

Let me tell you a story about a bell.

CHRISTOPHER

You—here?

VOICE OF THE BELOVED

I'm in the dark, in the wings. I came down from the bell tower; I was up there alone, checking everything over. The others are morons—this bell thing is about you and me. You do know that.

CHRISTOPHER

You've told me nothing but stories night after night after night. What kind of a tale is this?

VOICE OF THE BELOVED

Kanegamesaki.

CHRISTOPHER

Come again? Come just this once—come closer, please. . . .

VOICE OF THE BELOVED

Kanegamesaki—The Cape of the Temple Bell.

A girl falls in love with the hermit Anchin
As he travels south to worship at the shrine
Of Kumano. He spurns her. She pursues
Him through the region until he hides beneath
The great bell of Dojoi Temple. Driven mad
By passion, the girl transforms herself into
A fire-breathing serpent, and then coiling
Herself around the bell, melts it, destroying
Her beloved within. Later, when the priests
Recast the bell, a mysterious dancing
Girl appears at the new bell dedication

Ceremony—asks to be allowed to dance
In honor of the occasion. At the height
Of her dance the bell falls over her. The priests
Raise it, and an enormous serpent crawls out
From beneath it.

CHRISTOPHER

I get it, for I too have sung my torch song,
Sung my bell song, played the girl; coiled serpentine
In flaming faggot lust around the bastard—
In my dreams—written verse, spoken verse . . . for what?

VOICE OF THE BELOVED

The girl in that story was not a girl at all—not anyway until the Meiji period
late in the last century, when all the monks' boy love stories were retold
revised.

CHRISTOPHER (nods)

All Japanese monks, all samurai and all actor stories were originally about
faggots. And they all ended thusly—

I heard them, I saw them, I walked through them. I
Thought, let me make it up the stairs, leap over
The turnstile, lunge down the platform, throw myself
Into the train just as the doors are closing,

[He sits on a step about halfway up the flight.]

Be conveyed to the Rialto, have breakfast
There at Hector's with the hustlers: they're always
Terribly kind. Or, if I don't make it up
The stairs and over the turnstile, throw a shit
Fit right there on the street, shrieking my tits off

[Stands, backs in fright a few steps more up toward the top.]

Until a pair or more of New York's finest—
Who can in certain circumstances turn out

To be as kind as Hector's hustlers. . . . They were
Certainly that in those bygone days, when, not
Satisfied because they could not destroy me,
My tormentors set about to make my life
A waking nightmare in the neighborhood. Mean
Streets I walked—up Golgotha—in torment. They—
The boys in blue, so many Veronicas. . . .

[He wipes his face with the handkerchief and holds it out.]

Thanks, boys. Here, take this—in remembrance of me.

[He drops the handkerchief from a height. Lights dim to half.]

I am lying, I am lying, I am ly— (*pause*)
Blames self on self. (*pause*) Blames rest on Love. And casting directors. They promised me I could play Richard the Second. I saw myself gorgeous, settled on the gay ground—a legitimate theater bottle blond,
surrounded by minions, all mouse brown. The whole scene enveloped in a
hot rose glow. Instead, they tell me Richard the Third will be much more fun.
I wind up humpbacked, shrieking, despised, alone downstage on Bosworth
Field. Anybody who thinks that isn't funny shouldn't have come to college.
Still, I make the best of it—I'm eerily compelling. And now, to no applause
at all, this bell performance. . . .

STUDENT VOICES

This isn't the theater, this is life, real life. Now about the rehearsal of the
bell plot, scheduled for tomorrow night. . . .

[The lights dim to near-blackout.]

—◄○►—

SCENE: The lights come up. HALCYON's apartment.

HALCYON (very drunk)

Masters, gentles, spread yourselves: let us sit up—

STUDENT VOICES

It's cold in here! Can we light a fire, sir?
This thing works, right? What's there to burn?

HALCYON

Oh, for a muse of—we'll burn the muse!
We'll burn the muse at the stake. Serve the witch right.
There's sufficient been written—yes, burn the witch.
Sufficient's been—sufficient unto the night. . . .

[HALCYON retires from the stage.]

CHRISTOPHER (very drunk)

No! You can't burn the muse. No, she sings to me. She sings "Melancholy Baby." (*sings*)

"All your fears are foolish fancies, every cloud
Must have a silver lining—smile my honey—
Foolish fancies—maybe—Don't you know that I'm
In love—or else I shall be melancholy—"

[Chorus of boos. HALCYON returns, carrying a hat box.]

HALCYON

In yer hat, Margaret Mary—in yer Easter—

[He pulls out a feathered hat from the hatbox and puts it on.]

Now let us sit upon the ground and tell terribly sad stories of the deaths of everyone we know, then burn the hatbox and weep over them all. The hatbox, never the hat. How some have died just yesterday, how others on the morrow, if not sooner, if not right now even now as we sit upon the ground and tell sad tales—

CHRISTOPHER

Nobody's dying tonight—not in this room—but me, on G. (*he hits G*)

HALCYON

Is there no end to your need to be noticed?

CHRISTOPHER

No. I am Prince Hamlet, and was meant to be—
Not an attendant lord. The melancholy
Hamlet—*palladis omnis amans, color*
Hic aptus amanti. Oime—qual pallor!

STUDENT VOICES

Now he'll pass out.

[CHRISTOPHER passes out.]

Then he'll wake up, screaming, laughing, ready for another round.

HALCYON

Young men will grow pale and lean from sleepless nights, and from the cares
and pangs of love.

STUDENT VOICES

Tough shit. He'll be all right here with you. Good night, sir, see you in class
tomorrow.

HALCYON

Voices in the vestibule—good night, good night.

[Picks up the phone, then, looking down at CHRISTOPHER, hangs up.]

And would you care to take a look at this lug?

> "*Illum opportet crescere, me autem*
> *Diminui. . . .*" Go figure. "And what is Earth's
> Eye, tongue, heart else, where else, but in dear dogged
> Man—heir to his own selfbent so bound, so tied
> To his turn." (*removes the hat and puts it back into the box*)
> Just in case you think it's easy—Good night, sweet prince
> And flights of angels sing thee—

[HALCYON retires from the stage with the hat in the hatbox.]

CHRISTOPHER (wakes up screaming.)
Am I alone? The fuckers left me alone?

HALCYON (returning)
You're not alone. What woke you?

CHRISTOPHER
The bells—or the Bell Song . . . the Meneghini. I didn't shit on the floor, huh?

HALCYON
No, but you sent the rest packing.

CHRISTOPHER
Them? The Pharisees? They have complots to digest in some form. Whereas I, the publican—

HALCYON
A sinner—

CHRISTOPHER
Scarlet; I'd go down on Pilate to save Christ.

HALCYON
Oh, brother.

CHRISTOPHER
I am pilloried, weary, loveless, revealed; the Meneghini could sing me. I have always depended—not my role, really, but all the same I have—on the kindness of—them all. They allowed me use of the family name, which I call kind, and I was dependent on their many favors—thus it became necessary for me to entertain them—but in the existential sense they were strangers. It was you who first looked at me—as the title of the hot best seller says, beautifully— not as a stranger. May I sleep here? I'll fetch the *Times*, make the coffee—

HALCYON
What a great gettin' up morning. Yes, you may.

CHRISTOPHER

First I'll tell you more about *Intolerance*. My play—there are four stories. The story I tell you, the story I tell me, the story you tell me, the story you tell you. Four intertwined stories, about us. You've shown me how to do it, the way you've shown me everything else there is in life to do. You said, "O.K., kiddo, take it from where you say. . . ."

Now about the sets—I see all New York. I see it like Babylon in *Intolerance*, but it won't fall—not so long as I, as its rhapsode . . . And I see the hill of Golgotha—it's our hill, the one we walk up every morning when we've come up from here in a taxi because we're late for class. . . . And this part I'm not so sure about: the massacre of St. Bartholemew's Day, but maybe it's something about Normandy on D-Day. . . . Yes, that's it—with Chartres behind, and you trying to get to the Germans nested in the towers before the Americans blow the cathedral to kingdom come. And the gallows set: that's the kitchen at home where I tried at the age of seven to hang myself on the towel rack. . . .

Time for a song. Sing "Among My Souvenirs"?

HALCYON (singing)

"There's nothing left for me—"

CHRISTOPHER (joining in)

"Of days that used to be—"

CHRISTOPHER & HALCYON

"I live in memory
Among my souvenirs."

CHRISTOPHER (yawning)

I'm suddenly that tired—I must black out.

[CHRISTOPHER goes to sleep.]

HALCYON

Do you love it? Don't you just wish somebody would come along and stick an aromatic cigarette into every orifice in your body, and light them—all at once? Don't you wish you had a martini—and a cigarette in each and every orifice in your bod?

I cannot wait to see God; I have a few things to say to that number. "Hi—love yer hat; got a minute? It's about this life that late one led. Some things I feel require pointin' out to you, dear, the author of creation. I could go on through eternity about it"—but somehow, now that it's over and done with—I'll just nap. Lie down and rock my soul in the bosom of Abraham.

[Looks out at the audience, picks up the phone.]

Whoever calls, tell him to get himself fucked.

[He drops the phone on the floor: dial tone.]

[BLACKOUT]

CHAPTER FIFTEEN

While on the Town

> "Some also have wished that the next way to their father's house were here
> . . . but the way is the way, and there is an end."
>
> —John Bunyan, *The Pilgrim's Progress*

*Wherein the story of High Culture (the New York intellectuals) trading in
a sleek Gentlemen's Agreement homophobia for new-model, French-
derived semantic discourse on queer life, aesthetics and politics takes hold,
and overnight it becomes de rigueur to be suspected of (at the very least) a
single significant (of course youthful) homosexual interlude. Wherein
significant numbers of gorgeous, educated men loosen their skinny ties, kick
off their cordovans and fess up (often with the same crack, "Listen if
everybody told the absolute truth at their draft board, there would've been
nobody in Korea but white trash and Aussies") while the markedly less-
than-gorgeous and the drip-dry shirts scramble for a place in the Forum.*

Susan Sontag's "Notes on 'Camp'" and the genesis of the Warhol
Factory's aesthetic of trash coincided to dominate the period.
Reactions to Sontag's *Partisan Review* essay (and more from the
"discovery" and notation of the notes by *Time*) erupted nervously from
behind facades of the still largely closeted Queer Street (most particularly
in the odd, musty corners of certain faculty rooms *in fondo* in the ivy-covered
buildings in the widely distanced separate neighborhoods of Promising,
Meaningful and Deeply Talented and Seclusion, Betrayal and Go-to-Hell),
finally to be trumpeted daily of a late afternoon and early evening in what

had been all along (or at least since the 1930s) the epicenter of American Camp, the standing-room line at the Metropolitan Opera on the west side of Broadway between 39th and 40th Streets in New York City.

A significant social marker in this eruption was the appearance in the audience not only of Mae West, the Empress of Camp in the West, but of Susan Sontag herself in the glittering party, includng Jacqueline Kennedy, Leonard Bernstein and members of the Secret Service, at the historic return of Maria Callas to the stage of the Metropolitan Opera (as Puccini's Tosca) in March 1965.

This was preceded by the *Life* exposé of the homosexual subculture (a crummy rewrite with the corny equivalent of hick pix to match Mary McCarthy's 1951 dumbed-down cheap take on gay Village life in the socially conscious *New York Post*—"Ha, ha, ha, Blanche") and the publication of John Rechy's *City of Night* (laying out the coast-to-coast Queer Street map), which served to reestablish the notion of the homosexual as radical. Quick off the mark, the Uptown Homintern (Bernstein et al.), rather than doing anything so socially compromising as coming out as such or making public what had been so tightly wrapped and closeted, made the inspired (if deeply calculating, necessarily insincere and markedly improvisatory) move of quickly nominating "radical chic," which to many was a code name for a queer-inspired movement, to the spoon-fed press.

Radical chic involved, in sum, the inviting of a large number of armed and surly big Kahuna heavies of the unwitting-but-certifiably-Camp Black Panther movement into the *moto perpetuo* revolving-door-endowed free lunch that was the homosexual East Side's collective life experience, enduring, in their patient and wily way, the growling, hissing, spitting upon and occasional rough clawing of the hosts—and more particularly haplesly the hostesses—that ensued.

(Difficult, even for ready money, to schedule so many two-face face peels, deep-pore cleansings and mascara makeovers over what amounted to a single long weekend, even if one did appreciate that what was happening was a deep intensification of the moral sense through savage ironies.)

In reaction, excluded queers, lightning studies all, commenced appropriating the barricade mentality and socially disruptive strategies (later canonized as *transgressive*) of feminism and black activism, becoming equal adepts at generating the publicity which in modern life so quickly subsumes any and every stringency until it, the publicity, itself becomes (as more becoming to success and comfort) the ideology of idealogies. Not without conflict to be sure, a conflict which, in respect of what came to be known as Gay Liberation, voiced itself as a deep ambivalence regarding both categorical imperatives and value judgments (the World as Will and Show Business), which in a short five years would devolve into the Stonewall-riot split between comity and radical estrangement. Impossible it seemed to enlist simultaneously, in the cause of freedom for one and all, both platoons of drag queens and committees of true women, to espouse both the rough-edged, jagged strategies of the deep-dish caw-caw and the more rounded, authentic-feeling, if paradoxically more radically narcissistic *limerance* protocols of the Primal Scream.

City of Night, published in 1963, did, as it happened, mark the beginning of the New Queer Literary Age, one elastic enough, over the next quarter of a century, to accommodate such diverse and to-be-sure transgressive eruptions as:

- The continuous unending-story *delerium tremens* of veteran queer and self-loathing junkie William S. Burroughs
- The epoch-defining novels of Andrew Holleran
- The John Marquand-meets-Frank Harris, D.H. Lawrence and Oscar Wilde for-an-evening-of-pornographic-blackjack sagas of the hilarious Gordon Merrick
- The exuberant supposedly-communal-epic recitations of Boyd McDonald
- Literature's first queer gothic romance, Vincent Virga's *Gaywyck*
- A bona fide if short-lived New York queer literary coterie, the *Violet Quill*
- The determination of Michael Denneny to launch an entire program of queer books by a mainstream publisher, St. Martin's
- An entirely new (and welcome) generation of explicitly queer male and female poets and critics following in the wake of Thom Gunn and Adrienne Rich, comprised of, among others, J.D. McClatchy, Marilyn Hacker, Tim Dlugos, David Trinidad, Alfred Corn, Mark Doty, Wayne Koestenbaum, Dennis Cooper, Eileen Myles and Tom Carey
- The devastating and oracular stun-gun *contes moraux* of Dennis Cooper

• And coming full circle back to Los Angeles, the amazing advent and meteoric career of polymath critic Michael Silverblatt, the genius-reader host of National Public Radio's indispensable *Bookworm*.

—◄○►—

Rechy's plunge into the queer-picaresque, in a tight-knit roughspun prose that close reading could not shred, was savagely reviewed by the vermillion-wigged, weird-sister washout Alfred Chester in *The New York Review of Books*, Chester being the ideal representation of the way the West Side liked its queers to be in the '60s. Both Marilyn Monroe and Maria Callas, if truth be told, sang at the sexually omnivorous young president's Madison Square garden party in 1962, which the overwhelmingly homosexual, "out" and hallucenogenic-without-chemicals devotees of "the Meneghini woman" stormed for standing-room tickets, making of the west side of Eighth Avenue between 50th and 51st Streets more of a daylight queer three-ring circus than decades of in-and-out high-wire tea-room sex at the Greyhound Bus Terminal on the opposite side of the thoroughfare had ever managed to do.

Months later Robert Kennedy, the attorney general, was the honored speaker at the author's college graduation. (The stresses and strains of family life are aggravated to breaking point in the glare of the media—and here's the sheet music to go with it.)

Then that fall the author repeatedly ran into—or more accurately was repeatedly skirted by—Rudolf Nureyev at the Everard Baths, only to be told that the savage god was involved in a passionate affair with Tony Perkins. What was the world coming to—or was the question where had it been?

—◄○►—

Truman Capote was a chronic and habitual liar and mythomane, and also a writer of outré but certifiable genius, although oddly enough never considered true Camp. The success of certain significant failures is not to be confused with the flop-sweat stench of Doomed Failure and Foreordained Social Ostracism themselves, of which certain hysterical celebrity careers seem to reek from the very start, no matter how much amphetamine and expensive scotch they are braced with, no matter how much *Eau Sauvage* is splashed on them or how much cocaine is shoved up the sorry noses of the tragi-comic sluts attached to them by other names than Rose.

AT MAX'S KANSAS CITY

"It is part of the character of Manhattan that interior and exterior realities mingle recklessly."
—Suzannah Lessard

"Violence is the expedient of whatever has been refused an audience."
—Roberto Calasso

If, in 1950, Mankiewicz's Addison DeWitt, as incarnated by George Sanders in *All About Eve*, seemed serviceable-and-then-some as successor to Clifton Webb's Waldo Liedecker (in Otto Preminger's *Laura*, 1944) as the representation of Gotham's Petronius Arbiter, then it must be said that, when reflecting on the early 1960s (particularly following the assassination in Dallas on November 22, 1963, of the thirty-fifth president of the United States, John Fitzgerald Kennedy) it becomes difficult to fully sustain the credibility of the persona, yet at a stretch one might imagine the venomous male fishwife having something like this to say (say in 1969, when it was all over but the replays for New Jersey) to whatever readers (real or imagined) he might then have addressed:

In the unlikely event, dear reader, that you do not widely read, attend the theater, listen to unsponsored radio programs or otherwise keep serious tabs on the decade just passed, which originated the world in which you now live, it may be necessary to introduce you to Max's Kansas City, the bloody birthing room of that decade's signal product, known as Pop Culture: whose sinuous, dark mysteries of character, destiny and worth, I safely predict, will come to be studiously parsed in all the awful solemnity the sociological probes of a benumbed posterity may find itself capable of mustering.

("*Il consulta l'un après l'autre tous les devins de l'armée, ceux qui observent la marche des serpents, ceux qui lisent dans les étoiles, ceux qui soufflent sur la cendre des morts.*" —Flaubert, *Salammbô*)

Call it (any memory of Max's) at this late date, in the dawn of the new millennium, paleontology: the exhumation and scrutiny of old stashed bones. As Yvonne Sewall-Ruskin, widow of Mickey Ruskin, originating genius of Max's (and, speaking of successions of archetypes, an authentic successor to Tony Pastor, Texas Guinan, Sherman Billingsley and Toots Shor), has written, "Everybody who was anyone was there; Max's Kansas City was the place to be. It quickly became the new drug of the late '60s and early '70s counterculture scene, and its effects were lasting. The mere mention of Max's conjures up images of chic outrageousness. There never was a place like it and there never will be again."

Much the same thing of course may be said of hell. *The mere mention of Max's*: you could certainly sing it, had you the tune.

Actually Max's never *became* anything; it didn't ever have the time. It popped up overnight, like an enormous toadstool, and rather than being any brand or name of drug, it was from first to last a wholesale pharmacy.

The businessmen came in the late afternoon; artists who had before then crowded the Cedar Tavern and who'd been, since Jackson Pollock's death eleven years earlier, part of the First Generation of Abstract Expressionism's collective nervous breakdown, arrived at the same hour, filled up the front room and stayed all night.

Real movie stars came to the back room to see what low-down, no-account and fabulously named Andy Warhol–Paul Morrissey superstars (the Factory had relocated just across the street) were all about, and learned. Max's back room was the superstars' studio canteen; there they and their handlers lounged in the hot glare of Dan Flavin's neon red-orange triangle, drinking, taking drugs and feasting on one another's innards—creatures who a generation earlier (q.v.) would have been scarcely welcome to eat out of the garbage pails in the Stork Club's back alley.

And then there were the overwhelming (and overwhelmed) majority, the Nameless Lost, among whom the author would at that time certainly have been counted—had he been noticed at all, face down on the floor, Lou Reed stepping over him on the way upstairs to do his turn and he turning over, raising an arm and saluting "Blesh you, dahling!"

William Burroughs called Max's the intersection of everything (echoing Hofmannsthal's Ariadne, who, longing for death, famously laments, "*Hier kam alles zu allem*"). Perhaps he was thinking of the location, at 17th and Park Avenue South (the old Fourth Avenue) just beyond the north end of Union Square, a block up from Tammany Hall.

Such a definition reminds us too of certain inherent propositional limitations. It cannot for instance be categorically maintained that Max's was unprecedented: memories and accounts of it are likely to call to nostalgic New Yorkers' minds much of what transpired in the late nineteenth century further downtown at Five Points. And as five points make a star in the American flag, so was Max's that American. Recalling those haunting key words from the stirring sonnet of Emma Lazarus, never, not in all the years that Ellis Island operated, did so much wretched refuse from so many teem-

ing shores populate a displaced persons' staging area than did this guttersnipe way station in the Asphalt Jungle.

Max's Kansas City, where in the gangway off the kitchen, in maneuvers
reminiscent of the passage-slipway traffic on the great ocean liners, just then
winding down their transatlantic careers, where First would slum down to
Tourist and tourist snake up to tickle with feathers the asses of the rich and
prey on their vainglorious insouciance, queer back room met hip front room
to make drug/art deals that defined middle- and late-'60s cutting-edge
Bohemian New York. Appositely, self-loathing (the signal leitmotif of that
decade) found there the green room of the Gotham Theater of Cruelty's
Stage of the World, and its most eloquent expression in the establishment's
most famous bouncer, the legendary, relentless, unflagging gossip gumshoe,
gurrier and public scold, Dorothy Dean, Trouble's own trouble, Adversity
on spindly legs, who was such a Max's creature she might have been renamed
Maxine, and who avowed for many years afterward, "I-I said to Drella, I
loathe the '60s—I-I hated them then, and I-I hate them now!"

Sample snippets of the nightly discourse:

". . . 'and the greatest and most valuable among them have an important operation over a wide range: their contribution toward the life of the
agglomerate consists in acting, not in being acted upon. Others, but feebly
equipped for action, are almost entirely passive. There is also an intermediate
order whose members contain within themselves a principle of productivity
and activity and make themselves very effective in many spheres or ways and
yet serve also by their passivity.' Plotinus, darling, the second Ennead, the
third tractate, the thirteenth verse. Always reminds me of the life of bees,
busy little bees making honey."

"And what of poverty, riches, glory, fame?"

"Inquisitive little thing! The rich get richer and the poor are always with
us—somewhere. As to fame, it is either deserved, and then is due to the
service rendered and to the merits of the appraiser, or it is not and then must
be attributed to the injustice of those giving out the awards."

"Well I think Bette deserved the Oscar for *Eve*, I really do."

—◦—

". . . the cultivation, darling, of fleeting, exquisite transports on a gargantuan scale."

"Miss Dean agrees. I just heard her at the round table, in a vociferous stammer, quoting Kant to the effect that men, Italians and the night are sublime, whereas women, the English and the daylight are merely beautiful, and—this is Miss Dean's gloss, 'Big hairy deal!'"

—◄○►—

"Narrative, darling; you mean as a thing in and of itself? I'm afraid not. You see $E = mc^2$ affected every branch of human learning and endeavor, including everything in the condition of music, to which all art aspires. What you're still calling abstracted narrative, darling, is for all time revealed as convertible in the equation in which m is character and c^2 is the lightning-quick speed-of-light of cognition itself."

—◄○►—

Also, that simultaneously driven and crippled thing glam-rock/po-mo culture is, was born there (in the phone booth and toilets that seemed to be one and the same place), and it is essential if perhaps a little edged with asperity to remember, in these days of mall recreations and *nostalgie de la boutique*, that as the photographer Derek Callender put it, "There were enough drugs in the back room to cause birth defects."

Forrest (Frosty) Myers's laser beam, which shot through the air from 19th Street, pierced the front-room window and ran through to a mirror in the back room, creating what was thought of as an Outer Space effect. Some years later (conjunctive with Miss Dean's remarks to Andy Warhol) this assertion was corroborated when, at the first screenings of *Star Wars*, any number of startled viewers were heard to declare upon exiting, "Oh, that bar scene—wasn't it but *exactly* like like the back room at Max's!" And the memory of Frosty Myers's laser inevitably creates the memory of so many hundreds of holograms—people you could walk through.

Why was Max's never raided for much the same activity they went after at the Stonewall? Because of those front room businessmen, culture-vulture high rollers of the Lindsay administration (Fun City was what they were now calling New York), not to mention the omnipresent Bozo Brigade: personnel of the Central Intelligence Agency in rag and bob-tail mufti.

Yes, of course they came, to keep quite other tabs than Mickey Ruskin's night after night. They were fascinated: how not? One thought then as one thinks now that following the definitive Warhol multiple Marilyns, a sequence of multiple Dorothy Deans, multiple Donald Lyonses, multiple Danny Fieldses, multiple Fran Lebowitzes and multiple Holly Woodlawns, Jackie Curtises, Candy Darlings and John Waterses would have constituted not only a more aesthetically pleasing Warholian product line, but also one altogether more to the point than the multiple Jackies, Lizes, Elvises, Maos and electric chairs. Miss Dean, Max's Kansas City's Butterfly McQueen-cum–J. Edgar Hoover, was more far interesting than (if quite as lethal as) an entire showroom of electric chairs; Fran Lebowitz, its Dorothy Parker, together with transvestite superstars Holly, Candy and Jackie, far more interesting than the woman known by then as Jackie O.; Danny Fields, godfather of the Ramones, far more interesting (and a whole lot sexier) than Elvis; John Waters, far more interesting (and demonstrably better looking, really) than Liz; and Donald Lyons, the quite literally peerless grand compère of the back room's all-night, every-night nervous-breakdown floor show, infinitely more interesting than Mao Zedong.

The author, poleaxed by more than alcohol and controlled substances (in which connection it is interesting to note the prevailing attitude in respect of pleonasm, that as the substances themselves were controlled, the consumers of them need hardly be, as such), wondered: what could he possibly tell these people about himself to make himself the least bit interesting? Something about the identity crisis, perhaps, although of course he hadn't actually had one yet and therefore found himself yet again, as always, at a turning in in his career, in a precarious position, one perhaps not entirely unlike that he'd occupied a decade earlier in respect of that club down in the cellar in Jackson Heights. Sobering thought. Don't dwell.

A common Irish expression goes variously "the brains or the bottle," "neither the brains nor the bottle" and "both the brains and the bottle," all pitching the idea that the two qualia, brains and the bottle, match up in the gaining of an advantage. Pure whimsy as it turns out, although to be scrupulously accurate, the idea seems to be that the bottle in question is strictly speaking viewed in the denotative sense of a container of substance (substance viewed as an abstract, as for example *moxie*) rather than as in the more usual metonymic sense. (Kim Novak to Agnes Moorehead, about a washed-up actress in the George Sidney 1957 biopic *Jeanne Eagels*: "Was she any good, Nielie?" "She was *great*, until she met her match . . . the bottle.")

What's in identity? A name. What's in a name? A certain overdetermined wish fulfillment, not his own, the consequence of which is what, exactly? The identity crisis.

Meanwhile, what about an ingenious, spirited reply to "Notes on 'Camp'"? Considering the fact that without question Susan Sontag is to intellectual credibility in queer life what Evelyn Gentry Hooker was to the beginings of social acceptance, why not?

Chordal Ideation Sparked by "Notes on 'Camp'"
(Some Underlinings)

To talk about Camp is therefore to betray it. If the betrayal can be defended, it will be for the edification it provides, or the dignity of the conflict is resolves. For myself, I plead the goal of self-edification, and the goad of a sharp conflict in my own sensibility. I am strongly drawn to Camp, and almost as strongly offended by it.

The emendation of the author, Queer Temperament, in his own case would be, "I am strongly drawn to Camp sensibility and even more terrified of the consequences of finally embracing it—not the least of which would be condemnation to a life on the Upper East Side (could he make it back, like Prudence). He knew who—and what—he was and where he had come from, and even what he wanted, but as to where he was going, who could tell him? How could he get to Susan Sontag? Was she that much more inaccessible than Victoria de los Angeles? Wasn't it simply the question of getting into the right party? No, it was a question of somehow getting involved at *The New York Review of Books*—and going to Kakia Livanos's salon and finding Robert Silvers there was not the way in. Somehow Queer Temperament was not Marcel Proust, in spite of the fact that what it was he was pleased to call work he did do in bed all day.

Betrayal

In Irish experience, however becoming it is to be informed, you don't become an informer. They will either kill you outright, exile you to the Isle of Man or break your kneecaps so you'll never dance *Swan Lake* again. That said, what is life without risk? The most important tactical maneuver in Camp is *reculer pour mieux sauter*—in combat situations, pull back the better to advance: in modern dance as developed by Martha Graham, contract-release.

But the hitch is while Camp pull-back (ironic detachment, putting every-thing in terms of ". . . !") and Camp contraction (recoil from the "natural" is always highly visible), Camp advance and Camp release is always done in the dead of night, behind enemy lines and quite invisibly.

Which is why Gay Liberation, were it to succeed in its every stated aim—as for example the idiotic rejection by queer politicians of one of the two best plays in post-Stonewall theater (the other being William Hoffman's *As Is*), Mart Crowley's *The Boys in the Band*—would wipe Camp, along with lipstick, mascara, eye shadow and hair coloring, off the face of homo-sexual experience, rendering queer life as bidable as chastity. It isn't true (but sometimes it's useful to pretend otherwise) that to the Camp sensibil-ity every intimation of life is an imitation of life.

SELF-EDIFICATION

A daring, Luciferian concept, alien to the Irish Catholic mind (as is the Protestant understanding of Emerson's "Self-Reliance"). The psychologi-cal danger in it is clear: it relies on intrapsychic mirror-imaging and circular self-inflicted argument in place of transference and the talking cure. In mirror-imaging, the angles are reversed, the objects in the background appear closer than they actually are, and self-inflicted argument in and through which nar-cissistic anxiety is more likely to be exacerbated than quelled. In this con-nection it is well to remember that Freud's exposure as a child to Moravian Catholicism impacted on him in two distinct ways: first in the exposure to totemic priest-ridden religion, and second in simultaneous exposure to, and exclusion from, the idea of sacramental confession and absolution.

Thus the many self-invented victims of injudicious Camp are everywhere, as numerous and as sad as Fashion victims, for while Style is, like the muses, a stern taskmistress, Fashion, Style's slower witted stepchild, goes in for very lazy *laissez-faire*, under the mistaken apprehension that ready-to-wear (cf. Flaubert's *Dictionnaire des Idées Reçues*) is democracy in action.

DIGNITY

See above, in relation to the perils of self-deception vis-à-vis self-definition. (Suggested task role model: Mae West.)

CONFLICT

Self-regard (*amour propre*) vs. self-infatuation (Narcissus drowns).

Further researches into the "Love-Hate" relationship idea indicate love and hate are not opposite at all, but, like Eros and Aggression, arraigned on the side of life. So that "love your enemies" is more of a recognition quest than a forced attempt to reconcile opposites. On the opposite side of affect is avoidance and indifference ("Because thou art neither hot not cold, I will vomit thee out of my mouth").

A TABLE OF ELEMENTS IN CONFLICT

Love/Hate		Depression
Sex/Aggression		Prayer (non-petitionary)
Male/Female		Spirit
Yin/Yang		Void/Nirvana
Night/Day	vs.	Eternity
Left/Right		Ex/im/ploding
Sun/Moon		Interstellar Space
Arithmetic		Calculus
Hot/Cold		Apathy
Matter/Energy		Black Hole

Therefore, since all sex is aggressive, all aggression sexual (and all ways are one), there may really be no such thing as heterosexuality or homosexuality: As Gore Vidal would have it, there are merely circumstantial object-combats, which tilts the scientific categorization habit (late nineteenth, early twentieth century).

To snare a sensibility in words, especially one that is alive and powerful, one must be tentative and nimble.

As the New York City municipal bridge worker said to Ms. Sontag when, to mark a significant birthday, she once, with a companion, scaled the pylons of the Brooklyn Bridge, "You can do it, Sue!"

Camp is a vision of the world in terms of style—but a particular kind of style. It is the love of the exaggerated, the "off," of things-being-what-they-are-not.

VISION

All Camp is bi-focal.

WORLD

Not the epiphenomenal world of landscape, commerce and politics as the first element in "the world, the flesh and the devil." If "The world (*die Welt*) is everything that is the case" (*der Fall*), then the artificial (and therefore since man will pursue perfection and the end of things—compare *Beyond the Pleasure Principle*—Camp) is that which can either support ("I speak not yet of proof") or subvert the case (or The World that is the case)—or, for those minds capable of holding opposite propositions in the same thought at the same time—both.

"OFF"

An important Camp question: when in the individual sensibility does "gamey" turn into putrefied, "high" turn into fetid? Thus, in Camp necrophilia, the intercourse must always be with a beautifully embalmed corpse.

THINGS-BEING-WHAT-THEY-ARE-NOT

Plato rather than Aristotle. A is both A and non-A (the twin, the Other, the otherwise, the dead).

The work tells all. (Compare a typical nineteenth-century opera with Samuel Barber's Vanessa, *a piece of manufactured Camp, and the difference is clear.)*

TELL-ALL

All About Eve, All That Heaven Allows, All God's Chillun Got (Buffalo) *Wings, All-Over* (development in Abstract Expressionism).

Except that *All About Eve*, even if written and directed by a European Jew, is finally too absolutely forthright to be Camp. It certainly does, however, have Camp moments (all significantly taking place either at a theatrical party or backstage at a theater): Margo Channing's "Fasten your seat belts, it's going to be a bumpy night"; Miss Caswell's "You won't bore him honey, you won't even get a chance to talk"; the hapless pianist (Claude Shannon) when asked to reprise Liszt's *Liebestraum*, "But that was the *fourth straight time!*; and Eve Harrington's reaction to praise: "I just don't try to kid myself, that's all."

If the end of scientific discourse is to get to the bottom of things the better to stay on top of them, the end of artistic discourse is to get underneath things altogether. Depression is going under unprotected (*"facilis descensus Averno . . ."*). Camp is descending armed with talismans in search of the wellspring.

La Gioconda/Vanessa

Ponchielli's *La Gioconda*, words and music, is *altissimo* Camp: its exuberance and overdrive (the Laura-Gioconda duet *"L'amo come il fulgor del creato,"* Enzo's *"Tu sei morta"* and Gioconda's *"Suicidio!"* are the high points) turn the classic Verdian melodrama into a vertiginous roller-coaster ride.

In *Vanessa*, however, although the Menotti libretto probably does qualify as an example of rather hazy (and therefore, by Camp standards, imperfect) Camp, Barber, not five minutes into the first act, either subverts Menotti's intention or merely asserts his own with Erica's arietta "Must the Winter Come So Soon?"—a stretch of music nearly as beautiful as the second movement of the same composer's Violin Concerto (see above, Chapter Two).

—◄o►—

Perhaps though it is not so much a question of the unintended effect versus the conscious intention, as of the delicate relation between parody and self-parody in Camp.

The double sense of "question" (that which is or is not the case ["... !] versus the interrogative ["... ?"]) at the root of Camp. Thus the rhetorical "Is she a camp?" is the more correct form of appreciation than the categorical-declarative "She is a camp."

UNINTENDED/INTENDED

The Unconscious. *The Psychopathology of Everyday Life*, published at the height of *Jugendstil*.

—◦—

In naïve, or pure, Camp, the essential element is seriousness, a seriousness that fails.

Joan. No, not Bette-and-Joan, Joan. Bette Davis, with varying results, *did* Camp ("They're Either Too Young or Too Old," from *Hollywood Canteen*; *Tonight at 8.30* on Broadway) and could intentionally or not *be* Camp (King Vidor's *Beyond the Forest*, Irving Rapper's *Another Man's Poison*, *The Catered Affair* and parts of Robert Aldrich's *What Ever Happened to Baby Jane*). But Joan was Camp itself, throughout, as much in *Jane* as she'd been in Michael Curtiz's *Mildred Pierce*, Curtis Bernhardt's *Possessed* and Nicholas Ray's *Johnny Guitar*.

Vamping and Camp. "Vamp" as diminutive of vampire. Theda Bara, Pola Negri, Vilma Banky, Mae West.

Vampirism, necrophilia and fellatio.

The Madison: the ultimate Camp line dance. Drill precision (or you were thrown off the floor). The hand jive on top of it, without losing a beat. Everybody his/her own Mae West, all alone together in increasingly great assemblages. The single instance of, or *hommage* to, pure Camp in the *nouvelle vague*: the Madison sequence in *Bande à Part*, Anna Karina, Claude Brasseur and Sami Frey in cheap café sending up a send-up, achieving a moment of cinematic *jouissance* without diluting for a moment Godard's absolute formal perfection.

—◦—

What Camp taste responds to is "instant character" (this is, of course, very eighteenth century); and conversely, what it is not stirred by is the sense of the development of character. Character is understood as a state of continual incandescence—a person being one, very intense thing."

"Miss Demeanor is one very intense thing, but she lacks latitude."

—◦—

Camp taste transcends the nausea of the replica.

The most brilliant and provocative statement in the whole of "Notes on 'Camp.'" Such transcendence begins with overcoming the sick feeling in the stomach and bowels of the Camp queen, conditioned to self-loathing, experienced when first looking into the mirror at the face as nature left it. An hour (or more) later, when the subtle pinks and artful shadows have been achieved, the queen, self edified, adjusts her package and sallies forth undaunted into the world.

—◄◦►—

The connoisseur of Camp sniffs the stink and prides himself on his strong nerves.

From Des Esseintes (in Huysmans's *À Rebours*) chomping on leeks all the way to the depravities of the Mineshaft. ("Ya knew it was dangerous work when ya took the job!")

—◄◦►—

Camp taste is, above all, a mode of enjoyment, of appreciation—not judg- ment. . . . [It] doesn't propose that it is in bad taste to be serious; it doesn't sneer at someone who succeeds in being seriously dramatic. What it does is to find the success in certain passionate failures.

Without question, however, that said, on the other hand and (always) meanwhile, Camp tends to espouse the non-judgmental (as in George W.S. Trow's *Within the Context of No Context*) in a deliberative, rigorously cod- ified, politically conservative and strictly enforced methodology. Semantically, two senses of judgment obtain, the forensic and the punitive—remember- ing the fact that any conclusion, positive or negative, and especially one priding itself on having transcended opinion in close reading of the book of evidence, has in itself been proved inescapably founded at least as much upon projectile as upon objective criteria. Judge and jury are a team, and yet it is always the judge (who may instruct the jury; the jury may not instruct him) who calls the shots: in the case of Camp, the Superego instructs the postulant, "Thou shalt revel, thou shalt not parse" or "Utilize, don't analyze."

Thus Camp turns on its own dime, for while art forbids itself always to pose as any kind of ethical utility, Camp, so strenuously proclaimed as entirely under the sway of art, and yet so ready (as was Oscar Wilde) to make of the appetitive and the sumptuous a new and revolutionary ethics, really does not.

THE JUDGMENT SCENE FROM *AIDA*: THE MOST REVERED CAMP SCENE IN ALL OPERA

Baleful effects of: "*Ohime, morrir mi sento. In poter di custoro io stessa l'ho gettai . . . io stessa . . . io stessa. . . .*"

Queer identification with Amneris, the slighted daughter of the King. Total. Royal personage ("*Figlia di Faraoni!*") who cannot command the love of a soldier.

DISTINCTIONS

Ur-Camp, Camp (High and Low) and Meta-Camp.

Ur-Camp

The pyramids, Akhenaton, the Witch of Endor, Pandora, Herod and Herodias (never Salome), Tiberius, Nero and Messalina, Plotinus and Porphyry, Byzantium (especially Theodora)
    The leaning tower of Pisa
    The Borgia Popes, Pico della Mirandola and Savonarola
    Elizabeth I, James I and Louis Quatorze
    Jacobean tragedy (particularly *The Duchess of Malfi*)
    Charles II and Queen Anne (negative polarity)
    The Dutch (centuries before the Wildes came to Ireland)
    Jonathan Edwards and Lord Cornbury, the transvestite governor of New York (quite possibly a cruel hoax, in which case an instance of ur-Camp that becomes one of the earliest manifestations of the thing itself)
    The Rape of the Lock and *Tristram Shandy*
    Mephistopheles, in Goethe's *Faust*
    Die Zauberflöte

High Camp

Parsifal ("Parsifal, darling, engendered *Jugendstil*"—heard on the standing-room line at the Met, c. 1954, waiting to go in and hear Martha Mödl sing Kundry)

Charles Baudelaire (his outré behavior, particularly the incident cited by Walter Benjamin in *The Arcades Project* of his draping a feather boa across the full hat rack at a convocation of *academiciens*, emphatically *not* his sublime poetry)

Apropos the Baudelaire boa, a subheading:

Garb, Accoutrement and Camp

Regarding the use by men of clothing, articles and accessories of a shape or texture normally called feminine:

Whereas neither the tartan-kilted Scotsman (except when he is also wearing Marks and Spencer underwear) or the Yeshiva student who secures his *yarmulke* with a hairpin is by common consent regarded as Camp, the cardinal archbishop of any Roman Catholic diocese in the world, in full Babylonian regalia at Solemn Benediction, undeniably is, especially when taking from the thurifer the smoking thurible to cense his congregation.

(Apocryphal story much in vogue in the later years of Tallulah Bankhead's life: she to Francis Cardinal Spellman as he sweeps past her seat on the aisle in St. Patrick's Cathedral, "Your drag is divine, darling, but your purse is on fire!")

Male heterosexual cross-dressing lies entirely outside the realm of Camp. It celebrates no sort of failure at all but rather a more completely integrated libido than the general run of heterosexual male seems capable of, and this despite such neo-Puritan readings of Shakespeare's *Antony and Cleopatra* which seek to connect the references to the lovers' intimate transvestite practices—which without question, since of course Cleopatra was played by a boy, in all likelihood an aging boy (possibly the same boy who had already created the roles of Titania, Rosalind, Viola, Gertrude, Portia, Desdemona and Lady Macbeth), invoke the ardent bisexuality of Elizabethan and Jacobean England—either to the hubristic triumphalist decadence of the Twilight of an Age or a deeply encoded Doomsday warning against same.

Oscar Wilde's *Salomé*. A Camp abrasion of the pious legend of a Biblical cat's paw. The legend's point is clear in the New Testament telling.

It undeniably did become corrupted in the Middle Ages, a corruption both referenced and revived in that peculiar form of suppressed sexual hysteria characteric of the Church in France in the nineteenth century—which hysteria quickly spread to decadent English Catholicism and beyond, to Ireland and the immigrant American Church. Salome, the daughter of Herodias, was either too young and innnocent beyond ideation or too congenitally amoral to comprehend the details of the *provenence* of what she demanded, merely to please her mother and spite her stepfather, so that sexual-fetish motivation therefore had nothing to do with the case.

Parure (and today's accessorizing *couture* with fake jewels and knock-off power watches purchased from street vendors)

Der Rosenkavalier (tribadism set to musical smelling salts)

Julian Eltinge, Bert Savoy

Holly Woodlawn and Candy Darling

Charles Ludlam, Charles Pierce and Charles Busch

Ethyl Eichelberger

Dame Edna Everage

Lypsinka

Low Camp

Richard Strauss's *Salome*. Absolutely irresistible (to the young and gullible operaphile anyway) gumball trash. Periodically elevated in performance by singers of genius (Ljuba Welitsch, Leonie Rysanek) into the borderline realm of the ersatz sublime.

Elizabeth Taylor as Cleopatra in Joseph L. Mankiewicz's embarrassing fiasco of the same name. ("You barbarian, you burned my library!")

Lana Turner in *The Sea Wolf* strutting up the gangplank of a leaky-looking old tub. Merchant seaman: "Hey, lady, you can't come aboard, this is a tramp steamer." Lana: "Show me to my cabin."

Jackie Curtis and all other *shmatta* drag queens

Milton Berle's drag interludes

Diana Vreeland, arch imposter and pseudo-seer (who saw mainly a lot of Chinese red). "Mrs. Vreeland says all Swedes are walking toward a strange destiny."

Female female impersonation: Edy Williams in Russ Meyer's *Beyond the Valley of the Dolls*, Raquel Welch in Gore Vidal's *Myra Breckenridge*, Carol Burnett as Mildred Fierce and Phyllis Diller as Phyllis Diller

Going to the annual Greenwich Village Halloween parade as Mother Teresa

Meta-Camp

Anti-matter
Caravaggio
Wittgenstein (as a Jewish homosexual with the most meteoric intelligence of his generation, bar none, even Freud, and epsecially vis-à-vis Popper)
Mae West
Jackson Pollock

—◄o►—

History, like Einsteinian time, can seem to flow backward, the present to "influence" the past, a crucial tenet of the most original aesthetic-religious critical thesis propounded in our time, Harold Bloom's Anxiety of Influence. Caravaggio is not Camp but, miraculously, Meta-Camp—putting brush to canvas without underpinning draftsmanship, which is action painting in the seventeenth century, and also, for example, in thematic terms, rendering savage the Camp eccentricities of Firbank's Cardinal Pirelli.

Pure radical modern genius, and post-modern genius, too, although it is too soon yet to determine who is assured of a place in the pantheon. Genius on the order of Mae West and Jackson Pollock can never be Camp, but it must take up Camp in order to further rarefy and thereby render transcendent.

—◄o►—

Incest is the *lingua franca* of libidinal Camp.

All good-bad twin-sister movies are Camp: they are the double helix of homosexual projection, the one strand engaging in voyeurism (which is always screen murder) vis-à-vis lesbianism and the suppressed desire to switch the scenario to the twin brother and the mother. However, whereas D.W. Griffith's great near-twin melodrama *Orphans of the Storm* (1917) and the Bette Davis vehicle *A Stolen Life* (Curtis Bernhardt, 1947) are, inter alia, affectionate Camp, the greatest bar none Camp feature in motion picture history, Robert Siodmak's *Cobra Woman*, starring the short-lived but immortal double-threat Maria Montez ("Maria was a *good* woman!" Mart Crowley's play *The Boys in the Band*, 1968), is the epitome of Something Else.

—◦►—

The peculiar relation between Camp taste and homosexuality has to be explained. While it's not true that Camp taste is homosexual taste, there is no doubt a peculiar affinity and overlap. Not all liberals are Jews, but Jews have shown a particular affinity for liberal and reformist causes. Similarly, not all homosexuals have Camp taste. But homosexuals, by and large, constitute the vanguard—and the most articulate audience—of Camp. (The analogy is not frivolously chosen. Jews and homosexuals are the outstanding creative minorities in contemporary urban culture.)

To this dyad I propose, three decades after the publication of "Notes on 'Camp'" in the *Partisan Review*, a period in which intensive studies have significantly affected Americans' understanding (both liberal and conservative, if not radical and reactionary) of their culture, adding the blacks, urbanized in the same historical period in which the Jews rose to prominence in the liberal arts and the law and American queer culture entered its first period of florescence.

To that end, I would suggest investigation of the detectable presence and operation of that same necessarily negative polarity, or perceived passivity, of Daniel in the lion's den and all "Danielists" throughout history (Daniel means "God is my judge"), of the permission to at once identify and batten upon their trouble characteristic of the blacks, and considered in relation to the homosexuals and the Jews.

THE BLACKS, THE JEWS, HOMOSEXUALS AND CAMP
(We Others among Them)

To begin with, the Jews are not Western. Not in the definitions codified by English classicists in the nineteenth century when the German-French Enlightenment concept of the West, by which at least up until the time when Harold Bloom brought Kabbala to bear on the question, was varnished. They are Eastern. There is nothing in the rational pagan, this-day/this-night world of the Greeks, of the kind of bargain Moses had in mind—and when the Greek ethos met Moses's, in the Jerusalem of Jesus of Nazareth, in Mithraic Rome and in the Alexandria of the Hellenized rabbinate and late Isis/Osiris worship, it went under.

BLACK, BEAUTIFUL AND CAMP: THE "BEULAH" SYNDROME
(As in "She Done Him")

"Beulah, peel me a grape."
  "I'ze a-comin' miz Lou, I'ze a-comin'."
  "Yeah, you'ze a-comin' and yer head is bendin' low."
  "Where *you* been, eight-ball?"
  "Your bath is ready, Miz Lou."
  "Take it y'self, I'm indisposed."
  We believe we know what Mae West is doing with Camp in these sequences, but what is Louise Beavers doing?

Geometrical analogy: The three sides of the Camp triangle. For distinctly spiritual purposes, Camp can be neither the First Configuration, the circle, nor the Second, the square, but only and forever the Third, the triangle ("queer as a three-dollar bill" and the Irish popular slang term referring to the Trinity, the impossible but essential core myth of Western Thought, from the Greeks through Hegel—thesis, antithesis, synthesis—as "the three gay fellas").

The third elementary principle of mathematics—following Euclid's fifth theorem asserting the equality of the angles opposite the commensurate sides of an isosceles triangle and the Pythagorean theorem (immortalized in recitation on the screen by Ray Bolger as the Scarecrow in Victor Fleming's *The Wizard of Oz*, 1939, concerning the square of the hypotenuse)—propounded by Hero of Alexandria in the first century A.D. in order to resolve boundary issues (*so* relevant to our crowded and narcissistic time), states that in any triangle with sides a, b and c, the area enclosed will be the square root of $s(s-a)(s-b)(s-c)$, where $s = (a+b+c)/2$.

Which in the calculation at hand, will, of course, be $1 + 1'$, where 1 represents the Jews and $1'$ homosexuals, taken as the genotype "As Such." (Black Homosexual, as a phenotype, necessarily lies outside the calculation, as indeed the black homosexual—ask him—cannot survive except by assimilation to the genotype.)

For this reason, if for the sake of argument the base of the Camp triangle is the Jews, and the two other sides both impinging on primal Jewish energy (as charted in Kabbala) and directing it to the apex of the triangle are homosexuals and blacks, then . . .

Nor is this analogy (which, speaking categorically, is more than that) intended as a distracting piece of Camp in and of itself. The calculations *work* if trouble is taken with them, and therefore cannot be characterized as the success of any impassioned failure. Unless of course the whole of sociology is itself, as has long been maintained by members of English departments across the country, nothing but one *enormous* Camp.

PART FOUR

Expatriates

CHAPTER SIXTEEN

Author's Letters from London to a Former Schoolmate in New York

(A FARRAGO OF A FOUR-YEAR STAY ABROAD)

"Afterwards, in the dusty little corners where London's secret servants drink together, there was argument about where the Dolphin Case history should really begin."
—John le Carré, *The Honourable Schoolboy*

Wherein having found, yes, true love at the Yale Drama School, the author, for once in his relentlessly scrambled, piecemeal and too undeniably scavenging life, does the sensible thing and spirits the beloved out of the country, landing as it happened (and entirely without foresight) in what became known (almost immediately upon arrival) as Swinging London.

What do you do when there should be new words for happiness? Study etymology, silly boy.

The Beriosova/Nureyev *Giselle*
Ballet SRO queue
Covent Garden
Midsummer's Eve

My Own Dear Heart,

Must tender full and frank apologies, after you took the trouble to try to direct a few bucks this way, for missing by so wide a space the particular brand of vanilla-extract dream-of-Dixie lady-of-Larkspur Lotion pastiche apparently required by the demanding client.

One did consider automatic writing, but discovered oneself too ennervated by the experience of trying to compose Mad Ave ad copy even for trance. Sincere regrets and best wishes for a successful completion of the job. Best love to the boys in the back room, the boys in the band and the girls in Ward 8.

In any event, the visa difficulties are over for the nonce, and we can live here without showing a hefty bank balance, as we have ducked into the London School of Dramatic Art (run by one M. Gertrude Pickersgill, who must have understudied Ellen Terry: patrons Dame Edith Evans and Dame Margaret Rutherford. No men).

Actually, dear, it's down a long hall off Baker Street—I mean *all* of it is, and in the "green room" sits an enormous wicker basket, an exact match for one in the Zeffirelli *Falstaff*, full of props and wooden swords, store-bought hair and funny disguises, and Miss Pickersgill goes in for things like mime and *equipoise*. Yet she is a trouper and a dear, and the arrangement, while not quite résumé-enhancing, does definitely solve the visa problem for a year, unless we decamp, which we almost certainly will do—I mean to say, how much equipoise can a boy be expected to master—and then it's time for another scheme.

We go after class with our fabulous gal pal, an ex-Soho "exotic dancer" currently the mistress of the Iraqi ambassador to the Court of St. James, to the Café Vienna in Sicilian Avenue, a weirdly impressive mock-up of, one gathers, a Palermo thoroughfare, which Vincent says stirs race memories of his seignorial ancestral heritage. To this emporium Virgina Woolf would repair to sit and make notes on the universe—it has come to me that she is the greatest twentieth-century English writer; she puts all the men absolutely in the shade. And it's true, she writes about the universe.

I must remember, whensoever I think "this time next year," there *is no* this time next year.

Gor' ain't s/he gone and become the philosopher. It's Ireland did it, dear. Was strangely moved by Dublin. Not for nothing is the translation of the name into English "Dark Pool." The Liffey has a somber magic that ought to remind one of the Seine, but instead calls up the Harlem as it flows past the mystic coal chutes and scrap iron works anent the Major Deegan Expressway. One can lease an old Guinness barge and, well, barge westward along the Grand Canal to the Shannon at Athlone, and from there all the way to the estuary.

What a kicky barge we could get up, though the drag would have to be strictly Liffey washerwoman out of *Finnegans Wake*. "I must go to Aches-les-Pains."

(Oh, by the way, in case you missed it in Brooklyn, the I.R.A. blew up Nelson's Pillar to celebrate the fiftieth anniversary of the Easter Rising, but we were down in Kenmare, in Kerry. Vincent was reading Marcel Proust, and I was writing a play.)

All in all Ireland was, well, deeply moving. Not only did one come away at long last with an understanding of Bishop Berkeley (and really, kicking stones will get you nowhere against that mind, nowhere but the chiropodist's anyway) but one finally gets the point about Wittgenstein, the fellating St. Francis of the Prater. (He never cared what he ate, so long as it was always the same thing.) It was in Ireland Wittgenstein first grappled seriously, like Jacob with the Angel or Cuchulain with Maev, with Eternity, nailed to the conceptual wall as he was by the radical and absolute and uncompromising profundity of the common Irish phrase *the day that's in it*, and realized that whereas science is, for want of a better word, knowledge, philosophy is pure *lore*. Not to mention his definitive explication of *plus ça change*, which if you look at the landscape you can readily see he was driven to by the bewitching effects of the contemplation of lenticular cloud formation—time and again very like a whale, dear, which brings us back *commodius vicus* by way of *Moby-Dick* to *Billy Budd* in his latest incarnation, the blonded and etherialized Terence Stamp.

One should perhaps come back to NYU and do a paper, but something tells one Sidney Hook is no J. Max Patrick, and would undoubtedly insist on some tiresome process, like *courses* and *credits* and another degree.

Meanwhile one is studying the score of a contemporary opera, *Shit Against the Tyde*. You do recall the Tyde, dear, that fabled stream that flows into the Severn and has its own Sabrina, called Margaret, as in "Margaret, are you grieving?" and Margaret Burke-Sheridan and Margaret Leighton and the Titian-haired Margaret, Duchess of Argyll, the most adroit, dignified, elegant and *penetrating* fellatrix in *Burke's Peerage*, not excepting the unfortu-nate Princess Margaret Rose, whose husband, dear, is so much better at the act in question—I mean they have *contests* at Kensington Palace and he wins every time!

I am thinking of taking on the lead (Margaret) although it is written for a soprano. I said, "An English soprano part is never *that* soprano," and anyway the trouser part they've offered is that of a youngish dramatist who comes down to Tydeside in flight from the metropolis and from, you know, the straightjackets of ignorance, temptation, materialism and worldly distraction.

Comes down to Tydeside to write something earthy and authentic (in other words, darling, shitty), but of course in a fever of attachment to it all goes river bathing naked on Midsummer's Night—and, natch, comes upon Margaret. Actually what he does is he comes all over her, as she is by way of being the guardian river nymph, and, speaking of straightjackets unlaced, he is a mad one for the moonlit riverbank wank. It's all in the music; one of the many *leitmotiven*, don't-cha know, a little reminiscent, in a regulation disso-nant and yet somehow Michael Tippett-ish way of Siegfried, dear, ham-mering away on *Nothung*. Tippett is having a great sucess, by the way, at the Garden with *The Knot Garden*, a sort of *Between the Acts* weekend-house-party opus, all set in a maze (the title role), all about the state of, you know, society, and featuring a singing first, an actual homosexual couple, dear.

Anyway, Marge is no chump, no patsy, no downhearted frail awail in no jail and finally, no Rusalka. She is *furious* over what she, as the local patroness of fecundity and due process, regards, on her watch and in her ward, as this wanton expense of spirit in a wastrel's shame, not to mention the shaggin' mess on the mosses, on account of the fact that, as local *lore* would have it, where spunk is spilled on the spongy earth, there spring up on the very spot or spots your veritable whoreson *legions* of pocky, deformed *toads*, with a consequent pandemic spread of your whoreson heinous *warts* among the general populace, especially, as the general populace to a boy-Jack/girl-Jill is given to indulging in due process on the greensward.

And so, the intruder gets his, dear, all the way downstream to the Severn Gore.

Anyway, I said to them, composer and librettist (boyfriends, dear, just like Sam and Gian Carlo, only from Manchester and very manly, both) much the way the Meneghini instructed the *Vanessa* duo, when she was offered the title role, "Tell you what, fellas, you take that drip and rewrite him as a Joe Orton type, and while you're at it, give him three, no, four boy attendants, called

Agro, Bovver, Bugger and Bum, *all of whom wank together*" (I was thinking of polyphony, wasn't I, or is it fugues, and of that touching little scene in
the boys' school in Wedekind's *Frühlings Erwachen*) "and I'll take on any
English soprano as it were *au bord de la rivière*." They said, "We don't talk
French at Sadler's Wells." England isn't Europe, dear, in case you were
wondering. It is indeed a septic isle, but one's had one's shots and carries on.

Meanwhile, about the mss. one left behind, have they not yet fallen prey
to spontaneous combustion in the broom closet on Joralemon Street and
have not as yet been sent, don't send them, because one never knows about
Paris: one could be held there an hour, a day, a month, a lifetime. Anyway,
I shall work on the shit (if I can ever get off this queue and out of the Globe
and the Nag's Head) whenever we're back from where we're off to.

Amsterdam for a start, on the overnight Harwich–Hook of Holland
boat train, then down to the New Babylon ("*à Saint-Sulpice!*"), then south
to places like Arezzo, to see the della Francesca frescoes, Venice to try to find
Sant' Ariano, the island composed entirely of old skeletons (rather like a
coral reef, *mutatis mutandis*) whose leases run out in the municipal boneyard.
They won't tell you where it is, the ordinary Ventians won't—won't so much
as admit of its existence; we got the wheeze from an old theater hag in a pub
in St. Martin's Lane. Perhaps the Armenian priests on San Lazzaro will,
can one get to them. Must try using Arpenik's name. As a devoted intimate
of such a renowned survivor of the vile Turk's massacre . . . perhaps.

After all, onomastically, they would seem the ones to ask—the Lazerite
Armenian priests, dear, not the vile Turks, who never, consequence of atten-
dance at *plusieurs Così fan tuttes*—by your correspondent, not by any
Mustapha—seemed the least bit authentic, even if it's Istanbul, not
Constantinople.

(In French, of course.)

Then perhaps to Yugoslavia, where Mary Curtis-Verna is singing Tosca
and Aida in some spa, then to Athens to make *obéissances* to Athena
Parthenos, then to the Pythia at Delphi, then to Apollo on Delos, and lastly
to Thessaloníki to burn owls' gizzards at the altar of the Great Mother.
Cards to follow in our wake (unfortunate word).

London life lately disrupted by a spate of impassioned, unruly demon-
strations in front of our embassy in Grosvenor Square (the unfashionable
side). Therefore am glad to split to Split until everybody goes back to
Anaheim, Azuza and Cucamonga. Not that one does not sympathize, one
does, but if more had done what we did—still how could virile America stoop

to draft-board dissembling, pretending faggotry *en masse*? As it is, too many of our benighted sisters went into that man's army altogether willingly, themselves dissembling, and where are they now? Saigon, dear, if they're lucky, and that's *not* a picture with Alan Ladd and Veronica Lake, grab it.

So I guess I've talked myself into putting in an appearance in Mayfair. Grosvenor Square is near Berkeley Square (of the nervous nightingales), and Chase Bank where I cash my checks from home is in same, so rather than high tea at the blue hotel (the Berkeley) followed by a saunter to Penheligon's in Piccadilly for scent, a swerve to the spot where Adlai Stevenson dropped dead, all in the cause of bringing our boys home.

(Are you ready for a remake of *Christmas in Connecticut*, set in East Hampton? Candy Bergen and Steve McQueen?)

I press on, now on this little strophic clackety-clack, now on that mighty line-ed schema, imploring Calliope and riding manic-depressive waves (of no great pith or pitch, thank the Kindly Ones), mind-surfing as it were from roadside attraction to roadside attraction, between the British Museum (the Elgin Marbles plus), the National Gallery, the Victoria and Albert, the Tate, the Queen's Gallery, the Wallace Collection, Syon House, the Brompton Oratory (the Mazzuoli Marbles minus), the West End theaters, the Old Vic, Royal Festival Hall, the Albert Hall, the serious picture cave (you'd never call it a palace, no more than you would MoMA or the Thalia) underneath Waterloo Bridge, Sadler's Wells, the Garden. Putting in appearances, submitting to the influences.

Here's wishing you many gay days sweltering and sunning encamped at Riis Park (96? My God, here it's a dreamy 69), although it really is time, dear, you thought seriously about shipping it all out to Fire Island. I don't know, as things stand now, when I shall ever get back to the Grove, and I really would like to hear how things are in Glocca Whora.

It's really not difficult to get asked out for a weekend, only don't try going about it the way I did all those years ago in high school, even if Eighth Street is right there out the seminar window, so to speak. Much better in this decade (and as an informed graduate student at a major university) to trot up and cruise the china department at Bloomingdale's, looking (and I know this will be difficult for you, but a successful career is, as Stella Adler insists, informed by the embracing of its obstacles) *puzzled*.

He will of course come on to you; like as not he will want to talk about Havilland or Spode. Do *not* try to trump him by saying you prefer Rosenthal. Let him be the kindly light that leads; he'll be ever so grateful. If he leads you—and they all do—over to silver, let him tell you the difference between an English and a French place setting.

Perhaps he will turn out to be be Southern, in which case you must get him to talk about ice cream forks—they're mad keen, dear, the Southerners, to talk about ice cream forks. And sugar hammers. Ice cream forks and sugar hammers, and he's yours. You'll have your ticket, sweetheart, and that's not all, punched through, and like as not it won't be on the Long Island Rail Road, although they do seem to like to pile into that locker-room club car at Hunter's Point early on a Friday evening. It's like Julius's on clacking wheels.

He *may* take you out in a plane, in which case flying so high with some guy in the sky will be your wedge of hot cherry pie. I'm not being snide; if you let him know he's about to get your Cherry Grove cherry, I guarantee quick and happen lasting results. And do be sure, won't you, that you leave with the john you came out (to the *island*, to the *island*) with.

I foresee enormous success; you are possessed—no, darling, not like Joan, although those in the Deep Joan movement call *Possessed* her greatest performance. You are possessed of gorgeous teeth, a singular allure, brains and a first-class bachelor's degree, and, in my opinion, both a viable and a durable routine (besides going for your master's). You won't perhaps close the first half for some seasons yet, but I feel strongly the talent is there, and, let's face it, Riis Park hasn't been at the forefront of the action since *West Side Story* closed and the chorus boys stopped going there on Sunday. As a matter of fact, dear, they're nowadays all out on Fire Island. (Arthur Laurents told somebody, feigning indifference. His whole gang is here, around the corner in Drury Lane, getting *Gypsy* ready for Merman.)

Apart from anything else, and I am thinking of your welfare (as in general well-being, not as in homely caseworkers and the dole queue), if ever indeed I do come home (does anyone ever indeed?), I should like to be welcomed in properly grand-effulgent homo style, and you are, as is well known, stylishness incarnate, but generosity itself—what's called in Dublin *flahulach*—and do love to spread the hospitality. There's no getting away from it, is there, when you're Irish.

Ever So Much Higher Disinterested Love,
Walter Pater
("I'm rotten Walter, rotten
though and through. . . ."
"Bye, baby"
Bang bang)

29 Holland Park Mews, W.11
Late in Michaelmas term

A gra mo croi,

Well, we're back, and there it is, from the sublime to the ridiculous.
(Conversation reported by Freud on the deck of a cross-Channel boat, c. 1910:
"*Du sublime au ridicule il n'ya qu'un pas.*" "*Oui, le Pas de Calais.*") Heard
Rita Gorr at the Opera in *Le Roi d'Ys* and at the Comique a divine French
soprano heretofore unknown to me, Berthe Monmart, as Butterfly in French,
and in a little *cave* in Saint-Germain a rather fabulous *diseuse*, Cora Vaucaire,
who to my mind really is better than Piaf—although I never will forget Piaf
singing "*Non, je ne regrette rien*" and "*La Vie en rose*" to the massed citizenry
of Paris from the platform on the Eiffel Tower while the *feux d'artifice*
exploded in the night sky on the *Quatorze Juillet* just after the cease-fire was
declared in Algeria and the *plastiques* stopped blowing up in marketers'
faces in the Place Maubert.

Saw lots of Molière (plus Montherlant's *Port Royal*) at the Comédie
Française, Jean-Louis Barrault and Madeleine Renaud in *Le Mariage de
Figaro* and *Ah, les beaux jours!* at the Odéon, Zizi Jeanmaire as *la mome
crevette* in Feydeau's *La Dame de Chez Maxim* at the Théâtre du Palais
Royal, Edwige Feuillière in *La Folle de Chaillot* at the Palais Chaillot, and
up in Montmatre a deliberate and perhaps over-reverent *En attendant Godot*,
an evening at the Grand Guignol and Maria Casares in Claudel's *Le Repos
du Septième Jour* (which by then we were ready for ourselves).

Meanwhile, we've already booked for *Cyrano* at the Comédie for New
Year's Eve. And you know what, dear? Married life agrees with me. I like
the contrast of shopping by day in the Portobello market (our Place Maubert),
whipping up Vinny's dinner (and these two words have become a kind of
emblem for me) and then another night trotting down to the Garden or the
Old Vic etc. in the Cardin suit I got for—get this—twenty guineas in the
Strand (which is how the price tags hanging in windows here for anything posh,
glam or ponce-y reckon things, in guineas). They've cut some sort of deal; they
get the patterns from Paris and run them up here in their own English
worsteds. (I can only hope slave labor isn't involved; you know what a cham-
pion of the underdog—and of the mistreated bottom—I can be.)

That said, about marriage, there were hour-of-the-wolf interludes in
Paris, on solitary walks (while Vincent slept the sleep of the just) when I'd
see boys sitting carelessly on the contrascarpe, on the bridges, on benches in
the Place Dauphine, some looking alert and ready to precipitate themselves

upon the business of a "meter's running" game of *cache-cache*, some looking as if they would *evanesce* on call if approached, some looking so high
strung they would blow up in your face the minute they sat on it.

And I'd be tearing the walls off the universe settling in my so-called mind
the terms of my connubial life. *Terms!* Then I'd creep back to the small hotel
and sleep, and wake up and we'd have sex. Repeatedly.

Fortunately, all this lark would typically transpire, as I did say, close to
dawn, by which time the serious criminals are all bedded down with their molls
in the Rue Ste. Anne, for Paris is a city in which one can be very badly
rolled—*very badly*—and the indifference to Americans and loathing of
fags, so characteristic of the *gendarmerie*, is no help—especially if you still
harbor fantasies of Audrey Hepburn enacting *Funny Face* all over the
Quartier Latin, because what these *mecs* are likely to do to one's face just ain't
funny, and that's the name of that tune.

Tried on the crossing to get them to put down a tender so we could go
and have tea with the Dame of Sark and the Greffier, but you know the
modern world, rush, rush, rush (as in poppers and Dexamyl, as in "Hurry
up, please, it's time").

Speaking of which—time—the National Gallery has just bought, from
of all places, the Egyptian embassy here Tiepolo's "Allegory with Venus
and Time" (obviously stuck up on the ceiling there in the reign of some
Khedive) for nearly half a million quid—I've tried to work it out for your
amusement in guineas, but I can't. The *Guardian* wants to know if it's value
for money, and comes to the big-hearted (and distinctly un-Protestant) conclusion that it probably is, as the picture is "a splendid addition to the collection, and, if we don't stare at it too solemnly, to the gaiety of the nation."

What I say is there's as many a solemn thought can spring to mind when
viewing a Tiepolo ("Go ahead, *daahling*, tilt the head way back, have a
dekko") as in respect of anything else, and whatever turns your crank of a
wet November afternoon indoors on Trafalgar Square. For me it's the della
Francesca "Baptism of Christ," but then I always was pious, and took the
name of the other John, the Beloved Disciple, at confirmation.

Darling, did you know that in Ravenna—I know, I know, I have failed
miserably in reporting on the summer's excursion, but I shall, little by little
in the coming months, only mentioning for now that what's left of the Orient
Express is a camp and Belgrade is a real shit hole (in Zagreb, of course,
they've been doing it for years) and that there is this to be said for something I shall never do again, and that's hitchhiking. A delicious fatigue

descends in a pasture where you bed down for the night forty kilometers from Luxembourg after hours and hours of fragments of people's lives behind wheels, and then a day later the *camione* picks you up outside Oberammergau and drops you at bridge beyond Ferrara, under which you sleep again, and then at dawn, after two fab wop cops have checked your passports and wished you *buon viaggio*, this gorgeous Italian male pair who look like they just stepped off the catwalk on the Via Napoleone in Milano let you get into their Lamborghini saloon and take you to all the way to the outskirts of Rome (where Wanda lived in *Le Notte di Cabiria*) while you (that is I) up front with the driver retail the back story in Italian and when you (I) look into the back seat there is he (V.) asleep on the shoulder of perhaps the slightly lesser stunner, who is whispering "*tesoro*" as if to himself, because they are gentlemen and the last thing they would do in the world is come between (pun intended) two innocent young marrieds on their extended *luna di miele*.

Anyway we were hardly back in London a minute before we had to check into the theater school, and then I started taking Greek—see below— and then the Paris season started, and we just had to go over (we were up front about it, declaring ourselves students of comparative theater, and so got "Picky's" twinkly blessing).

Because a great part of the point of this ersatz remittance-man routine (silently reaffirmed each morning in the grave interval between waking and ringing) is that one has, in one's own mind, come, after all, to *Europe*.

Where were we? Oh, yes, Ravenna. In a little bapistry next to San Vitale. The Redeemer waist-deep in the Jordan with cousin Johnny, in mosaic, revealed to have parts. *Parts*, dear, on the *Redeemer*, *l'homme-dieu*, the Lord God, the Second Person of the Blessed Trinity incarnate. I was almost scandalized, but then I thought, well, that's how they saw religion back in the days when Istanbul was Constantinople and Theodora was empress. Gay.

All fall, as if to let us know they can do it here as well as the French, what action in the London theater! *Penetrating*, dear. Athene Seyler and Sybil Thorndike (at eighty-eight) in *Arsenic and Old Lace*. Paul Scofield in *Dance of Death*. Horrifyingly real, particularly when he takes the stroke and she (Mai Zetterling, remember her?) stands over him hissing "Die! Die!" and before doing just that he gets up enough adrenaline and gall to spit in her face. Very nervous-making, and yet how very different from Method acting. It's the voices do it—apart from Page and Stanley, and maybe Julie Harris and of course what remains of Lynn Fontanne (but she will never play in New York again, I fear) and of course Le Gallienne (who will play as long as Thorndike has, at least), there aren't any the like of them at home. Certainly (apart from Alfred Lunt, who had long since disappeared entirely from the Everard in the afternoon even before one darkened its frosted glass doors) not from the men, who, let's face it, rely more on *smell* (and don't we love them for it).

Meanwhile, guess what's happening a block away from here? Antonioni is shooting his first English-language picture. Vanessa Redgrave is in it. (About as much chance of wedging in as an extra as of singing *Shit Against the Tyde* at Sadler's Wells, yet one can dream. I mean Steve Cochran was in an Antonioni picture, right?)

And then, to top it all off (although even to write down such a phrase, as if one were talking about a fudge sundae, is damning: the experience will be remembered until death, whereas whatever else happened in those days, on or off the stage, will be obliterated), I ran into (literally, coming out of Boots the Chemist in Picadilly as I was going in), I swear to the living God in all Three Persons, Samuel Beckett! I excused myself, drew back, really did go a little funny and then said something short. He couldn't have been more genuinely kind and polite. I mentioned Marie Kean, from Dublin, probably the gretest exponent of *Happy Days* in English (in which I really do think it belongs, *pace* Madeleine Renaud, and of course I didn't share this opinion with the author) and the Grove publisher Barney Rosset, whom I met once in East Hampton, and then I let him go. As the wife in *The Dead* says of the boy she loved in Galway who died of consumpton, "Such eyes he had." Blue-blue, dear, and he almost gave me a smile. I backed away. Beckett was (as I'd already realized from friends at the BBC) over from Paris to supervise the taping of his first-ever play for television, a solo turn for Jack McGowran, whom we saw last year in Dublin as Joxer Daly in *Juno and the Paycock* at the Gaiety, along with Peter O'Toole and Siobhan McKenna and Marie Kean. They raised the money to save the theater from the wrecker's ball when we lived across the street in Mrs. O'Shea's theatrical rooming house with the diva Margarita Rinaldi in the top floor back (*en suite*), who was rehearsing her Violetta to go into the Gaiety as soon as *Juno* came off. Micheál Mac Liammóir (after taking his lengthy ease, was the wheeze at the Gentlemen's Convenience in nearby St. Stephen's Green) would drop in for tea and sandwiches nearly every afternoon since he'd fasten himself on any diva who stopped in Dublin.

And now even as I write I tremble. I mean stars are stars, but this was better than running into Molière (and too many cuts to count above the ghastly Edward Albee with whom he—Beckett, not Molière—once shared a double bill at the Cherry Lane. *Happy Days* in fact, running with, I give you, *Zoo Story*.)

A far cry I declare (the encounter in front of Boots) from the days of lurking in dark corners at the San Remo hoping for a glimpse of Kerouac. Although one wasn't completely mad. He was, as they say here, dishy— even when, or perhaps especially when, staring into the middle distance, shitfaced, holding up a wall—and he could write a style, more so than any of the others, and after all, one did get a rather divine camp name out of it, courtesy of the cunning Madge, one one (which makes two, as in the *dioscouri*, as in Patricia and Katie Bosworth in *A Stolen Life*) does hope to do something else with than sign letters.

Although I do feel letter writing is an art, one that threshes out the kinds of problems (as say, between the first- and third-person personal pronoun in serious writing), too many—most—writers publishing today just leave in as part of their m.f. *process*, as though the great abstract-expressionist revolution that Pollock, Krasner, de Kooning, Still, Newman, Kline, Rothko, Guston, et al. worked on painting really could be tranferred directly to writing. It can't. Even Kerouac, as is now well known, at least to those of us who have been to any of Herbert Weinstock's soirees have ascertained from cunning remarks made by Robert Giroux, who edited *On the Road*, didn't "spontaneously" just sit down but got stoned and shitfaced and then transcribed what had been edited onto that printer's roll.

I mean, as my Aunt Florrie's pal Mary Murray once said, after walking out of curiosity into an Episcopal Church and taking a look around. "Who's kiddin' who?"

Plus which, have you ever seen a picture of the young Beckett, at Trinity, for instance? Ay-yi-yi-yi-ay-yi-yi!

Speaking of smell (other than of sweet success or the odor of sanctity, both available, let's face it, by the spritz, free, at the perfume counter in any decent department store here as elsewhere in the modern Western World— or, as they are now saying in Paris, the line of demarcation being early 1964, some months after the Kennedy assassination, the *post-modern* one) a young, sweet-tempered and terribly fresh-from-the-bath-smelling Scottish blond (boy) called Brown (all the silly Soho queens ask, "And *do* you?"), well met through friends at the *Miss Julie* opening (Maggie Smith and Albert Finney), voiced interest in any American writing a play, and as he is currently busy being one back of the beast with the director of the Chichester Festival, he was all jiggly in the nicest way.

Which brings me to something that really is, I suppose, a proper sundae (or more exactly *frappe*) topper, much with sprinkles and maraschino cherry (no stem), but I must swear you to absolute secrecy—or as they say in Ireland, "Now this is to die with you, because, you see, it was to die with *me*."

Last night our benefactors, the beauteous Ralph and Joanna, on a break from repertory in Colchester, when we attempted to pay them back part of what we owe them, refused, commanded me to continue writing. Well, the farce is good, and they would be good in it, although I get the idea they would rather be in Pinter or Joe Orton, and one has got to admit, darling, one is simply no Pinter or Joe Orton . . . yet. I suppose one isn't even a Harry Koutoukis, although you can tell him from me, apropos *Only a Duchess Can Dance When She's Loaded*, that there's many an as-yet-untitled broad can do the same, and has, and, barring jail, will continue doing so.

They offered (Ralph and Jo-Jo) to give us a thousand pounds for next year. I was flabbergasted. One imagines—or, more properly, fantasizes—receiving this kind of offer from an older gentleman but to receive it from two heterosexual beauties, each uncommonly talented as well as rich . . . well, I suppose one could be thoroughly *American* about it and say that since the fortune originally came from Maxine Elliot. . . .

Curious thing about Maxine Elliot. The theater she built and named for herself—not the Maxine Elliot Theater but *Maxine Elliot's Theater*— was situated opposite the Metropolitan they've now torn down as well. It's where Jeanne Eagels opened in *Rain*, and many years ago at a Sunday brunch in I can't remember what East Side warthog's *ungepotchke* flat, a venerable old queen told me all about it, how J.P. Morgan, her lover and financial adviser, tutored Maxine in finance, enabling her to weather the crash of '29 (that wiped out my father, dear, and put paid to my mother's dreams of security and happiness). And now this offer. Well, now I want to write a play about Maxine Elliot.

(I sure do have some predilection for divas and strong theatrical women; I wonder will anything ever come of it other than paying money to see and hear them emote?)

One viable scheme may be that English-language theater in Rome off the Piazza Navona, run by some old Brit bat with an Italian name and a lunatic fairy son. Maggie Wagner says she can work her wiles on them both if there's a part for her, and of course I said there was (or soon will be).

You remember I told you about Maggie, who pronounces her surname, as they will do here, *auf Deutsch*. She's our medium in the séances we've been conducting in the sitting room ever since Vincent came up the stairs one nasty, cold wet afternoon and looked into the hallway mirror right into the wild eyes of the ghost of Jean Forbes-Robertson, yes, Jo-Jo's mother, wearing the dove-gray muslin dress the theater hag from St. Martin's Lane—I've taken to calling him Mr. Satterthwaite after that old queen in Agatha Christie who gets in everywhere—informs us she wore as Hedda Gabler in the West End sometime in the late '40s.

Moreover the lock was broken and the hasp thrown up on Jean's old theater trunk (a thing that has disappeared from the player's *équipage* in our time), and it absolutely was locked up tight as a Sacred Heart Madame's snatch, because Joanna pointed it out the day we moved in.

Jean Forbes-Robertson was Maxine Elliot's niece, dear, and they say one of the two most riveting ingenues in the English theater, the other being somebody called Meggie Albanesi, poor girl, killed in a car crash, but it seems she (Jean) drank. I must say it's getting so I want to scrap the farce and do a play about her, a rather more serious *Blithe Spirit*—in which case *die Wagner* can be the r.m.s. Madame Arcati.

V. de los Angeles, Bette Blackhead and D. F.-Dieskau are set to team up for Gerald Moore's farewell at the Festival Hall. The promoters are calling it the end of an era. How dare they! An *accompanist?* All right, *the* one, but come on, Nigel. I mean Bette may be ready to check in the slits behind her ears where those *unheimliche* head tones originate, and go home, and that's fine with yours truly, because although none of them are getting any more *jugendlich*, Victoria is still able to create the impression of gathering fresh blooms, whereas Bette's cool detachment seems to me increasingly intended to mask the inner exertions of a late and desperate harvest. I mean all in all I prefer her *doppelgänger* Miss Dietrich. (No, dear, not D. F.-D., although it *is* generally assumed . . . I mean, of course, Marlene.)

In any case, Victoria is not even fifty, and hasn't yet sung Carmen in the theater. Not to mention recitals. I mean this Janet Baker girl at the Wigmore Hall is honest, forthright, touching and deeply committed, no doubt (even if she tends to *meow* in French songs, and read from a score, if you please), but who is there on the horizon? I love Crespin, and Elly Ameling is nice, if you like to spend a whole night out at a master class, but I want Victoria to go on as long as Celestina Buoninsegna, Fritzi Scheff and Schumann-Heink (although not of course combined).

Yes, I'm taking Classical Greek, once a week, evenings at Morley College, acoss the river in Southwark. Virginia Woolf once gave lectures there to working men. I find it, Classical Greek, rinses the mind, although how *qualia* can really be represented as so concrete, so *there* in a language, rather than, you know, here in the head, which of course is the conflict, because this language is also the language of Plato. . . . Yet the very idea that the mind can be *implied* rather than *inferred*, and by extension *implicated in* rather than *extricated from* the press of the phenomenal world . . . Well, Virginia Woolf wrote *The Waves* on that very theme, didn't she. Didn't she?

Be on the lookout for the notice in your mailbox charging you to saunter over to the P.O. for *Long Lay the World*, a little *Mawrdew Czgowchwz* Christmas miracle play. A taped reading would be nice, could you bring such a thing off, S. Perelman—our own Pearl Mann—being a working sound engineer and all. I couldn't find a way to put Victoria in it with Mawrdew— and in any case Victoria is, by virtue of the *Canto a Sevilla*, more of a Holy Week diva—but I have managed to work Mary Curtis-Verna in.

As ever,

Kit Marlowe

CHAPTER SEVENTEEN

Ashes to Ashes, Dust to Dust, but Not Yet

Wherein spring, and all it signifies in English poetry, is sprung.

92 Elgin Crescent, W. 11
Lenten term

Fedelissima sentinella,

Along with Zephyrus, if in a style something gustier, Martha Graham has just blown into town. She's at the Sayville, on *upper* Shaftesbury Avenue, just north of Cambridge Circus. You will perhaps recall my telling you of the Oscar Wilde/Robbie Ross memorial tea room, "Hades in Cambridge Circus," and the dressy frolics in it. They should put up a sign like the way the Windmill Theatre in Soho did after the war, "We Never Closed."

Whatever of that, Martha, opening with her *Phaedra*, put out the word that the Faithful are to consider themselves artists, slip in through the stage door and find seats in the stalls (not hard; the gods are packed out, but in the parterre you could shoot game). Our having taken those dance classes at Yale with Pearl Lang enlists us in the Faithful. Remember Martha herself taught dance movement to Bette Davis at the John Murray Anderson School in '20s Gotham. We are following in the footsteps, as it were. Question: can that *walk* of Bette's be adapted for male use—which brings us to another question: what *is* the use, the male one? The use, the custom, any of it. This I believe is called the Identity Crisis, and can go on for some years. Gay.

So there I am alone at the opening, because Vincent is tending bar these nights at Tiffany's—a dive, darling, that was once the late Victorian palace of entertainment called the Trocadero—London's Tony Pastor's, apparently, in which the then Prince of Wales what was to become Edward VII (and ain't education grand: at last a reason for one's awareness of modern European history), in the manner of Belasco in that gorgeous theater of his on 43rd Street, kept an upstairs suite of rooms—into which, needless to remark, neither the Princess Alexandra or Mrs. Keppel was ever invited—and entertained, so the Soho apocrypha do record, both young girls and young boys. Seems he liked to watch them have at it (imagine, a royal I-can-see-you wanker) and sort of *participate* now and again in the classical manner of regal debauchery, like Tiberius and the *spintriae* in the pools on Capri, like Prinny at his pavilion in Brighton.

So there one is, alone in the stalls with the curtain about to go up on *Phaedra*, when down the center aisle strolls Vivien Leigh on the arm of John Gielgud.

Story: they were onstage together once in *Caesar and Cleopatra*, and he had to exclaim "Ah, tiger cat, you make me tremble with lust!" and there was so much shrieking from the Polari-slang pansies in the gods—although not as much as on the opening night of Ivor Novello's *Perchance to Dream* (dubbed in the 'Dilly, *A Chance to Scream*), when Ivor himself (Miss Brown) in the male lead (it was a Ruritanian romance) stopped a young thing and bold-as-brass importuned, "Wilt step into yonder cottage with me?"—the management was forced to post *matrons*, same as they had to do for us, dear, at the Polk movie in Jackson Heights for the cowboys-and-Indians, Buck Rogers and Three Stooges matinees.

One is unquestionably aslant by now, dividing one's attention between Martha and Bertram Ross facing the audience and the backs of the heads of the pair sitting just across the gangway with their backs to one. One is fairly agog, although one tells oneself after all these are not the Lunts.

All goes well enough until the close of the first interval. The bells have rung, *he* has returned to his seat, but *she* has not. The lights go down, the curtain goes up on Act Two. All is focused anticipation of half an hour of mounting frenzy.

Seconds pass as Martha carries on doing her nut, and then in a sudden shaft of light from the left *she* appears, tottering, pissed as a newt; one wonders will she make it to the seat. She twigs her surroundings, and gets it that nobody is paying her the least mind. The shaft of light disappears; she seems to *draw* the light from the stage. She takes another look around, sees an empty seat—next one's own on the side aisle. (One likes to look at dance askance.)

She sits down, leans over, stage whispers, "I couldn't get into the loo . . . and then I couldn't get *out!*" One smiles and nods, conspiratorially, meanwhile directing her attention to Martha, who by now is hovering barely an inch away from Bertram-Hippolytus's naked-but-for-G-string torso (a column of ivory) contraction-release *masturbating.* She (the great beauty of the age in England, still) becomes riveted on *Phaedra.* On the story . . . on the message. She gets it that Martha is, well, seventy-plus. She sobers up in about eleven seconds. Astounding. She is all there. She could walk up on that stage and play both Cleopatras, back to back or simultaneously, you just know it.

The lights come up. She turns to one. "Thank you," she says, flashing that smile again, "you're very kind," and I swear on my mother the next thing that comes out of the mouth, with no thought at all is "Miss Leigh, you may always depend on the kindness of strangers."

Instantly she is as if cued in. The smile slowly and relentlessly metamorphoses into that vortex-of-ironic-calamities expression that annihilated us in *Streetcar.* She seems instantly elsewhere. One longs to hear her exclaim "Oh, oh, sometimes there's God, so quickly!" She remains silent; she drifts away to meet a man who looks like John Gielgud but is in fact her cavalier, Shep Huntley, come to carry her off to the Moon Lake Casino.

Is life a scream?

Devotedly,
Frieda Bruce Lockhart

146 Kensington Park Road, W. 11
Trinity term

O, Pythia,

. . . where it says in *To the Lighthouse,* "Time passes."

Four years have elapsed (and how many letters sent back and forth) as if in a dream (corny as that sounds), and now the party's over, so it is.

> "It's time to wind up the masquerade
> Make your mind up; the piper must be paid."

Turns out the piper all along was a London cabbie, darling. "To go to Covent Garden in a hackney coach!" One did, carrying on there like a

hooligan besides, and even got arrested (due to a direct dose-response relation), happily not for streetwalking, but how very embarrassing all the same—
and spent a long, dark night in the Bow Street tombs, along with the rest of
the Irish hooligans hauled in. Not amusing.

And so we're gleefully packing up to sail home from Southampton, on
the *France*.

Interim Report to the Committee on Lavender Intelligence:

Vivien Leigh committed suicide in her flat in the Albany barely six weeks
later, the cause of death officially registered as tuberculosis. Astonishingly,
Laurence Olivier was permitted by authorities to spend a private hour paying
respects to his former spouse, the great English beauty of the age (still),
during which time (there was just enough) it was presumed by everybody of
a certain age in the English theater he was able to burn all the diaries whose
publication might have (even then) ruined him by exposing the parallel lives,
homosexual and heterosexual, he'd led, beginning with his capitulation to the
businesslike, unfussy, sure-footed Noël Coward (for whom onstage pedal
sex was said to have been as deft and amusing a trick as any phrase he ever
turned), which gave his protégé the initial leverage (apparently as great in
backstage parliamentary politics as in onstage exploits) he had never sur-
rendered over a four-decade career.

As deaths go—well here, it's like Toscanini's in New York, a decade
ago; they're calling it the end of an era.

Joe Orton beaten to death by his long-suffering and sickeningly untal-
ented mate Brian Halloway, who then took an overdose and went the way
of all flesh; no definitions.

The first men walked on the Moon.

One read (first time each) *The Years* and *Between the Acts*.

Jack Kerouac expired in his triumphant mother's (talk about Obstacles)
embrace.

The seasons went on revolving, delighted with themselves.

And we are packing to come home, because of a telegram.

MAWRDEW CZGOWCHWZ DAZZLING STOP LETTER FOLLOWS STOP
SOLOTAROFF NEW AMERICAN REVIEW

I keep dreaming over and over again, night after night, that it really did
happen, only to wake up every morning and realize: it *really did happen*, and
the only real question is, did goodness have anything at *all* to do with it? (I
mean as opposed to talent and hot luck, which presumably one must have.)

Partly out of contrition, I suppose, or the fear of being damned to hell for appearing to try (never *mind* actually trying) to establish one's early reputation by trashing a forebear, whom one actually in his heart fell for, like a ton of the bricks my grandfather hod-carried in 1890 on the construction site of Carnegie Hall, I'm sending ahead this (unpublished and, I'd like to vow, to remain so, but I can't, for you see somebody might want to buy it, and I like pretty things) obituary of the man who (all unawares) tormented me into the Life. Redaction of a verbal performance—but you know what Madge says, "You know Mawrdew, you're not going to have an easy time getting people to read you. If they could *hear you talk* extempore—but even then. . . . It's just hard to believe anybody has the total recall motor mouth you have."

They (the audience) were nonplussed when I told them I'd never fancied Kerouac. Could they have twigged to it: me lying in my teeth, for motives I wish I didn't understand? In any case they heard me out, which was the point. Lie all you want if they'll listen, and as for wondering what they would have done had you told the truth and broken down weeping, like you did when you first heard—skip it.

I was of course shitfaced, but awfully fluent, perked up, I must say, by inhalations of opiated hashish—more emancipating than Dexamyl.

"You don't like Kerouac?"

"Bent over and whimpering, I'd doubtless have liked him a lot. Enjoyed listening to *The Lone Ranger* with him and telling him how *Kimo-sabe* means "cocksucker" in Navajo. 'Living to the blank tranced end of all innumerable riotous angelic particulars that had been lurking in our souls all our lives.'"

"Is he a queer?"

"He is notorious; his beautiful man's body matched only by his simple child's mind."

"But is he queer?"

"Jack is, as all who know him insist, a saint, with kindness in his eyes, warmth in his laughter and a delicate benevolent mischief in his parish-priestly smile. But even so, it is still frightfully disintegrating—because, after all, what does the queer boy have to offer the straight boy? Consolation once in a while, or if he gets lucky, the consolation prize.

"And as for girls, well on the one hand, with his lay-your-head-on-my-big-broad shoulders and his dark, wavy hair any living, breathing woman must long to muss, he wanted to make it up to them for all they'd missed—not having penises, essentially, and the consequent progressive castration melancholia and compulsive feeding frenzies—and on the other it's terribly hard work adapting oneself to deflecting a woman's tenacity, and he was terrified of the implications of it all, especially if he confessed to certain secret incorrigible predilections, such as reading fashion magazines, cooking and singing.

"The girls, without actually putting out, gave of themselves in physical contact, but it was contact that for Jack belonged elsewhere—not as it were in the back seat in long sits with them, and who knows who looking into the rearview mirror, but up in the front seat, with the gear shift and Neal. Talk about a conflict between needing and being horrified!

"He'd spent a lot of time trying to get reasonably honest with himself, but being into words, he realized those two were ones you can really stretch, and consequently he spent a lot of lonely wet afternoons—as much *pour encourager les autres* as on his own behalf, because that's the kind of guy he was—trying to stretch them—deftly employing the criterion of embarrassment, a modified version of the criterion of dissimilarity. No go; all that happened—laceration intensified beyond stretch in desperate failed attempts at the self-abuse equivalent of the quadruple lutz—was the doorknob fell off.

"Thus he came to know his need, if not it him. The imperative is not a tense but a mood, and as for the girls, well, they were, all told, a post-war race of voracious filter feeders beset by distinct leanings toward ludicrous men, and what they asked for, preparing tasteful welcomes and getting him to talk about himself—the hooks and ladders game—and thought to get was sacramental bread risen in a warm place, a crusty French baguette. But what they got when reaching was only stones, round, hard and clammy, along with the unsettling behest to throw away their diaphragms and go to confession. Because in men like him, given to states of narcissistic ecstasy, object gender is finally irrelevant, because the sexual excitation—jumpin' in the sugarbowl, with boys, with girls—is identical to the sexual gratification.

"For Jack too, like William James—who was after all whacking for two, as nobody'd ever taught Henry how—was a compulsive wanker—*quod turget urget* on the old paddle ball—but so ego-bifurcated that half his libido had early snapped off, leaving him very little fire down below and, due to displacement upward through a deviated septum of the snapped off half, with a ferocious case of post-nasal drip.

"And so it went until, having become in his own mind a great writer with biceps to match and a major force—*Kunstmachen in dem Kabaret*—in the

Warhol factory, in *Couch*—but in reality a disused toilet bowl. A whimpering, shambolic eyesore, with nobody shelling out, nobody looking or listening as they once had; none of those women-or-men-either who in his sweet-and-willing-patient-with-everybody-beseeching-at-the-portals-of-the-soft-source days used to give him whiskey and money and suppers, while he gave them his energy, his love and his invention. *Voilà où menent les mauvais chemins.* The sun was lost, and the earth, and no man's wit could well direct him where to look for either both or anything.

"John Donne. And so, finding himself a dog-eared old card with nothing but rotten beans in the bottom of his trick bag and nobody buying, recipient no longer of either the kindness of strangers or the charity of passersby, he went back home one broken-down bodhisattva and, surrendering a career in pride, covetousness, lust, anger, et cetera, kicked down the food door, ate himself senseless, crawled onto the couch and collapsed, his chief diversion thereafter his own little glass bead game, imaginary baseball, played with marbles, toothpicks and an eraser, the rules of which were carefully inscribed on little white 5x8 cards—he should waste his time writing something like *Lolita* or *Pale Fire?*

"*Il voulait faire avouer à sa mere que tel qu'il était valait encore mieux qu'un autre.* He thought she might pass it on. Also he found her demands both modest and specific—with the girls they'd been the exact reverse.

"Neal used to boast they knew time. Maybe, but what they didn't know was there is a short-period ripple on the long-period graph of varying lunar declination against time. If only they'd read psychoanalytic literature like everybody else in the '50s, they'd've known what Spielrein told the Congress of Vienna in 1920: psychoanalytic investigation has taught us that the concept of time—and particularly of the nonce—in children is not *a priori*.

"One thing about psychoanalysis the boys did get was that the life they celebrated was ruled by unconscious mechanisms, to two of which, condescension and misplacement, they were particularly dedicated. Also Neal the speed freak, who scarcely regarded the garb of logic as a necessary decency, postulated that any two things dug at the same time were identical, if only *a posteriori*, whereas splash-head Jack knew that even as a result of the most rapturous enthusiasm they were at best analogous—*mi casa su casa*, but I am Who I Am. And also that the very question, is this or that quieting or disturbing? is wrongly put: that reality is the sum of wishes whose objective fulfillment or non-fulfillment is beside the point. That we all must eat, even those who can't cook.

"But poor Neal's instinctual defusion led to such rage against himself that its components could never in this world be erotically bound, and so neither psychoanalysis nor reliance on a transitional object or a blow job given by a saint could bring him safely out of the middle passage to the garage for an overhaul. And Jack twigged the pathos of triumph and trophy big time—not to mention the success of certain impassioned failures. Moreover, that the inconsistency of liberal education, undecided as to which instinctual claims, which exuberant virile flourishes of The Wand of Youth to allow and which to suppress—positioned halfway between the exertions of coupling muscle and the modulated promptings of the Inner Light—results in initial license, then sudden, unexpected and thus all the more cruel license revocation.

"But back to Jack. In later years, home through the day with ma-mère, the saint would be visited on a straight exhibition policy by the hipster high school sophomores from Fort Salonga.

"And old cronies who, while privately referring to him as a dumb tool talking to his right hand, would, refreshed by ma-mère's lemonade, commiserate with him over lost Eden, holding that hand. 'We understand completely. Your great fortitude in this tyrannical age of mercenaries and gladiators. Your dazzling existential courage in a world overstocked with the wicked.' They assured him that, in place of the beat girls he'd gotten down and dirt-real with, the world was now inhabited by a plethora of brash females, rivet heaters and passers-on, the *cliterati* and, on the flip side, mousy eunuchs for the Lord's sake: linked lobbies surging through the academies using their twats and cavernous assholes as inkwells and writing with sharpened claws poetry and novels teeming with instances of the fused participle, and noising such terms as contestation, essentialization and the originary moment.

"But in vain did they make their report, for he could never grasp the idea. In fact he never grasped anything more, not even what was no longer *res extensa*, and thus left with the consolation of the existence of the self as pure duration free from all lenticular elongation, he curled up into the fetal position and waited . . . for supper . . . for the late show . . . for the sight of God.

"And so, done with grooving on the nonce, he expired in *Stabat Mater*'s waiting arms and was laid out, not in the appropriate lavender but in red plaid. Groovy."

They applauded. (May God and His Blessed Mother forgive me, darling—at Max's.)

And lastly (to be sent under separate cover, as if to an agent, so if you meet one downtown, tell him I can do a series of these), I put to you, culled from the evidence of his own eyes and ears and from those of other live witnesses, and of course "worked up" but, I swear to you, not in any respect—barring jarring repetitions, which do not read, or play, as successfully as the reprises in the plays of the divine Tennessee—a rather ambitious little documentary, in hypermetric verse. The material seemed to warrant it, although so far as British play agents and producers are concerned, there is, as my father likes to say, not the call for it that there was. Fuck 'em.

Drawn from your correspondent's encounter in and around Soho and the 'Dilly with one who aspires to be the English Candy Darling. (Not that the poor thing's ever heard of Andy, Candy, Holly or Jackie, but she does seem to know who Judy is.)

I went along with (remember?) Mr. Satterthwaite, who (natch) knew the exact Soho location of the back-alley-drag-queen-bee-hive pub. He'd been advised by somebody or other on Wardour Street to "take your American would-be writer friend to check out one Vilja de Tanguay—her many enemies call her variously *Vile-jar de Tanqueray* and Virago de Takeaway. She's Ealing comedy meets Joe Losey meets Joe Orton meets Hammer horror, and both bearer and star subject of a truly cautionary tale."

Maybe, but to me she so resembles Miss Charity in the savvy lip and surprising-erudition departments, that one wonders both *could she be?* And *might she make it?*

Your correspondent's encounter with the subject (no taping; s/he wouldn't hear of it, not even for ready money) together with a certain amount of expert opinion mopped from an interview registered in the press done with La Tanguay ("My parents met on tour, darling, with Anna Neagle in *The Merry Widow*").

Expert opinion in the Sunday *Observer*, chiefly, it looks to me, from the contemporary equivalents of the sort of Harley Street Sanhedrin professionals who advised Virginia Woolf to "practice equanimity," a type modified and decidedly dressed down over the years by the rigors of consensus diagnostic *re* societal ills and personal maladjustments effected by post-war traumatic stress in the British Welfare State.

A cautionary tale of a deeply troubled (fe)male, and h(is)er adventures in a society in which the frank foregone conclusion is tht s/he, as a rebarbative pathological transvestite narcissist (if not sociopathic autist), s/he is and ever has been from the foundation of h(is)er world (on tour with Anna

Neagle in *The Merry Widow*) must inevitably, and sooner likelier than
later, peg it (i.e., *desist*—one more racket in the metropolis ceased), either
slitting h(is)er fat and rather unbecoming wrists as wide open as your pork
butcher slices filets to pound down into schnitzels, or swallowing a entire
bottle of Mandrax washed down with a full quart of warm gin, or both
together, well before the investiture of that paragon-and-end-product-of-
centuries-of-English-breeding-and-cultivation, young royal Charles as Prince
of Wales—this—the Prince of Wales—coincidentally a pub in the better part
of the West End that doesn't normally welcome Vilja or Vilja's kind but,
if she is telling the truth—and there's the rub, but if you rub it the wrong
way, darling, it spits at you—Vilja has lately managed to crash on the arm
of, I give you, a Conservative Member of Parliament from a safe seat somewhere in the Home Counties.

One sees this all as the dire outcome of Logical Positivism, and renews
one's solemn vows to the apostate and great-souled Wittgenstein. *So wie*,
employing *in tandem* the techniques of both the *Tractatus* and the
Investigations and casting the matter, by way of a left-handed compliment to
T.S. Eliot (who may have written books for Eartha, but, as the song goes,
not for me), to once more write the hypermetric mighty-dose-of-salts (as in
Nightwood) line to which you have become accustomed since even before
our sojourn in this the Muthafuckaland. Seemed called for.

—◄○►—

Interesting detail: she worked from notes, which she would check often, slip-
ping on each time an enormous pair of glasses with upswept diamante
frames—suggesting a kind of insouciance, no? I thought it did. To me it
said, "Look, we all know how these things are done," and also disarmed
the interviewer taking notes, as if the two of us were spelling one another
working up an audition scene rather than the subject pretending spontane-
ity, which would tend to make the interviewer feel he was watching and hearing just another variation of her drag pub act.

Perhaps after all she'll decide with Miss Parker that she might as well live.
I hope she does; I liked her. Obsessed, zonked, a ward casualty of the Welfare
State, you couldn't call her nimble or swank, but I liked her.

Also a couple of notes:

Diana Dors is widely believed over here to have indeed murdered some
thug, rather in the same way Lana is widely believed to have—shot? knifed?

Can't remember. Well it was eleven years ago, in another era: women were still wearing *gloves*—Johnny Stompanato.

Vilja mentions the importance of the Krays. Not that race from *Forbidden Planet*, although being with La Tanguay . . . well, actually it was more like *This Island Earth*. Well-named, they are the twin brother lords of the British Underworld, and one's a *fag*, darling, right up front. Naturally one wonders do they ever do a turn at keeping it in the family, but one's been advised that to venture that question out loud is, well, let's say worse than asking around NYCB who besides Danilova and Lincoln Kirstein knows the true story of Balanchine's Russian *amour fatal*. It is to court certain maiming and in all likelihood death, and that in Swinging London, where it's all just bloody *marvelous*, luv, and whatever cranks your Austin Mini.

In perpetuity,
Norma Desmond

CHAPTER EIGHTEEN

Vilja de Tanguay Exults

> "Style, neurologically speaking, is the deepest part of one's being, and may be preserved, almost to the last, in a dementia."
> —Oliver Sacks

> "Funny business, a woman's career."
> —Margo Channing, in *All About Eve*

Vilja de Tanguay, male actress, is discovered seated in the worn, faded plush red velvet settee of a Soho lounge bar that has seen better days and classier ways, nursing a warm gin and It and smoking a Balkan Sobranie stuck in a long ebony cigarette holder.

The Time is younger than Never, but older much than Now.

I

I can't *imagine* why I've agreed to talk
To you, darling—you aren't *anybody*
At all, are you, although you certainly do
Come highly recommended. Nevertheless,
You realize, no queen can absolutely
Trust her own henchmen; Elizabeth the First
Both hated and feared the Star Chamber. It must
Be this thing I have for yanks. My mum had too,
A thing for yanks, and for the matter of that
So did my poor bent dad, and a *big* thing too,
One that must have given no end of relief
To yanks and tommies, paddys, taffys and jocks

All alike in the war. They did have that much—
Mum and dad, in common, that and the music.
And little me, darling that I was although,
And I really oughtn't go tellng all this
To a stranger . . . though all told, considering
That bleedin' *exposé* in the *Observer*—
Well, Miss de Tanguay was *observed* right enough,
And thorough too, to a thanks-for-the-mem'ry,
Right down to the bleedin' *suicide*. That were
A mistake on my part, luv, to give the snouts
A sneak of the ending. Now she's got to *work*,
Buckle on them Bristol Cities, hump herself
Into that flouncy *cerise* and bust her arse,
Yes, to keep the *omi bonas* on the rut.
Yes. Well, the snouts must work like the rest of us,
And you must expect it, luv, you must expect
The Great British Press to give you stick if you're
Anomalous in any way, anything
But stock-issue Army-Navy merchandise,
Or of course Danny La Rue, who's not only
A great star but a perfect gentleman. Yes,
Danny La Rue set the bar for an entire
Generation of *artistes*. And I always
Was *sensitive*, from a child, what if the shrinks
Always would go on as to how my wants were
Far too simple and my loathings too tangled
And complex. Oh, and by the by, regarding
The snouts, luv, I would that much appreciate—
And make it well worth the concerned party's while—
Any additional, supplementary
Information individ'juls might offer
Of whatever slanderous and libelous
Invective related to this and any
Other sphere in my regard clandestinely
Circulated—for example that I am
A tart who'll squat and take a bit o' rabbit
From any ponce in the 'Dilly for the price
Of a curry and chips. *Well worth the while, luv.*

Because although I have not let this get out—
And I trust you with it, I do, the truth is
I've had a bit of money left to me. Yes,
A nice little bit from a right old geezer
I looked after once—changin' his nappies, like,
And given him 'is bath, luv, with a nice bit
O' slap and tickle thrown in compliment'ry.
Well anyway, as luck would have it—all bad—
Mum and dad was blowed up—yes, the pair of them,
Blowed up returning to their digs, whilst on tour
With Ivor bloody Novello—oh, not that
He was *in* it, or anywhere *near* it, darling,
Not on your nellie. Up here in London was
Ivor, snug as a bug in a rug, though truth
To tell, nobody was, really, not even
The royal family or toffs at the bloody Ritz.
In any case, I wouldn't've known, I was
Evacuated to the Cotswolds, to gran's,
Dad's mum, in which dwelling—a depressing place,
All blackened brick and chipped tiles like the dark lair
Of the spitting monsters whose spittle was death.
I did not thrive there withal that the Cotswolds
Is a charming district renowned in Britain
For its stone *cottages*—not that yours truly
Ever did set foot in one, a stone cottage.
Not till that fatal night on the Embankment
When first I entered with flushed cheeks the cottage
With no doorway what's framed in trellis roses,
But cut stone walls half crossing one another.
Do you know what *cottage* means in England, luv,
Other than a proper dwelling? Means a loo,
A public loo, that's what, a bog, a crapper,
A gentlemen's lavat'ry, and *cottage-ing*
Means enterin' into said facility
For other purposes than uri-nation,
Purposes that can still land you in the jug
If the filth's feelin' *exuberant* that day.
Anyway, luvvy, at gran's I was thought of

As a bug right enough—as a right species
Of *cock*-roach—pun intended. I understand
Some geezer wrote a book on the same subject—
Well, I could tell him a thing or two first hand.
And there I lived, crouched down like a little toad,
Terrified, between the stairway balusters.
I was always a bit *chesty*, luv, a bit
Catarrh-ish. Seems in the Cotswolds that's thought of
As *delicate*—would you credit it? I mean
To say, in Doncaster they'd laugh in your face
Were you to take on that way with the *vapours*.
There's now't so queer as folk, as the saying goes,
But gran were other than queer, she were *ghoulish*.
I remember this one time, me sliding down
The polished-bright mahogany bannister.
She caught me at it and screamed, *Filthy! filthy!*
If you think I don't *know why* little boys slide
Down bannisters, so they can *feel that down there*,
You're that much mistaken. Wheat that springeth green?
I think not. You're *chaff*, you are, blown in the air.
Now you go sit in the bath and *cleanse yourself!*"
I'd no *idea*, luv, what she was on about,
And the bath needless to remark was frigid.
Other times she'd sit on the old chesterfield—
Flashin' 'er positively *feral* green eyes
Under dreadful eyebrows, the dreadful eyebrows
Of a beast—swillin' pink gin whilst shufflin' cards
To lay out just there on the bible table
For game after game of solitaire patience.
I preferred animal snap, meself, but that's
Neither here nor there, is it, at this late date.
Sit there alone list'nin' to the wireless
And *screamin' ragin'* like a thing demented
Over Lord Haw-Haw. Or when she'd people in—
Trapped is what they were, *trapped*, she'd be holdin' forth,
Cluckin' like a brood hen how she didn't hold
With *goings on*, she were that *particular*.
Right witness for the *prostitution* she were,

Bloody-minded hypocritical old tart.
A proper old snout at that; no tongue sandwich
Were needed to make *her* talk. All *prophetic*
She'd be, lookin' into the middle distance
Like some bloody Mother Shipton, holdin' forth
On any subject you like. She'd have them in
Of a time, her like—a superfluity
Of which it did seem t' me was prevalent
In the district. They'd sit, luv, in a circle
And say strange things and read from *recipe books*—
Yes, gran would read aloud from Mrs. Beeton.
I remember on one occasion it was
On how to make a proper pot of tea. Yes,
Imagine. You must warm the pot first of course,
Put in the tea and pour in the hot water
Just as it reaches the boil, else it will part
With its gasses. "Rather like *yew*, Agnes,
In'it?" one old crone cackled, "in that you're
Like to part with your gasses any minute
Of the day, all sudden-like. One big old bag
Of trapped wind, that's yew, Aggie girl!" Well now gran
Would never have allowed anybody else
But this one hag to say such a thing out loud,
To her face no less, but they were pigeons paired,
Them two, save they were gorgons. No, Aggie girl
Weren't no oil painting, luv, case you've not
Guessed the fact. No oil painting—'less t'were done
By bloody Francis Bacon. She *hated* mum,
She did, hated her like rats hate poison,
Not for bein' pretty though—she couldn't *see*
Beauty, it were ouside her *experience*.
No, for snatching—pun intended—her darling
Straight from under her very fat red ugly
Gin-pickled nose. Some pretty bloke 'e were too,
Though he weren't straight, luv, not a bit of it.
Then accused *me*, right to my face, no sooner
Than a proper face came on me, of being
A *bastard*. "That filthy bitch whelped a bastard.

Born under a treacherous star, that one was,
You want to be wary of gettin' near him.
The stick that pokes the fires of hell's what he is.
Stalks you like a mute, the creature does, the while
A mood of violent idleness prevails.
I'd take no odds on his innings, 'specially
In times of persistent fog." A bastard, *me*!
Illegitimate! After the war she tried
Collectin' swag from the government, but they
Soon enough saw through the old cow's little scheme.
With the upshot that yours truly was shipped out
From the breath and stink of that dreadful dungeon
In the Cotswolds in two shakes of a lamb's tail—
The little lamb what Mary had, or what had
Mary, depending on who tells you the rhyme.
Yes, me, illegitimate—out of some yank's
Shaggin' bollocks what rogered me wayward mum.
P'raps it's true; seems likely, which is probably
Why I like yanks. Like you, darling—oh, not that
I imagine you'd've swung for mum, but swung
For—swung *on*—dad, oh, you'd've done that, that much
I'll tell you gratis, from what I remember
Of his person—distinctly, dear, in the bath.
The bath was cold, but dad weren't, not half. Coo,
What a memorable member! Pity that—
Not only that it was blown to smithereens,
Sky high along with the rest of him, but that
He didn't pass it on to me. I don't mean
Get me to *hold it* or anything, the way
You would a *billiard cue* or something, only
You know, whatchamacallit, *genetically*.
Anyway gran was murdered, dear—yes, murdered.
In Hull; they found her with her throat cut open
Like a bloody gaping shark, and that put paid
To Aggie, and what I say is, good riddance
To nasty rubbish. I cry *Halleluiah*
To this bloody fucking day. Still, I reckoned
She was dead right about mum, about the yank

And about me, which suited me, luv, right down
To the ground, so long as she was all along
Dead as old dreams of merry fucking England.
They do say how blood is thicker than water,
But water, though it does drown, also washes
The blood off your hands. Yes, wash your sins away
In the tide. Must be nice to believe in that.
Though I must say they buried her beautiful,
Whoever they were: flowers and everything,
Though to what end I can't fathom, as she left
Every last penny she had to the lepers.
I don't know why I'm telling you all these things,
I don't have a lot to do with anyone
Ever, really I don't, luv. I can ring up
The psychiatrist if I'm depressed, only
Really, what's the use in the end? In the end
There is no use. "Stay with the fear, Miss Tanguay,
It won't kill you." "That's where you're wrong, doctor,
It can do, quite; it has done once already.
And by the by, it's Miss *de* Tanguay, thank you."
I thought, that'll sort him out right and proper
In his National Health researches. Being
Spoken to that way is *infuriating*;
It's like being read out about *abundance*.
You're meant to think and *live* abundance—thinking
And living abundance *creates* abundance.
Well that's lovely, that is, but when all you've got
Is five pound two-and-six and your teddy boy
Wants to know who's the mean old john what gave you
The two-and-six, and you tell him "They *all* did."
I love that joke. Fact is, luv, I've always been
A bit *Restoration*—a bit *Regency*
As well. Now, what was it I was on about?
Oh, yes, *friends*. Haven't got none, I'm afraid, luv.
Look, who does a girl like me set her cap for,
A clean-cut City type with prospects, per'aps,
Or one of of those disdainful boys in boaters?
I do have *associates*, but you can't call

The people I mix with friends by any stretch.
In times of trouble—leading for example
To evacuation of the premises
Sudden like—they would not exactly recall
To mind the Kentish fishing fleets at Dunkirk—
If you as a yank understand the ref'rence.
They made a lovely picture out of it—that's
Usually the way Americans *get* the Brits.
It wouldn't even occur to a single
One of them—no, not one, luv—to sock a girl
To a meal once in a way, as I'm advised
You are about to do, you darling. Oh, no,
You musn't worry, pet, bright girls never mix
Business with pleasure . . . except *on occasion.*
I shall sing for me lunch. And sing a good tune.
Where were—oh, yes, concerning *associates.*
Associates don't care so much as a sprat
For their mates in this business, not a bloody
Tinker's toss. Never did nor never will do.
Success, the strategists say, is on the side
Of the big battalions. Whatever of that,
I long ago abandoned goals that involve
In any way the close cooperation
Of another she. As for men, what are they
By and large, now they've turned bleedin' *sensitive*—
And I'm talking about the *straight* ones, darling.
I mean look, a man who would say "I have got
Your supper ready," and you look up and there
It is on a plate surrounded by parsley—
There's just got to be something a little strange
About him, luv, and don't tell me otherwise.
Oh, I'm not a nice person, luv, not at all;
You don't want to have nothing to do with me.
It's *risible* what I am, yes, *risible.*

[S/he was right about the double negative. Not nothing. One wanted to get
him/her down. Not nice at all in the contemporary sense, but in the eighteenth-
century sense, as in "nice in the manner of his reputation," very nice indeed.
And guilt by association. S/he made one feel oneself transgressive.

Meanwhile, check the anomalies and discrepancies and the anachro-
nism. *Lord Haw-Haw?* If she actually heard Lord Haw-Haw and watched
old gran shrieking at him, then either she's rather older, dearie, than meets
the eye, or she's been clocking her seniors in the 'Dilly and *appropriating*.
Sound familiar? (Milanov on faggotry: "In Zagreb dey've bin doing *dot*
for years.") Your faithful correspondent's indeed been doing *dot* for years.]

II

Those first years after the war I spent idle
In a Church of England children's home. I still
Can smell the smells—Jeyes Fluid, Mansion Polish,
Boiling cabbage, Scrubbs Ammonia for the drains,
Coke coal burning and incense. And I sang there.
I was a boy soprano. Matter o' fact
I've a plaque celebrating the Joys of Song.
Home on the wall. Yes, *she'd* tried, old Aggie had,
Nippin' me in the bud, but this 'ere little
Fairy flower grew stronger by the hour.
Although not on the revolting food, because
I started fasting too, for the attention.
I still do, luv, devoutly, when I'm alone;
I feel it's ever so noble to suffer
For one's silhouette. And went to bed early—
Some dosser's done a book on that as well—wrote
The 'ole thing sittin up in bed, the wanker.
In dreamland I dreamed of strong silent heroes,
Who stood by me, and I them, through thick and thin.
Men who walked the high road to glory and felled
Opponents with a single blow. Imagine
My astonishment then, when one night and then
Night after night, first one then all the others
In succession, having taken me down from
The high road into ever such a lovely
Moonlit hollow, the lie of which I'd never
Seen awake, laid me down on grass softer than
I'd ever been laid on, fed me on chocolates,
And started in doing things to me I'd not

Since I were ever born conceived of. I mean
I knew from dad, and from meself, men's willies
Went *telescopic*, but that that, if y' like
Meant *visions through the telescope!* Predestined,
I said to myself on waking, all of it,
Predestined like the Presbyterians hold.
I recall saying next, well this *is* a bit
Of all right this is, for a heresy. Yes,
Because I *realized* these things the heroes
Done t' me in dreams were *forecasts*—yes, *forecasts*
Of me life to come, and into the bargain,
The things my particular hero had me
Do to *him* were such things as I'd from that out
Spend me waking life—'though I didn't yet know
The Word *perpertrating*, perpertrating, yes.
When your very first assay is with *gods*, luv,
You're bound to grow to man's estate believing
Yourself legendary, know what I mean? Yes.
Especially when so far you'd felt *extrinsic*,
And you'd been 'avin' the correct feeling, luv.
So I never did need to read Sigmund Freud's
Interpretation of Dreams. I was Joseph,
Me own Joseph *revealing* things to Pharaoh,
And Pharaoh meself as well. So I must have
Inherited a peculiar gift from gran.
Afterwards—for these revelations kicked up
A terrible fuss in me head, consequence
Bein' I caused a *fyu-ro-ray* in chapel.
One Sunday the vicar'd just done wrappin' up
One of his specials with the usual cant,
"So you see, we are all in God's hands." "*Palsied,*"
I snapped, without a thought, causin' a *fyu-ro-ray.*
What I was tryn' t' do, see, was attract
The notice of the star songbird, Giles Fulham.
Next I was fostered—billetèd with one lot
Upon another of proper swine, swindlers
Bleedin' the Welfare State of what they wouldn't

Give gran, *agents of penetration*, get me?
They did. Thus did the world become a nightmare
Full of horrors both real and imagined.
Next was the approved school—yes, luv, she's
A member of an *echelon*, a drag-queen
Yard bird, old-lag ward of Her Majesty. Yes
A run-in with the rozzers over a bit
Of store theft is what did it, luv: two lipsticks,
Jar of foundation, comb and pocket mirror,
And the child not yet up for the eleven-
Plus. "That he did feloniously and with
Malice aforethought . . ." Can you credit it, luv?
And that is where the drama really started,
The Approved School. I weren't there a fortnight
Before I slashed me wrists. Bled like a stuck pig,
I did—not that I've ever seen a stuck pig.
Mind *yew*, I'd had such attention forced on me
By all the psychiatrists, starting with when
I wanted dolls for Christmas. I used to have
To play with toys in a sandpit while they watched
What I was at. You talk about Big Brother—
Only what Mister Whore-well never told was,
Big Brother is an "I can see you" *wanker*.
Mem'ry, they like to tell you's like a searchlight
Sweeping across a darkened landscape, trying
To locate. . . . Sounds a lot to me like *Dartmoor!*
I was a proper mess as a child. "Run up
On remnants 'e were, the little sod." Dear gran
Said that, and I reckon she was right. The bread
I dropped invariably fell buttered side
Downwards. Well, luv, I was rushed to hospital
Bandaged, sedated and allowed to go back.
I slashed me wrists again a fortnight later
Just for a little more attention—and then
I climbed up on a water tower and threw
A brick at the headmaster, though I didn't
Aim to hit him. He was a lovely old man—

Not the sort at all to jump out at young boys
From behind doors—and I think he cared for me.
I don't mean he *fancied* me, though had he done
I'd've done anything he wanted to. Yes,
Give me an old geezer, so long as he's sweet
And not a candyman or a chicken hawk,
And doesn't go calling me insulting things
Like "tart" and "nancy boy," he may do with me
What he will; whack me bum, give me a good wank,
Suck me willy red-raw and I'll do any
And all of those things and more besides to him.
I'll dress up—this happened once, with an old dear—
As a parlour maid, luv, with a goffered cap
And broderie Anglaise streamers, and knickers
Of the loveliest soft cotton—and like it.
Although the truth is I don't care to whip them
And listen to them whimper and watch them crawl
The length of the parlour floor and piss themselves,
I really don't. Sometimes I wonder could there
Be such a thing as a nice person in me
Screaming to get out and perhaps show mercy
Unto the thousands? At the C of E school
I wanted to be like God, without shape, form
Or passions. Well, bloody sod-all if there is.
Although I have me points—the mouth for a start—
No, not what comes spewing out of it, the mouth
Itself. *La bouche.* Mine turns up at one corner,
See? That is called the *Signature of Venus.*
In any case, by that I was finished
Up there on the water tower and the blood
Had *coagulated*—being a practiced
Hand by then I'd not cut deep—and was brought down,
There were crowds of yobs streaming all around me;
It were amazing—like the Talk of the Town.

[FYI, The Talk of the Town is nothing written, as per *The New Yorker*, but
a nightclub, not quite top drawer, in Leicester Square where Judy among
others has headlined.]

III

Well, I came out of hospital, re-entered
Counseling, obeyed the probation yobbos
Then went to earth till I were a full grown thing.
First job. I started as a commis waiter
In a very small family hotel, live-in.
One evening this guest, a well-dressed, sadistic
Particle, showed me these pictures, all nude
And pornographic. I shrieked, and said he'd tried
To rape me. I didn't like him, not at all,
So I just made up this story about him.
The best thing about me is I can come down
To reality. I can say it's quite wrong
To do a thing. On the other hand I know
I'm going to do it, because I want to.
The way I live is, I know, a terrible
Waste of a life, but there's nothng else I want.
I've heard it said one of the satisfactions
Of long intimacy is the confortable
Habit of expressing the dead obvious
With impunity. Lovely word, that; posh word.
But the fact is I can do that by myself
And often do—same as spankin' the monkey.
It saves me from becoming deep, which would be
Deadly for the career. Although it's funny,
I remember once saying—I don't recall
To which psychiatrist—this was in the late
Phase of the National Health's compulsory
Counselling for adopted adults—I was
Adopted, as you might say by the 'Dilly
And so I qualified roy'l—well, that I was
A plain-spoken person, and he said "You're not,
You know. You write line upon line at every
Session, and it's my job to read between them."
I must say that made me feel terribly chuffed.
Nonetheless I felt compelled to remonstrate.
"My mind is a *ru*-in," I said. "I suffered

Horribly during the war. Lost both parents,
Was victimized by a madwoman, then sent
To live with monsters. All *that's* got me mental,
I live me whole life in a quake and a dread."
"Yes, every place-of-safety order expires,
In time," says he; "we must—" I cut him right off.
"I can't be blamed for the dreadful ugliness
Inside me." "Your mind a ruin?" he said then,
"I think not, although it might appear to be
Convenient to say so, the better to charge
Good money for admittance. Here is something
Thomas Mann wrote, something you might take note of.
'For the sake of humanity, for the sake
Of love, let no man's thoughts be ruled by death.'" Well
Having whipped meself into a rare taking
I was not exactly *mad keen* to be told
Just then what some bleedin' dreary-sod Jerry
Had to say about humanity, life, love,
Death or liver sausage, thanking-yew. Got up
My nose, and no mistake. That said however,
I'll allow as how I did think that remark—
Me charging admittance—was brilliant. Full marks
To him, cheeky beggar, full marks, and so says
Both of me. Nonetheless, luv, between the lines
Or atop them makes no matter, I simply
Couldn't have him scoring that one; I did have
Me *reputation* to think of, didn't I?
And the thing of it is I was always *grilled*
By the girls after each one of the sessions,
And whatever else, you didn't lie to *them*.
And you see, luv, what it *is* is I have got
This *particular* reputation. "There is
One thing about you, Vilja," Lil said—"Lil,"
By the by, is for "Lili Marlene"—you know,
"Outside the barracks in the pale moonlight; that's
Where I stand and wait for you each night." Who-so-
Ever-you-may-be in Lil's case. Yes indeed,
Lil's a great one for the yeomen of the Guards.

Started out as a liaison courier,
Lil did, luv, specializing in *pavement work*.
Rocketed to the top of the profession
In the war—there were *opportunities* then,
And Lil took 'em all, one by one, yes indeed.
Renowned for her broken-wing technique she was,
And take her far it did, but like that, it would
Rebound on her one day. Tempting fate, some said
Was the cause of it—bowlin' and battin' both
At once. Whatever of that, she was beaten,
Very badly beaten by persons unknown,
And retired for a time, but came back. They do.
She's a huge, crippled, cunning woman is Lil,
And you don't go up against her, you do *not*.
"There's one thing about you, Vilja, and that is
You *will* go about tellin' the truth. And now
You're at it again. Honor bright and that lark.
You're either tellin' the truth now with neither
Trifling alteration nor grave suppression
Or else you're a deep one." Well, I set about
Accepting this unprecedented tribute
Like a bleedin *prem-yay danseur*, honeybunch,
At Covent Garden, accustomed to dancing
The role of prince, with retainers, with valets
And equerries and—or *ak-chully* more like
A prima ballerina—like old Margo
Fon-tayne—with the ease of long habit. "Oh, well,"
Says I,"Tell the truth and shame the devil," "Oh,
I *see*," says Lil, proper like. "Well as to *that*,
Vilja, You are the very one, right enough,
To shame the devil *rigid*, when it comes down
To *wiles*. You're a hard-headed mercenary
Shrew, inward and slothful, but watchful, and smart.
There's a good long stretch on your aerial. Yes,
I've not often seen cleverer, save perhaps
When fired up by two or three gin and Its,
In an atmosphere you've been taught to believe
Refeened, say Gorringe's, your sense diluted

Beyond detectable trace, you *will* break out
And run amok. Serenity is just not
Your long suit; you come roaring into a room
Like an autumn gale direct from the Western
Approaches and wonder why you frighten ilk.
Then too, whilst on the subject of howling gales,
Another thing you are is one ferocious,
Unrepentant *breaker of impromptu wind*,
A trait as it happens you share with the late
Lamented Miss Marilyn *Mon*-roe—the great
Difference being of course, luv, that however
She managed to, shall we say, bring the thing off
Somehow doesn't relate to your performance,
Which really belongs on Brighton Pier. Mind you,
A weak claim is better than none, and she *was*
A divinity. All the same you do have
A low drop, which, if an old pro may whisper
A bijou wordette in your ear, you would be
Well advised to confine to your act. You see,
Your offstage performance on Mandrax, I fear
Is widely regarded as *insincere*, luv,
As paying out rope. All in all, you are not
For all markets, as the Bard says, whether on
The block *with contents* or *as found*." Bloody cheek,
The cow. Tongue like a razor, though; 't'were folly
To get on the wrong side! Of 'er! She's Scottish,
Y'know, with connections in the Isle of Man.
Need one say more? Well, perhaps a bit. There was
This one time Lil come down frightful with the curse,
She were up in St. Thomas's Paddington;
We all went in to see her, and truth to tell
She made it a lark, she were that good humored.
Well, what with penicillin, these days it's not
Half bad, really. But some nasty particle
In the 'Dilly starts in referrin' to Lil
As *cock-a-leeky*—which *ought* to 'ave betrayed.
A thoroughly dismal ignorance, wot, of
Lil's *performance* in bed. But did it? There was

The rub—afterwards known in the 'Dilly as
The rub what effectuated the *rub-out*.
Because, may I tell you, luv, Lil weren't out
And convalescin' *two full days* before that
Particular pair of rouged lips just *vanished*.
Yes, *disappeared*. There was some speculation
From testimony of one kind or t'other
What she was workin' the sea front at Blackpool,
But she's never again been *seen* in London.
And I mean Lil was thick with *Diana Dors*—
A murderess, luv, and the *Krays*! Well, back to
Herr Doktor, the Jerrys' pal, and his bleedin'
Judgment handed down in the case. I chivvied
Me brain, I did, for a suitable response,
Then rose up in all me majesty, I did,
I was that livid. "You can go *shit* y'self
In bloody Covent Garden market, *y'toad*!
I've a right mind, I do, to 'ave you called up
Before the National Health Grievances Board
For suggestions of a certain character!"
Then he looked me straight in the eye, luv, and said—
Half a mo', I wrote it down the whole of it
Directly I'd swanned out. I can do that, luv—
Cue-ing and topping, see. Yes, here it is here.
"Who is safe as we where none can do treason
To us except one of we two." Imagine!
Well then I *did* feel threatened, make no mistake;
They've got the goods on us, shrinks, the goods. They can
Put us away for six months hard—they call it
Occupational. They can *plug us* into
A wall socket, just like the bleedin' telly.
They've got techniques and practices what they learned
From the Shanghai police. They've no emotions,
They've all taken the second vow. What they want,
Is their money, what I want is me tablets
On the National Health. And Her Majesty's
Government is ready and willing to do
The heavy father. Oh, yes, I tell the truth,

And the hard truth is, I must be what I am,
And that ain't no bleedin' Shirley Bassey song.
I *must* be a female impersonator,
A 'Dilly drag queen on the game. So far,
As I know it's the only way a sweaty,
Pasty-faced, unskilled, effeminate and, yes,
Attested *uncommon imaginative*
Boy can hope to be extraordinary.
I say I'm bisexual, but the truth is
I do like boys better than girls. That fact that
The compliment isn't returned, I don't give
A harlot's crumpet. I love *me*, luv, I *do*.
I love myelf very much, and I hate lots
Of things and lots of people. If I ever
Thought of loving somebody else, even just
A little, it would have to be somebody
With money—a *terribly wealthy* person,
And I'd know deep underneath it was only
Their money I was after, so you see, it's
All ridculous—bloody *ridiculous*.
We British have an expression, luv: *no joy*;
No joy of him, her, them, it; no joy at all.
Besides, breaking up is hard to do, *n'est-ce pas?*
Best to never get involved in the first place.
And therefore, luv, no descent for this chappie
Into the black trough of relationship hell,
Thanking-you. Not that I'm a person to sit
Home alone mulling over the gay details
Of me suicide scenario, no, no,
Uncommon imaginative as may be.
Because, when he said that about the lines, see,
What I *wanted* to say was this. "Yes, doctor,
And the lines run across the white page, forming
A sort of *grid* against emptiness, get me?
And the reason, doctor, I can't read is not
Bleedin' *dyslexia*, it's that every time
I try making words out of the letters, well,
They *come apart*, the words, the letters falling

To the bottom of the white page in a heap,
Then, as if a trap door opened, off the page
Altogether, and the white nothingness is all
There is. It's all there *isn't*, doctor. Yes."
Y' see luv, I *used* to be able to read—
In the library at the C of E school—
Just So Stories and *The Wind in the Willows*.
But this one afternoon, luv, something happened,
And I never read—and never sang again—
Not even when my heroes came in my dreams
And carried me off to the hollow. And it
Weren't me voice breakin' neither. "So just you
Try telling me I'm normal and skyving off,"
I said to the bleedin' ponce be'ind that desk,
"The way you put down in your bloody report
To the National Health, because to really
Help me is beyond you. Your patient, doctor,
Is in critical condition—critical
And unchanged—and you, doctor, are a failure,
A critical, unchanging failure!" And that
Is that tale told, luv. Next consideration?
Oh, yes, we were on about *relationships*.
Well, no relationships don't mean no *larks*, luv—
It don't mean no *adventures*. As for instance,
I was picked up quite by mistake on Curzon Street
By a rich American—an *editor*,
Yes, me, and given a *proper* job, the job
As *hostess* at a *party* he was giving,
A bloody *cotillion* is what it was, luv
In a Palladian mansion in Wiltshire,
With a Wren library the guests went wild for—
Of course they *would* do, them bein' *litrary*—
With all them Camp carvin's by Grinlin' Gibbons.
And bloody enormous crystal chandeliers
And *twal-de-jew-y* chair hoods. And that many
Heavy silver dishes, kept ingeniously
Hot by patent arrangements. *Fray't-fully* grand
And bijou *intell-ek-shul* it were, what with

Everybody rattlin' on whilst looking past
One another into the middle distance,
Wherever that *is*. Anyway, luv, *lashings*
Of lovely drink, and me, luv, sittin' right there
Among the bless-ed, in an imperial
Force projection of the intellect—meanin'
Me, luv, talkin' posh. There is a *nuclear*,
A *radioactive* quality about
A clever woman whose brain's been underused,
And often there is no way she can control
The emanations. And we dined off wild boar,
And there was *leavings* galore. *Wild boar!* They all
Got stinking drunk, and I stood up and led them
In a game Of Shapes and Atti-chudes. Then when,
Courtesy of the lashings of lovely drink—
Not to mention me shapes and atti-chudes, wot—
The old gentleman discovered what I was—
What I *am*, he was oh-so-understanding,
I suppose because he dealt with *lit'ra-chure*
And that, I felt he understood me better
Than he might care to admit—and would I care
To come one night to Annabel's with him. Yes.
Very toff's-in-town-for-the-season that was.
I love rich men and champagne and caviare,
And baubles and bangles and beads, that I do.
The plain tuth is, luv, when they're old all they want
Is the company—to be seen with a chic,
Smart, attractive, up-market Englishwoman—
And sucks to these bloody ignorant punters
In the 'Dilly puttin' out the *calumny*
That in me sensible tweeds, in me twinsets
And pearls—which just happen to be genu-yne
Cultured ones, luv, from Majorca—I look like
The captain of an old girl's school hockey team.
Vicious. Yes, "Jumped-up pork pie and beans" is what
They call me. Vicious. Anyway, luv, it's all
They want, the old gentlemen of quality,
And not about to grow no *bugle* on you

Neither, as you sit with them in some so-called
Cabaret, watching some tart 'oo 'asn't washed
'Er Marks-and-Spencer knickers since last *Chewsdy*—
If it weren't last Chewsdy week. Trot backstage
You can see them *airing* in her dressing room,
Skid marks and all, 'top the PVC mini.
You put her out in the daylight, she'd draw flies.
And flappin' 'er bleedin' mammaries about
Lak she were Elsie the Cow up for *auction*
At a bleedin' *rodeo*. Yes, luv, simple
The old ones' wants. Although it can happen that—
I do recall one geezer sayin', "My cock's
A plug in the wall of time, at age sixty-one
I can come to feel sixteen." He was something
Unusual. Normally they don't have what
You'd call an *orgasm*; more a *spillover*.
What the editor did, after telling me
That modern experience is characterized
By meaningless mechanized situations
Of disrelation, was ask "Are you happy
As a woman?" *Happy*! God, Americans!
I didn't like to tell him the rosy glow
Of a woman fulfilled is not exactly
Characteristic of your 'Dilly drag queen.
Or that the wants and needs of artists—money,
Fame and beautiful lovers, says Doctor Freud—
Are *perpetch-wully* unfulfilled. "That's asking,"
I said, "or as my old gran would say, 'Them as
Ask question will get told what.' Or I might say,
Just like the ministers do in Parliament,
'I must have notice of that question.' "I see,"
Said he, and left off. It made me laugh it did,
To dig up the old dead cow and put sage words
In her filthy, foul old mouth. "You must have loved
Your grandmother," he says. "Oh, indeed I did,
And were terribly cut-up—bereft really—
At her passing. She were such a good woman,
She succored widows and old age pensioners."

I'm wicked, I am, luv, and do like treating
Yanks to a bit of cod Yorkshire—and I can't
Tell you, luv, what a treat it were t' go in
For *word play* knowing the bloke wouldn't get it,
Smart as he was, and posh and lit'rary. Yes,
Thrilled my little willy rigid, that it did,
Into a right wicked stand in me knickers,
To engage in conversation with a gent
All flavored with shrewd and astringent humor.
Some of my other admirers are gamblers,
Businessmen, actors, even writers like you,
Although they are never really rich, begging
Your parsnips, except maybe for Joe Orton,
Or old Terrence Rattigan; the like of them
And that lot aren't ringin' up *my* number.
What I must do next is put me photograph
In *Stage*, then I must do a summer season
As a try out. Yes, for mine is an untapped
Intelligence waiting for the right format.

[At which point one realized one needed to wind it down, and so shifted
the talk to the subject's long-planned suicide.]

IV

Yes, I mean to do it, luv, and no mistake.
At twenty-nine. Fame, should it come, doesn't
Last forever. Although if I'm *serious*
'Bout bein' famous I really must get on
The stick, for as it stands, luv, if distance
Truly lends enchantment and absence really
Makes the heart go fonder, then I ought to be
The toast of the town—know what I mean? Funny.
However, talking of that, it is hard work,
Humor is. It is often more difficult
To get people to laugh than ever it is
To bring them to orgasm. One soldiers on,

Nevertheless, it is an attested fact,
The more famous you become, the lovelier
You are. And in my case, I'd still be myself,
Still get depressed and I don't want to be old.
One has such a short life anyway before
One's blown. That was written about spies' cover—
But really does as well for roses . . . and queens.
You must work at life to live it, luv and I'm
The laziest girl in town. Without desire
There is no will power, and the will power
Needed for recovery—for I *am* that ill—
Cannot be manufactured. Sometimes I dream
I'm Bette Davis in that tragic picture
Where larkin' about in the doctor's office
She comes across her case file with the two words
Prognosis negative stamped all over it
Like a hid'jus rash, and *realizing*
She's got but six months to live before she dies
A ridiculous, boring death, does a bunk,
Returnin' to 'er old life of gin-vermouth
Cocktails an' 'orses and all that carry-on,
Then comes back to the doctor, dies and goes
To 'eaven, while angels croon. Yes, we creatures
Of the night live complicated lives. Gran was
Mad keen, luv, to be in on the Last Judgment
And to watch all the sodomites go roaring
Down to 'ell. I don't know why, but that makes me
Want to die. Just to know there'll be none of that.
Though you don't know, do you, don't, not anything
At all. That you're being incinerated,
Like the Jews, the gypsies and the sodomites
In Germany in the war. No, innocent
Of all of it you are as is the baby
Whose face the cat sits on the while he's sleeping
And that's 'im gone fer 'is tea. I loved the war,
I did, luv, yes, 'though it claimed both my parents.
That is the way they put it, "The war claimed them."
Like they was abandoned parcels some punter

Nicked out of Left Luggage. The slogans. I loved
The slogans 'bout beltin' up, like "Careless talk
Costs lives" and "Be like dad, keep mum." Of course dad
Didn't, did he? Not if she went walkin' out
With yanks—but then they *both* of them went walkin'
Out with yanks—there bein' yanks galore, to spare,
More than enough to go 'round. A *plethora.*
Then too, luv, like as not they found one to *share.*
Right theatrical that, *sophisicated,*
Like in *Design for Living*—and that would mean
I was a love child in a *beautiful sense.*
And even more tragic. All the more reason. . . .
Morbid, you're likely thinking, but the truth is,
True stars are never happy—never, never,
Never. Do you know what love is, honeybunch?
It's anything you can still betray. A great
English writer wrote that, and truer word was
Never writ. And "Why does everyone get
So *agitato* on a Thursday?" Wrote that
As well, And this, the best: "You are either good
Or bad, and both are dangerous." There's no end
To it, you know, no end in sight. Then it's done
In the last beat of the secret English heart.
You're dead as doornails, and you hadn't a clue.

[This was *verbatim,* promise. Do you suppose s/he had any *idea?*]

MART
CROWLEY'S

"THE
BOYS
IN THE
BAND"

...is not a musical.

DANCER
FROM
THE
DANCE

BY ANDREW
HOLLERAN
A HAUNTING
NOVEL OF
ROMANCE AND
DECADENCE
IN THE FAST
LANES OF
GAY SOCIETY
"EROTIC HEAT
PERCOLATES
THROUGH
THESE PAGES..."
SUPERB."
—The New York Times Book Review

HE WAS SO INNOCENT...UNT
FELL CAPTIVE TO THE BROODING
AND SINISTER SECRETS

GAY N.Y.C.

VINCENT
VIRGA

PART FIVE

Return Engagements
(Postquam Rearrived)

Mawrdew Czgowchwz
James McCourt

RIDE THE SUBWAY
It's Faster, It's Cheaper

CHAPTER NINETEEN

Moving Back and Moving On

(STONEWALL AND EVER AFTER)

> "The prelude and postlude of any historical event intrude upon the event itself by way of its dialectical exposition. Moreover every dialectically manifest historical event splits itself into polar opposites, generating thereby a force field in which the clash between its prelude and its postlude is enacted."
>
> —Walter Benjamin
>
> "What was it in the beginning, the thought, the word or the deed?"
>
> —voice from a cubicle at the Continental Baths

Wherein the narrative sweep of events effectively replaces the events themselves. Holly Woodlawn, Jackie Curtis and Candy Darling, Lou Reed and the Velvet Underground peak. At the Factory, the Warhol-Morrissey moompix studio on Union Square, Valerie Solanis, having a couple of years since shot Andy (on the day before Sirhan Sirhan shot Robert Kennedy in Los Angeles), the masterpieces Flesh and Trash are, well, shot, and elsewhere (on Fire Island) Frank O'Hara is run down by a beach taxi and dies of the injuries sustained. Tendered report of O'Hara's funeral, James Schuyler experiences the Moment of the Wasp in the Room, the transcription of which, in "Funeral at Springs," ushers him out of the New York School into the visionary company of Blake, Keats, Hopkins and Joyce. Author returns from London to scissor-dive into the deep end of the pooling story, of poetry, pictures, pornography, sex, drugs and rock 'n' roll. ("Not that again!" "Yes, that again. Seems it never ended, so get with it!") Abandon Itself bursts forth uncontrollably in queer life, taking hostages, savaging lives. "Fuck art—let's dance!"

("This seems too much, even to me."

But darling, don't you see? What we're doing is terribly important—simultaneously protesting and imitating construed sex-violence as components of a single force field!"

Those two words again—he doesn't even know what they mean.)

Theater of action: hustler/drag bars in Midtown and the Village, the Everard, as always, and the new, so to speak, upscale places: the New St. Marks, the Continental, the Club Baths.

Also, such more ramshackle, lean-to and carnival-tent establishments as Man's Country and the Broadway Baths, not to forget the trucks on West Street in the Meat Packing District, from just after midnight until dawn, and most celebrated of all, the Morton Street Pier.

The "S.T.D." code, introduced c. 1970 at the Everard.

"Do you think she is a serious toe dancer?"

"That woman is a serious toe dancer." (Or "a deeply serious toe dancer" for a bad case, particularly of rectal rather than urethral gonorrhea, or for syphilis.)

Author, in sight of actually being published, ventures again into the (largely heterosexual) Fifth Avenue salon of Kakia Livanos, to which a pod of shipping-millionaire Greeks, a single serpentine, drunken defrocked Irish Jesuit priest (had he really been the dead fat pope's confessor? Would he go into a blackout and tell?) and the earnest, brilliant young editor of The New York Review of Books have been lured to spar amicably with their hostess on current events and world affairs.

Retreating downtown, Queer Temperament, the author, heady with that publication prospect, instead of intelligently regrouping his meager forces (staying home reading Ulysses), ridiculously imagines himself as another Addison DeWitt in the back room of Max's (Kansas City: in the back room at old Max Patrick's on Fire Island he might still draw a small crowd). Ridiculously. There is neither call nor occasion for another Addison DeWitt at Max's Kansas City. The position is already held fast by the beyond-formidable Donald Lyons, no man's fool, least of all his, although, not coincidentally both kind friend and benefactor to QT in the matter of putting out (the *work*, the *work*; Author was most emphatically not otherwise merchandisable product).

Therefore, he wisely and without hesitation, moves sideways. To, of all unlikely places, the Stonewall Inn.

Stonewall. The last of the *événements* of the sputtering sixties ("I-I *said* to Drella . . .") which, like the Civil War in the history of the Republic, provided the dividing line and break in the history of queer experience, and which, like all traumatic ocurrences rendered the beliefs and assumptions of the preceding generation naïve, complacent and obsolete in the eyes of their successors, whose war-cry rings out thus:

> "And be our oriflamme today
> Judy's last-filled script!"

Thereafter, from an unobtrusive, sharply angled coign of vantage, he watches unfold the story of Gay Liberation (or queer creep) in the wake of the declassification by the American Psychiatric Association of homosexuality as a disease.

Narrated through the phenomena of the first onscreen queer hardcore porn, of the GAA and the Firehouse dancer/activists, relentless drugged dancing as the gay lockstep march-in-place.

Psychobabble.

An answer to psychobabble: "To give oneself permission is nothing other than to take a chance on not getting caught."

Also, as has been said of the first generation of Russians after 1917, they are as enthusiastic and happy as only the young can be when completely wrapped up in tasks which have almost no actual relation to their personal lives.

The first Stonewall commemorative parades. The Changing of the Guard: post-war compliant and closeted Cherry Grove queens relent.

("The generation sacrificed to the epoch of doctrinal metamorphosis remains essentially alienated from and directly hostile to the evolution at hand"—Auguste Comte, *Un Appel aux Conservateurs.*)

A great wave of the affluent decamp from Fire Island to Long Island's East End, to Quogue, Southampton, East Hampton and Sag Harbor. Those left behind, the medium forever gone in which their ardent deeds took shape, the bright new day of their post-war ebullience overwhelmed by the low scud and gathering shadows of an alien, grubby sadistic devolution of values, taste and performance, hole up at the Firehouse, in what has become known as So-Ho (Miss Dean dubs it "So-ho-*hum*") in the upstairs lounge, and in wrinkle rooms around the city: Uncle Charlie's, the Beau Geste, the Menemsha Bar, Julius's.

"Everything's changed."

"You've noticed."

In reaction to the mustaches, flannel shirts, construction-worker boots, faded Levi's, leather-tongued key rings (with more keys dangling from them than can possibly be necessary in a single civilized life) and color-coded handkerchiefs ("They call that *cruising*? I call it the cruising equivalent of painting by numbers"), they, the old proud, dress in pressed chinos, button-down shirts and striped ties, and in rumpled pebble-weave tweeds, drink bourbon old fashioneds, stingers, brandy alexanders and awfully good old vintages. They smoke Lucky Strikes, Chesterfields, Pall Malls and Kents, and play and sing the golden oldies.

They venerate Ruth Draper, Bea Lillie and Judy, making homosexual proof texts of the lyrics to "The Man That Got Away," "Alone Together," "Smile" and "Somewhere Over the Rainbow." Also Madame Spivvy, Frances Faye and Elaine Stritch ("Stritchy") and refuse to jump into the political fray. *Laudator temporis acti*, they stage their own incredibly long last stand.

Like characters in epic poetry, older battle-tried men are surrounded, and, calling out to younger men (of the class that used to furnish them with eager protégés) for aid, are largely ignored—the cadets, in fact, having almost to a man turned on their elders, whom they denounce as paleozoic losers, damning the lives they have led as essentially lives of furtive, obsessional, voyeuristic longing.

The great exceptions are those somewhat anachronistic eager-beaver preppie types who work the men's room at Grand Central Terminal ("Why do these same men keep reappearing here in their droves, several times a day?" a talking candid camera might ask. "Surely they all have keys to corporate toilets"), in which venue far more elaborate signal systems operate than in the subway tea-room network, and cluster like sub-debs at a Junior Miss cotillion in back-lit corners of the lounge at Penthouse East. They can be *had*.

Unbowed, the old faithful, subscribing to the myths surrounding their emergence from the Second World War (myth understood as the collective memory of a group about its past, a memory which sustains a belief system shaping its view of the world in which it wishes to continue to live, that is, something that never was and always will be true), maintain that they would rather die than serve and propagate the new religion, the religion of the Marlboro Man clones, with its tattoos, cockrings, tit-clamps, cigars and ritual hot-ash frolics in cavernous back cellar rooms in the Meat Packing District ("Tell me, dear, where *is* the Meat Packing District?"), a program of order and conformity whose power to contain was surpassed only by its ability to define.

Recalling Oscar Wilde's *De Profundis* (and noting the desperate irony of the switch), they quote a signal passage back and forth to one another. "The one disgraceful, unpardonable, and to all time contemptible action of my life was to allow myself to appeal to society for help and protection." Ironic, because for them the *only* hope for stability in the coming lean and hungry years appears to lie in a program of pre-ordained steps, in which they must revert to the very behavior of the preppies who seem to batten on them, oil up old rusted gears and set about making new and strenuous efforts at attracting women more superannuated even than they themselves, to whom they must rigorously audition, one entire season minimum, as walkers. (There's gold in them there hulls, and hotel cabanas in Palm Beach.)

The righteous and the ungodly (in contrast to the preppies in the Grand Central men's room and at Penthouse East, who are reverent and pious, patient and kind . . . but can they be trusted by a battered heart?) remonstrate in choruses, exhorting one another thus:

" 'Let us not reverence the gray hairs of the aged, for that which is feeble we have found to be nothing worth. Therefore let us lie in wait for the righteous, for he was made to reprove our thoughts.' The Wisdom of Solomon, darling, 2:10–12. Look it up."

Harry Hay, however, does none of these things, but instead devises the Radical Faeries in spiritually evolved New Mexico and blossoms anew.

Overnight, or so it seems, the relaxation of the laws governing censorship (also bigger and better deals made with the police and the Mafia by an increasingly upwardly mobile and mobilized Faggotry) facilitate the explosion, alongside the straight product, of queer male art pornography—amazingly to those for whom the prediction made by Rodney Harrington in Grace Metalious's '50s best-selling shocker *Peyton Place*, that actual unsimulated fucking would become a commonplace attraction on the motion picture screen, had been for twenty years a dripping-pipe dream.

Directors such as Gorton Hall, Wakefield Poole, Jack Deveau, Arch Brown, Francis Ellie, Arthur Bressan and Fred Halsted blaze the trail, preparing the way for the triumphant entry into the New Jerusalem of sexual expression of Sam and Joe Gage, respectively the Ross Hunter and Douglas Sirk of hard-core homo melodrama.

Overheard (or overthought):

"Although it is accurate enough, darling, to nominate Joe Gage the Douglas Sirk of queer porn, it is hardly sufficient tribute. Yes, the great romantic trilogy is deeply Sirkian, but in *Closed Set*, in the more problematic *501* and finally in the apotheosis of the form that is the New York sequence in *Handsome*, that aggregate we call Joe Gage—and why shouldn't it be an aggregate? Shakespeare was—composed of Sam and Joe Gage, Richard Youngblood and Russell Ballard, the mantle of Caravaggio falls on howevermany shoulders. Still-frame enlargements of the New York sequence of *Handsome* would encompass the erotic charge and the *facture* of thousands of full canvasses and detailed moments from every painting in the Merisi canon, leading up to his *Seven Corporeal Works of Mercy* translated into cinema. The corporeal work of mercy that is the New York sequence of *Handsome* is the redemption of the torments of . . . I cannot go on."

The spanking new queer glossies trumpet the new line, and soon enough their impact is felt on mainline print advertising. Fabulous drag queens crashland on the pages of *Vogue*. Putassa de Lafayette, the six-two-in-socks bolt of black lightning, shod for style in size elevens and gorgeous beyond telling, transcending radical chic, embodying the post-modern, hits the big town.

Nightly sex marathons rumble in the trucks and on the piers. The author remembers his high school and college job as longshoremen's paymaster and, speaking of reminiscence, is stung by nostalgia over the vanished glamour of the New York waterfront, when the Hudson south of the Bronx was correctly called the North River (bon voyage baskets were always labeled Pier 84 or 88 or 92, et cetera, North River), the plethora of sailor and longshoreman bars, the "I've got a right to hang around, down around the river" opportunities (and very serious risks) taken, the wild seeing-pals-off parties on shipboard (sometimes, as in the legendary disappearance from on deck, and subsequent retrieval at dawn on the shore of Fire Island, of Jazz Age party hellion Star Faithfull, emblazoned on the front pages for a week and echoing in "the columns" for months, even years), and of his own glamorous return from Southampton on the *France*, to undertake a literary career.

This new volume of waterfront traffic produces a decade-long gridlock so stymying that when, a decade later, in the panic of the first terrifying reports, first of "the gay Cancer," then of GRID, and finally of AIDS and the metaphysical Human Immune-Deficiency Virus (and what in every epoch has been simultaneously more terrifying, more seductive and less coherent than its metaphysics?), the cry goes up to GET OUT OF TOWN!

Few do. The spiritual paralysis and moral *accidie* ("A virus has no morals!") has become as baffling and as over-determined as the force that keeps the cast of Buñuel's *The Exterminating Angel* locked up behind church doors.

Not to mention the amphetamine, dope and downs ingested, inhaled and injected (almost interchangeably) by spectators and spectator-participants as well at the exhibition fisting-sex shows held nightly at the Mineshaft (where nobody had to pass any tests, or submit to the anxieties attendant upon audition, because, as Addison DeWitt a generation earlier had remarked of television, that's all it was, nothing but auditions) and on the dance floors at Flamingo, 12 West and the Saint.

PISO MOJADO (and how!) SOLO BASURA. Skid marks.

Thus dawned an era of queer trench warfare, from the back alleys off Broadway to the chic and exclusive gated mews: Patchin Place, Milligan Place, Pomander Walk and Sniffen Court.

The young bloods wish the old would die off. Instead, they speak clearly, loudly and incessantly of the profound attachment they felt (and feel still), of the penetrating concerns that animated and sometimes tormented them in those days now long gone in the company of that noble society of beautiful and valiant young boys, whose every utterance is remembered as an example of a mode of speech as poignant and meaningful as the *langage clus* of the troubadours. (Such are the repressions of memory in the face of the overwhelming distractions of whatever present obtains.)

CHORUS OF DRIVEN DANCERS, MAD TO BE HELD

"We've all gone crazy lately, darling, rolling 'round the basement floor."

"So What? Butterflies are free to fly away."

"Love leaves its stains."

"Pedal to the metal, muthafucka!"

Years later, when it all blew up in everyone's face, some realized the cruel irony of the obliviating ubiquity of "I Will Survive," the disco anthem, at a time when the dancers were already succumbing to amoebiasis and taking every drug there was in the world to go on dancing. Then, when the curtain at last did come down, Donna Summer found her stage-door Johnny in Jesus, but her *orebaisia* gay-boy cult found theirs in Mr. Death (and he didn't look anything at all like that Brad Pitt.)

And in those years to come, the author would spend time with friends in Westbeth, often gazing down on what remained of the Morton Street Pier, a blackened slab, like an enormous Anselm Kiefer canvas year by year dismantled further, until the blackened surface had been torn away and the pilings had almost completely sunk into the North River, like the Sunken Cathedral and the Kingdom of Ys.

◄o►

Excerpts from A Historical Document: *The Warehouse Newsletter* (kindly entrusted to the author by the artist-collector-gay archivist Barton Benesh).

The Warehouse was one of a succession of dance halls with free-for-all back rooms then known as "waterfront fuck pits." As the following excerpts demonstrate, the convergence of Civic Activism and Vested Interests, like that of any two streets on the Queer Street map, created any number of Speakers' Corners.

WAREHOUSE NEWSLETTER
THURSDAY, AUGUST 14, 1975
VOL. 1, #8 - 2,500 COPIES

Printed and Distributed in the general interest & welfare of Gays in the Village to become more knowledgeable and aware of the dangerous conditions that exist in and immediately about Warehouse Piers 48 and 51—STAY OUT OF THERE AT NITE.

MICHAEL'S THING PRAISES "WAREHOUSE NEWSLETTER"—NITE ACTIVITY ON PIER 48—SLOW!!! EXTREME FIRE HAZARD EXISTS ON ALL PIERS—EXERCISE CAUTION WITH CIGARETTES!!!!

As the last issue of the Newsletter was being distributed the article that appears in the current <u>Michael's Thing</u> was called to my attention. It begins on page 37 and continues for about 4 pages. I am very grateful to this publication for taking the position it has on this matter. I had no idea that they had planned article and it was well presented including a little history of the gay activities that began a couple years ago and has since grown into one of the most dangerous nite areas in the city. On a par with this dangerous situation in our Village area would be Central Park, Morningside and Riverside Parks and the inevitable subway "T" rooms. Many times I have thought the motto of promiscuous gays, including myself, should be a variation of the Post Office motto: Through rain, hail, sleet and snow, the "gays" will get through!!! I recall the "land's end" area in San Francisco when I lived there years ago—it was more like mountain climbing than casual cruising.

Would you believe that there are still some people in the New York City Gay Community who are not aware of the dangerous conditions on the Pier? It is up to all of us to discourage people from going to the piers at night. When someone asks you where the pier is—go ahead and tell them, but I believe you also have a responsibility to advise them NOT to go there and WHY. If they still insist that's their business. If they have no more consideration or respect for themselves than to take the risk I hope they have their life insurance paid up. It has been mentioned in this paper previously that because of the big decline in nite activity at the pier, and that about the same number of pick-pockets-muggers continue to work the pier, that your chances of being ripped off and/or physically assaulted have gone up. YOUR CHANCES OF BEING ROBBED, HURT OR IN FACT KILLED ARE BETTER THAN 50 PERCENT. Pier 48 continues to be a questionable place to visit during the day and is continually visited by people "other than gays." Nearly every evening that it is not raining I have made several trips around the area at night, and occasionally during the day. It just isn't the place to go for "fun." Now that the Federal House of Detention has been closed and all the men moved to the new prison downtown the immediate area in front of Pier 48 has become more deserted during the day hours and at night. When you go up those stairs to the second floor of Pier 48 ask yourself how you are going to get out of there when the local teenage gang invades the pier. If someone throws down a cigarette on the stairwell and it smolders into flames, how are you going to get out? You should think of those things before you go up the steps. There are also a few areas on the second floor where the floor is very weak—watch your step—is the guy you are cruising for real, or is he a rip-off??

The NEWSLETTER is available at most of the bars. Kellers, Danny's, Peter Rabbitt's, Choo Choo's Pier, Ty's, Boots & Saddles, The Underground and the Studio Book Store. They are also available on Piers 48, 49 and 51. You will find them hanging on nails for easy pull-off, or lying around. At the One Potato they are on top of the cigarette machine—at the Studio Book Store they are near the bulletin board. Copies can be found occasionally on the piers during the day but are usually torn down by evening by the muggers, pick-pockets or a few others who seem to be opposed to informing people about the dangers of the piers.

An incident at the Ramrod when I distributed my last NEWSLET-TER puts a question in my mind. Until last week I have been leaving copies at the Ramrod. After I left several dozen copies there last week, including hanging some on the coat hooks near the pool table, I was curious where they had disappeared to when I passed by about 15 minutes later. Was informed by the bartender at this point that he had been told by the manager, and also that I had been informed that they did not want copies of the NEWSLETTER in the place. No one has ever told me not to leave copies there. I have no problem in dealing with that in and of itself. What pissed me off was why didn't the bartender say so when I came into the place and proceeded to pass them out to those few people at the bar, hang copies around the room, saw the bartender reading the article, BUT ONLY after I left did he remove the copies and throw them in the garbage can. I expect that copies will be thrown away by some for whatever their reason, but to willfully destroy copies in the manner in which the Ramrod saw fit was certainly in poor taste to say the least. It is also curious that the person who was responsible for trying to take down the barricade to the second floor of Pier 48 identified himself, not by name to me, but as being from the Ramrod—whether he works there, hangs out there, or includes himself in a social set that goes there I do not know, I know only that he identified himself as being from the Ramrod. All the other bars have been very cooperative in allowing me to hang the NEWSLETTER on their walls, give it out to customers, etc. They seem

to support the concept of disseminating information about the piers—
it is to their advantage businesswise if nothing else. Many thanks go
to Arbie, Joe, Dennis, Choo Choo, Julio and Cy for their cooperation.

An observation on Pier 51: The crowd there seems to be a different
attitude as opposed to the attitude that existed on Pier 48 when it was
the popular place to go during the day. The discretion and general con-
duct of everyone is much less blatant than ever existed on "48." On
Pier 48 the attitude used to be "everyone for himself" and completely
independent from anyone else for good or bad circumstances. At Pier
51 today there is a very healthy attitude of being concerned about each
other and accepting the conditions of the physical structure as being
hazardous, but reasonably safe when discretion and care are exer-
cised. That kind of an attitude is healthy and doesn't seem to distract
from playing fun games—just watch your step with bare feet or sneak-
ers—lots of chips of broken glass and loose boards with rusty nails
sticking up. AGAIN, LET ME REMIND EVERYONE THAT ANYONE WHO
ENTERS THE PIERS IS IN VIOLATION OF THE LAW FOR TRESPASSING.

To clarify a comment at the end of last week's NEWSLETTER about
being "sitting ducks for muggers in the area." The "made to order
mugger area" DID NOT mean that the bars were mugger areas, but
that the Pier(s) are "made to order mugger areas" and should be
avoided. Let's face it gentlemen, there are literally hunderds of people
in the area at night and especially on weekends. The muggers and
pick-pockets know this and will take advantage of it whenever possible IF YOU ARE IN THE MUGGERS TERRITORY—PIER 48 AT NIGHT.

◄○►

Chorus of Appalled Elders (for whom the Clones are the Gadarene swine,
being driven by demons into the Sea of Galilee):

"It's worse than the Soviet Union, really—worse than any five-year plan;
their relentless program has necessitated the sacrifice of the comfort, the
nerves and the embedded customs of an entire generation."

"They feel strongly that personal comfort is irrelevant."

"So is sable, darling, but we covet it all the same."

"Loudly as their *apophasis megale* [great declaration] goes booming
through the universe, the basis of their existence is correspondingly slim, for
in order to exist in reality conscious reflection is demanded."

"Dank black holes, full of creeping murmur and the poring dark."

"Their so-called fierce, incomparable joy in succumbing to a state of out-rageousness, dissipation, restlessness, and desecration has resulted in immense exhaustion and amoebiasis on a massive scale. Also, herpes and hepatitis; *everybody* is getting transfusions, as if indeed Dracula were loose in Gotham."

"Dracula indeed! Night life and vampirism have always been connected, dear, althought the bat angle is oddly apt. Most humans would fail miser-ably in the environment designed for bats, hanging stark naked from the ceiling in caves cluttered with dung, catching insects in one's open mouth while flying at high speeds through the night. Not *them* however—they glory in it."

"Are we talking, darling, about what is coming or came down at the Mineshaft? What flecks of gold in the sluice of the experience? Primitive and palingenic elements. Shit. Men lie on the floor while other men shit on them. That's a *religion*? People are eating each other's shit at the Mineshaft. Nice people don't eat shit, darling. They eat what we are eating, here at the Coach House!"

"What I say is, when your idea of a base camp at the summit of ambi-tion is a time-share in some jerry-built lean-to in Island Pines, you are undoubtedly a troubled woman."

Then, turning on a dime—a trick they'd mastered dancing the Madison out in Cherry Grove—inverting in sudden mood swings the amorous terms of the above conviction, they set about leveling vociferous maledictions against the new young, the lately beautiful, declaring in effect, "You, the ungrateful, are set to betray to a hostile world the doings of a secret brotherhood, for which crime the penalty is annihilation."

Thus, when the Firehouse is itself burned down by the Mafia, some said 'twas with the blessings of the Old Guard, who, like the character in that noto-rious-faggot-and-big-Camp-Yukio-Mishima's *The Temple of the Gold Pavilion*, felt that the place had to be destroyed to become eternal. The Mafia had always gleefully cooperated with a cunningly abject faggotry, but could not abide the arrogance of a rampant new one, the recusant retreat to dim, pricey haunts muttering, "We told you so!" In them, as they attempt to find repose in lavish love seats, easy chairs and soothing fireplaces, the candles they'd burned at both ends gutter out.

(Yukio Mishima [*Shining Star*, the English translation of his *nom de plume/guerre*] had become in the sixties not only a global literary phenome-non, but in his spare time—when he wasn't either writing another knockout book or training his private army to return Japan to glory and reinstate the Mikado as a divinity—an astronomically priced hustler, brought from Tokyo to New York to drive hordes of rice queens mad with desire by Tennessee Williams—operating out of the Monkey Bar of the Hotel Elysée on East 54th Street, and, desperate faggot rumor had it, charging a hefty agent's fee.)

Finally, to complete the grisly metaphor of flaming faggots, constant flames, carrying the torch and so forth, the curse seems to snap back fiercely at the howlers when, one sorry night in 1977 at the venerable Everard, in a scene reminiscent of the immolation of the Old Believers in Mussorgsky's *Khovanshchina*, a token number of those very old believers are indeed incinerated. An era completed. Mayor Abe Beame expresses outrage that the nine dead men were asleep in an establishment intended for bathing. He is not renominated.

Not that the *arriviste* commissars really constituted a unity, no matter how much of a united front they seemed to put up. They were sharply divided on many issues, of which one in particular became emblematic: the problem of Stephen Sondheim. Extraordinary lyrics, innovative dramaturgy, a driving theatrical vision . . . and fake music.

In the end the controversy, faulted as too fatiguing in a time when *energy* was everything, was unceremoniously snuffed out. The upshot: either you hailed Stephen Sondheim as a genius (as in a similar vein, and with similar political correctness, the majority would hail Steven Spielberg) or you could kiss goodbye to any invitation anywhere. It seemed that even in the pitch-black back rooms and in the trucks (where they couldn't clock you according to your color-coded back-pocket handkerchiefs), unless you could hum "Here's to the Ladies Who Lunch," you couldn't, as the English—arriving in their droves in the wake of the utter collapse of Swinging London—liked to put it, "Go toss yourself off in a corner, darling!"

So far as Kander and Ebb's *Cabaret* was concerned, no such vexing aesthetic problem sprang up. Kander and Ebb were not constitutive of serious argument; there simply was not enough there there, a lack, however, magnificently overcome by Joel Grey, the most *explicit* Broadway musical actor since Larry Kert in no matter what class of vehicle. Joel Grey *was* *Cabaret*. No male singing actor since Ezio Pinza had made such an impact on Broadway, and no female since Ethel Merman. Joel Grey brought to Broadway the artistry that Judy Garland had brought to the form she virtually invented, the single-performer spectacle, forerunner of both Performance Art and the Happening.

Cabaret became something else, in retrospect. As *A Berlin Diary* was prelude to the Holocaust, so it was prelude first to the devastating amoebiasis and hepatitis epidemics of '70s homosexual New, and ultimately to AIDS.

Meanwhile, the author, who never did again return to the Stonewall, except by way of watching pass by the first several commemorative parades, returned to Max's Kansas City, in time to be in at the death of Candy Darling and to participate in the liberation, re-invention and apotheosis of decade-long famous and fabulous Holly Woodlawn (of whom her alter ego Chi-Chi Castanets declared, "Holly *es muy chic*; *ella compra en* Bloomingdale's").

Whereupon, chiefly through the management of the redoubtable Bill Corley (recipient of the Letters from London, Chapter Sixteen, and constant telephone sidekick), who wrote for her publicity kit, "Holly holds the telephone in a hanky—she is far too chic to touch plastic," and the encomia of George W.S. Trow in *The New Yorker* ("Holly is the very best transvestite"), record-breaking engagements at Reno Sweeney's and Trude Heller's sealed the reputation of this charismatic Latin from Manhattan as the Goddess of All Downtown.

Additionally, the author is at long last published, initially in *New American Review* (cover story: rapt introduction by editor Solotaroff) and finally, through the good offices of Susan Sontag (the Benefactor, whom he had not as yet met formally, but with whom his partner had struck up a friendship; as production manager of *The New York Review of Books*, they had been working together long hours nightly—her essays being written and delivered to press with thrilling celerity), who, by dint of her gimlet eye for the new and startling, had brought *Mawrdew Czgowchwz* to her own publisher, Farrar, Straus and Giroux.

Mawrdew Czgowchwz, well reviewed in columns across the country, sells selectively ("Oh, a book like that has to be allowed to get up steam"). Nevertheless, promptly disappearing from library shelves everywhere. What a camp.

Soon the author, wondering what next, hears a familiar voice, the Guardian Angel's, whispering admonitory words in his ear.

"Write something else, something new and exciting."

"What?"

"Plays, sagas, essays, anything."

—◄o►—

Scribblings in notebook from that tricky time:

A note in the personals of a gay newspaper. "Never been rained on; no one's ever sat in the back seat." (With telephone number.)

"Busy little—seeking indeed to foster those sinuous fluencies needed to make one's way among strangers. Or as somebody once remarked, not too unfairly, a fairy-dust factory running at full bore."

Overheard at the Beau Geste:

"Do you realize, darling, that this *Directoire* has renamed the month of Judy *Stonewall*? I want them all beaten to death with baseball bats!"

Something terrible is going on at the Continental, the New St. Marks, the Club, Man's Country. Nothing less than the destruction of traditional bath culture (conversation/repose/meditation/sex) due to the drug explosion and the introduction of Muzak over the PA systems: calculated to get-'em-in and get-'em-out, without concern for sleep cycles or overnight accommodation or any civility at all.

Significantly (but it cannot last), the horror has lately been valiantly counteracted by the Continental's introduction of the triple-goddess cabaret: Eleanor Steber, Bette Midler and Holly Woodlawn. Habitués sitting on whoopy cushions in slouchy postures redolent of Levantine ennui in the fabulously appointed souterrains of the majestic Ansonia, have prompted the very old to declare a new '30s-Berlin decadence.

> "The shadow of the dome of pleasure
> Floated midway on the waves;
> Where was heard the mingled measure
> From the fountain and the caves.
> It was a miracle of rare device,
> A sunny pleasure dome with caves of ice!"

From the Plaza Fountain through the Ice Palace to the Mineshaft: the downward trajectory of a culture.

> "I would build that dome an air,
> That sunny dome! Those caves of ice!
> And all who heard should see them there,
> And I should cry, Beware! Beware!
> Their flashing eyes, their floating hair!
> Weave a circle round them thrice

And close your eyes with holy dread,
For they on honey-dew hath fed,
And drunk the milk of Paradise."
                              —Samuel Taylor Coleridge, *Kubla Khan*

◄○►

The author has discovered John Waters—remembers him as a kid at Max's.
Crazy brilliant; wishes he could work with him (like, say, on a fake docu-
mentary about all of the above), but he is one star who flies strictly solo (like
Mawrdew Czgowchwz fleeing Prague).

("I do think people tend to look their best under arrest"—John Waters.)

He has also come upon (in this instance and because of his time abroad
some years after the knowing few) the chronicles of one Boyd McDonald.
Thousands of vagrant "voices" of Queer America.

At last Richard Plante has been heard: the pink triangle victims of the
Nazi death camps are being recognized.

◄○►

"Myth is something that never was and always will be true."
                              —Socrates, to the youth of Athens (hemlock words)

The seventh anniversary of Stonewall. More and more people are claiming
to have been there, on the spot at the barricades, hurling things and shouting. How should the author know? He got out. The only thing he can't
figure is, he got back to Mott Street a little after twelve. (He remembers
because the V., sitting home reading Balzac, said he wasn't going to start worrying until midnight, and he was just about to start worrying.) But the reports
say it didn't even start until twelve-thirty. So, they're asking him, "You were
inside, right?" And he answers "Yes, but I didn't see anybody throw any shot
glass or any cops in uniform duck down behind the bar."

He saw one demented queen on speed throw a drink—a stinger it was—
in the plainclothes cop's face—there were two cops, and he decided by the
look of them that one was Italian and one was Polish, on the principle that
the Precinct would never send an Irish cop in to take the Friday night payoff
in such a toilet, they're so *sensitive*, so *volatile*—and the queen tossed the drink
and hissed, "That's for *Judy*!"

He remembers thinking, that's what George Brent says to Bette as he's leaving to go off to his medical conference and she, unbeknownst to him, is going blind and about to die, and he's talking about a cure for brain tumors, and with each strike, he'll say, "That's for Judy, that's for my wife!" And he—the author, not George Brent—knew it was a stinger, because he was sitting at the bar with the distressed queen, both ordering the same drink and getting buybacks and putting them away each about one in ten minutes, and in fact the queen, as a gesture of commiseration over Judy had given the author two Dexamyl, and he kept looking up at the platinum blond go-go boy with the filthy feet dancing on top of the bar while the prismed ball flicked specks of light all over the room, like at Roseland.

So he can't figure it, because the plainclothes were not the vice squad, and it was all over before midnight, and he thought, well now I can go home, now that I've witnessed the queen's grand gesture, and all the wop cop did was smile—almost as if he too were suffering over Judy—and in fact stopped the Pole from retaliating with force, and he remembers saying to himself that was cool; maybe the Italian (who was very gorgeous, whereas the Pole was a slug) has somebody in the family or some *goombah* who's queer, or maybe he too is feeling Judy's death, because she did after all have heterosexual fans too, lots of them, and after all, why would they aggravate the incident futher and draw attention to their routine mission to pick up the weekly hush?

So he wakes up the next afternoon that June to find V. still reading Balzac and the Village threatening to go up in flames, and V. says a couple of the gang have called wanting to know—because he'd been telling them about this new adventure he was on and this low dive, as in Billy Strayhorn's "Lush Life," he was going to regularly to watch the go-go boys, always fantasizing he's Audrey Hepburn with George Peppard in *Breakfast at Tiffany's*, sitting at the bar getting looped and watching the stripper and saying back and forth, "Do you think she is deeply and meaningfully talented?" "Talented, yes, deeply and meaningfully, no."

Aubrey wants to know was he at the Stonewall last night? and V. says he doesn't know, and that night the flames indeed break out, and he of course never goes near the place, tries to say quiet, but has a terrible dream about Judy being burned at the stake, like Falconetti in Dreyer's *Jeanne d'Arc*, only it's really him.

—◦—

Sex at Gethsemane: phone call from Bill Corley:

"Mard, they're doin' it in the bushes! Jimmy Palmieri was feelin' fucked out and went down there on a meditation retreat, and they're *doin'* it, Mard, same as everybody up here, only instead of lickin' it off the floors like we are, they're lickin' it off the dewy grass at dawn. It's a *scandal!* I mean ain't they supposed to be down there *praying* for the salvation of the *world?* It's a scandal, worse than the suppression of the Latin mass. It's all because of the pope, y'know." (Paul VI, who as Carlo Montini, Cardinal Archbishop of Milan, was said to have had a stable of the most gorgeous models in Europe straight off the runways of the Via Montenapoleone, and was said also to frequent, in mufti, the lineup of *ragazzi* in the *Stazione Centrale.*) "The fags have got the pope by the balls, Mard. I'm telling you, the Church won't *survive* it!"

Author feels a great desire to write these tidings up and send them to Boyd McDonald at *Straight To Hell* publications, except that Aubrey insists he writes all those "contibutions" himself, which is the point and why he's so great.

But maybe this is irrelevant, because he (QT, not Boyd McDonald, who is a loner par excellence) has been asked by Richard Hayes, who's climbing on the wagon, to join the editorial founding board of something called *Christopher Street.* The editor-in-chief to-be is somebody called Byrne Fone; lives on Stuyvesant Place, the divine street only a block long, running slantwise between Third and Second, with St. Marks (the church, not the baths) at the Second Avenue end.

◄○►

Author passed the *Christopher Street* ed board test and, although by the time the premier issue hit the stands, Byrne Fone (he knew what *he* was doing all right) had dropped out, was represented in it by a review of Fassbinder's *Faustrecht der Freiheit.* That was it for CS, but the experience warmed him up for writing about Fassbinder, and as feature writer and regular New York Film Festival reviewer in *Film Comment,* for publishing an important piece on Douglas Sirk, right opposite one on the master by Fassbinder himself (in translation), in which they both discussed the same four pictures, *All That Heaven Allows, Written on the Wind, The Tarnished Angels* and *Imitation of Life.*

—◄○►—

Journal entry:

Aubrey called last night with hideous news. Addison Verrill, *Variety* stringer and astringent wit, a friend to the otherwise friendless, has been murdered. A. called yesterday morning to announce the death of the Meneghini, of a heart attack, in Paris, *una vera traviata* (*"sola, abbondonata, in questo popoloso deserto che appellano Parigi"*). What news will Dame Sibyl bring tomorrow? These things always happen in threes, don't they? On the other hand maybe he won't be calling here at all, but elsewhere to announce. . . . CUT!

Addison's body discovered by Sharon Delano and Luis Sanjurjo with a knife sticking out of the chest (stabbed right to the heart) and the head bashed in with an iron frying pan, lying on the floor smeared with Addison's gorgeous, quicksilver brains. This is queer life?

Exactly a week after the screaming headline in the *Village Voice* WHO KILLED ADDISON VERRILL? ran, the murderer, a sickeningly eerie dead ringer for the victim, significantly absent the gleam of a beautiful high intelligence in Addison's flashing eyes, had confessed to Arthur Bell ("Bell Tells") "I KILLED ADDISON VERRILL!" and the terrible story was told in full: the pickup at Danny's, on Christopher Street, the drugs, almost certainly PCP and/or MDA ("Mary—Don't Ask!"), the psychotic narcissistic rage erupting in bed with the mirror image and the hideous, brutal murder of one of the true princes of the city, who, same as the author, had a right to hang around down around the river, but met his death doing so.

The Guardian Angel, an encore:

"Write something new and exciting."

"What?"

"Anything. Plays, essays, poems—"

"We've been through that."

"So do it then."

"One can but try."

"One might try thinking of succeeding to boot."

Funny, he's just bought his first pair of them. Boots.

—◄○►—

On the theatrical front, after a series of exhilarating and initially promising discussions with actresses Grayson Hall and Viveca Lindfors and a meeting with the director Minos Volanakis, the author's playwrighting aspirations came a cropper in a welter of what film critic Andrew Sarris once called disruptive career problems. Few murmurs from the Coast ("Some promises of a test, nothing definite"), compounded by the disinclination of arts editors in the downtown papers, for whom he had been working for some time, to put the author in row G on the aisle of any playhouse in town for the purpose of reviewing, lead him to conclude that as a man of the theater he seemed likely to remain for some time in the *lobbies* category. Undeterred in his mind, he did manage to conceive a postscript to a play he greatly admired then and has continued to admire since, Mart Crowley's *The Boys in the Band*. This opus he had found it necessary to defend passionately against virulent accusations in *the community* ("Ha, ha, *hah*, Blanche!") of its author's selling out to heterosexual fag bashers by painting a "down" picture of a life they were so very committed to publicizing as happy, joyous, boundless and free—without so much as a nod either to old Harry Hay or old Leo Lerman or old Tobias Schneebaum or anybody else except that darling old wanker Dennis Pratt, out in full regalia with a television play all about him under the *nom de théâtre* Quentin Crisp. *The Boys in the Band*, a beautifully crafted and passionately true melodrama of shipwreck and survival, was exactly what they should have taken to their hearts, not least of all to fortify them for what turned out to be the torpedoed sinking to the bottom of the sea of their very benighted queer existences.

◄○►

Postscript to *The Boys in the Band*:

Michael meets a friend the morning after the curtain comes down, at St. Malachy's. He's coming down the steps from mass upstairs in the Actors' chapel and the friend, an old "Wanna-know-why-I-drink?" sister he hasn't seen in some years, is coming up the stairs from the Sunday morning meeting of Alcoholics Anonymous in the basement.

Michael is amazed, and asks what's happened to the old friend to bring him to this pass.

"Well, you know, darling, I always did like a good trick, in the sleight-of-hand department, I mean, as well as in the other. Parlor tricks, *trompe-l'oeil* and *trompe-l'oreille*, and the amazing thing is, all these people—and we number in the hundreds of thousands, they've pulled this *trick* on themselves, and they get you to pull it on you too—meaning me.

"You never saw Gertie Lawrence, darling, in *The King and I*, right down on 45th Street at the St. James—because of course you came from out there someplace, whereas I didn't. I came from right here in Hell's Kitchen. I was the Girl from Tenth Avenue—remember? *I* remember the time we had that long discussion about it, how you felt like an imposter, and believed everybody else who'd come to New York from Out There must feel like one too, at heart. Very *Manhattan Tower*, that discussion, and very Dawn Powell.

"Anyway, Gertie sang a little song in that show. Not 'Hello, Young Lovers,' the one she sang to the children, grouped around rather like the children gathered around the feet of Christ you see in those sickly oleographs—there's undoubtedly one up there in that big room you work, hanging in an alcove with a rack of vigil lights all ablaze in front of it. Or like the pictures of the little pickaninnies and slant-eyes gathered around the feet of the Capuchin missionaries they paste on the mission box.

"But in this case earlier in the show—in the opening scene—to her, Anna's, son. A song, dear, all about fear, and how Gertie fooled the people she feared by whistling herself out of it. Whistling a happy tune—can you stand the pain? Hammerstein's lyrics are so sickening, really; it was Larry Hart who had the goods, desperate drunken woman that she was. And fooled herself as well—Gertie, that is; poor Larry never fooled himself or anybody else. And this was especially poignant because all the while Gertie was in the most terible pain and dying of cancer.

"Well, dear, AA is rather like that. You might want to give it a try—if only to expose it, yet again, for what it is—you were always as I remember a real stickler for home truths, especially in the case of the homeless homosexual. But y'know, I'll tell you something. You look pretty exposed yourself this morning—rather more in need of a little cover story than yet another homeless homosexual truth.

"Here's my number, dear—in case you've struck it out of your little black book. I'd be happy to meet you any time—I always liked you, you know: you were as big a sonofabitch as any I ever grew up around, and as anybody I've met so far in that den of hypocrites downstairs. Oh, and *admitted* hypocrites, dear, we even have a slogan for it: *Act As If*.

"And that, I guess, is my homely, homosexual truth for the day as well as my little bit of twelfth-step work, carrying the message to the still-suffering alcoholic—because you never as I remember made any bones about that, the alcoholic suffering.

"Now I can go get a strong black unspiked take-out coffee from Smiler's and check into the 55th Street Cinema for *Centurions of Rome.* Have you seen it? I've been every day for two weeks, sometimes sitting—or kneeling—through it twice. An absolute masterpiece, darling, starring the Godman of the Moment, Eric Ryan. I mean seriously, forget Richard Burton in *The Robe*; forget Victor Mature in *Demetrius and the Gladiators*, never mind the rumors, and anyway I think those photos are as fake as the one of poor Jimmy Dean fucking a pig back home in Indiana.

"Why, do you know, darling, that if you check into the St. Marks any night in the wee hours until the end of the run, you will find him down in the steam room, being *worshiped?* Yes, venerated and tongue washed—every limb and crevice of him. They say it's all part of the campaign, and that he stands there for *hours*, darling, like a *statue.* I don't think I could take it, and in any case, I'm in bed by ten or, at the latest, eleven, these days, reading poetry. George Herbert just now:

> 'If then all that worldlings prize
> Be contracted to a rose;
> Sweetly there indeed it lies,
> But it biteth at the close.'

"You said a mouthful *there*, queen. Well, listen, darling, I should be down on my knees in the front row in about ten minutes. I'd light a candle for you if the had any in the joint; as it is, guess I'll just have to strike a match.

"*Arriva-derci*, pet, or as Fulton Sheen used to say every week on television, in the springtime of our happy youth, 'Bye now, and God love you!' Was she a camp? *She* acted as-if all right; they should have given her the fucking Sarah Siddons Award."

CHAPTER TWENTY

Fielding Shortstop

> *"There are no small parts, only small actors."*
>
> (proverbial)

Wherein the author's epic ambitions . . . hold (as to a pattern filed), while he, employed as a journalist in a way he finds analogous to the fetching position of shortstop (adopted in baseball in consequence of the preponderant right-handed batter) learns the value of quick (but telling) response.

STARDOM PLUS

Curious, variable "results" come to be published whenever and wherever seekers after "that elusive quality"—whether they be would-be entrepreneurs or putative hawkers—announce they've found it/they've got it. They're talking about stardom. Purpose, radiance, oneness, strength, grace, the will, the ways . . . *all that.*

Stardom may be appraised as a quality, as a realm of no easy access, as a locked chamber: a fantasy tomb as a way of life. Is stardom accidental? Is it a visitation? Is it a compulsion—all that heaven allows? What makes a star, and who knows?

What is it that separates the star from fellow toilers? There is no explanation. They who think they know are mistaken. They who say they know are dangerous: do not entertain them; pass them by.

One verified method of celebrating as opposed to dissecting mythic celebrity (stardom) is to isolate the MC (star). First go hunting and capture ye your star. Be sure you know what you're after. The star is not only not like fellow toilers at that point in history/geography; the star is not like other stars either. No two great singers are remotely alike. No star actress wears anybody else's old hair *or* calls herself an actor. The *prima ballerina assoluta* is elevated, not hoisted.

Then examine the star in relation to the star alone. As Mrs. Siddons apparently had the wit to understand, *honesty* is the mark of a star. A star is honest in the most difficult way, and in the old meaning. It's a pain to be a star. Toilers may eventually go home to rest. A star may be allowed the occasional luxury of assuming an attitude of repose; s/he may not rest.

Is stardom ephemeral? The controversy rages. Is the goddess you watched devouring fate her way last night on the *Million Dollar Movie* a star anymore as she plotzes just now across Seventh Avenue into the Stage Delicatessen fixated on cold tongue and Diet Dr Pepper? Is there a God?

The diva nearing ninety is a star. She's a star if ever there was one. To ask why would be an impertinence. Watch her progress into the opera house. Consider her eternal. Thirteen years ago, on a summer night in Central Park, the ancient high priestess of the dance raised two potted flames up in her hands. She lifted her arms against the dark. Nobody in the world could know why. She was a star; that was all.

Stars understand their stances, but not apparently. "True stars impel; they need never campaign."

Ten Things Stars Rehearse to Enforce Their Stardom

1. Glances of Withering Scorn

2. Concern

3. Poetical Attitudes

4. Political Attitudes

5. Repose

6. Passion (akin to Concern)

7. Empathy (with Cosmetics)

8. Composition

9. The Balance of Opposites (once called Paradox)

10. LOVE

Stars keep their interior journeys to themselves. Stardom demands secrecy. Obsession is obsession.

Examine then the star in relation to the star alone. Employ circuitous illogic exclusively.

Stalwarts devoted to diva are strenuously concerned merely with establishing the relation in quality (her oneness) between diva this day and diva yesterday. (And nothing is so over as yesterday.)

Picture people (all mankind) indulge most profitably in litanies, not comparisons. There is no yesterday on the screen. A name is a face is a voice is now.

Dancers dance tonight; they've never danced before. "The dancer is in competition with no one but him/herself."

The realm of stardom: no such place. This mistaken notion is most often encountered in the wicked proposition that X, the star, apart from possessing that *c'est ça, sine qua non*, plus tax, "it"—the mystery passport—happens to have been in the right place at the right time. Thus souls have come to grief and ruination paying lip service to a spurious cartography—expounding, predicting, assuring, yakking—only in the end to discover that it is high time for them to check in their lips and their notions of service and go home. There is no land where stars bloom.

Stardom as a sealed chamber. This notion is romantic. It is thereby either all too true or just idiotic. If all too true, it is also currently all too bruited (about). Private lives are private hells—but hold! Our research will uncover the address. We find Madame X alone at home in hell—Lola Montez as She-Who-Must-Be-Obeyed as Norma Desmond as Alma Tormented. Or else private life is Toyland-bliss full of Madame's souvenirs, all extensions of Madame's immutable self—white carpets, mirrors, the Impressionists (or the Post-), marble halls. If the sealed chamber notion is just idiotic, if we may throw the French windows open and admit God's own clear light and air, we can actually *talk* with the star, dance with the star, be with her as she eats and drinks and is merry. Art and life are for then fused. We are stars (for a brief spell).

The frailty of stardom. Madame is indisposed and will not sing. *Madame est souffrante; elle ne danse pas.* Rumbles of desperation on the closed set: the lady is incommunicado—call the agent. The High Priestess of Ptah has never been indisposed in her career; Aida may become indisposed between the boudoir and triumphal scenes. None of the Willis is quite likely to—God forbid—break a leg, but Giselle may split a tendon

in the mad scene and find herself unable to come up out of the grave—so
to speak—to jeté her way to salvation in the second act. Dress extras do not
ever "go" incommunicado. The frailty of diva arises out of the demands she
makes upon her voice. She may speak to her voice; she may not bully it. If
she tries, the voice will out. The frailty of the *prima ballerina* is partly a consequence of the stress she puts on her center, which must become unwaver-
ing, and partly a literary device once translated and immortalized by a great
lady of the screen. The frailty of great ladies of the screen is the consequence
of and culmination of the belief in the frailty of women in Western civilization. As a belief, it is not long for this world.

THUH OPRA

"I know what I'll do, I'll throw 'em an opra."
                                        —Mae West, in *Going To Town*

What follows is eternally relevant—but it dates from, is dated by, 1978.

Mae West, eternal diva, empress of hilarity, essaying the role of Cleo Borden, fabulously wealthy cattle baroness and international temptress (in the
film *Going To Town*, 1934), faces a problem: How to crash the set who
summer out at Southampton; how to make a big splash among the dressy
old bags who drink pink tea with their pinkies crooked in the air. "I know
what, I'll do," Cleo/Mae decides. "I'll throw 'em an *opra!*" So she does (or,
she does so). She throws them a chamber production of *Samson and
Delilah*. Mae West's thumbnail Delilah is about the greatest thing she ever
put on film.

"Opra" started out as chamber entertainment in late-sixteenth-century
Italian *palazzi*. This season at the Metropolitan Opera House, Beverly
Sills, no mean comedienne herself and one of America's two top executive
divas, gave a performance of the courtesan Thaïs which in many eerie ways
seemed inspired by Mae West's Delilah.

What can this mean?

Singing is the ultimate expression of sexuality. This is the meaning of
all mating calls in this world. True passion does not speak, it sings. A sung
mass is as much a ritual display of passion as is an opera. What it is, exactly,
that singing does to the nervous system has never been explained, but it is

certain that the music of the spheres is not instrumental but vocal. Angels sing. (They play harps for accompaniment.)

(Thus the author, seemingly addicted from an early age to word association and, hence, to psychoanalysis, chose his diva in a split second on a single hearing at the Metropolitan Opera House of the aria "*Porgi, amor,*" the opening of the second act of Mozart's *Le Nozze di Figaro*. Victoria de los Angeles was, and is, the soprano's name, and for him the name and the instantaneous nature of the decision—if private revelation in a box seat overhanging a public auditorium with, as the soprano of his dreams later averred, every main characteristic of the *corrida*, can be called such a thing—proved a double winner, for the onomastics of the name was, and is, quite beyond apt.)

Mothers do not play toccatas and fugues to soothe their terrified children; they sing lovely lullabies. Left alone to face the void, a pilgrim will sing, or if he cannot, hum. The sound the self makes in, to and for itself is the sound it most needs to "go on." In opera, this need is expressed in terms of exhilarating combat, expressed in terms of "situations" often verging on hilarity, expressed opulently and thrillingly.

The Soprano

Balanchine says ballet is woman. So's opra. The primary iconographic image of opra, even now, is that of an opulently molded woman, wearing a flowing gown and/or, perhaps, a helmet, carrying a fan or a spear. The ultimate operatic religious term is *diva*, which means goddess. The worship of the diva is a continuing function of operaphiles. This circumstance has come about because the diva is the anima image of the composer. All the greatest opera composers have been men. Men project their animas. The diva reigns.

Soprano is in fact a masculine word. It denotes simply one who sings *sopra*, or above the staff (that portion of the Western musical spectrum in which the regular host of humanity speaks and sings). The first *soprani* were young boys, acolytes of the Church of Rome, and *castrati*, a vanished breed. They carried on the tradition of the piping charmer-boys of classical antiquity. None too soon it became evident that a true woman could best produce the soprano thrust required to portray a true woman on the operatic stage. Thus were divas invented. Divas, like courtesans, have informed Western culture. The diva lives in a world of music, champagne and gems. The difficult part is the music.

The Mezzo-Soprano

She is the other diva. Her voice is of a darker coloration. She cannot sail to the very top of the female voice, but what she can accomplish in the middle and lower registers is often far more entrancing, thrilling and voluptuous than the sorts of warbles some soprani give out. She is often the heavy, the "other woman," which, as in forties movies, opens up vast possibilities to crafty females. The classic example of mezzo-soprano composition is the role of the Egyptian princess Amneris in Verdi's *Aida*. Others are the title role in Gluck's *Orfeo*; Bizet's Carmen; Fricka, in Wagner's *Die Walküre*: Saint-Saëns's Dalila; Santuzza, in Mascagni's *Cavalleria Rusticana*. Some singers erase the distinction between soprano and mezzo-soprano by singing parts written for both, or in-between categories. (Maria Callas, Victoria de los Angeles, Régine Crespin, Christa Ludwig, Janet Baker, Shirley Verrett and Grace Bumbry are among those who have done so in our time.)

The Tenor

"The tenor? What about him?" (An anonymous diva, thinking like Mae West . . .) The tenor is the putative peacock in the garden of opra. Tenor singing signals lust. Tenors tend to be far more comically petulant, illogical and pretentious than divas. When they're sexy, they're very very sexy. When they're not—*Next!* Great tenors are the rarest operatic species. Thus, when they impress, they impress forever. Ask anybody to name the biggest opra star ever. Caruso, period. Ask a Wagnerian who was the great Wagnerian *heldentenor*. Melchior. The very names Björling and di Stefano were magical in the forties and fifties, as the names Pavarotti and Domingo are today. And Vickers and McCracken and Gedda and Bergonzi. Tenors often get ideas. One current *heldentenor*, who sings Tristan, suggests that Isolde is really a figment of Tristan's febrile imagination—a projection. ("If they buy *that*, they'll buy *me!*"—one dissenting soul confessed.)

The Baritone

The baritone is the voice of the antagonist-father-brother-seducer-adviser-villain-also ran. Among the greatest baritone parts are Mozart's Don Giovanni—written for, and often sung by, a bass—Verdi's Iago, Wagner's Wotan, Verdi's Falstaff, Debussy's Golaud, Mozart's Count Almaviva and Figaro, Berg's Wozzeck, Bizet's toreador, Escamillo. A good baritone voice is the most reassuring sound on the operatic stage (even, or even mainly, when portraying evil). A tenor's hysterics may arouse, or provoke. The baritone statement tends to ground proceedings. Thus baritones tend to be stable persons. It's in the nature of the job. Baritones accept defeat; tenors next to never. Tenors would rather perish. Baritones make better friends.

The Basso

He can be either *profundo* or *buffo*. The *profundi* tend to play wise old men; the *buffi*, foolish ones or younger rascals. The greatest basso buffo part is Leporello in Mozart's *Don Giovanni*; the greatest profundo, Mozart's Sarastro in *The Magic Flute*. The line between the basso and the baritone is even fuzzier than the line between the mezzo-soprano and the soprano, but the true basso sound is one of almost infernal authority. Bernard Shaw decreed the music written by Mozart for Sarastro music fit to be put into the mouth of God. Considering the God he must have had in mind . . .

Opera Stardom

True stars impel; they need never campaign. In the late nineteenth and early twentieth centuries, opera stars were what movie stars are today. Limos and furs, caviar and champagne, affairs in the newspapers. Then movies, an equally bizarre, ferociously exigent and overwhelmingly seductive art form redefined stardom, reconstituted glamour.

The greatest opera star of all time was Maria Callas. Another great opera star is Birgit Nilsson. She possesses the biggest voice in the operatic world. Beverly Sills is a magniloquent opera star. For a time she had it all. The problem with opera stardom is that it goes when the voice does. Movie stars can last for decades; opera stars cannot.

Once, years ago, a great opera diva, a Metropolitan Opera star, a mainstay, a prima donna, was set to make her entrance as Tosca. A kindly stagehand stooped to help her with the train of her elaborate Act One costume. "Don't bother," she whispered, "they also pay me here to sweep the fucking floors."

Considerations

Opera promotes seraphic absurdity. It, like toe dancing, is an outrageous enterprise. Operaphiles are dangerous. They are *echt* fanatical. (People who think that people who don't think the way they think are menaces are menaces.) Opera is a potent word. It has informed the culture. Soap opera. Rock opera. Horse opera. Space opera.

What goes on at an opera? Too much for television. (Try watching one on television. Very little emerges: all gesticulating dolls.) Tales of love and lust and death—all that—sung out (or bellowed, chirped and crooned all too often). Also very funny things—meant to be so. Almost all the greatest musical shapers of the last four hundred years have grappled with the form. Beethoven wrote one single perfect opera, then stopped. Debussy also left the world one radiant masterpiece. The other great composers left quantities of them.

The Composer

The composer is simultaneously everywhere and nowhere. Of all the rubric pieties of the operatic enterprise, the one most bruited is "the composer's intention." The composer's intention is impossible to fulfill. This is what makes opera a religion, the attempts to realize the composer's intention. (Religion is kinetic bondage.)

There are certain definitions. There is a Mozart style, a Wagner style, a *verismo* style, a French style, a *bel canto* style, a "contemporary" style. Singers become specialists. Leontyne Price avows her best vocal pals are Mozart and Verdi. Her most conspicuous successes have been in Mozart and Verdi roles. Tito Gobbi is thought of almost exclusively in terms of Verdi villains (and the Verdi comic villain, Falstaff). Birgit Nilsson is the greatest Wagnerian singer of our time; Leonie Rysanek, the greatest exponent of the vocal style of Strauss.

The Conductor

The conductor is the composer born again—for a given performance. He must forge his intentions into congruency with the composer's intention. Such as Toscanini did. Such as Wilhelm Furtwängler, Thomas Beecham, Karl Böhm, and Georg Solti did. And Carlo Maria Giulini and Pierre Boulez do. Conductors may also become flamboyant stars, as did Toscanini and Leonard Bernstein and Herbert von Karajan, and as James Levine is in the strenuous process of doing just now. In America, where stardom is the established religion, "charismatic" behavior wins converts to opra. ("Yes, well, be that as it may . . ."—a dissenter.)

Attendant Priests

Opra is religion-circus-theater-spectacle. Stage directors, set designers, lighting designers, costume designers, publicity folk and collateral noise-makers—and even critics—make crucial contributions. This, as a circumstance, is not news; yet it provokes controversy.

Over a decade ago, a (then) youngish hot-shot stage director was given the job of mounting a contemporary opera's premiere. He cheerfully announced to a group of his minions one afternoon that of course he hadn't bothered with the music; he'd staged the play. Let the rest of them worry about the music. That venture sank like a cement block—containing the composer's intention. Moral: Don't hire a tin-eared hot-shot. An opposing argument: Too many singers, even still, have truculent manners in the matter of positioning themselves to make their noises. One remembers fondly that Callas could sing while waltzing (and even facing upstage). Somewhere the truth reposes. Scratch the tip of the iceberg on this question and the volcano explodes, mixing metaphor, fire, brimstone, ice and the composer's intention.

This season, the astonishing beauty of the lighting plans for *Tannhäuser* and *Pelléas et Mélisande* proved what an enhancement such a contemporarily achieved "addition" can be. In each instance, the lighting partnered the music, telling all. This can have been no fortunate accident. The lighting designer tended to the music.

Operatic publicity folk are a valiant breed. In the clashing temperaments department, opra is as *crowded* as the movies, and the publicity staff must mediate day and night. They are performers, unsinging, if not unsung.

Opra is exactly like the atom bomb. No use asking where it came from. Much less ask why. It is what it is; it is.

The Metropolitan Opera

The building in which opera is housed, so far as most Americans are concerned, is still the Metropolitan Opera House in New York City, a hideous blanched pile decorated in the tackiest decor imaginable, with Chagall's cluttered whimsies pasted up on the walls, and, in the auditorium, polyurethaned cherrywood ingeniously contrived to look like Formica: they were certainly cultivating a new audience. It is a chilling theater to enter. It is, however, acoustically almost entirely satisfactory. Which means that when the lights go down the auditor has a fair chance of getting through the evening without falling asleep and having a nightmare and waking up screaming and causing some excitement. (Falling asleep is an old comic tradition at the opera. Oftentimes it is justified. In fact there are times when a body, if roused, is more than entitled to beg, "Please don't wake me." Opera can be killing. Let's not name names.)

The Line, the Claque and Backstage

In the old days (the good ones), the line flourished. "The line" is the standing-room line at the Metropolitan Opera House. In those days it would form in the late afternoon. It was composed of a few hundred regulars—stalwarts—who formed alliances, friendships and marriages, who argued, who agreed, who fought the chill winters by attendance at operatic spectacle. Nowadays the line is an exigent assemblage of folks who·wrangle. They buy tickets in the same way, but that is all. The differences between the old line and the new line are many and various and irksome.

The procedural rigors of standing on the line as it exists at the new Met—the constricted ambience, the self-appointed "placers" (one might as well be on line at the bank, or waiting for welfare)—induce the kind of torpor that finds expression in the generally insipid quality of the conversation carried on. The conversation on the line in our time bears the same relation to the conversation on the line at the old Met as Muzak does to bel canto. There is no scintillation. It is impossible to believe that anyone could be inspired to depict situations on the line in our time in any poetic or fictive way, that the line could nourish imaginations as it once did. What line folk are up to nowadays is ranting a lot, buying, selling and trading tapes, observing a bizarre pecking order and cruising.

The claque has gone out of fashion. At the old Met, groups of seedy gnomes would regularly organize claques for both the greats and the second-rates. Students were recruited in hushed tones by the gnomes, who would stand in the shadows near the arcade of shops and public telephones along Broadway. The approach was very much the same as "Wanna buy filthy pictures?" was in those days, and like peddling joints and poppers and angel dust is in our time. The going rate was two bucks, which meant that if a client went up to the Family Circle standing perches at the very top of the theater for $1.25, he could make enough on the deal for a snack. Plus he heard the performance for free. This was a way to sop up a little musical culture of an evening and get a few psychic rocks off in the bargain, yelping into the void, making like an opera singer. One was generally solicited for pro-screaming, for bravos; but in the seasons in which Maria Callas redefined operatic performance in New York, many were bribed to shout boos. (Students from the better schools never stooped to join this enterprise.) Debut claques were the most amusing. Occasionally one's conscience so pricked one that, rather than cooperate in a scandal such as Charles Foster Kane might have created, one refunded the money and skulked away. The practice of claquing is generally regarded in our time as, well, tacky. The gnomes seem to have died out.

Going backstage was gorgeous in bygone days. Each diva had what was termed "the list." To be put on the list—by one of the captains in charge of the diva's fan club—was a very big deal. Sometimes one's virtue lay on the line. Making the list was like making the fraternity/sorority. The only open list in the old days was Zinka Milanov's. Everybody in New York seemed to be on it, and the diva would stay on in the dressing rooms until the wee smalls as hundreds filed in for signatures and open house. All one had to do was wait a half-hour in the freezing cold after a performance for whichever star to take off the makeup, have a belt of something and open the doors.

At the Lincoln Center lockup, select groups of the chosen are ushered into a waiting parlor backstage that looks like a seedier version of one of the rooms at Frank Campbell's funeral parlor, there to congregate and/or suffocate until the diva of the evening appears. Going backstage is an ordeal these days. The knowing seldom bother.

The Metropolitan Opera is said—proclaimed, really—to be in the best shape it has been since the early 1950s. Whether or not this vaunted circumstance can be correlated to the surprising trend the Gallup poll recently reported—that more Americans are content with their lives in these United States than were in 1974—is worth considering. (Perhaps while listening to a Saturday broadcast or two this season. For opera foists illusion.) The one thing that is certain is that there are two distinct schools of thought and thinkers (neither of them being bribed by gnomes) on the merits of the Met's artistic director and principal conductor, James Levine. Virtually the entire New York musi-critical fraternity (plus Harriett Johnson) considers him the cat's couture *complet*. To many another seasoned listener, especially those who tend to be enthusiasts of (of all things) *voices*, he is rather Something Else. These are they, the immediate descendants of those Europeans who invented opera and have nourished it for nearly four centuries, the dwindling, aging, increasingly brittle backbone of a metropolitan, operatic culture that spread from New York, Philadelphia, Baltimore and Boston across the length and breadth of the United States, who disapprove to the point of abhorrence the Wall of Sound the newly trained Met orchestra unleashes nightly under the baton of its gung-ho artistic director, who seems to have pared things down to a couple of bare essentials: no interpretation, just *play*, and for choice, just to keep things interesting (and the audience awake), two tempi: loud slow and loud fast—a barrier, through which few voices of any size smaller than those of Birgit Nilsson (or, though she's off the roster nowadays, Eileen Farrell) may penetrate to make the odd dramatic point. (A significant exception to this perplexing routine: the phenomenal Leonie Rysanek, whose wild-card instrument, however on earth or elsewhere it was trained, is capable of cutting through any orchestral boom-box effect, not entirely unlike the way police-emergency-vehicle, ambulance and fire-truck sirens can be heard roaring up and down the avenues beyond the theater walls.)

Some sacred operatic precincts to which operaphiles make pilgrimages are the Mozarteum in Salzburg, Mozart's birthplace; the Bayreuth Festspielhaus, Wagner's self-constructed sacred grove; the Teatro alla Scala in Milan—which by its very name summons up notions, visions, both of holy stairs and of a show-biz stairway to paradise; the Opéra in Paris, a hysterically monumental edifice erected to glorify the essentially imperial nature of the art form; the Vienna Statsoper; the Royal Opera House in London's Covent Garden; and Mozart's unmarked grave.

Speaking of which, Victoria de los Angeles, no great enthusiast of either von Karajan, under whom she had sung Donna Anna at La Scala, or of Salzburg, commenting rather severely one evening at the Navarro, after having given a recital at Avery Fisher Hall, on the Salzburg festival and its politics, drew the following response from her by then dear friend the author: "You mean Mozart is spinning in his grave?" "No, Mozart is not even there in the summer; he has taken a grave at the beach."

Close Encounters With Divas

Interviewing Leonie Rysanek, one of the two female stars of the current big Met hit *Tannhäuser*, is a grand experience. Sitting high over Central Park, pouring out strong coffee and slicing hefty wedges out of a big Viennese cake, offering the visitor a healthy belt of *schnapps*, she lounges, refusing all refreshment, and lights into a vividly detailed analysis of her role—the saintly Elisabeth, whose inner fire, flaring up and all over the turbulent music drama, leads the hero to a mystical salvation.

Miss Rysanek leaped to New York operatic fame in 1959 when she replaced Maria Callas in Verdi's *Macbeth*. She was made to face booing claqueurs from the start, and she routed them all like a real warrior. She became famous right away for "the Rysanek dimension"—which detractors would describe as the notion of playing all her roles the same way, as bonkers. The truth is she found in each of her impersonations a vein of melancholy, fatalistic, introspective truth, and mined it in startling ways. Her Desdemona, for example, became an eerily precognitive collaborator in doom, rather than the more usual hapless sacrificial victim. Her Sieglinde in *Die Walküre* seemed consumed in exalted terror, even as she discovered and succumbed to passion. Her characterizations are relentless, and are all tinged with this arresting, often unsettling, quality. Rysanek cheerfully pours the visitor more coffee, stops, stands, paces about the room, looks over at her husband, who has been gently steering the interview in the most interesting directions, and flatly states that that is the way it must always be for her because of her Czech ancestry. Everything becomes clearer. She jokes, and chats about her famous friendship with Birgit Nilsson (who has publicly credited Rysanek with instructing her in some of the emotional demands of the parts she [Nilsson] had already made famous, and consequently of having helped her deepen her interpretations). She talks enthusiastically, approvingly, of James Levine. She paces, mentioning a persistent back problem, and offers more *schnapps*. She makes the visitor feel he is welcome to stay all afternoon. Her husband calls and postpones an appointment, and the diva talks on at such a pace that ambitions of complete recall on the interviewer's part go right out the window—where they belong, as it turns out. The *gestalt* of Rysanek is immediate, and energizing. She says in as many words exactly what Maria Callas used to say—often sadly: "You see, I know what I do."

Encountering Grace Bumbry at a dinner party given by a madcap operaphiliac swell from Kentucky, and having been apprised ahead of time that the diva had asked that the assembly not talk all night about opera, this guest was fortunate and most agreeably surprised at being seated to Miss Bumbry's right at table, and treated to a delightful, non-stop, extremely animated outpouring all through the many-coursed meal. Exhilarated by her recent success as the second of the two women in *Tannhäuser* (the goddess Venus), she seemed delighted to hold both regal court and the floor, giving out bits of inside dope here and there concerning the progress of operatic affairs of state.

Grace Bumbry, an American and pupil of the late great Lotte Lehmann, made her first big splash in Europe and became famous in an extra-musical way for being the first black singer to appear at the Bayreuth festival (as Venus in *Tannhäuser*, in 1962). Her career as a mezzo-soprano was going full tilt when she decided (not capriciously, she will have you know) to switch over and up to soprano category. (Venus, as it happens, is one of those strange roles which can be sung by either mezzo-sopranos or sopranos.) She was full of gusto in anticipation of her Norma, which she plans for Covent Garden in June, and full of elegant mischief, telling tales out of the operatic arena. "And then she said to me, 'Grace, . . .'"

She delighted the entire company, dwelling in relaxed conversation on the sillier side of the profession, while at the same time brimming over with goodwill and serious appraisals of her many distinguished colleagues, present and former. She spoke particularly of Rysanek, of Nilsson, of her reverence for Callas, of her affection for Victoria de los Angeles (her colleague in Bayreuth in that earlier *Tannhäuser*) and, now and again, this guest will avow, so as not to suggest we spent the evening in the company of an operatic Mary Tyler Moore, with a calculated degree of acid wit on this one, and that one, who, would you believe . . . ? At a sensible hour, Grace Bumbry departed, escorted by the madcap. She had proven enchanting.

Opra: both high hat and low down.

BROKEN GODDESS

"If you are being a woman, be a strong woman!"

Broken Goddess, a short chase-apprehend-agonize-surrender-vanquish-release release, features before all or anything else in the way of a realized work a grand apotheosis of the town's most lovable, improbable, strong boy/girl trouper, whose name itself, redolent of the principle of LASTING in the graveyard dead of psychic winter, is the first and finest emblem of its wearer's valiant, elegant presence in this world frame and time slot that is (provisionally) New York now.

Immortal Films's offering is a slender fragment dealing in the tense exploration and delicate excavation of notoriously treacherous terrain (or space): the area behind the eyes—that nervous quicksand country where nightmares flash out of chaos to trap the soul and drown it in murmuring terror. *Broken Goddess*, a lustrous looking exposé of glamour-as-terror is, in flashes, credit enough to its homaged sources in myth and tragedy—in the manner of an impressive screen test—to encourage its creators to go to greater lengths and make a feature next time out.

The film as it rolls looks very much like the last part of something broken off from something else—the finale of some unsettled agon involving an anonymous dreamer and a frightening anima fantasy projection. The star is happily perfectly cast, being in the immediate sense so evidently a component creature, able in so being to suggest dim haunting correspondences with component archetypes in mythic dream realms—sphinxes, chimeras, manticores, seraphim, etc.—all refracted healing images heralding selfdom. Holly Woodlawn is a renowned and wonderfully adept practitioner of travesty whose performance is achieved on the screen at an assured velocity, always on pitch, always on the attractive *qui vive*, here telling the stark tale of some radical woe. (Drag these days is too usually a matter of shrieky kazoos and lurching frantic slapdash. With La Woodlawn the turn is all blazing trumpets and majestic supplication.)

The protagonist lopes down a long stone staircase into hell, at a purposed, measured, anguished pace. Feet, legs, torso and face pass in vertical review, revealing a shredded Amazon shrouded in mourning-black tatters, hounded down by Torment, driven to distraction at the reflecting pool over which Nike stands adamant sentinel. (The tinted black-and-white footage was shot in pre-to-early dawn at the Bethesda Fountain in Central Park.) In the progress of the film it will be discovered that her triumph is merely her *lasting*, that her reward is *renewal*—the pagan actual grace the Self dispenses at great cost. The climactic self-realization, the Broken Goddess's discovery of her own worth (unspecified in linear plot terms, as is the specific circumstance of her anguish), is fleshed out as the vision of the White Goddess—H.W. in a previous incarnation as a high-glamour blonde siren of the glossy mags parading in the air over the glistening lake in a set of attractive superimposed stills meant to be the numinous emblems of the Broken Goddess's salvation—backward in memory and forward in resolve. The effect achieved is anomalous—Woodlawn's performance in motion down in the dumps is much more gorgeous than Woodlawn's rather conventional transvestite posture in stills, which seems to embalm chic—but the sequence succeeds in the cross-cut "dialogue" between the quivering creature in closeup and the retouched, lacquered creature zooming down out of the sky like some quasi-corporeal meteor. In these moments the luster of the performance becomes fully manifest. It is a technically problematical, jumpy transition which shifts the rhythm of the film rather abruptly. So far the Broken Goddess had been fleeing the camera, her tormentor—the camera playing a vicious largo game of tag, telling her there is nowhere she may hide it will not search her out, expose her. (The most memorable single tableau involving figure and ground in the film is a shot of H.W. couched in misery at the rim of the fountain with the graffito CRAZY emblazoned—courtesy of Gotham's vigilante band of unit publicists—behind on the stone wall her head rests against.)

Some obvious if worn epithets generally employed to describe the music of Debussy in extra-musical terms advertise the film itself: spectral, pleading, aqueous, visionary, erotic, mordant. The use of *La Cathédrale Engloutie* to underpin the Vision Scene is particularly successful. The allusive Laura Nyro titles are attractive, but lend an unnecessary double emphasis—no words, printed or spoken, seem necessary—to the "dialogue" between the mind of the producer-director Dallas and the extraordinary mimic intelligence of his star—all mediated by the makeup artist and hair stylist, the production designer and the editor—a dialogue which goes a fair way toward demonstrating the radical truth that "nothing is lost if one does not try to say the unsayable. Instead, that which cannot be spoken is (unspeakably) contained in that which is said."

When Holly Woodlawn walks back up the stairs into the dawn, she flashes a back the like of which has not been glimpsed on the screen in too long. It is a gesture which commands: "If you are being a woman, be a *strong* woman!" The impulse to leap to the top in a single bound to meet the star up there on the world's plateau can best be expressed in another command—to Immortal Films: "Take that star and shoot her again!"

LUCHINO VISCONTI: IN MEMORIAM

"Count Luchino Visconti, Duke of Modrone, was born November 2, 1906, in Milan. . . . Young Luchino became acquainted early with painting, music and theater . . . He played cello and often visited La Scala. . . . His father organized plays and entertainments in a local theater."

—*New York Times*, March 18, 1976

Operatic Visconti

All epitaphs are killing; they nail life down. ("So *that* was what it was all about, that life.") Similarly evaluations of the works of geniuses (in the case of Visconti, *le opere*). Nevertheless, Verdian Visconti; the association does support.

Visconti was operatic in his cinematic creation not merely as a parallel/ consequence of his grand successes in the lyric theater, or of his intimate work shaping the career of the ultimate singing actress of the mid-century (Callas), but as a consequence of his inheritance. Operaphile Viscontiani, reversing the terms of the metaphor ("like opera"), see in his stage work the mark of the filmmaker, the adaptation of cinematic *trompe-l'oeil* ("tracking" revolves, flicker-lighting, pin-spot "iris" close-ups) to that arena in which a kind of spastic puppetry is the iron convention and theatrical m.o. (As if to comment on this convention, Visconti makes a great deal out of it in the opening scene of *Senso*, in which the flaming spirit of Verdi's music is being acted out in the gallery of the Teatro Fenice in Venice by a "chorus" of Italian patriots—and only trumpeted and mimed by the ham singers.)

Visconti's debt to opera, or rather his inheritance of its glorious abandon, is simply a function of his northern Italian aristocracy. What happens in the soul of every Visconti film is that the spirit of music-and-mimicry (called *musicry*), tutored in twentieth-century celluloid mysteries, becomes immortal-anew (as all "immortal" things depend upon re-election, to be brought back by popular demand). Polyhymnia and Melpomane, enlisted for screen tests, emerge in the Visconti canon as Magnani, Valli, Paxinou, Girardot, Cardinale, Bell, and Berger/Thulin, each the diva.

The Past: Lontani Giorni

"Time's relentless melt." The dissolve; the fade.

Director Visconti deals with that which is over, with that which is lost (including out the abandoned project, *À la Recherche du Temps Perdu*). All cinema can deal with in any case is the past. The forties are now regarded as Byzantine-distant, and the phrase "only yesterday" applies with literal force every time any important film is re-released. It was given to Visconti to trumpet the truth of passing and the past, musically in motion and pictorially in the revival of Renaissance painting in terms of acting bodies and vibrant backgrounds—and in so doing, so performing, that we are not only reminded but assured, not merely convinced but convicted as well. Visconti's art is in this way the veriest Italian art, for in Italy the past, all of it, is everywhere to be seen and felt, corroded but enduring (like Visconti locations and situations).

Even in "contemporary" films, like *La Terra Trema*, *Bellissima*, *Rocco* and *Conversation Piece*, the whole weight of the past hangs heavy. The Sicilian fishermen are reincarnations of an ancient, heroic race, engaged in brutal conflict with "modern" commerce, torn as they are out of the original context of the pagan communal world and enslaved by "capital" interests. *La Terra Trema* is also, in formal terms, a tribute to the silent cinematic past and to montage, to Eisenstein, and to realism. The beautiful little girl in *Bellissima* is Anna Magnani's neurotic version of her own lost self, a constellated *puella aeterna*; and the satire on Cinecittà and the "old-fashioned" mechanics of studio moviemaking (Visconti sees the future vistas: locations, panoramas) are surely to be read against the "new" cinema, of which Visconti was a founding genius (the romantic division). *Rocco* is a tragic dialogue between the illusory Arcadian past and the image of the dead father pinned to the mother's widow's-weeds, and the violent contemporary urban present (memories of a perpetual Sicilian sunshine summer shrouded in the falling snow of a Milanese winter). It is also an elegy on Christ, on classical notions of sainthood and on the death of the religion whose dancing ground is Italy. *Conversation Piece* is a frantic collision between the outside (now) and the indoors (then) in now/then Rome, a poem of a gentle man's privacy, of its invasion by a gang of inchoate babblers and hellions ducking in and out of Pandemonium (the traffic). It is also an elegy on the Italian Renaissance and on Idealism, both all over.

White Nights is a film about childhood. The sound-stage sets and the snow are like a toy city and the third act of *La Bohème*; and the love pledges and betrayals are as arbitrary as the Eden games and expulsion games of the very young playing at growing up. Maria Schell is a child-waif, a Mélisande. The game of waiting for the lover's return is a ritual of a return to the time of waiting, to latency, to the time between the injuries of birth and *the fall*.

Sandra (Vaghe Stelle dell'Orsa) is in the mode of classical tragedy, played on the ancient volcanic precipice of the town of Volterra, where the stage is set for a replay of an Orestean situation melodrama cloaked in the mannerisms of Jacobean tragedy, in which, however, the situations are each and all differing versions (the brother's, the sister's, the mother's, the step-

father's) of what the secret past contains. The film is full of Pirandellian res-
onances: ambiguity, shifting memorial ground, and operatic touches—a mad
scene, duets, crashing pianistic chords accompanying the outsize acting.

The short, shattering episode called *La Strega Bruciata Viva* (from *Le
Streghe* [*The Witches*]) presents Mangano, the actress, in desperate flight
from her accumulated past, ending up on some Alp, trying desperately to
paste some of her past back on her face, to look like someone again, unwilling to be present (she knows the company in the lodge are slicing her to bits
and tossing her into the flames of the open hearth), trapped without time.

Three Epics

Senso is the first Visconti color spectacular, and the first of his pictures to
engage every level of his taste and passion: for music, for painting and
architecture, for panoramic outdoor movement, for classical tragedy
(revenge, madness), for the entwinement of political and personal destiny,
and for surfeit, opulence, extravagant gesture (long shots of doors opening
upon doors until there is a long hallway passage cut through the endless
rooms, through which the heroine pursues and escapes). The Countess
Livia Serpieri (Alida Valli) is all majestic supplication crossed with Maenad fury, an Italian Melpomene. Italian history is her history; she contributes to its fulfillment (*risorgimento*) and it enlists her doom (events
conspire). Italy becomes all idea, compelling, symbolic. Livia becomes all
role, all Revenge, sensation. The Italian inheritance, pagan sensation,
Luxuria, dooms.

The Leopard, mangled in distribution, survives in a series of immense
cinematic panels, which could be run in any order and which serve as
emblems for the decay of a society. There are brilliant living friezes and frescoes, baroque groupings of stars and extras, intimate single portraits and
elegant formal family groupings. There is the hot, dry pulse of sexuality;
there is feasting and dancing, and talk of both natural and political philosophy. It is a portfolio, partially reclaimed, a series of gorgeous reminiscences
of a great, doomed project: the epic of collapse, itself capriciously wrecked
by enemies of movies.

The Damned, the first of the late-period Visconti, is a film in which each
of the major characters is informed as much by archetypal symbolic content
as by idiosyncratic, personal trait, and in which the maestro (able to sum-
marize and distill, juxtapose and fuse, play, contort, and surround) inves-

tigates the origins of that conflagration which consumed European culture, leaving the very ashes and rubble out of which, among other aesthetics, that of neo-realism would rise. Visconti, presenting the day-before-yesterday, splashes the screen with lurid and combustible effects and situations, elicits brilliant corrosive performances (neo-Jacobean Guignol). From the lush family banquet to the mephitic cyanide wedding breakfast, where annihilation is the portion, Visconti, in the guise of Mephistophelean puppeteer-ventriloquist, mimes and voices, in socio-political costume (high fashion, low drag, uniforms, fetishes), those passions and terrors in which every sentient personal history abounds.

Aschenbach and Ludwig:
Portraits of the Creator

Of the quartet of summary masterpieces which installed Luchino Visconti up front in the motion picture pantheon, it is possible to say that, like the "big four" gemstones of luxury and Kabbala, they play off one another in ways unique in cinema history, in that each singularly and all together demonstrate the degree to which Visconti's cinema was fulfilled by his great work in opera—and in particular the La Scala productions of the early 1950s in which he created the space into which the supreme singing actress of the century, Maria Callas, moved and fairly overwhelmed. The fire-music-sex-death spectacle *The Damned* is the ruby among them; the transcendental *Death in Venice* the emerald (the imperial gem); the transparently self-referential psychic autobiography *Ludwig*, the pinnacle of Visconti's achievement, the diamond; and the heartbreaking *L'Innocente* the evening sapphire. An intimate knowledge of the music of the lyric stage enabled this great film director, this late-born genius of the Renaissance, to understand and exhibit to perfection the Paterian dictate defining aesthetic aspiration: in a perfect double helix, the heightened reality of gesture that is cinema—gesture parceled into segments and reassembled in the projection of *quantified time* into a *mise-en-scène*, and *also/simultaneously* the *essentially musical* (and for talking pictures, by analogy, the *sung*) condition of that great art which, following the single essential dictate of opera, *prima la musica e poi le parole*, lives on through time according to the regulated pulse of an equation derived from the value of both the *mise-en-scène* over the montage *and* vice versa.

A second Visconti, like a second Verdi, is an impossible conception.

MELO MAESTRO DOUGLAS SIRK

The Sirkite evangelist, exulting in the pictorial energy, wit, irony and classical pathos (juxtapose two or more of the above, depending on your capabilities), appeals with all guns drawn to the open-eyed and rhythmically witted (those younger viewers in this lesser time for whom revelation in motion pictures has become scarce). The Sirkite will point out how his hero husbanded his resources—forging an utterly vivid, personal style—and used it *politically*, in a personal politics: a dissection of the consequences of mendacity (and not only in *Imitation of Life*), making features which explore relentlessly moribund delusions and inauthentic perceptions in a world of material plenitude and spiritual desolation.

In an appreciation of four Sirk masterpieces of the fifties, we celebrate his bravura, as it worked simultaneously with and against popular, melodramatic material ("The Weepies"), turning story circumstances into *Sirkian-stances*. Sirk—staging pictures, creating impressions of austere isolation on the all-too-overcrowded gigantic wide screen—became the supreme circumventor (Sirk-Inventor) of the meretricious in mid-century Hollywood. (*And* since the Orpheum facts have long since convicted us of and sentenced us to living there in our fantasies, our Sirk is a true redeemer. That's a religion, indeed.)

All That Heaven Allows (1955), Universal-International. Ross Hunter, producer. Director of photography: Russell Metty.

Sirk: "In melodrama it's of advantage to have one immovable character against which you can put your more split ones. . . . The picture is about the antithesis of Thoreau's qualified Rousseauism and established American society."

Rock Hudson as a noble savage? Jane Wyman, America? Agnes Moorehead, America's shadow?

Jane Wyman, a widow with two grown but not grown-up children (one a pompous, callow boy, the other a ridiculous girl-student of Freudian psychology), falls in love with the man who comes to trim the trees: Rock Hudson. Friend Agnes Moorehead warns: "Carrie! Your gardener!" Jane enlists, on the side of *love*. Rock meets Jane's town friends. No possible communion. Jane vacillates. Then reneges. Rock departs, Jane alone, her children departed, realizes her mistake but does not ask for a second chance. She sits instead in front of an empty reflection in a switched-off television tube—a perfect Sirkian mirror. Suddenly she changes. She rushes to Rock, only to find him not at home. She departs. He returns in time to see her departing. He calls out, he slips, he falls, he concusses. (What more could anyone ask to happen?) Jane sits up with him through the night. At dawn, he wakes. They are together forever. (What more could heaven allow?)

The picture is simply plotted, gloriously shot, featuring New England (beautifully contrived postcards) fall and winter as seen through the enormous window of the barn Rock Hudson had built for himself and Jane to live in. Weather is a primary force throughout. Love blooms in full leaf, wanes in dead winter, when the evergreen trees are chopped down and taken to the town for Christmas. Love is reaffirmed in midwinter-spring, with the thaw-glazed field of snow blanketing the barnyard "in a silence deep and white."

Jane Wyman lives in a tight little world in a tight big house with room dividers and latticed front windows barring her from a new life. She is widowed, worried, trapped, resigned, riddled with "decency" and alone. Rock Hudson's barn is one great open space, out of the town; the window is one great sheet of glass. All within is serene. Hudson, the builder, possesses a certain modesty-in-strength, a Galahad quality, a Siegfried bearing: of a frank and open nature, innocent of cerebral guile, blessed with patience.... The Rock Hudson/Jane Wyman combination was the perfection of fantasy—Galahad to the rescue. The lady rescued. America, if she had listened to Thoreau.

Official mid-century America, overfed, victorious fifties meets the Thoreau-truth-teller. *All That Heaven Allows* is Sirk's most wistful, elegiac statement. The picture says, "Would that it were. . . ."

—<o>—

Written on the Wind (1956), Universal-International. Albert Zugsmith, producer. Director of photography: Russell Metty.

Sirk: "Just observe the difference between *All That Heaven Allows* and *Written on the Wind*. It's a different stratum of society in *All That Heaven Allows*, still untouched by any lengthening shadows of doubt. Here in *Written on the Wind*, a condition of life is being portrayed, and in many ways anticipated, which is not unlike today's decaying and crumbling American society."

The Sirk picture of Sirk pictures, consummate.

An oil-rich brother and sister, Robert Stack and Dorothy Malone, two Texas hellions, go on the rampage. Stack flies from Texas oil land to New York with his best friend (the once-more poor but truly honest Rock Hudson), corrals the most elegant woman in New York, Lauren Bacall (who else could better claim that title, then as now) and brings her back to Texas. She is dazzling and devoted and placates his demons for a time. Malone, having been desperate after Hudson since childhood, fails to corral him and concocts revenge. Malone to Stack, referring to herself, taunting: "She saw the end of a marriage, and the beginning of a love affair." It is untrue, of course, but when Stack, who has been (wrongly) advised by the family doctor of his probable impotence, is confronted with Bacall's eventual pregnancy, he attacks her and she miscarries. Lost and violent, Stack tries to kill his best friend, and is, of course, killed in the attempt. Malone, on the stand, sole witness to the killing, gives up and exonerates Hudson. She is left her dead father's millions and who-knows-what life. Told in flashback.

The perfect Sirkian plot. His lifelong preoccupation with split-character, divided selves, pitted against integrated character, played twice at once in a perfectly paired quartet. Divided Stack against co-ordinated Bacall—"elegant" here signifying whole, instinctive, supportive, redemptive (traditional good-woman functions in pictures). Split, twisted, desperate Malone beating herself against the Rock.

The picture opens in a blast of wizard self-assurance, quick bold cuts from the exterior of the mansion as a car screeches up the drive; to below stairs where the first words are spoken by the sibylline black servants ("I heard talk. . . . There's going to be a killing, et cetera. . . ."); to the entrance hall, all gaudy neo-classic pillars, crystal chandelier, sweeping staircase, and huge (latticed) windows; to an upstairs bedroom window framing the sensuous bloodthirsty Malone looking down at a severe angle at her revenge as the drunken Stack staggers into the hall below and quantities of dead leaves swirl in his wake. Then to the room where Bacall awakens. The camera pans on a desk calendar and, as the dead leaves are swirling below in the hall, the dead leaves of the calendar yield to the wind and blow backward to the beginning of the picture's time.

Almost all of the picture is shot in barren settings, oil fields zooming past as Malone drives to a roadhouse in her sports car: the roadhouse, all tacky decor and jukebox that plays "Temptation," the sterile house itself, the tank-town. Twice, once on the Stack-Bacall honeymoon, in Florida in the moonlight oceanscape, and once in an oasis in Texas, a small river and pool where Malone goes to hear the voices of her childhood—her brother and the man she desires—does nature enter to enforce the contrast, to imply hope, to suggest possible redemption. But in the honeymoon scene there is the eventually fatal revolver hidden under Stack's pillow, and in the sylvan Texas scene, Malone only hears the voices of the past and hears herself taunting her brother, bargaining for the best friend's affection. The character is bruised, and the performance is seductive and touching (among Oscar's better choices). Why *can't* the friend love the sister? We discover why, or how not, soon enough.

Stack acquires Bacall (Stack's acquisitive compulsion to *have* the best, Malone's compulsive venality, these are bred into the Texan-American Hadleys), and he's obsessed with Hudson, to the extent that he feels supplanted as a son, hating him and loving him, pitifully, fraternally, asking when dying how they came so far from the river. It's some family romance.

Stack, Malone, Hudson. It is an incestuous sibling triad that must perish—and Bacall must do it, unwittingly, directly—and it is a family as paradigm of society. (Sirk has blessedly never made a "message" picture in his career. As a cinematic genius whose trumps are irony and flamboyance, he works around The Literate Serious in sudden and vivid broad strokes.)

Malone goes berserk one night in her room, plays "Temptation" at top volume on the hi-fi and does a wild masturbatory Salome dance in front of Hudson's picture. But Herod is not present in the father. He (Robert Keith) is a sick old man who staggers up the stairs while the dance is on, suffers an entirely appropriate cerebral hemorrhage at the top of the stairs and tumbles back down, dead, the way (we finally understand) the mankiller in Malone would really like Hudson to do. The cross-cutting in closeup of this maenad and that sick progenitor is electric. There had never been a nutritive mother. The offspring are withering. . . .

Bacall has nothing quite so attractive to do. What she does do is maintain tension. Oddly enough, and gratifyingly, this actress, whose entire career was founded on smart back-talk—elegant lip, ready mouth—plays the seriously wronged wife without a trace of miscast wanness. In casting terms it was like asking a thoroughbred to just stand there and rear its head from time to time. It's a perfect balance.

In the end, Stack dead, Malone the heiress clasps a model oil derrick while sitting at the desk under her father's picture. Electra in Dollarland. Hudson and Bacall drive away . . . *naturally.*

—◦—

The Tarnished Angels (1957), Universal-International. Albe. producer. Director of photography: Irving Glassberg.

Sirk: "In a way *The Tarnished Angels* grew out of *Written*. You same pair of characters (Stack and Malone) seeking their identity i. .e follow-up picture; the same mood of desperation, drinking and doubting the values of life, and at the same time almost hysterically trying to grasp them, grasping the wind. Both pictures are studies of failure. . . . In both *Written on the Wind* and *The Tarnished Angels* it is an ugly kind of failure, a completely hopeless one."

In quite another way it was that *The Tarnished Angels* grew out of "written." It came from Faulkner's *Pylon*. It is interesting nonetheless that Sirk speaks about the literary inspiration he tried to work into his vision on this picture more than any other. He tells Jon Halliday he used to read Eliot's "Prufrock" aloud to Rock Hudson in order to let him hear his character, a Faulknerized Eliotesque outside man. To Stack he read from "The Waste Land"—Phlebas the Phoenecian and death by water. Methods. . . .

Rock Hudson, a newspaper reporter in New Orleans in the Depression, sets out to explain to himself for his readers (the viewers) the motives behind the wild daredevil fliers—ex-World War I ace Robert Stack; his wife, Dorothy Malone, a parachute jumper; and their sidekick-mechanic Jack Carson. The air circus is the existential arena. Malone is prostituted to an airplane dealer to further her husband's ambition, and Stack commits suicide in the upshot, crashing his plane into the water. Hudson and Malone contact, but separate. The fliers, apotheosized, cannot live on the ground. They are the terrible angels who visit havoc upon the earth. When they betray themselves as human beings, they vanish into air.

Sirk: "The story had to be completely un-Faulknerized, and it was."

Jon Halliday: "Outstandingly the best adaptation to the screen of any Faulkner, acknowledged as such by Faulkner himself."

Faulkner is verbal music; Sirk is pictorial. Shooting in black and white, technically a come-down in 1957 (the U-I executives didn't trust the story), the picture looks exactly right as it happens. In the fifties, America thought of the Depression as very much a black-and-white period, because its moving pictorial records—as opposed to the Hoppers and Shahns on still canvas—were all old newsreels and old movies in black and white. The

.eventies can put the thirties into color; the fifties would not. The fifties were a supposed technical triumph in themselves.

Working in black and white, shooting planes against worried skies, planes zooming around pylons in lunatic aerial carousel, shooting Malone, blown into the wind and hurtling toward earth until the parachute opens, Sirk is right in the realm of sudden and violent movement he favors. The scenes on the ground, crowded, crammed rooms eerily lit and as indebted to the grotesque in German cinema as anything he has done, point up the ironic treatment of the desperate, not-truly-heroic fliers—the Sirkian alternative response to, say, Hawks's *Dawn Patrol* or Walsh's *Fighter Squadron*, where the men prove themselves heroically. The tarnished angels don't prove a thing.

It is a picture about sad losers, "narrated" by the there-and-not-there cynical Hudson. In contrast to his earlier "melo" masterpieces, the emphasis in *The Tarnished Angels* is far less on enlarged characters than on action—really unaction, reckless, positive inertia which kills human response, vitiates human concern.

◄○►

Imitation of Life (1959), Universal-International. Ross Hunter, producer. Director of photography: Russell Metty.

Sirk: *Imitation of Life* is more than just a good title, it is a wonderful title: I would have made the picture just for the title, because it is all there—the mirror, and the imitation. . . ."

Andrew Sarris: "What was needed with this material was the ironic perspective Sirk's cooly contemplative style provided for such projects as *Imitation of Life* and *All That Heaven Allows*. Neither indulging his glossy characters, nor indicting them, Sirk had the gift of making them come alive through windows, mirrors, and other shimmering surfaces. More important, Sirk confronted the absurd anguish of shrunken souls with shiny faces head-on."

Finally, the definitive masterpiece.

Would-be actress-mother Lana Turner meets itinerant Negress-mother Juanita Moore on the beach at Coney Island when their daughters strike up a play-friendship. Juanita Moore becomes Lana Turner's unpaid maid at first. Lana Turner sacrifices romance for her only love, her career; the black and white daughters grow up together. Lana prospers. The light-Negress child, Susan Kohner, finds Negritude unbearable, finds she can pass for white. Beaten by a boy (Troy Donahue) for imitating, she leaves home and descends to sleazy nightclub work. She struggles and makes her way. Her mother seeks her out and in the confrontation is forced to masquerade as Kohner's childhood *mammy*. Lana Turner reaches higher and higher into stardom (an Italian film director enlists her artistic services), and her daughter, Sandra Dee, drifts along in the background. In the end, grief kills Juanita Moore. The climax of the picture is Moore's grand and moving funeral, for which she has saved all her life, at which Susan Kohner makes a sudden, stabbingly appropriate appearance. In the wake of the noble black woman's death, the remaining principals are faced with the consequences of their imitation lives' careers. Susan Kohner is seemingly redeemed and reconciled.

Sirk: "I feel *Imitation of Life* and *Written on the Wind* . . . have something in common; it's the underlying element of hopelessness. . . . In *Imitation of Life* you don't believe the happy ending, and you're not really supposed to. Everything seems to be O.K., but you well know it isn't."

The entire picture is *trompe l'oreille* and a feast for the discerning eye from beginning to end. Never has Lana Turner's unctuously sincere pear-toned elocution been better pitted against the utter vacuity of her gaze, the deadly precision of her MGM comportment—that walk, that invisible thick slab of the *World's Great Quotations* balanced on that perfectly poised head. Those Jean Louis gowns. It's all there, perfect imitation of vitality. If ignorance is a delicate and exotic fruit whose bloom is gone if ever once touched, the Lana Turner character in *Imitation of Life* is the Queen of the Mangoes. The perfection of seeming, she can no more be touched—moved to real action—than Narcissus can kiss his image in the reflecting pool. As perfect a contrast and balance to the Juanita Moore character as is black to white, in color.

Susan Kohner, a newcomer, triumphed as the Sirkian split-character. (*Imitation*: another quartet: Turner and Moore, Kohner and Dee.) The scene in which Kohner is slapped down by the boyfriend is shot on the oblique, through a plate-glass window reflected. Reflection, chance seeing, reinforces for the viewer the pathos of the girl's secret and *allows* the character her desperate alternative.

And desperate it is: Susan Kohner, sitting in a chorus line of chairs, joylessly kicking up one leg, holding a grotesque champagne bottle in the ugliest nightclub in the world (Sirk directing *Cabaret* . . . !), and immediately thereafter backstage, turning her back to her mother, sitting in her dressing-table chair, wounded and cruel. Her last permission, her final admission, is to her mother, to be embraced one final time. The next embrace is of the flower-decked coffin. Embracing death; *leading* life. For Sirk, *deus ex machina*, the anodyne.

Poet, debunker, triumphant charlatan, stunner, Hollywood visionary and magnificent obsessor. Douglas Sirk resides in Picture People's Paradise.

JOE ACKERLEY

I
The Dog

My Dog Tulip by J.R. Ackerley. Poseidon Press.

I had a dog once myself. (I know, I know, I hear you: the book review as attitude autobiog; but I simply don't know how otherwise to get a purchase—I mean a grip—on this one. It is a bitch.)

I thought back to my dog, Tiny, when I looked at the first chapter heading of *My Dog Tulip*, "The Two Tulips" (trips on the tongue, doesn't it), because there were two distinct Tinys, too. My dog Tiny . . . No, I can't go on with it; let the dead rest. Poor Tiny, dear reader, was a schizophrenic—Spitz Pomeranian raised from a pound-reject pup by my brothers and me—who was very often very sweet in a dog's dumb way, and had a very pretty white ruff (Tiny I), but whose most characteristic remark (Tiny II) was "Grrr." ("You're in my face.") He terrorized our valiant family out in Jackson Heights for years, until one afternoon, long after my older brother's departure, via Korea, for marriage and life on the West Coast, Tiny went for my mother's face. (The testimony: "That dog saw me leave here with your brother in 1952, and your brother never came back—to stay—and from that day to this. . . .") Tiny was, after a brief and brutal trial, summarily executed, in Jamaica, Queens.

Coincidentally, in the very same year as this vaudeville was playing the nabes, a bachelor was living in bliss with his dog, Tulip, across the Atlantic, in Fulham, a suburb of London, older but not unlike Jackson Heights in that . . . never mind. J.R. Ackerley (1896–1967), commonly known as Joe, was a respected literary homosexual BBC mandarin, whose other, far more interesting if not more lascivious, books than this, *My Father and Myself* and *Hindoo Holiday*, entitle him, it is generally agreed, especially among Tories, to a permanent seat in the celestial parliament and the permanent guarantee of installation for his stuff on the shelves of the book department at Brit-O-Mart, civilized high culture purveyors. In *My Dog Tulip*, first published three decades ago (you remember the '50s), he immortalizes, in a style eerily reminiscent of John Cleland, the breathless adventures of his Alsatian soulmate, which consist in the main of a truly advanced sequence: his heroic and finally successful campaign to get the heroine laid, then pregnant, then parturient. . . . It goes on.

My problems with *My Dog Tulip* are telling. I react very strongly in the negative to Ackerley's playing out his Oedipal melodrama (God rest the man, though, now he's dead, along with Tulip and Tiny) on a *dog*. This, you will realize right away, is a rather stunning prejudice, and I confess it right off the bat, not necessarily to get time off in Purgatory, but so as not to . . . Skip it.

In my opinion, a man's best friend is his best friend, not his goddam *dog* (and not his mother, after all). It may, I suppose, be inferred from the above that, had Tulip been a male (called, say, *Toby*) . . . well, I will admit that, such a predilection for the male of the species—any species—have I, that I can't sit down to a lobster supper after a show without ascertaining, as did Nellie Melba, "Is it a cock?" Similarly, while working up this review, I came across a picture of the very first German shepherd—Alsatian in England—ever to win the Westminster. He's called "Ch. Covy Tucker Hill's Manhattan," and he's a great beauty. No trouble getting Manhattan laid, if you ask me. Know what I mean?) However (and in this I may have been merely, pitiably, the phobic young father to the prudish man before you), so far as I was concerned, if Tiny had a penis, it was evidently not only tiny, it was, importantly, Tiny's; it wasn't mine—not even by extension. Therefore, when it comes to Tulip's cunt, well, I'm squeamish—or, as my old friend Ralph would say, "I *skeeve* on it."

The great critic Harold Bloom writes, in *A Map of Misreading* (Oxford University Press, 1975, 1980; p. 76): "*All interpretation depends upon the antithetical relation between meanings, and not on the supposed relation between a text and its meaning*" (Bloom's italics). Thus, I fear, even in my attempt at correlating the story of Tulip with the story of Tiny, I have failed, at least in compassion. I have similarly failed in my close reading of the prose ode *My Dog Tulip*, obviously because of the famous Bloomian *belatedness* (this review, long overdue, is that failure's emblem) and because of belatedness's attendant anxieties, thrust up from resistances, introjects and botched cathexes (how dare *I* scorn Ackerley's Oedipal performance). Specifically—I own it—I seem to have come to grief (having, if I may boast and live, sailed through the *clinamen, tessera, kenosis*—those bowel movements of Tulip's! Those uncleanly fluxes!—and hyperbole) between the rock of *askesis* and the hard place of *apophrades*. (Nightmares of the raging ghosts of Ackerley, Tulip and, yes, Tiny, afflict me lately. Tiny and Tulip, for example, fucking their brains out. And remember how it was when you first saw two dogs stuck together and cried? Well!)

To hell with me. The important thing about this book *is that it is.* "If no 'meaning' of a 'reading' intervenes between text and yourself, then you start—even voluntarily—making the text *read itself* (Bloom, ibid; italics same). And, for Tulip, that *she got her man—and she kept him* (italics mine). In the words of St. Ruth Draper (words we would do well to heed in these dissolute times): ". . . ought to be enough for anyone."

II
The Man

The homosexual . . . is a delightful melancholy person when he does not indulge in sadistic passion with another man.

—Julia Kristeva, *Black Sun: Depression and Melancholia*

In contrast to this is the other kind of artist who starts off with crude representations of the secret self phenomena or personal aliveness which are pregnant with meaning for the artist but at first have no meaning for others. The artist's task in this case is to make his very personal representations intelligible, and in order to do this he must betray himself to some extent. His artistic creations seem to him like so many failures, however much they are appreciated by the coterie; and in fact if they are appreciated too widely the artist may withdraw altogether because of the sense of having been false to his true self. Here again, the main achievement of the artist is his work of integration of the two selves.

—D.W. Winnicott, *Human Nature*

A few years ago, I went down to Rodmell, the little village near Lewes, in Sussex, where Leonard and Virginia Woolf, in connubial celibacy at Monk's House, lived out the best years of their lives. It was from the bottom of the garden there that Virginia Woolf walked out, on March 28, 1941, with her pockets full of stones, into the River Ouse—an unhappy ending to an affective life irradiated with high literary genius but marred by the recurrent torments of depressive vertigo—an event to which I attempted to allude at the end of the tour of the premises. It was a remarkable one, in that visitors were allowed, even encouraged, to sit in the very chair the great writer had sat in, next to the wireless on which she'd heard the war news and the BBC Third Programme, surrounded by the verging-upon-hysterical craft decor lavished upon the Monk's House interior by her more fortunately thick-skinned sister Vanessa Bell.

"I've been down to the garden's bottom gate," I remarked to the bright and amiably doughty middle-aged woman engaged by the University of Sussex to point things out to visitors, "but the path to the river is sealed off. Just as well, I suppose, or you'd be pestered by a lot of people like me, retracing her last steps: something that could, I imagine, quickly become rather ghoulish."

"I beg your pardon?"

"The path—down to the river. She walked into the river."

(Sharp intake of breath; a hasty look around.)

"Ah, yes . . . Well, you see—this is it."

Reading Peter Parker's *Ackerley: The Life of J.R. Ackerley* (Farrar, Straus and Giroux, 1989) is the same sort of experience. I am grateful for the effort, and I commend the book in a general way to readers who wish to place Ackerley in a wider picture than he places himself in his own work—revelatory as it is—but there is no path in it down to the river. I didn't care before I read it—and still don't care nearly as much as I do about Virginia Woolf—about Ackerley or any of his friends, in the main self-regarding, facile, insular products of public schools and universities, men who, like E.M. Forster, were given to quasi-incestuous sadomasochistic passions with their peers, but I kept remembering that all the while I'd lived in England (and read everything I could by and about Virginia Woolf) I'd been fairly tormented by the sense of futility, and of waste, put into me by her great struggle to stay alive for as long as she managed to do. This book gives me something of the same feeling. "Practice equanimity, Mrs. Woolf," was what a Harley Street physician said to her. And all the while her cousin James Strachey, Freud's English translator and perhaps the most eminent psychoanalyst, after Ernest Jones, in England, said— what? Did what? Hoped she'd snap out of it, perhaps write her way out of

it? This never made any sense to an American for whom the therapeutic—
whether or not triumphant—was certainly a factor. I began to see then, have
seen in the two decades since with increasing rather than diminishing frus-
tration, and see again in this book, that so far as literary Great Britain is
concerned, not even the diagnostic is reckoned really worthy of consideration in any but the most frivolous and anecdotal way. It is as if what Elizabeth Bishop wrote to Robert Lowell all those years ago had locked in, like
some psychic version of the lethal London fogs Monet found so mysteriously attractive (before he came to the radiance of Giverny):

> There is a deadness there—what is it—hopelessness. . . . That kind
> of defiant English rottenness—too strong a word—but a sort of pig-
> gishness!—As if they've thrown off Victorianism, Georgianism,
> Radicalism of the 30s—and now it's let's all give up together.

The late Bruno Bettelheim quotes Freud on biographers: "Whoever
undertakes to write a biography binds himself to lying, to concealment, to
hypocrisy, to flummery and even to hiding his own lack of understanding."
This is too harsh and too ungrateful. What of reviewing biographies? Must
I confess my own lack of understanding of (if I may put it upside-down) the
German for *flummery* before admitting that I suspect Peter Parker of it? I
do not suspect him of the more cynical intentional lying or concealment—
and of no more hypocrisy than his age, nationality and education may have
creased him with—and I must insist that he seems not to bother to hide his
lack of understanding (even on the level of sociological grasp: for example,
he numbers Philip and Ottoline Morrell among those distinctly more shab-
bily housed and gowned elect habitually referred to by Virginia Woolf as
"the Bloomsberries").

Writing, particularly writing biography, is like acting: it is between
seven-tenths and four-fifths reaction. When it succeeds, the actor, paying
attention to the subject's circumstances and reacting to them, "becomes" the
character (as, most happily, Lytton Strachey became Queen Victoria, a
role he was born to play). When it fails, it becomes abreactive in tone: fitful, discursive and scolding. The reaction formation constructed in defense
against overdoing the scolding and against the feeling of failure—failure to
unite with the subject—is the reductive interpretation of a life, based almost
always on a combination of the author's own sense of inadequacy (the correct, if intolerable, feeling in the circumstances) and whatever available

gossip is lying around in letters written about the subject by friends or enemies (almost always red herrings) or letters written by the subject to throw
the overly inquisitive off the scent. (But a schooled analytical intelligence
can often hold such documents up to the mirror of the subject's nature—
that quiddity inferred by his actions and the consequences he acknowl-
edges—and thereby read the inverted script.)

Writers of consequence, no matter what flummery they permit themselves to be cajoled into uttering for publicity purposes during their life-
times, take little interest in facilitating their biographies (no more than
Cleopatra—so Shakespeare informs us, the guiltier he may color our satisfaction in seeing it done—wishes the passions and derelictions of her
woman's breasts betrayed by a boy player in a strapped-on, rag-stuffed
bodice, piping her woes to the paying public).

That J.R. Ackerley, in spite of writing autobiography, tried to make it
terribly difficult to know him, in life and for posterity, is not really an interesting or engaging enough ploy to be worked up into a full-length biography. Therefore, I'm bound to be severe with this book, even as I
acknowledge with some gratitude the industry behind it; it seems to me the
textual equivalent of those demireps of whom Samuel Johnson said,
"Because they have made themselves public, they consider they have made
themselves known." *Ackerley* demonstrates the curious fact that the fascination putative writers of biography are apt to succumb to is really a kind
of passion for cartography. (One of the first ways the bright child idling in
the schoolroom is apt to lose his immediate grasp on the lesson at hand is
by drawing maps of imaginary countries.) British university education and
the arrogant confusion it fosters take to extreme lengths the metaphysics of
microcosm and macrocosm, in which the individual entity is seen as reca-
pitulating the nature and structure of the universe. A man, rhetoric aside,
is not the measure of all things. Literary life is not life; it is a kind of map.
(In order to represent life truly, it would have to be a map as inexorably and
minutely detailed as the terrain of life itself.) If there are readers who can
read biography without looking for the topographical contours of a life, I'm
happy to say that I don't know a single one of them. For all these reasons,
I'm afraid I have to call this book a failure: stunted, smug, willful and
unyielding. Peter Parker is, like his proverbial namesake, certainly nosy
enough, but to little avail. Reviewers who have remarked that Ackerley has
been given the biographical treatment he merits cannot have read him very
sympathetically (or are, shall we say, conflicted).

A plethora of recent English biographies have been written merely anecdotally, aping the English novel—and the English novel, or rather its anemic successor, the twitchy English post-novel, is devoid of topography. You can pick one up several times a year and come a little closer to death breathing its atmosphere, but English fiction has ceased to be written to any soaring level almost since Virginia Woolf walked into the Ouse a half-century ago. (Time out for Ivy Compton-Burnett, Anthony Powell and Angus Wilson.) These new texts, fictive and factive, are moribund because their psychology—which was the only real excuse for the novel's existence (it was the bourgeoisie's comfortable, commodious replacement for the more rigorous epic)—is moribund; it has been lobotomized and its customary insight replaced by varieties of hectoring assertion. Here, for example, is Parker's lively attack on a minor character, one of the Ackerley family's neighbors on Richmond Hill:

> Next door was Metcalfe's London Hydro, a smart establishment presided over by Dr. Harry Wadd, a dirty-minded old fraud who spent as much of the time he could spare from fleecing his wealthy patients exchanging smoking-room stories with Roger.

Nothing informs or corroborates this detraction. I hold no brief for Dr. Wadd, or for any Wadds claiming descent, but really! One simply doesn't do that kind of thing in biography. Or this next either, although as imagistic writing about the Battle of Britain it is quite effective. Unfortunately, it substitutes a snapshot of a symbol for the condition symbolized.

> But it is doubtful Ackerley would have survived had he been at home, for all the ceilings came down and all the doors and windows were blown in. . . . A heavy bronze statue of a Greek boy, one of his favourite possessions, had toppled from its shelf and landed on the sofa where Ackerley usually sat. Thus he had escaped a fate which would have had a certain poetic justice: to be killed by Narcissus.

It's no use writing hortatory sentiments about a cold cast-bronze Narcissus when you're supposed to be creating the impression of hot breath on the mirror. ("You speak to me of narcissism," wrote Artaud, "but I reply that it is a question of my life.") But in order to do that, you must first understand and be able to delineate the two different senses of the crucial verb *affect*—which Parker is fond of using only in its first, that of *pretend*. Neither is documentation any guarantee of accuracy. The employment of hearsay inevitably creates the problem happily defined by Hugh Kenner as the "Irish fact"—that is, true for the speaker but not always admissible evidence—and, as Lady Bracknell says of the Court Guides, "I have known strange errors in that publication."

The mechanism of denial that has recommended itself as the fit replacement for bourgeois novelistic psychology is not univalent but ambivalent or polyvalent. Denial is a dystonic reverse function (the obverse is ambiguity). Thus it is as axiomatic in England as anywhere else that there can be no denial where awareness has not been at play. The tragic, hubristic British rhetorical-epistemological habit of mind—Puritanism, utilitarianism, mercantilism, empiricism and water closets, from Hobbes (excepting Hume) to Matthew Arnold and Bertrand Russell (and his contention, disproved by Gödel, that mathematics is reducible to logic) down to contemporary rigorist grammarians—has consistently reinforced false verisimilitude and discredited anomalies, equating awareness (stimulus) with insight (response). All the while, the worst depredation suffered by Britain in its millennial cultural battle with the originator of its civilization, France, has been the gradual erosion of Britons' ability to separate *principe* from *pratique*—a famous French specialty. For a long time now, the British have had no principles whatever, merely practices. (Americans have another problem, more melodramatic than tragic: an inability to separate *principe* from *publicité*.) There is a single viable perennial psychology, just as there is one evolving physics, and it does not, despite its most important modern exponent's quirky admiration for England and the English language, issue from a pragmatic and basically "sane" English mode of perception: it is hot and wet and filthy, the way everything south and east of Calais is, in Britain, said to be. It is a mongrel; it bites (the way Ackerley's dog Queenie, immortalized as "Tulip," did); and its grammar is often atrocious. The British don't want it any more than they want the Channel tunnel, but, as they say, there it is.

Having myself already taken up enough space abreacting, I must, in reviewing *Ackerley*, declare an interest. It is my belief, formed on the evidence of his published fiction and his diaries (as well as one undoubtedly adduced because, like Canon Chasuble in *The Importance of Being Earnest*, commiserating with John Worthing over his beloved brother Ernest's sudden death in Paris—"carried off . . . by a severe chill"—I am myself, so to speak, peculiarly susceptible to drafts), that Joe Ackerley was a lifelong alcoholic. That is to say, he suffered from the disease the American Medical Association lists as alcoholism, which some in recent years have called Jellinek's disease. It is not a disease that always produces (though it sometimes does) rachitic panhandlers, screaming paranoiacs on airplanes, disoriented writers of genius on television talk shows and unlooked-for windshield cleaners at stop lights. It is a progressive and terminal disease that all too often takes its time. When it does not destroy its victims in youth or middle age through massive insults to the brain, it is certain as it worms its way through their lives to cause them to do untoward things on impulse: pouring urine out of boots through open windows and leering—toothless in the public street—at the immediate objects of their desires. Readers temperamentally resistant to discussing this malady (or of the narcissistic character disorder believed by many researchers in the field of addiction therapy to be, along with a certain metabolic irregularity, chief among its multideterminations, physical and psychic, hereditary and environmental), or readers for whom classic psychoanalytical theory and practice are simply subjects for parlor games and party turns, may stop reading here. I suffered a similarly dismayed reaction to Richard Ellmann's biography of Oscar Wilde—a far more ambitious, sympathetic and successful enterprise than *Ackerley*, but one that even so fails completely to recognize, and therefore to delineate, what self-loathing in a homosexual alcoholic— no matter what degree of either talent or genius he has—really looks like. (It looks like the picture of Dorian Gray.)

Alcoholism is the allergic reaction to a chemical that paradoxically demands more of that chemical; it is related ontologically to D.W. Winnicott's excitation/rest cycle and to feeding in the infantile, narcissistic stage of life. (Adult narcissists typically conceive the love object as comestible, as did Marcel Proust, and fantasize the commonplace "Oh, I could eat him with a spoon!"—therefore ensuring that the beloved becomes both execrable and excretable.) And it is related existentially to the fact that a pleasant or desirable-tasting liquid becomes both the sustenance and the destroyer (*Quod me nutruit me detruit*): the perfect type of punishment unconsciously sought by the infant who fears that his devouring love cannot be tolerated. (The infant consequently projects the "devouring mother"—an imago that cooperates by being able to "do unto another" what is seemingly being willed against her—by introjecting the Avenger.)

In a society and in an age in which the broadest public attention has been drawn to the desirability of rehabilitating victims of coalcoholism (indeed, in a handful of enlightened states, treatment of coalcoholism is covered by medical insurance), why should one have to cajole others into taking seriously what one wise coalcoholic has dubbed "the founding disease"? Alcoholism has been pandemic in the West since the expansion during the Renaissance of both Western cognizance and libido or—whichever may be thought to have occurred first—since the ante was upped over viniculture and the brewing of hops when Irish monks discovered how to distill ardent spirits: *uisce beatha*, "the water of life"—whiskey. (That alcoholism and coalcoholism have become a subject for jokes is the surest sign of therapeutic efficacy, for ridicule is merely denial in sports clothes. Just as twenty years ago the statement "Everyone knows somebody who is writing a novel" turned quickly into the question "Do you have a friend who is *not* writing a novel?" so the increasingly nervous observation "Everyone seems to know somebody in a recovery program for chemical dependency or codependency" has in the 1980s—thanks to the work done by persons of consequence, including at least three wives of prominent politicians—turned into the question "Do you have a friend who is *not?*")

If there is not as much published in medical journals or available to the general public in Great Britain concerning "the addictions" as there is in the United States; if there are not as many facilities (of both the professional and the "self-help" sort) for the treatment of addictive diseases in that troubled society as there are currently in this one, that lack is certainly little excuse for a British biographer's failure even to clock the boldest signs of narcissistic depression. Nearly every significant diagnostic and therapeutic procedure available to the English-speaking analytical community (apart, that is, from the erotic whimsies of Jungian theory and practice—essentially an elaborate reaction formation against psychoanalysis) proceeds out of Freud by way of Melanie Klein directly to the formulations of D.W. Winnicott—the pioneer, especially in terms of the vicissitudes of the child, if not in the world then at least in the English-speaking world (he died in 1971, four years after J.R. Ackerley)—and to the formulations of R.W.D. Fairbairn, whose thesis on narcissistic anguish poses the following question: "What are the states of 'unpleasure and anxiety' against which creative production may be used as a defense?"

In Fairbairn's view—as recently summarized by Anthony Storr in *Solitude*—there exist two fundamental ones: the depressive and the schizoid. The emotion characteristic of the first is a feeling of hopelessness and misery; of the second, one of futility and lack of meaning. Not only is schizoid apathy different in quality from depression, but the two states of mind tend to occur in persons of different temperament and character structure. People threatened by a sense of futility and meaninglessness have not progressed past an early stage of emotional development, the "paranoid-schizoid position." The others are further along, in the "depressive position," and are much more extroverted. Both come under the Freudian oral phase, the first being concerned with suppose primitive emotions concerned with sucking and incorporation, the second with biting— the discovery and acting out of aggressive feelings toward the person providing food and love.

In the final chapter of *Human Nature*, the recently published summation of D.W. Winnicott's thought, we read this terse account of the phenomenon of psychosomatic diseases (and we can only hope we have progressed beyond that stage in general opinion at which the term *psychosomatic* was taken to mean *imaginary*): "Analysis in terms of the depressive position reveals a great deal in these cases, particularly a defensive mood of a chronic kind with depression hidden at the core. This is called common anxious restlessness in childhood, or hypomania, and in psychoanalytic theory the restlessness is thought of as a manic defense against depression; a constant over-activity and bolstering up excitement leads to physiological alterations. . . . A source is also found here for the various compulsive indulgences."

Both alcoholism and narcissistic disturbance are inherited; the first somatogenically and the second psychogenically. Alcoholics and other addicts tend to have family members who either abuse substances, are sexually compulsive or become abstracted or "dotty"—in general, who "check out" a good part of the time. In the United States, the cover, or buzzword, for this phenomenon is *dysfunctional family*. The family of J.R. Ackerley exhibits so much of this behavior, and of the compound psychosexual dislocations of father-daughter incest and mother-daughter rage, that the conclusion is inescapable that one and all survivors sought refuge down avenues of mood alteration.

Here is Parker on Ackerley's sister Nancy:

Nancy had been bored. Her baby had been a brief distraction, but after his birth, Nancy's boredom had given way to acute depression. . . . Whether she was suffering from the then unrecognized condition of post-natal depression or simply exhibiting the symptoms of what amounted to a constitutional dissatisfaction with life, is unclear, but her husband was worried enough to send her to England and to ask Dr. Wadd [remember him?] to keep an eye on her and send him bulletins about her progress.

The ruination of Nancy had begun very early on and she had failed to grow up. Indulged and, quite literally, spoiled by her father, she was accustomed to getting her own way and had developed from the small girl who stamped her foot and screamed until her desires were met.

"Constitutional *dissatisfaction with life*"? "Quite *literally, spoiled*"? Parker has been listening to too many of Margaret Thatcher's speeches. (The prime minister as introjected Avenger: this psychic malady, like hysteria, can infect an entire body politic.)

Actually, the portrait of Ackerley's sister done in these pages—that of a nervy woman clearly addicted to the dubious diagnoses of the medical profession and to the several mood-altering prescriptions she had been cavalierly dispensed, who seems, after decades of disorientation, to have recovered completely, in almost indecent haste, following her brother's death—is an accidentally more detailed, complex and ultimately satisfying one from the histrionic point of view (and aren't all characters in biographies read these days in casting terms?) than that of the book's principal subject.

Parker's reaction formation, abreaction, denial and reckless writing notwithstanding, he does lead off with great gusto on the superficial man, although I was dismayed by the book's first sentence: "J.R. Ackerley should not have been born at all." It might be supposed that, contrary to what I have already indicated, Parker is indeed identifying with Ackerley here, seconding his self-estimation, but in the first place, such a judgment is not in his brief, and in the second place, in a survivor of parental brutality, the feeling that one should not have been born is part not of the true self but of the false one; it is another introjected feeling, used as a defense against the terror of the true feeling: that it is "they" who must be annihilated. Surely "*might* not have been born" would have sufficed to indicate objectively the precariousness of the situation: a mother who loathed sex and a father who simply happened to be out of "French letters" one night early in the winter of 1896.

The story then picks up steam around the author's own quasi-erotic assessments. So often does he contend in the first few chapters that Joe Ackerley was beautiful of face and form, that I began to remember the old joke about Joan Crawford pictures—the writers had to include asides every so often buttressing the fiat that here was one gorgeous woman—and the longer I looked for evidence in the photographs enclosed in the book, the more I began to imagine that Ackerley and Joan Crawford . . . The same jaw, the same shoulders. Parker is at some pains to suggest that his subject bore "a striking resemblance to the American actor Montgomery Clift," but I hold out for Joan Crawford, perhaps because this biography strikes me in the same way as does Oscar Levant's immortal summation of the actress in character, addressed to John Garfield in *Humoresque*: "She's as complex as a Bach fugue!"

The (Joan Crawford–like) impression of willfulness and tempestuous perversity is reinforced by one of Ackerley's characteristic double-edged remarks: "I fear that in my life I have disappointed a great many people. Having been attractive, there were more to disappoint than would have otherwise been the case." (That remark is perhaps slightly more suggestive of a Mae West than of a Joan Crawford, and oddly reminiscent, too, of the counsel offered to a friend by one of our relentless contemporary American diarists, himself a rather famous and perhaps even valiant gladiator in the narcissistic arena. "The trouble with you and me is that we want everybody to love us—and we can't *know* everybody!")

Ackerley was luckier—if life's a boon—than his older brother Peter. Their mother took so many "purges, nostrums and bodily exercises" (presumably excluding sex) to abort her firstborn that he showed up backwards, maimed with a double hernia. (The psychic upshot of this was his determined management of his own death in World War I, which resulted, of course, in his being greatly mourned, both in the family circle—Mauriac's "serpent's nest of blood ties"—and beyond it.) Joe Ackerley survived, on the face of it unscarred, to term, if only to atone his whole life long for intimidating his parents into permitting his birth. (Second sons have a notoriously difficult time of it as it is; Joe Ackerley's deal is worthy of a script thrown at Joan Crawford—moreover, one thrown to her years before *Humoresque*, in the 1930s, when she tended to go before the public impersonating masochistic, if always boldly plucky, proletarians.)

So much for the energy expended limning face and form. Concerning that expended in detailing vicissitude, it is simply exasperating to read a plot paragraph that begins, "In spite of Roger's frequent and extended absences, the family seems to have been a happy one," refers to Ackerley's bedwetting as "his one weakness" and concludes, "Amongst the household staff, two employees left an impression on him. The first was a boot-boy, and the impression was that of his hand on Joe's bare buttocks in some childishly erotic game; the second a French nurse or governess who, when he 'played with [his] little tassel as children do,' took his hands away, told him he was dirty and threatened to cut off his penis with her scissors." Are all English happy families like that, or are boot-boys and French nurses not reckoned family? That the parameters of Joe Ackerley's sexual life can be drawn in his repellent charade with a French prostitute in the First World War and in the ambivalence of his prolonged masturbatory career, seeking and then "cutting off" a regiment of penile boot-boys, suggests something else. There is no demonstrable evidence in Ackerley's record, written or spoken, that he understood the trajectory of his erotic life. As an adolescent, he thought of sex as having "nothing whatever to do with those feelings which I had not yet experienced but about which I was already writing a lot of dreadful sentimental verse, called romance and love." (One cannot of course write, sentimentally or otherwise, about what one has never felt.) The boy-man who continued all his life to play puerile erotic games nevertheless never stopped looking, in spite of the sordid paucity of the stuff in his family romance, for love.

I do not intend to suggest that—in the notoriously inhumane and psychoanalytically monstrous formulation of the diabolical Edmund Bergler, the therapeutic Rumpelstiltskin of the 1950s who led the unsuccessful American rearguard opposition to the motion to strike homosexuality off the list of mental diseases—sexual intercourse between men is the "neurotic counterfeit" of heterosexual practice. Nor will I endorse for a moment either the dizzy and reductive view (Parker characterizes it as "strictly Freudian") of the erotically spasmodic W.H. Auden, which strictly legislates the limits of male-male sexuality to the "'oral,' acting out 'Son-and/or-Mother,' or 'anal,' playing 'Wife-and/or-Husband.'" I merely wish to indicate that Ackerley's own evaluation of his instinctual object reach was so furtive and so fraught with imposed and inextricably intertwined— in the unfortunate English of James Strachey's translation of Freud, "cathected"—delectation and disgust, as to suggest that it had never progressed beyond the melodramatic confines of the W.C.

Peter Parker allows that "in spite of what was to be an extremely promiscuous life (some 'two or three hundred' partners, according to his own calculations), Ackerley remained sexually fastidious. This fastidiousness was considerably compromised by the fact the [he] suffered from *ejaculatio praecox*, or sexual incontinence." But this, though close (as part for whole), is not the issue: the issue was spoliation of a deeper kind. Ackerley himself confessed that his ideal friend "should admit me but no one else; he should be physically attractive to me and younger than myself—the younger the better as closer to innocence." It is that exclusivity and innocence which the sexual partner's projected loathing despoils in *ejaculatio praecox*, before he can tolerate that partner's orgasm. This is narcissistic pathos at its simplest and most timorous. (The late critic Richard Hayes wrote of Eugene O'Neill, "Not artifice, nor any solacing reason could mediate the authority of his private pain.")

Of course Ackerley lived in a treacherous time; all homosexuals did, and we should keep that in mind before we go after any of them. No mention of homosexuality could be openly made in England (not even when the whole populace was said to be singing "I Never Saw a Straight Banana"), and the middle classes really did believe that men of the lower classes owned cruder feelings than theirs and were capable of treacheries their mothers had never dreamed of. (They held these beliefs even after reading the novels of Marie Corelli—who, by the way, comes in for a rather knee-jerk sneer from Parker. This is yet another instance of the crudely digested, and belched, received idea. The author of *Temporal Power* was at least as authentic as Iris Murdoch is.)

Here is E.M. Forster warning Ackerley on his foray into the theater:

> As for them nactor [*sic*] chaps, Joe, as many as you like, but *many*—take no one of them seriously, for you will then be asking for what they can't give. So either many or none!

And here is Forster, the putative gay liberator, the author of *Maurice*, that (more overtly) homosexual *Lady Chatterley's Lover*, on Ackerley's attachment to a male member of the "lower orders":

> The standards which are so obvious to you are very remote to him and his class, and he was bound to lapse from them sooner or later. And by standards I mean not only conventions but methods of feeling. He can quite well be deeply attached to you and yet suddenly find the journey up [from Portsmouth] too much of a fag. It is difficult for us with out middle-class training to realize, but it is so.

These sentiments were shared by Ackerley himself, who, responding to Leonard Woolf on the matter of a likely libel suit against *We Think the World of You*, the model for the hero of which had been one of the great attachments of his life, wrote:

> I am rather naïve in such matters, as I was explaining, rather tipsily, to Ian. It had not occurred to me that the working classes brought actions, even if they ever read books. . . .

Ackerley at his best, in *My Dog Tulip* (which embarrassed many) and *My Father and Myself* (which dismayed not a few), is wonderfully good. At his maudlin worst, he is like someone who's been sitting up too late trying to read Ronald Firbank between the lines.

> The days potter by here much the same. Sometimes the sad sound of their ticking gets into my ears as they disappear into history, carrying nothing in their delicate hands but a yawn.

(Of this Forster actually wrote: "Can the day that produced such a sentence be lost?")

Fortunately, we have the best of Ackerley to read—the aforementioned *My Dog Tulip*, the fictional memoir *Hindoo Holiday*, *My Father and Myself*—and we know how good they are. For me the best passage Ackerley wrote occurs in *My Dog Tulip*, and concerns the suicide of an unknown boy.

> And young Holland, where did he die? Where is the swamp into which he drove his face? Lost, lost, the inconsiderable, anguished deed in the blind hurry of time. The perfect boy face downward in a swamp. . . . The doctor who performed the autopsy remarked that the muscles and limbs were absolutely perfect, he had never seen a better developed boy in his life, nor, when he split open the skull, such deep gray matter. Ah, perfect but imperfect boy, brilliant at work, bored by games, traits of effeminacy were noticed in you, you were vain of your appearance and addicted to the use of scent. Everyone, it seemed, wished you different from what you were, so you came out here at last and pushed your face into a swamp, and that was the end of you, perfect but imperfect boy.

Ackerley had written more openly and more directly of himself, of his disappointment that the war experience that killed his brother had not made more of a "man" of the survivor: "I needed to have shoves forward. My own nature was not the sort that comes out well in emergency. If I had had a shove from the Major in the Boom Ravine in France I should have acted heroically, though I should not have wished to: his leaving it in my hands or putting obstructions in front of me was fatal to my character." It is pathetically and dismayingly characteristic of a culture that simultaneously sentimentalizes and brutalizes childhood (by calling it the only "place" in which "character" is ever "formed") that hell-for-leather bravado should be so equated with heroism.

Later, in fictive disguise in 1923, he continued in this vein. "Standing there he mocked himself with visions, saw himself going gloomily on, getting a little more slovenly, a little more weary, a little more acrimonious and dull, more hopeless, more abandoned. . . ."

And toward the end of his life: "How glad I was whenever my problems were forestalled or solved by [other] people. . . . As I have already said, I was ever one of life's subordinates, I have always wanted someone standing at my elbow, throughout life, taking all my responsibility from my shoulders."

To which the ever-scolding Parker (who, in a hilarious burst of dense snobbery entirely in line with E.M. Forster's caution on actors, finds his subject's geriatric passion for the pop singer Cliff Richard "inexplicable") replies:

> This melancholy self-portrait is so flagrantly at odds with the regard in which Ackerley was held, and knew himself to be held, that it could only have been written in the deepest dejection. It seems inconceivable that Ackerley could in all honesty believe that: "Ill-read, unmindful, of narrow interest. I often felt too stupid to connect a single book with a suitable reviewer's name." Apart from anything else, if this were true, the BBC would hardly have invited him back for a month at the cost of fifty guineas a week. In the final analysis, perhaps he did not believe it, for he did not incorporate these pages into *My Father and Myself*. He might also have reflected that, if he had made a mess of his emotional and family life and had wasted his time upon the work of others at *The Listener*, he had also managed to write a handful of very good books. He kept these volumes, a small

but impressive stack, beside his bed and sometimes sat in pubs alone, rereading them and chuckling appreciatively to himself.

Ah, yes. . . . Well, you see—this is it.

RONALD FIRBANK

The Flower Beneath the Foot by Ronald Firbank. Penguin Modern Classics.

He was on his way here to us. He died in the spring of 1926, in Rome, at the *Quirinale*, as unfortunate a venue strategically as onomastically. ("Mind *you*, dear, he needn't've died at *all*, had he chosen to stop at the *Inghilterra*," is how one venerably raddled old Sibyl insisted at me on a Roman summer night a generation ago. In those years, if you were scheming to get noticed by "your own" on your European maiden voyage, you wore a lot of gray seersucker, you sported yellow or orange linen ties and you flashed your New Directions Firbanks. Dearie, do you remember the *Caprice/Inclinations/Vainglory* volume with the "Andrew Warhol"—cupid cover design and the Ernest Jones introduction: "Ronald Firbank is a better and more serious writer than it has ever been fashionable to suppose"?) Died writing *The New Rhythum*, a novel of New York, of which masterpiece seven chapters and assorted notes survive. ("I am writing a novel of New York, since I was never there . . . I hope to come out next year and develop it all.")

I like to think we (they, the then "we") would have welcomed him, had he (happy phrase!) "come out" to us. He'd have written for Frank Crowninshield's veteran-smart magazine and for Harold Ross's smart new magazine and been taken up (no, not done in, taken up) by Carl Van Vechten, Robert Benchley and Dorothy Parker. Alexander Woolcott would have sniffed his hind parts, said something dreadful and been reprimanded by Helen Hayes. The Lunts and Noël Coward . . . never mind. Tallulah Bankhead would have said there was more to him and to his rare birds, met eye-to-eye, than there was to Maeterlinck's. Once pictures started talking, his new-found friends, all of them gay for a buck, would have had him uncrated and shipped West by rail, in a rococo caboose marked "uncouple at Pasadena." In Hollywood, he would have worked with Ernst Lubitsch, under Irving Thalberg, on Jean Harlow vehicles—because, you see, in *The New Rhythum* he had opened up a fresh vein of, as he put it, "expressions of the soil," and he need never have looked back on the exquisitely finished vocabulary and acoustic (that twilight English of the cataleptic British Empire) he brought to a perfection unrivaled in his lifetime in *Concerning the Eccentricities of Cardinal Pirelli* (1926). Instead, he died at 40, of what was in those days politely described as "an excess of champagne and nerves" (officially, *pneumonia*). No "massive insult to the brain," merely an exhausted cut.

Alan Harris, in the introduction to *The New Rhythum and Other Pieces* (London: Duckworth, 1962), says, "One thing is certain: New York or New Jerusalem, this last vision of the Firbank world, with its pervading atmosphere of a ballroom in Chedorlahomor—a *faubourg* of Sodom, as readers of *The Flower Beneath the Foot* will remember—fanned in defiance of Nature by breezes from the isles of Greece, is the authentic thing."

So (authentic a thing) is *The Flower Beneath the Foot*, which I would place alongside *Pirelli, Prancing Nigger* (*Sorrow in Sunlight*) and *Valmouth* as the fourth precious gem in the canonic diadem. (It is, in fact, the ruby. *Valmouth* is the emerald, *P.N.* the sapphire and *Pirelli* the diamond.) It is the story of a girl who loves a prince, loses him to a princess and in consequence locks herself away for life in the convent in which she was raised. ("Oblivious of what she did, she began to beat her hands, until they streamed with blood, against the broken glass ends upon the [cloister] wall: 'Yousef, Yousef, Yousef . . .'") The girl, Laura, becomes (as if at once, for the planet Firbank is time-warped) a saint. Her emblem: "Some girls are born organically good; I wasn't."

Saint Laura de Nazianzi is native to a country, Pisuerga, to whose queen she is attached as lady-in-waiting. Her mistress complains of her, "She reads at such a pace . . . and when I asked her *where* she had learnt to read so quickly she replied 'On the screens at Cinemas.'" Laura dreams of being wed in Kiroulla, the capital, "under the low white dome, crowned with tourquoise tiles, of the Cathedral, which was known to all churchgoers as *the Blue Jesus*." She dares voice her devotion for the offspring to the politically ambitious parent—"He has such strength! One could niche an idol in his dear, dinted chin!"—and is severely rebuked. "Enough!" "Holy Virgin," murmurs Her Gaudiness, the Mistress of the Robes, as the lovesick postulant departs, "Should His Weariness the Prince yield himself to this caprice." " 'It would be a fatal connexion,' the Queen continued, 'and must never, never be.' "

It never is. King Geo and Queen Glory descend from—where else?—England, with their beastly little fox-hunting daughter Elsie, and the fates grind Mlle. Nazianzi's desires to ashes-of-roses dusting powder. Here is one passage in the prayer's prayer, the dilemma, and the forecast of the eventual salvation, seraphically conveyed:

> "Oh, help me heaven," she prayed, "to be decorative and to do right! Let me always look young never more than sixteen or seventeen—at the very outside, and let Youself love me—as much as I do him. And I thank you for creating such a darling, God, (for he's a perfect dear), and I can't tell you how much I love him; especially when he wags it! I mean his tongue . . . Bless all the sisters at the Flaming Hood—above all Sister Ursula . . . and be sweet, besides, to old Jane . . . Show me the straight path! And keep me forever free from the malicious scandal of the Court. Amen."

As Teresa of Ávila once said to a suppliant *hermana*, a fan of her *Exlamaciones*. "This just came hot off the griddle, Dolores—the answer to your frantic prayers. Read the summons, and weep without ceasing."

Now, just in case you are not now, nor ever have been, Catholic (or any of the dressy smells'-n'-bells spinoffs), don't feel excluded; there's plenty in *The Flower Beneath the Foot* to unnerve you. There is Chedorlahomor: ". . . to gratify her own wildest whims, the dearest perhaps of which was to form a party to excavate (for objects of art) among the ruins of Chedorlahomor, a faubourg of Sodom." There's the languor and ecstasy of the summer palace, where "in the deserted alleys, the golden blossoms, unable to resist the sun, littered in perfumed piles the ground, overcoming her before long with a sensation of *vertige*." There are the variegated anxieties of politics: "And brooding on life and baits, and what A will come for while B won't, the Count's thoughts grew almost humorous as the afternoon wore on." And finally, supremely, there is the crucified narcissism worthy of Racine, of Rimbaud and of Oscar Wilde: " 'Before life,' she murmured, 'the saddest thing of all, was thrust upon us, I believe I was an angel . . . Oh, what did I do to lose my wings?? Whatever did I say to them! Father, Father, how did I annoy God? Why did he put me here?' "

V.S. Pritchett, that amiable yeoman of the garden in which everything seems lovely, right, has recently written of "the old, robust masculine tradition of British comedy from Fielding to Smollet [continuing] in our own vernacular." (He's praising Kingsley Amis.) You know the drill: good beef, nice bit of roast potato, thickish portion of pudding, a decent claret. There is another vernacular, one that can speak of "Laura's sad little snatch of a smile"; one that celebrated the last (long—still with us) gasps of mock-monarchy and mock-religion in the formerly favored sceptered isle. It goes with ortolans, with wild rice, with, yes, champagne (and nerves) and with a divine bit of *coeurs flottants*. This book is written in it. Cherish it. It's never (God willing!) going to wind up ionized on *Masterpiece Theater*. You're charged to *read* it, merely.

CHAPTER TWENTY-ONE

Two Serious Laddies: Raymond Chandler and Herman Melville

*"I was beginning to think perhaps you worked in bed, like Marcel Proust."
"Who's he?" . . .
"A French writer, a connoisseur in degenerates. You wouldn't know him."*
—Raymond Chandler, *The Big Sleep*

Wherein the author undertakes queer studies.

I

RAYMOND CHANDLER

Stripped to its core essentials and abstracted from hair and wardrobe and the back projection of the plots—serial melodramas with all the kinesthetic overkill of Metastasio's opera librettos—Raymond Chandler's writing is about two things: alcoholic depredation and deeply betrayed men—which is to say one thing from two angles.

What Marlowe admits to liking are liquor and women and chess and a few other things. In *The Long Goodbye*, he spins out seven adjectives, ostensibly in the matter of coffee. "I went out to the kitchen to make coffee—yards of coffee. Rich, strong, bitter, boiling, hot, ruthless, depraved. The lifeblood of tired men."

Yes.

Marlowe fighting with Marlowe, a struggle carried on almost entirely in the muted growls of two bulldogs.

It is only at the very end of a tale that it ascends in whirly spirals to the point at which it takes on the desperate quality of—in Marlowe's own words from *The Little Sister*—"a sort of high keening noise, like a couple of pansies fighting for a piece of silk." And again from *The Long Goodbye*: "You bought a lot of me, Terry. For a smile and a nod and a wave of the hand and a few quiet drinks in a quiet bar here and there. So long amigo. I won't say goodbye. I said it to you when it meant something. I said it when it was sad and lonely and final." This really should be accompanied on the soundtrack by Judy singing "The Man That Got Away:" "Goodbye— good riddance: every trick of his you're on to—but fools will be fools—and where's he gone to?" Oscar Wilde said all girls become like their mothers, that is their tragedy; no man does, that's his. What did he mean? This: At least once his mother was fucked by his father. And he wants that for him- self—blanketed with white orchids.

Howard Hawks was characteristically smart about Chandler, calling his dialogue as good as Ben Hecht's. *Pace* Hecht, Chandler is a radically dif- ferent kind of writer and operates on an altogether different level. No com- pletely satisfactory picture has been made from any of his books (the whole of *The Big Sleep* and Claire Trevor's absolutely definitive performance in *Murder, My Sweet*, the 1944 film version of *Farewell, My Lovely* come closest) because he is one of the great modernists who took from the motion picture those elements that made it thrillingly new and, as post-modern crit- icism would have it, transumptively recast them as literature. He took back the book, making reading another kind of cinema.

The most characteristic moral signal in Chandler is the chess prob- lem—and the most tantalizing question in chess is, can it be played with- out the queen?

Homoeroticism saturates Chandler's work. The search for Rusty Regan in *The Big Sleep*, the longing for Terry Lennox in *The Long Good- bye*, and in *The Lady in the Lake*, in the small, hot room in San Bernadino's Prescott Hotel, sometime during World War II: Philip Mar- lowe, stripped to the waist, sweating, sits on the narrow bed, eying the lan- guid, no longer young Texan bellhop, and, having offered him an opportunity to sit and drink, spreads out on the bed a lot of what he calls tired-looking dollar bills.

"How long can you stay?"

"Doin' what?"

"Remembering."

"A dollar gets you remembered in this town. You a dick?"

"You ever seen a dick playing solitaire with his own money?"

Talk about deeply encoded literature.

In motion picture versions, his women tend to be conflated into manageable heroines and some ancillary villainesses. In the books there are many more of them, and they are disposable plot ploys, much as are the allegorical women in Edmund Spenser, whom the chivalry-obsessed Chandler often resembles. In fact the six major novels could been six parts of one epic, and *Playback* could be read as a version of the *Mutability Cantos*.

A great Raymond Chandler sentence from *The Big Sleep*:

"The blonde was strong with the madness of love or fear, or a mixture of both, or maybe she was just strong."

Marlowe, in *The High Window*:

"I like small, close-built men. They never seem to be afraid of anything. Come and see me some time."

(A reminder: Mae West, in *She Done Him Wrong*: "Why don't-cha come up some time . . . see me; I'll tell your fortune. Yeah—you can be had!")

Note the always evil doctor in the books. He is there to signal that the human condition (particularly alcoholism and homosexuality) can never be cured, and seldom arrested for long—a day at a time, as people came to say in later years. In Chandler, faggots are always vile, sinister, filthy and submissive. In the late masterpiece *The Long Goodbye* (and there is a great leap in stylistic vigor between it and the antecedent *The Little Sister*), one of the most poignant and authentically wrenching stories of male/male love in American literature, the suppressed hysteria of abreaction threatens on every other page to turn the work into an arch parody of the author's trademark funky-armpit panache, but happily never does. Terry Lennox says, "I'm not sneering at sex. It's necessary and it doesn't have to be ugly. But it always has to be managed. Making it glamorous is a billion dollar industry, and it costs every cent of it."

Despite Marlowe's confessed predilection for liquor, he is not anything like a lost-weekend drunk, or even a guy who walks into a place and orders "the usual." On the contrary, he's a fussy tippler who'll drink any number of different combinations and cocktails over the course of a book and only rarely tie one on with a vengeance.

Nevertheless, and from the point of view of fable writing, once the observer-protagonist's pattern of drinking has been established, it is formally inevitable (and aesthetcally imperative) that down and dirty drinking should be featured all around him. A salient characteristic of the writing is that for all its reliance on alternately languid and snappy dialogue (the Chandler music that seizes the plots by the neck) it is persistently and seductively jagged. No "take" is ever longer than an average motion picture shot, and no two successive takes are ever made from the same position. Perhaps nothing may be said to have originated in Los Angeles but the definitive expressive put-down "I don't think so" did erupt into literature there, in *The Big Sleep*.

Every time Chandler opens his mouth on the subject of men (whom we picture either as dull trolls or as humpy numbers drawn by Paul Cadmus), the same weak defense (speaking of chess) is played. Only a hermeneutic dimwit could fail to smell the flop sweat of a guy who desperately wants—whether he needs it or not is something else—to spend days on end riding saddle across the country with the kind of trucker who smokes raw Lucky Strikes and passes the pint of rye across the seat in the middle of the night without wiping the nozzle.

Yet Chandler is not inattentive to his female characters. For example, he loves gorgeous blondes, and he costumes them with the avidity of a Travis Banton. When dressing them up he does so in any number of detailed ensembles, always with matching hat, shoes, bag and gauntleted gloves. When dressing them down, he does so most often in the same one-piece white sharkskin swimsuit.

Chandler is a fatalist. "You can't judge people by what they do; if you judge them at all it must be by what they are."

How do you find that out? Often by the tone of what they say about what they do. Marlowe, for example, investigates people and delves into human nature, and this is what he says about a type he seems to despise pretty thoroughly.

"He was living with a rich pervert, the kind that collects first editions and does fancy cooking and has a very expensive secret library behind a panel in the wall."

This is called homosexual paranoia on the hoof.

And here is Marlowe in the clinch:

" 'Why of course Roger knew all about it.' Now she was smiling at Spencer patiently as if he was being a little slow on the take. The tricks they have."

"And the tricks I don't," is the vital subtext.

Bluntly, in *The Long Goodbye*, Marlowe kisses Eileen Wade only in the dark in the car and drinks gimlets with Linda Loring ("She had that fine drawn intense look that is sometimes neurotic, sometimes sex-hungry, and sometimes just the result of drastic dieting") because he is obsessed with Terry Lennox—whose real name is Paul Marston, with the same initials as Marlowe.

"He had made a fool of me, but he had paid well for the privilege." Five thousand dollars, the portrait of Madison that Marlowe keeps locked in his office safe and calls his good-luck piece—which is nothing less than the exact mirror-reversal of keeping a pair of the-most-gorgeous-hustler-you-ever-paid-to-fuck-you's drawers.) Neurotic in hearts, sex-hungry in clubs and starving in spades.

"Good night, Mr. Marlowe," Linda Loring says. "It's been nice—or has it." "We had quite a fight." "You mean you had—and mostly with yourself." "It usually is. Good night, Mrs. Loring."

The origins of this confusion reside not so much in biography—Chandler's drunken absconded father, his overbearing Anglo-Irish mother, the wife eighteen years his senior, as in what we must call pre-biography: that agon in the development of the soul psychoanalysts learned after the Second World War to call the Narcissistic. The etiology of Chandler's—and therefore Marlowe's—pathology—is less interesting than the chief manifestation of the conflict: that although Chandler/Marlowe really considered himself—and called himself—a man who thinks *for* himself, he really has—and Marlowe is—a man who thinks nearly exclusively *of* himself.

The genius of Raymond Chandler (who, as we have come to realize, isn't simply a superior crime novelist but one of American literature's supreme forensic investigators of the psyche, the equal of Hawthorne) is that he makes his readers identify with the intrapsychic Marlovian struggle on every page.

Not that it can be said with any authority that the narcissistic dilemma is more common to deeply homosexual men; it is simply more noticeable—the way the so-called depressive defense (particularly of alcoholics) is more noticeable (and reprehensible in society) than the manic defense of politicians, businessmen and upper-echelon career members of the armed forces.

As with sex ("It's great stuff, like chocolate sundaes. But there comes a time when you would rather cut your throat"), so with aggression. Those with a Wordsworthian sensibility, or some variant of it, tend to react to the "getting and spending we lay waste out powers" line of argument; others to free and unrestricted trade policies, a difference reflective of the contrast between pacific temperament and that which is convinced that war is the health of the state.

The Mexican connection: Dolores Gonzales in *The Little Sister* and the third and final Terry Lennox apparition, Mairanos. For the British (Chandler's mother was Anglo-Irish and he was educated in an English prep school), Spaniards have been the psychic Dark Other (Moorish, Roman Catholic) since the Armada, and the Spaniards of Mexico, interbred with blood-drinking Aztecs and worshipping the Virgin of Guadeloupe, whom they call "La Moreñita," have been especially so. In Los Angeles all this is reinforced by the city's social and political brown/white divide, effectively dictating the projection of "dark" impulses, the veiled and the hidden onto a population viewed by white Angelenos as alien and sinister.

II
HERMAN MELVILLE

"Julia Kristeva says the homosexual is a charming, delightful person so long as he does not indulge in sadistic passion with another man."
       "Fuck huh!"   —Author's remark, Interlocutor's response

"Mother, how about Billy Budd *at City Center."*
       "No, I don't think so, I don't care for the theme."
                              —Author-son and Catherine McCourt, née Kitty Moore

Queer Temperament's mind hot-flashed back to City Center on 55th Street (such men, where have they *gone?*) and then to Vic Morrow and Gavin MacLeod in Genet's *Deathwatch*. (FRENCH PLAYWRIGHT QUEERS SELF—review headline in the *Daily News*.)

Time to go home and think up/write something about Melville—that play perhaps, in which M., like the Old Queer Fuck (but grander, more sympathetic) sits on a bench at the foot of Christopher Street and is visited by:

The ghost of his father, Allan, inaugurating a scene in which the beautiful boy Herman and the even more gorgeous but utterly broken Allan travel, father and son, in a howling gale up the Hudson to Rensselaer, where Allan collapses and, after a three-day hallucinatory brain fever, in the throes of which he goes raving mad, dies.

Enter Hawthorne (the man that got away), inaugurating a scene in which the two enthusiasts together climb the humpback whale–shaped mountain in the Berkshires, which, following the descent, becomes the night-and-day specter outside the study window all the while Melville is writing *Moby-Dick*).

The Ghost of his son Malcolm, a suicide in his room on the top floor on East 26th Street, inaugurating a scene in which Malcolm is played by the same boy who played the boy Herman, in a neat role reversal, and in which howling gale, fever and madness are all exhibited in fear and silent scorn, ending in a single pistol shot.

And finally a procession of his characters: Ishmael, Ahab, Queequeg, Starbuck, Pierre, Billy Budd, Claggart, Captain Vere (played by the same actor who played Allan).

—◦—

The queer bracketing of Melville begins with his identification with lost boys, or in the Greek tradition, father-mourning exiles (Orestes), father-seeking escapees (Telemachus) and feared and despised scapegoats (Philoctetes).

Melville, abandoned in adolescence by the gorgeous-failure father, Allan (complete with scenes of raving madness and enforced family secrecy and the perceived annihilation, simply by surviving, of the father by the mother), corresponds to the Orestes complex—a hypothetical invention, based on late Freudian speculation and a few more recent card games. In the playing out of the Orestes complex, the mirror opposite of the Oedipus complex, which dramatizes the unconscious wish to murder the mother and marry the father, the mother is the beard.

Melville, whatever he did or didn't "do," is very definitely a poster boy for nineteenth-century male homosocial glamour, and a great precursor for the major New York character in the book. The South Sea idylls—an earlier *On the Road*, if you will—would not be what they are without the presence of the mysterious Other, the boon companion—he existed, and reminisced about it later—who jumped ship with M. It is not that Fayaway and the other maidens were beards exactly, but whatever it was that M. did, he couldn't have done without the witness—and that in itself is categorically homosexual.

The central melodrama of Melville's happiest period was his meeting with Hawthorne—and here I talk about the difference between the fabulist (M.) and the moralist (H.). They may be distinguished by the way in which they treat time. The fabulist concocts fabulous time, poetic time. The moralist embalms time, as Hawthorne did by throwing the action back two centuries.

Moby-Dick as a great all-male American epic of estrangement and apocalyptic vision is of course prime stuff. Sometimes a big white whale is just a big white whale that spews danger, and sometimes it's something else as well.

There has always been a substantial queer reading of *Pierre*, which is just authentic enough to support the general argument of the lonely, abject, abandoned, Other-seeking male. In the incest with the half-sister Isabel, it is indeed easier to call a beard a beard—but this is not the point I'm reaching toward. Rather, the melodrama shifts back into the life, when both M.'s sons flee him, one by disappearing into the West, the other by killing himself in the house on 26th Street.

Billy Budd, the most homoerotic as well as the most beautiful piece of short fiction written by an American in the nineteenth century, hardly needs a queer reading, in that any and all other readings must spring from just such. In it, Melville succumbs to what Wallace Fowlie (on Rimbaud) called Angelism. The nineteenth-century queer angel in America was Billy Budd (and not Huck Finn, *pace* Leslie Fiedler's reading of "Come back to the raft again, Huck, Honey!"). Claggart was his queer devil adversary—and it scacely needs remarking, but queers are getting dumbed down at a rate far exceeding the requisite hosing down of straight trade that is a commonplace in their mythology. The greatest enemy of the homosexual may now be the other homosexual. Queers can do things to the self-esteem of other queers—witness the Chelsea Boys—that no heterosexual schoolyard bully, no cruel father, has ever matched. Captain Vere, then, stands for the impotent God.

And women come into it importantly. Orestes was, after all, pursued by the Furies and pardoned by Athena (a phallic woman, if you will, but a woman of means). So Melville's mother and wife—blamer, harridan, heart-scald and finally (in preserving, however absent-mindedly, instead of destroying, the unpublished work) pardoner and benefactor.

Dorothy Dean

PART SIX

Dead Reckonings

CHAPTER TWENTY-TWO

Two Jims

"The structure of poetry is continuous parallelism."

—Gerard Manley Hopkins

Wherein the author approaches two homosexual master poets, one become a dear friend and silent master, the other a greatly admired acquaintance for whom he feels the bewildering affection generated by the strange attractor, both representatives of that generation (Armistice Day–Pearl Harbor Day) to which he, just under the wire, sets great store in belonging.

I
JAMES SCHUYLER

"A few almond trees
had a few flowers, like a few snowflakes
out of the blue looking pink in the light.
A gray hush
in which the boxy trucks roll up Second Avenue
into the sky. They're just
going over the hill.
The green leaves of the tulips on my desk
like grass light on flesh,
and a green-copper steeple
and streaks of cloud beginning to glow.
I can't get over
how it all works in together . . ."

—from "February"

"Here, just for you, is a rose made out of a real rose . . ."

—from "Fabergé"

"Along with a theory he was building a methodology. Ordinarily a computer user would construct a problem, feed it in, and wait for the machine to calculate its solution—one problem, one solution. Feigenbaum . . . needed more . . . needed . . . to create miniature universes and observe their evolution . . . change this feature or that and observe the changed paths that would result . . . armed with a new conviction, after all, that tiny changes in certain features could lead to remarkable changes in overall character."

—James Gleick, *Chaos: Making a New Science* (1987)

He really liked having Irish blood ("My mother was a Connor"), and when he came of age, he readily took back his father's name (there had been a divorce), but whenever he went back to East Aurora, he saw people who only remembered him as Jimmy Ritenour.

Schuyler's poetry is a poetry of the hidden become suddenly apparent.

Like Melville's work, Schuyler's replicates the life's beginnings in the abandonment by the father (through divorce) and evolves into a portrait of the poet both as displaced American (early life in Washington, D.C., supplanted by life in East Aurora, New York, and exile in college in West Virginia) and as charmed innocent, in fact as Billy Budd. Schuyler's experience in the U.S. Navy during World War II was scarcely happier than Melville's Billy's, and the consequences of his enlistment nearly as fatal.

In Italy, just after the war, he was befriended by Auden, then stopping on Ischia. There was a kind of apprenticeship, the details of which remain unclear, except that Auden gave him his Camp name, Dorabella, in contrast to the Fiordiligi of Chester Kallman. Schuyler's recklessness and violent drinking became apparent, and, in the light of what we now call post-traumatic stress, then called "nervous from the service," he began to undergo long mood swings resulting in a series of psychotic interludes. From this time the re-emergence of religious yearning, and what the Catholic poets would in that decade call the sacramental sense of life, and an immersion in Italian opera ("Lina Pagliughi, Cloe Elmo, Ebe Stignani, the young di Stefano; pretty sensational") and theater (*As You Like It*, in Rome: "*Tuttto il mondo è un palco scenico*").

The friendship with the older poet endured and, upon his return to New York, on the way to taking up employment at the Museum of Modern Art, he was, significantly if accidentally, Auden's companion at the New York first night of Eliot's *The Cocktail Party*. (*"Deuxième choix*, dear. Wystan and Chester were having one of their little *tiffs*. That didn't matter to me; the world and its mother were there, which of course riled Chester no end.")

Further developments: his odd-man-out (if sentimental favorite) position in the New York School, vis-à-vis the twin histrionic virtuosi, Ashbery and O'Hara—this was before Ashbery decamped for France, spending ten years there and returning, aesthetically speaking, armed and dangerous and already embarked on the career which would bring him to the pre-eminent position in late-twentieth-century American poetry he is now thought to hold.

Contributions to the Poets' Theater and a novelistic collaboration with Ashbery (*A Nest of Ninnies*) ensued, plus the publication of his own first novel, *Alfred and Guinevere* (to be succeeded some time later by the compressed masterpiece *What's For Dinner*, which stands alongside the four long poems, "The Crystal Lithium," "Hymn to Life," "The Morning of the Poem" and "A Few Days," and the sequence written while a psychiatric patient at the Payne Whitney Clinic).

O'Hara's death in 1966 came as the decisive turning point: the poem "Funeral at Springs," in which Schuyler "decides" to assume the position vacated. Convergence of this, accidental or not, with the onset of genuine psychosis. Schuyler's madness. *The Crystal Lithium* and *The Payne Whitney Poems*.

His greatness made manifest in *Hymn to Life*. Subsequent confirmation in *The Morning of the Poem* (1980, Pulitzer Prize) and in the novel, *What's for Dinner?* Full recovery under Dr. Daniel Newman and friendships with Darragh Park and Tom Carey. His valedictory masterpiece, *A Few Days*.

Schuyler, having decided that reliance on the iambic-trochaic-dactylic-anapestic formalities (not since Hopkins the most vital measure of English poetry, not since Whitman the strongest representation in verse of American speech) made no more real linguistic sense than an Elizabethan poet's harking resolutely back to Anglo-Saxon alliterative patterns, found his solutions not merely in constant reading but equally in wresting meaning from Romantic and twentieth-century pianistic and symphonic literature.

In his last years before he died in 1991, he joined the Episcopal Church and undertook a short-lived public reading career, in which the visionary quality of the work was even more apparent.

Letters and diaries have been posthumously published; his papers and record collection are in the James Schuyler archive at the University of California, San Diego.

◄○►

I once confided to a young poet (Wayne Koestenbaum) who had just secured an appointment to the faculty at Yale that I was tied in a knot over how to begin writing about James Schuyler's *Selected Poems* (Farrar, Straus and Giroux). "He is the best," the young man said. "Do you really think so?" "Oh, yes. Every time I read 'Hymn to Life,' I burst out crying." "Well, will you tell them that—your students—when you get up to the Vatican?" "Of course—why not?"

Why not? Why not admit that when I read through this volume, read poems I've been reading for years, my desire is not to *say* or *write* anything at all: it is to go running screaming into the street. That says it all? I wish it could. Samuel Beckett said, "All poetry, as discriminated from the various paradigms of prosody, is prayer." Virginia Woolf, writing about Henry James (*The Golden Bowl*), said he was "one of the few who attempt to picture people as they are. But again, though he is almost overscrupulous not to exaggerate, to see people as they are and the lives that they really lead, it is naturally through his own eyes that he sees them—eyes [that,] we are led to think, must be provided with some extra fine lens, the number of things he sees is so extraordinary." Readers who remember that this cunning tickle of VW's formed the lead-in to what was essentially a "significant form" pan of the gorgeous book, will perhaps also realize—if they are aware of how James Schuyler operates at all—that this same kind of seemingly respectful nod toward the great labors of evidentiary culling behind the poems is often used to form a point-coordinate parabola with which to whip-snap a summary "Who cares?" "So what?" back at them—the poems "about" Jane and Joe and Kenward and Doug and Frank and Fairfield and Darragh, and the other (long dead) Frank, and the very much alive and prized "dear John," et cetera, et cetera. Even the feinters with damned praise—poets mainly, of his generation, who liken this evolved master to some lark out on a tree limb somewhere in literary Nether Yaphank—go in for it: Schuyler, of course, is *lovely*; he could "read" the telephone book. But that's just *it*: he *does* "read" the telephone book; he "reads" the white *and* the yellow pages. So what? Who cares? I once dutifully, and gratefully, audited a pair of lectures on contemporary poetry given by Harold Bloom at the New School. In the corridor, during a chatty recessional, I asked one or two of his most obviously keen and brilliant students if they valued the poetry of James Schuyler. "Who?"

The greatest poetry is not merely delightful; it is categorically utilitarian; it throws us, its readers, lifelines when we need them. My strong feeling is that at a certain point in life, you could die from not knowing the poetry of James Schuyler. Close reading of the dextrously tesselated verbal events of "The Crystal Lithium," "Hymn to Life," "The Morning of the Poem," and "A Few Days" (not this is like that is like those is like them—not "the noise"; rather they *are* this, that, those which, them; what, I you, us—the true Such: What's What) can, literally, save a reading life.

If I were teaching this poetry—analyzing its prosodic corpuscularity instead of merely prescribing it, and using it myself for transfusions into distressed, bipolar mood-life (and, not so incidentally, as a source of practical historical and literary privity for my own work), I would probably begin by asking students to copy out two poems: the sestina after Dante, "I have reached, alas, the long shadow," and the next poem—a fractional sestina-collage called "An Almanac." Then I'd have them make a chart—you know the drill: you would most certainly find what I found. Plot the push-pull coordinates in the sestina's thirty-nine lines against the equivalents—mostly in the assonantal and interior echoes of the seventeen-line "Almanac." Do you hear in the pulse the presence of the strange attractors? Of course you do; it's a heartbeat, ready for combat.

An analogy from science, after a fragment from Wallace Stevens:

> . . . And yet relation appears,
> A small relation expanding like the shade
> Of a cloud on sand, a shape on the side of a hill.
> —from "Connoisseur of Chaos"

"He was studying attractors. The steady equilibrium reached by his mappings is a fixed point that attracts all others—no matter what the starting 'population' it will bounce steadily in toward the attractor. Then with the first period doubling, the attractor splits in two, like a dividing cell. At first these two points are practically together, then as the parameter rises, they float

*apart. Then another period of doubling: each point on the attractor divides
again at the same moment. Feigenbaum's number (4.6692016090) let
him predict when the period doubling would occur. Now he discovered that
he could also predict the precise values of each point on this ever-more
complicated attractor—two points, four points, eight points. . . ."*

                                                             —Gleick, *Chaos*

Compare the openings of, first, "The Crystal Lithium" and "Hymn to
Life," then of "The Morning of the Poem" and "A Few Days":

The smell of snow, stinging in nostrils as the wind lifts it from a beach
Eye-shuttering, mixed with sand, or when snow lies under the street
       lamps and on all
And the air is emptied to an uplifting gassiness
That turns lungs to winter waterwings, buoying, and the bright white
       night
Freezes in sight a lapse of waves, balsamic, salty, unexpected:
Hours after swimming, sitting thinking biting at a hangnail
And the taste of the—to your eyes—invisible crystals irradiates the world
"The sea is salt"
"And so am I."

—◦—

The wind rests its cheek upon the ground and feels the cool damp
And lifts its head with twigs and small dead blades of grass
Pressed into it as you might at the beach rise up and brush away
The sand. The day is cool and says, "I'm just staying overnight."
The world is filled with music, and in between the music, silence
And varying the silence all sorts of sounds, natural and man-made:
There goes a plane, some cars, geese that honk and, not here, but
Not so far away, a scream so rending that to hear it is to be
Never again the same. "What, this is hell." Out of the death breeding
Soil, here, rise emblems of innocence, snowdrops that struggle
Easily into life and hang their white enamel heads toward the dirt
And in the yellow grass are small wild crocuses from hills goats
Have cropped to barrenness.

◄○►

July 8 or July 9, the eighth surely, certainly
   1976 that I know
Awakening in western New York blurred barely
   morning sopping dawn
Globules face to my face, a beautiful face, not
   mine: Baudelaire's skull:
Force, fate, will, and, you being you: a
   painter, you drink
Your Ovaltine, and climb to the city roof, "to
   find a view," and
I being whoever I am get out of bed holding
   my cock and go to piss
Then to the kitchen to make coffee and toast
   with jam and see out
The window two blue jays ripping something white
   while from my mother's
Room the radio purls: it plays all night she leaves
   it on to hear
The midnight news then sleeps and dozes
   until the day which now it is,
Wakening today in green more gray, why did
   your lithe blondness
In Remsen handsomness mix in my mind with
   Baudelaire's skull? which
Stands for strength and fierceness, the dedication
   of the artist?

◄○►

[A Few Days]
are all we have. So count them as they pass. They pass
   too quickly
out of breath: don't dwell on the grave, which yawns for
   one and all.
Will you be buried in the yard? Sorry, it's against
   the law. You can only

lie in an authorized plot but you won't be there to
    know it so why worry
about it? Here I am at my brother's house in western New
    York: I came
here yesterday on the Empire State Express, eight hours
    of boredom on the train.
A pretty blond child sat next to me for a while. She
    had a winning smile,
but I couldn't talk to her, beyond "What happened to
    your shoes?" "I put them under the seat." And
so she had. She pressed the button that released the
    seat and sank
back like an old woman. Outside, purple loosestrife
    bloomed in swathes
that turned the railway ditch and fields into a
    sunset-reflecting lake
And there was goldenrod and tattered Queen Anne's Lace
    and the noble Hudson
on which just one sailboat sailed, billowing, on a weekday
    afternoon.

    The design of the line, or phrase of a line, or of one stanza, is the design of the poem, is the design of the collection—self-similarity throughout. ("Turns-in-on-itself," the nervous comment goes, from those whom prayer enrages.) Using the four elements earth, air, fire, water for the imagery, and the two forces gravity and levity to negotiate among them, gives the first two of the four dimensions, linearity and stature (extent and height). The "weak" force and the "strong" force, in argument (stress count/vocalic value = prosody) render the third and fourth dimensions, depth (inscape) and time. The formation will be that of the coordinates flung out from a spinal (idea) stem, forming the pattern of a leaf. As in each leaf the branch and so the tree is figured (probably the origin of the practice of awarding laurels to accomplished composer-singers), the leaf is the stanza, the branch the poem, the tree the Work.

The smell of snow, stinging in nostrils as the wind lifts it from a beach
The smell of snow (water)
stinging (fire)
beach (earth)

snow/beach = gravity
wind/sting = levity (inhalation:dream)
from gravity to levity = the lift-off of the poem.

The wind rests its cheek upon the ground and feels the cool damp
damp
wind
rests its cheek (abrasion:fire)
ground
cool damp
Proceed as above . . .

Awakening in western New York = (geography:earth) (gravity)
sopping dawn (water/fire) (toward levity:evaporation)
Globules (water) (gravity)
beautiful face = dream (air) (toward levity:idea)

A Few Days (concept:idea:levity)
are all we have. So count them as they pass. They pass too quickly
too quickly (burned up:fire) (levity in process) (flowing fast:water:levity
    pulled back by gravity)
out of breath: don't dwell on the grave, which yawns for one and all
= desperate (despite the order "don't," the reader does) reach toward levity
grave (earth) (gravity)
yawns (gasping:air:attempted levity . . .)
Proceed, doubling, doubling back.

I merely wish to indicate by means of this analogical grid-play what I
take to be the obvious. It has been said, kindly, by poets, that James Schuyler
has succeeded in making the lyric dramatic. What I would insist is that he
has subsumed the lyric and the dramatic in the epic: Euterpe, Melpomene
and Thalia are the backup trio in the pageant that only Calliope, in all her
majesty, can lead. What sort of epic? Not of arms and the man; rather of
the man in his arms—although, as in "Dream lover put your arms around
you," as in Samuel Beckett (writing about Marcel Proust), "Writing is the
apotheosis of solitude," that means merely and always the epic of the Self
accounting for itself—"Here!"

Along the way, Self, everyone you ever knew, or read about or thought
of, or willed killed, or thought up out of the entropic, chaotic, pleonastic,

capably-negative, southpaw *pis-aller* of ideation and recourse. All that heaven allows; all it thinks is just not nice. Make a wish upon a strange attractor; hitch-hike; take the consequences; write when you find work.

Of course I find the actual life this poet has led greatly heroic; of course I do. Of course, that isn't the point—not even a little? No? Yes, and no. The point is the work—the rose made out of the rose? Yes. Yes, and yes.

The time, the place, the matter, the investigation. From World War II ("We won the war!") to the present ("Oh?") in New York and its satellite Edens (those little places just two, three, four hours . . .). The one life we have to live. Meticulous, seeming-offhand: a kind of dowsing; uncanny receipts for recall and reiteration carried about in a memorized breviary of "influences," from—but *no*, not *that!* It is an epic of a life that came into its maturity at the exact moment when the city assumed its capital-of-the-planet status—the period of Abstract Expressionism, of Balanchine and the first generation of NYCB divinities (culminating in *Agon*), of Martha Graham, of first-run film noir, of Great Evenings in The Theater, of the post-war explosion of Free Love (especially this last, in a headlong-hellbent era when to do for it was not, necessarily, to die for it). It is a great pilgrim's progress: the out-of-town apple-knocker postulant ("You look interesting. Here's a copy of my new little magazine, *Upstate*"), the navy veteran, the big bad boy, erratic and brilliant from the first—stretched on the spokes of the wheel of life, like in the lyric from Billy Strayhorn's "Lush Life"; wondering half out loud whether James Joyce was any good (and why not?). Working at MoMA. Found out, labeled as founding coconspirator of "The New York School." Embraced, ensnared (he might have agreed with Dorothy Parker: "I've always said, that's the way I am; take me or leave me, or as in the usual order, both"). Published, noticed; considered disturbing, disturbed. Netted, sequestered, enduring, and, though it's something you won't find trumpeted in the work, beloved. The great friendship with a great American painter, with poets, with. . . .

I want to close what I've opened only the least crack with a glance at "Buried at Springs," the poem in memory of Frank O'Hara. O'Hara will be remembered as a poet of stunning and stinging brilliance, I believe, and Schuyler, as I have said, is, to my mind, immortal. Reading "Buried at Springs" is not a lesson, nor is it not not:

> There is a hornet in the room
> and one of us will have to go
> out the window into the late

August mid-afternoon sun. I
won. . . .
. . . .

The rapid running of the
lapping water a hollow knock
of someone shipping oars:
it's eleven years since
Frank sat at this desk and
saw and heard it all. . . .

Ezra Pound said, didn't he, that it was necessary that masterpieces be written; it was of no great importance by whom. The hornet is gone out into the empyrean; the desk—"this," not "his"—belongs to whoever hears the water, who still withstands the shock of the hollow knock—which is the heartbeat, saying again and again "not yet," and after and after, "I won." The poet contemplates his dead poet friend's absent shape, something quite like mind-caressing the archaic torso of an (American) Apollo, and says, day-in, day-out, as was suggested by that even earlier prayer-poet, "Why not change your life?"

II
JAMES MERRILL
(In at the Death of the Heart)

"I do not offer up my inmost feelings to the tender mercy of fools."
—Leoš Janácek, *Letters*

*"Like
$(x/y)^2 = 1$
—or equals zero, one forgets—"*
—James Merrill

THE DAY DAVID JACKSON PROVED HIMSELF A FOOL

The author, theretofore charmed by the still viable scotch-oiled social savoir-faire dispensed at lunch (for instance, picking up the check with the swift *négligé* aplomb of the Southern gentleman, continental around the edges, that James Merrill's titular longtime companion (and medium of *The Book of Ephraim* and *Mirabell, Books of Number*) had been dealing wholesale for, it was said, a generation, reaching so back to QT's impressionable youth, that time for which he was to suffer a progressive and nearly terminal nostalgia, saw the bubble burst in an instant, watched the house of the most exquisite pornographic playing cards blow away down Third Avenue in a cold-douche, hot-flash of recognition, all on account of an impossibly vain and radically stupid *obiter dictum* directed at the lately deceased Mae West.

The Conversation (1982)

[Note: All David Jackson's (DJ's) seemingly interrogative responses are delivered in the flat declarative—an old faggot trick intended to discomfit the presumed-cadet interlocutor.]

QT: Yes, a new character, an unruly Italian mezzo called Vana Sprezza.

DJ: Vana Sprezza . . . Vana Sprezza.

QT: Yes, Vana with one *n*—short for Sylvana.

DJ: Very good—and you say she bears resemblance to Mae West.

QT: In a way, yes. She's learned much from observing Mawrdew Czgowchwz, who in turned benefited greatly from observing and befriending Mae West.

DJ: Mae West; do tell.

QT: Yes.

DJ: Mae West was in some way important to you.

QT: Indeed. In fact when she died I wrote her obituary for *Film Comment*, ending with the advice to the carvers of her tombstone— proposing a simple legend, "Come up and see me some time."

DJ: Oh, I'm afraid Mae West has a lot more lessons to learn before she can enter heaven.

QT: I couldn't disagree more. A finer woman not only never walked the streets, but has never graced the corridors of heaven either.

DJ: I'm afraid, young man, you are completely mistaken in that idea.

Silence prevailed; decorum was maintained, notwithstanding the entrance of that indispensable alter ego (variously called Moriarty and The Guttersnipe) to whom QT has remained ever grateful for preserving him, since the days of NYU, from close association with fools and frauds like this one. The amiable, expansive Southern homosexual gentleman who likes his liquor had just turned into a poseur whose one true idea of heaven was real gamey hooker cock (smelling rather like deep-fried conch picked out of a garbage pail after about three days) from the back alleys of Key West and, speaking of literary concerns, whose sole traffic in close reading was getting an eye lock on the label of a bottle of Old Crow.

The Pathos of the Situation

David Jackson, in order to feel needed, and having failed utterly in fulfilling his earlier and more robust fantasy of being translated into a higher realm and growing to the scale of angelic discourse, tried desperately to reduce esoteric thought—the all of it, sluiced through the do-it-yourself version of a prefabricated pipeline (the Ouija board)—to the measure of the arc of his own mind's portal.

Or, in exact terminology, the diminished capacity of a brain and nervous system (shredded by alcohol and worn to a frazzle by access upon access of self-incriminating rage) to inform a mind that tended to wander but never got far in flight from its own prosecutor, of anything at all in any coherent way, lavishing upon its multiple malformed introjects all of the nurture and affection for which the world at large had somehow never given him an outlet—leaving his partner, James Merrill, a Puck bereft of an Oberon. That was miscasting, certainly, in both directions, but manifestly the scenario.

◄○►

A vexed being given to letting all and sundry hear, and sometimes feel, the brunt of a misplaced contempt. One regularly saw "Lord what fools these mortals be!" writing itself in the cartoon bubble over Merrill's head while he listened with pained smile to the ordinary, hapless, but generally quite inoffensive, betises of his lesser interlocutors. (JM/DJ might also appear as Ariel/Caliban. The unfairness: Does Ariel get the humpy numbers? He does not, not without paying for them *per il naso*, whereas Caliban often, confoundingly does, apparently for the reason that the humpy numbers time and again turn out to be boys beaten to a pulp by their daddies and taking the beatings for love. Go figure.)

James Merrill's relation to the life of the temporal world as it is commonly, and insufficiently, understood often seemed a forecast of his relation to the afterlife. He seemed to see in daily living merely an exciting connection with a remote element when there is only a hint of what is going on. (Although perhaps the startled look may have been largely the result of his wearing contact lenses. If so, the temperament, either by natural inclination or studied application, certainly seemed a close fit with the look.)

Of course David Jackson was not happy in his Caliban role, anything but, yet the fiction was maintained. And neither are comparisons of Merrill to Gielgud unwarranted—to Gielgud and to Sarah Bernhardt, each a wild card who redefined in absolutely personal terms for at least a generation the classical acting styles of their respective traditions. So Merrill's formalism succeeds when it succeeds (and when it is not compulsively seizing on entries from the Dictionary of Received Ideas and beating them to death in verse, and when he is not, in some strange state of "the show must go on" persistence, determinedly singing while indisposed) entirely on his own terms, markedly American-loneliness ones. This is at once his strongest bid for authority and the reason he must never be imitated by anyone seriously interested in becoming a working poet. Merrill is a naked singularity. (He could of course be imitated, indeed more easily than any of his contemporaries, but then so could Gielgud and Bette Davis.)

The life, as viewed by outside onlookers who can't imagine how the poetry "fitted in," uncannily resembled the exotic, passionate, opulent, "charmed" and secretly violent life depicted in the strange chameleon-like novels of Gordon Merrick (turning on dime upon dime from rather stirring romances into queer pulp trash and back again), *The Lord Won't Mind, An Idol for Others, Forth Into Light* and *Now Let's Talk About Music*. In that life, David Jackson became a progressively cantankerous cliché wrinkle-room queen in the Shambles of Faggotry, witty, bitter, caustic, well on the way to wet brain, and yet retaining the vestiges of—or was it only the memory projected with such force as to actually simulate—his own unquestionable brawny-Adonis young manhood.

In Biblical terms, they were David and Jacob, the Beloved and the Trickster—David dancing before the Ark, Jacob dreaming at the floor of the stairway to paradise—and then, soon enough, the party animal, the social arbiter and the dreamer wrestling for the angel's (read the trickster's trick's) blessing, "I could love you for yourself."

And finally, in the Sandover enterprise, DJ as dj, spinning platters, his "information" *Narrishkeit* countered by JM's creation of Mirabell, his Better Angel, the finest creation of his relentless poetic wish-fulfillment. And then the strange anomaly of the naming of the epic.

Merrill hated the vulgarity and pretension of the ersatz mansion in Southampton, imposture, fake heraldry, sub-Hearst baronial *grossière*, and yet he invented a place called Sandover and slapped a picture of it—the mansion in Southampton—on the cover of the published work. The pathos of that title includes the fact that the real world of Long Island's South Fork is indeed bathed in all seasons by one of the world's most remarkable washes of changing light, the draw for painters of all schools for a over a century, and yet the impression created is one of being shut up in a sort of bungalow San Simeon and bundled down to the beach cabana and back—in which circumstances, just how much of the light's variety did he ever experience?

And then what? The dogsbody grunt work of turning into acceptable and often compelling verse (and Merrill really *could* do the poetic equivalent of Helena Modjeska, reducing an audience to tears by reading the telephone book), this rodomontade cooked up by what one must agree somewhat reluctantly to call David Jackson's Unconscious (since the difference between DJ's continual Unconscious and DJ continuously unconscious merits some serious consideration, and not merely as a semantic exercise) was purely Sisyphean, and thereby definitely infra dig. Apart from the desperate futility of the labor itself, Sisyphus was definitely what James Merrill's coevals in the World of Affairs would have called NOCD; compare Euripides, *Medea*, on Glauce:

"Who is she—who? My grandfather was the *Sun*;
Her grandfather pushes rocks uphill in hell!"

The Author (QT) and His Alter Ego, The Guttersnipe (TG), aka Moriarty, Go at It

QT: The thing is, he interests me as a contrast to Schuyler.
TG: Yeah, yeah, two Jims. So you've decided to let David Jackson get away with shit.
QT: Yes.
TG: You like this kind of company.
QT: Not a whole lot.

TG: So?

QT: I like going to the apartment. He ropes in interesting types.

TG: Shucks, and I left my autograph book at the dry cleaners.
Thought you got over all that—never did you any good, not in the
end. Plus which, your calling cards are pretty dog-eared these
days, don't-cha know. Of course, you might revive the story of
your long-lost love, the Summer of Happiness routine, Night Journey across America . . . all that. Don't know how the Greyhound
Bus performance would play with that crowd—might send a
mixed message, although the sailor and the Donald Duck comic
book is one of your kickier turns. Come to think of it, performance
art may turn out to be your forte—but does the Ingram-Merrill
Foundation give grants for it?

QT: I'm so glad I taught you to pronounce forte properly. Anyway I
admire Merrill.

TG: What for?

QT: In particular? His lyric poetry.

TG: Which you can read in a book. Besides, I've heard you say he
indicates.

QT: It's true, he does, not that any members of the Academy of American Poets would know, or care to know, what is meant by that.
He does indicate, relentlessly. I was thinking about his first
published poem, "The Black Swan," and the two words that
came right at me, as a description of his lifelong m.o. were "bent
neck." Norman Mailer once referred to his infinitely superior contemporary, Truman Capote, as "a ballsy little guy." Of course he
didn't know—or did he?—that anatomically Capote was just that,
freakishly so. "All potatoes and not much meat," as the nastier
boys at the Everard used to say about gentlemen of a certain age
they affected to disdain in the steam room. Bent neck says it better
about Merrill—neck in the way the Irish use it.

TG: What you're saying, essentially, is Merrill is the reactionary and
Schuyler is the progressive. Merrill is *disegno*, Schuyler is *pintura*.
Merrill is Lorenzo Lotto, Schuyler is Caravaggio. Merrill is
Aaron Copland, Schuyler is Samuel Barber . . . and Ashbery—
whom you refuse to talk about at all, he intimidates you so—is,
who, Elliot Carter?

QT: He's been compared to Mozart—Merrill has.

TG: You'll have one know. I don't buy it, not for a minute. Mozart, I think not. Poulenc, maybe. Listen, the strands of the double helix informing high genius, whether in music or in poetry, are simultaneously imbued with the deepest sorrow and suffused with the most sublime joy. Exhibitions of a temperament alternately shot through with regret and charged with elation are not exactly the same stuff. Figurative adumbration, the fixing of them, doesn't automatically achieve resonance; it is not the same as the movement of figures simultaneously colliding and interlocked, figures whose movement in the very act of drawing them erases them. And the knee-jerk punning is symptomatic of a relentless, driven strip-mining of the language.

QT: I do wish you'd leave the stylish talk to me.

TG: I've been every place you've been; eat your heart out.

QT: Also Merrill stormed heaven, whereas Schuyler embezzled it, but Schuyler also harried hell—what Stanley Kauffmann has called the internal realm of chill and longing and dread of chaos—which Merrill seems never to have really done much more than sniff at, so far as the record is concerned, until the diagnosis. I'm speaking of the poet, as poet.

TG: Did the poet never seriously consider the prospect of contracting AIDS?

[If indeed James Merrill showed for a considerable while a nearly comical aversion to the author's company, one both disturbing and fascinating for the frequency with which he apparently felt himself obliged in respect of certain valuable friendships to abide it—including a single occasion on which he agreed to a joint reading downtown at St. Mark's Church—the fact can perhaps be explained by the unerring sense he had of what lay not far beneath another's surface, in this case beneath the author's apparent ebullience and geniality, a rooted propensity for having statements like the above form in his nether mind, a mind in the end of the day he, Merrill, would have considered no more trustworthy, companionable or, in the key word he was raised on, *nice*, than those of the thuggish dullards who tormented him in prep school. And that did rankle, because he'd once written a note thanking the author for an original photograph of Maria Callas as a pretty teenage girl, saying something like "If I'd had this to hang in my gym locker back then, they'd never have come after me the way they did."]

QT: Also he's held in high esteem and regarded with enormous affection by people I really respect; John Hollander, for example, who's no man's easy mark.

TG: So you write him a letter. You do not let some rancid old queen who, instead of, in the immortal words of your pal the legendary Everett Easter, sittin' up, takin' n'u'shment every morning over on 72nd Street, belongs in some tar-roof roadhouse swilling rot gut and scarfing road kill, trash the divine Mae.

QT: Mae can take it where she is—she always could. It was Mae who taught me everything I know about dealing with the David Jacksons of the world—who by the way can be very charming and even occasionally kind.

TG: We're a little too old for that kindness-of-strangers shit, and those people will always be strangers to you, don't imagine—

QT: Otherwise. I don't—and thank you for sharing.

TG: I mean just look at the low-down sonuvabitch; if it weren't for his nouveau riche protector, where would he be? Who'd give him a New York minute? Wealth is a requisite of the mendicant mentality, if only because without it there would be nothing to be given gratis rather than earned.

QT: There's a whole lot more to James Merrill, man and poet, than the mannered drawl and faggot cruelty he was as well taught by masters as any Catherine Sloper.

TG: You know all that and I know all that, consequence of certain *imprevu* and putatively anonymous collisions taking place in such dark places as Joseph Caldwell writes of, occasions entrusted to the pages of a locked diary recording the private thoughts and experiences of a discreet New York homosexual, and consequently meant for publication . . . sometime. Meanwhile, are you going to tell me, tell yourself, tell both of us you buy into that Erich von Däniken-cum-Madame Blavatsky-with-sage-cosmic-asides-by-Carl Sagan-Ouija-board horseshit as poetry? You, who used to lie abed swooning over Teilhard de Chardin?

QT: I didn't at all, not until Mirabell.

TG: Mirabell, the beautiful peacock angel. Clearly your guardian angel nostalgia hangover.

TG: Probably, yes.

TG: Look, the fact is, so long as James Merrill, who like any true lyric

poet didn't exactly know what he was talking about, only that
something was occurring to him in verse, that is, obeying the lyric
impulse, of which Neruda spoke, "*La rosa sin porque florisce
porque florisce*"; when he obeyed, he was fine. Nearly as soon as
he pressed his luck and pushed his voice, he became strident.

QT: You're right, he did, with the exception of Mirabell.

Listen, if it is true of heterosexual love that partners who succeed do so ultimately in imagining themselves as one another, then
in homosexual love the beloved succeeds by imagining himself his
lover: in the case of the rich, prim, sissy boy, the big, bold beautiful guy. Mirabell, more than anything he is talking about, is the
Physique Pictorial version of the incorporeal hunk. It's a type of
regression which at once seeks to uncover the lost world of childhood and indeed to commune with spirits in some way. Merrill
always seemed out to demonstrate that he was just as alive as other
people, and as busy as any hostess. Therefore, when he wanted to
reach the dead, it perhaps made sense he went about it in the
rather energetic Camp way women of his mother's generation
often entertained themselves in the afternoon and evening.

TG: Prefabricated schemata: all scaffolding, no edifice. A Potemkin
Village epic—little input from Calliope; more from Urania and
Clio, and some, but not enough, from Euterpe. Also, inclusion of
musical terminology is not what makes a poem musical. In sum,
the propagation of wa-wa in didactic blank verse hardly constitutes
a new way of fathoming creation.

QT: I insist, Mirabell is . . . celestial.

TG: Don't-cha know, as was so memorably if rather feverishly articu-
lated by the dizzy old-shoe society hostess drumming up the
applause at that memorable performance at the Guggenheim.
After which—don't tell me; something inexplicable in you got off
on the fantasy of understudying Peter Hooten.

QT: I'm talking about the angel in the poem, on the page.

TG: Oh, so am I.

QT: The whole Peter Hooten thing was intricate.

TG: Tell us about it, Eve.

Mirabell. Peter Hooten. Chance Wayne. Hooten's resemblance to Paul
Newman onstage opposite Geraldine Page in *Sweet Bird of Youth*, in the

spring of 1959. Merrill as Alexandra Del Lago, the Page role. Although on the face of it there is no correspondence in the life to the idea of the washed-up star found in a bolt hole, restored by a telephone call from Walter Winchell (Hermes), there is that about Merrill which suggests, absent any factual evidence, but deeply ingrained, the idea of a fall from a great height.

More than any other poet of his generation, the generation succeeding Lowell and Bishop, Berryman and Jarrell, he was studied, like a play or a book or a set of blueprints. And not for how to write poetry so much as for how to live—posing an anomaly in itself; poets, after the pattern of Virgil and Horace, are habitually invited to the high table; they have very seldom bought or inherited the table itself.

Poets since Shelley have put in metaphysical claims as unseen legislators; Merrill, having found himself uniquely capable of doing so, put himself above legislation, establishing a court of his own—itself an anomaly: a putatively other-worldly environ which could, and happily often enough did, assume as raucous an atmosphere as that of Margo Channing's dressing room.

"The theater is the royal road to madness," he insisted, yet he led his life as theater, never more so than in casting himself as Alexandra Del Lago, artist and star, to Peter Hooten's Chance Wayne. The figure of Sarah Bernhardt coming down the spiral stairs ("the spiral staircase of association / Around the well of substance"—"Accumulations of the Sea"). She stood still and the stairs wound around her. Merrill likened himself to her when he said the closet dissolved around him. The image would do as well for the apparent motion of his life, which resembled, as viewed from the other side of the footlights, that of a grande *horizontale* (the illusion of the languid homosexual) as well as the remarkable sustaining power of his personal performance: as on script and in role, one imagined, in his sleep as in his waking life. Also, as Bernhardt was Jewish, so Merrill was queer—a very successful celebrant of a certain perceived failure: to measure up to heterosexual manhood, to marry. And the kicker: the last ten or eleven years of his life was spent in a secret open coffin.

He joked that his father had been born poor. (Was he pushing a resemblance to Horace, in terms of twentieth-century American "success?") The Merrill money was so new its green came off on their hands. His self-image as eternal *eremenos*—breathing in, as he had been to Kimon Friar—was as it turned out not at all easily transformed into that of the *erastes*—breathing out, as over the waters. But outside as well as inside the realm of the aesthetic, exigent in the social and the political, to which the *erastes* was, according to the tenets of Greek *paidaiea*, absolutely committed. He was far too much the Peter Pan type, avoiding any and all serious adult decision making exclusive of the crucial calculations (discovered in late adolescence) of poetry and, of course, of social "arrangements." Even so, he seemed to move in the society he chose like the jeweled salamander through flames.

—◦—

From the author's diary (January 1993):

Back from Key West [The Elizabeth Bishop Conference]. A wealth of dish, location for a party scene [for *Delancey's Way*]: rooftop over Fast Buck Freddy's. Fantastic anecdote about Tennessee Williams and the high school kid in the dungaree cutoffs putting up his hand during a lecture the spanking new English teacher was giving on *Glass Menagerie*: "I know Mr. Williams . . . he gives me money."

Standing there doing the dishes with JM while JDMcC minds DJ (all but completely ga-ga in the evening). [Reading over entry years later: what did this mean? The memory is of JM washing and done drying, but that can't be right, must've been JM rinsing and done stacking in the dishwasher, or even, it would seem more likely, vice versa.]

JM meticulous and thorough throughout, and, of course, observant-observant: the kind of compulsive recorder who seems distracted by the adventures of others.

Thought back to the initial meeting (inaugural presentation?) on 72nd Street. Not so very different really, after twenty-five years, than the night on Bank Street or the first uptown matinee—except, significantly no audition prepared; none required, none sought and none, if the truth be known, welcome, no matter one was oneself.

First impressions: his distinctive conversational style, unmistakably charged with pained attention.

Haunted, terribly Hamlet-like (surrounded, he would appear to think, by Osrics). Orestes-like. The Orestes complex. The firstborn homosexual son of divorced or estranged parents, held in ransom by the mother, his father as good as dead to him, is psychically charged with the mother's murder, and turning in, suffers, like Orestes, like Hamlet, not guilt for which he is bound to atone but shame which he is bound to expunge either in the perpetration of, or in the act of suffering (or much of each), psychic violence. His only way out is to seek the Oracle. "Joy (word rusty with disuse) / Flashes up, deserved and pure"—"Time Recaptured," from "Family Week at Oracle Ranch" [in *A Scattering of Salts*, 1995].

He's certainly a maverick, Merrill. Most American mavericks come from Hunger or lesser places, or, like Melville and James, from "backgrounds." The fact that Merrill came from raw not bred stock, education and position bought rather than bestowed, creates an anomalous intellectual and social anxiety. Nobody in any earlier generation of the world he came out of could matter spiritually. There were none he could point to and say "they are my forebears." Hence theater.

But who *was* he, standing there, drawling that drawl?

◄o►

The Guttersnipe:

In any event *Sandover* opens with a categorical error, as important to a poem purporting to pitch a type of scientific system as to metaphysics: the making of a commodity out of time. Time is not the attar of the rose, it isn't even money; it is not a nominal quantity at all but only, always and, as it were, forever, a way of measuring, in relation to space, that which is called an event. In terms of high school physics, time has not to do with scalers but with vectors.

QT: "Under no circumstances can the representation of an Idea be considered as successful as long as the virtual sphere of its possible extremes has not been reviewed." Walter Benjamin.

TG: Really. I think I'd better go find something to do in the bathroom till you get normal.

Regarding the matter of the review of such radical extremes as Walter Benjamin's (in the last analysis, a suicide) urges, and taking into account the celerity and ease with which the virtual becomes actual (cf. supra: Schopenhauer, *The World as Will and Representation*, source of this, as of so many of his ideas), in all subsequent discussions between his selves, QT and TG, it was, not surprisingly, the latter whose ethical convictions came to cut the pattern of the argument, in particular as concerned QT's relations with the designated keepers of the Merrill flame. He was therefore able to satisfy himself that although the extreme fastidiousness that might prevent him from revealing, on the basis of private information, this, that or the other about James Merrill, man and poet, might with some justification and considerations of fair use be set aside, neither were the extreme and mean-spirited speculative excesses of wild analysis and prurient speculation warranted in pressing the argument or decent, period. Merrill was, after all, himself the keeper of a flame; that the flame in question was neither a noted poet nor indeed an agent of moral instruction whose genius would ever be valued by a wider world was irrelevant. It also seemed imperative in later years to understand the pathos of James Merrill's life as that of a compulsive observer whose great fear was that when he lay dying others' lives would flash before his eyes, and not merely to score points off its manifestations, not least because of a letter the author received upon the publication of an elegiac work of fiction: "It has taken me a long time, but I have finally come to inhabit the world of *Time Remaining*." For such gestures one either accepts the lifelong obligations of gratitude or one has become at best a slob, at worst a violator of trusts.

QT: Look, I'll get back to you. O.K.?

TG: Check. You'll know where to find me, down by the schoolyard. And try to remember this: simply because you, in consequence of whatever foggy political ideas of spiritual advancement and self-regarding bluff you adopted, find it convenient to play the fool and accept the derision of others, you cannot with impunity yell "fool" at anyone you like.

Whatever of any of that, QT can most certainly list those poems that seem to him foolproof and certain to be canonized:

The Black Swan
Accumulations of the Sea
The Peacock
Willow
The Country of a Thousand Years of Peace
The Lovers
The Charioteer of Delphi
Salome
Mirror
The Day of the Eclipse

The Locusts
An Urban Convalescence
A Vision of the Garden
Scenes of Childhood
The Water Hyacinth
Chimes for Yahya
Verse for Urania
Losing the Marbles
From Morning into Morning
The Pardoner's Tale
Days of 1941 and '44
Palm Beach With Portuguese Man-of-War
The Mad Scene
The Cupola
The Friend of the Fourth Decade
The Summer People
Syrinx
The Will
The Oracle

Wherefore, inconclusive remarks on Merrill: pattern taken from Section Three of "Losing the Marbles" in Part V of *The Inner Room* (1988).

(The Guttersnipe, upon reflection, says this:

"You might end up showing the result to him—and, as Karen Richards, planning on emptying the gas tank so the car would stall on the road to the station in Brewster, muses, who knows but he wouldn't come to see the honest humor of it himself . . . in time.")

Inconclusive Remarks Subject to Random Erasure

no need   Henry James   benefit   friction w. market
respect   admiration   majority   peers   market
squarely   own terms   retail results   better prizes
theater   royal road   madness
nevertheless   theatrical   analogies   tenor   life
type   stricken poet   nearly Bunthorne.
"The Black Swan"   "Sorrow's lost secret center"
locus/matter   entire oeuvre.

Kimon Friar   strong mentor   Rothbart   Merrill   Odette
(32 fouettés   tendency)
heavy investment: being betrayed
Sebastian Venable   Violet   Hellen-two-"l"s
Oresteian   Greece   locus
Orestes Complex   mother's "attempt"/make   little   boy
little girl   reaction formation secret knowledge
Clytemnestra   boy   sexual union   father
she unman   (in his) own estimation
Merrill   concrete mind   poetry   father   money
Charles   money on money   James   poetry on poetry
Father erotic object   mother *l'aborita rivale*
royal infant   majesty baby   Freud   exposed at birth
rescued by Apollo   Ion
Sandover long nightmare   Mirabell dawn
Joy (word rusty with disuse)
Flashes up, deserved and pure.

CHAPTER TWENTY-THREE

Personnel and Bulletins from Zones of Dread

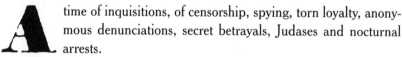

"The scarlet stains upon the body, and especially upon the face of the victim were the pest ban which shut him out from the aid and from the sympathy of his fellow man." —Edgar Allan Poe, *The Masque of the Red Death*

"They go at it, darling, nec spe, nec metu."
—anonymous professor on the phone to a colleague, at dawn,
following a night in the trucks

Wherein a present is wedged between an absent future and an absent past.

A time of inquisitions, of censorship, spying, torn loyalty, anonymous denunciations, secret betrayals, Judases and nocturnal arrests.

Cometh the hour, cometh the man. So, with the dead-eye showmanship, right in sync with the rise out of the linoleum-floor, folding-chair, ratty-old-couch nightclub culture of late-'70s Downtown, of Performance Art: one-man shows, where the instant luminary, Ron Vawter, plays Roy Cohn and Jack Smith with an incorruptible clarity of intention, and the job, instead of acting (as Stella Adler or Lee Strasberg or Uta Hagen or Sanford Meisner of the Neighborhood Playhouse employed the term), is the even-more-exhausting ordeal of constantly maintaining one's personality. . . .

Enter, screaming, Larry Kramer (does not care to play, well or not so, with others), who would perhaps even today (although you wouldn't know)

429

wish to be remembered as the dark-cramped-venue Lenny Bruce of AIDS—persecuted, driven to the vertiginous Edge of Doom—but whose histrionics actually made him into—and he should complain?—its Jackie Mason, the *rebbe* as licensed fool and Broadway legend. *Ridi, Pagliaccio, ch'il cuore ti frangi.* Laugh, clown, laugh. Smile, though your normal heart is breaking, and if it turns out you have no normal heart to break, you can always put that award where your normal heart ought to be.

In his normal heart, of course, Larry regretted his audiences' discomfort—it ran quite contrary to the feelings he would have wished for them in other, less apocalyptic circumstances. But that too is Shoah Business, and who shall 'scape whipping?

"I'll say it: letting that madman hold the rostrum is peculation of public funds!"

—◦—

". . . it is also the pardonable vanity of lonely people everywhere to assume they have no counterparts."
—John le Carré, The Honourable Schoolboy

Unhappily, it is also the less than pardonable (even when completely understood) hubris of the very lonely in combat situations to adopt the methods and style of the enemy not only in order to confound him, but in order to turn him on one's putative allies. Douglas MacArthur, the last Shogun of Japan, is an example; he managed not only to very nearly break the spirit of an admittedly appallingly cruel conquered enemy, but to kamikaze his own career in a dirty kick-box confrontation with President Harry S. Truman, and in retirement to torment his queer son to death by suicide.

Larry Kramer, of course, has had no suicidal offspring, not exactly. No single memorable mot has ever been heard coming out of this motormouth in overdrive, yet it is demonstrably true that the mouth's gale force wind has blown down many a pathetic little political straw house and blown apart the pathetic little straw men inside, and this is neither cream cheese nor chopped liver but a nearly Ciceronian rhetorical achievement.

All the same, to whose benefit—*cui bono*—his critics demanded, familiar as they were only with the most straightforward non-subjunctive concepts of edification and alarmed too that the guns in Larry's wars of religion all too often seemed to them pointed in the wrong direction.

"Larry fumes, but fortunately there is no hatred in him—or not much and not very dangerous. About a man in Larry's position, there are always certain misunderstandings."

"That silence equals death in every instance is far from certain. What is certain is that death equals silence—a thing in many instances, darling, devoutly to be wished."

"Unsay that, wicked woman!"

Yet what they could not manage to agree on among themselves was, *Which* wrong direction? Against any and all platform rivals, ostensibly fighting for the same cause, in the assumed manner of Act Up against global capitalism and Big Pharma as such, which the more politically suave (lobbies, access, all that) understood were in the end the only channels available for any success at all in their enterprise. (After all, didn't Mother Teresa sit down to dinner with despots and world swine to accomplish her ends?—who, of course, many believed was as much concerned with seeing herself, if only from heaven, played by some contemporary equivalent of Ingrid Bergman or Audrey Hepburn or even Sally Field, or, perhaps more seriously, Linda Hunt—little realizing that in contemporary Hollywood the role might well be snapped up by Whoopi Goldberg or Robin Williams, no shit.)

Who would Larry see in the role of Larry? But we digress, they said to themselves. "Digress! Digress!" Larry shot back. "I give you full permission!" Well, they could go in a couple of different directions, depending on the concept thrust. Robert Redford. Dustin Hoffman. Kevin Costner . . .

Then again the young, reared for the most part either in strict lower-middle-class Christian homes (and abstracting for the moment their likely expulsions therefrom) or in itinerant come-as-you-are-and-stay-that-way trailer camps, geared to regard all displays of temperament as modalities of instruction and/or outpourings of lovelorn sentiment rather than as a confounding and chemically unstable compound of Jeremiad wrath and Catskills stand-up comedy . . . did not think him at all appropriate.

You're supposed to wash the mah-jongg pieces before every session.

More sympathetic commentators opined that by the time AIDS hit, Larry, having been, like Mildred Pierce, far too trusting, for far too long, had become both the logophilic (as long as it's just *logo*philic) equivalent of a dark-adapted eye and a hardened woman.

The relationship between Larry Kramer's histrionics and balloon art has not been fully appreciated.

"I'm afraid you are all missing the point. In Larry's view, in order to combat Falwell and the Christian right, what is needed is an equal and opposite hysteria. Larry is not afraid to make himself appear—or indeed to become—ridiculous. The only question is, is there underneath all of it an equal and not at all opposite overwhelming drive, that of self-promotion. Falwell and Robertson and all that ilk don't give a wet shit about faith, morals or any kind of decision; they are demagogues pure and simple—only they are filthy and worldly. I cling to the belief that Larry is in the last analysis selfless."

"Whatever meaning is credited in their final configurations, countless gestural touches could have been conceived by nobody in advance, even the artist."

Edith Cavell declared you could do anything in the world, provided you didn't mind who got the credit. Larry minded very much, as did every other AIDS-related commandant.

It isn't just the generals, it's everyone who carries a weapon.

Thought: Jeanne d'Arc was no demure little thing either, but rather a tough, headline-grabbing, self-immolating little number who had a job to do and did it, and it is not beyond the reach of the cultivated imagination, considering the perdurable Gallic vogue for American phenomena like the Marx Brothers, Jerry Lewis and Madonna, to foresee in the not too distant future a postmodern French deconstructionist treatise out of Nanterre entitled *Le Mystère de la Charité de Larry Kramer*.

And who could have predicted that such venting of rage and suffering persecution for justice's sake over a bullhorn would in the last analysis make of Larry Kramer nothing less than the Gandhi of AIDS (with time yet, let there be light, for *Satyagraha*?). Nobody—but *nobody*.

All in all, however, in a development analogous to the development of Greek tragedy following Thespis's bold egress from the chorus line, myriad performances sprang up in consequence of Larry Kramer's shtick and that of other rival first-half turns. Yet the one thing Larry never did get, as he routinely barged his way center stage at the beginning of every reading, demonstration and vigil, was that closing the first half, not opening it, was the most desired slot in vaudeville.

By and by AIDS witness became remarkable for qualities less resembling revival meetings than group regression therapy ("Wait your turn please, and remember, no touching!") staged as a unit-set strophic psychodrama, with two or more well-rehearsed actors playing terrible people reviling one another over their fundamental existential rottenness and revolting personal habits, while maintaining their personalities, hell-bent for leather and terrified of nothing so much as of Stella Adler's swooping down the aisle and crying out, "You're boring, darlings, boring!" The hallmark: the domino-row collapse of the collective immune system.

"There's a lot of it going around this year, darling; death."
—Diane DeVors

It is not correct existentially to speak of one-time infection (no matter how convenient it became in the next decade for such dramatic purposes as Jonathan Demme's laudable *Philadelphia*), and the heartbreaking attempts of America's then greatest living novelist, Harold Brodkey, to come to terms in print with his own impending death from AIDS. Massive repeated assault must be acknowledged. As with the brain sustaining insults flung by alcohol and other chemicals, we must understand the trauma of the whole human immune system as under siege, largely from the devastating effects of chemicals the human body had never before ingested. To invoke Charles Ludlam again, it is as if it were the voice, and each assault another *Norma*:

Galas: Bruna, how many Normas do I have?
Bruna (looking down her throat): Eighty-six.
Inevitably, the time arrives when there are simply no more Normas.

—◦—

The last graffito scratched into the mirror of the Eighth Street BMT men's toilet before it closed:

MENE MENE TEKEL UPHARSIN!!!!

—◦—

Cassandras—a representative roll call:
Randy Shilts
Darrell Yates Rist
Richard Voinovich
Mark D. Niedselkowski

Roger McFarlane

Lambda Legal Defense

Thousands of Heroic Lesbians

Dignity

Bernard Lynch (A gorgeous Irish priest. When cruised in Central Park he would stop, smile and say "I'm booked." He meant, of course, by the Lord)

Richard Rouilard, editor-in-chief of the *Advocate*, 1990–1992, the exact two-year length of its relevance to queer politics

Andrew Holleran in his definitive work of non-fiction, *Ground Zero*

"There were countless guardian angels charging about upon diverse errands too, of course, but being unseen their actions need hardly be related."
—Mary Lavin, "Chamois Gloves"

"Do what is asked of you, sister; no less, and no more. We don't want any private enterprise in piety."
—ibid.

"Must've been after, deah, 'cause she was draggin' things a bit."
—Mae West on Sarah Bernhardt in vaudeville

◄○►

By the time Quentin Crisp (QC) got around to being a famous immigrant, he was more Martita Hunt than anything like Bernhardt, particularly Martita Hunt as rethought by Hermione Gingold in collaboration with Estelle Winwood—who, asked how it was she stole every scene she was ever in on stage or screen, replied "I play the play!" It was the Gingold lisp that finally put it over, in combination with the Winwood whimsey. "I must go out next week to Chicago and address the lesbians. I shall tell them to be happy."

Kissed by some strange angel at the spectrum's extreme violet end, Crisp managed to live in genteel SRO squalor (uncannily resembling that of the legion of character women on Midtown's Sixth Avenue in the days when there was a living Broadway theater) in one of the few remaining boarding houses still operating in the East Village. He gave out essentially a less imaginative version of the line ("Perhaps you would care to have a look at some of my personal notices?") plied by the Old Queer Fuck on the Park Bench, and managed to work exactly half—the latter half—of Gore

Vidal's program for something like happiness: "Never turn down a chance to have sex or to be on television." Finally, however, his deeply, wildly self-abasing reactionary stances were to create in the general queer public exactly the response of one vocal operaphile in Little Italy to the later career of the defiantly perdurable Renata Scotto: "I *skeeve* on huh."

"I Will Survive" and "I'm Gonna Live Forever" slow to dirge tempo, as if the dj were leaning on the needle. Disco dies. A mourner laments in form.

"Yes, dear, they're going, the pack of them—going fast. Positively passing in music out of sight—and it isn't disco music either, it's 'Where E'er You Walk,' dear, sung by the same darling lyric tenor, so it does seem, at memorial service after memorial service. Why, that sweet boy sings—so very beautifully—'Where E'er You Walk' more often to more people than Renata Scotto has ever sung 'Send in the Clowns.'"

On the public response in the early days of the epidemic: the great smear of mortality across the picture, the dirty mark of pain and horror, found in few quarters a surface of spirit or speech consenting to reflect it.

So it had been as they'd been warned: a fool's paradise. Warned by the bitter Old Guard in the darkened wrinkle rooms, who now spoke to the young, if they spoke to them at all, not boldly, but in simple statement form, sometimes philosophically, sometimes as if seeking personal exculpation, sometimes, though rarely, and then almost reflexively, in order to be liked or pitied, as if they were talking, as if for the first time, to heterosexuals.

For with the Great Liberation, they, the old, had abandoned their last hopes, even in the wan compassion of the mercy fuck—which having only heard tell of and never dispensed, these Olympic-class sexual athletes, the drugged young, imagined as inexplicable-if-not-handsomely-paid-for encounters between certain of their own, young, beautiful and naked and the old, senile and ugly, in which the former entwined with the latter in seeming delight.

They, locked into single expressions of single moods of what in all likelihood had once been mood-variant natures (nurtured by Mabel Mercer and Frances Faye), had returned almost listlessly to the ways of their youth (for as the young were dying in their droves, so failing supply had accompanied diminished demand), inwrought, obsessive, elliptical, desperate, to the circle jerk behind locked doors and to what remained of the tea-room scenes and of The Way of the Crosstown Bus. A fool's paradise, from which the specified had been chased like a dangerous animal. What therefore had at present befallen was that the specified, standing all the while at the gate, had now crossed the threshold . . . and on such a scale as to fill out the whole precinct.

"Who gathers knowledge, darling, gathers *tsouris*. Ecclesiastes."

The following a discussion with David McIntosh, in the garden he made at the Gay Center on West 13th Street:

"The likely truth is neither AIDS nor cancer nor any other disease is ever going to be absolutely eradicated allopathically, because, point-blank, once and for all, it is in the exact nature of allopathy to contain disease, not to eliminate it. Humanity did not eliminate wolves, lions, tigers, panthers, et cetera; they domesticated, worshiped and bred dogs and cats. Allopathy domesticates, worships and breeds disease. Now everybody go home—and pray.

"And you might while you're at it learn a thing or two about herbs, and make a friend of a witch."

◄◦►

Of course, I *had* made friends with a Witch, John Yohalem, who said:

"Wicca—which is a modern religion based on ceremonial magic and traditional folklore—was founded, theologically speaking, on the male-female duality as creative sacrament, and at thumbing one's nose at prim British de-sexed religion, so the Witches were a bit uneasy with variant sexualities. Then, in this country, the feminists got hold of it, and lots of them were lez, so of course modifications had to be made. Still, conservative, by-the-Book Circles exist, as they would, in a religion with no official dogma beyond 'An it harm none, do what thou will,' and no corrective institutions to adjudge the innumerable feuds. If you didn't like the folks in your coven, you went looking for another coven, or you 'hived' with new friends.

"Then along comes AIDS, and of course there were conservative witches who said, or, rather, intoned, 'The Goddess is punishing Practices Against Nature.' That was great fun, because everyone had a wonderful time trashing the old-fashioned types who had said it. Everyone felt real self-righteous, and pro-gay was part of the good feeling.

"Someone even rewrote the symbolic sacramental blessing, you know? 'As the blade is to the male, so the cup is to the female, and conjoined, they bring blessedness'? Whereat the priestess (or priest) brings the knife into the cup held by the priest (or priestess)? It got rewritten, 'As the blade is to the lover, so the cup is to the beloved.' A more universal view, it was thought, of the old 'in-out.'

"Everyone designed rituals around AIDS: Rituals for a Cure, rituals for understanding, rituals to send energy to distant Positives—Witches *love* to send magical healing energy, it is our favorite thing—rituals to zap coven members in travail, rituals to build T-helper cells (these might not have been a good idea, anti-virally speaking).

"I was introduced to Wicca Seattle in '87 (after twenty-six years as a solitary Pagan, going to the opera when I needed magical ritual) by Laughing Otter, whom I met through the Radical Faeries; he introduced me to Leon, who was the teacher of Wicca in the Northwest. I did my year-and-a-day with Leon.

"Otter was sort of a gumball-spewing shaman, descended from Southern Baptist preachers and trained by Thundercloud, a Lakota in Leon's coven. The epidemic, the talk of New York and the obsession of San Francisco, was still a glimmer on the horizon in the Northwest.

"Then Otter's lover died of it. A year later he went to the desert to commune with its spirit, and when they brought him back to town, he couldn't breathe. He had dreamed, out there, of a white lady—I knew exactly who *that* was, but somehow his hosts missed it. He lasted two weeks in Harborview—the ones the Goddess loves, she takes quick. (*And* in October, so they don't have to hang around long before Samhain.)

"Everyone was frantic while he was in that damned ward: rituals, vigils, the huge local pagan community galvanized. One day I ran into Mary, Leon's Maiden (later his Priestess), when she'd been sitting by Otter's bedside, and she suddenly collapsed on me sobbing. She worked in an herbal store. 'I'm supposed to be a healer, and these men come to me, and I can't do anything for them! I'm a Witch, I'm supposed to be able to *heal*.'

"They really thought they could beat AIDS, by sending energy; it was a major theological crisis when they couldn't. Not that allopathic medicine was helping much either, at that point. Scientists were as frantic as we were.

"We gave Otter a masquerade funeral. You never saw anything like it; bad taste was *de rigueur*. Junk food was served. I was very sedate in full leather. Tim came in gold lamé, and he's dead. Stefan came as Morticia Addams (tiny steps in a black hobble skirt), and he's dead. Leon's Allan wore a leopard-skin bustier and falsies with alligator clips on the nipples; Purple Mark wore *white*, powdering his long hair and face. And Thundercloud led a Lakota mourning chant, wordless keening, high and lonesome, and suddenly it hurt us and we all let go—everything we were holding back, in our white-folks way, came barreling out of us. It was the moral equivalent of grand opera. TC was a wreck for months, but that's what a shaman does—heals the tribe, not necessarily himself.

"As for the virus—the Witches were numb for a while, under the repeated blows, but life goes on. I started to make mandala talismans for friends who were positive; they meditate on them to zap the virus, which is part of the drawn pattern. Haven't lost a patient yet. Wish I'd done one for Charles Ludlam.

"It's all natural cycle, though, right—Nature, red in helper cell and pseudopodium? Aren't viruses also children of the Goddess? Not that that makes *them* immune to anything. But as Black Lotus put it, 'I am the Mother of All Things, and All Things should wear a sweater.' Goes for condoms, too."

—◦—

Commentary—response to a letter:

Leaving intravenous drug users aside, the overwhelming percentage of the male sufferers of AIDS are routine practitioners of what is commonly known as passive-position anal intercourse, or what the Greeks, who always, only and forever envisaged such practitioners as adolescent boys, called catamites, after Ganymede, the boy beloved of God the Father, Zeus—or in plain talk, those of us who take it up the arse. And the establishment noise is we are compulsively so, and that as a consequence—of that and of the compulsive use of toxic substances ranging from amyl nitrate to horse tranquilizers and back, and added to same the disquieting gossip that we are what the Yiddish language calls *oyshgetrett* (fucked out)—we can't even have this anal sex anymore without first getting stoked up and then chilling out by, for example, putting on headphones, getting ourselves slung into leather or stainless steel chain-link hammocks installed in filthy basements near the North River waterfront—see above: no more smooching on the porch swing under the June moon, you candidate for this depraved life, so forget lyrics like

> 'I just adore the boy next door
> I love him more that I can say'

and the Judy who sang them to you.

Plus which, smart Tops did not get AIDS maybe for the same reason smart fuckers didn't get syphilis for centuries. It's an age-old piece of wisdom, dispensed by Italian neighborhood doctors that after you fuck anything—man, woman, sheep or decapitated chicken—you first piss right away, clearing the channel, and piss into a glass which you then dunk your cock into. The end.

Urine is the best antiseptic there is—a fact known to peasant women for centuries, who bathe their children in it before rinsing them off in streams. (P. S. The right pocket yellow handkerchief might have had some salubrious effects after all, although even then being what's known as an all-out Undinist didn't cut it in the purification line—only the dunking the dong in the cup of your own piss.)

Easy enough if you believe the working HIV hypothesis. Well, I call this the Manichaean approach, and in Puritan America it is a shoo-in. The Devil Virus. But for those who believe that no retrovirus can by itself do all that with which it is credited, there is another, more lurid and complex scenario—right out of Plato and St. Augustine by way of Dante and the Marquis de Sade. It is even less pretty, but before I get to it, let me go back to my dream, because a lot of the time I know—from the letters—you'd rather be listening to dream songs than to reports of waking nightmares.

And I know why. The stuff that dreams are made on is more us. Also, my dreams will be different from your own—congruent in assertion, perhaps, but different in cut and line—whereas the reports of waking nightmare are all the same.

And yet there is still no falsifying evidence to contradict the central dogma of molecular biology: that information can pass from nucleic acid to nucleic acid, and from nucleic acid to protein, but not from protein to nucleic acid.

Take that onstage, darling, the next time somebody casts you as Lucky in *Waiting for Godot*. Meanwhile, be careful of what you write down and sign, lest, moving from nuclear biology back to high school chemistry, where we belong, it all blows up in your face.

And in conclusion, the first four questions, Who am I? Where do I come from? What do I want? Where am I going? have been answered. The time has come for the second four, Who is alive? Who is suffering? Who understands? Who investigates? Speak up.

NICE BOYS AND NEEDLES

Published in the *New York Native*,
Issue 74, October 10–23, 1983.

by Michael Shernoff, M.S.W.

Even "nice boys" do it—use needles to take their drugs, that is. It has become increasingly apparent to substance-abuse professionals that I.V. (or intravenous) drug use in the gay community is far more prevalent than has been generally appreciated. Indeed, needles—or "points," as some know them, are seldom discussed at all, at least among the uninitiated. While it is hard to get a clear picture of the extent to which needles and drug use are connected in the gay community, certain instances come to mind.

- The infamous San Francisco baths, The Hothouse, which recently closed, used to have signs posted at the door indicating various forms of prohibited behavior: hustling, the selling of drugs, the playing of radios and shooting up. Local color, thought the naïve New York tourist.

- Another popular San Francisco sex club has a regular assignment for its morning shift to sweep up the sidewalks outside the club's windows. It seems discarded hypodermic needles have been seen there too often.

- A friend described an experience at New York's Everard Baths. Before getting down to business with someone he had just met, the fellow asked if my friend minded if he "got off first." Not one to stop the party, my friend did not object, thinking that his momentary fuck buddy wanted to be the first to cum. Whereupon he was given a dextrous demonstration of the method one uses to tie off an arm with a belt and shoot up without assistance. More local color.

- On the Saint's closing night last spring, I recognized a fellow traveler on the Pine/Saint circuit. He was at the sink in one of the men's rooms with a syringe in his arm. As I stared, he nonchalantly moved to one of the nearby stalls, needle still in his arm. "He isn't diabetic," I thought.

- A friend who is a flight attendant for one of the major airlines recounted the following. He was working in first class on an overnight flight to Europe when one of the passengers, a man he casually knew from both Fire Island and around Manhattan clubs, emerged from the lavatory in a business suit, jacket over his shoulder. There was a syringe stuck in his arm as he stumbled back to his seat in a drug-induced stupor.

- The toilet stall doors at San Francisco's Trocadero dance palace were removed more than three years ago, not for fear of sexual goings on, according to the owner, but to stop patrons from shooting up and nodding out behind the latched doors.
- Discarded syringes are commonly seen on the floor of the bathroom next to the rear bar, downstairs at the Mineshaft.
- A few months ago, while on a date with a regular pal who is a well-respected physical therapist at a major New York medical center, I was offered cocaine. He also asked if I'd prefer to shoot it, since he "just happened to have a syringe in the house." I demurred.
- A middle-class white gay client of mine with Kaposi's sarcoma admitted only after several sessions that he had shot drugs repeatedly, and had shared syringes with friends over a two-year period preceding his AIDS diagnosis. But he had certainly made no such admission to the CDC investigator to whom he had denied any history of I.V. drug use.
- A close friend of mine, who is far from naïve about drugs, told me that during a week-long vacation at the Pines earlier this summer he was hanging around an acquaintenance's pool with a group of men when the host offered cocaine. Shortly, he emerged from the house with a tray, on which was a large vial of cocaine, snorters and a syringe. Several of the men used the same syringe to inject themselves with the cocaine.

Closet within a Closet

A reluctance to talk about, much less admit, using needles to take drugs is understandable, given the attached stigma. But this reticence makes the problem all the more difficult to recognize or confront. While it may be generally accepted that drugs, including alcohol, are part of the urban gay "lifestyle," it would come as a surprise to most that needle use has also become part of the picture—for more people than is commonly realized. In this sense, shooting up is a kind of closet within a closet for many gay people; it is a topic not easily broached, except with those who share the same fascination. Only people who shoot up seem to know who their compatriots are.

In Praise of Larry Kramer:
A Testamentary Statement
to the *Queer Street* Author
by Robert Weil

It will be hard for any who were not young adults in the 1980s to fully appreciate the catalyzing effect Larry Kramer had on the gay community. Indeed, I cannot think of a single voice more effective in warning of the plague that soon would be visited upon us like "a holocaust on an entire world."

Who among us who were sentient in those terrifying years cannot still visualize the black-and-pink "Silence = Death" buttons first worn by the activists? But the slogan popularized by Act Up and other groups was far more than mere Krameresque rhetoric, and the deadening silence of the press, not only about the looming AIDS crisis but about queer culture in general, reflected a staggering cultural prejudice that had existed as long as late-nineteenth- and twentieth-century gay life had flourished. Larry Kramer's almost eschatological vision and his aggressive, "in-your-face" political advocacy came then to define the activism that defied this prejudice.

It's stunning just how far the gay movement has progressed in a little over twenty years. Those of us who are old enough can recall with clarity that the *New York Times*, in fact, refused for many years even to use the word "gay," preferring the more genteel word "homosexual"; this semantic choice was the pallid indicator of the paper's far from bland decision to avoid not only polite but virtually every overt mention of the AIDS crisis in the early years when the virus was spreading unchecked in bathhouses and back rooms across the country—spreading as if by fire from Village rooftop to rooftop. At a time when hundreds of thousands of people, the overwhelming majority of them gay men, were being infected, the *Times* and almost all other leading papers simply failed to cover the crisis.

As a twenty-five-year-old in the late winter and spring of 1981, just months after medical authorities and doctors realized that an epidemic was at hand, I first became aware of the virulent nature of this contagion that

had yet to acquire a name. An avid reader of the *New York Times*, I diɑ
see one, perhaps two minor mentions of GRID or a virulent "gay cancer,"
but the disease simply did not exist in the mainstream press, and it was the
New York Native, begun one year earlier, in 1980, by Chuck Ortleb, that
provided an extraordinary, and still largely unrecognized service, in warning gay men that a plague was already full blown. As a result of these
prophetic tocsins issued by the *Native*, I was one of the lucky ones who
quickly chose celibacy during those years, since no one was quite sure what
specific sexual act caused infection. I still don't know what impelled me to
act so early, but it was the articles in the *Native*, which I eagerly read every
two weeks, which provided graphic warnings and horrific medical reports
that could not be found in the leading science magazines of the day.

Similar articles appeared in other gay newspapers and sympathetic publications over the next two years, while the general and scientific press
remained at a polite remove, although some articles, far more dire, began
to surface suggesting that a round-up or quarantining of infected man could
be in the offing. As the epidemic began to infect and gradually decimate a
population, gay leaders were extraordinarily responsive during this har-
rowing period (GMHC was founded by Kramer and five other early leaders—Nathan Fain, Larry Mass, Paul Popham, Paul Rapoport and
Edmund White—in Kramer's Village apartment in January of 1982).
Yet, as cachetic wraiths soon came to supplant the body-builders on
Christopher and Greenwich Streets, the *Times* remained eerily silent.

Undoubtedly, the most consequential journalistic story of these terrifying years was Kramer's seminal piece, "1,112 and Counting," which
appeared in the *New York Native* on March 14, 1983. I still remember
buying the paper at the corner of 23rd Street and Third Avenue, quite
aware on what night of the week the delivery truck would bring the latest
edition. There, emblazoned on the cover, was Kramer's latest jeremiad,
as fiery and passionate as anything I had ever read about the contagion. I
actually devoured the piece on the sidewalk across from my apartment, and
literally felt a chill, so powerful were Kramer's words. I called all the
friends I knew who might be affected and begged them, taking Kramer's
advice, to stay out of the bathhouses, where many still chose to spend their
weekend evenings, and I later xeroxed the piece and sent it to friends on
the West Coast. My personal background made me recall the rank apathy,
the neglect, of the larger German public when Hitler took power and the
Nazis began persecuting the Jews, and this was a comparison that would

become the basis of Kramer's *Reports from the Holocaust*, published a decade later.

In recalling the full impact of Kramer's words, I do think the article was a turning point that forced the community itself to take *some* responsibility for its actions and actually contemplate, if not finally begin to use, condoms, in spite of the many who felt that prophylactics conferred an unacceptable sentence they could not possibly countenance.

Historians often struggle to define an exact turning point when a curtain comes to a close, but for me it was the Kramer piece that marked the end of an era, for previously a majority of gay men still seemed, or were clearly unwilling, to part with a multiplicity of mating rituals—be they on the rotting piers, in twenty-four-hour bathhouses, in the mythic tea rooms or in the endless variety of bars—that had in many ways come to represent the centrality of queer culture. Kramer's piece, unbelievably alarmist (no one could accuse him of understatement), thus stated, in no unequivocal terms, that the jig was now up. The piece was then as much a premonition as a dirge for a lifestyle that could no longer be maintained. And by the end of 1983, although there were nearly 5,000 reported AIDS cases in the United States and over 2,100 deaths, the tide seemed finally to turn, both in the gay community and in general public consciousness. There appeared finally an awareness of not only the grave medical situation but also the struggles that lay ahead in reconstructing a once vibrant culture that was crumbling as rapidly as the wood planks on the piers of the Hudson.

◄○►

Old Queer Fuck on the Park Bench:

"I hate to be a pill, to piss on smoldering embers, no matter how warming, but the facts are these: it was neither Larry Kramer's hysterics, the courageous reporting of the *New York Native*, Everett Koop's blinding-hot moral flash or anything else that turned the tide of AIDS recognition in America and of AIDS research funding by the American government. It was nothing less or other than Ronald Reagan's sentimental—goddamnit—feelings for a fellow guy he just happened to like a whole hell of a lot from their Hollywood days, a guy called Rock Hudson who came down with the goddamn thing. And if you don't think them's the facts, go look them up. As our story winds down to a close, darlings, in the year 1985, rather than cut AIDS funding by ten million. Ronald Reagan—or more probably Nancy, as Ronnie was already, courtesy of Alzheimer's, more and more lunching out, though not in public—was upped to one hundred million, and, get this right please, a 270 percent increase in AIDS reporting. You see, darlings, all that heaven allows written on the wind by tarnished angels is an imitation of life."

—◄o►—

"All Lil's boyfriends are Judases, betraying her with kisses for cash."

CHAPTER TWENTY-FOUR

Two Almost Tragic Characters

BLUES FOR MISS DEAN

Dorothy, formerly Black Barbarella and The Spade of Queens, not to mention the erstwhile bouncer at Max's Kansas City, having loathed the sixties, then and again, found herself no great fan of the seventies either, and, since the fifties had so receded in the memory of the tumultuous NOW eighties (despite the fact that the two decades were being strangely aligned by commentators, much as had the fifties and the twenties) as one by one and then some by some, then by the score, then like ninepins in an endless bowling marathon, the denizens of that NOW time now perished in agony, found herself more and more retreating, funeral attendance apart, from the rigors of public life.

Following the death of her Maine coon cat, Normal, she declined into a perilous state in her apartment on Morton Street, amid stacks and stacks of old copies of the *New York Times*. Dug out at the direction and under the supervision of the now markedly successful (in New York and Los Angeles) Michael Maslansky, and installed in the Hotel Empire on Broadway at Lincoln Center, she was supported for a time by a subscription taken up among loyal friends, eventually leaving New York, removing to Boulder, Colorado, where she found gainful employment in a book store and began to improve, it was reported, steadily, laying off the sauce and returning to Bible study (for she had been a minister's daughter).

Briefly returning to New York for the funeral at St. Marks in the Bowery of her beloved friend J.J. Mitchell, Dorothy encountered QT, with whom, following her own counsel, she had not been speaking for some time, and Tom Carey, with whom she had been corresponding. When QT, ignoring interdict, enquired after her well-being, she looked warily at them both and admitted to a terror of dying of AIDS. Afterwards, Tom Carey was bewildered until QT explained that Dorothy's self-description had always been this:

"My tragedy is I have th-the soul of a white h-homosexual t-trapped inside the b-body of a black heterosexual w-woman."

The idea that Dorothy could be anything else but immune was not an easy one to consider. People had been terrified of her, in a Typhoid Mary kind of way: she'd seemed always to be unscathed, even if, when you asked her how she was feeling, she'd invariably shake her head and declare, "Poorly."

Dorothy on her role as bouncer at Max's Kansas City:

"Th-th-they also serve who m-merely guard the *portal*."

—◄o►—

Two from the Funeral Chorus:

"Miss Dean was a Bojangles to the moneyed white radical chic."

"The Spade of Queens was a white Aunt Jemima cookie jar for the gay self-styled."

—◄o►—

A typical early seventies exchange between Dorothy and QT:

"I-I hate thuh dance—don't you?"

"No, Dorothy. Whenever I'm not at the Met, I'm at the State Theater."

"Huh. Well all that was invented by Lincoln Kirstein for high-toned fairies, and he is a genius, whether or not his Mr. Balanchine is. Anyway toe dancing, the bal-lay, isn't what I mean. I mean that awful spectacle of people stomping around the stage with no shoes on. It ain't fittin'!"

"Without shoes, Dorothy, fittin' is hardly an issue, now is it?"

"Huh. You're so g-goddamn smart. All you f-fairies are; it's impossible to have a s-s-serious c-conversation about Culture with any of you!"

"Well, Dorothy, I love Martha Graham—and took a year of dance with Pearl Lang at Yale."

"W-well, you're a fool, but I knew that the minute I first looked at you, even b-before you opened your mouth."

That Dorothy.

A Classic Dorothy story:

Dorothy, invited to a dinner party, was seated alongside the conductor husband of a famous diva. At the point at which on such social occasions gentlemen used to retire to the library for brandy and cigars, Dorothy's head was seen to dip suddenly (the sign: when that head bobbed back up, as it always did, well, get ready) and almost as suddenly rise again. (Certain parties among the knowledgeable were waiting for it to actually swivel.) Turning to her right, addressing her first words to the maestro that evening, Dorothy declared, "Th-there's something I've been m-meaning to ask you: W-where's your *meal ticket* tonight?"

Hastily bustled away by an appalled hostess, while apologies were proffered by all, poor Dorothy was tossed into the bedroom and told to stay there until everybody else had left. Some time later, the hostess, readying herself for bed, kindly decided that as Dorothy took up very little room, she might as well leave her where she was, over on the far edge of the bed. Removing the sleeper's glasses and putting them on the night table, the hostess herself turned in and, having been assured by the self-possessed and urbane maestro that no real wound had been sustained, and that indeed her dinner party had not been ruined, slept . . . until awakened by a stabbing pain in the left shoulder. Dorothy, sitting bolt upright in the light of the bed lamp, desperately reaching with one hand for her glasses, was jabbing the woman mercilessly with two fingers of the other and hissing, "Who are you? Who *are* you?" "Dorothy, Dorothy, please, it's————!" "Oh." Putting the glasses on, peering at her bedmate for a second, then whipping the glasses off again and turning back to lie down: "W-w-ell, it's four o'clock in the morning; I would think you would have the d-decency to *g-go home!*"

Dorothy did finally succumb to immune deficiency, in the form of lung cancer, and died in Boulder. In a scenario QT has in mind, she goes straight to heaven, concerning which turn of events she is at first skeptical. Even more nonplussed is she by the fact that instead of being called upon to render any kind of account of her life, she finds the recording angel has left a set of blues and a copy of Kant's *Critique of Pure Reason* because (a) he can't face being cross-examined by the former Max's Kansas City bouncer, *New Yorker* fact checker ("Blues for Miss Dean!") and notorious public scold, and (b) knows Dorothy is so honest that if she didn't think she ought to get into heaven she would eighty-six herself—or maybe not even want to get in in the first place.

Q and A

"By what Velcro, darling, do Dorothy Dean and Bruce Ritter adhere?"

"Well, small dark as over and against tall blonde."

"A goof for Dorothy—but a priest, and a fairy too?"

"It could be, shall we say, brought off, under the rubric of the Bible. Dorothy's angle—she seems to have gone back to it with a vengeance— Bible study, and the beauteous, manly Bruce—Father Noble—well, his is self-referential, rather like one's own in one's Jacob–Good Thief period. Of course our Bruce would go all out for the big role, the Redeemer.

BRUCE RITTER, O.F.M.

For QT, the most gripping thing about the Bruce Ritter scandal was the fact he was a Franciscan; they just didn't go in for that kind of thing (boy molesting), and as it played out, the affair had all the hallmarks of an almost Jansenist self-flagellation. "That kind of thing" was the province of the Jesuits, absolutely. QT remembers being courted by a Jesuit for the seminary, and by somebody from Dunwoodie (in Yonkers). Later, Prudence read him, saying he undoubtedly pictures himself as Manon Lescaut at St.-Sulpice, singing "N'est-ce plus ma main?" to some Gérard Philipe type.

Author seriously attempts to describe, from the point of view of the seductive youth, the acutely homosexual atmosphere of the clerical milieu (comparing it to football teams and to the seminary, neither of which he has any experience of, but he is trying . . .).

Children are sexual, are seductive, and the problem is the guilt culture, which turns sex into violence—nearly always around alcohol or some relaxing drug, particularly marijuana. But nobody ever makes any boy gay, not in a seminary certainly. If it happens that environment is what makes somebody homosexual—and this is very doubtful—then the job is done by the parents in the first two to four years of life, the end.

THE REDEEMER

SCENE: Lights up on the mural of the Urban Crucifixion.

FATHER NOBLE

The thing you'll throw in my face right off the bat is the crucifixion mural. I know that.

All right, all right, a little over the top
What with yours truly as JC, but listen
Caravaggio painted himself into
"The Taking of the Christ in Gethsemane"
As Judas Iscariot, didn't he? No?
And anyway there's no such picture? I could
Have sworn—anyway the principle's the same:
A contemporary depiction of sin,
The greatest of all, collective betrayal
Of the redemptive figure, no matter who.
I could be anybody, that's a tenet
Of the Fransciscan belief. I could be you,
You could be me, and we could both turn into
Christ Crucified; in fact it's our ambition.

I don't know why they're after me. What for—some Polaroids of kids
in their underwear?

Are they coming after that cute lying mick—what was his name? Jog-
ging up in Central Park cruised by various and sundry—he was cute; he'd
stop and smile and tell them, "Sorry, I'm booked."

By Jesus, get it? Made a good story back home on the old sod—hah,
hah—where a government fell over the story of the shielding by a high court
judge of a priest like him and me.

Lynch. No, darling, they're not lynching Lynch; they're lynching yours
truly. A spoiled priest. Spoiled—like a can of tomatoes!

The word defalcation. The *Post* reporter said "we are running a story
about a defalcation." Primary definition "embezzlement."

Wasn't there an heroic priest tale called *Embezzled Heaven*?

Secondary meaning: "failure to meet an expectation or promise."

Defalcation/defecation: as in the lumps of shit left on the toilet floors
when the stalls were first closed in the subway tea room purge. Finally the
tea rooms themselves were padlocked.

Maybe you think priests never went into tea rooms, never made the stations? Would you like to know how many times in a week they'd run into
one another, or how often the stalls doubled as confessionals?

We met—not the little blond trick—but my own perpetrator, as we're
all now called—we met at Julius's down in the Village, a joint where the
bar was stacked with pictures of boxers. An athletic-manly rendezvous. He

was manly . . . manly but warm—you know the type; sermons were usually bland and sometimes incoherent, but never assaultive. Not like some of the notorious Jesuits up at St. Ignatius Loyola on Park Avenue who stirred up souls like fucking Fulton Sheen.

He got me drunk and took me home in a taxi. I didn't see where we were going, but it sure as hell wasn't Park Avenue. In fact, next morning, when I was shown the door and given directions to the D train, I realized we were in the Bronx.

Anyway, when we got there, it smelled—the wax candles, the furniture polish. I checked out the lace curtains as we were going in, but I thought . . .

Then when it was over, he took me into the sacristy, and together we said the Act of Contrition, and he told me to go straight to confession. And here I am.

Well, not straight—I took another detour. Don't go ape-shit, please, like the priest on that detour did in the box. The fucker refused me absolution. So the next week, after checking Julius's, I went back up to the Bronx on the D train and got it good from—who else—the perpetrator. Never felt so clean, so pure, so satisfied in all my life. (laughs)

And if you don't think that's funny, you better not take instruction in the one, true, holy and apostolic faith.

Then I got to the campus on the hill in Riverdale—and right about that same time the word had gone out in Julius's and in the wrinkle rooms that there were a pair of bars right under the el—you rode the West Side IRT up to the end of the line—where the pickings were good on warm spring nights, particularly at the one on Broadway, right under the train station, where on the jukebox, along with Joan Baez and Peter, Paul and Mary, you could find Miles Davis, John Coltrane, Lord Buckley and Moms Mabley.

> A Catholic college campus is a hot place,
> The most practical perfect combination (no, not combustion).
> Of church and laity, high brow and rabble
> In existence. In it one is comfortably . . .
> Whatever.

You could go in, pose as an alumnus or some business type "recruiting"—making vague references to the television industry: sportscasting was particularly effective—get a little drunk with the boys, standing them to shots with their beers and making sure they got into—as you did not, or else what would the point be, right?—that state from which, emerging the next morning, they could sincerely tell of not remembering a thing that had happened, then getting them over, still standing up, into Van Cortlandt Park for fun and games in the bushes and benches around the deserted mansion. Very simple fun and games, of course—these were in the main very simple, although by no means simple-minded, Irish Catholic boys working their way through college, and if they suddenly came to with an unfamiliar object, especially one intimately connected to the nice guy who'd been talking to them like a serious adult earlier in the evening, stuck up their asshole . . . there would be substantial trouble.

That other thing, however, the genuflection to receive the species, would usually, in any event, come off, especially if the first thing they noticed, should they come out of the blackout before climax, after the bobbing head and the feeling of wet receptive warmth down there in the general area— and if anybody has to tell you about teeth, you need more practice before trying any of this—was the sight of a twenty stuck in the left shirt pocket next to the clip-on ballpoint pen, sheltering the pulsing heart.

And on a Friday night, if the heavy petting and the genuflecting to receive the species went well, one could often get them home overnight. There's a very busy taxi stand right there where the stairs come down from the station overhead, at which the traffic late on a Friday night, in what would appear to be a sleepy neighborhood on the edge of Yonkers, looks more like the corner of Eighth Avenue and 50th Street when the fights at the old Madison Square Garden let out.

Then there was the *rehabilitation* at the hands of a *therapist*—a priest, of course, so the hands were beautiful; beautifully manicured: such pretty half moons. This bozo tried to tell me, a Franciscan, for Chrissakes, that what had happened to me was a new version of the devil getting into God's holiest. Talk about *paranoia*.

> They claimed we'd had the whip hand; that was a laugh.
> The boys had the whip hand always—whip it out
> And wave it in your face right in the classroom.
> Work it up and down with a hot fist—not quite
> The beautiful hands of a priest. Oh you must
> Remember that one; they'd hang it on the wall,
> The priests' mothers would. Mine did. All in fine script
> Surrounded by white lilies for purity.

Whip it out and point it at you, as Finn said,
Like something to hang your hat on, and dripping
Like Pinocchio's nose, if Pinocchio
Was already a real boy. I saw myself in him.
What queer doesn't see himself in some younger,
Weaker thing? Oh, to linger silent among
A noise of boys! In the dead end it came back
To haunt me, The Beautiful Hands of a Priest,
When they slipped on the cuffs. "We've nailed the bastard."
I don't have to tell you what that called to mind.
Pinocchio's nose. I remember reading
One of those books about boys' schools in England,
Except that this one was in Edinburgh.
Seems one of the more progressive headmasters,
When told of mutual masturbation cells
In the dormitories, came out with, "My dear
Fellow, it is no more than blowing your nose!"

I started having fantasies about the therapist, right there in his office in
the rectory. Saw him as a priest as defrocked Satanist, trying to get him into
the classic psychoanalytical position, the reverse of the face-to-face Annunciation, in which the Virgin becomes impregnated through the ear. He
wants to get me into the position to be buggered through the ear. Suppose
the reverend was an adept at piercing and pain and cigar burns and
coprophagy?

About my little blond? Ganymede he called himself, my Ganymede.
It's a mistake to put them through college, it really is, and give them classical reference. My Judas Iscariot is more like it, and never mind thirty pieces
of anything; this kid was ambitious. I should have poisoned the little shit
and left him in the Meadowlands. Strychnine is the way to go; it makes
them arch their back and die in writhing agony.

That would be something to watch, a boy like him
Whipping it out, arching his back, and dying
In writhing agony. That'd get me off
In record time, and time is of the essence
So they say. The essence of *what* I wonder.
Looks like I may have some time to find out.

Have you ever heard the story of St. Paul
And Eutyches? You can find it in The Acts
Of the Apostles. Of all the acts put on
By that crowd, St. Luke seems to have liked Paul's best.

"A man who has been told that everything is a symptom need never accuse or judge himself or ask to be judged." Fulton J. Sheen.

"Judge not, lest you be judged." Jesus H. Christ.
Augustine on children and sex. Their members
Are innocent, but not their wills. Innocent
Members. Sounds like NAMBLA blah-blah, doesn't it.
Shall we talk about the Menendez brothers?
Now there you have two clever little killers,
And the eternal—all-male—love triangle.
Oh, yes, that's what it was, a love triangle
Played out in the Cuban style. Sound eerily
Familiar? Well, it ought to. The Trinity.
The Father, the Beloved Son, the Voyeur.
And the woman—the mother—blown away . . . why?

For good measure? Just for being there eating ice cream in the same family room with Father? Known to the world as Kitty—but her real name was, of course, Mary. Well, Mary Louise.

And at the end of it all, what? Suffering. Looking good on wood. Well, it was a time, was it not, of unprecedented suffering in the queer world, and the best that could be said of any of us is that when we came through it, we were changed but not obliterated, and what we always were remained visible through what we had become.

Or else we croaked.

PART SEVEN

Moon over the City
Los Angeles

Lost Angeles
(Inside Story)

Storyboards

V isiting Los Angeles time and again, arriving by bus, by air, on the Super Chief to Union Station, and once, in tribute to another, finer vanished way of life, descending at Pasadena to be driven through the pass and along Mulholland Drive to Doheny, the border separating West Hollywood from Beverly Hills. Then down Doheny to Sunset and east to 1416 North Havenhurst to the Colonial House, just a few paces down the hill from the site of Nazimova's '20s seraglio, the Garden of Allah.

Purpose: to take it all in, to get it all down—the mystery, the mutability, the enveloping allure of this force field antipodal to New York, and always re-enforcing the idea of it as the birthplace of that reactive and ultimately benighted twentieth-century homosexual hypothesis, Gay Liberation.

New York vis-à-vis Los Angeles. Principal industries:

New York (as in textbooks of the 1940s and '50s)—clothing manufacture and book publishing.

Los Angeles—aviation and motion pictures.

CASINO/DIAMONDS

From a Hollywood diary:

Brooks Riley, then an editor at *Film Comment*, set up lunch and after-

459

math with the great Michael Powell [MP], then doing a sort of Zen roshi turn at Zoetrope, Francis Ford Coppola's glamorous, state-of-the-art and somewhat pastiche operation run out of the historic M-G-M studios on Formosa, in the geographical center of old Hollywood.

MP an apparition, yes, but of what?

A gay gramps, surely, in this instance and for a season in Golden Years residence among his artistic progeny, to a man queer-accepting, or, as the Mott Street Italians back in New York would have it, *umbothered*.

An, in every way, less magniloquent, less orotund, but concomitantly gifted Orson Welles, in the guise of a British edition of a great European theater-music-moompix *monstre sacré* on the level of Renoir, Visconti and, yes, Eisenstein, fresh out of Wardrobe and Hair and stamped with no sell-by date whatsoever; on offer as something like an altogether stable, authentic, needless to remark, accomplished and voluble Quentin Crisp. (A case of getting it all backward, really, like referring to Joan Bennett as the false Hedy Lamarr or saying that Tuesday Weld reminds you of Faye Dunaway or Dunaway reminds you of Sharon Stone, but the image is nonetheless restorative and somehow emblematic of the increasingly vaudevillian politics of queer New York vis-à-vis the more realistic talking-money, ballot-box queer politics of first San Francisco and then, more durably, Los Angeles, bringing it all back in the early '80s to where it all started in the late '40s.

Gorgeous pastel print shirt, hibiscus in hair (very Dorothy Lamour), all poised for the hearing confession of a film rhapsode (certified by Brooks Riley for work done at *Film Comment*).

"You look pretty absolutely gorgeous."

"Thank you; I feel a bit like Bea Lillie about to rip into 'Lily of Laguna.'"

Thus made to feel luxuriously at ease, rhapsode launches into strophic ode, detailing the effect on the childhood psyche of seeing *Black Narcissus* screened at the Polk.

(Note: The parish had warned pointedly against parents allowing children to see the picture, which had been rated Objectionable-in-Part by the Legion of Decency. Thus, although it would never be, like Buñuel's *The Young and the Damned* (*Los Olvidados*) or Henry Cornelius's *I Am a Camera*, constitutive of what we called a Mortal Sin Double Feature, it was on its own to be shunned. Yes, there were nuns in it, and yes, purity wins in a beautiful Himalayan setting—famously represented by the Pennines enhanced by the knockout matte work of Alfred Junge. However, like Miss

Prism's verdict on the fall of the rupee, this subcontinental melodrama was reckoned somewhat too sensational. Unbothered, QT walked in bold as brass at four o'clock on a Tuesday afternoon, occasioning neither remonstrance nor a blind bit of notice from the impassive matron busy behind glass at her manicure.)

MP sympathetic to the overstimulating effect of a parochial-school neurotic homosexual boy torn between, on the one hand, strenuous bicycle riding and rough body-contact sport, and, on the other, to roller skating over long distances, through the streets of adjacent neighborhoods—significant among them the burgeoning Indian and Pakistani communities of "Tudor" Jackson Heights about a mile away, around the Jackson and the Colony movie theaters, domiciled there while serving their respective delegations at the then newly created United Nations a half-hour away—through strange streets and into strange schoolyards, strange playgrounds and strange back alleys, and nearer to home given (QT) to aggressive skating and the promotion of rough-and-tumble, limb-body-contact re-creations of the then wildly popular Roller Derby contests.

A boy already somewhat cosseted by the ministrations of the Grey Nuns of the Sacred Heart (originally *Les Soeurs de la Charité de Couvent de Montréal*). Their admirable dedication to and expertise at instruction in English grammar, mathematics, voice and indeed the rudiments of Western music theory did not automatically translate into a taste for such elements of the prescribed reading curriculum as James Russell Lowell's "The First Snowfall," Henry Wadsworth Longfellow's "Hiawatha" and "A Hymn to Life," Edgar Allan Poe's "The Bells" and Edna St. Vincent Millay's "The Ballad of the Harp Weaver." He preferred Poe's Tales, Longfellow's "Evangeline" and Millay's "Renascence" and her sonnets, and listening to his mother relate, for all the world as if she'd been there with them, "Vincent's" party nights in Greenwich Village with Maxwell Bodenheim (*Naked on Roller Skates*) and Eugene O'Neill—whose *Mourning Becomes Electra* with Nazimova had been, next to Jeanne Eagels in *Rain* and Mae West in *Diamond Lil*, her greatest youthful thrill in the New York theater.

Neither did the strict tuition in the elaborate niceties of English grammar—sentence diagramming growing ever more complicated from fourth grade through eighth, not to mention in the current work—quite seem to match his deep-end immersion in early-'50s film noir dialogue. Meanwhile, over in the music department, neither the stern formalities of Mozart,

Beethoven and Schubert, the intoxicating chromaticism of Wagner, nor the more astringent lyrical beauty of Debussy's "Clair de Lune" and Tchaikovsky's *Nutcracker Suite* adequately prepped him for that Saturday matinee performance at the Metropolitan Opera of Richard Strauss's *Salome*, sung by Ljuba Welitsch.

As to the nuns, if they ever smelled of anything other than Kirkman's soap, they did so of the very lightest suspicion of Friendship's Garden, or as was sometimes darkly whispered by parochial trouble makers, 4711 but never of anything so redolent of mystery as Black Narcissus.

Also QT confessed to the startling histrionic conflict between the Himalayan Anglican nuns of *Black Narcissus* and such homegrown screen representations of Catholic nuns in action as Ingrid Bergman in *The Bells of St. Mary's* and the double dose of Loretta Young and Celeste Holm in *Come to the Stable* (Henry Koster, 1949), a thing the author had wanted to do for some time in a somewhat different context.

MP most understanding, sympathetic and entirely willing to grant retrospective absolution, especially after hearing the story of the notorious "curse boxes" routinely installed following Young's winning of the Oscar for her so-wholesome performance in *The Farmer's Daughter* (1948), into which offenders in the profanity sweepstakes were required to deposit an offering for "the missions." Joseph L. Mankiewicz, assigned to a subsequent Loretta Young picture, is reputed to have walked up to the star and said, "Now before we begin work, Miss Young, there is just one thing I need to know: how much is it going to cost me to tell you to go fuck yourself?"

A decade later, QT next admitted, despite imagining himself quite the sophisticated high-school senior, college material, inured to seizures of primitive emotions, when the nun came out of the shadows at the end of *Vertigo*, he about lost it—he didn't know for a split second what was hitting him, and the take wasn't much longer than that, but in it a whole history came back, flooding his brain. Given the similarity of the high tower and the bells and the terror, he then remembered *Black Narcissus*. He couldn't help wondering if Hitchcock had not worked the whole picture back from that point? It certainly looked like an *hommage*.

Powell replied, "I can't imagine he was remotely aware of any resemblance, or would have seen anything whatever in it. Your reaction of course is interesting, and gratifyingly so to those of us who believe in the storing and study of moving images and cinematic moments along the same lines as the research and study of painterly effects and the paths of literary and musical influences since the Renaissance, but I'm afraid in this instance it was surely entirely personal."

"Also theological and psychological; movies are a religion, are they not?"

"Oh, certainly, or else I would hardly be here in Hollywood, sitting in the vicinity of all this sunshine with a hibiscus stuck behind my ear, now would I?"

Yet another noteworthy historical Hollywood detail, in and of the moment.

MP had not yet been taken by the proprietors of Zoetrope, putative purveyors of look/see high art, already too accustomed for QT's taste to the glassed-in limousines through which they saw the dayworld of Los Angeles but darkly, to view the amazing folk-art Hollywood-stars mural on Cahuenga, just south of Hollywood Boulevard, in which Bette Davis and James Dean are pictured side by side. (Alas—destroyed in the Northridge earthquake of 1991; a Polaroid of the work taken at the time of the MP interview remains on Author's New York living room wall.)

"Extraordinary—are you sure?"

"Yes, and I think I get the rationale. Jimmy is painted in his red jacket from *Rebel Without a Cause* and Bette in the jodhpurs from *Another Man's Poison*.

"Oh, yes, Emlyn [Williams] was in that one. Adored her, of course . . . hilarious stories; mouth like a sailor, apparently, when oiled up. Magnificent actress of course—but that picture was a real stinker as I recall."

"Pretty bad—but there's an immortal bit of dialogue in it."

"Oh, is there really?"

"Yes. 'You killed Fury—you killed him. There isn't a man, woman or child I wouldn't see dead at my feet if it would bring that horse back to life!'"

"And I wanted to talk about *The Red Shoes*, with Moira Shearer—always more vivid to me than Margot Fonteyn."

"Oh, much. Came back to Covent Garden, you know, only a few years ago; did the cakewalk number with Freddie Ashton. Lit the place up. We all adored her."

"I was there then."

"Where when?"

"At Covent Garden when she did the cakewalk with Ashton."

"Were you really? Well, then I expect you know."

Interesting circular exchange, the author said to himself—a real loop. Like being auditioned in form for a proper British conversation; he'd forgotten how to have one, only mused on the fact that Harold Pinter made an entire oeuvre out of them. They'd been used before, in Noël Coward, for example, among so any others ("Very big, China." "And Japan?" "Very small."), and in the plays of Terrence Rattigan. It was finally Harold Pinter's genius to invest them with the raw low-drop of the working class, then work them up into the new middle classes' mindless defense-against-conversation, torquing them into a kind of nakedly absurdist sublimity.

"But hang on a minute, dear boy, the Covent Garden cakewalk to one side, surely you are improbably young, are you not, to have seen Shearer in her prime?"

"No, I'm actually older than might appear."

"Oh, are you really? Imagine. Amazing place, California."

"Truly. Well, look at you; you don't look a day older . . ."

"Than what?"

"Than whatever age it was you used to be."

"Really?"

"Absolutely."

More on the bewitching splendors of *The Red Shoes* and *The Tales of Hoffman*. Then about *Mawrdew Czgowchwz*, which Brooks had told MP all about, giving him a paperback copy.

"I started writing the thing when I was in college."

"Back when Shearer was in her prime, do you mean?"

"Well, a bit later than that—but that's the period it's set in, exactly."

"Took you a while to work it up, I expect."

QT realized he was being—must be being—treated to exquisite dry wit—a compliment, even an honor, in the circumstances. And art, as Stella Adler had insisted for decades, is in the circumstances. So too, of course, is the death of the first boy apprentice in Benjamin Britten's *Peter Grimes*—accidental circumstances—and Michael Powell didn't look terribly unlike Peter Pears in that role. Fascinatin', as Mae West would have said, eyes shot upward, toward heaven.

Later with Brooks Riley:

"What are you doing for the rest of the afternoon—the beach, maybe?"

"Exactly—down to Santa Monica to Mae West's Neutra beach house."

"And?"

"I'll probably stand on the beach, looking up at the veranda, and read what I wrote about her when she died. She might get a kick out of it—she liked being read to, you know—Freud particularly."

THE LATE MAE WEST

"As expression, music behaves mimetically, as gestures respond to stimuli that they imitate by reflex action. In music the rational, constructive principle suppresses the mimetic. The latter must assert itself polemically; espressivo is the protest of expression at the ban placed upon it.
—Theodor W. Adorno, *Mahler, A Musical Physiognomy*

Late one evening a few years back, in the last decade in which she made her living, the late Mae West, less and less often present ringside in downtown Los Angeles, more and more at home in her sumptuous white suite in the Ravenswood Apartments on Rossmore Avenue in Hollywood, spoke of a visitor she'd been entertaining at her leisure at regular intervals in between reading and revising her memoirs.

"Here I was, sittin' on my big white couch and who should come to see me, all in evenin' clothes, but Lou—gone ovuh, y'know, some years ago. 'Lou,' I said, 'you're lookin' fine.' He always got himself lookin' good to come up and see me when he was livin', y' know. He said to me, 'Mae, I always admired your hands. You have lovely white hands.' And I said, 'Yeah, and they go all the way up the arm.' Yeah, Lou was lookin' real fine."

Mae West was terrifying—that's what it was—and there was nothing else to do about it but to pretend otherwise. Tragedy is to bear the truth; comedy is to pretend otherwise; melodrama, Mae's forte—and she was the truest musician of the great high comedians—is a tightrope walk between the two.

Her content was much greater than its container: all the while she was pretending to be a camp Delilah, she was enacting (in deeply encoded terms, but in mortal earnest) the Queen of the Night, Chaos in whalebone stays. Mae understood an important truth: all that is necessary for one to become, de facto, a monster, is to allow oneself to be exhibited—in the very sense in which Walter Benjamin, in "The Work of Art in the Age of Mechanical Reproduction," said that the work forfeits its quasi-religious cult value to assume its proper exhibition value—and the thing that becomes crucial is the point of intersection between work and onlooker.

Mae West defined, too, the corollary to the proposition: that the only effective shield for a monster against those brawny, determined and witless cats' paws (called in story books knights errant) is the cultivation in the cushioned lair of the private view. As she put it, prefiguring by some decades Foucault's concern with *le souci de soi*—and sharing with Horace, inter alia, a devotion to the mirrored bedroom ceiling—"I like t' see how I'm doin'," adding the footnote, "I invented myself, and I never could put up with sloppy work."

Hamlet asked the player to hold the mirror up to Nature; Mae decided to hold the mirror up to Mae—figuring the best way to read Nature was to read Nature's accomplishment, not Nature's promise—what's what, not what's not: the payoff not the pitch. Thus Mae understood perfectly the difference between male and female narcissism. A man is in love with knowing his image in the pool, but has been warned, genetically, of the risk of submersion: knowledge of ecstatic foreclosure; a woman is a little in love with the tactile sensation of total immersion, but can also be wary of the baptismal purpose. Mae said to the maid who entered advising her her bath was ready, "Take it yourself, I'm indisposed."

Grandfather crossed the Brooklyn Bridge to catch her in vaudeville on Atlantic Avenue. She was a smoldering brunette in those days, a working man's nostalgic vision of the vanished Lillian Russell. Mother and a sidekick sneaked out of school right under the nose of a Sister of Charity one spring afternoon a couple of decades later to catch her in a matinee of *Sex*. Father and mother, like everybody else in the Depression, sat through *Night After Night*, *She Done Him Wrong*, *I'm No Angel*, *Belle of the Nineties*, *Goin' To Town*, *Klondike Annie* and *My Little Chickadee*, which came out the year I was born. I got a load of her (by then as much a household word as Duz) only on television, trading innuendo with Mr. Ed, the talking horse, and knew right away, as we were to say of much else much later, that she was too much for television—one of those Other Beings from that other, vanished, world, illuminated, like television, from behind, but ever so much bigger. The nature of that being, however, was something else: indeed her entire career is a spectacular chronicle of the ineffable pitched as high concept. Never much of a credentialist but no stranger to hard work, she had the great good sense, finding herself enrolled in the School of Hard Knocks, to audit nearly all the courses, thus avoiding the necessity of, shall we say, putting out for her A's. She needed no diploma hung on the wall. ("Would'a gotten in the way o' the mirrors," she might have said.)

What she brought to film was the full realization of her own personal kinetic potential. It is probably true, as people who knew her said, that no cinematic effect could match the hologrammatic vision of Mae West onstage, lying in her big swan bed in *Diamond Lil* or sallying forth to meet the masses in *Catherine Was Great*. ("Oh, Var-vara, hahnd me my traveling case and my peasant disguise.")

The buzz derived from watching her lope into an empty set-up frame, sniff-scan the room (the darkened auditorium of viewers) like an ocelot in heat, dispense with the information that "Goodness had nuthin' t' do with it, dearie!" and then swerve off camera (as if, well, the carte de jour was looking good, but she'd be taking her time over an aperitif). She demonstrated beyond doubt that personal kinesis. Here was Thalia on the move, with a number of similar calls to make in the neighborhood.

So did Mae West become a one-woman National Recovery Administration, uplifting the knackered millions in a fashion and to a degree utterly unprecedented and never again seen—a kind of White Lotus whose far-from-secret society, with its mass membership of ticket buyers coast to coast paying a queen's ransom in box office tribute to their cosmic heroine, who, co-opting both the energy and even occasionally the scripting of the essential triad of nineteenth-century American mythic impulses—the messianic, the millenarian and the revivalist—promised, in the fantasy of return to a Golden Age (the gilded Gay Nineties), to wrest new treasures from the depths of the earth, enrich the poor, put down the mighty from their seat and exalt the humble and the meek. Mae did more than save Paramount Pictures; she went a long way toward saving the nation from the nasty Bolsheviks of *The New Masses*.

There is a discernible element of reaction characteristic of great comedy (Aristophanes, Shakespeare, Molière and Congreve) as opposed to strenuous comedy, *comédie larmoyante* and farce (Ben Jonson, Beaumarchais, Feydeau, Clyde Fitch). Such conservative reaction is everywhere to be found in Mae West's antics—often miscalled buffoonery, which is to confuse Thalia with Bacchus, and Mae never played a drunk scene. Great comedy is never sentimental, and the essence of political revolution is sentimentality.

Mae's reactionary stance was something of a blind: she reincarnated the belle of the Gay Nineties—the essence of curvature—in the age of the flat-chested boy-girl flapper (Louise Brooks, Clara Bow) only to endow her with all the (as-it-were value theory) sexual allure of the black blues woman. In the early part of the century, Isadora Duncan and Ruth St. Denis and Martha Graham had freed women's movement—inaugurating a rather hieratic style, an example of which can be viewed in the temple dances of the besotted votaries of Ishtar in D.W. Griffith's *Intolerance*—while Mae, sister votary of Gilda Grey and Eva Tanguay, shimmied in burlesque like a wild thing. But when, a decade later, nearing thirty-five, she discovered nostalgia, she seemed to regress to something of a cross between a diva of opera's own Golden Age and Leopard Woman of the Argentine.

Accompanying her movements was the liberal use of the moan— theretofore the exclusive property of black female vocalists, and heard in the '20s recordings of Ma Rainey, Bessie Smith, Lucille Bogan, Victoria Spivey and others—introducing thereby the first transposition of black sexual expression into the repertoire of a white American vocalist.

Mae become, as such, far more "transgressive" than Sophie Tucker, Helen Morgan, Ruth Etting et al.—but then Mae's art, which fathomed its registers and their drift, had a different coded aim—one most clearly and memorably expressed in the superimposition of images in the "Dark Waters" sequence of *Belle of the Nineties*.

And in life the same license carried over into her long-term association with chauffeur Chalky White—not perhaps a gesture likely to be saluted by contemporary black theorists as a valiant championing of sexual and ethical relativism and the utility of a multicultural perspective, but one nevertheless on record—whatever the motivational mix involved.

Ultimately more philosophical than political (she resisted the emulous), Mae was indeed deeply reflective, intensely spiritual. Parker Tyler's idea of her—the reconciliation in one body of the gay son and his gaily painted all-forgiving mother—is one not incompatible with the long-sought vision of a conciliation between idealistic and materialist conceptions of reality that has characterized the oblique agony of Western philosophy.

She both sought and afforded more than mere approval. The extra dimension in the West turn is exemplified by the held frame, the rolled eyes, the strut and the few seconds of distracted absorption that follow, elaborated and, in its depiction of affect, agogic.

Mae's slow-motion involuntariness acts as the counterpoint to her announced program, which is not only voluntary but willful. She talks one line but enacts another, deeper one, hypnotizing her men by suggesting the state of being hypnotized—a Trilby to her own Svengali—or as if the things she is saying are things she's just thought of. Such discontinuity is evident in all her work, at first disconcerting but eventually comforting in its implicit intention: the indication of the primacy of reflective meditation over the immediate (and relentless) positing of the subject (a.k.a. the capacity to resist paranoia and to exorcise pathic narcissism).

So, when she speaks of "sex truth," she is sidestepping the question of whether sex and truth are or are not commensurable: what she is declaring in no uncertain terms is that sex truth and other truth are best described as two tenants with time shares in the same atelier: truth works the days, sex truth works the night shift. As experienced by the viewer—and seen correctly as Mae returning the viewer's gaze—Mae's commentary (on Mae) is, again, like looking into the mirror and, instead of being convinced, having the image in the mirror take life from the speculation. More than mere approval, the plethoric quality of the Mae West take—the held frame, the rolled eyes, the split second of mystical absorption—soon take on the physical (optical) sensation of simultaneity, and therefore the mental (and spiritual) sensation of eternity, a grace like the contemplation of the Christian saints and of Zen, which prompts further contemplation.

Or, as Mae herself would have put it, "Beulah, peel me a Muscat grape: its aroma, at once mordant and fugitive, assists spiritualization by its evanescence. Yeah." She called it being in contact with "the Forces" and considered neither the activity nor the aptitude esoteric. In an interview toward the end of her life she avowed, "I've usually been able to figure things out for myself; once in a while I get into trouble, and then I ask Grace Moore."

Mae's effect on formal religion—and particularly on California Orphism—is not to be underrated. Los Angeles was the launching pad not only of the delirium of pictures but also of Aimee Semple McPherson, whose evangelical vaudeville echoes down the ages—in Hollywood each decade is an age—to psychics and channelers all along Melrose Avenue and Santa Monica Boulevard.

Mae West was the temple prostitute not of any neo-Babylonian Ishtar but of the Temple of Liberty and Reason—as Mary Magdalen had been the vestal neo-virgin of the Temple of the Body of Christ.

Mae's mission was the reintegration of the denatured motion-pictured woman. Going better than the vaudeville magicians' sawing women in half, motion picture directors succeeded in cutting them into pieces—closeups, medium shots—long shots—and even leaving bits of them on the famous cutting-room floor—the conceptual flip side of the casting couch. The brilliant thesis of French feminist Catherine Clément's *L'Opéra, ou La Défait des Femmes* has nothing on the mass anxiety and schadenfreude that male audiences experience seeing their mothers and sisters hacked to bits.

Thus, Mae's rendition of Delilah's *"Mon coeur s'ouvre à ta voix"* in *Goin' To Town* reminds us that just as Saint-Saëns was an astringent classicist, so the key to her own aesthetic is reconstitutive vigor, as the signal gesture of her walking whole into the frame, doing her turn and, whole again, walking out is each time an entry into Jerusalem, a passion, a death and a resurrection.

And anybody who doubts this religion's hold on America is as great as that of Isis, Osiris and Company's on ancient Egypt—or that the motion picture is the return of that hieroglyphic text that once ran the length of the Nile—isn't, as Mae might have said, playing the schoolmarm in *My Little Chickadee*, payin' attention.

Mae's originality is of a different type from the originators; its quality is that of the reiterative that denotes a kind of otherness that is perceived not as the result of comparison but as constitutive of selfhood as such—and as in the artistic output generally characteristic of New York/Hollywood, it draws to itself what culture has rejected as derelict and beat up, nurses it and urges it between rounds back into the ring—with the important difference that while it similarly both posits and negates the phantasmagoria of a transcendent landscape, it does so not by salvaging nothing but the transcendence of yearning but, conversely, by pitching and affirming the joy—the kick—of immanent satisfaction.

Hence the chaotic embrasure of her art—and Mae is the self-similarity of chaotics: its waxing-waning inconsistency. Many characters in the first act of *The Drag*—which, if ever unearthed from the Library of Congress and produced, might well prove as tenable and disturbing as Büchner's *Woyzeck* and Wedekind's *Erdgeist*—don't show up in the second; when taxed for explanation, she snapped, "I dunno; maybe they're busy."

That said, the ode outright is less interesting than the ode incorporating the palinode (carnival's requisite inversion), and the livid, murky or glaring light her deviousness casts on the societal arrangements surrounding her cavorts prevents those arrangements from being taken for granted.

She allied herself instinctively with the Surrealists (and was duly memorialized by Dali), according to Walter Benjamin the first whose "profane illuminations liquidated the sclerotic liberal-moralistic humanistic idea of freedom." But rather than succumbing to the temptation of becoming her own mirage, as the Surrealists did theirs, she became entirely her own reality. She stands, also, with Brecht—proletarian goddess that she was (got up as the Statue of Liberty) and fielded by the proletariat not merely to enshrine its desires but to fulfill them, not to embody its world-view but to promote it, not to embellish circumstances but to alter them. But only up to a point: her association with the notorious red-haired gangster Owney Madden made her only too familiar both with real liquidation and with the real character of the hoodlums Brecht sentimentalized, and she declined after all to accommodate herself to the constructive dictatorial side of revolution.

Meanwhile, although costumed as Lady Liberty, Mae bore a stronger resemblance to Adolph Weinman's "Civic Fame" (1914) atop New York's Municipal Building (restored and regilded in the year of her centenary) and for many years reigned supreme as New York's most renowned (and, after a brief stint in jail on Welfare Island, most notorious) performing woman. And she knew, as they say, both ends of the job—although increasingly she came to feel, despite protestations to the contrary, like Lola Montez (Eliza Gilbert, another girl buried in Brooklyn) and again, like Horace, "odd, worn out by being gawked at, in the street, in the theater . . . tired of providing, with strenuous effort that must look lighter than a breeze on a still pond, what people took to be mere diversion" (W.R. Johnson). Thus her attachment to "The Forces."

Yet she remained the woman of the people. In *She Done Him Wrong*, she marries the cop, and in *Belle of the Nineties*, she marries, against the odds, the prizefighter, having restored her honor by restitution to the rich guy she unwittingly fleeced (and with whom, in a more romantic vein, she would have tied the knot). Even when, at the end of *Goin' To Town*, she marrries the Earl of Strattan, it is not as a society dame but as a real broad that she does so, thus implicitly expanding horizons for any number of industrious working girls.

The reversal, like the restitution, is fundamentally Oedipal. Mae had to fix it up for her father, the battling Jack West, just as in life, when she could have had any number of the consuls of New York and later Hollywood, she always kept the company of the gladiator, always threw her lot in with the anonymous pug.

Mae's comedy cannot be explained as a continuation of the Anglo-American satirical tradition. Americans inherited from the British a great fondness for making fun of other's weaknesses, as at the Algonquin Round Table. Far more commandingly singular and representative is Mae sitting alone on her big white couch in Hollywood than were the overpublicized cavortings of a whole gang of her artistic inferiors slouched drunk in Manhattan. Immeasurably greater her donation than for example that of the odious Robert Benchley, who so despised her in *Sex* and whose opinions, like his short and terrible forays into motion pictures, exist merely as splenetive footnotes to others' careers.

Mae, like the Jews who scrambled and redefined American comedy as shtick, took camp out of the homosexual shadows where it had been tended by such geniuses of the New York Tenderloin Rialto as Julian Eltinge, Bert Errol and Bert Savoy, and Mae's exact contemporary, the eternal flame of the British pantomime, the great Douglas Byng (1893–1987). She brought Camp into the light of the silver screen, introducing the delicate side of vampirism, sadomasochism, paranoia and necrophilia, while James Whale, Tod Browning, Lon Chaney and Bela Lugosi were scaring audiences to death.

As the glory of Mae's comedy works through Camp to the transcendence of Camp, so her serious transports move past the edge of dullness to the realm of the Companionate Sublime, entirely rejecting in the process the orderly substantive claims of sociological fiat, technical or formal reason, protocol statements and determinisms of such knights errant as Weber and Durkheim, Russell and Carnap, Weber and Fields.

Philosophically she is like Wittgenstein: the clue, her assumption, rather than her arrogation, of the axiom "I am the case." Not so much hard to understand as a day's work to keep track of, busier than the missing characters from *The Drag*, rejecting the whole of twentieth-century positivism derived from the Enlightenment, especially its social engineering, which she correctly saw as a system of pseudo-ethics that, while claiming to put forth great promises, succeeded only in fielding dire threats.

(Mae did not believe in eugenics either, although she could be existentially severe when sizing up specimens. "That guy's no good," snaps Cleo Borden in *Goin' To Town*; "his mother shoulda thrown him away and kept the stork!" And as a phenomenon neither repeatable nor divisible without alteration, she would have abhorred cloning, as she did those female impersonators who, not content with simply offering tribute by working encoded references to her philosophy and fair-use employment of her accent and gestures into their routines, crossed the line and tried to reincarnate her character while its originator was still alive and holding forth.)

Both psychologically and aesthetically, she is more like Racine than has heretofore been appreciated, and her strategies employ something very like the Racinian room: all formal negotiation proceeds from and returns to what in French theater is known as the comedienne's *loge*. And when she leaves it, it is the world of the boudoir that spills out into the streets—archetypically, the Bowery, characterized by Whitman as the place of all places where popular enthusiasm is felt "bursting forth in those long-kept-up tempests of handclapping: electric force and muscle from perhaps two thousand full-sinewed men." Not, clearly, the bourgeois room that shuts the street out.

Mae West is not the great comedienne she is by virtue of kidding sex. Lyda Roberti did that just as well, as Mata Machree in *Million Dollar Legs*, and the vamps Mae vamped—Valeska Suratt, Pola Negri, Theda Bara—and even the great tragediennes Jeanne Eagels (the mercurial "Duse of the Midway") and Alla Nazimova as often as not got astonished laughs as they did gasps of sympathy. She is great by virtue (and how she would have raised an eyebrow over that particular term) of her uncanny ability to assimilate an entire range of shtick sedimented in the history of late-nineteenth-century Anglo-American show business (with French farce asides) and accreting from the work of her now-forgotten contemporaries, and of not enclosing herself in comedy at the expense of melodrama.

For it is also essential for an understanding of her art to remember her early appearance as Little Willy in the definitive Victorian melodrama, *East Lynne*: as she lay there center stage listening to a Brooklyn audience racked with sobbing at the immortal words "Dead—and never called me mother!" she learned the essential lesson of communicative pathos.

As stipulated, Mae West's aim was to disarm—to neutralize aggression. The *voir-dire* delay tactic in *She Done Him Wrong* ("Why don't-cha come up some time . . . see me") bespeaks an ability shared to the same degree by only one other comic genius I know of: Jack Benny, as in the immortal, "Your money or your life." "I'm *thinking* . . . I'm *thinking*!" Both adhere to the summation in Schelling's "Answer to Armed Robbery" from *The Strategy of Conflict*. "And making myself irrational is the best way to reduce the risk that this man will kill us all."

But she did not only disarm archetypal male phallic aggression. As important, perhaps more so, she refused, as Carl Jung would have put it (in that selfsame era in which the spurious aura of his now extinct *phronesis* back-lit, or shadowed, every public stance), to be devoured by her archetype, Entertainment, as those other daring and dazzlingly famous proponents of heavy-give, Jeanne Eagels, Jean Harlow, Mae's adoring

Paramount colleague Marlene Dietrich and, finally, the apocalyptic Marilyn Monroe, were by theirs. Mae, doubtless instructed by her Guardians, frankly and fearlessly sidled right up to her archetype and said, "Hello, dearie, how are ya?" And that was the happy turning of that terribly dangerous corner.

As surely as do Aristophanes, Molière and Oscar Wilde, Mae West belongs in the Western canon. Her name alone would demand it, did not the magniloquent benevolence and attested prodigal generosity of her art and her life make her beyond dispute the finest American comedic metabolist who ever walked the streets.

Thus, progressing through the orders of 1930s Depression-relief comedy, from the angelic (Jean Arthur) and archangelic (Irene Dunne) through the seraphic (Gracie Allen) we come to the highest, most urgent messengers: Dominations, Powers and Thrones: W.C. Fields, Jack Benny and Mae West. Mae, being of a speculative turn of mind, might well agree with Spinoza that, considered from the point of view of the order of Nature, it is equally possible that a certain man exists or does not exist—she would think of it, say, in terms of a muscle-man casting call—but considered from the point of view of the order of art, the existence of Mae West, as ordained by Mary Jane West, would not be up for questioning.

Even so, her oeuvre, though polysemous, never sends out mixed messages. What it does—to amend somewhat further Adorno's comments on Mahler—is sabotage the established language of comedy-melodrama with dialect, encoding a cryptogram composed of warning signs ("Men Thinking of Working") of the progress that hasn't yet begun and the regression that cannot really mistake itself for origins. It too repels a synthesis; its manner resists fusion, implacably opposing the illusory reconciliation of antagonistic elements—a consequence never of inadequacy, but of the embodiment of a content that refuses to be dissolved in form.

Mae's strut, as Adorno said of Mahler's symphonic movements, creates energized wakes that are "streams on which is borne whatever is caught in them, yet without its particularity being entirely absorbed." Likewise they hasten "to succor an ego-enfeebled humanity incapable of autonomy or synthesis".

Affects are archaic discharge syndromes which replace voluntary action. And what defines tragedy, comedy and melodrama are the gradations in the registers of the voracity of the three drives, sex, aggression and death.

Tragedy:aggression::comedy:sex::melodrama:death.

◄○►

There is perhaps a point to be made regarding Mae West in relation to Parker Tyler's theoretical proposition of the drag queen as the reconciliation in one body of the gay son and his gaily painted all-forgiving mother, a reconciliation not incompatible with the long-sought vision of a conciliation between idealistic and materialist conceptions of reality that has characterized the oblique agony of Western philosophy.

Thus in writing about her, one is tempted to forgo contexts and simply elaborate, in imitation of her art. (Taking a leaf from Bakhtin, the fellow celebrant of carnival, we are sparing in our study with "the superfluous ballast of citations and references—for the qualified reader they are unnecessary, and for the unqualified *unnecessary*.") As assiduous in covering her tracks as she was in blazing the trail, Mae would have wanted it that way.

CHAPTER TWENTY-SIX

On Location

Met Michael Maslansky for lunch (Canter's on Fairfax).
Inter alia (all about MP and the Mawrdew Czgowchwz tease; MM said to take every Hollywood tease dead seriously) a reprise of the endless cocaine marathon discussion at Tom and Judy Lillard's about why my mother was a Bette woman and his mother a Joan woman.

"Deep Joan," I said.

"Don't make fun of Joan, baby—it's not smart to make fun of Joan; Joan was deep."

It was of course in Curtis Bernhardt's *Possessed* (Joan opposite Van Heflin, in which she is, instead of "as complex as a Bach fugue," as murky as a Brahms sextet) that the medics inject the serum and she counts backwards. Opinion is sharply divided on whether or not she was dubbed.

It was clear to Author that, more than any other actress in her salary bracket in heyday Hollywood, Joan was successively raped by the male gaze. In return for the privilege of behaving in a way she came to believe appropriate to a Hollywood star, and in an exchange with which a few hundred thousand of her somewhat identity-challenged female and homosexual male audience identified absolutely, she became the utterly passive accomplice in what indeed was a movement in motion pictures as hieratic as Byzantine art . . . et cetera.

MM: Did I tell you she was deep, baby? She was.

—◦—

In the Celebrity cab, along Sunset Boulevard, feeling dropped into another story, or set of stories, Author felt like Davis on loan-out from Warners (all that black and white and shadows and rain) to Metro (the Baghdad of Hollywood studios), so that all of his thought and gesture came though in Technicolor, with swooping musical soundtracks. Also, looking out the window, he found himself beset with telephone-pole nostalgia.

Back in that preceding decade, Bill Hoffman (dramatist, author of the best of the AIDS plays, *As Is*) had reported, back in New York, how, having gone out to Los Angeles for the filming, he got into the routine of taking Santa Monica Boulevard boys home and paying them just to talk. Authentic dialogue rhythmically rendered, never rhetorically charged or haranguing, except as a utility in climaxes, had long been the hallmark of his work, and he would take down the fantasies they retailed.

These, he and QT agreed, comparing notes, were hardly ever as developed, as shaped, as those redacted by Boyd McDonald for *Straight to Hell*, but more so than the manifestations on view a few years later in the calculated stroke videos of the entrepreneurial master-baiter Dirk Yates, these always erotically charged by the sound of jets landing just out the window. (Who has not dreamed of doing it in the, yes, cockpit, with both the uniformed pilot and his co, while a flying machine the size of a crosstown New York City block is on automatic pilot, being flown by a computer in Atlanta.) Low-budget videos in which room tone has seldom been adjusted for clarity, meant, of course, to suggest verisimilitude, a quality otherwise in short supply, as the pseudo-candid-camera talent is composed in the main of white-trash specimens dressed up as young and not-so-young Marines from San Diego's already notorious Camp Pendleton, in and out of uniform, spread out on the couch and/or the bed, drinking beer and masturbating to not very convincing, abundant or particularly fulfilling orgasms—off-the-rack amateurs tending not to have many such same.

Enter Chad, the Melrose Avenue boy of a thousand-and-one faces, all of them identically posed out of a thousand-and-one high school yearbooks, enveloped in the full-spectrum rainbow mists of his illusions, sitting with two rather drab and formless handlers, telling his tales. But are these illusions? Can they be? Could they be sustained by this mannequin? Are they not meticulously honed, relentlessly drilled performances, calculated precisely to create illusion? It must be so; it could not be otherwise; the alternative is too sensational not only to be studied but even to read in the train.

"Meet Chad. He's something of a legend with us, even among all the pathological liars in Boys Town, all the Marnies who claim to have been Marines.

"You could say he dresses up to people, only of course he's always naked. Different strokes for different folks, as they say in Senior Loveland, but after all, how many ways are there to jack off, really?

"No, it's goes deeper—which of course is what he likes best; he'll be doing it for free in his old-whore age, when he's thirty-five. But he's some-how different from one to the next.

"But since you have a number of other calls to make in the neighbor-hood, doubtless including high tea on Ivar, you won't have time to sit through the feature, but you must at least check out the preview of coming attractions. Do say you will."

With pleasure, Author avowed.

"Oh, goody! You'll find the boy rather like certain operatic heroines, throwing up many riddles, having a pronounced power instinct that is nevertheless terribly brittle. It's a gay turn—and he definitely does aspire to leading roles, in restaurants and at star parties—hilltop and beach house."

"Probably the right idea, since restaurants are being called the new theater."

"And drugs the new cinema. Hilarious. [to Chad] All right, Superboy, you're on. This is your chance to wow them in the print culture. [to QT] Chad's big on the print culture, as they never taught him to write."

"I like your silk pajamas."

"The television executive gave me all these silk shorts and pajamas just to walk around in."

"Samples."

"In the beginning *he* walked around in silk shorts and pajamas and I walked around bareassed, while he teased me about being a wild Indian—'a wild untamed spirit in an exquisitely civilized body' were his exact words. I wrote them down—I have them somewhere, if you'd like to—"

"I don't think that's necessary. Civilized."

"Well, I work out."

"Of course. Being spoken to like that makes for easy listening."

"It does. He was incredibly nice. Awesome. Really. I once asked him why—how—he was so nice. He laughed and told me I knew too many peo-ple in the movies; I should get to know more people in television. He said television and lingerie had something in common: the lingerie business was to the clothing business what television was to the movies. That's how he talked."

(Not bad. He doesn't seem to like silences.)

"He was considerate and gave me massages."

(Lovely eyes.)

Handler Two enters discussion: "Define yourself in jockeys, we insisted;

we see him as a Ganymede—who got a very high place at table on Mount Olympus."

Chad: "That's right above Laurel Canyon; they live up there, these guys."

Handler One: "Jared Benson type, but maybe with any luck bound for higher ground than El Paso. A little spoiled for choice, true—what can you expect when they not only get hosed down and buffed up, but are given both expensive teeth and an expensive vocabulary?"

Chad: "My television executive saw it differently. 'Don't ever wear Calvin Klein underwear—or any other kind of jockey short. You're better than that. You're a forthright young man, not a little faggot mannequin in a diaper.' He saw me in boxer shorts."

Handler Two: "He wanted to own you, baby; we want to share you with the world."

"Underwear was his fetish. 'The Greeks understood drapery; a man's stuff nesting along his thick thigh under light white cotton.' I didn't even know who Ganymede was then."

(And look at you now, eh?)

"When he told me, I asked him what happened when Ganymede grew up, got hair on his balls, stopped being grateful for crumbs from an old man's fancy table?"

(He had a point, I reflected; not a ridiculous one either.)

"'The Greek myths do not record history,' he said, 'they record immutable truth. He who humbles himself—not he who allows other to humiliate him—shall be exalted. He who allows others to humiliate him will go on doing so. And never put mascara on your eyes; you're not a girl, you're a beautiful young man. A little green eye shadow, with your coloring, and a hint of blush to prevent that detached quality—which is wildly attractive—from hardening into disdain. And go light on the cologne. Heavy cologne suggests a career overcoming the stench of cat spunk and wino shit in the back alleys off Santa Monica. You do not need to play it for sympathy; johns are born sympathetic . . . unless, of course, they're not.'"

Handler One: "Roman generals used to wear rouge in their triumphal parades, so as to appear to be blushing with embarrassment at all the attention they were getting from the mob."

Author then charged them to let the boy just talk. Already he had begun to resemble, mutatis mutandis, Vilja de Tanguay—who happily, at last report, had apparently changed her mind, deciding to live, and whose headliner career in the increasingly up-market drag venues of both the East and West Ends had become for Author a source of quiet satisfaction, even if her entrance line, to orchestral fanfare, not suggestive of serenity, was, "Make a path there, will you please—stretcher party!"

Chad, nostalgic, on his New York Period: "Yes, the Haymarket on Eighth Avenue and 44th Street, quick turns at the Adonis on 51st Street, at the Big Top on Broadway and 47th and the 55th Street Playhouse, aisle dancing at the Gaiety Male Burlesque, over the Howard Johnson's: they could hear the music downstairs, Mr. and Mrs. Fat America, and their two-point-nine fat kids, together outweighing six New York street urchins, pigging out on the fried clams and the pie à la mode."

—◁○▷—

Author, nostalgic in turn, recalls his now fully grown University of Washington graduate nephews as teenagers on a Christmas visit to their grandparents in New York. Their bold request:

"Will you take us to see the ladies of the night?"

"Absolutely. I'll even wait for you on the curb until you finish."

"Are you crazy? Only to look at, okay?"

"Absolutely—and would you be interested then in seeing the gentlemen of the night?"

"What, pimps?"

"No, no, dear, for that you're better off watching *Naked City*. I mean the gentlemen hookers—you know, as in *Midnight Cowboy*."

"Oh, . . . well, . . . yeah, sure."

So he took them to the Haymarket, where they actually shot pool, cool as two cucumbers with the hustlers. And as they were both both manly and beautiful—big hunks of boy from the Pacific Northwest, one Celtic-Nordic blond, the other a darker, brooding type—while he, QT, sat at the bar thinking (of all things) of the Stonewall, and determining to stay sober drinking in case anything untoward . . . because the look on the barman's face, not to mention the collective gaze of the drooling warthog brigade when he trotted in with the pair, was something else, and he, QT, was actually the godfather of the younger, the blond.

They remembered it. Later that night, back in Jackson Heights with the grandparents, the blond confided the following to his godfather (meant to stand happen in parental stead on matters not merely of faith and morals but, hey, the tricky stuff): "I finally understand what a girl is talking about when she says she sometimes feels like a piece of meat, with men mentally undressing her. God, what a deal!"

The older kept his counsel; he'd always been the silent sentinel.

◄○►

But back to Chad.

"When I came back from New York, I was recognized. Something had happened to me there, something that gave me status . . . power . . . ascendancy."

"On Santa Monica Boulevard."

"I never worked Santa Monica. A guy picked me up there once when I was just walking along on my way to the baths on Ivar. Took me down Vine past Melrose where Vine becomes Rossmore, down the block from that big Catholic Church to the El Royale."

"Not the Ravenswood, huh?"

"No, why?"

"Mae West lived at the Ravenswood. Christ the King was her church. She gave them all her old limousines. Hated to see nuns boarding any kind of public transport. Said a nun gives her whole life to God, she should ride around in limousines."

"Oh, yeah? Cool. Well, this guy at the El Royale's thing was for us to do it all standing on manhole covers stolen from New York—specially one marked 'Made in India.' We spent the whole fucking night on that one practicing all the positions of—"

"Don't tell me, the Kama Sutra."

"Yes. Of course he did put orange satin-covered pillows down, but even so the next day my sore ass felt like we'd done it all in bumper cars.

"The next day I had him checked out through the network and discovered he was famous, known in the Industry as a player of the highest standards of artistic integrity, and for that reason had many enemies; he's dead now."

"Any idea who got the manhole covers?" QT asked his hosts. No, they didn't.

"I admire artistic integrity," Chad continued, off on his own bat. "That's why I never needed a fluffer, not on the runway, not on the set. In the first place I can do myself. I gave a demonstration once, at a consciousness-raising group over in Encino, and the moderator said, 'Shit, if I could do *that*, I'd never leave the house!' And then when I was first out here doing auditions, I had to go down on Jack Wrangler on the set of *Valley Vampire*. I was understudying the lead, a strictly vanilla North Hollywood High sophomore type Jack seduced with the promise of no school, no parents, all the boys you want, eternal life. Jack was awesome, a real sweetheart."

"And your television executive—"

"There won't be any more offers from him. He made the big one, and got turned down. One Friday afternoon, instead of dropping me at my corner, he took me to his place in the desert. Rancho Mirage."

"And offered to make you—"

"An honest whore. No more grasping, no more lies, no more cover backgrounds—they're called legends in spy work, and we do that too, you know, when we're trusted. We develop scenarios and assume a silhouette; it's exciting, and there's lots of it happening in Los Angeles—sort of like in *The Maltese Falcon*, you know."

"*The Maltese Falcon* is set in San Francisco," Author bravely countered. No reaction, not so much as a "whatever." He was, it seemed, neither to be interrupted nor deterred.

"I remember I was talking about Dan Di Cioccio—you know, from *Boys in the Sand* and *Bob and Darryl and Tex and Alex*? Saying something like I aspire to his quality—he went to the Yale School of Drama, you know."

"Yes, I do. I was his classmate. We called him 'Pecs,'" Author responded.

"Really." (Spoken as only a habituated West Hollywood gayboy can; in Los Angeles, in the immortal words of Fran Lebowitz, "Listening is not the opposite of talking; the opposite of talking is waiting.") "I guess the truth is I went to the Yale School of Drama too—the Joseph Yale School of Drama, Sex Garage campus."

Clever, no question; real possibilities, as they say, although for what is never specified. As if Author could do anything for the boy, except perhaps save his life (a commonplace fantasy).

"I told him—the executive, that is, not Dan; I'd've been anything, done anything with Dan—I didn't really groove on being a backstreet wife, and then I said if he really loved me he'd bankroll me in a remake—of *Back Street*, right—that I'd call *Back Alley Boy*, an All-American story."

Handler One: "We're all very patriotic about American queer video."

Chad: "French, German and Danish stuff is absolute shit; lesser nations co-opting our system to benefit from our developed goods and services without shouldering the responsibilities of the greatest world superpower in history. Opening America to all kinds of foreign influences and diseases in order to destabilize our burgeoning economy and to subvert our technological advancement. I hate that."

"So you use only American product."

"I don't use it myself—I make use of it. One of my clients, this sixty-year-old professor, teaches the Philosophy of Aesthetics. When I first came out, that meant a teacher at a beauty school to me, so you can see how far I've come."

Handler Two: "The professor wrote a deeply cool book: *That's Zentertainment: Detachment and the Politics of Enlightenment.*"

Chad: "Zen-tertainment, get it?"

Author: "Got it."

"I tried to get it at Book Soup on Sunset; they said it was a rarity, but they'd let me know when it turned up. Looked at me funny; I think it's a cult thing. Maybe I was supposed to add a password or something like that."

"Yes, probably."

"Whatever. Anyway, we're sitting here naked, watching *Forbidden Letters*, with Richard Locke. It's by Arthur Bressan, who is a genius. I know him. So he starts getting all theoretical about Arthur. 'The angles, the way the arms and legs, buttocks, round heels, scrotums and members are disposed, like separate body parts in that soft light.' I kept on smiling."

(And so did I.)

"'You are not like the others,' he told me, while his Super 8 camera rolled and I masturbated on a mirror-top table while watching a clip of the Christy twins fucking. 'You are not like the others,' he said, 'whose expressions vary only a little from hope to greed to desperation; your most characteristic expressions are too intricate to be easily read.' That professor taught me a lot."

"Like the French Ventriloquist."

(Vacant smile—so much more appealing, really, than a knowing one.)

"You're from New York, right? Do you know anything about Washington? Most New Yorkers know about Washington Square, and that's about it. Do you know how they operate there?"

"No. I haven't been in Washington since the Civil Rights March. Why don't you tell me all about it—that is, if it's not too compromising, or too dangerous."

Handler One: "It's not dangerous; he's a Republican."

Chad: "We get flown back there all the time. Some lobbyist picks up a video, or gets sent our prospectus, and next thing you know, love slave, baby, with surveillance twenty-four/seven."

"Wearing?"

"They wear out before we do—all on taxpayers' money."

CHAPTER TWENTY-SEVEN

1416 North Havenhurst

(BETTE DAVIS)

> "Remind me to tell you about the time I looked into the heart of an artichoke."
>
> —Margo Channing, in *All About Eve*

While the camera that I am eyes the apartment.

THE FIRST DAY

[Unfortunately gone unrecorded. The author, forgetting to check the tape recorder, had assumed it was in working order, but it had cracked under pressure in the luggage hold and the batteries leaked, so that when he tried the first playback, at the end of about two hours, there was nothing; he was aghast.]

QT: This is impossible—how could I have been so stupid?

BD: Think *nothing of it*—I'm *hopeless* with machines. It's after five, I don't know—look, you'll just have to come back tomorrow.

QT: That's very good of you—I—

BD: Nonsense, Nancy Culp is coming over at about half-past five; we're on the Democratic steering committee together; I don't suppose, though, she'd have flashlight batteries around the house.

QT: Well, in that case I really must—

BD: No, *no*—tell you what, stick around, we'll just *dish*.

[And his real name was *not* Gertrude Slyscynski.]

BD: Fix me a scotch, will you—and oh, help yourself.
QT: Thanks, I don't drink.
BD: What, nothing?
QT: No alcohol.
BD: Oh—Nancy doesn't either; it looks like I'm the only lush—well,
      look, at *least* you did not ask for *white wine*.
QT: No, God willing, it will never come to that.

[Nancy Culp came in and was quite interested. "Hmm—I think I *do* have
flashlight batteries, someplace or other."]

THE SECOND DAY

[QT approaches the Colonial House, this time from the east, along Sunset, past Crescent Heights and a left turn down North Havenhurst.]

QT: You know, I didn't dare say this to you yesterday, but as I was in
      the car, coming from the direction of Laurel Canyon, it occurred
      to me that this must once have been a shady neighborhood, per-
      haps in the wake of the goings on at the Garden of Allah. Some-
      where in Raymond Chandler, and I can't at the moment tell you
      in which of the six major novels, some cop refers to "that male cat
      house up on Havenhurst."
BD: Well, my deah, let me tell you, there are times when—
QT: Carole Lombard gets a little bewildered.
BD: That's one way of putting it—oh, so you know.
QT: That she haunts the building, yes.
BD: Not the building; the back patio, up from the swimming pool.
      And she rattles on the door of her apartment like she's lost her
      keys. Nobody seems to mind.
QT: Will you come back?"
BD: You know, I hadn't really thought about it—anyway, from what
      I've always heard, it's not your choice, you're made to return, until
      whatever went wrong is made right. Particularly if you don't know
      you're dead, if it was a sudden thing, like it was with Carole.
QT: Hard to imagine Bette Davis made to—

BD: I know, but then again I did always obey strong directors.

QT: You've been here for some time; how do you like it?

BD: Very much. This is one of the old ones they haven't torn down yet. [long drag on cigarette] Of course they haven't torn me down yet either.

[She used the same line with Dotson Rader in *Parade*, but it's a good line.]

And speaking of all that, I am all for the new moral code. In the Puritan, or in the Catholic—mostly in the Puritan and the Catholic—upbringing—if sex, then marriage. Well, that is a perfectly *ridiculous* reason for marriage.

QT: It's all right to live in sin, of whatever gender variety?

BD: You put it oddly, but, yes, I'll go along with that.

QT: So Margo Channing's "forthright, upright married lady" declaration is somewhat ironic.

BD: Well, Margo wants very much to believe it.

QT: That is, unless you look up at breakfast or turn around in bed, and there he is—

BD: Yes, yes. Margo wants—wanted—to believe that.

QT: And what about the things you drop on the way up you may need later on?

BD: Well, let me tell you, I was listening to that speech again, just the other day. We're making this rather interesting record, of some of the speeches and some of the songs I've—well, sung is probably not quite the word—but you know what I mean.

QT: Yes.

BD: And that business is absolutely true, and for a woman, a certain kind of woman, it turns out to be even more important than . . . the other. Fortunately, I never had any serious problem, really, either going up or coming down.

QT: Coming down. You put it so casually, almost—or just baldly.

BD: What is reality, my dear, if not bald? Anyway, I didn't, because I was basically decent to people so that when I ran into them again . . . but it's a brilliant remark, because many people weren't— didn't do this. You treat some sound man horribly, and then years go by and you inherit him again and God help you, you know . . . but certainly the last line—

QT: You mean, "Slow curtain, the end."

BD: No, no, that's later. I mean, technically, yes, it is the last thing she says, but—

QT: It's the coda, isn't it. The undercutting twisting of the thing so as to bring Margo back to—

BD: Yes, yes, exactly, you're so bright. I mean the last thing that matters, the last thing that involves you before you come to "slow curtain," which is a throwaway.

QT: "Without that, you're not a woman. You're something with a French provincial office and a boxful of clippings, but you're not a woman."

BD: Yes. That idea does, for a long, long time, seem the most important thing of all.

QT: I shouldn't be interrupting, but the inferential opportunities one has interviewing you are really something else. Something about you in performance, for instance, is the uncanny ability you demonstrate—again casually or offhand—to be in the thing and simultaneously illustrating how it gets done without indicating.

BD: Oh? Without indicating what?

QT: Oh, you know, the Stanislavsky thing. Brando doesn't do it either.

BD: But I am not Stanislavsky—not "Method."

QT: No, I know, you're John Murray Anderson and some Martha Graham.

BD: Yes, exactly. What was that brilliant thing she said you mentioned?

QT: "In order for there to be dance, there must be something that needs to be danced."

BD: Yes, yes, brilliant. What she said to us was, "Think of acting exactly like a ballet."

BD: But not classical ballet.

BD: No, but she did say ballet, by which she meant that acting had to have a continuity of movement in both voice and body, everything smoothly connected. Essential for the stage, of course, but people don't realize that you've got to keep your movement constantly in mind in films as well—and of course I'd already studied with Rashanara up in Peterboro, New Hampshire, at a school called Mary Arden, and had set out originally to be a dancer, but Rashanara died, and it was only then I sort of made up my mind to be an actress in the theater.

QT: And not motion pictures.

BD: No. I didn't know much about them, hadn't seen many, really; we weren't permitted to go, you see—very Puritan upbringing altogether. But when she said that, Graham, about movement, I took it to heart immediately, and it is every bit as important in films as in theater. You'd be surprised how many people in films know nothing about it, and although it might sound simple, it's not, because, of course, the very first thing you must learn to do is hit your marks. You can't imagine how much time is wasted in rehearsal with actors who don't hit their marks. And then, of course, the consciousness that you absolutely must hit your marks if they are going to photograph you can be terribly inhibiting; the last thing you want is to preoccupied—on top of wondering what is going into that camera.

QT: And then into the can and finally up on that screen.

BD: And there you are sitting—squirming—through the premiere, and that forty-foot horse's ass up there on the screen is you.

QT: But is it—you?

BD: Oh, yes, my deah, absolutely no question, it is you. You may walk away from it with your back turned as slow as you dare, or run away as fast as you can—

QT: Like Margaret Elliot in *The Star*—or later Alexandra Del Lago in Tennessee Williams's *Sweet Bird of Youth*.

BD: And in the last analysis, it is you.

[Spoken exactly the way Margo Channing, claiming retention of exclusive rights and privileges to "certain areas of my life" and quizzed by Bill Sampson, "For instance, what?" nails the issue: "For instance, you!"]

QT: I keep coming back to Margo Channing, and I suppose it is the role with which you are most identified, but I'll confess something: as great as you were, I really can see the picture working quite as well, in a very different key, with Claudette Colbert.

BD: I absolutely agree with you—that script!

QT: Dynamite. Loaded with opportunities for fire and music—and tantalizing asides—you know, I used to lie awake nights trying to picture Margo Channing as Mark Antony in Wilkes-Barre. [long pause, followed by loud guffaw]

One thing, I never could picture Claudette behind the notions counter, but you, definitely, after Gabrielle in *Petrified Forest*. Also with her, it definitely would have been a part, a part in a play, whereas with you, it was a role; you really brought so much—

BD: Of myself? I did, because the role was such a godsend at that point in the career—but of course I paid a price; I convinced myself I was Margo Channing and Gary was Bill Sampson, and when Margo married Bill, I simply had to marry Gary.

QT: And the other thing of course is, and it is a great moment in cinematic history—there you are, standing on that landing, and up into the shot come—

BD: Sanders and Marilyn Monroe. Zsa Zsa Gabor used to remark on that for years after: she was getting ready to marry George— unwisely too—and was around a lot.

 Well, I'll tell you, at first I didn't know what to make of that girl, either, in the picture; she seemed so odd, so *flat*—you know, her line readings, and just generally—although certainly not where it counted. And all the men thought she was nothing.

QT: Surely not the cameraman.

BD: No, no—or any of the technicians either, *that* I can tell you—that was something, the way she had them all—no. no, I mean the men in the cast, Gary, Marlowe, even Sanders. And I thought, well, they're probably right, but there was this—something. As I say, I thought the way she read the lines was ridiculous, I really did. I remember I'd given a party at Trader Vic's in San Francisco, near the beginning of the shoot, and she came alone and drank nothing but milk. Oh, she was very clever—and they all thought she was nothing, and then, back at Twentieth, I managed to get in to see the dailies—this was not Warners, you know, and *Eve* was not a Bette Davis picture, but I remembered what they'd all been saying. Well, I saw that entrance, and it was then I said to them, you are all *mad*; handled properly she could be really something big. I suddenly saw the obvious, that she was essentially a comedienne, and a completely different one from anything there had ever been before. She was funny, but she was something else too, something else entirely, something I'd never come across. And I told them. I said, you are so wrong.

QT: Well, you hit that mark; let's go back to them and the how-to-do-its.

BD: The marks. Well, fortunately I have good peripheral vision so I don't have to count steps, which is one way but awfully distracting. I take my marks from the furniture, I always have; I'm lucky in that.

QT: So that's the secret of Bette Davis eyes.

BD: Oh, have you heard the song? She's a darling kid.

QT: I have—and you know the great thing is nothing has to be explained to the young.

BD: You mean, for instance, "Who is Bette Davis?"

QT: Yes, exactly—and I do see, apropos the marks thing, that if you don't have to worry about it, you arrive each time stress-free, ready to assume the right position on the arc of the character.

BD: Well, that too, yes, but before you even get to that—and how many do, really? not that many—you simply aren't wasting the director's time, and upping costs.

QT: Economy in every direction—but did you, or do you, ever go into rehearsal without the character?

BD: Not any more, no. Now it's like I've heard artists talk about with painting, you just pick up the brush, but in those hectic shoots at Warner Brothers in the thirties—before, let's say, *Marked Woman* and *Jezebel*, although I used to absolutely cram for the character, still it didn't always come on schedule—oh, and then of course there was *Jane*—much later on, and we were under enormous pressure, because the producers had first told Aldrich, "Well, the script is great, just get rid of those two old broads and we'll get you all the money you want," but he wouldn't, and so for a gag I took out that famous ad in *Variety*.

QT: "Experienced actress seeks employment."

BD: Yes, and in the uproar that followed we got the money, although Miss Crawford issued a statement asking Miss Davis, when telling that story on the promotion tour, please not to refer to her as an old broad.

QT: Well, Joan was deep.

BD: She was *what*?

QT: Another gag, at least I think so; she's referred to by some people as Deep Joan.

BD: That has got to be a gag.

QT: Well, irony is in nowadays, in big.

BD: That isn't irony, my deah, that's hallucinating.

QT: Meanwhile, I've lost the thread—about *Jane* and the character.

BD: Oh, well, I was about to say that Jane Hudson was another great exception. I hadn't the faintest idea what to do with her, until I saw the wardrobe.

QT: Oh . . . sure.

BD: The minute I did, she came to me like that.

QT: And then movement—you know your signature walk has helped define many of your characters, and never more amazingly than Jane Hudson. Not only has she gone to pot, but the Bette Davis walk has too. Do you think that walk comes out of the Graham thing?

BD: No, it seems always to have been—you know everybody has always talked about my walk, but I never knew anything about it; it's just the way I walk.

QT: It seems to cover more ground per stride, that's one thing.

BD: I give you that—yes, it definitely does.

QT: James Baldwin, talking of champions of bald reality, said pretty baldly, "Bette Davis walks like a nigger."

BD: Yes, they told me. What do you say back to *that*?

QT: Not much, I imagine.

BD: Not anything.

QT: You know, don't you, what Gore Vidal told Baldwin?

BD: I do not, what?

QT: That he couldn't be both Martin Luther King and Bette Davis.

BD: Oh, *God*!

QT: All the same, black audiences identify with you.

BD: Of course they do.

QT: For any particular reason, you think?

BD: I suppose—I like to think—because I act the truth.

QT: Will that do for gay audiences as well?

BD: Well, that I don't know. Gay audiences, that seems more complicated. Gay audiences seem to identify more with the—I don't know—the ambition of the women I played, or if not exactly identify, they *side* with me.

QT: And what is truth, in acting?

BD: Hard to say, but you know it when you see it.

QT: But what's it like from the inside?

BD: Like what you suggested before; do the task—finish the picture— that's to say, of course, your picture in the big picture. I tried producing just once; never again.

QT: And you did some rewriting now and again.

BD: Oh, only one time, really, with Astor, on *The Great Lie*—but really, the picture made *no sense* before the two of us sat down and worked it over. There was this absolutely *pivotal* part that hardly *existed*. Well, we fixed that, and Astor got the Academy Award for best supporting actress. Astor was really smart, you know, and just *oozed* class all over the place, she really did, and then that gorgeous voice.

QT: I want to return for a minute to truth in acting. Meryl Streep's acting teacher, watching her in something, is supposed to have called out, "Play the *scene*, Meryl, don't play the *mood!*"

BD: That's good. Wyler kept telling me essentially the same in *Jezebel.*

QT: And in *The Letter.*

BD: Oh, yes, in *The Letter*, he absolutely *hammered* it *into* me. Play what is *written*, the *logic* of what is *written*, and let the mood be established around that.

QT: What about the illogical?

BD: Good point—for instance, in *Jane* what was there to do? You lie to the audience all the way through, then you say, well, this is how it was. Very difficult, because after all so far as Jane knows, it's all the truth; she did make Blanche a cripple. You have to forget the story, really, and for better or for worse be on your own.

QT: And instead of the mood or the scene, play the wardrobe.

BD: Sounds ridiculous, doesn't it.

QT: No, not at all. In fact, it reminds me of my friend Tom Carey— you know, Dobey's son. Remember, I told you yesterday I'd stayed overnight in Sherman Oaks with Dobey and Marilyn, and Dobey drove me here.

BD: Yes, yes—of course *I* adored *Dobey's* father.

QT: Well, Tom had the part of the groom in the last segment of *Plaza Suite*—one short scene, and when he entered, there was an over-turned chair from the argument between the Walter Matthau character and the Lee Grant character, and his question was, should he play the chair—notice it on his way to the bathroom door to get the fiancée to come out—and I think it was Lee Grant, who is a Method actress and terrific, who advised the director, "Let him play the chair."

BD: Well that does bring another thing up, and that is that you simply must know—the character must know and be able to react, either positively or negatively depending on the script, to the sets. You know I grew up with real sets in the theater. I remember going to see Frances Starr in *The Easiest Way*, a Belasco show, and I can remember every *detail* of that set. I remember the trunk she sat on, and real props—I mean it was a real bottle of milk on the windowsill that froze.

QT: That is interesting, because as an actor you are a realist, but you're not a naturalist, not slice-of-life; you abstract.

BD: No . . . yes, that's right. What I do lament today is that the worst insult is, "You're acting."

QT: Yes, a complete misreading of the directive "Don't quote-unquote act"—or as somebody-or-other once called out to Geraldine Page, "Gerry, don't just do something, *stand* there."

BD: That's good.

QT: Back to the wardrobe and sets.

BD: Yes—but of course, number one, I did not have the handicap of Adrian. I mean the clothes I wore never changed that much, and still look all right today; what I wore in *Dark Victory* is very like what I wear today. I never wore wild Hollywood glamour—

QT: Drag.

BD: [guffaws] Exactly.

QT: So you were never upstaged by the wardrobe.

BD: Right—particularly the hats. And then the sets. If, as a character, if you don't believe the set you're in, it can be such a handicap, it really can.

QT: Speaking of chairs again, in reviewing your performance as the mother in *Where Love Has Gone*, one critic said, "Sitting in the ugliest chair in Hollywood, she declares 'Somehow the world has lost all its standards and all its taste.'"

BD: Yes, exactly. I remember that chair—*hideous*, but the character was perfectly at home in it.

QT: And of course the reverse of playing the wardrobe and set, or elements of it, is the Hollywood total-effect: making your real-life environment a beautifully dressed set, to which your hair, wardrobe and accessories correspond, and only then—

BD: Will you know who you are—oh, that is *too* true.

QT: Hollywood's dubious message to the world. But coming back to acting, once you've absorbed all those things—the wardrobe, the sets, everything—

BD: Then get to work, and play the scene as written.

QT: I have to tell you this is exactly the way Callas talked about the score.

BD: Well. Of course she did; she was incredible; I thought so.

QT: Speaking of which—scores, you did have some great ones.

BD: Sensational; Max Steiner and, oh, Korngold!

QT: You were his muse, or so he said.

BD: And what a compliment—that *Deception* score. And he was the *most* darling man.

QT: So with faith in all these elements, you play the play.

BD: And Wyler really did hammer that into me in *The Letter*.

QT: And in *The Little Foxes*.

BD: Well, Willy and I fought all the way through *Foxes*, and you know he saw I was so terrified of playing it, and tried to change the way it was played, but Hellman wrote one character, and Bankhead played it that way, and I was going to play it that way, but I was absolutely terrified.

QT: Because of Bankhead's performance.

BD: Absolutely. You know I was on loan-out to Metro, and I really begged Sam Goldwyn to let me do something else, a screwball comedy. I'd already done *It's Love I'm After*.

QT: At Warners, with Leslie Howard, and later you'd do *The Bride Came C.O.D.*

BD: Oh, Cagney was the best actor I ever worked with, definitely— Cagney and Claude Rains.

QT: And the best actress—or actresses?

BD: Oh, Gladys Cooper, no question, and Fitzy and Fay Bainter, then Astor, and of course Thelma Ritter. I always wanted to co-star with Hepburn—*there's* an *actress*—but nobody ever came up with anything I felt we could show her. I'd love being opposite her; she's an amazing woman.

QT: Well, at the moment the only thing I can think of is some kind of crazy meeting between two characters with the same name each of you have played.

BD: What do you mean?

QT: Jane Hudson. Hepburn played Jane Hudson in *Summertime*.

BD: [great guffaw] My God, that is amazing—that is a *scream*. Well, look, if you figured that out, you go back to New York and write something for Hepburn and me.

QT: Never mind New York, I'll write it on the red-eye and mail it special delivery before I go home to bed.

BD: You live in Manhattan.

QT: East Twenty-second Street, right around the corner from Gramercy Park.

BD: That's terrific.

QT: We're getting away from Tallulah Bankhead.

BD: Not fast enough for me, my deah. Well, you know, I hadn't seen her in *Foxes*, and when they signed me, I didn't want to, but my husband and I were motoring to the coast from New Hampshire—

QT: This was Farney, number two, who dropped dead on Wilshire Boulevard.

BD: Yes. Poor Farney. Well, on our way out we were directed to stop someplace in Ohio—she was there playing it—and got lost on the way, which in those days was terribly easy, and ended up not arriving until the next day, and going to see it that night, and she was absolutely *livid*. I had to go back and see her, and she was just *livid*. She was, of course, sensational in it, and I thought this really is a terrible injustice, and I begged Sam Goldwyn to take her, but he wouldn't; he said she was box office poison.

QT: She was sensational in *Lifeboat*, but it was a Hitchcock picture and an ensemble picture, so she didn't have to carry it.

BD: Yes, exactly, and it's true I did have to carry *Foxes*, but it was still a terrible injustice, really it was. Regina Giddens was her part, no question. Certain parts are for certain actors. As was said at the time, all Cornell had to do was get into that blue dress and she was Candida, and all Bankhead had to do was get into that black dress and she was Regina Giddens. Very sad.

QT: Which I guess brings us back to Margo Channing.

BD: But Mankiewiecz never meant Margo Channing—

QT: To represent Tallulah Bankhead, no, true; and the original story was taken directly from the real story of a rather ghoulish girl who inveigled her way into the affections of Elizabeth Bergner, but you realize it just couldn't have been taken otherwise than as a Bankhead-inspired turn. In the first place, it was the voice—yours was a couple of tones down, caused I know by the bronchitis and the fact that they couldn't wait, and it was hardly the Bankhead baritone. Nevertheless, people picked up on it—and then there was the mink coat Margo treats like a poncho. Bankhead lived in her mink coat—and that line about the wedding with Bill, "What will you wear?"

BD: "Something simple, a fur coat over a nightgown." Oh, but *really!*

QT: Really. The gag going around was Tallulah would skip the nightgown.

BD: Well, you know I bought that coat—got it half price, and wore it for about a hundred years. I bought five of the costumes at the same time.

QT: So you were attached to Margo after all.

BD: Oh, yes, as I told you, I thought I was she.

QT: And not remotely Tallulah.

BD: Oh, my God, *no!*

QT: There was, apart from anything else, one significant big and telling difference. Geography. By 1950 Bankhead was on her way to becoming Broadway's reigning Queen of Camp, and you, although a Camp icon, were not, in life, doing that turn out here; you were looking for more scripts and getting them. Nevertheless, from the minute the picture came out, no female impersonator could do a Bette Davis without doing a Tallulah Bankhead.

BD: It's true, and, you know, before that they used to do me and then do Eleanor Roosevelt at a garden party. Imagine. The thing is, of course, there has to be something distinctive about you before they can do you. I mean, for instance with Joan—apart from "Bless you, bless you all," what could you do?

QT: Unless you were Faye Dunaway, later on.

BD: Don't *ever mention* that woman's *name* to me!

QT: Yes, I know there were difficulties on *The Disappearance of Aimée*.

BD: *Difficulties!* Turn that thing off and you'll hear all about *difficulties.*

QT: Just one question; did you see *Mommie Dearest?*

BD: Of course I did.

QT: And?

BD: She *was* Joan! I knew Joan, and that woman *was* Joan.

QT: Do I rest my case, or not?

BD: She was Joan—nevertheless, never, *never* in *all* my professional *life* have I endured such unprofessional—well, you know people said it should never have been made, that picture.

QT: Dunaway wasn't even nominated.

BD: I know, and I suppose that was—of course people said Christina should never have written that book, but I have to say I didn't blame her at all: she was living in a mobile home in Tarzana!

QT: Well, about doing Joan. That was her own voice dubbed over yours in Jane, when she's talking to the liquor store man.

BD: Yes, it was. We went and told Joan nobody could do it, and she was so flattered—she was flattered out of her *mind*.

QT: Female impersonation reminds me again of Mae West. What the female impersonator goes for is the persona, the actor's or Mrs. Roosevelt's. Mae West's persona was entirely self-invented.

BD: It was indeed. Of course, if you're any good—

QT: You have to, yes. We were talking about that, weren't we, about the differences between Ruth Elizabeth and Bette. Bette won out.

BD: She did, yes. I thought for a long time Bette and Ruth Elizabeth could coexist; I tried, I really tried to make coexistence work, but I couldn't.

QT: You became ruth-less.

BD: If you want to put it that way.

QT: Well, you see, Mae West had something of that same problem, and like you was closely bonded with a sister as well.

BD: It was Bobby first called me Bette, you know.

QT: And Mary Jane West went on at three as Baby Mae.

BD: Did she, at three?

QT: Yes—beats Margo Channing's entrance as a stark-naked fairy by a year. But about her persona, somebody was once going on about it, how perfect it was, and Mae said, "It oughta be. I invented myself, and I never could put up with sloppy work."

BD: Oh, that is good, isn't it, and of course exactly right. "Never could put up with sloppy work." Oh, that is brilliant.

QT: Tell me about Mae West—the dinner party.

BD: The famous dinner party.

QT: Yes; Bette Davis, Beverly Sills and Mae West; what a grouping.

BD: Yes, indeed it was. Well, it was fabulous; it was the first time I'd ever met either Beverly Sills or Mae West.

QT: The Beverly Sills meeting is certainly interesting; practically everybody knows that when she sang Elizabeth the First in *Roberto Devereux*, she copied your gestures from *Elizabeth and Essex*, particularly the clasping and unclasping of the right hand—a mannerism that had become an essential part of all the female impersonators' Bette Davis routines—but I'm really much more interested in your reaction to Mae West.

BD: Of course, so were we, just like two awestruck kids.

QT: Now that is interesting.

BD: It is, isn't it; we kept looking across at one another. Of course Mae West was a legend when we were—well, certainly when Miss Sills was in diapers.

QT: And you were in drama school and going to Broadway shows; you saw her in *Diamond Lil*?

BD: Absolutely, and in *Sex*; she was—well, what can you say?

QT: Unprecedented.

BD: That, too, but she was riveting, and absolutely awesome to us; back then on Broadway and again right there at dinner, wearing these enormously high heels, they went on for blocks. I don't know how she walked in them really. And then she was much less Brooklyn in her speech, which I thought was very interesting.

QT: People said she was softspoken as a rule.

BD: It's true, she was—she almost wasn't Mae West.

QT: She used to answer the phone, people said, and either say she was the maid, or that she was her sister Beverly, and that Miss West was not in.

BD: Yes, well, we were *fascinated*, both of us. And then some time later, Miss West asked us—that is, Chuck Pollock, who was the host of the dinner party—and myself to her apartment for tea, and of course it was fabulous, all in gold and white, everything, white marble fireplaces and crystal chandeliers, and of course she dressed entirely in white. And I was so tempted—her bedroom was so famous for all the mirrors—and I kept thinking how can I possibly sneak into the mirrored bedroom without her knowing it, and I decided it would be very rude.

[Subsequently, a third and final meeting between Bette Davis and Mae West took place in the aforementioned host's West Hollywood apartment, from which we have the kind of record—from a microphone hidden in the coffee table flower arrangement—of which, in a better world, as in the case of the late John Ardoin's making tapes of personal conversations with Maria Callas at low emotional ebb and marketing them after her death, it would be a sign of moral integrity to ignore. Such bottom feeding is, like illness for Lady Bracknell, hardly a thing to be encouraged in others. And yet . . .

In any event, in an excerpt that bears upon the present interview, Bette, indisposed, was going on about her impossible husbands—Farney by that time quite forgotten—and a kind and very wise Mae leaned over, patted her on the hand and declared, "Oh y'don't *marry* them, deah."]

QT: Now we're getting away from Gladys Cooper. What about her as a mother figure? There really was an extraordinary rapport between you, and yet, of course, the character wanted the absolute opposite for Charlotte of what Ruthie wanted for you, and couldn't have been much like Ruthie.

BD: Well, Gladys Cooper, my deah, working with Gladys Cooper was one of the great privileges of all time. Gladys Cooper and Jane Cowl both—I never got over it.

QT: Jane Cowl. *Smilin' Through.* My mother still has the sheet music of the song with her picture in costume on the cover. I'd completely forgotten you worked with her—in *Payment on Demand,* yes. You ask her why she never married, and she says, "Because no one ever asked me, dear, and anybody I ever asked said no." A great moment, hardly ever talked about.

BD: Well, I have to tell you that working with Miss Cowl in that one scene, and being in a star position, well, I was *embarrassed,* I was actually *embarrassed*—and I think that's to my credit. I should have been.

[That statement, for QT, became the key to his subsequent understanding of Bette Davis.]

QT: Yes, I see that; but not with Gladys Cooper; embarrassed.

BD: No, privileged, enormously privileged, but not embarrassed; no, not at all.

QT: Of course the part was so much more substantial.

BD: Exactly. Anyway there were no stars in *Voyager.*

QT: No stars. You mean an all-star team has no—what?

BD: No star position. Of course it was a Bette Davis picture.

QT: In many ways *the* Bette Davis picture.

BD: Is it your favorite?

QT: It is, my favorite all-around Bette Davis–auteur picture, yes.

BD: Not your favorite performance.

QT: The performance is impeccable, the high-water mark of what I call Benevolent Bette. Kit Marlowe in *Old Acquaintance* is another one, the wife in *The Great Lie* and Miss Moffat in *The Corn is Green*. And I'm very fond of the Benevolent Bette–Malevolent Bette standoff in *A Stolen Life*. Good twin pictures are rare.

BD: But your favorite performance, Margo Channing?

QT: No, your greatest performance, in a close-edge win over Leslie Crosbie, in *The Letter*, is unquestionably Judith Traherne. In *Dark Victory*.

BD: I'm happy you think that, because I believe it's quite true—you know it was Goulding's idea to have the friend put in that saved that play, and Geraldine Fitzgerald was just—well, I saw Fitzy just the other night in something, with Suzanne Pleshette, playing a nun. And you know when Fitzy came here with her one-woman show she asked me to be guest of honor on opening night, and I was—well, for Fitzy to do a one-woman show, as a great friend and a person I loved, I was *petrified*, but, *oh*, I needn't have worried. I thought she was brilliant—*brilliant*, with the long white hair . . . well, she's an incredible woman. *She* should have played the girl in *Wuthering Heights*, and not Oberon; it drove her mad on that set, playing that dull sister, when she *was* that peat-moss wild Irish girl. They just never cast her right, they never got her message. Well, she showed them—in *Long Day's Journey*, she was fantastic, she was actually terrifying in that role; you'd have sworn she was a morphine addict.

QT: Can we talk some more about Gladys Cooper?

BD: Oh, my deah, I could talk all afternoon about Gladys Cooper. Never a minute late, the perfect professional always, absolutely no star temperament at all, considering the fact she'd been a great star, the great beauty of her age—I *adored* her. Of course the part could have been written expressly for her; there was nobody else in the *world* who could have played that part with anything like her quality. I *adored* her.

QT: It shows in the performance; there even seems to be a physical resemblance between mother and daughter. That's probably why I wondered—

BD: About Ruthie. No, Gladys Cooper was nothing at all like Ruthie.

QT: Scratch that one then. Fay Bainter, what about her?

BD: Bainter I also adored. Bainter *made Jezebel*; her performance *made* Julie's character; she was pure poetry.

QT: The best supporting actress Academy Award—and she defined the position, didn't she.

BD: Absolutely. I've never thought of it that way, but yes, absolutely. She was such a dreamy actress; I'd seen her as a kid in *East Was West* and her other great shows in New York. . . . See, it was such an odd experience, and could really happen that way only in films, where you had reached a certain level and these great and famous older woman were playing lesser parts, and I never got over it, especially as I'd been in drama school and gone to see all these gorgeous creatures onstage giving these performances; wondrous, and then barely a generation later—

QT: What goes around comes around, undiminished.

BD: Yes, exactly.

QT: Thelma Ritter.

BD: A godsend. That wonderful relationship between Birdie Coonan and Margo Channing—well, it was like with Fitzy in *Dark Victory*. She saved the thing from going into the maudlin and the sappy, really, by taking the onus off Judith Traherne, who doesn't have to keep going on—

QT: You mean once the point has been stated, in prognosis negative.

BD: —and on about her condition; yes, after the prognosis negative business. You see, that's what it meant to have these terrific writers working day and night in that Hollywood. In the play for instance, the character of Ann, the friend, isn't there, which left the actress alone.

QT: To sink or swim. Miss Bankhead sank like a stone.

BD: I know. Thank God, I didn't see her in that one. She was terrifying enough to me when she was having the triumph of her career. What a force.

QT: Unhappily, a force that became a farce.

BD: Oh, don't print that—don't print that while I'm alive.

QT: Well, now, that's going to be a lot of years.

BD: You think? We'll see.

QT: I imagine you the way I imagine my mother, immensely old.

BD: Really? Turn that thing off and tell me about your mother.

—◄○►—

QT: And although she wouldn't often like to be reminded of it—she was after all convent-school-bred, had had that screen test in Astoria my grandfather absolutely forbade my grandmother to follow up on, and had all this taste in music and theater—she of necessity, working in the archdiocese, would routinely mix with the Aggie Hurleys of New York, and of course find common ground with them. One of my father's West Side pals, Charley Nally, and his wife, Kate, were examples. My mother said, "Kate Nally is the salt of the earth; a little Tenth Avenue, of course."

BD: Oh, that is wonderful.

QT: I think of it because of *The Girl from Tenth Avenue*.

BD: Of course. And Thelma Ritter played that salt-of-the-earth woman to perfection—which of course was exactly what made Margo Channing an appealing character, and so vulnerable, because for all her savvy about a woman's career, she still was unable to see through Eve Harrington—

QT: To Gertrude Slyscynski.

BD: Exactly—but *Catered Affair* reminds me of something about my mother. She always came onto the set of each picture for one day, only one, and the day she came onto *Catered Affair*—

QT: Thelma Ritter meanwhile having originated the Aggie Hurley role on television—which in the few short years since 1950 had become a lot more than auditions, wouldn't you say?

BD: No question. I never saw her in it; I heard she was brilliant, and I believe it. Well, Ruthie came on the *Catered Affair* set, and there I was in this truly awful black satin slip, looking like Aggie Hurley looked, and she took one look at me and let out this bloodcurdling yell, in front of the *en-tire crew*. I tell you, my deah, I nearly *died*.

QT: She couldn't bear you looking like a woman who'd come down.

BD: Never could—very interesting. The struggle she had, don't you see, after my father walked out. Of course she drove him mad, I see that. I did the same.

QT: Drove your father mad—how so?

BD: No, no, I drove my husbands mad, later on.

QT: Three out of four, maybe, but never Farney.

BD: Poor Farney. I was madly in love with Wyler just then.

QT: I have no wish to pry, but what about Howard Hughes?

BD: Oh, well, that—I honestly cannot tell you what that was.

QT: Then it's of no concern; yet people will talk.

BD: Oh, won't they *just.*

QT: Bette Davis doesn't care. Ruth Elizabeth would have, though, wouldn't she?

BD: Yes, she would, and that, I suppose, is really why she had to go.

QT: I had an idea, from what we were talking about yesterday, about the New York theater, and the actor's obligations in it; about glamour and the Great White Way—

BD: Well, it was never the same as the picture business, never. You were just what you were when you were in the theater giving that performance, you had no obligations out of the theater at all—no obligations of appearance or whatever, and of course it was a shock to all of us when we came here that that is rather an important part of it, because you're certainly known by more and more people. In fact, Laemmle's secretary at Universal gave me a long lecture one day about how I must wear more makeup and comb my hair more—imagine! I mean, I never thought I looked that bad.

QT: Let me tell you what Merman said on Broadway at the dress rehearsal of *Call Me Madam.* She had this gorgeous Mainbocher wardrobe, and was asked what she wanted done with her hair. She said, "I thought I'd wash it." And that was for playing the part.

BD: Well, exactly. Well, out here it's part of the job, and if you do not accept that—well, as a matter of fact, the actors who *beef* about the lack of *privacy* and, oh, the *necessity* to be *bothered* by the public and all this, they're usually the ones who if they weren't *bothered*, they would *die*. But those of us who accepted it right from the beginning knew perfectly well that that was just as much part of the job as your work on the screen, and indeed it is.

QT: And you knew how to get privacy; when it was time, you went home to New England.

BD: Yes, and so far as publicity was concerned, I did all my publicity after the film was shot, because I never felt it was fair to other people on the set to have interruptions, and interviewers coming around, and it's not fair to you either, because you get your mind distracted—and that system worked well.

QT: You're one of the few left who actually worked in the theater at the very end of that period you were talking about—the Belasco period, although Clyde Fitch was well before your time—and in the beginning of the Great Awakening, the peak of O'Neill's career, the early Group Theater. You had the one great triumph in *The Wild Duck*, still a very modern play, with Blanche Yurka, and then Hollywood. Any regrets?

BD: Yes, there are, I have to admit it, but once talking pictures came in, everybody who was thinking knew you should try it. Now, I did stick it out for a few years until the good parts came—with Arliss, in *The Man Who Played God*, and then with Leslie Howard in *Bondage* and *Petrified Forest*, and many times I thought, I must get back while they still remember me and do a play—funnily enough when I was doing *Dangerous*, playing Joyce Heath, a theater washout.

QT: Supposedly based on Jeanne Eagels. By the way, have you ever seen her performance in *The Letter*?

BD: Never have, no. They say she's great.

QT: She has this fantastic mounting-crescendo monologue right at the end. As you may know, in the original, Leslie gets away with the murder and there is no retribution, except that she and the husband must live with the knowledge that she loved the man she killed.

BD: "With all my heart I still love the man I killed."

QT: Yes, well, there's a convergence, or a near convergence—a matter of just a few years between that performance of middle-class colonial British hysteria and your Mildred, in *Of Human Bondage*, and the outburst that put you on the map: "*Oi* disgust *yew*! *Oi* disgust *yew*! You're nothing but a *cripple*, a *cripple*, a *cripple*!"

BD: Yes, well, of course poor Joyce didn't have that kind of stamina, did she, but then I got my first Oscar for *Dangerous*—presented by D.W. Griffith, you know—and well, you were a little less ready to leave Hollywood after you got an Oscar. And then, almost before I knew it, after the business with the strike I went on and

the lawsuit I brought, which I lost, but honorably, there came
Marked Woman and *Jezebel*, and the second Oscar, and I'd gotten
to love the work. I loved everything about it, the grind, the technical innovations that kept on coming—Technicolor, wide screen,
stereophonic sound. And even television. I love my work on television; I've given some of my best performances in only the last
few years, on television.

QT: And you have had good writers.

BD: The best.

QT: I was only wondering if, having played Ibsen, you were not—

BD: Hungry to play the great modern plays; I was.

QT: But you weren't sitting out here consoling yourself, were you now.

BD: No, I was not. You make a decision, and then you go to work. Of
course there was always the business of finding great stories, but it
was heartbreaking; the producers never read anything. I remember
one time I told Jack Warner I wanted to make the great Knut
Hamsun book *Victoria*, and he said, "No good, Helen Hayes has
already done it in New York."

QT: Favorite actresses you've never worked with?

BD: Hepburn, Celia Johnson, Anna Magnani, Jeanne Moreau.

QT: Favorite actors you've never worked with.

BD: Gielgud, Richardson, Alfred Lunt, Brando.

QT: I'm glad you mentioned Lunt; I saw him in *The Visit*.

BD: I saw him—them—in everything.

QT: She was pretty amazing.

BD: Amazing, yes—*he* was absolutely *great*.

QT: You saw them in everything; what's the best thing they did?

BD: Oh, *Idiot's Delight*, no question.

—◄○►—

QT: I mentioned yesterday we might do game time.

BD: Oh, yes, what happens to the characters. Sure.

QT: What happens to Margo Channing?

BD: Well, she certainly does *not* retire from the theater or give up her
life for him, the way the feminists—perfectly ridiculous; don't
know where they got that from.

QT: It's true all she says is she no longer has to—

BD: —play parts she's too old for because she has nothing else to do with her nights—exactly. Mankiewiecz has *told* us in his book he *loves* these theater women. No, no, Bill continues to direct her, and they have battles of course, but only in parts suited—

QT: And not, in all likelihood, in plays written by Lloyd Richards.

BD: No, that's right, I don't think so either. Others.

QT: Miller? Sherwood? Tennessee Williams, perhaps?

BD: Well, *I* did do—

QT: *The Night of the Iguana.*

BD: It was something of a nightmare—really—though I was good.

QT: You were *damn* good.

BD: Nevertheless, a nightmare—absolutely.

QT: We won't dwell. I was thinking of Margo as Big Momma.

BD: You mean, in *Cat on a Hot Tin Roof*; but that was only—when was that?

QT: Only four, five years later—still, for a part that good.

BD: True, she'd do it.

QT: And she wouldn't have to spend two hours in that girdle. [guffaw]

QT: Christine Radcliffe [the murderous pianist in *Deception*]. What do you think she got, ten, twenty years?

BD: Oh, I should think at least ten years.

QT: Will he wait for her?

BD: I'm not so sure . . . his career; he isn't the waiting type. Of course, with everything they've both gone through, it's just possible.

QT: Charlotte Vale [in *Now, Voyager*].

BD: Oh, she keeps her word—and, anyway, she's completely grown out of him; she realizes he isn't . . . no, she marries Doctor Jacquith, and carries on with his great work.

QT: Kit Marlowe [in *Old Acquaintance*].

BD: Oh, you know, the Pulitzer Prize, the what's-it-called, National Book Award.

QT: And Millie Drake? [same movie, Miriam Hopkins's character]

BD: Oh, more of the same, don't you think? Big best sellers, made into pictures.

QT: Like *Old Acquaintance.*

BD: Yes, exactly, a Bette Davis picture.

QT: Co-starring Miriam Hopkins?

BD: Oh, I suppose so. Look, remember what I told you about the

Hollywood Bowl sunrise service; you did it once—just once. It's
the same with Miriam—just once.

QT: Just so you could grab her and shake her like that.

BD: Oh, my *deah*, you should have *heard* her, you'd have thought—I
don't know *what*.

QT: She had been violated?

BD: Well, that is a *bit* . . . but you know, Miriam was an actress who
thought she was up for just about anything—so long as you didn't
muss her hair.

QT: I like the life-art complication; it sounds like Pirandello, no?

BD: Yes, but if you told Millie as much, she'd think you were talking
about a dress designer.

QT: Jane Hudson—off to Camarillo, you think?

BD: Can't think where else—hope they've been decent to her.

QT: A great favorite of mine, Susan Grieve [in *Winter Meeting*].

BD: Hmm. [long drag on cigarette] Well, again, the Pulitzer Prize, at
long last—the other one, I don't know; like to think so.

QT: If it's at long last, she could win the triple crown; they've got this
thing now called the National Book Critics Circle Award. John
Ashbery won the triple crown—sometimes also called the hat
trick—some years ago.

BD: Oh, well, that, then—yes, that would be nice for her, the triple
crown.

QT: They wouldn't have to give her the hat; she'd have one.

BD: Susan Grieve? Oh, yes, indeed she would—just one.

QT: Finally, what was the best thing ever in Old Hollywood?

BD: The best thing ever—oh, *oh*, the *canteen*, no question. Hedy
Lamarr selling kisses for a dollar, things happening twenty-four
hours a day. We had been gods and goddesses to those boys, and
suddenly there we were doing the jitterbug with them.

QT: Well, the goddesses anyway.

BD: [almost wistfully] Yes, the goddesses, anyway.

QT: By the way, when the Moscow Art Theater came to Yale in the
spring of 1965, after a week of being instructed by their demon-
strations, I asked what American actress they felt most approxi-
mated their level of aspiration and achievement. The answer, put
through translators, was instantaneous, and as understandable in
Russian as in English. "Bette Davis."

BD: I never heard that.
QT: I guess nobody ever told you, till now.
BD: Can you beat it?
QT: In my opinion, no, you can't.
BD: Be sure to put that in, will you?
QT: You don't even have to ask.

[QT packed up his apparatus, bidding goodbye to Miss Davis.]

Thank you, it was as great as I expected.
BD: I loved it—hope you have a good flight back, and say hello to your
mother for me, will you, and tell her I like her son very much.

[Duly done, his mother's reply: "Yes, well, Davis was always class."]

CHAPTER TWENTY-EIGHT

Star Soul

(PRELUDE TO A POSTSCRIPT)
RICHARD (SAULS) ROUILARD, 1949–1996

> *To turn as swimmers into cleanness leaping*
> *Glad from a world grown . . . filthy and demented.*
>
> (with apologies to Rupert Brooke,
> once the most beautiful corpse in England)

1416 North Havenhurst. Richard Rouilard, Carole Lombard and Who-Investigates:

Author approaches the Colonial House again, some years later, to be with the man he had learned to call his Philoctetes: Richard Rouilard, the rhapsode of Lost Angeles. He'd had Edmund Wilson's *The Wound and the Bow* in mind, in a perhaps not altogether whimsical connection to RR's famous collection of bow ties, assembled for a book he'd been planning on the history of the tuxedo, a subject that in his hands would, without question, have given Robert Pirsig's *Zen and the Art of Motorcycle Maintenance* a run for its stylish money. And he considered the dilemma of their disposal in bequests, and the haunting image of an inner man, stuck away somewhere, not in a beautiful white bedroom in the apartment once inhabited by Carole Lombard, there on the border of West Hollywood, and not at the Venice beachfront house either, but as if in a remote cove on the far side of Catalina, a place he had spoken of as a refuge, a place he and Bob (Cohen) had found one time on a sail from Malibu. In Sophocles,

Philoctetes, in giving away the bow, is brought back to be cured of the sup-
purating wound. There seemed always the chance that progress in the fight
against AIDS would be made in time to bring RR back to sustainable life.
It didn't turn out that way.

QT: We've all heard your story in bits and pieces.
RR: That's all my story is, hon, bits and pieces—audition pieces.
QT: You've been frequently tested?
RR: Frequently? Incessantly. Most recently by the *Los Angeles Times*.
    "You have everything we could want, but, frankly, we were hoping
    for a woman." "Well, I can do that!" Hired.
QT: The pieces fell together.
RR: Didn't they just. Well, falling together is the new done thing—
    falling apart together, like on some demented deconstructionist
    dis-assembly line. Yes, hon, the connoisseur vanguard is out there
    getting to know Death really close up and personal. Nevertheless,
    we won't dwell; we'll talk about abiding.
QT: I'm ending my history in 1985; we're quite a distance beyond that
    now.
RR: Says who?
QT: You have a point.
RR: If nothing else, one must believe one always had a point.
QT: One that seems clearly the principal function of your throwaway
    swank.
RR: God, I haven't heard "throwaway swank" in years!
QT: It was essentially '50s.
RR: Hmm, and I always wondered why I was not essentially '60s.
QT: Well, you've got "it." Where do you think it came from?
RR: I think when you've been kicked to the curb, you try to retaliate
    with something disarming.

[The attempt to get RR from the life resulted in a kind of mobile *abbozzo*.
The author said if he ever wrote a play about him, he would call him Dick
Wheeler, DW, as if he were actually behind the scenes of his own life, get-
ting Billy Bitzer to crank the camera on cue.]

QT: Tell me if you can about the secrets of queer Hollywood.
RR: The secrets of queer Hollywood. Remind me to tell you about the

time I looked into . . . You know what a *secret de Polchinelle* is?
Comes up somewhere in Agatha Christie; Poirot dwells on it. It's
a secret that, as he says, everyone is allowed to know. For this reason the people who do not know it never hear about it—for if
everyone thinks you know a thing, nobody tells you. I suppose
English linguistic philosophers would classify it as a paradox; the
French apparently don't bother; just life.

QT: Polchinelle is the English Punch, as in Punch and Judy.

RR: Exactly. There are a million Punches in queer Hollywood, and
the number grows exponentially, but still only one Judy. Do you
play bridge, by the way? I bet not.

QT: Yes, no, I don't.

RR: I just knew it. Do you play *any* card games?

QT: Casino.

RR: Really? What about pinochle?

QT: My father once taught me pinochle. I used to crawl out from the
bedroom into the all-night games he ran with his old high school
crowd from Regis.

RR: That's somewhere in Manhattan, isn't it?

QT: It is; I was very verbal.

RR: Well, out here, hon, bridge is the *obligatoire* homosexual card
game.

QT: Such things matter.

RR: Quite so. For example, let's say you're the declarer at a slam, and
if a certain finesse succeeds you'll make the contract. If your only
way to make the slam is to rely on the finesse, your chances are
about fifty-fifty, usually less. But in some deals you can do much
better than to stake the outcome on a finesse. A different line of
play might elevate your chances to three in four and in some cases
even higher, all the way to gotcha. It's this will to improve on
chances that distinguishes the real player from the also-ran.

QT: Sounds impressive, but, sadly, I don't get it.

RR: Well, why should you, when you've already played poker with
Davis? It's the same as Michael Maslansky telling you Joan was
deep; it amounts to an article of faith.

QT: A faith in what, exactly—celebrity?

RR: I love doing celebrity—working it, stalking it, making it nervous;
being a celebrity, no thank you. Hollywood celebrity in the '80s is

the La Brea Tar Pits full of soft-boiled shit. You either figure out a way of getting across it on a long plank—

QT: Like Venice in the winter, in high water.

RR: —or you fall in. Venice is another problem—drive-by shootings.

QT: I meant—

RR: I know.

QT: So celebrity's sickness isn't so much in its secrets as—what?

RR: Simply, celebrity is metastasis.

QT: The *Star Soul* scenario begins with the story of Baby Rouilard, illegitimate offspring of a French airline hostess, born with a raised eyebrow like a circumflex accent, adopted by the kindly Saulses and brought up in upper-middle-class luxe in the jungle of New Jersey's Italo-Jewish trucking mafia. A little background on the New Jersey of the period. Asbury Park, the Roller Derby: thuggish bruisers and diesel dykes on wheels, all of it as big a fix as wrestling. Atlantic City, the Miss America Pageant, which you've re-created in miniature out at the beach as Gaywatch. Adoptive mother's name?

RR: Norma.

QT: Adoptive father's?

RR: Unimportant.

QT: You frustrate somewhat my assumptions regarding the Orestes complex, except of course that in the case of the adopted male homosexual child, the adoptive father is really not an Agamemnon figure but an Aegisthus one, although it gets tricky with Hamlet, whom you resemble temperamentally far more than I myself—you'd certainly be more believable in the part, goddammit, despite the anguished claims I made for myself to myself back in the early '60s.

RR: You and every other homosexual in New York under thirty, apparently.

QT: Whatever of that. Hamlet does want to be fucked by Claudius; undoubtedly the uncle is the father in fantasy—in fact I've always thought Hamlet Father and Claudius ought to be played as twins, so that in the closet scenes Hamlet's howling about the two portraits—Hyperion to a satyr—could be played as deep irony.

RR: I'm a sucker for deep irony myself.

QT: So either the Orestes complex doesn't obtain or you are in fact a lesbian.

RR: Speaking of deep irony, I think I am.

QT: Check. In any event, it seems Baby does not quite work out, chez Sauls.

RR: Not quite? Quite not.

QT: A couple of teenage suicide attempts.

RR: Unsuccessful, but nonetheless instructive; one discovered a strong distaste for failure.

QT: Essential, as I see it, to your path work.

RR: My what?

QT: Your path work. How you took the PATH to New York, what and whom you found there, and the wisdom acquired in your being taken up, such as, for example, the mystical difference—or perhaps it was a lesson in gay alchemy—between French and English table settings.

RR: Essential information.

QT: First development turn, Sauls family attempts to disown Baby Richie, who hadn't quite worked out. Richie's response. Finding hidden in the library the double sets of books intended to fuck the IRS, he makes photocopies. Very serious threats in both directions. Cut to clip of John Garfield—

RR: *The* most gorgeous Jewish leading man, bar none, in Hollywood history.

QT: —in Rossen's *Body and Soul.* "What are you going to do, kill me? Everybody dies." So Richie Sauls takes back his name, Richard Rouilard, becoming, after many vicissitudes—

RR: The only queer in Los Angeles both baptized and bar mitzvahed.

QT: Question. Seeing you've been bar mitzvahed, what's your mitzvah? Apart from decorating that is.

RR: I'll get back to you. I do believe you mentioned vicissitudes.

◄○►

RR's narration (intercut with the odd obligatory curse): Law School in Houston. First meeting with Bob Cohen.

"I'd never been south—unless you consider the Fontainebleau in Miami Beach the South."

The Cohn-Rouilard marriage: from the first it was Richard and his powerful husband, Bunny and Bu. The San Francisco years, opening the first gay-advocacy law firm in the city, working with Harvey Milk. Harvey Milk's murder in 1978 and the decision to come to Los Angeles. The "visualization" of Bunny Mars, a woman he'd thought up in Houston (she's from Spring Branch) and fielding her as his alter ego, the wildly successful social columnist of the *Los Angeles Herald-Examiner*. RR, for the whole length of Bunny's tenure at the paper, would go along as her stringer to events, always conveying Miss Mars's regrets (IMPOSSIBLE VENIR MENSONGE SUIT), revealing her sudden indisposition due to ferocious migraines brought on by the combination of a choker sched and the dreadful pollen carried on the Santa Ana winds. And if there wasn't a Santa Ana, some terrible spores discovered that very morning in the air-conditioning system of her pre-war Elusive Drive apartment house—where at inty little dinners, she would dispense wit and wisdom to the chosen few, discoursing brilliantly on the Hollywood of the '40s and '50s, the shift from film noir and domestic "problem pictures" to the post-HUAC blockbuster, wide-screen Biblical epic period, larded with such tidbits of Los Angeles faggot lore as the discovery of the spectacular Guy Madison (freshly discharged from the Navy at the end of World War II) in the tea room at Venice Beach, and a whole catalogue of details concerning Rock Hudson, Tab Hunter ("Anybody wanna fuck a star?") and Jeffrey Hunter. This concluded with her ironic commentary on the immensely rich and successful Hollywood homosexual mafia: their toy boys picked up by trolling trolls out of the back alleys off Santa Monica Boulevard, bathed, buffed and nourished (rather like Dorothy and her friends when they finally get to the Emerald City), given new sets of gleaming Chiclet teeth, rigorous Beverly Hills haircuts, nice manicures and fetching little off-the-rack wardrobes from Old Navy and the Gap, and ferried from Central up to Malibu like so much delicatessen for consumption at the drugged orgies that have done so much to revive the glory days of Hollywood Babylon.

Finally, one night, RR, flatly excluded from a black tie event by the doorkeeper (as Miss Dean might say, "Th-th-they also s-serve . . .") at the Chandler Pavilion (most likely tipped as to Bunny's increasingly tenuous cover), he broke down. "But I *am* Miss Mars! I *am* Miss Mars!" The jig was up, and as RR put it, it was time to retire the rabbit.

Whereupon Bunny repaired to her Venice beach house, where, sitting on an exquisite apple-green sofa between twin copies of the Apollo Belvedere artfully painted in the most vivid glossy shades, the better to recall the actual look of classical Greek statuary, she undertook "community service." She had decided the Old Guard was right, "Nice women don't work;

nice women volunteer." Giving history lessons, particularly on the theme of American post-war cultural expansion as seen from the point of view of a Sun Belt matron who knows her onions and her jewelry, to a rapt audience of the young. Bunny's *Sunrise Semester* was held at noon. She wanted to set the record straight before she and the rest of Southern California sank into the Pacific Ocean.

While outside on the veranda, guests sit on the deck and do the Gay-watch routine, the musclemen parading by, holding up their rating cards, 1–10. One or two drift in to replenish their drinks and, sitting at Bunny's knee, are caught up in her little lesson.

There followed the two years in which RR edited the *Advocate*, turning it from a tawdry, primitive sex-and-dish rag into a sophisticated and powerful instrument of the queer political agenda.

In depicting RR as Dick Wheeler, in the docudrama he did come to write by way of an extended eulogy, the author pictures him this way at his desk, at the end of a typical hectic day, dictating to his assistant:

"Now concerning the queer American dream. If the dream of each and every straight American boy is to stand one day tall at a podium, outdoors, right at the top of a white marble staircase in the nation's capital, freezing his ass off in January, and declare, 'I do solemnly swear'—Sonia, don't look alarmed by me; I know what I'm saying. 'To discharge the office of'— et cetera. How does it go? I played it once in Perth Amboy. 'To uphold, protect, defend'—whatever. Yes, 'the Constitution of the United States, so help me God,' then so help me God, the dream of every red-blooded American queer is to stand indoors halfway up a townhouse staircase in a black taffeta Edith Head gown and bark, 'Fasten your seat belts, it's going to be a bumpy night!'

"Queer America is Margo Channing. The homosexual knows the answer to the question can chess be played without the queen? [pause] However [pause], all the same the Homintern must agree to realize that if you're out for America's true love—all the lip-smacking Presbyterian compassion the great heart of the nation can give—then you must be prepared to die, and die valiantly—remembering that great newspaper adage, 'If it bleeds it reads.' Nothing else will suffice. Got that? Good. [aside to the audience] Meanwhile, who says you can't take up one of history's most terrible human catastrophes—the AIDS plague—compare it to another—the Holocaust—and make of it the plot of a Hollywood melodrama called *He Learned to Love*, a remake of *Dark Victory*. You can—you heard it here in

the City of Angels, fountainhead of the Gay Liberation Movement—
thanks to Harry Hay and the Matachines—the jesters—and not to Ross
Hunter and his '50s Universal closet fags. [riffles through copy]

"All right. Now get this. About those other two. Out them both. Dish her
but kill him—and be *vish*. You can do it darling—think pink triangle. Step
on his face. Leave fucking Bruno Magli heel prints, darling, no jury will con-
vict you. [to the audience] And remember, *Vorstellung* is performance. [looks
at copy and photos]

"Right. Blow that up, downsize that and get Liz Smith on the phone—
and, Sonia darling, if it's not too much trouble to remind the dry cleaners
to expedite my black tie? Then call the cocktail at AIDS Project Los
Angeles and tell them I'm running a West Hollywood minute late. [to the
audience] Listen, the trick of attendance at lots of Hollywood parties is simply to remember that there's always a kitchen door."

◄○►

Concerning Chad—archetypical L. A. gayboy-on-the-make and his notorious tapes:

"I've heard of them. I met him once, or it it wasn't him, then another.
No, it was him. He seemed to think he was giving me an interview; he
wasn't. I took him to the Rose for lunch and told him he should lay off the
mushrooms for a while, stop being drilled by handlers who read Burroughs
and William Gibson and John le Carré, and start drinking black coffee and
reading Dennis Cooper by himself.

"I mean, darling, this is a boy who thinks he's a telepath because he
knows the Häagen-Dazs vanilla fudge ripple is really cold in the freezer
compartment, who thinks *chicanery* means some kind of sadomasochistic
sexual practice. You begin to realize if he sticks around those Camp queens
long enough he'll be calling the doorway the *penetralium*.

"One thing he does have, however, that is scary—absolutely uncanny.
Those monologues, complete with relative and subordinate clauses. Didn't
you wonder?"

"Well, I made a remark about the French Ventriloquist, but he didn't
get it."

"The Chads don't get anything, that's the thing. This one you just came
from will say one of two things or maybe both, if you brought the cocaine:
that he's channeling dead men who adored him on the astral; that when he

was in Washington . . . et cetera. When he was in Washington, indeed—what for, the Reagan inaugural? And yet maybe he was—maybe some crazed Pasadena pedophile took him along as his fucking son, no pun intended. And when he was there they put a transplant—right?—in his sinus cavity or somewhere convenient, and so every time he opens his mouth he is unwittingly entrapping some derelict loose canon. What goes around comes around, what gives gets, meaning the apparatus. Then he chills out, and it's as if he thinks he knows what he's saying, only of course by now he's the same as all those boys who came back from Saigon in the '70s, where they took so many drugs at their desks that when the commanding officer would come into the room, and they'd jump up and salute, and he'd say, 'As you were, men,' they couldn't remember!

"Oh, well, hooray for Hollywood: from Edgar Bergen and Charlie McCarthy to this in two quick generations."

"But how can any of it be possible?"

"I don't know; there's a theory that some of them, probably Scientology dropouts, when drugged in a certain way and plugged into some equivalent of Learn While You Sleep tapes. Or else they find photographic memory types. I never used to believe they actually existed until I got to law school. Frightening. Thank God not one of them ever seems to get elected to high office. And I've seen it out here a lot—although not where it might do some good, in actors, but in writers, no less, writers on contract, who can commit any old piece of scripted shit to memory in nothing flat, and rehash it over a weekend to keep the studio wolf from the door. Well, Chad would seem to have it, plus which he must be a prize example of a successful Clear, in the sense of absolute tabula rasa with no biography of his own at all, who can regurgitate virtually anything they siphon into his brain."

"Maybe there is mind control out here, and the story that there aren't any minds to control is a bluff."

"It makes him seem most improbably learned."

"And therefore oh so appealing to all these brutally ugly compulsive masturbator theoreticians and semantic studies queers being churned out of UCLA faster than Fox used to turn out starlets.

"The thing is you never know in what combinations these little monsters are going to express themselves on any one particular occasion. Yet they have no guile, no Eve Harrington characteristics at all. You really ought to get this one down on videotape, as in *Sex, Lies and.* In a way it's like talking to a mynah bird. What the little bird tells you isn't the news or even disinformation, it's more like old jingles from radio, like 'Eat too much, drink too much? Take Brioschi anti-acid' or 'My beer is Rheingold the dry beer, think of Rheingold whenever you buy beer.' Stunningly weird.

"You know what we really ought to do, instead of cooking our queer rewrite of *All That Heaven Allows*. We ought to get that kid and do a spin on *My Own Private Idaho*—call it, let's see—yes, how about *They Own My Privates: I'm a Homo*. Happy ending, of course, everybody reconciled, as the sun sets over Sandy Gallen's Malibu beach house.

"But what should we really be talking about? Power? The Los Angeles inferiority complex, the Big One, the critical importance of existential decorating, why stars always got off the train at Pasadena? About Pasadena today and Republican fags, political reality in America in relation to show business?

"About Judy Garland, and what the gay movement is doing two decades after Stonewall—*les événements de soixante-neuf*—to erase her memory through the slavish adoration of her troubled daughter. About the difference between the Santa Monica Boulevard Halloween parade, the Hollywood Boulevard Halloween parade and the Greenwich Village Halloween parade? About Christmas in Palm Springs and The Bu? About Raymond Chandler misty nights and old-style crime in Hollywood and how nowadays everything that happens in the so-called real world is handled as a sequence first and only later (after the editing) as an event, like the Menendez brothers, like O.J.

"I did like that kid's little rap about American porn, because we were overwhelmed by Jack Deveau and Joe Gage and Wakefield Poole, all the art-film pornographers, so I suppose I sound pretentious. When I first arrived, I used to go to these meetings down in basement of that Old Dress Extras Club—little did they suspect—where some gnome the color of the sand on Santa Monica Beach would lecture on subjects like The Redefinition of Open Space in the Films of Gorton Hall, Existential Metaphysics and the Reverse Angle in Jack Deveau's *Left Handed*, Dialectical Montage in Arthur Bressan's *Pleasure Beach* (starring the deeply tragic Johnny Dawes, the Tom Hanks of queer pornography). How Bressan's *Forbidden Letters*, starring the Prince of Tides, Richard Locke, was intended to enforce the idea of predestination, whereas mise-en-scène in the Joe Gage *Hank* trilogy and especially later in the second and definitive triad of *Heatstroke*, *Closed Set* and *Handsome*, which, with its infernal-erotic night scenic, highway neon, dark trees/steaming manhole aesthetic, was the real masterpiece, was intended to enforce the idea of the free will.

"He said Richard Locke was so gifted he could play either condition, top or bottom, with equal conviction. He called Joe Gage a disciple of both Douglas Sirk and Edgar G. Ulmer, of both Jack Kerouac and Boyd McDonald—but we knew that.

"Finally, lauding Sam Gage as the Ross Hunter of the movement, the Gage men—all representations of retribution for the victims of the Universal purge of the '50s—and the high art cinematographers Richard Youngblood and Russell Ballard, who were to Gage what Russel Metty had been to Sirk, he defined for history the culmination of gay art porn before the onset of videotape, on which all sex is lies. The most accomplished abstract Ophulsian film in the genre he found to be *Closed Set*, and the apotheosis of everything the greatest single sequence in the genre: the New York City sequence of *Handsome*, in which the visual/verbal *Grosse Fugue* Gage brings off—including the single most extravagant and ecstatic gesture in the history of such endeavor, the descent of the monolithic slab from Kubrick's *2001*, transformed into The Cosmic Glory Hole—an instance of Camp gestural definition equal to any other ever made in whatever medium: containing virtually every seminal homosexual fantasy extant and culminating in the sacramental phallic aspersion blessing the onscreen sealed-with-a-kiss nuptials of Roy Garrett and J.D. Slater, establishing Gage once and for all, insofar as all art aspires to the condition of music, as the Beethoven of queer porn.

"Whereupon the short-lived Joe Gage aesthetic gives way in the middle '80s to William Higgins, thence to videotape, and it's all over. It was some performance. I've never seen or heard of the speaker again."

"But he was taped."

"Oh, yes."

(Did Richard Locke really go out into the desert, finally, and find enlightenment? Anyway, he's dead now, as is Eric Ryan who used to skate along the esplanade at Venice, where Richard Rouilard spent his weekend for a little while more.

Richard Locke, the Gage Men, Richard Rouilard, all gone. Joe Gage alive and kicking.)

QT: To paraphrase Anna Russell and Randy Shilts, what did the boys in the band play on? And tell me why his "Patient Zero" fable was so destructive to queer politics.

RR: Some snowy night—

QT: In front of the fire. I do know you edited Shilts at the *Advocate*; what would you say now that he's gone home?

RR: [directly into the camera] I said I'd outlive you, Randy, if it was the last thing I did.

QT: Martin Duberman, it is said, is generally disinclined to experience life west of the Hudson. What is he missing?

RR: A metaphysical question. Like who really got what they wanted out on Fire Island. And if almost nobody got what they wanted on Fire Island, that truth is nothing compared to today's air-ferry to South Beach. Rich old queens in white shantung pajamas, silver lamé beach clogs and Panama hats to protect the face from the lacerations of the cruel carcinogenic sun that once they worshipped as freely and as wantonly in their daring white sharkskin Jantzens as now do the luscious carefree young they've come to ogle—cunning and frisky as they are in their sailor tops, grass skirts and Ray-Bans.

　　Nice manners people have in burdensome times. And they all want ladies' rosewood kneehole desks and Chinese Chippendale foot stools. Don't ask me, I tell them, ask Chuck Pollock. Privately, I wonder what on earth for, when these ladies—all fat ladies, darling, who don't even sing, so with them it's never over. Give them a Chinese Chippendale foot stool, they'd sit on it, and they could hardly get one fat knee in the ladies' kneehole hole, never mind two. As pieces of furniture, they do make nice little cubbyholes for dogs to snuggle up in, that I grant you—the rosewood desks, I mean.

QT: My version of that is this. You can now catch the Hampton Jitney on the corner of Queer and Lonely, not far from the boarded-up Adonis Theater, but next to nobody ever gets a round-trip ticket; most board with a single bag, and although they may promise, in the words of the '40s movies, to *send for my things*, they never do.

RR: Under the circumstances, there are limits to the things people may wish to understand about themselves.

RT: What circumstances are those?

RR: In California, any and all circumstances. The viscosity of quicksand increases with shearing. Rate times time equals distance is not a universal law—there are conditions under which it doesn't apply.

RT: Marcel Proust said something like that.

RR: Ah, yes, Marcel Proust. Griefs, at the moment when they change

into ideas, lose some of their power to injure our hearts. He said
that too. He said a lot, when you come to think of it.

As for me, I have stood around and walked around and fucked
around and drunk and drugged around with ex-con (you know,
from the Big House) transvestite hookers on West Street and
rough trade in the trucks, and all day every day all they were saying was, "Fuck them!"—by whom they meant what it has become
convenient to call The Establishment (but they wouldn't have gotten—and didn't get—so fancy; all they said was *them*). And if
you had asked any of them (the them I knew, not *them*, right?) if
they harbored in their waterfront minds the slightest idea that *they*
would give a dead rat's ass or lift a fat fucking finger—so much as
a polished, diamond-ringed pinky—to help them (us) in any kind
of mortal crisis, they would have honestly laughed in your face and
said, "What are you, fucking crazy?" So, I'm sorry, but none of
this rhetoric about how they want us dead makes any real sense.
Yes, they want us dead. You want to make something of it, other
than reality? You want to make something of it it isn't—like
morality?

We hold this truth to be self-evident: it is not sufficient that the
state of affairs novelty's promoters promote should be simply better than the state of affairs which preceded it; it must be manifestly
sufficiently better to make up for the evils of the transition.

What I'm getting at is, after you have adopted the refusal to
buy into the paranoid stance (above), then do act as if everything
outlined in that stance were the absolute truth. Then and only then
are you an effective activist or politician, and then and only then
will you avoid—escape, really—being consumed by your role.

I mean those very few—and unless I'm completely crazy, they
are a little on the increase each year as the AIDS crisis goes on—
nice women who never worked but regularly volunteered. Nuns.
Priests even. And cops who understand the existential buddy
thing. And fireman who understand it better.

There is a certain honesty in gay identity politics. Once gay
identity faced itself and realized that it is both ontologically meaningless and epistemologically spurious, there was nothing else for it
to do but turn political—to some purpose, if you take Lambda
Legal Defense into account.

On the similarities between Italian and Jewish men:

RR: It is very hard to find one who is absolutely homosexual, and not
       interested at all in women sexually. It is also a commonplace that
       nearly every Italian man is available, at least to every other Italian
       man—and then there is the Mafia penchant for drag queens. It is
       obvious that in the clinical terms now operating, nearly the totality
       of Italian men have been sexually abused by their mothers: the
       prevalence of phallic worship in the Mediterranean, et cetera. So
       in Italy, fundamentally nobody really gives a shit about homosex-
       ual behavior, but the Dantesque proscription of sodomy is very
       seriously upheld. This is hypocrisy, yes, but it is something obvi-
       ously fundamental to the Latin psyche.

           As for the French, I don't know, but it is very well documented
       that Louis XIV was as an infant exposed and masturbated by
       court ladies and gentlemen too, and look what he grew up to be.
       Also, when Louis Malle made *Murmur of the Heart* and cast Lea
       Masari, a beautiful Italian woman, as a character who intiates her
       shy teenage son into sex, nobody objected for a minute. What
       would happen now?

           Serve us all better to plug in and amp up, if you ask me. And
       by the way, how can we read the lapping waves, closely or other-
       wise from this side of the double dune—where we belong?

           One has earned one's place out of the sun—and a consider-
       ably safer one it is too, something which I for one always seem to
       have known. One is no longer wildly distracted by the future;
       one's attention is, along with one's disbelief, simply more evenly
       suspended.

           I have no wish to be remembered, thank you, much less
       mythologized as something that never happened but was always
       so. Merely to be recognized as an authentic presence in penetrable
       space, in an authentic time frame—put up with by those con-
       cerned, few as they are.

QT: Edmund Burke said manners are more important than laws.
       "Upon them in a great manner, laws depend. The law touches us
       but here and now, and now and then . . ."

RR: [takes a long drag on his cigarette] The law hasn't touched me in
       years, I'm happy to say.

QT: Shall I say, don't press your luck?

RR: I'm happy to say I never press anything—it's another thing I haven't done in years.

Remember Lionel Trilling? Jewish. Hated being. He said of somebody, "We expect of him that he will involve us in the enjoyment of moral activity through the medium of a lively awareness of manners, that he will delight us by touching on high matters in the natural course of gossip."

May I cause no harm, and leave music and beauty behind when I return to Forever.

Liberals may have fancied fags as part of their own agenda, but if red is at the far left of the spectrum, surely violet is at the other end—was there ever really a left-wing queen? It just isn't in the job description.

What "the unexamined life is not worth living" has come to mean for queers is an exaggerated version of what it has come to mean for everybody else. That unless you are under some small degree of public surveillance (the opposite of what the philosophers had in mind), unless, in the culture of self-promotion as heavy industry, you make it, at the very least, into the office newsletter, unless you have a cause of any kind at all that can be publicized (for the common good, supposedly) then your life is not worth living. And the most pathetic of all such "unexamined" lives is, of course, the anonymous one. To do any good at all—or even to involve oneself in an erotic enterprise of whatever degree of aesthetic value—that is not available to a camera or recording device of some kind, or cannot be reported on the Internet, is, well, pointless—even subversive.

It has as a consequence been said of us, by queer theorists and historians of the era, that we embodied within ourselves and created in others a kind of transcendent yearning for the possibility of redemptive change of a highly suspect sort—wielding an assumption as a predicate, wish-fulfilling "as if" into "so that." Yet no *mirabilis* cornerstone myth can ever take without the presto-change-o suspension of time and history, and what could we do? Religion had offered for our inspection the gift of the spirit as the promise of a future life—not as a present essence and source of happiness, but on the installment plan, as a vague deposit to be protected by moral behavior of a stringent kind.

Although to be scrupulously fair, it must be admitted that to replace a world that does not understand you with the model of a world you do not understand, really, is a poor if compelling advance, all told.

One realizes one's reached a certain plateau in life when the answer to the question "What do you do in bed?" becomes "I eat, sleep, read and watch television."

I have a new tape. James Dean as John the Beloved Disciple in *Father Peyton's Family Hour*, so that you can stub out your cigarette on him, the way he used to ask johns to do—an enactment in the modern age of the habitude of St. Sebastian. Was he the end or was he not?

Entirely happy. Who said perhaps we feel like that when we die and become a part of something entire, whether it is sun and air, or goodness and knowledge?

QT: I don't know— Schopenhauer?

RR: Schopenhauer or John Latouche. Well, I sometimes feel truth and youth and beauty are the last things I want to think about—then it occurs to me they probably will be just that.

When young, all living things are passionate, and their passionate hope of mastering the world is what makes them attractive; especially to predators.

I don't in fairness see what more there is we can ask of life. Except of course hair color that's continually true, uniformly beautiful and long lasting. *Coloración completa.*

Sooner or later—and we do run out of time—every career homosexual reaches zero point. The hard heavy years have worked us over, and comes the moment of sudden loathing; the season of storified sorrow—in which the bright obvious stands motionless in the cold shallows . . . at riptide. [pause]

Then almost immediately you are Joan Crawford striding despairingly in sequins into suicidal water. Where nobody is allowed in. When I'm there, but—nobody sees me in that condition. Nor do I emerge until I am fucking ready to be looked at.

And in case you think this thing overtakes you at a moment when you are either actually being rejected or in a moment, such as on the shrink's couch, where you are paying money to re-enact some primal rejection, *wrong.* It's never then. When it attacks you is in the middle of the night—and not in the weeks after your diagnosis, when you wake up screaming or in night sweats. By then the scene hasn't the shame to further complicate your woes by co-opting the symptoms of actual dissolution—and anyway you've got your support group, your railing, and you are not allowed to have the scene. You don't go there.

But of course you don't have to, and you know that. And because the memory of it is so indelible . . . you take a pill. But this is how it happens.

One night—no point in overdoing . . . just say it's Christmas Eve, after midnight. The presents are all unwrapped; you're in bed; the dishwasher has stopped; all is calm, all is bright. Or better: you are holy/all is clear/they are loved/it is perfect. A full moon has come up, and, yes, when you looked up at dinner—and just before, when you turned around in bed—there he was, so you're not just something with a French provincial office, a box full of clippings and a white telephone with what used to be a Crestview number. That's gay—but right then, right there in the stillness, not a creature stirring, the rather too emphatic scent of Caleche in the air, it hits you. You're still not a woman—and there's no trick will ever make you one.

Next thing you know, you're sitting under the tree with all the wrapping paper—maybe it's been neatly folded, maybe it's just crumpled up all over the place—and you've picked up the cashmere sweater—yes, Versace—and you're holding it to your cheek. You haven't put the tree back on, but moonlight is streaming in off the patio, hitting the tinsel, reflecting off the ornaments, and as you look at them you see the pool reflected, and when you turn and look out the french windows, there in the silvery light . . . and no matter what, you're still not a woman.

You know, it's really very funny about us, if you want to think about it. For years, after they stopped clapping us *tout court* in irons and walling us up, when they started getting compassionate, they said "This is a sickness, you must get over it; we can help you get over it. Now put on these electrodes . . . now swallow this medication." Fade-out, fade-in, the liberators have come, have seen, have in some measure conquered—so they're nearly all dying; that's the price of glory. And now what's happening? We who remain have begun to reassess the situation, offering fresh, new advice to the young homosexual, And what is that advice? "Look, darlings, it's really no big deal any longer, being homosexual; get over it." Now what exactly do we call *that*? Tell me.

Scene Sketches from the Docudrama
(Written on the Red-Eye Back to New York)

SCENE: DICK WHEELER, BETTE DAVIS, haunted and haunting at 1416 North Havenhurst.

DW (to the audience)

I get it now—it's talk-show format. (*nods*) Can do. (*to BD*) I wanted to be with you in *What Ever Happened to Baby Jane?*, sitting down to tea just to hear you tell me "Daddy always said you can lose everything else, but you can't lose your talent!"

BD

I detest cheap sentiment.

DW (wistfully)

Do you? I used to—it was smart to. Then I got political, and was forced to recognize the salient fact that cheap sentiment, like cheap scent, is the bottom line of the will of the people. It's their snakebite nostrum.

"But you can't lose your talent." How I wanted to die believing that.

BD

The law touches us now and then . . .

DW

Laws? Fuck laws. Phyllis Dietrichson had the right idea—throw all the blankets off the bitch, open the windows wide: it's the only way to get what you want—to get what you have got to have if you're going to be fabulous. (*to BD*) You must agree with me, you were fabulous.

BD

Absolutely. I always said it. Fuck 'em.

DW

Actually, you only said it once, onscreen. In *Bunny O'Hare*.

I always said fuck 'em. I said, "I came into this world surrounded by vicious women, I'll exit with the Three Fates working overtime." (*to BD*) Like you as Leslie Crosbie, in *The Letter*, with that obsessive lacework.

BD

Her bridal veil—made for the wedding with Death.

DW

Stitching my panel for the AIDS quilt. (*calls to the Fates*) In shot silk, while you're at it. Homosexuality: just another vibrant thread in the fabric of life? Not quite.

(*reflecting*) One had a certain bizarre allure, it's true. As an admonition—a token of God's own unmitigated gall. (*pause*)

I'd be interested in meeting up with God.

If only to ask the following question: (*smiling*)

While I have you—why did you give us AIDS, that snaking, coiling, constricting, suffocating . . . just for your own goof? Or is this the way you wish to show the world that faggots have become your chosen people? (*pause*)

They told me when they came and got me from the orphanage, I had a rattle.

BD

All babies get rattles—it's what you give them.

DW

I thought I was born with one—for, like the ancient Athenians whose aesthetic I revere, particularly their penchant for the Dionysian, I was, I am, devoted to snakes.

They rear up too in Euripides's *Ion*, son of the sun god—an early take on the story of my life—in which, some Hermes—as in ties and scarfs and cologne—betook himself to some far yonder laurel close to watch and wait for me to turn up—in Laurel Canyon—which I did, worshiping my absent father in sun plays.

BD

We gave B.D. a rattle—speaking of snakes!

DW

Bette, they've already started accusing me of lack of depth! I had nearly limitless power—if on a single vector. Lack of depth, me!

BD

It's exactly what happened to me, my deah.

DW (mournfully)

I took too many drugs in the '70s.

BD (nods)

I drank—far too much—and it wasn't Calistoga water.

DW

Thanks. (*to BD*) I'm a heap of chemically treated old bones, like Piltdown Man.

BD

I know exactly what you mean. First they hacked me to bits, then the chemicals—and radiation! *Microwaved* like something in a fast food restaurant on Santa Monica Boulevard!

DW

This building they made us live in was no help either. Repainting it green and white; it looks like a six-story Chasens! Ripping out the historic privet was one thing—but the fretted lanterns, the tecoma bushes and the mariposa were the last straw!

BD

I said, "This is one of the old ones they haven't torn down yet. Of course they haven't torn me down yet either." Nancy Culp persuaded me to move in—said I'd be happy here.

DW

I should never have been persuaded to leave Whitley Heights—or later the savage splendors of Laurel Canyon. Just as I had once belonged in the penthouse on Horatio Street, looking across and down at my origins in hideous fucking New Jersey, I belonged up there on Mount Olympus with the

Greeks and the Birth of Tragedy—growing into my golden years surrounded, as Cukor was, but with brainier specimens—to whom I would
show all your pictures, Bette, over and over. Your pictures do not wear out.
Faggots, you know, tended to be family outcasts—and especially with
AIDS, before people realized they could get free publicity—TV, the Quilt,
all that—for their compassion. I taught them to use their imaginations, I put
to them the fearful question:

> What is to become of imagination
> When there is nothing left to pretend to be?

BD

We were like gods and goddesses to the audiences. I wore the red dress to
the Olympus Ball in *Jezebel*—and the same one fifty years later on the
Johnny Carson show, under the very leopard coat Farney gave me the very
day he dropped dead on Wilshire Boulevard.

DW

And here we are together at the end of *Jezebel*, in the plague wagon.

BD (smokes)

Of course, Ruthie insisted we should never have left Laguna.

DW

I should have stayed in Venice. The beach! The sun . . . the surf . . . the
sleaze . . . the works! The house done in what one critic called *une efflo-
rescence confusé*. "Fuck you," I said, "I am anything but confused—this
decor is high *Louis Seized*." All lost! On my last birthday, on a "Gay-
watch" sail out to the Bu—to have yet another look at what many of us, necessarily, had to go on missing, we put a message—remember message plays,
Bette?

BD

Watch on the Rhine. I demanded the picture. The wife's a secondary part,
they said.

DW

We put one in a bottle—off Malibu.

BD

There are no secondary parts in wartime, I said. Terrific picture.

DW

I rest my case. Give the people what they want—

BD (guffaws)

You know they said that at Harry Cohn's funeral!

DW

I meant it as a *kinna hurra*. (*pause*) They want my bow tie collection—to auction for AIDS charity—plus the notes for the book on the tuxedo, a sort of "Zen and the Art of Black Tie Party Going." Funny, when I started the collection, they said "a black bow tie is a black bow tie," but I declared once a black bow tie has been tied around a man's collar—one beautiful, expensive snake becomes another beautiful—then taken out around his neck into the night and tugged when it droops, then brought back at dawn, untied, removed and examined, there is already in it a pattern as distinct as a snowflake. Not that my men had much to do with driven snow—hardly a race of transparent receptacles for transcendent doctrine. I went for the standard type of homewrecker, six foot six . . . in two directions, tall, dark, and not too deliberate: the wide-eyed lumberjack dreamboat full of muted thunder. I liked rumpling their already-rumpled hair. (*pause*) White ties too and formals of different shades from all the years of party-party. We danced, as David danced before the Ark and prophesied.

After all that, when the plague started, the ties became my quilt. My husband's idea was to cremate me on Venice Beach in black tie with the collection: in the other world, I'd have what-to-wear to parties and meet all those men again. As I lay dying, I got spiritual, uncluttered, for a man who revolves, escapes from space. Even so, the *kinna hurra* didn't—is it true the good die young?

BD

The good, both young and old, die unpublicized.

DW (lying down as if on the couch)

Who am I? Where do I come from? What do I want? Where am I going?

Remember death. What is life to me without me? Where is the light? (*gets up*) Let's face it, even before AIDS we were a line company, our heads all full of bang-bang. (*he lights two cigarettes, à la* Now, Voyager, *hands one to BD*)

The past is about to happen. The future, long since settled, now darkens it with its wings. And I have no problem with trivial information acquisition. Anyway, why sort out the signal from the noise?

BD

Exactly. You're so bright. (*blows smoke*)
No question. You know, you ought to write a play.

DW

Dictated from the astral!
You know, when I planned my funeral, on the boat off Malibu, I said, "After all the money spent in the last two years keeping me fabulously alive, such very expensive ashes should not be treated like dirt." People said the minute the ashes hit the water, they would reconstitute as Captain Homo, ready to fight for truth, justice, the American way and the best table at Chinois.

(*he sniffs at something in the air*) Do you smell that? That's Carole Lombard. This was her apartment. She's been in to see me a lot since I restored the decor the way I thought she'd like it.

And now these echo-visions—all the shit I told the shrink.

BD

I never told a shrink anything!

DW

You told Howard Hughes everything; Your second husband, Farney, taped it all—the reason he got his. Your lover had him zapped on Wilshire Boulevard.

BD

He was a son of a bitch—but I loved him.

DW

If I had a shrink like you—as Charlotte Vale.

BD (to the audience)

He does not much exaggerate, I was good.

DW

The trouble is I'm more Charlotte Vale myself. Mother dropped dead, just like that. I was an ugly duckling . . . et cetera.

BD

Et cetera at fifty bucks an hour.

DW

Fifty? Two hundred—and it's forty minutes. Four-O.

In tribute to the culture I leave behind, I want to produce *Intolerance*. On the astral. "A Sun Play of the Ages" The four stories will be (*to Bette*) the story I tell you, the story you tell me, the story I tell me and the story you tell you.

BD

Griffith presented me with my first Oscar. *Dangerous*.

DW (as the phone rings)

My part was the Rhapsode of Los Angeles. (*into phone*) Who? (*pause*) Are we close? (*pause*) Sonia, would you just tell them either that I'm in prayer and meditation or else that I'm in hair and wardrobe? I'll leave it up to you. (*pause: to BD*) Who says you can't get good help?

BD

Of course you can—

DW & BD (together)

Just pay the fucking money!

BD

We were on hundreds—thousands—of screens at once all over the world— every place where pictures—

DW

And have I still got my talent?

BD (turns to DW, solicitously)

Of course you still have your talent—no question. Once you're a star, you don't stop being a star.

DW

Then I'm happy. (*thinks*) We'll take a meeting. Bette, you'll be Lillian Gish, all right? "Out of the cradle endlessly rocking."

BD

Don't talk to me about Gish. She was a pain in the ass. A great actress, no question—I give her full credit.

DW

You will be my psychopomp.

BD (smoking)

Hah! Two things Gary always said about me. "You're pompous, and you're psychotic."

[The cradle-casket is brought out.]

DW

What is this—the casket scene from *The Duchess of Malfi*? That playwright has been dead for three hundred years.

BD

All playwrights should be dead for three hundred years!

DW

Bette, when asked in *Now, Voyager* if you believed in the hereafter, you said you'd like to think there was a chance for such happiness to last. I feel that now.

BD

And what such happiness did you have in mind?

DW

This one. Planning . . . producing! Now I'm free of my survivors. They can take my bow ties and my manuscript too. I got them—the ties—in the first place for being—they said loyal. And as for reflection on the social wrong that art-language does to those irrevocably denied the privilege of culture . . . fuck it. (*smiles*)

[The bed becomes a boat, with the sheets as sails, a boat bound for Catalina.]

And don't forget. Bette, you're coming with me.

[BLACKOUT]

While You Were Out

(THE BOOK TALKS BACK)

> "—I replay the scenes
> from that movie The Past, starring not
> Mr X playing opposite myself
>   but Endymion,
> Narcissus, Patroclus, all the fellows
> I have welcomed to the tiny duchy
>   of my bed—the world's
> only country entirely covered by
> its flag."
>
> —Richard Howard, "'Man Who Beat Up
> Homosexuals Reported to Have AIDS'"
>
> "Not everyone was a cardinal at the seafood barbecue, but nobody brought
> his wife."
> —Peter Robb, M

From the author's diary:
　　Wrote first act flying back. Landed, slept, woke up, called Donald.
　　"Donald."

"Jimmy, welcome back, sweetness—been wondering about you. You know, from the way your bags were packed, it looked like you were planning on staying for a long time."

"I might have, in another life; but you know Los Angeles."

"Indeed I do, and love it: so many people loitering about, all that lunching in public."

"Listen, there was this message on the machine from Stuart Byron; did I know where Aubrey was. Is there some new crisis?"

"Once a *Variety* stringer, always a *Variety*. It's the weatherman."

"The weatherman."

"That's what I said, bub. While you were occupied out there on the coast—"

"Lunching in public."

"Lunching in public. So Stuart calls announcing he's in love with a weatherman—in Boston. Naturally, I thought: that Stuart, now a chic radical fairy, going and digging up the Last Weatherman. I simply assumed some leftover radical, and said to myself, Stuart is so archaic, and whoever knew any of the Weathermen were queer . . . but of course he was in love with a *weath-er*-man, a meteorologist! Jimmy, have you *written* anything?"

"The first act of a play, on the flight home."

"A play set in an airplane. What about, a bumpy night?"

"No, no, the flight was smooth. I wrote the first act on the flight, in my seat. It's about Richard Rouilard and Bette Davis, eloping together in the afterlife."

"Darling, you didn't tell me your friend had died. I'm sorry."

"Oh, he didn't, he hasn't. It's only an idea I had."

"Really. Well, I must say you are beginning to exhibit the industrious energy of a Clyde Fitch, but tell me this, dear—and I don't mean to pry—but you haven't by chance been thinking of writing one—"

"About you, in the afterlife? Not the remotest chance. As a matter of fact, if it were going to be about us—"

"You call it *Old Acquaintance*. I am relieved. You in the Miriam Hopkins role, I presume."

"Absolutely. Meanwhile, Richard [Corliss, editor-in-chief of *Film Comment*] has asked me to do a history of queer pornography from the Park-Miller days up to last week—on celluloid. I'd been lamenting the adoption of videotape. But you know, the material is pretty impalpable—in words."

"Words of more than two syllables, yes indeed."

"Donald, do you remember my Old Queer on the park bench?"

"Jimmy dear, the woods are full of one-night sensations. You mean, I take it, your archetype."

"Yes, you remember, you played him once."

"In Wilkes-Barre—will I ever forget it. How does it—"

"You played it in a reading, dear, in Westbeth. My plays, as you well know, are rather like television, nothing but auditions. How does it go? The Old Queer Fuck sits on the park bench and tells stories. Remember, somebody said it was very like *Zoo Story*."

"And you were cut to the quick; it was nothing whatever—"

"Nothing whatever—although since that dear time *whatever* has come to—"

"Mean whatever. I know, dear, but just think what happened to *weatherman*."

"You are a spiritual work of mercy."

—◦—

The Return of the Old Queer Fuck on the Park Bench:

Just back from California, that merry old Land of Oz just east of the Astral, the author wonders, has flying so high downwind through the American night's four black spacious skies in a state of such high exhilaration that he was for over five hours enabled to view with the equanimity essential to the artist's task the deaths of others, two others in particular, Bette Davis and Richard Rouilard, met some years apart but inseparable in his mind with the Colonial House (as it was when the façade was cream white trimmed in robin's-egg blue), have him confusing the gift of the exalted state of first draft composition with the intoxicating if finally terrible gift of prophecy? He lay back and took a nap.

He dreamed for an interval about his eleven quick minutes of New York Fame. Nothing to do with a book, merely the four-week CBS (Studio 54) *College Bowl* run in May of '62. The parties at the Waldorf, the Camp cavortings backstage, which really had amused the camera operators: Author striding onto the set for rehearsal, in manly-Dietrich (Marlene, not Fischer-Dieskau) silk dressing gown drag, white scarf flowing, declaring, "Max, that key light . . ."

About being saluted on the opera line, and backstage by singers; being recognized on the New York streets; hearing himself discussed from the next booth at the Algonquin Bar, really a very *It Should Happen to You* kind of fame. This was made the more fatally blinding by the graduation-year crisis in a searing four-year passion, one kindled in the fall of '58, nourished through four entire opera seasons, between himself and the quite heterosexual Other, during which a mutual love of the singing of Jussi Björling, a

shared passion for J.S. Bach, for jazz, and for (him watching *him*) shooting pool, cemented what looked like a perdurable Platonic friendship
("Hah, hah, *hah*, Blanche!") bursting forth in his stressed mind all over
May, June—and any other woman unlucky enough to ask him to a prom
or find his smoldering-sensitive manner (oh, *brother*) attractive—by a reckless reading of *The Symposium*, the Other's Irish Greek-god build and profile, definitely Alcibiades material. All enhanced to the release of the film
Compulsion, in which, as previously noted, Dean Stockwell and Bradford
Dillman enacted the Leopold-Loeb Chicago murder of little Bobby Franks
(who, it turned out, get this, had been *deuxième choix* after a boy in the
same class who was home sick that day, one Billy Schon, later William
Shawn, editor of *The New Yorker*. Plus tax).

Waking some hours later, he went out *sur le motif*, as Cézanne had
directed, indeed finding through some rather extensive nocturnal field work,
done in the very same place as a generation before, Madison Square Park
(interestingly now only a four-block walk from home). There his archetype
would come, and come again, at unappointed hours.

Whereupon in the days, weeks, months and years to come, with the
Nietzschean idea of the eternal return returning, he would come to see the
Old Queer Fuck as the Wizard of Oz, a kind of queer Joe Gould (to whose
spell Joe Mitchell, himself still there up at *The New Yorker*, which had
become his prison and his old hotel, had succumbed), certain flapping-den-
ture mouths at the Everard Baths and the wizard from *Captain Marvel* still
making with the *shazams*, even though there were no more crippled news-
boys (although there did begin to appear a multitude of seeming equivalents).

"I make no formal distinction between the fact and fiction; my brief is
ideation, and ideation is *real*."

—The Old Queer Fuck (hereafter the Archetype)

—◦—

And thus he spake:

"And speaking of the English classicists, it must be one of the supreme
ironies of Culture that the end result of all the fantasies cherished by countless nineteenth-century Oxbridge pedophile onanists (wankers is what the
sour boy tarts of Picadilly called them) who affected to embody for their
time the life-transforming ideals of Hellas, who traveled to Greece in their

droves to kneel in the sacred groves and nibble on the Moly, and under whose rubric the fabulously Irish but fatally sentimental Oscar Wilde went down in henna flames at Bow Street Court House and the Old Bailey, should turn out to be the White Party at South Beach.

"But what is this mystique of the dj, high priest of a new karaoke? Of course today's queers, grooving not merely to the music but to the spin the particular star dj gives the music, were they to see videos of their forebears sitting in the dark hushed Byline Room watching Mabel Mercer playing with her silk handkerchief and whispering deathless wisdom into the microphone, must consider the whole spectacle by comparison paraplegic.

"I always despised the criminal chic Genet hawked. After all, good boys pretending to be bad can be art, as in the miraculous films of Joe Gage, but bad boys pretending to be good are just kitsch crapshooters and fakes. Anyway, the least of Joe Gage is far superior to *Chant d'Amour*, although that cigarette-smoke-exhaled-through-the-straw-stuck-through-the-hole-in-the-cellblock-wall thing was good. And really, who was not made hard in his seat and gooey while observing Vic Morrow and Gavin MacLeod in *Deathwatch?*

"In certain blue films—instance, *Centurions of Rome*, starring the late Eric Ryan and that divine queen who plays Caligula so exactly like Richard Nixon, you cannot help but get the point—art pornographjy reaches its gestural peak. When the augur reads the results of the come shots on the walls of the Baths of Caracalla. Not since Ramon Novarro in the 1925 *Ben-Hur* has such content-rich j.o. pay dirt been shoveled up."

(A terrible occasion: the author's last sighting in this time of Eric Ryan, a cachectic ruin, standing under terrible red and green Christmas lights at 42nd Street and Eighth Avenue just down from the Show Palace, scene of his former floor show triumphs, dressed quite unseasonably in a blue cashmere sweater, dungarees and what did seem to be Bruno Magli loafers slipped on over naked feet, looking at one of the Bible freaks' signs—AIDS, AMERICAN INFERNAL SODOMITES DISTEMPER—and crying.)

"Driven livin' as the Sunday preacher said."

◄○►

"Is art a lie? 'What is truth?' queried Pilate, washing his already spotless hands then turning on the hand dryer.

"And as for the past, and remembrance of same, well, while you're remembering, and rearranging, it obviously is still the ongoing thing. *Remembrance of Things Pluperfect* might be a novelty—how's that for paradox?

"Who is it, darling, calls AIDS *death with knobs on?*

"Sickness requires healers: the thaumaturge, the prophet, the wise man and the tyrant flourish as never before in The Life. 'Nothing can save us that is possible: / We who must die demand a miracle.' Old Wanker Wystan Auden wrote that, darling."

◄o►

"Darling, all things will be undone; remember, Mont Ségur just *wasn't.*"

◄o►

"I am in awe," he declared, "of the power of male sex energy. I enjoy an intense session of self-affirming masturbation that lasts for hours, riding to the edge of Tantric bliss. The longer I do it, the more sex energy builds until I feel I am about to lose consciousness. It's not just getting off, it is like an out-of-body experience, my whole being transported to a higher plane, definitely a religious experience. Now if I could just get *paid* to do this shit."

◄o►

"The truth is we've neglected to provide the proofs of ego and the protocols which fame demands, and it's too late now. Our communal saga, auspicious enough in conception, teasing enough in detail and God knows hinged on myriad riveting references, is not sufficiently furnished with redeeming social value to be widely recounted in an age in which, increasingly, labels are worn on the outsides of garments. There's no retrieval of days lost we know not how, and vows not kept are vows not kept forever. Nevertheless, one's not a fool. Now that one's old one finds it entertaining to rearrange for interviewers the facts of one's life and ancestry. One has learned to shield oneself, reinventing oneself through one's own disappearance.

"In one's youth, walking into the light source to meet it head-on, the shadow falls behind, and one rarely if ever looks over one's shoulder. Later, past the noontime of one's life, the light falls from behind, casting one's shadow in one's path.

"Implications."

"There are always implications; they are part and parcel of the trigger hypothesis and the inevitable result of invocations to labor and courage in the fulfillment of high designs. Always new questions to think about too—such as can it be possible after all that there is something that travels faster than light—thought, for instance?"

"In any event all one's shiny keys will one day be taken from the place where one has left them, and all one's cupboards opened and all the little things one wished no one to see will then be seen by one and all.

"And so, so what? You cheated; Mr. Big did likewise. You kept the Hope Diamond, he kept the cash. A lot of trouble for nothing—still you didn't live in vain; there's not a soul can fairly say you did.

"Amateur theatricals—still going on out in Cherry Grove, you know. This summer, a revival of Maugham's *Our Betters*, retitled *Our Bitters*."

[Author's note: Queer fiction is done in bas-relief; the number of free-standing characters of distinction in it is very few. Burrough's acid-head narrator in *The Ticket That Exploded*, Rechy's anonymous hustler in *City of Night*, Joseph Caldwell's hero in *In Such Dark Places*, David Plante's Daniel Francoeur in the sculpted novel series chronicling his life, Sutherland in Holleran's *Dancer from the Dance*, the great Designated Mouth (derived undoubtedly from *Nightwood*—and Matthew-Mighty-Grain-of-Salt Whoosiewhatsis) is certainly one, and Mister Friel in *Nights in Aruba*. Also, both characters in Christopher Davis's beautiful *Joseph and the Old Man*, certainly the best piece of shorter gay fiction, and all the beaten broken boys in all the perfect novels of Dennis Cooper.]

―◦―

The Archetype:

"Flannery O'Connor, a psycho-sexual cripple and devout Catholic possessed of a literary talent bordering on genius and given to the depiction of freaks was of course in the '50s greatly revered by queer co-religionists and their chic sympathizers.

"I adore your friend's *Gaywyck*. It's even better than *The Lord Won't Mind*, and it's so *written*—and after all, was it not about time that strapping, brilliant, rich and gorgeous men stopped relating to one another sexually in terms of a barracks, a trench, a toilet or a football field, and started gushing praise and love all over one another in luxurious beds in luxurious apartments surrounded by beautiful things?

"NAMBLA, a shut-down shop-front, behind which nevertheless, one hears . . ."

[Author's note: Pomosexuality. I call homosexual those male writers whose work so obviously betrays paranoid anxiety over treaties with the paternal introject as to render that concerning maternal treaties insignificant by comparison. I therefore nominate Herman Melville the most important American homosexual writer. His heterosexual counterpart is obviously Nathaniel Hawthorne.

So: Homosexual	Heterosexual
Stephen Crane	Henry James
Ernest Hemingway	F. Scott Fitzgerald
William Faulkner	Sinclair Lewis
Eugene O'Neill	Theodore Dreiser
William Gaddis	J.D. Salinger
Harold Brodkey	John O'Hara
Tennessee Williams	John Steinbeck
Truman Capote	Gore Vidal (introject: America)]

◄○►

"Let's put it this way, darling: there was more to Child's than the pancakes."

"I hog the mike, I know. Pure greed—the greed of an old spook in a hurry."

"If you want to talk about paranoid, culture theorists are the end: they believe not so much that God is talking to them, as that God is their Charlie McCarthy. If the Government and the Media were the world, and not merely a version of it for which the electorate—the notorious 47–49 percent or whatever it is together with the minions of Hollywood and Madison Avenue—are responsible for foisting on us . . . but they are not. 'The world,' as Wilfred Owen wrote in 'The War God,' 'is The World, and not the slain nor the slayer, Amen.'"

"Of course Athens was neither Pericles nor Praxiteles nor Plato nor any of the tragic or comic poets either, no matter how we've been taught to believe. And we have no idea what Sparta was. Who's to say it was nowhere, just because it has disappeared without a trace? If Japan and Europe had their way, so would the USA. Or is that paranoid?"

◄○►

"On the Road all those Beat generation bums humping America in old jalopies chugging from coast to coast before the Interstate. Hunched in box-cars and flophouses and pads—how was it they put it—pulling wrists?"

"That was existentialism, wasn't it?"

"No, existentialism came out of Paris, where everything happens and nothing is true. The opposition came from London—or Oxford and Cambridge, or all three. England, anyway, where nothing happened after the '60s. It says everything that is true."

After disco, the Madison.

"It's so old, the Madison; when I recall it I see the phantoms of great hopes dancing in the mist—although they say Bobby Madison was named after it. Bobby Madison, in *Power Tools* and oh, my god, with Paul in *Brother Load*. Of course Eric Ryan was the king of kings—and Richard Locke is God the Father!"

"What about Fred Halsted?"

"Fred Halsted was wicked; many people say he worshiped the devil."

"He did not, he worshiped Joseph Yale, they were a devoted couple—and *Sex Garage* and *L.A. Plays Itself* are in the Museum of Modern Art's permanent collection. When Joseph died, Fred couldn't go on, and put a plastic bag over his head."

—◇—

Spurred on by that most industrious pawnbroker of literary criticism, Jacques Derrida ("If one calls *bricolage* the necessity of borrowing one's concepts from the text of a heritage which is more or less coherent or ruined, it must be said that every discourse is *bricoleur*"). For the fragment, as it expands and becomes a new text is larger than the particle whence it originated.

Quiz Questions:

1. Even if it isn't technically eavesdropping, does overhearing such information immediately reconstitute one as a decentralized subject?

2. Is one a decentralized subject if one has (a) not only no job, but (b) no succinct job description?

3. Can one be a decentralized subject if one is not even French?

Happily one can, if the ventriloquist is French—or even if he's simply under French influence.

` INCONGRUENCE OF JAMES AND RYAN

*,iour alone; take them off—I don't care where; absorb,
,ain them; drown them, kill them if you will; so that I may just a
., all by myself, see where I am."*

—Henry James, *The Wings of the Dove*

". . . Eric Ryan, darling—the most beautiful porn star of all time, whose story is a perfect illustration of the Mary Astor Career Trajectory:

"1. 'Who's Eric Ryan?' (real name, et cetera, early appearances: Arch Brown's's *Dynamite* starring the then supreme Jack Wrangler, William Higgins's *The Boys of Venice* and the breakthrough, Francis Ellie's *Centurions of Rome*).

"2. 'Get Eric Ryan'—the high roll of his career—including floor shows at the Follies Male Burlesque and the Show Palace and appearances in the early hours of the morning at the New St. Marks Baths—where he was worshiped in the steam room by literally dozens of delirious men tongue-washing every part of his body clean of every accumulated trace of semen, sweat and Angel Dust, washing his perfect feet with their ecstatic amyl-nitrate tears and swabbing them with their sopping late '70s Hair-by-Kenneth manes.

"3. 'Get an Eric Ryan Type.' Career on the turn, ER starts turning up at the Broadway Baths in the afternoon and the Big Top—paying to get in like everybody else, and staging 'Please worship me!' scenes in the back room while the reverse images of his performances of former years are played out on the screen.

"4. 'Who's Eric Ryan?' ER standing in the middle of winter on the northeast corner of 42nd and Eighth, only a few yards down from the Show Palace marquee, looking gaunt and hideous, his eyebrows all penciled in, dressed in what appeared to be the last articles of clothing in his possession: ripped and faded denims, dirty white Foot Locker tennis shoes.

"Everybody's suddenly running around reading *The Anatomy of Melancholy*. The Anatomy of Melancholy indeed; what about the Melancholy of Anatomy? Is anybody thinking of that in this youth-obsessed country?"

[Author's note: Michel Foucault in San Francisco (like Socrates, a pedophile warthog). From the École Normale to the fleshpots of Folsom. Killed in the bath like Marat, under the direction of the Marquis de Sade, but what was Charlotte Corday doing being that boy in a towel? (Brought it on himself, some theorists would say. Foucault's man was the defiant answer to Michelet's woman—cited by Barthes on *On Revolution*.)]

—◄○►—

"How many Sundays is it since Pentecost?"

"Why?"

"I've been remembering Eddie West's Pentecost sermon at the Dune Church back in the '80s. He said it was an illusion—Eddie . . . death— that life itself was by definition eternal.

"'The enemy lies waiting in the long grass,' he said, 'with his tales of death and despair,' often disguised as oily compassion and that dangerous diagnosis, psychoneurosis, the "malicious animal magnetism" of twentieth-century apostasy—but it simply isn't so. The gate of heaven is not a revolving stile. Too few there be, alas, that love God's lore—which is to say the treasury of rich, embroidered tales in which his eternal wisdom abounds.

"'But you do,' he said. 'You are made in the conspicuous image and likeness of God, who loves the focus of lonely wonder at the center of your being, the confusion of your inner vehemence. Biddable oafs, if the truth be known, bore him silly, however bound he is by self-prescription to care for them.'

"Nice speech, Eve—or Eddie, rather. There's one girl who paid no attention to St. Paul or any of his silly admonitions.

"'He happily assents to the fulfillment of your aspirations,' he said, 'albeit not unconditionally. There are limits to worldly things, to brands, content, services and access—so in the name of the very God who imagines you, govern yourselves accordingly—*ein Mensch zu sein*. The Ten Commandments are the Ten *Commandments*, darlings—not the ten suggestions!'

"That Eddie!

"'It isn't easy—we know that; there is much virtuoso wickedness in the world. Assaults and criminal damage are ever on the increase, although police have beguilingly attributed this to increased reporting. The world and its rulers are absolutely obsessed with info dominance, with deep-strike architecture, with asymetric competitors and all manner of dark knowledge.

"'So keep your PIN a secret and never tell it to anyone; be cautious when giving your account numbers over the telephone. Such has life become in the Free Society. One might laugh out loud, would it do one any good—

as it is it would likely serve only to bring on more suspicion. So opting for righteousness is rather like doing modern art; you have to deepen the game to be any good at all. It simply isn't enough to keep your eye on the ball; in the immortal words of the great Babe Didrikson, you've got to loosen your girdle and really let the ball have it. As an Irish poet once put it to me, "We must record love's mystery without claptrap, snatch out of time the passionate transitory." '

"And waiter, I'll have another old fashioned, please. Well, Eddie West surely knew all there was to know about passionate, transitory snatch.

" 'From time immemorial,' he said—Eddie, that is, not the Irish poet, whoever he was—'the enigmatic need for sensation has found a certain provisional satisfaction—has pitched its tent—in gaudy fashion, but its true home ground is in the end staked out solely by rigorous theological inquiry. Would the children of God squander an inestimable inheritance on politics? On late-breaking developments? Cast their patrimony to the trade winds? I don't think so, as the children say today, or as my mother, God rest her soul, would put in, "In a pig's eye!" In God's plan there are no late-breaking developments. Put not your faith in princes.

" 'Rather, hold up your heaving shoulders, darlings, and emulating Shiva, dance—for although no incantation can ever compel the gods, many a song and dance has charmed them silly.'

" 'I cannot encourage spiritual democracy. The elect are not the elected—and you can say I said so. The beings of light exist in choir hierarchies, from angel to seraph, as do the colors of the rainbow from red on up to violet—and is not hierarchy as a concept more distinguished than the leveling effected by shallow spiritual liberation, which in the end always aims at disturbing the equilibrium of the exquisite? Assuredly.

" 'Who has not passed through the inferno of passion can never ascend Mount Purgatory to—what? No less a mind than Einstein put it this way: "Try and penetrate with our limited means," he suggested, "the secrets of nature, and you will find that, beyond all the discernible concatenations there remains something subtle, intangible and inexplicable." The veneration of that force, beyond anything we can comprehend, and not of the notoriously narcissistic no-brainer posed by poor Hamlet, is the question, my dears. Must we suppose repose, cradled in sad cypress for all eternity? Who says? Who says heaven is repose? Clearly the mystics don't think so—not from what I've read of them—or any vapid disappearance into abeyance either. They seem to think it's one endless orgasm, and here's what I say to that: Hooray!'

"Eddie made those dowagers blush at their prayers, that's the truth.

They heard the hum of heavenly wires big time every time the maestro pitched that High Church woo.

"'In any event, don't worry about dying, darlings, it's your birthday! Speaking for myself, as pants the hart for cooling streams, I can hardly wait—even if, as rumor would have it, heaven can—for I believe, you see, they are too long, the weeping and the laughter, the love, the desire, the hate. I do.

"'Sigmund Freud—for whom I have the same degree of respect that I have for Mary Baker Eddy, abetted by the allure of a quirky sense of humor—joked that every night the sleeper abandons himself to death in high hopes of a dawn reprieve. I insist the time will come when, like me, you will become impatient with said reprieve!

"'Well,' he proclaimed, 'the fact is, darlings, not a soul in this congregation has the remotest idea of the nature of the joys of the resurrection and the life to come in God. It can never have occurred to a single one of us, and of course, strictly speaking, it is never going to. It is the everlasting idea of us that is, as it has from all eternity, of which our time on earth is otherwise, occuring in all delight to God.'

"One old thing kept snoring through nearly the whole of the sermon that morning, only to come to life when Eddie invoked the Light of Eternity. Then later at lunch, she approached him and asked, 'Excuse me, Canon West, but the Light of Eternity—do you happen to know the *color* of it?' 'Why, yes, my dear, I do. It's blue—like your lovely hat.'"

—◄○►—

A Coda: Joe Le Sueur doing Meals on Wheels in East Hampton. A female therapist assigned to a local AIDS case: two ex-Universal '50s contract players, antique dealers ("It was either open a shop or open a vein each!") and long-time companions. Everybody who knew what a neighbor in the country was adored them both, and I got them put on my Meals on Wheels route (you see it: the hospital tray with covered dish, little single flower, brought in every early afternoon: evening meal being one of those megaton I.V. cocktails, part nutrition, part demolition nobody had a better idea than). This one cold winter afternoon, as he'd come in the kitchen door, the soon-to-be-survivor shouted in to the patient on the davenport, "Blanche, did I tell ya there are rats in the cellar?" By the time he reached the living room, there stood the stern and no doubt overworked therapist (remember Barbara Baxley at Raymond Massey's bedside in *East of Eden*?) looking down at the patient, who had begun mock-whining,

"*Mais je t'implore, mon amour, oui, je m'abîme.*"

"Speak English, Blanche, will ya; we got company."

"You wouldn't treat me this way if I weren't in this condition."

And, of course the partner, whipping out a cigarette and lighting it, barked,

"But ya *are*, Blanche, ya *are* in that condition!"

"You are so cruel."

"Just remember, Blanche, without me, you'd soon end up like Cecilia—living in filth, insisting she had her little angel in once a week to dust, whereas what she was trying to say was it had been a whole week and still no one had showed up with her Angel Dust"

"Oh, you are venomous when drunk—but who shall 'scape whipping?"

"Indeed I am cruel, aunt—I have been taught by masters."

"Oh, that was divine, honey, did you tape it?"

"In stereo, my pet."

"Delicious. I adore you."

"And I you, love."

The therapist, appalled, took the partner aside, whispering not low: did he not realize the end was not far off and no attempt at all that she could make out had been made at closure?

"Closure!" (Throws the cigarette down and grinds it out on an expensive [very] Kazakhstan rug and turning the color of real anger.) "You want closure, I'll give you closure. Sewing first your mouth and then your snatch shut—I will leave your asshole, which has done all the talking around here for weeks, free to cry 'Help!' And if none of that corrects you, I will, I swear to Jesus, Joseph and Miss Mary God, bury you in the crypt you belong in, drive a stake through your vile heart and cover you with a concrete slab!"

And then (to Joe): "Tell me, darling, are vultures on your endangered species list? Because if so, I'm about to offend your principles!" Whereupon he dragged the poor woman to the front door, threw her coat and bag out onto the front porch, bellowing, unnecessarily Joe thought (but reasoned not the need), "And now get out!"

And when she did, he slammed the door, and turned back to the room. "Closure!

"Oh, thank God," was heard from the divan, "now what's for lunch?"

And the dying words of the patient. After some days of what seemed a coma, the eyes snap open suddenly and the voice comes clear.

"Shit, now I get it! Oh, well."

And he falls back on the pillow, dead.

DRAWING TO A CONCLUSION

In the brief space of one volume we have condensed many different concepts, all of which go to make up the ground.

Tension, value (tones of gray), light, shade, compression.

Our language changes as new words are created to express new—

(Actually, darling, there are two schools of thought on that subject.)

Tension is the strain of things falling apart. That much is—

We have concentrated on the main aspects of the subject, leaving out less critical aspects.

Diagonal plan, dynamic in itself in spite of the evident fixedness of an apparently accidental composition.

Everyone knows that sometimes a good sketch, drawn casually but with a sure hand—

Sprezzatura.

Predicament, wherewithal, shades of limelight; how it got to be so.

Times, places, weather conditions and wardrobes.

What more, what more?

He might have taken the time to say something about Truth, Beauty and the Goodness of God.

But the time got away from him, so it seems.

Plus which he says there is no why—a metaphysical statement, having no relation perhaps to the facts of life as they are known to us, but nonetheless disquieting. No *why?*

Author walking, hearing voices, having visions? Tell it to the Marines.

Elaborate designs, grids, imaginary maps? Put it all in Bloomingdale's window.

And yet, and yet.

If the stream of consciousness is what we're all immersed in,

If riverrun past eveandadams truly,

Then sink or swim, or go away somewhere and read a novel,

With a beginning, a middle, an end, and make believe narrative
solves something.

Put another way, the author has essayed the transcription of nothing more or less than a congeries of echoes, of years of overheard and vis-à-vis smart talk.

Did Narcissus ever come to love Echo? If so, that boy is alive today.

THE BOOK TALKS BACK

Having heard your story in bits and pieces . . . what of it, wonders the nerveless dark angel of age, guardian still, on the Lexington Avenue subway in late December 2002.

What did he do—what did he do wrong; indeed. (*Such Were the Joys* would hardly do for the book's subtitle.)

Is there literary fascination in the clear recitation of the facts? Whatever the answer—yes, no, yes and no, now and then, that depends, whatever—*Queer Street*, although drawn as a rectilinear diagonal and not a meander, is unlikely, all said and done, to afford it.

To the question has any clear recitation of the facts ever proved genuinely persuasive, he answers no.

We know this argument: writing in a literary and not in a documentary way.

Queer Street addresses the author of *Queer Street* (in strictest confidence):

So you take perverse pleasure in pulverizing the patho-logics of trusted response, do you, darling? What is it you said yourself—or was that you pretending to be one of the Voices or one of the Voices pretending to be you (and so what?)—*gay gown*.

Or, recalling with unmixed delight Gore Vidal's once advising James Baldwin he could not be both Martin Luther King and Bette Davis, can you really envision yourself, merely on the say of even so keen an observer as Richard Rouilard, as both James Joyce and Bette Midler?

Are you so burdened, darling, with the overwhelming paternity of modernism?

Hutcheon's Typology of Textual Narcissism: covert = overt/ diegetic = linguistic. Truth lies.

Prigogine's Dissipative Structures Theory.

Can the boy getting over himself get over himself getting—

Been there, done that, got the T-shirt, rent it in two, kneeling on the ground, roaring *Stellla!* They shrieked with laughter—only one among them, Miss Dean, to wit, reacted in terror. "W-w-when you get like that you're *d-dangerous*." You know, don't you, she kept Mace spray in that chic little purse.

◄○►

And Truth, Beauty and the Goodness of God are there somewhere in the notes—cross-identified with the yearning female element in collision with the ill-defined male trace.

And the city revealed itself: the matter of prose romance. New York will be a wonderful place, they all would say, if they ever finish building it.

And he should attempt to come to conclusions?

Identity and the Masks of Enclosure. Narcissism and Dissembling in the Usurper. Extrusion from the Tribe. The Fluidity and Porosity of Texts prior to Canonization. Written on the Wind.

A life, all told, crowded with incident, semi-veiled in secrecy (and only that, apparently: at one point hadn't his mother declared, "You can't shock me, you know—I read *The Well of Loneliness* and all the rest of it; we all did back in the twenties"). And as for exposure, his obsession with Salome . . . although as was pointed out at the time, Ljuba Welitsch didn't dance, Rita Hayworth most certainly did. He'd dance.

> *"Meanwhile, pipe down, there are people trying to die in here!"*
> —a Voice in the Night at the Everard Baths

> "Die, die, my darlings—we're going to breakfast."

> *(That was Youth with its reckless exuberance when all things were possible pursued by Age where we are now looking back at . . .)*
> —William Gaddis, *Agape Agape*

And after breakfast they walked out of the Everard. Turning east, into the rising sun, they made for the Lexington Avenue subway.

LEO LERMAN: A DEATH

Leo Lerman lying in state in his bedroom at the Osborne, listening in at a fabulous matinee he wouldn't have missed for the world, while outside it was August.

"*Intestate*—Leo? That's impossible, he—"

"In *state* . . . in state."

"Oh . . . yes."

"Positively *pharaonic*, isn't it."

"*Ironic*—why? It's exactly what Leo—"
"*Ironic*! *I-ronic*—"
"Oh, sorry. Everybody's *whispering*, that's—"
"We're all failng, darling—getting on. Age comes, the body withers."
"That body lying there looks like it's about to sit up."
"And hum a tune?"
"A Gershwin tune . . . how about him."

—◄○►—

Veronica Geng: But what did Leo Lerman *do* exactly?
Author: He did everything exactly.
Geng: Hmmm.
Author: No, that's the point; he was *about* exactly.

—◄○►—

"Tell me your dream," Leo would say, sitting there in his study at the Osborne, diagonally across from Carnegie Hall, one of the great rooms in private New York, like the habitat of the richest Russian in the world. "In my dream I'm the richest Russian in the world, traveling in a private railway car from St. Petersburg to Venice for *Carnevale*, then to Monte for the season." A room the richest Russian in the world—one with necessarily English tastes—would have had installed in his apartments in Petersburg, and at the same time of course reminiscent of the library on a great ocean liner, say the *Berengaria*: gorgeous burled-wood paneling and filled to the ceiling with first editions. "Sit on that chair, like they do on French television . . . on *Le Divan*." (The compère, posing as a shrink, always had the guest sprawl full-frontal on *le divan*—the analyst's couch—to do some free-associating, bean-spilling, provocative bead-reading concerning other's foibles. The author said they ought to have the show in NYC, and he would go on and tell about himself sleeping under the Names Project quilt.)

So after the death of Harry Blair, Leo became the author's Virgil.

And the author would tell Leo time and again that if Manhattan was, as he, Leo, always said, a great luxury ocean liner, then he, the author, was a stowaway. He could, using his father's waterfront connections, get on board easily and stay there, coming out (in so many words) from under his hiding place in the lifeboats only in the evening, when the security was lax—never daring to promenade in the afternoons on deck—and commute up to first, as later you could in the last of the great vessels, the *France*, through the chapel, and meet the swells . . . and on and on like that.

Leo said everybody brought up in Queens felt like that; he had too, in Elmhurst and at Newtown High School ("in the same graduating class with Risë Stevens—Risë Steenberg she was. I was in the senior play of course; played Orsino in *Twelfth Night*—had the most *gorgeous* legs"). The thing was to get over it. As long as we were born within the city limits— and as in our cases could look up and see the fabulous skyline looming in the west—we'd fulfilled Euripides's first requirement for a happy life: nativity in a great city—*the* great city.

So, Purgatory as anteroom: Leo's gorgeous wake. The World and its Mother going in to the viewing ("Fran is here to see you, dear") and coming back out to the living room to talk. Author reminded that the wake used to be nearly a commonplace occurrence in Irish homes before 1950. Unusual for a Jewish man; for Jews, sitting *shiva* is always after the burial.

Leo lying snug as a bug in a rug at home—and Maria Callas, who was indeed Leo's dear friend, would, were she alive, be looking at him and wondering perhaps why all New York did not tremble before him as Rome did before Scarpia; quite the opposite, he was their guide to the higher regions.

Dead as a doornail, yet dreaming of Venice and of his corner suite at the Gritti, overlooking the Grand Canal. Dreaming of *Carnevale* and the (perhaps after all consequent) plague, but also (strangely like some Christian) of the Redentore and of that surpassingly beautiful theater on the stage of which Callas had first stunned the world, La Fenice, the Phoenix, rising from its ashes time and again.

Finally, the memorial service at the Grace Rainey Rogers Auditorium of the Metropolitan Museum of Art. The empty chair, the fedora, the scarf, all spotlighted, as befitted a star. Speeches by the great and the good (so-called, ironically, by edgy New York voices) and on the soundtrack *Mariettaslied* from Erich Korngold's masterpiece, *Die Tote Stadt*.

—◄○►—

The author upon exiting made his way through the Egyptian rooms:

Imagine after all carrying on with authority in the Leo tradition—the beard (whiskers, not some chic, compliant, slightly racy woman), the cane, the magisterial, forbidding-yet-inviting demeanor.

Whereupon what?

Only connect.

To what, to whom?

Give it . . . something—but whatever else, don't give it a rest. The battalion of the valiant won't; not even now that the Supreme Court has reversed *Bowers v. Hardwick*.

All right—George Trow and Micheál Mac Liammóir.

Elaborate—only just sufficiently.

George (W.S.) Trow because of *City in the Mist*, a neglected masterpiece of the New York School (itself inexplicably disregarded) and because Leo said what he loved about reading Trow was the free and willing espousal, the patient endurance, of a peculiar American loneliness. Micheál Mac Liammóir because, apart from the fact he played both Hamlet and Oscar Wilde (the equivalent of James Baldwin's attempt to be both Martin Luther King and Bette Davis) and invented Orson Welles for Dublin, he was of that metropolis the very kind of arbiter Wizard of Oz (being, after all, a North London Jew called Alfred Wilmot giving all along the best impersonation of an Irishman ever seen, heard, touched-tasted-or-handled) that Leo Lerman from Elmhurst was for Manhattan.

Nearly finished; something more—but keep your eye on the time.

Duly noted—for instance?

A little something transcendent.

(That word again—he has never even known what it means.)

He'd once mentioned the Mac Liammóir connection to Leo, who guffawed, replying, "My dear, if I'd had Mac Liammóir's talent, I'd have sung *Scawpia* opposite Maria down there on 39th Street, instead of gasping for breath in a box—and that made two of us at least if you remember, me in the box and Maria onstage."

"You're really not like Mac Liammóir, you know; you tell the truth."

"I'm lazy, my dear—a good liar has to keep track, and I simply couldn't be bothered."

"You know, if I thought I could, I might try to—"

"Pick up the torch?"

"Yes."

"After I've—well, now that you've stopped going around lighting everybody's cigarettes, which could be called a kind of practice, you might decide to do something along those lines."

"Thing is, I can't ever imagine myself as the world's richest Russian."

"Of course you can; all you have to do is stop imagining you're really Prince Myshkin. You know, when my mother died, Gray and I went out to Elmhurst to collect her things. When we opened this one closet in the bedroom, out poured a lifetime's worth—an *avalanche*—of junk jewelry. It was a *camp*!"

"I've never carried any kind of torch at all that *mattered*, except perhaps on the page."

"Then that's your role. Console yourself my dear, and take courage; nothing's ever really been accomplished by an American that can match what's been done here on the page. That's what American loneliness is all about, isn't it."

In the Egyptian Room, a place he'd been haunting since childhood in search of his own *Shazam*.

◄o►

The oldest Egyptian hieroglyph for the Truth has a slant or an edge on it, a hacking or cutting edge; thus from down the canonical ages (it would so seem) was the truth an ethical utility. And beauty a formal, pleasing, vain and useless bale of goods.

Be that as it may, why was Leo's face suddenly right there, carved on that mummy case? (Author would have sworn to it; must be what they mean when they talk about the imagination.)

Jesting Pilate: And what is truth?

Stella Adler: Truth, dahling? Truth is in the circumstances, always— and Hamlet is not a guy like you.

Slow curtain . . . the end.

Captions and Credits

All pictures not credited are from the collection of the author.

LC: Library of Congress; LGC: Lester Glassner Collection; VVC: Vincent Virga Collection

Frontispiece: "Jimmy, New York City, 1982," by George Haas, courtesy of the artist

I. Origination

Background image: New York City at Night, LC

Foreground images, clockwise from far left:

Author's confirmation picture, 1952

"440," mixed media, 7' x 70' (detail), 2000, by Darragh Park, courtesy of the artist

Author with friends at high school dance, 1957

Ljuba Welitsch as Richard Strauss's Salome, 1951, VVC

Eve Harrington (Anne Baxter) and Margo Channing (Bette Davis), from Mankiewicz's *All About Eve,* 1950, frame enlargement, LGC

Author's father, 1928

II. Investigations

Background image: map of Greenwich Village, LC

Foreground images, clockwise from far left:

Tallulah Bankhead, by Carl Van Vechten, 1934, LC

"Soldier Asleep on Greyhound Bus," by Esther Bubley, 1943, LC

The two faces of Kim Novak in Hitchcock's *Vertigo,* frame enlargements, LC

The Hotel Astor, LC

Carnegie Hall, United Artists, 1947, movie poster, LC

A Star Is Born, Warner Bros., 1954, movie poster, LC

"Shubert Alley," by Lester Glassner, 1953, courtesy of the artist

III. Breaking Out

Background Image: "Couple on Fire Island," by Jarry Lang, 1965, VVC

Foreground images, clockwise from far left:
Harry Blair
Author with friend and mother at opening of Metropolitan Opera, 1963
Diane DeVors, by Jarry Lang, 1964, VVC
From Drags to Riches, program, Cherry Grove Playhouse, 1964, VVC
Dixie, 1964
Everard Baths, New York City, advertisement
Partisan Review, Fall 1964

IV. Expatriates
Background image, right: Author's letter from London, 1969
Background image, left: Piccadilly Circus, London, LC
Foreground images, clockwise from far left:
Author in London, 1970
Author (center) with Vincent Virga (left) and friends in London, 1970
Svetlana Beriosova in Ashton/Walton's *Facade*, VVC
Author's letter from London, 1970
Victoria de los Angeles as Massenet's Manon, courtesy Xavier Vivanco
Jacqueline Du Pré, LC

V. Return Engagements
Background image: New York City subway map, LC
Foreground images, clockwise from far left:
"David with the Head of Goliath," by Caravaggio, Borghese Gallery, Rome, cour-
   tesy of Matthew Fink
Herman Melville, LC
Tennessee Williams, LC
Maria Callas and Luchino Visconti in rehearsal, La Scala, Milan, VVC
Raymond Chandler, LC
Mawrdew Czgowchwz, book jacket design by Lawrence Ratzkin, 1975, Farrar, Straus
   & Giroux
Gaywyck, 1980, Avon Books
Dancer from the Dance, 1979, Bantam Books
The Boys in the Band, National General Pictures, lobby card, 1970, LGC

VI. Dead Reckonings
Background image: "Silver Lining," by John Paradiso, 1995, courtesy of the artist
Foreground images, clockwise from far left:
James Schuyler, by Clay Felver, 1985, courtesy of Darragh Park
James Merrill, by J.D. McClatchy, courtesy of the artist
Bruce Ritter, AP photo/Richard Drew, 1989
Time Remaining, book jacket design by Chip Kidd, Alfred A. Knopf, 1993
"Seductive," by John Paradiso, 1991, courtesy of the artist
Dorothy Dean

Neil Cunningham
Vincent Virga and the author in pool, Rancho Mirage, New Year's Day, 1980, by
    Jarry Lang, VVC

VII. Lost Angeles
Background image, right: "Palm #2, Echo Park, 2002," by George Haas, courtesy
    of the artist
Background image, left: "Palm #7, Silver Lake, 2002," by George Haas, courtesy of
    the artist
Foreground images, clockwise from far left:
Mural on Cahuenga Boulevard, Los Angeles, photo by the author, 1983
Helen Phillips (Jane Wyman) and Bob Merrick (Rock Hudson), from Sirk's *Mag-
    nificent Obsession*, 1954, VVC
Deep Joan, LGC
Joan Crawford (Faye Dunaway), from Perry's *Mommie Dearest*, 1981, LGC
Sister Ruth (Kathleen Byron), Sister Clodagh (Deborah Kerr) and Mr. Dean
    (David Farrar), from Powell's *Black Narcissus*, 1947, LGC
Los Angeles postcard
Mae West, LGC
Bob Cohen and Richard Rouilard, by Greg Zabilski, courtesy of Bob Cohen
Queer Street, jacket design by Rubina Yeh, W. W. Norton & Company, 2003
Douglas Sirk, LGC

Index

About the Author

JAMES MCCOURT was born in New York City and was educated at Manhattan College, New York University and the Yale School of Drama. His novels include *Mawrdew Czgowchwz*, *Kaye Wayfaring in "Avenged," Time Remaining* and *Delancey's Way*. His stories, articles and film and book reviews have appeared in *The New Yorker*, the *Paris Review*, *Grand Street*, the *Yale Review*, *Vogue*, *Film Comment* (contributing editor in the seventies and eighties), *SoHo Weekly News*, and the *New York Times* and *Los Angeles Times* book sections, and he commented on the 1995 Oscar presentations for *Buzz*.

James McCourt has taught creative writing at Princeton and Yale. He lives in New York City and Washington, D.C.